Dynamic Econometrics
for Empirical Macroeconomic Modelling

Dynamic Econometrics
for Empirical Macroeconomic Modelling

Ragnar Nymoen
University of Oslo, Norway

World Scientific

NEW JERSEY • LONDON • SINGAPORE • BEIJING • SHANGHAI • HONG KONG • TAIPEI • CHENNAI • TOKYO

Published by

World Scientific Publishing Co. Pte. Ltd.
5 Toh Tuck Link, Singapore 596224
USA office: 27 Warren Street, Suite 401-402, Hackensack, NJ 07601
UK office: 57 Shelton Street, Covent Garden, London WC2H 9HE

Library of Congress Cataloging-in-Publication Data
Names: Nymoen, Ragnar, 1957– author.
Title: Dynamic econometrics for empirical macroeconomic modelling /
Ragnar Nymoen (University of Oslo, Norway).
Description: USA : World Scientific, 2019.
Identifiers: LCCN 2019943684 | ISBN 9789811207518 (hardcover)
LC record available at https://lccn.loc.gov/2019943684

British Library Cataloguing-in-Publication Data
A catalogue record for this book is available from the British Library.

First published 2020 (hardcover)
Reprinted 2022 (in paperback edition)
ISBN 978-981-124-947-1 (pbk)

For any available supplementary material, please visit
https://www.worldscientific.com/worldscibooks/10.1142/11479#t=suppl

Desk Editors: V. Vishnu Mohan/Sylvia Koh

Typeset by Stallion Press
Email: enquiries@stallionpress.com

Dedicated to Kjersti-Gro

Preface

This book is a result of teaching time series econometrics to students of economics at the University of Oslo. But why write a textbook when there are already excellent books available? Self-scrutiny shows that one reason has been quite practical. Each term, I seemed to end up with half a dozen lecture notes, with interpretations, simplifications (at least that was the intention), remarks and "extra material" that I thought were relevant and important to bring to students' attention. At some point, the idea to try to consolidate all this material by writing a textbook became more than a thought.

One point that can motivate students to become interested in macroeconometric modelling is the duality between the equilibrium concept used in dynamic economics and the stationarity of time series (individually and jointly). At the same time, students often explain that they have problems with seeing that connection because they are not used to working with difference equations. Hence, although courses in modern macroeconomic theory appear to place quite high demands on the students' ability to master differential equations, there seems to be a gap that needs to be bridged. Apparently, and understandably, saying that difference equations are "just" differential equations in discrete time is not of much help for many students.

Hence, I have included a separate chapter on the theory of stochastic difference equations, which hopefully will help the reader acquire familiarity with the theory of difference equations needed to be comfortable with the exposition in the rest of this book. One intended side effect of this choice is that throughout this book, we can apply the perspective that time series are generated by systems of stochastic difference equations. This gives a common analytical framework for presentation of single equation and multiple equation models, of VARs and of recursive and simultaneous equations models, and of stationary and non-stationary time series.

Another perspective which is important to convey in the teaching of econometrics is the system perspective. Real-world economic variables are part of large, complex and dynamic systems. Even in the cases where the research question can be answered by the use of single equation modelling, system thinking is usually needed in econometrics (e.g., validity of conditioning, and validity and relevance of instruments). When the modelling purpose is to construct a usable macroeconometric model, the system perspective and multiple equation modelling becomes more evident. Stability of economic equilibria, and stationarity of variables are phenomena that are system properties. Hence, an attempt has been made in this book to use the system perspective as a red thread, starting with two simple models from economic dynamics in Chapter 1, and ending in Chapter 12, which is about model-based economic forecasting.

The selection of topics is another difficult decision in the writing of a textbook. Readers who know how fast time series econometrics as a field is expanding in terms of methods, models and techniques, will find that the list of topics in this book has indeed been narrowed down. For example, the statistical inference framework is frequentist, even though, over the last decades, Bayesian methods have gained ground in the quantification of macromodels. A main reason for this choice is that the focus of the book is the specification, estimation and testing of empirical macromodels, which in many ways is different from the quantification of parameters of a specification that has been theoretically derived. Both approaches have roles to play in macroeconomics. However, when a young person asks about the background needed for acquiring skills in the building of empirical macromodels, my answer is that knowledge and understanding of the methods that have been included in this book are an essential part of that background.

There are a number of people who have contributed, influenced and helped with this project, some over a long time period, others during the final stages of writing the book. As a PhD student, I learnt a lot from Harald Erik Goldstein and Anders Rygh Swensen, and that learning has continued during the years we have been colleagues at the University of Oslo. Another colleague who has had a huge long-term influence on this book is Gunnar Bårdsen at NTNU in Trondheim. Together, we formulated an approach to empirical model building that resulted in two operational macroeconometric models (for Sweden and for Norway). Gunnar and I have also co-authored two textbooks in Norwegian, and it goes without saying that the experience from writing those two books has been important for this book project.

Talking about actual macroeconometric model building: Even longer back in time, in the mid 1980s, a modelling group led by Eilev S. Jansen was formed in Norges Bank [The Norwegian Central Bank]. I was lucky to become a team member, and learnt a lot, not least through the group's contacts with the international research and modelling community.

A number of people have helped with improving the manuscript at different stages. Eilev has read the whole manuscript, and has contributed a lot. Other colleagues and students have read longer or shorter parts of the text, and have delivered valuable corrections, comments and advice — thanks to André K. Anundsen, Gunnar Bårdsen, Bjørnar Drejer, Fernanda Winger Eggen, Marte Marie Frisell, Harald Erik Goldstein, Malin Jensen, Kjersti-Gro Lindquist, Markus Sageng Gyene, Anders Rygh Swensen, Genaro Sucarrat, Alexander Sanner Skage, Mikkel M. Walbekken. Finally, I would also like to express my thanks to V. Vishnu Mohan and Sylvia Koh at World Scientific for excellent work with the typesetting and final preparation of the book, and to David Sharp for initiating the project.

The errors that remain, even after all this effort, are my own responsibility. For corrections, additional exercises, and access to the datasets, please visit the book's website: http://normetrics.no/dynamic-econometrics-for-empirical-macroeconomic-modelling/.

The supplementary materials are hosted at the link: https://www.worldscientific.com/worldscibooks/10.1142/11479.

Veneli, 30 September 2018

About the Author

Ragnar Nymoen is a Professor in the Department of Economics at the University of Oslo. He has worked as an economist in the Research Department at Norges Bank, and has published papers in macroeconomics and econometrics. Nymoen teaches econometrics at the bachelor, master and Ph.D. levels.

Contents

Chapter 1

Introduction to Dynamic Macroeconometrics

In this chapter, we illustrate several typical properties of dynamic systems by the use of two simple and well-known economic theoretical models: the cobweb model and a textbook macromodel of the Keynesian type. Several concepts which play central roles in the book are illustrated with the aid of the example models. Those concepts include dynamic solution, stability and instability of solutions, equilibrium correction, exogenous variables and dynamic responses to shocks. The chapter ends with an overview of the book.

1.1. Introduction

One hallmark of macroeconomic systems is that the adjustment to a shock (i.e., impulse) spans several time periods. Using terminology invented by the Norwegian economist Ragnar Frisch, whose contributions defined macrodynamics as a branch of economics, we can speak of *impulses* to the macroeconomic system that are *propagated* by the system's internal mechanisms into effects that last for several periods after the occurrence of the shock.[1]

Because dynamic behaviour is an important feature of the real-world macroeconomy as we measure it, a dynamic approach is needed both when the purpose is forecasting, and when the objective is to analyze the effects

[1]Notably, one of Frisch's influential publications was titled "*Propagation Problems and Impulse Problems in Dynamic Economics*" (Frisch, 1933). Frisch's contributions to dynamic theory began even earlier, in Frisch (1929), and in the form of influential lectures in USA (see Bjerkholt and Qin, 2011).

of changes in economic policies. Hence, both fiscal and monetary policies are now guided by dynamic models.

Consider, for example, the use of monetary policy in economic activity regulation, with the central bank sight deposit rate, i.e., the interest rate on banks' deposits in the central bank, as the policy instrument. It is interesting to note that no central bank seems to believe in an immediate and strong effect on the rate of inflation after a change in their interest rate. Instead, because of the many dynamic effects triggered by a change in the interest rate, they prepare themselves to wait a substantial amount of time before the change in the interest rate has a noticeable impact on inflation. The following statement from Norges Bank [The central bank of Norway] represents a typical central bank view:

> The effect of changes in interest rates on inflation occurs with a lag and may vary in intensity. In the time it takes for a change in interest rates to feed through, other factors will also have an impact resulting in changes in inflation and output.[2]

The models used in fiscal and monetary policy analysis need to be quite detailed, and with complex dynamics, in order to meet the requirements of the model users. However, to start studying dynamic econometrics in a systematic way, we can use much simpler models. In this introductory chapter, we look at the *cobweb model*, which illustrates several properties of dynamics that we will meet again later in the book. Section 1.2 presents the cobweb model and its dynamics. In Section 1.3, that model is used to draw the distinction between stable and unstable dynamics, which is important in all system analysis. Two other concepts that are central in the book, *stationary state* and *equilibrium correction*, can also be defined with the use of the cobweb model, see Section 1.4.

The dynamics in Sections 1.2–1.4 is of the deterministic type. However, to make our models applicable to real-world data, we need to include random variables, which we do in Section 1.5, which leads to a simple example of estimation with *time series data* generated by the cobweb model, see Section 1.6.

An attractive property of dynamic models is that they generate the kind of *autocorrelation* that we observe in real-world time series data. Loosely defined, autocorrelated variables are to a certain degree predictable from

[2]Norges Bank's web page on monetary policy. Copied 3rd November, 2016.

their own past. The cobweb model generates the so-called *negative* autocorrelation, while many macroeconomic variables are dominated by *positive* autocorrelation. In Section 1.7, we use a macroeconomic model of the Keynesian type to illustrate positive autocorrelation. At the same time, this provides an example of an open system (of equations), where there are non-modelled, or exogenous, variables.

Section 1.8 gives a brief introduction to the concepts of correlation, regression, exogeneity and causal effect, which are all central in macroeconometrics. The chapter ends with an outline of the content of the book.

1.2. Cobweb Model Dynamics

Our first example of a dynamic model is of partial equilibrium in a single product market. Let P_t denote the price prevailing in the market in time period t, and let Q_t denote equilibrium demand and supply in period t. The model consists of the demand equation (1.1) and the supply equation (1.2):

$$Q_t = aP_t + b, \qquad a < 0, \tag{1.1}$$

$$Q_t = cP_{t-1} + d, \quad c > 0, \tag{1.2}$$

where (1.1) is a static demand relationship: If the price is increased by one (unit), the demand is reduced by an amount a in the same period. Hence, time plays no essential role in this part of the model: the short-run response of demand with respect to a price increase is the same as the long-run response. However, on the supply side, time does play an essential role: if there is a price increase in period t, the supply does not adjust with the amount c before period $t+1$.

In terms of economic interpretation, equation (1.2) may represent a case of production and delivery lags so that today's supply depends on the price obtained in the previous period. The classic example is from agricultural economics, where the whole supply, for example, of pork or of wheat is replenished from one year to the next.[3]

A different economic interpretation (see, e.g., Evans and Honkapoja, 2001) is that (1.2) captures that the underlying behaviour of suppliers may be influenced by expectations. We then imagine that underlying (1.2) is

[3]For a concise textbook presentation, see Sydsæter *et al.* (2008, Section 11.2).

another relationship, namely,

$$Q_t = cP_t^e + d,$$

where P_t^e denotes the expected price in period t. If we assume that information about period t is either unavailable or is very unreliable in period $t-1$, when expectations are formed, suppliers have to set $P_t^e = P_{t-1}$, which brings us to the dynamic supply function (1.2).

According to Frisch, equation (1.2) clearly qualifies as a *dynamic model* of the supplied quantity since "one and the same equation contains entities that refer to different time periods", namely Q_t and P_{t-1}. What about the model as a whole, i.e., the system given by the static equation (1.1) and the dynamic equation (1.2)? Is it a static or a dynamic *system*? To answer this question, we consider Figure 1.1.

In Figure 1.1, the downward sloping line labelled D represents the (initial) position of the demand equation (1.1). However, care must be taken when interpreting the supply curve. To understand why, consider the quantity supplied in, for example, period $t = 10$ when we assume that $t = 9$ represents a stationary initial state. By stationary (or equilibrium) state, we

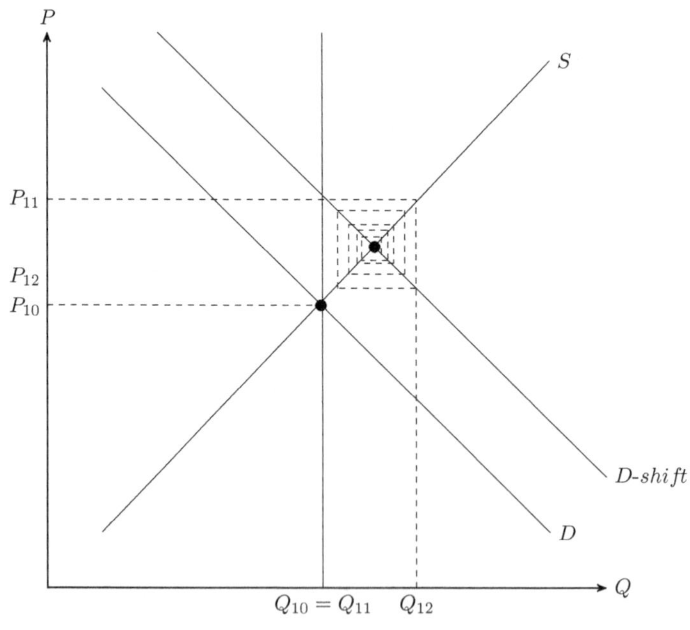

Figure 1.1. Deterministic dynamics: Cobweb model.

mean that both quantity and price have been constant for several periods, hence, for example, $P_9 = P_8 = \cdots = P_{-1}$ and $Q_9 = Q_8 = \cdots = Q_{-1}$.

According to (1.2), supply in period 10 is given by

$$Q_{10} = cP_9 + d,$$

since supply is a function of the predetermined price P_9 (not of the price P_{10}). The supply in period 10, which we can call the short-run supply curve, is therefore completely inelastic with respect to the price in period 10.

The inelastic short-run supply curve is indicated by the vertical line from Q_{10} in the figure. The long-run supply curve is defined for the stationary situation characterized by $P = P_t = P_{t-1}$ and $Q = Q_t = Q_{t-1}$, and is drawn as the upward sloping line labelled S in the figure. Hence, while on the demand side of the market, the derivative of Q with respect to price is the parameter a both in the short-run and in the long-run, there are two different supply derivatives: The short-run derivative is zero, while the long-run derivative is c.

We next turn to the market system's response to a shift in demand which we assume occurs in period 11, represented by the dashed demand schedule labelled *D-shift*. Because of the dynamics of supply, it matters a lot whether the demand shock is permanent or temporary. We first assume that the shock is permanent, and leave the analysis of a temporary shock as an exercise. Even though demand increases in period 11, and because of the inelasticity of supply, the quantity traded in the market in period 11 does not change. Hence, $Q_{11} = Q_{10}$, but the market clearing price increases from P_{10} to P_{11}, i.e., from the old intersection point to the period 1 intersection point between the new demand curve (i.e., *D-shift*) and the short-run supply curve.

The price and quantity pair (P_{11}, Q_{11}) does not, however, represent a new stationary state. Instead, in period 2, the supply will have increased, according to the short-run supply function. With a downward sloping demand curve, P_{12} must therefore be lower than P_{11}. In the example in Figure 1.1, with the slopes being what they are there, P_{12} is nevertheless higher than the initial price, P_{10}. The consequence of the price reduction from period 11 to period 12 is that in period 13, the supply is reduced compared to period 12, and the price rises again. As the figure indicates, the dotted lines that connect the sequence of price and quantity pairs make out a cobweb pattern, and we can imagine that the dynamic adjustment process continues until the new stationary state is reached as indicated by the intersection between the (long run) S-schedule and the *D-shift* line.

1.3. Stable and Unstable Dynamics

With the aid of computer simulation, we can generate data according to the cobweb model, and graph the data in time plots. In Figure 1.2, the two first panels show the time plots of price ("Price dynamics" in the figure) and quantity ("Quantity dynamics") which correspond to the cobweb figure. Initially, the system is assumed to be in a stationary state, and the two plots therefore commence as horizontal lines. In period 11, the demand gets a positive shift, illustrated in the last panel of the figure, and this triggers the dynamic responses in the two first panels. We see that both the price graph and the quantity graph are oscillating in the periods after the demand shift. In time series analysis and econometrics, this kind of erratic behaviour of time series variables is referred to as *negative autocorrelation.*

The solutions shown as time graphs were obtained from the so-called *final form equations* associated with the dynamic model (see Wallis, 1977). A final form equation expresses a current endogenous variable in terms of exogenous variables and lags of itself, but of no other endogenous variable. In Exercise 1.1, you are invited to show that (1.1) and (1.2) imply the two

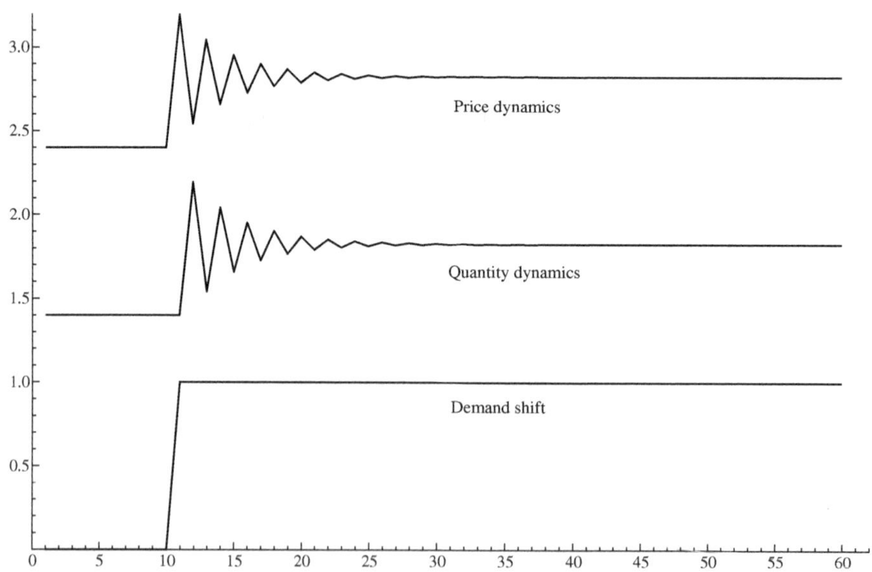

Figure 1.2. Time plots of price and quantity variables that are generated by computer simulation of the cobweb model.

final form equations:

$$P_t = \phi_1 P_{t-1} + \frac{d - b_t}{a}, \tag{1.3}$$

$$Q_t = \phi_1 Q_{t-1} + \frac{da - cb_{t-1}}{a}, \tag{1.4}$$

where the *autoregressive* parameter ϕ_1 is defined as

$$\phi_1 = \frac{c}{a}, \tag{1.5}$$

and b_t, is defined to be b_0 for $t = 1, 2, \ldots, 10$, and $b_1 > b_0$ for $t = 11, 12, \ldots, \infty$.

By looking at the second terms on the right-hand sides of the equality signs, we see that the final equations capture that when b_t shifts, the price is affected first in the same period as the shock. The increase in quantity happens with one period lag due to the delayed response of supply to the market price changes.

In terms of mathematics, equations (1.3) and (1.4) are two first-order linear difference equations (see Sydsæter *et al.*, 2008, Chapter 11). The second terms on the right-hand sign of the two equations are called the *non-homogeneous* parts of the difference equations. Because of the way we have defined b_t, both are functions of time. The first terms in the two equations, $\phi_1 P_{t-1}$ and $\phi_1 Q_{t-1}$, are the *homogeneous* parts of the equations.

Note that the autoregressive coefficient of the homogeneous parts is the same in the two equations. This means that the dynamic properties of P_t and Q_t depend on one single ratio, namely, the ratio of the two slope coefficients, $\frac{c}{a}$. In Chapter 3, where the theory of difference equations is reviewed, it is shown that the condition

$$-1 < \phi_1 < 1 \Leftrightarrow -1 < \frac{c}{a} < 1 \tag{1.6}$$

implies global asymptotic stability, which means that the system consisting of P_t of and Q_t reaches a stationary state from any given initial condition (starting point) as t grows towards infinity.

A stationary state for P_t can be denoted by P^*, and is a parameter that does not depend on time. Stationary states (i.e., equilibria) generally depend on the non-homogeneous part of the final equation, as Figures 1.1 and 1.2 illustrate. In Figure 1.2, P_t and Q_t exhibit dampened oscillations. The oscillations are due to the negative sign of the autoregressive parameter, $\frac{c}{a} < 0$. The dampening is due to the parameter values used in the computer simulation of the model solution, which were chosen to be $c = 1$ and $a = -1.3$. Hence, consistent with Figure 1.1, the supply schedule has a steeper upward slope than the demand curve's negative slope.

There is nothing (in economic theory) hindering that the demand curve has the steeper slope. In that case, with $\phi_1 = \frac{c}{a} < -1$, the system will not be globally asymptotically stable. The dynamic process is unstable, and the oscillations are not dampened; instead, the fluctuations will increase with time as we move away from the period when the shock hit. If $\phi_1 < -1$, the effects of a shock increase with time. Therefore, it is the custom to refer to $\phi_1 < -1$ as the case of *explosive* solution paths. Equation (1.6) implies that $\phi_1 > 1$ also gives rise to explosive solution paths (but without the oscillations). Positive ϕ_1 values are not economically meaningful in the simple cobweb model, but in other models, positive autocorrelation is a typical property. Below, we will look at a macromodel which has $\phi_1 > 0$ as an implication, and where $\phi_1 > 1$ is a possibility.

It remains to be seen what happens to the dynamics of the cobweb model when $\frac{c}{a} = -1$, i.e., the slope of the demand curve is the same as the slope of the long-run supply curve (but of course with opposite signs). In this case, with $\phi_1 - 1$, the dynamic response that follows after a shock is characterized by non-dampened oscillations. Hence, although the dynamic response is not explosive, it is still *unstable.*

The other unstable value that the autoregressive parameter can take is $\phi_1 = 1$, but this value is ruled out by the economic interpretation of the cobweb model. However, for other models, the economically meaningful "candidate" for instability is $\phi_1 = 1$.

1.4. Stationary State and Equilibrium Correction

We can seek a solution where $Q_t = Q^*$ for all t, and $P_t = P^*$ for all t. Such a solution must satisfy $P_{t+1} = P_t = P^*$ and is only possible when $b_t = b_{t-1} = b$. It must also be a solution of (1.1) and (1.2), hence

$$Q^* = aP^* + b,$$

$$Q^* = cP^* + d,$$

which can be solved for the static equilibrium (or stationary) state (Q^*, P^*) as

$$Q^* = \frac{ad - bc}{a - c}, \tag{1.7}$$

$$P^* = \frac{d - b}{a - c}. \tag{1.8}$$

Subject to the stability condition (1.6), we can obtain an equation that shows how $\{Q^*, P^*\}$ are interpretable as attractors to the changes in P_t and Q_t. We use the final equation for P_t, and substitute the expression for ϕ_1:

$$P_t = \frac{c}{a}P_{t-1} + \frac{d-b_t}{a}.$$

Add and subtract P_{t-1} on the right-hand side of the equation:

$$\begin{aligned}
P_t &= P_{t-1} + \left(\frac{c}{a} - 1\right) P_{t-1} + \frac{d-b_t}{a} \\
&= P_{t-1} + \left(\frac{c}{a} - 1\right) \left[P_{t-1} + \frac{1}{\left(\frac{c}{a} - 1\right)} \left(\frac{d-b_t}{a}\right)\right] \\
&= P_{t-1} + \left(\frac{c}{a} - 1\right) \left[P_{t-1} - \frac{a}{a-c} \left(\frac{d-b_t}{a}\right)\right] \\
&= P_{t-1} + \left(\frac{c}{a} - 1\right) \left[P_{t-1} - \left(\frac{d-b_t}{a-c}\right)\right].
\end{aligned} \tag{1.9}$$

Finally, if $b_t = b$ for all t, we can use the definition of P^* to write the final equation as

$$P_t = P_{t-1} + \left(\frac{c}{a} - 1\right) [P_{t-1} - P^*].$$

By using ΔP_t to represent the change in P_t from period $t-1$ to period t, i.e., $\Delta P_t =: P_t - P_{t-1}$, we can write the final form equation as

$$\Delta P_t = (\phi_1 - 1)[P_{t-1} - P^*], \tag{1.10}$$

which is an *equilibrium correction model* equation, usually known by the acronym ECM.

Below, we will reserve the term ECM for the case of stable dynamics. In the stable case of $(\phi_1 - 1) > -2$, an initial positive disequilibrium $(P_{t-1} - P^* > 0)$ will lead to $\Delta P_t < 0$. The price fall is larger in magnitude than the deviation from equilibrium, which leads to $P_t - P^* < 0$, and hence $\Delta P_{t+1} > 0$, and so on. The signs of both the disequilibrium terms, and the price changes will change in each period. However, due to the stability assumption, $(\phi_1 - 1) > -2$, the oscillations become dampened over time.

The same steps applied to the final form equation for quantity gives

$$\Delta Q_t = (\phi_1 - 1)\left[Q_{t-1} - \left(\frac{ad - b_{t-1}c}{a - c}\right)\right], \tag{1.11}$$

and, for the case when there is no change in b

$$\Delta Q_t = (\phi_1 - 1)\,[Q_{t-1} - Q^*], \tag{1.12}$$

showing that there is an equilibrium correction equation also for Q_t with the same equilibrium correction coefficient as in the ECM for P_t.

1.5. Random Fluctuations

So far, we have analyzed deterministic dynamics of the type often used in dynamic economics, with the difference that we have used discrete time, whereas continuous time is common in theoretical analysis. However, the hallmark of econometric models is that endogenous economic variables are modelled as random (i.e., stochastic) variables. In the context of the cobweb model, this entails that we introduce two random shocks: ϵ_{dt} (demand) and ϵ_{st} (supply):

$$Q_t = aP_t + b_t + \epsilon_{dt}, \qquad a < 0, \tag{1.13}$$

$$Q_t = cP_{t-1} + d + \epsilon_{st}, \quad c > 0. \tag{1.14}$$

The random variables $(\epsilon_{dt}, \epsilon_{st})$ are typically specified with zero means, and with fixed variances. It is the custom to refer to (1.13) and (1.14) as structural equations, and to assume that the two structural disturbances are uncorrelated.

A *reduced form equation* expresses a current endogenous variable in terms of exogenous variables, and of lags of itself and of other endogenous variables. The reduced form of (1.13) and (1.14) is not difficult to find. Equation (1.14) is already a reduced form equation. The other equation is obtained by re-normalizing (1.13) on P_t and then substituting Q_t with the right-hand side of (1.14):

$$P_t = \frac{c}{a}P_{t-1} + \frac{d - b_t}{a} + \frac{\epsilon_{st} - \epsilon_{dt}}{a}, \quad a < 0, \tag{1.15}$$

$$Q_t = cP_{t-1} + d + \epsilon_{st}, \quad c > 0. \tag{1.16}$$

The current period price variable P_t depends on the deterministic demand shock (b_t) and the two current stochastic shocks, ϵ_{st} and ϵ_{dt}. The current quantity, however, only depends on a single within period random shock, namely, the unpredictable supply variation ϵ_{st}. These are the consequences of the adjustment lag in supply, the main economic behavioural assumption of the cobweb model.

The final form equations can be found by following the same steps as for the deterministic version of the model. They become

$$P_t = \phi_1 P_{t-1} + \frac{d - b_t}{a} + \frac{\epsilon_{st} - \epsilon_{dt}}{a}, \tag{1.17}$$

$$Q_t = \phi_1 Q_{t-1} + \frac{da - cb_{t-1}}{a} + \frac{a\epsilon_{st} - c\epsilon_{dt-1}}{a}, \tag{1.18}$$

with notation $\phi_1 = \frac{c}{a}$ for the common autoregressive coefficient in the same way as for the deterministic final form above. In Figure 1.3, we have added the price and quantity dynamics with random-shocks to the graphs with the deterministic solution in Figure 1.2. The stochastic solutions are shown as dashed lines, while the deterministic ones are shown as solid lines. We see that the random shocks add to the volatility of the series. However, the deterministic oscillations dominate in the first periods after the demand shift in period 11. As the system moves away from the period of the demand

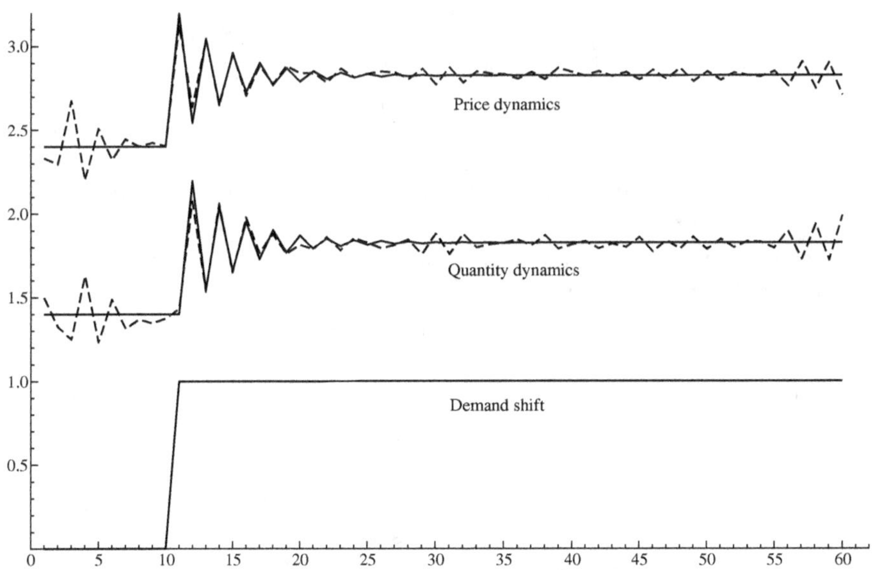

Figure 1.3. Time plots of stochastic and deterministic price and quantity variables generated by computer simulation of the cobweb model.

shock, the effects of the random shocks gradually dominate the fluctuations in the graphs.

1.6. Estimation of Cobweb Model Dynamics

We can use the data plotted in Figure 1.3 to give a first example of the use of ordinary least squares (OLS) to estimate the coefficients of a dynamic model equation. The graph in the first panel of the figure is the time plot of 59 computer-generated observations of P_t, from period 2 to period 60. Assume that we did not know what the value of ϕ_1 used in the data generation was. Can OLS be used to estimate ϕ_1 with a reasonable degree of precision?

To find the answer, we can formulate (1.15) as an regression model equation, for example, as

$$P_t = \beta_0 + \beta_1 P_{t-1} + \beta_2 S11_t + u_t, \tag{1.19}$$

where β_0, β_1 and β_2 are coefficients to be estimated, and u_t is the error term of the regression model. $S11_t$ is a so-called step-dummy (or step-indicator) which captures the shift in the demand function. Hence, $S11_t$ is defined as

$$S11_t = \begin{cases} 1 & \text{if } t \geq 11, \\ 0 & \text{otherwise.} \end{cases} \tag{1.20}$$

OLS estimation of (1.19) by the use of the 59 observations gives

$$P_t = \underset{(0.053)}{-0.755}\, P_{t-1} + \underset{(0.128)}{4.22} + \underset{(0.027)}{0.745}\, S11_t, \tag{1.21}$$

where the numbers in parentheses are standard errors of the estimated coefficients (see Exercise 1.3).

The slope parameter values used in the data generation were $a = -1.3$ and $c = 1$, implying that the true value of the autoregressive parameter is $\phi_1 = -0.769$. Hence, there is an estimation inaccuracy, but it is only minor in this case.

However, it is far from obvious that OLS should work this well. One reason for being sceptical towards the estimation is that the regressor P_{t-1} cannot be exogenous in the sense that you know from introductory econometrics. In the main model taught in introductory courses, often called the "IID cross-section model", the regressor is uncorrelated with *all* error terms, and that assumption drives the result that the OLS estimator is unbiased (see Stock and Watson, 2012, Chapter 14). In the final form equation of P_t, the situation is different. Although P_{t-1} may be uncorrelated with current and future disturbances u_{t+j} ($j = 0, 1, 2, \ldots$), it cannot possibly be uncorrelated with past disturbances, i.e., u_{t-j}, $j = 0, 1, 2, \ldots$. This follows once we recognize that time flows in one direction from past to present. Therefore, all the shocks that have occurred so far in history must necessarily be "baked into" P_{t-1}, and as a consequence P_{t-1} is correlated with the past regression errors.

The partial dependency between P_{t-1} and the regressions disturbances defines P_{t-1} as a *predetermined variable.* This concept, which characterizes the lagged regressor as a hybrid, partly endogenous, partly exogenous, is central for understanding the possibilities and limitations of estimating dynamic econometric models like (1.21).

Predeterminedness implies that the OLS estimators may be consistent. Consistency of an estimator means that as the number of time periods in the sample increases, the distribution of the estimator gets more and more tightly centred around the true parameter value. Asymptotically (i.e., for an infinitely long sample), OLS estimators are therefore unbiased even though they are biased for any finite sample length. For models like (1.21), the OLS estimators of the coefficients will be consistent if and only if the equation disturbances are not autocorrelated. In the data generation, no autocorrelation was secured by generating the 59 error terms as independent standard normal variables. Hence, a possible explanation of the small estimation error for ϕ_1 that we have observed in the numerical example is that the sample size is large enough to allow the consistency property to "shine through" in the estimation results.

Later in the book, we will review closely the statistical theory that underlies why we have reason to be optimistic about the possibility of estimating the coefficients of dynamic models. Also, why the condition about no autocorrelation in the error term (often called no residual autocorrelation) is crucial.

1.7. Business Cycle Dynamics

The cobweb model's negative autocorrelation, with dominant short-run oscillations for both price and quantity, can be relevant for markets and sectors of the economy where supply is inelastic in the short run. As mentioned above, markets for agricultural products are examples of this, although in modern economies supply can be replenished by trade also for perishable products. A market which has huge macroeconomic influence, and where short-run supply is inelastic, is the housing market. Housing supply is necessarily fixed in the short run (it is a stock), but net housing demand can change a great deal, and rapidly. The implication is that housing prices have a potential for volatility. Another example is the market for foreign exchange under a floating exchange rate regime. Since the net supply of domestic currency is fixed, day-to-day variations in the net demand will determine the exchange rate (Rødseth, 2000, Chapter 1)

However, in markets for manufactured goods and for services, short-run fluctuations in output are mainly demand-driven, and prices follow relatively smooth time paths (due to mark-up price setting). In those parts of the economy, positive autocorrelation in output will be more typical than negative autocorrelation.

As an illustration of positive autocorrelation at the macrolevel, we consider a stylized model of the Keynesian type for a closed economy. The equations of the model are

$$C_t = a + b\,\mathrm{GDP}_t + cC_{t-1} + \epsilon_{Ct}, \tag{1.22}$$

$$\mathrm{GDP}_t = C_t + J_t, \tag{1.23}$$

$$J_t = J^* + \epsilon_{Jt}, \tag{1.24}$$

where the symbols are defined as follows:

- C_t is the private consumption in period t.
- GDP_t and J_t represent gross domestic product, and capital formation (i.e., investment). The three variables are defined in real terms.
- a–c are parameters.
- ϵ_{Ct} and ϵ_{Jt} represent random shocks to consumption and investment with zero means (i.e., mathematical expectation). For simplicity, we assume that they are uncorrelated.

If $c = 0$ is imposed as a parameter restriction in the consumption function (1.22), the model becomes a static macromodel. However, it is reasonable to assume $c > 0$, as it is realistic that private consumption is smoother than income, at least for annual data, which is what we have in mind. The parameter b is the short-run propensity to consume. It is non-negative by assumption, i.e., $b \geq 0$.

Finally, (1.23) is the general budget equation, and (1.24) says, very simply, that J_t, representing investment (capital formation), is fluctuating around the equilibrium value J^*.

The final form equation for private consumption becomes (Exercise 1.4)

$$C_t = \frac{c}{1-b} C_{t-1} + \frac{1}{1-b} \left[a + bJ^* + \epsilon_{Ct} + b\epsilon_{Jt} \right]. \tag{1.25}$$

We see that

$$\phi_1 = \frac{c}{1-b} \tag{1.26}$$

is the autoregressive coefficient in this final equation.

With $c > 0$ and $0 < b < 1$, it is implied that $\phi_1 > 0$, and private consumption is therefore positively autocorrelated.

In the same manner as for negative autocorrelation, positive autocorrelation can be stable, unstable or explosive. As seen from (1.26), stable dynamics requires $c < 1 - b$, which is not implied by the assumptions about consumer behaviour that we stated above. As the cobweb model also illustrated, dynamic stability is a system property, which requires system thinking and system analysis.

If $c \geq 1 - b$, dynamics will be unstable ($c = 1 - b$), or explosive ($c > 1 - b$). With explosive dynamics, we can imagine that consumption is in an initial stationary state, but as soon as there is a small disturbance, consumption will start to move away from that starting value. Unlike the cobweb case, the explosive path will not contain a deterministic oscillating component, but move steadily away from the initial value.

Figure 1.4 shows the time plots of the three variables of the model. The time series were computer-generated, and we have used parameter values $b = 0.25$ and $c = 0.65$, so that the plots illustrate stable dynamics. We see that the volatility of the investments series is clearly reflected in the time plot of GDP. In fact, since J_t is autonomous and fluctuates randomly above and below $J^* = 40$, the only "source of" positive autocorrelation in the two simultaneously determined variables GDP_t and C_t is the smoothing of consumption, which is clearly visible in the time plot of C_t.

Returning to the theoretical model, the stationary state is obtained by solving (1.22)–(1.24) for the case where all shocks are set to zero and $C_t = C_{t-1} = C^*$. Hence, we find expressions for C^*, GDP^* and J^* from the static equation system:

$$C^* = a + b\,\text{GDP}^* + cC^*, \tag{1.27}$$

$$\text{GDP}^* = C^* + J^*, \tag{1.28}$$

$$J = J^*. \tag{1.29}$$

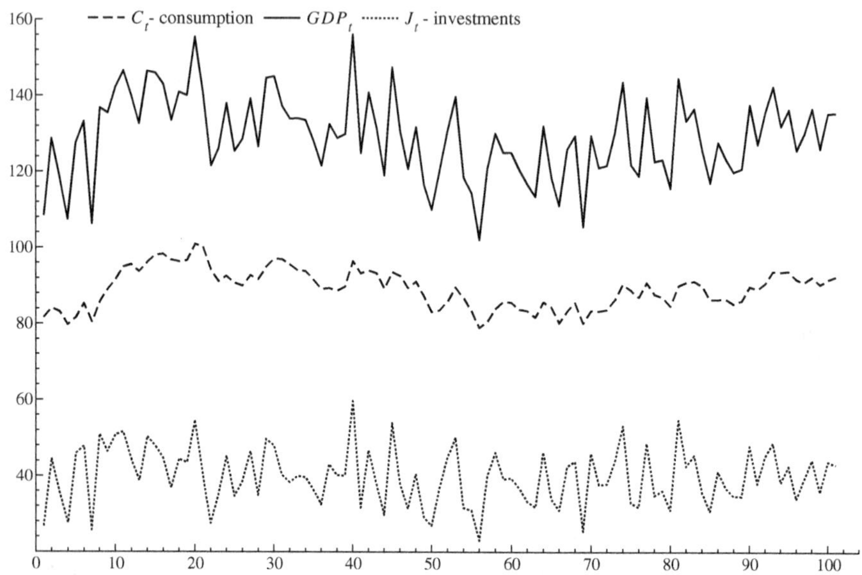

Figure 1.4. Time plots of computer-generated data for the variables of the Keynesian model (1.22)–(1.24).

The solution for C^* can be expressed as

$$C^* = \frac{a + bJ^*}{(1 - b - c)}. \tag{1.30}$$

This solution is only meaningful when the denominator is strictly positive, which is implied by positive and stable autocorrelation:

$$0 < \phi_1 < 1 \Longrightarrow 0 < 1 - b - c < 1. \tag{1.31}$$

In the case of stable dynamics, the final form equation for C_t can be reexpressed as

$$\Delta C_t = (\phi_1 - 1)\left[C_{t-1} - C^*\right] + \frac{\epsilon_{Ct} + b\epsilon_{Jt}}{1 - b}, \tag{1.32}$$

which has an equilibrium correction interpretation, but without the "overshooting" that characterized the cobweb model: Since $(\phi_1 - 1)$ is positive and less than one in absolute value, the correction taking place in period t is less than the disequilibrium in period $t - 1$.

Box 1.1. RBC and autocorrelated output-gap

Other macrodynamic models can have completely different theoretical interpretations than the Keynesian. Appendix A contains a Real Business Cycle (RBC) model, and a simulated series for the (log of) GDP minus trend, the so-called output-gap.

As noted, in the generation of the time series plotted in Figure 1.4, we have chosen parameters $b = 0.25$ (short-run marginal propensity to consume), and $c = 0.65$ (habit formation). The calibrated autoregressive coefficient ϕ_1 is therefore 0.714, meaning that on average one-third of the disequilibrium from last period becomes corrected in the current time period.

1.8. Causality, Correlation and Invariance

Some introductory books in econometrics liken econometric estimation with laboratory studies where the focus is on how a treatment, measured by variation in a variable X, causes an effect or response, in a variable Y. The research interest is then on the causal mechanism, from X to Y: However, unless the variation in X is carefully controlled in a laboratory experiment, the estimation of the causal mechanism needs to be based on much more than "mere" data and statistical methods. Specifically, as the reader may be well aware of, correlation alone cannot distinguish between cause and effect. With reference to Figure 1.5, if we imagine a dataset with observations of Y and X, and that we calculate the squared empirical correlation coefficient r^2_{YX}, that number can be close to 1, but that does not imply that X caused Y. Instead, Y may have caused X as illustrated in Figure 1.6. The correlation coefficient r_{YX} is the same in the two cases. However, the slope coefficients of the two regressions corresponding to Figures 1.5 and 1.6 are not identical.

By solving Exercise 1.6, you are reminded that for the two-variable systems in Figures 1.5 and 1.6, the relationship between the two slope

Figure 1.5. Two variable system with (one-way) causation.

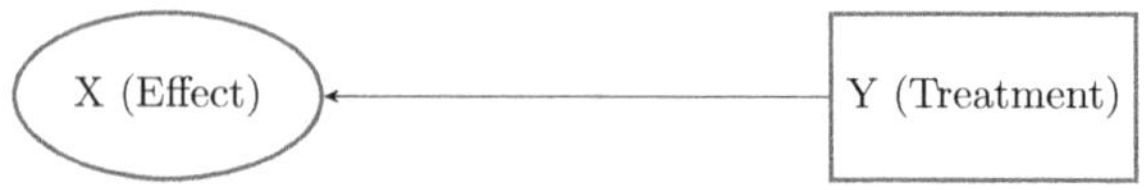

Figure 1.6. Two-variable system with reverse causation. r_{YX} is invariant to the direction of causation.

coefficients that we can estimate is

$$b = b' \frac{s_X^2}{s_Y^2}, \tag{1.33}$$

where b corresponds to Figure 1.5 and b' corresponds to Figure 1.6. s_Y and s_X are the empirical (sample) standard error deviations (i.e., $s_Y = \sqrt{s_Y^2} = \sqrt{1/T \sum_{t=1}^{T} (Y_i - \overline{Y})^2}$, for Y). We use the symbol T for the sample size (number of periods).

By itself, the fact that the estimated numbers for b and b' are different is of little help when it comes to settling the causality issue. However, it seems reasonable to require of our tentative causal relation that it remains more or less unchanged when other parts of the system undergo changes. Without that kind of *invariance*, the relationship will be of little value when we attempt to use it to predict the effects of changes, see Box 1.2.

Box 1.2. Invariance and persistence of economic relationships
The importance of judging the degree of persistence over time, and the invariance with respect to shocks, of relationships between economic variables, was one of the many fundamental issues that were raised and tackled, in principle, in the treatise "The Probability Approach in Econometrics", by Haavelmo (1944); see Morgan (1990), Bjerkholt (2007), Hendry (2018) among others. Chapter 2 of the treaty was titled "The degree of permanence of economic laws", which also introduced the term *autonomy* in this context. Much later, invariance and autonomy became integrated in the conceptual and theoretical developments related to the role of exogeneity in econometric models, see Chapter 8.

With the invariance requisite brought into the picture, equation (1.33) points to one interesting possibility: namely that at most one of the two regression coefficients is stable (invariant to shocks), when the ratio $\frac{s_X^2}{s_Y^2}$ changes. If b is invariant in this way, b' cannot be invariant, and vice versa. Hence, invariance can be investigated empirically over a sample that contains shocks. This is at least something: If invariance in "one direction" can be established over a sample where there has been interventions (i.e., policy changes), there is some reason to hope that the invariance may also hold for the next change that we want to estimate the effect of. Realistically speaking, relationships between economic variables cannot be invariant to all types of shocks. Invariance is a partial and relative property. Econometric relationships and models are products of civilization, and as such, they will be disrupted sooner or later. Nevertheless, invariance (partial as it may be) is a valuable property of an econometric relationship.

Correlation, regression and causation have been on the minds of statisticians, econometricians and philosophers since the start of the previous century. The initial position may have been that causality *was* correlation. But the statisticians Karl Pearson and George Udny Yule showed that there were important exceptions. The most important ones are called *nonsense regression* and *spurious correlation*. Yule's (1926) nonsense regression has become better known among time series econometricians as *spurious regression* following the influential work of Granger and Newbold (1974). It denotes the case where standard tests for the existence of a relationships are used in data situations where they do not apply. As a consequence, the tests may strongly indicate a relationship which is not in the data. Spurious regression is a main theme in Chapters 9 and 10.

While the spurious regression phenomenon is due to a serious underestimation of the probability of Type-I error when testing the null hypothesis of no-relationship, spurious correlation is about interpreting a relationship that does in fact exist. Spurious correlation can be explained by comparing Figure 1.5 with Figure 1.7, where we have introduced a third variable, Z. If the reality is that both X and Y are influenced by Z, the correlation

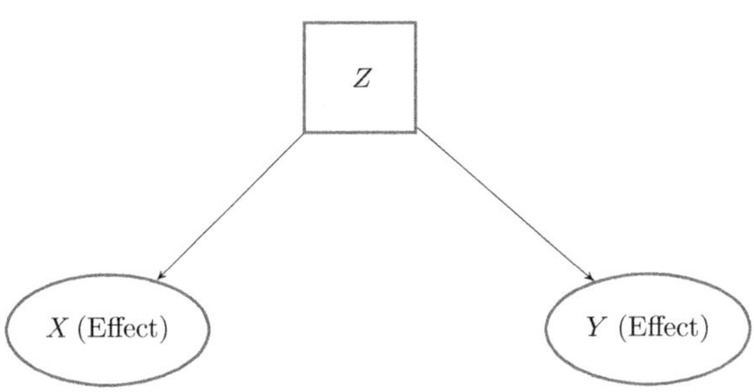

Figure 1.7. Spurious correlation: Two variables with one common cause: omission of Z may lead to wrong conclusion about causation between Y and X.

between X and Y in Figure 1.5 can be called spurious: that correlation reflects that the two variables have a common cause, not that there exists an independent relationship between them. When the situation is as shown in Figure 1.7, it leads nowhere to try to affect the Y variable by taking control over X. Instead, the key is to model the relationship between Z and Y, to become able to use it to make predictions about how Y responds to a change in Z.

Box 1.3. Find out more about causality and exogenity
Aldrich (1995) is a very readable journal article about Pearson's and Yules' contributions to correlation analysis. Causality in macroeconomics is treated in depth in the book by Hoover (2001). A modern philosopher who has written about causality and exogeneity in economics is Cartwright (1999, 2007). Judea Pearl is a central figure in the causality debate, see his "Causality blog": http://causality.cs.ucla.edu/blog. Exogeneity is the topic of Chapter 8 below.

Later in the book, we will present statistical methods that allow us to analyze the degree of invariance of empirical relationships, and in some cases the methodology makes us able to reach a conclusion about the direction of causality within the realms of the models that we are investigating. However, in macroeconomics, it is just as important to be able to analyze systems with two-way dependence (i.e., two-way causality), as depicted in Figure 1.8. Both the cobweb model and the macromodel above are examples of joint dependency between endogenous variables, and of dynamic forms of interdependency. For example, the dynamic responses to a demand shift

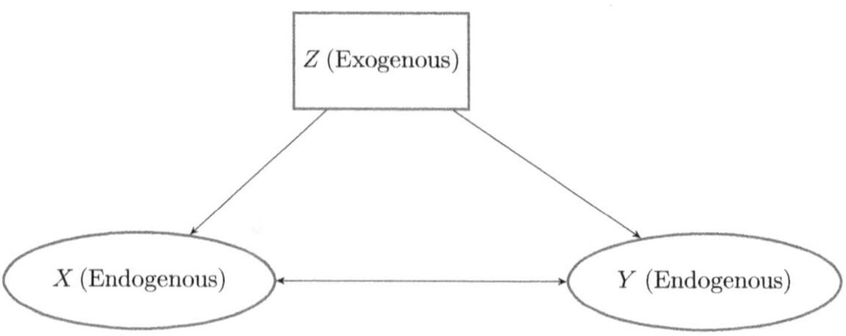

Figure 1.8. Mutual dependence.

in the cobweb model, which we discussed at the start of the chapter, can be interpreted as an example of change in the Z variable in Figure 1.8.

The Keynesian macroeconomic model above is another example of joint dependence since income depends on consumption and consumption depends on income in the same period. Hence, the joint dependence is represented by a simultaneous equations model (SEM). The exogenous variable J_t in the model is represented by Z in Figure 1.8.

In the same way as the term "cause" can take different meanings, and as the conditions for causal analysis can hold under some changes to the system (e.g., policies) and fail under others, there are several concepts and connotations of the meaning of "exogenous variable". When we study macroeconomic theory, "being exogenous" means that the variable in question is determined outside the model. The model is open in the sense that the number of equations is fewer than the number of variables.

Also, in econometrics, the concept of exogenous variable sometimes refers to being determined outside the model, but for some purposes we need to be more precise by using a relevant concept from a wider family of econometric exogeneity concepts, as explained in Chapter 8. Underlying these concepts is, however, the idea that a variable may be regarded as exogenous if we do not distort the answer to the research question we have posed by conditioning on that variable.

1.9. Overview of the Book

Econometrics as a field of knowledge is a combined discipline, as illustrated in Figure 1.9. It combines economic theory with mathematical statistics. Empirical econometric models in particular not only require data for specification and testing, but both producers and users of econometric models need to have knowledge about data sources, and of the main strengths and limitations of the measurement system.

With the exception of Chapter 2, where we review econometric background about models and estimation method for *cross-section data*, the data type that we have in mind in the book is *time series data*, where the variables are observed for several time periods. However, there are several concepts and methods that we cover, which may be of interest for researches who estimate models with the use of *panel data*, which combine cross-section variation and time series variation.

The statistical theory of stationary time series is well developed and is the foundation of applied time series analysis. It also gives the basis of

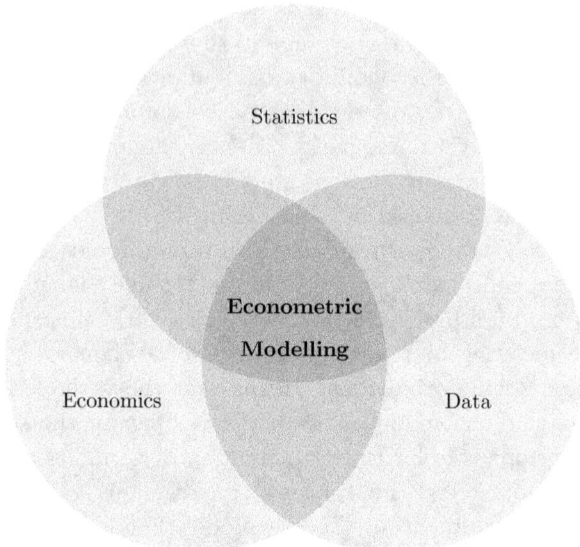

Figure 1.9. Illustration of Econometric Modelling as the intersection of the fields of statistical theory, economic theory and the information in observed data.

econometric models for stationary time series data. This basic theory is presented in Chapters 3 and 4. In Figure 1.9, it can be represented by the intersection between the area labelled Statistics, and the area labelled Economics. Applications of these models to real-world data, we can imagine as belonging to the intersection area labelled Econometric Modelling, where statistics, economics and data combine to become empirical econometric modelling.

Chapter 2 contains a review of the concepts and theory from statistics and econometrics that we assume that the reader is familiar with. That chapter covers, in a concise way, regression models and the estimation of structural equations estimated by instrumental variables. It also introduces matrix notation for econometric models. Chapter 3 is also a background chapter with a presentation of the necessary theory of linear difference equations.

Chapter 4 defines a stationary times series variable as a stochastic process which is mathematically expressed by a linear difference equation which is globally asymptotically stable. Although much of the basic concepts and theory can be learned from studying the simplest case, a first-order autoregressive model, AR(1), applied modelling requires higher order dynamics.

Chapters 5–7 cover the statistical and econometric analysis of stationary economic systems. These chapters contain the core econometric tools and results for building empirical econometric models of stationary systems of time series variables, both single equation models and multiple equation models. The vector autoregressive (VAR) system in Chapter 5 is both an important model in itself, and a basis for the econometric models in Chapter 6 (single equation models) and Chapter 7 (multiple equation models).

In Chapter 8, several important concepts of exogeneity are defined. Weak exogeneity is perhaps the fundamental concept, since without it, consistent estimation of parameters of interest is impossible. Most often weak exogeneity, characterizes a valid conditioning variable in the regression model, but can also refer to a instrumental variable, and to a non-modelled variable in a multiple equation econometric model. Other concepts are relevant when the research objective is forecasting and policy analysis. Invariance, which was mentioned above, is a concept which is closely connected to exogeneity.

In Chapter 9, the theory is extended to non-stationary time series. There are two broad forms of non-stationarity, deterministic trends and unit-root non-stationarity. Deterministic non-stationarity includes, in addition to the (linear) time trend t, t^2 and higher order polynomials in t, and impulse indicator variables and step-indicator variables. Deterministic non-stationarity can be incorporated in the stationary framework of the earlier chapters, and, in practice, statistical inference is unaffected by this kind of non stationarity.

Non-stationarity due to unit-roots is another matter. Models with unit-roots are important since they are able to reproduce typical properties of real-world time series. However, the statistical inference theory is affected, notably when we test for relationships between independent unit-root non-stationary variables, i.e., the spurious regression problem which was briefly noted above.

Chapter 10 is about cointegration which can be regarded as the "flip of the coin" of spurious regression. Unit-roots make inference about relationships between variables hazardous when standard critical values are used, but the problem is greatly reduced by using modern, non-standard, distribution theory. Series that are cointegrated have several representations that are known from the stationary case, notably equilibrium correction, VAR and moving average. And vice versa, equilibrium correction implies cointegration. The VAR representation of cointegrated variables is known as a cointegrated VAR. Dynamic models of the cointegrated VAR can be developed, and represent a major increase in the scope of econometric modelling of stationary systems.

Empirical model specification involves many choices and decisions, for example, about sample length, variable transformations, order of dynamics, significance levels, small or large final model to report, etc. If we can use computer algorithms to automatize some of these many decisions, we can speak about semi-automatic modelling in econometrics (Hendry, 2018).

A long-lasting debate in econometrics is whether it is best to go specific-to-general, or whether general-to-specific is to be preferred. In Specific-to-general: start from small model, and enlarge if it fails. In General-to-specific (Gets): start from a large model, and reduce it to a smaller one with the aid of statistical tests. Both types of searches use economic theory and both make use of several statistical tests, and practitioners use both.

In Chapter 11, we discuss automatization of modelling decisions with the use of the algorithm *Autometrics*, which is part of the program package PcGive that we refer to in the book, (see Doornik, 2009; Doornik and Hendry, 2013a). The main purpose of automatic variable selection is to find the data generating process (DGP). Another usage, perhaps less obvious at first thought, is to robustify a theoretically specified model against the biases that will otherwise affect the parameter estimates, i.e., unless the *a priori* specification should happen to be identical to the DGP. In Chapter 11, we provide examples of both usages.

Forecasting is an important purpose of statistical econometric model building. Chapter 12 discusses the role of empirical macroeconometric models in forecasting. There are several good reasons for doing model-based forecasting, especially when the number of variables forecasted is relatively large. For example, model-based forcasts obey the accounting identities that are specified in the macroeconometric model. Macroeconomic forecasts of cointegrated variables also are themselves cointegrated. None of this "internal order" on a set of forecasted variables is possible by relying on assembling statistically sophisticated univariate forecasts.

Nevertheless, model-based forecasts frequently experience failures in the sense that the forecast errors are larger than there was reason to believe on the basis of the model's performance within sample. The chapter therefore aims to elucidate the weak spots of model-based forecasting as much as its strengths. As we shall see, the same features that make a model attractive, such as economically interpretable long-run relationships and equilibrating adjustment, make the model-based forecasts vulnerable to *structural breaks* in the economy. Hence, it is not only model specification that requires the active decisions of the model builder, but the use of the model in forecasting also depends on the intervention of the model user to aid the model's adaption to a new reality after a structural break in the economy has occurred.

Figure 1.10 shows the chapters that we have briefly reviewed, and some of the relationships between them. The solid lines indicate the "route map" that simply follows the numbering of the chapters. The dashed lines indicate alternative routes through the book.

For readers who have background in an introductory course in econometrics, which covered both regression models (estimated by OLS) and structural model equations (estimated by Method of Moments/Instrumental Variables), the material in Chapter 2 may be well known. The use of matrices to represent those model equation types may, however, not be covered by an introductory course. In any case, it is definitively possible for readers with a good grounding in econometrics to jump to Chapter 3.

Often, a first econometrics course gives an introduction to dynamics, for example, under the heading dynamic regression (models). For readers with that kind of background, it may be possible to skip Chapter 3, and move directly to Chapter 4 (as indicated by the dashed line) where the concept of stationary time series is defined, and the properties of stationary time series are presented. However, Chapter 4 (and indeed the rest of the book) makes many references to mathematical concepts and results in Chapter 3, so the reader should at least be prepared to use Chapter 3 as a reference.

As noted above, we view both single equation econometric models (Chapter 6) and multiple equation models (Chapter 7) as models of the VAR (Chapter 5). It is possible to pass from Chapter 5 directly to Chapter 7, but note that one important class of multiple equation models consists of conditional model equations and marginal model equations, hence there is a close connection between Chapter 6 and Chapter 7.

On the other hand, it is possible to go directly from Chapter 6 to Chapter 8 (exogeneity) since the main discussion in Chapter 8 relates to parameters of interest in single equations models. However, as explained in the chapter, exogeneity is also relevant for multiple equation models.

The discussion of Gets modelling and automatic variable selection (Chapter 11) refers mainly to regression models, so it can be read after Chapter 6 as indicated. However, the chapter also refers to non-stationarity

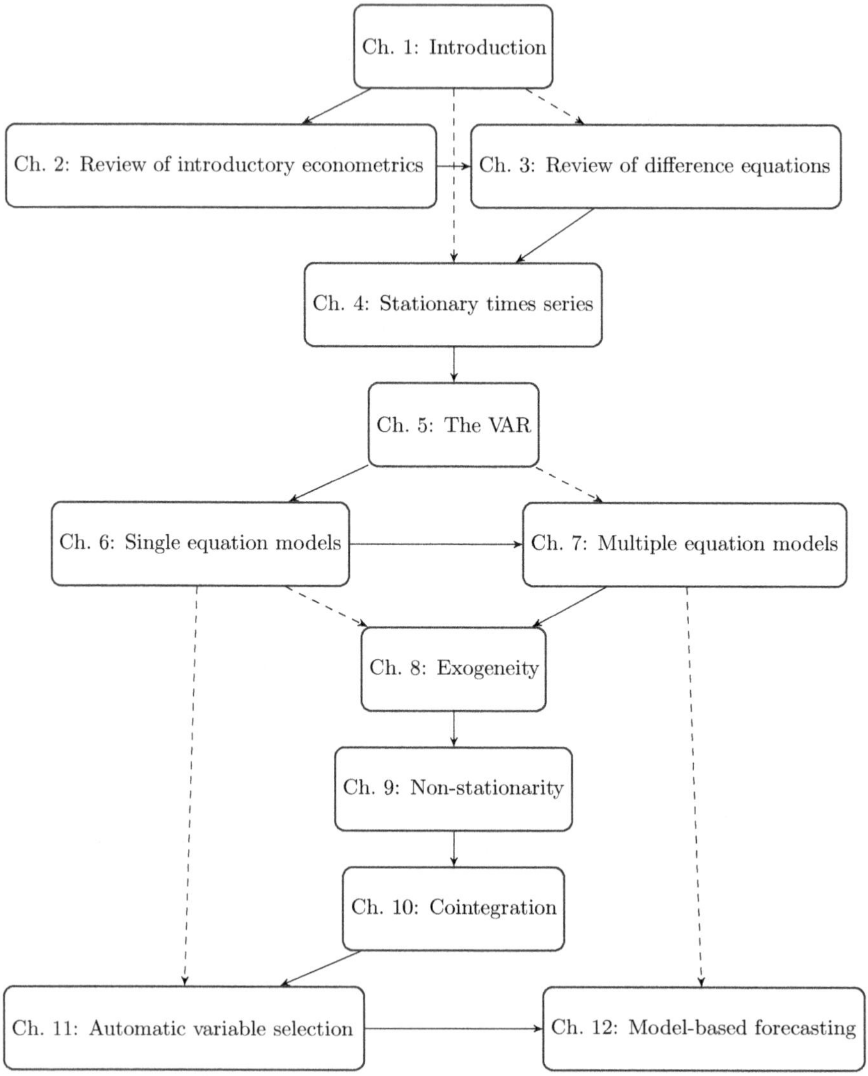

Figure 1.10. The main chapters of the book, with some of alternative "route maps" indicated by dashed lines.

and cointegration, so an even better choice is to simply follow the ordering of the chapters. The last chapter of the book discusses forecasting from a system perspective. Since the exposition makes use of the simplification that the model parameters are known within the sample (estimation theory is tuned down), the chapter can be read, for example, after having been through Chapter 7), as indicated.

1.10. Questions and Answers and Statistical Software and Datasets

There are exercises at the end of each chapter, and Appendix C contains answer suggestions to all the exercises. The questions are a mix of theoretically exercises, and computer exercises.

The book mainly makes use of the *OxMetrics* software programs *PcGive* and *PcNaive*, which have been developed by Jurgen A. Doornik and David F. Hendry at the University of Oxford over a number of years. Information about the latest version of the *OxMetrics* program family is available at: www.timberlake.co.uk/software/oxmetrics.html.

In addition, *Eviews* is used in the solution sketches to a selection of the computer exercises to demonstrate the replication of results from different programs, and to show that most of the exercises do not require a specialized software. Eviews is at www.eviews.com/home.html.

The datasets used in the examples, and in the exercises (at the end of each chapter) can be downloaded from the book's website: http://normetrics.no/dynamic-econometrics-for-empirical-macroeconomic-modelling/

1.11. Exercises

Exercise 1.1. Show that (1.3) and (1.4) are the final form equations for the system

$$\begin{aligned} Q_t &= aP_t + b_t, & a &< 0, \\ Q_t &= cP_{t-1} + d, & c &> 0. \end{aligned}$$

Exercise 1.2. Explain how Figure 1.1 is affected if the assumption $-1 < \frac{c}{a} < 0$ is changed to $\frac{c}{a} = -1$.

Exercise 1.3.

(1) Estimate (1.19), using the dataset *dgp_demandandstoch* in one of the formats provided on the book's webpage. Use the variable labelled P_STOCH as the price P_t, and the series named STEP11 in the database as $S11_t$ in the text.
(2) Estimate the model using the first 19 time periods. What are the main differences compared to the full sample results?

Exercise 1.4. Derive the final form equation (1.25) from models (1.22)–(1.24).

Exercise 1.5. Use models (1.27)–(1.29) to derive the expression in (1.30), and a solution for GDP*.

Exercise 1.6. Show that for the 2-variable systems in Figure 1.5 and Figure 1.6, the relationship between the two slope coefficients that we can estimate is

$$b = b' \frac{\hat{\sigma}_X^2}{\hat{\sigma}_Y^2},$$

where b corresponds to the relationship shown in Figure 1.5, and b' corresponds to Figure 1.6. $\hat{\sigma}_Y$ and $\hat{\sigma}_X$ are empirical (sample) standard error errors: $\hat{\sigma}_Y = \sqrt{\hat{\sigma}_Y^2} = \sqrt{1/T \sum_{t=1}^{T}(Y_i - \overline{Y})^2}$), hence $\hat{\sigma}_Y^2$ is the variance of Y (and similarly for $\hat{\sigma}_X$).

Exercise 1.7. As a first example of real-world time series, we will look at data collected from the Fulton Fish market in New York (see Graddy, 1995; 2006). The dataset we use involves aggregated daily prices and quantities of whiting for the period 2 December 1991 to 8 May 1992.[4]

(1) Download the file Fulton.zip provided on the book's webpage to get the access to the dataset fish.xls (or one of the other data bank formats provided). The variable definitions to note are as follows:

- *pricelevel*: the average daily price of whiting in USD.
- *price*: the natural logarithm of *price level.*
- *tots*: total quantity sold (Daily aggregated quantity in pounds)
- *qty*: the natural logarithm of *tots.*
- *stormy*: A dummy (indicator variable) which is 1 if the weather at sea was stormy, and zero otherwise.
- *mixed*: A dummy (indicator variable) which is 1 if the weather at sea was mixed, and zero otherwise.

[4]The dataset was downloaded from http://people.brandeis.edu/~kgraddy/datasets/fish.out on 6 July 2018.

A dummy variable for public holiday has been added to the dataset following the analysis in Hendry and Nielsen (2007, p. 200)[5]:

- *hol*: 1 if trading day is on or close to a public holiday. Zero otherwise.

(2) Investigate the two time series *pricelevel* and *tots* for signs of autocorrelation.

(3) What about *price* and *qty*?

[5] Two other existing analyses of this dataset are Angrist *et al.* (2000) and Graddy and Kennedy (2010).

Chapter 2

Review of Econometric Theory

In this chapter, we give a review of the main concepts and estimation methods that we will use below. We also introduce the matrix notation that will appear in later chapters, and give some useful results from matrix algebra that we will refer to in this book. The context is the independent and identically distributed model which many readers will be familiar with from courses in probability, statistics and introductory econometrics. Both regression models and structural relationships (i.e., between two or more endogenous variables) are covered. We end the chapter with an intuitive introduction of the regression model for time series variables, which is one of the main models of this book.

2.1. Introduction

As noted in Chapter 1, empirical econometric modelling is a combined discipline. In this chapter, we review several of the statistical concepts that are useful for specification of econometric model equations.

Structural econometric model equations can be regarded as joint probability density functions written in equation (i.e., model) form. Regression model equations are conditional probability density functions written in model form. Hence, the system perspective should remain "in the picture" even when we are concerned with the specification and estimation of a single equation model. The point is perhaps easiest to acknowledge when we think about instrumental variables: Logically, a candidate for being an instrumental variable must belong to the same larger system as the variables that we have singled out for modelling are taken from. Also, regression model equations can be interpreted in the system perspective as conditional models of the larger system.

However, it is also true that the specification of the larger system is often a big challenge, and there is usually a reason why we focus on a single equation in the first place. More often than not, this has to do with the difficulty of representing the full system. There are also research purposes where a partial (which could mean conditional) specification is a reasonable starting point. However, sooner or later in an empirical modelling project, the larger system usually has to be addressed. For example, a qualitative sketch of the wider theory is much better than simply taking instruments out of thin air. Likewise, when estimating a regression equation, the focus is often on the invariance of model coefficients with respect to regime-shifts elsewhere in the system. Also this analysis requires that the wider system is accounted for, at least in qualitative terms.

Having defined regression models and structural models with reference to different types of probability distributions, we briefly review the common estimation methods: ordinary least squares (OLS), method of moments (MM) and instrumental variables (IVs), and maximum likelihood (ML). All three estimation principles will be used later in the book. We also include in this chapter the matrix notation for econometric models, and the main results of matrix algebra that we will refer to in some of the later chapters.

Even though this chapter contains a review of statistical concepts and estimation, it is not a substitute for the "Review of Statistics" chapter that you typically find in textbooks in introductory econometrics or for the careful presentation of estimation methods and hypothesis testing that you also find in those books. Instead, the aim is to provide the reader with a relatively concise "warm-up" chapter that will help refresh knowledge of introductory econometrics, and of matrix notation and algebra. If the material in the chapter is completely new to you, the best advise may be to pick up one of the textbooks in introductory econometrics (perhaps one of the books that is listed at the end of the chapter). To this chapter, there is a quite large set of exercises, that may also aid the reader to assess her knowledge level.

2.2. Probability and Random Variables

The following sections review some of the essential statistical concepts and estimation theory.

2.2.1. Experiments, random events and variables: The need of a model

A random variable attaches a value to each single event of an experiment. The experiment can be literal (like in coin tossing). However, in econometrics we are usually not in control of the experimental design "behind" the random variables. But we can, nevertheless, regard the real-world data *as if* they were generated by a (large) experiment (which we call the Data Generating Process (DGP)), and we can build models of the experiment with the aid of mathematical statistics.

When we start studying statistics, simple experiments are used, such as coin-tossing or the probability of having a girl baby. In these cases, the DGP and model are so simple that it is easy to overlook the more general message, namely that a statistical model is always formulated for a purpose, which may be about profits, research or fun (if it is allowed to say that). Hence, there is an instrumental aspect of model building, which means that it involves decisions, and that it requires knowledge and skills.

Consider the example where the purpose is to estimate the probability of a girl baby. In this case, the Bernoulli model (or Binomial model) can be used, even though the Bernoulli model is clearly not a realistic DGP for the biological process of childbirth. But, for the specific and limited purpose of estimating the probability that a baby is a girl, that DGP, is relevant.

The models that we use for estimation are based on assumptions that need to be reasonable simplifications of the real world. Because if they are overtly wrong assumptions, all the inferences we make based on the model become misleading. It does not help if our estimation procedure is formally correct, if the formalism is built on assumptions that are unreasonable. At the same time, all models are simplifications and therefore "wrong". They cannot be accurate descriptions of the real world, because then they would stop being models. This is a paradox that we have to live with as econometricians: All models are wrong, but we, nevertheless, need models to draw inference-based conclusions about those aspects of the real world that we have chosen as our business to investigate.

Sometimes, different models have many similar implications for the research problem, and the choice of model may then not be so important. However, in particular in macroeconomics, the policy implications of the approaches that we can choose between are quite different. The decision on a model therefore becomes a matter of some consequence. In such cases, econometric methods can often play a role in the specification of a relevant model for policy analysis, see e.g., Bårdsen and Nymoen (2009), and Akram and Nymoen (2009), who looks as the importance of wage and price setting when the model usage is to aid monetary policy analysis and decisions.

Returning to the basic concepts of statistics: An event represented by a random variable can be a simple result (boy/girl child) of an experiment, or a composite result (number of girls from three births). Heuristically, a random variable is therefore a function of the simple events of an experiment. For the variable "Number of girls," the value set is $\{0, 1, 2, 3\}$. A discrete random variable can take a finite number of values. A continuous random variable can in principle take an infinite number of values. The two terms, random variable and stochastic variable, are synonyms for the same concept.

2.2.2. Distribution functions

Let X denote a random variable (discrete or continuous), and let x denote a value of that variable.

Definition 2.1 (Cumulative distribution). *The cumulative distribution function (cdf) $F_X(x)$ gives the probability P that a random variable X is less than or equal to the outcome x:*

$$F_X(x) = P(X \leq x). \tag{2.1}$$

For a discrete variable, the cdf has a characteristic step-function shape, starting in 0 and increasing in steps until it reaches the value 1 for the highest value in the value set.

The change in the discrete cdf takes place at the point where the discrete variable goes from a lower to a higher value. The change in the cdf corresponds to the probability distribution which gives the probability p_x for a value x:

$$p_x = f_X(x), \tag{2.2}$$

with properties: $0 \leq p_x \leq 1$ and $\sum_x p_x = 1$.

For a continuous variable, the probability of a given value is zero. To represent the change in a continuous cdf, the *probability density function* (*pdf*) is used:

$$f_X(x) \geq 0 \quad \forall \text{ ("for all") } x, \tag{2.3}$$

The pdf is scaled in such a way that the area under the function is 1:

$$\int_{-\infty}^{\infty} f_X(x)dx = 1.$$

The probability for $P(X \leq a)$ is then

$$P(X \leq a) = F_X(a) = \int_{-\infty}^{a} f_X(x)dx. \tag{2.4}$$

Conversely,

$$f_X(x) = \frac{d}{dx} P(X \leq x) \tag{2.5}$$

confirming that the pdf $f_X(x)$ represents the change in the cdf.

2.2.3. Moments

If X is a discrete random variable, the *expectation* is given by

$$\mu_X = E(X) = \sum_{i=1}^{k} x_i f_X(x_i). \tag{2.6}$$

If X is a continuous random variable, the *expectation* is given by

$$\mu_X = E(X) = \int_{-\infty}^{\infty} x f_X(x)dx. \tag{2.7}$$

Box 2.1. Rules for the expectation

1. $E(a) = a$, for a constant a
2. $E(bX) = bE(X) = b\mu_X$, for a constant b
3. $E(a + bX) = E(a) + E(bX) = a + b\mu_X$
4. $E\left(\sum_{i=1}^{n} X_i\right) = \sum_{i=1}^{n} E(X_i) = \sum_{i=1}^{n} \mu_{X_i}$ for n random variables

The *variance* of X is given by

$$\sigma_X^2 = \text{Var}(X) = E[(X - \mu_X)^2] \tag{2.8}$$

$$= \int_{-\infty}^{\infty} (x - \mu_X)^2 f_X(x)dx \text{ (for the continuous case)}, \tag{2.9}$$

and the standard deviation is given by

$$\sigma_X = \sqrt{\text{Var}(X)}. \tag{2.10}$$

Box 2.2. Rules for the variance

1. $\text{Var}(a) = 0$
2. $\text{Var}(bX) = b^2 \text{Var}(X) = b^2\sigma_X^2$
3. $\text{Var}(a + bX) = b^2 \text{Var}(X) = b^2\sigma_X^2$

It is common to use the term *location parameter* as a synonym for expectation, and to use *scale parameter* as a synonym for variance, or for its square root, i.e., the standard deviation.

The best known distribution function of all may be the standard normal (Gaussian). It has first-order moment $= 0$ and second-order moment $= 1$, usually indicated by $X \sim N(0, 1)$. Figure 2.1 plots the pdf and cdf of the standard normal distribution.

The degree of non-symmetry in a distribution, skewness, is measured by the third moment:

$$\text{Skewness} = \frac{E[(X - \mu_X)^3]}{\sigma_X^3}. \tag{2.11}$$

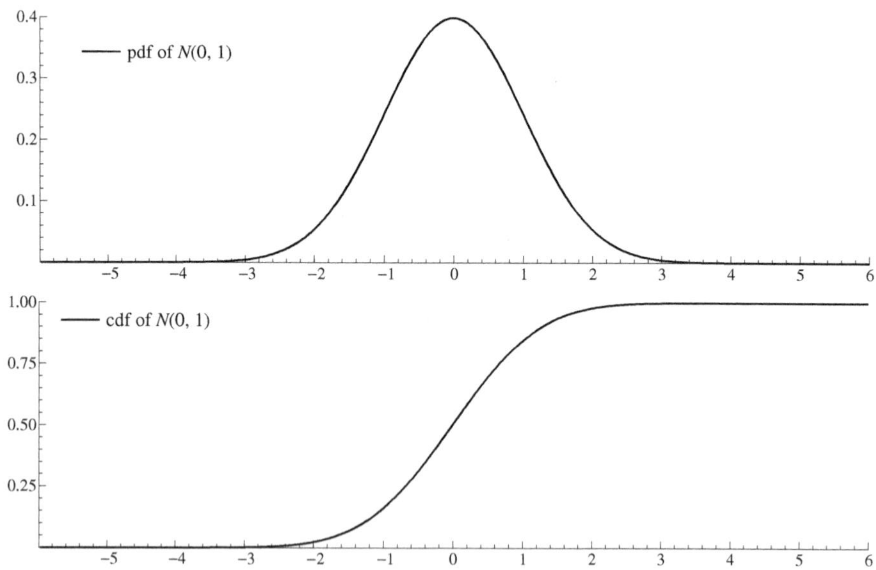

Figure 2.1. The standard normal distribution $N(0, 1)$: (a) pdf and (b) cdf.

Kurtosis, the fourth moment, is given by

$$\text{Kurtosis} = \frac{E[(X - \mu_X)^4]}{\sigma_X^4}. \tag{2.12}$$

The normal distribution is often used as a reference. It has Skewness = 0 and Kurtosis = 3. Kurtosis > 3 implies the phenomenon of *fat tails*, also called *heavy tails*.

Investment strategies or prediction models that assume a normal distribution when the distribution is in fact, heavy-tailed, can lead to huge financial losses (or gains) because the probabilities of large impact events are underestimated. It has become known as the *Black Swan Problem*, after the best selling book by Nassim Taleb. In econometrics, the degree of kurtosis is a concern because the significance of t-values and other common test statistics may be overestimated if they have fatter tails under the null hypotheses than the formal inference theory in use will have us believe. Assume, for example, that with reference asymptotic theory we use critical values of the $N(0,1)$ distribution to judge the significance of a t-test. However, unless the sample is fairly large, the true distribution of the t-value may be better approximated by a *t-distribution*, because of their fatter tails, as indicated in Figure 2.2.

While single black swans may be the nemesis of stock operators, builders and users of macroeconomic models often come in touch with structural

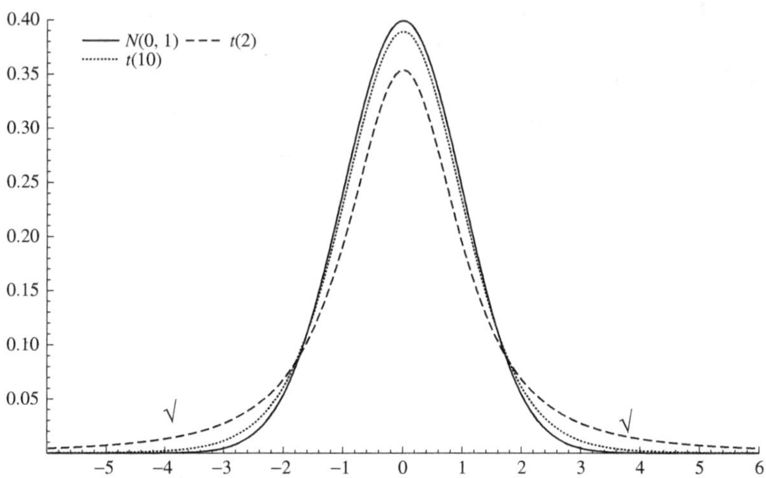

Figure 2.2. $N(0,1)$ pdf together with pdf for Student's t-distribution with 2 and 10 degrees of freedom (with a single black swan indicated in each of the tails).

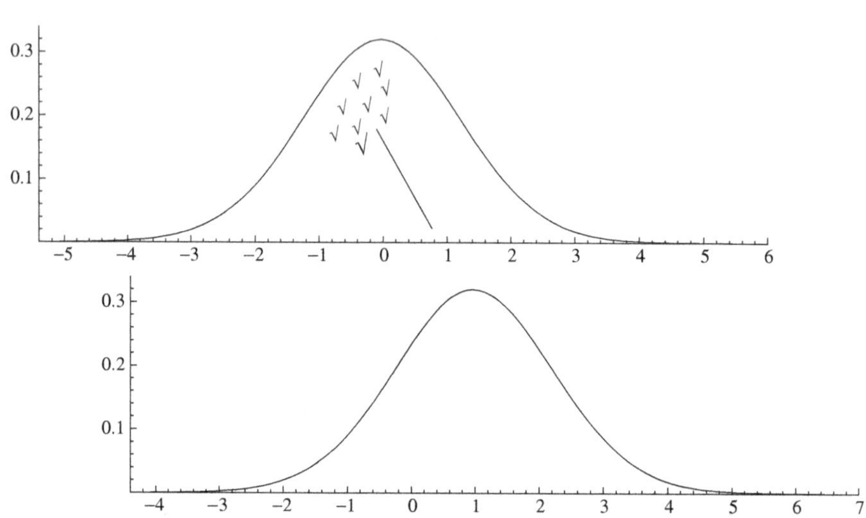

Figure 2.3. Location shift (flock of black swans). The upper pdf of $N(0, 1)$ gets its location parameter shifted to unity (the pdf in the lower graph). The flight direction of the swans is indicated by the straight line.

breaks in the "big experiment", the real-world DGP, that cause the first moment of a variable's distribution to change. Hence, the black swan analogy needs to be extended to a flock of black swans, that we can imagine lifting the location of a distribution from one point on the real line to another (Hendry, 2018; Hendry and Nielsen, 2007, p. 32), as illustrated by Figure 2.3. Location-shifts in the DGP, although they can be treated *ex post* by the use of indicator variables, and (better) by progress in modelling (Eitrheim *et al.*, 2002), their short-term impacts are to cause forecast failures, because they may be near impossible to detect in real time. In Chapter 12, we will have opportunity to explain this point at some length.

2.2.4. Functions of random variables

When $Y = g(X)$ is continuous, and the inverse function $X = g^{-1}(Y)$ exists, we have the powerful result:

$$f_Y(y) = f_X\left(g^{-1}(y)\right)\left|\frac{dg^{-1}(y)}{dy}\right|. \tag{2.13}$$

The reason we use the absolute value $\left|dg^{-1}(y)/dy\right|$ is that $dg^{-1}(y)$ can be a declining function, while a pdf by definition is non-negative for all values of the random variable.

2.3. Statistical Concepts for Modelling of Relationships

The main part of this review chapter covers models where time does not play an essential role. We therefore commence by numbering the variables by an index i, which is a popular choice of index for individuals in a random sample.

We assume $i = 1, 2, \ldots, n$ pairs $\{X_i, Y_i\}$ of random variables. The key to be able to give econometric treatment to the relationship between the two variables is that we assume a joint cumulative distribution function (i.e., a "statistical law") for the variables.

For ease of exposition, we assume that both X_i and Y_i are continuous variables. Combinations of the two types of variables in a model usually represent no problem, in particular when the explanatory variable in the model is a discrete random variable. However, in the case of a discrete endogenous variable, care must be taken when specifying the distribution function; see Hendry and Nielsen (2007, Chapter 4) for details of the *Logit model.*

In our case, with two variables X and Y, the *joint pdf* can be defined as

$$f_{X_i,Y_i}(x_i, y_i) = \frac{\partial^2}{\partial x_i \partial y_i} P(X_i \leq x_i \text{ and } Y_i \leq y_i) \tag{2.14}$$

with the following two main properties:

(1) $f_{X_i,Y_i}(x_i, y_i) \geq 0, \forall x_i, y_i,$
(2) $\int_{-\infty}^{\infty} \int_{-\infty}^{\infty} f_{X_i,Y_i}(x_i, y_i) dx_i dy_i = 1.$

The first property corresponds to non-negative joint *point probabilities* in the case of random events and discrete variables defined over such event sets. The second property is the counterpart to the requirement that discrete probabilities by definition sum to one.

The joint probability density function is equal to the product of the two *marginal* pdfs if and only if X_i and Y_i are independent variables:

$$f_{X_i,Y_i}(x_i, y_i) = f_{X_i}(x_i) f_{Y_i}(y_i), \text{ in the case of independence,} \tag{2.15}$$

where the two marginal pdfs are $f_{X_i}(x_i)$ for X_i, and $f_{Y_i}(y_i)$ for Y_i.

A *conditional* pdf is also defined in the same way as in the discrete variable case, for example, as

$$f_{Y_i|X_i}(y_i \mid x_i) = \frac{f_{X_i,Y_i}(x_i, y_i)}{f_{X_i}(x_i)}, \tag{2.16}$$

when the conditioning is on a value x_i that the random variable X_i can take. Conditional densities represent genuine statistical distribution functions. For example,

(1) $f_{Y_i|X_i}(y_i \mid x_i) \geq 0, \forall x_i, y_i,$
(2) $\int_{-\infty}^{\infty} f_{Y_i|X_i}(y_i \mid x_i)dy_i = 1,$

and the conditional distribution function is obtained by integration:

$$F_{Y_i|X_i}(y_i \mid x_i) = \int_{-\infty}^{y_i} f_{Y_i|X_i}(z_i \mid x_i)dz_i.$$

Since a conditional distribution function has all the mathematical properties of an ordinary distribution function, it can be characterized by its *moments*. The first two moments are the expectation: $E(Y_i \mid X_i = x_i)$, which we will often represent by the symbol $\mu_{Y|X}$:

$$\mu_{Y|X} \underset{\text{def}}{=} E(Y_i \mid X_i = x_i), \tag{2.17}$$

and the variance $\sigma^2_{Y|X}$:

$$\sigma^2_{Y|X} \underset{\text{def}}{=} \text{Var}(Y_i \mid X_i = x_i) = E(Y_i - \mu_{Y|X})^2. \tag{2.18}$$

Here $\mu_{Y|X}$ and $\sigma^2_{Y|X}$ are different from the corresponding moments of the marginal distribution (the exception: the case of independence). For joint distributions, covariances are also defined:

$$\text{Cov}(X,Y) = E(X - E(X))(Y - E(Y)), \tag{2.19}$$

where $E(X) \underset{\text{def}}{=} \mu_X$ is the marginal expectation of X, and $E(Y) \underset{\text{def}}{=} \mu_Y$ is the corresponding first-order moment of Y.

In econometrics, we are sometimes interested in the third- and fourth-order moments. As noted above, the third-order moment measures skewness, and the fourth-order moment is called kurtosis, and measures the probability of realizations outside the usual range of variance of the variable. In standard statistical inference theory, the fourth-order moments of the variables are assumed to be finite. This means that extreme values (i.e., outliers) are so improbable that they can be ignored. The Gaussian (i.e., normal) distribution is fully characterized by the two first moments.

Hence, if we start from a model formulation based on the normal distribution, but discover empirical outliers, we need to answer the question about how the extreme values are to be interpreted, and further treated in the econometric investigation. One possibility is to regard them as temporary shifts in the location of the distribution. In this case, we do not really interpret the outliers as extreme observations from the same distribution, but as evidence of changes in the first-order moment, the expectation. In practical modelling, this boils down to "taking out" the extreme observations by the use of impulse indicator variables (aka, binary variables or "dummies"). This can be thought of as a way of robustifying the inference, since the extreme observations do not influence the estimation of the parameters of the model that we are interested in estimating. The other possibility is to regard outliers as evidence that the joint probability distribution of the data is non-normal. This leads to non-standard inference, which may be difficult in practice since non-standard means exactly that: It is not included in the standard software packages for example. Advanced users will nevertheless be able to work around the problem, for example, by the use of bootstrapping methods (see Kennedy (2008, Chapter 4) for an introduction).

The linear relationship between Y and X that we want to estimate is

$$Y_i = \beta_0 + \beta_1 X_i + \epsilon_i, \quad i = 1, 2, \ldots, n, \tag{2.20}$$

where β_0 and β_1 denote the coefficients, or parameters, of the relationship. ϵ_i $(i = 1, 2, \ldots, n)$ are n random variables that we do not have observations of. They are called disturbances, or model equation errors, or simply error terms.

Equation (2.20) is not yet a complete specification of an econometric model. To complete the specification, we need to say more about the assumed properties of the disturbances ϵ_i $(i = 1, 2, \ldots, n)$.

When the specification of the properties of the disturbances refers to the *conditional* probability distribution function of ϵ_i $(i = 1, 2, \ldots, n)$ for fixed X_i, we obtain the linear *regression model* between Y_i (called regressand) and X_i (regressor).

When the assumptions about the properties of ϵ_i $(i = 1, 2, \ldots, n)$ do not refer to the conditional distribution of ϵ_i given the regressor, but to an simultaneous (joint) distribution function, the interpretation of the model equation (2.20) is changed. It is not a regression model, but is known in econometrics as a *structural equation*. The parameters of structural equations can only be estimated consistently subject to *identifying assumptions* that we review below.

Hence, we have two different econometric models with the same model equation, namely (2.20), but where the difference lies in the relationship between X_i and the error ϵ_i. Both model classes, regression equations and structural equations, are important models for empirical econometric modelling. The choice between the two model types will be guided by the purpose of the modelling exercise. In empirical macro economic modelling, with multiple equations, regression equations are typically combined with subsystems that consist of structural equations.

We commence with a review of the simple regression model, and then review estimation of a single structural equation.

2.4. The Simple Regression Model

In the canonical econometric regression model, the statistical interpretation of the coefficients β_0 and β_1 are clear. They are the parameters of the conditional expectation function between Y and X.

2.4.1. The specification of the regression model

The complete specification of the regression model consists of the model equation (2.20) and the following assumptions:

a. $E(\epsilon_i \mid X_j) = 0$, $\forall i$ and j (the symbol $\forall$ is used as short-hand for "for all");
b. $\text{Var}(\epsilon_i \mid X_i) = \sigma^2$, $\forall i$;
c. $\text{Cov}(\epsilon_i, \epsilon_j \mid X_i, X_j) = 0$, $\forall i \neq j$;
d. β_0, β_1 and σ^2 are constant parameters.

The notation $\mid X_j$ means that the assumptions refer to a conditional probability distribution. It would have been more precise to write the assumption as, for example, $E(\epsilon_i \mid X_j = x_j) = 0$ to be clear about the conditioning on a particular value (i.e., x_j) taken by the random variable X_j. However, when there is little danger of misunderstanding, we will use the simplified notation in the list **a**–**d**, which many readers already will have recognized as the *classical assumptions* about the disturbance in a regression model.

If we take the conditional expectation with respect to X_i (using i as the subscript for the conditioning variable) on both sides of the model equation (2.20), and use assumption **a**, we get

$$E(Y_i \mid X_i) = \beta_0 + \beta_1 X_i, \tag{2.21}$$

which we will refer to as a *linear conditional expectation function*, since we can imagine that each time we give a different argument (value of X_i), we will get a unique value of Y_i. Another common name for (2.21) is the *population regression line*, or the *population regression function.*

Assumption **a** deserves a couple of comments. First, note that it implies

$$\mathrm{Cov}(\epsilon_i, X_j) = 0, \quad \forall i, j.$$

This is a consequence of the result from statistics, saying that if the conditional expectation of one variable (ϵ_i), given the other (X_j), is a constant, the covariance between the two variables is zero (they are uncorrelated variables). Assumption **a** states that the conditional expectation of ϵ_i given X_j is constant (in fact zero).

A second remark draws the attention to how subtle the distinction between assumptions of regression models, and the implications of those assumptions, sometimes are. We can start from the definition of ϵ_i as the difference between Y_i and the conditional expectation of Y_i given X_i, and take the expectation of ϵ_i conditional on X_j:

$$\begin{aligned} E(\epsilon_i \mid X_j) &\underset{\text{def}}{=} E\{Y_i - E(Y_i \mid X_i) \mid X_j\} \\ &= E(Y_i \mid X_j) - E(E(Y_i \mid X_i) \mid X_j). \end{aligned}$$

If we set $j = i$, we obtain

$$E(\epsilon_i \mid X_i) = E(Y_i \mid X_i) - E(Y_i \mid X_i) = 0 \quad \text{for } j = i, \tag{2.22}$$

which says that the regression disturbance ϵ_i is, by definition, always uncorrelated with X_i. Hence, **a** appears to be an implication, not an assumption. One way to defend its classification as an assumption is to note that the result in (2.22) used the general definition of the conditional expectation function. That function needs not be linear, as assumed in (2.21). Hence, one way of interpreting assumption **a** for the case of $j = i$ is that it requires that the functional form of the conditional expectation function is correctly specified.

What then about assumption **a** for the case of $j \neq i$? The short answer is that this is indeed a genuine assumption that is equivalent to the assumption about independence between pairs of (X, Y) variables. We return to this point below when we present an equivalent, much used, way of specifying the econometric regression model.

Assumption **b** is called the *homoskedasticity assumption* about the regression disturbances. The parameter σ^2 refers to the conditional distribution, so we could have used the notation $\sigma^2_{Y|X}$ here (see Exercise 2.5). However, in the specification of regression models, the notation without explicit conditioning is usual.

Assumption **c** is a statement about mutual independence between the random regression disturbances, and it is also equivalent with an assumption about mutual independence between the pairs $(X_1, Y_1), (X_2, Y_2), \ldots, (X_n, Y_n)$.

Assumption **d**, the constancy of parameters assumption, is not always included in the specification of a regression model. However, if you give it a minute's thought, you can see that it is quite essential in order to have a useful model. If the regression coefficient β_1, for example, varies a lot (much a like a random variable), our regression model will not be very useful for producing results about how much Y_i changes when X_i changes.

Failure of parameter constancy in practical modelling can be due to omitted variables, or to a wrong functional form. The statistical regression model says nothing about how Y_i and X_i are measured. If the functional relationship between Y_i and X_i is nonlinear, the estimation of a linear model (without transforming the data) will often lead to loss of constancy for β_1 and σ^2, while transforming one, or both, of Y_i and X_i to, for example, natural logarithms, will often improve things in the direction of more stable parameters (so that **d** again becomes a tenable assumption).

There are usually several aspects of variable transformations to consider in any applied econometric project. It is no exaggeration to say that the choice of functional form is an essential step in the modelling process.

Sometimes, as noted, the specification of the regression model is presented in another, and equivalent, form.

2.4.2. An equivalent specification

The classical regression model specification above was for the conditional distribution of the unobservable error term in the model equation. An equivalent formulation of the regression model is to start with the joint probability density function of the observable variables, and to be clear about the model equation's close connection to the conditional distribution of one of them (i.e., Y) given the other (i.e., X):

a*. The pairs $(X_1, Y_1), (X_2, Y_2), \ldots, (X_n, Y_n)$ are mutually independent and identically distributed, IID for short.

b*. The conditional distribution of Y_i given X_i has expectation $\beta_0 + \beta_1 X_i$, and variance σ^2 which is the same for all i.

c*. The model equation is $Y_i = \beta_0 + \beta_1 X_i + \epsilon_i, \ i = 1, 2, \ldots, n$.

d*. β_0, β_1 and σ^2 are constant parameters.

In this formulation, **a*** implies that the ordering of the variables does not matter, it is up to us how we organize the data. For example, instead of $(X_1, Y_1), (X_2, Y_2), \ldots, (X_n, Y_n)$, we can think of the variable set as

$$\{Y_1, Y_2, \ldots, Y_n, X_1, X_2, \ldots, X_n\},$$

where in general there is dependency between Y_i and X_i, so that the conditional expectation is non-constant (hence $\beta_1 \neq 0$), and therefore

$$\mathrm{Cov}(Y_i, X_i) \neq 0 \quad \forall i,$$

but where all the other variable combinations are independent:

$$\mathrm{Cov}(Y_i, Y_j) = \mathrm{Cov}(X_i, X_j) = \mathrm{Cov}(Y_i, X_j) = 0, \quad i \neq j.$$

Hence, we have in particular:

$$\mathrm{Cov}(Y_i, Y_j) = 0, \quad i \neq j.$$

If we insert the model equation from **c*** we get

$$\mathrm{Cov}(\beta_0 + \beta_1 X_i + \epsilon_i, \beta_0 + \beta_1 X_j + \epsilon_j) = \beta_1^2 \mathrm{Cov}(X_i, X_j) + \mathrm{Cov}(\epsilon_i, \epsilon_j) = 0.$$

Clearly, for $i \neq j$, $\mathrm{Cov}(X_i, X_j) = 0$ from assumption **a***, and therefore assumption **c** of the first version of the specification follows, i.e., $\mathrm{Cov}(\epsilon_i, \epsilon_j) = 0$ for $i \neq j$. Note that no conditioning is needed here because of the independence between the two X variables.

Above, we saw that **a** can be interpreted as an assumption about correct functional form of the model equation. Hence, $E(\epsilon_i \mid X_i)$ is also implied in the equivalent formulation that we now consider. Moreover, independence between the disturbance and the regressor for the case of $j \neq i$ can be shown by utilizing that the ordering of the variables is arbitrary by the assumption of independent sampling:

$$\begin{aligned} E(\epsilon_i \mid X_j) &= E\{Y_i - E(Y_i \mid X_i) \mid X_j\} \\ &= E(Y_i \mid X_j) - E(E(Y_i \mid X_i) \mid X_j) \\ &= E(Y_i \mid X_j) - E(E(Y_i \mid X_j) \mid X_i) \\ &= E(Y_i \mid X_j) - E(Y_i \mid X_j) = 0 \quad \text{for } j \neq i. \end{aligned} \tag{2.23}$$

It remains to be shown that also assumption **b** of the first version of the specification is covered by the second one. Express $\mathrm{Var}(\epsilon_i \mid X_i)$ as

$$\begin{aligned} \mathrm{Var}(\epsilon_i \mid X_i) &= E\left\{\epsilon_i - E(\epsilon_i \mid X_i) \mid X_i\right\}^2 \\ &= E(\epsilon_i^2 \mid X_i) - 2E(\epsilon_i \mid X_i)E(\epsilon_i \mid X_i) + (E(\epsilon_i \mid X_i))^2 \\ &= E(\epsilon_i^2 \mid X_i) - (E(\epsilon_i \mid X_i))^2. \end{aligned}$$

By the same argument that led to (2.22), the second term in the last line is 0^2 for all i. Hence, we see that $E(\epsilon_i^2 \mid X_i)$ is just another way of writing the conditional variance $\mathrm{Var}(\epsilon_i \mid X_i)$ in **b**, which is equal to σ^2 by assumption **b***.

2.4.3. The Gaussian regression model

As many readers will know, for the above model specification, OLS estimation can be shown to give estimators that are unbiased, e.g., $E(\hat{\beta}_1 - \beta_1) = 0$, when we let $\hat{\beta}_1$ denote the OLS estimator of β_1.

The OLS estimators have known distributions in large samples, which can be used for inference. For example, the null hypothesis $H_0 : \beta_1 = 0$ is against the one-sided (e.g., $\beta_1 > 0$) or two-sided ($\beta_1 \neq 0$) alternative.

However, in order to do so called exact inference in finite samples, the above specification can be extended by assuming that the conditional distribution is Gaussian (i.e., normal). We then replace **b*** and **c*** by the more specific assumption of conditional normality:

$$(Y_i \mid X_i) \overset{D}{\sim} N(\beta_0 + \beta_1 X_i, \sigma^2), \tag{2.24}$$

where $\overset{D}{\sim}$ reads "distributed as", and $N(\beta_0 + \beta_1 X_i, \sigma^2)$ denotes a normal distribution with expectation $\beta_0 + \beta_1 X_i$ and variance σ^2.

It follows that the error term $\epsilon_i = Y_i - \beta_0 - \beta_1 X_i$ is also Gaussian with expectation zero, and with that same variance σ^2:

$$(\epsilon_i \mid X_i) \overset{D}{\sim} N(0, \sigma^2). \tag{2.25}$$

This version of the model is also attractive for pedagogical reasons. For example, from the properties of the joint probability density function of (X, Y), which is the bivariate Gaussian distribution, we have (see Exercise 2.6):

$$\beta_1 = \frac{\sigma_{XY}}{\sigma_X^2}, \tag{2.26}$$

$$\beta_0 = \mu_Y - \beta_1 \mu_X, \tag{2.27}$$

$$\sigma_{Y|X}^2 = \sigma_Y^2 \left(1 - \frac{\sigma_{XY}^2}{\sigma_X^2 \sigma_Y^2}\right), \tag{2.28}$$

where σ_X^2 and σ_Y^2 denote the unconditional variances, σ_{XY} denotes the covariance between X and Y, and μ_X and μ_Y are the expectations of the two variables. $\sigma^2_{Y|X}$ is the conditional variance of Y given X. As noted above, we often use the simplified notation $\sigma_{Y|X} \equiv \sigma^2$ in the regression model specification, which is also the interpretation of σ^2 in the way it appears in (2.24) and (2.25).

Note that the expression for the conditional variance can be written as

$$\sigma^2_{Y|X} = \sigma^2_Y(1 - \rho^2_{XY}), \tag{2.29}$$

where

$$\rho_{XY} = \frac{\sigma_{XY}}{\sigma_X \sigma_Y} \tag{2.30}$$

is the theoretical correlation coefficient, which is larger than -1 and smaller than $+1$:

$$-1 < \rho_{XY} < 1, \tag{2.31}$$

so that the conditional variance is always positive. All of these parameters are population parameters. We next review their estimation.

2.4.4. Estimation of the Gaussian regression model

We now turn to the estimation of the parameters β_0, β_1 and σ^2 for the model equation (2.20), and the statistical specification in **a**–**d**. The conditional distribution function $f_{Y_i|X_i}(y_i \mid x_i)$, when the conditional distribution is normal, is

$$f_{Y_i|X_i}(y_i \mid x_i) = \frac{1}{\sigma_{Y|X}\sqrt{2\pi}} \exp\left[-\frac{1}{2}\left(\frac{y_i - \beta_0 - \beta_1 x_i}{\sigma_{Y|X}}\right)^2\right], \tag{2.32}$$

where π is the number Pi ($\simeq 3.1416$). Due to the independence assumption of the regression model, the joint pdf of $\{Y_1, Y_2, \ldots, Y_n \mid X_1, X_2, \ldots, X_n\}$ is

$$f\{Y_1, Y_2, \ldots, Y_n \mid X_1, X_2, \ldots, X_n\} = \prod_{i=1}^{n} \frac{1}{\sigma_{Y|X}\sqrt{2\pi}} \exp\left[-\frac{1}{2}\left(\frac{y_i - \beta_0 - \beta_1 x_i}{\sigma_{Y|X}}\right)^2\right]. \tag{2.33}$$

We can bring our notation in line with the notation of the regression model by setting $\sigma_{Y|X} = \sigma$ as noted.

For known parameter values β_0, β_1 and σ^2, equation (2.33) can be used to calculate the value of the joint pdf for any given values of the random variables.

But we can also turn the question around and ask: For n given values of (Y_i, X_i), what are the most likely values of the parameters β_0, β_1 and σ^2? In this interpretation, (2.33) is called the *likelihood function*. To answer the question, it is easier to work with the log-likelihood function, obtained by taking the natural logarithm of the expression in (2.33), and write it as

$$\begin{aligned}\mathcal{L}(\beta_0, \beta_1, \sigma^2) &= \sum_{i=1}^{n}\left[-\frac{1}{2}\ln(2\pi\sigma^2) - \frac{(Y_i - \beta_0 - \beta_1 X_i)^2}{\sigma^2}\right] \\ &= -\frac{n}{2}\ln(2\pi) - \frac{n}{2}\ln(\sigma^2) - \frac{\sum_{i=1}^{n}(Y_i - \beta_0 - \beta_1 X_i)^2}{2\sigma^2}, \quad (2.34)\end{aligned}$$

where we used capital letters Y_i and X_i to denote both random variables and realizations. The first-order conditions for the maximization of the log-likelihood can be solved to obtain the maximum likelihood (ML) estimates $\hat{\beta}_0, \hat{\beta}_1, \hat{\sigma}^2$ for an individual sample. The same expressions are interpreted as ML estimators when the random variable interpretation of Y_i and X_i is used.

Equation (2.34) can be maximized in two steps. First, find the values $\hat{\beta}_1$ and $\hat{\beta}_2$ that minimize the residual sum of squares RSS $= \sum_{i=1}^{n}(Y_i - \beta_0 - \beta_1 X_i)^2$. Second, take the minimized value of the residual sum of squares:

$$\text{RSS}^* = \sum_{i=1}^{n}\hat{\epsilon}_i^2 = \sum_{i=1}^{n}(Y_i - \hat{\beta}_0 - \hat{\beta}_1 X_i)^2,$$

as a fixed number in the *concentrated* log-likelihood function, and obtain the value $\hat{\sigma}^2$ of σ^2 that maximizes:

$$\mathcal{L}(\hat{\beta}_0, \hat{\beta}_1, \sigma^2) = \frac{n}{2}\ln(2\pi) - \frac{n}{2}\ln(\sigma^2) - \frac{\text{RSS}^*}{2\sigma^2}, \quad (2.35)$$

where $\mathcal{L}(\hat{\beta}_0, \hat{\beta}_1, \sigma^2)$ denotes the concentrated log-likelihood function.

The first step of the maximization is simplified if we make use of a *reparametrization* of the model equation obtained by adding and subtracting $\beta_1\mu_X$ on the right-hand side of the equation:

$$Y_i = \beta_0 + \beta_1\mu_X + \beta_1 X_i - \beta_1\mu_X + \epsilon_i,$$

and defining a new intercept:

$$\alpha \underset{\text{def}}{=} \beta_0 + \beta_1\mu_X \quad (2.36)$$

allowing the reparametrized model equation to be written as

$$Y_i = \alpha + \beta_1 (X_i - \mu_X) + \epsilon_i, \quad i = 1, 2, \ldots, n. \tag{2.37}$$

The term reparametrization is fitting since one of the parameters (i.e., the constant term) of the model equation has changed, but notably without affecting the error term. Therefore, the statistical properties of the Gaussian regression model are unaffected by the reparametrization of the model equation.

Reparametrizations will appear frequently in the book. They need to be distinguished from variable transformations, which are also very useful operations in applied modelling, but which will in general change the disturbance of the model equation. Later in this chapter, the reader will be reminded of *weighted least squares* (WLS) estimation, which is a special case of *generalized least squares* (GLS). Weighted least squares involve variable transformations that change the statistical properties of the model equation. The motivation is to solve a problem (e.g., heteroskedasticity) by reinstalling classical properties in the regression error.

However, OLS is sufficient for estimation of the conditional expectation of the Gaussian model. In order to simplify, we write the residual sum of squares to be minimized as $\sum_{i=1}^{n}(Y_i - \alpha - \beta_1(X_i - \bar{X}))^2$, which amounts to replacing μ_X with the mean $\bar{X} = \frac{1}{n}\sum_{i=1}^{n} X_i$.[1]

The two first-order conditions for the minimization of $\sum_{i=1}^{n}(Y_i - \alpha - \beta_1(X_i - \bar{X}))^2$ are as follows:

$$\sum_{i=1}^{n} Y_i - n\hat{\alpha} = 0, \tag{2.38}$$

$$\sum_{i=1}^{n} Y_i(X_i - \bar{X}) - \hat{\beta}_1 \sum_{i=1}^{n}(X_i - \bar{X})^2 = 0. \tag{2.39}$$

Equations (2.38) and (2.39) can be solved for $\hat{\alpha}$ and $\hat{\beta}_1$, respectively, to give

$$\hat{\alpha} = \bar{Y}, \tag{2.40}$$

$$\hat{\beta}_1 = \frac{\sum_{i=1}^{n} Y_i(X_i - \bar{X})}{\sum_{i=1}^{n}(X_i - \bar{X})^2}, \tag{2.41}$$

[1]Under the assumption of a bivariate Gaussian distribution, μ_X is then seen to be estimated by its ML estimate.

where $\bar{Y} = \frac{1}{n}\sum_{i=1}^{n} Y_i$. By using the definition in (2.36), the estimator of β_0 becomes

$$\hat{\beta}_0 = \hat{\alpha} - \hat{\beta}_1 \bar{X}. \tag{2.42}$$

We have now shown that the OLS estimators of the slope coefficient and (the two versions) of the constant term are identical to the ML estimators when the assumptions of the model are valid (identical and independent normal distributions).

The last parameter of interest to estimate in this model is the variance of the error term, σ^2. In this step, we do as noted above and maximize the concentrated log-likelihood function (2.35) with RSS* treated as known. The first-order condition is given by

$$\frac{n}{2}\frac{1}{\hat{\sigma}^2} - \frac{\text{RSS}^*}{2}(-1(\hat{\sigma}^2)^{-2} = 0 \Leftrightarrow \frac{n}{\hat{\sigma}^2} + \frac{\text{RSS}^*}{\hat{\sigma}^4} = 0,$$

which gives

$$\hat{\sigma}^2 = \frac{1}{n}\text{RSS}^* = \frac{1}{n}\sum_{i=1}^{n} \hat{\epsilon}_i^2, \tag{2.43}$$

as RSS* is the sum of the squared OLS residuals $\hat{\epsilon}_i = Y_i - \hat{\beta}_0 - \hat{\beta}_1 X_i \equiv Y_i - \hat{\alpha} - \hat{\beta}_1(X_i - \bar{X})$.

As many readers will be aware of, $\hat{\sigma}^2$ is a biased estimator of σ^2, while an unbiased estimator is given by

$$\tilde{\sigma}^2 = \frac{1}{n-2}\sum_{i=1}^{n} \hat{\epsilon}_i^2. \tag{2.44}$$

For moderately sized samples, the difference between the two estimators is small, and in practice it plays little role whether $\hat{\sigma}^2$ or $\tilde{\sigma}^2$ is used in the calculation of the standard errors of the coefficient estimates, and the conventional *t-values* of the coefficients, for example,

$$t\text{-value} = \frac{\hat{\beta}_1}{\sqrt{\widehat{\text{Var}}(\hat{\beta}_1)}}, \tag{2.45}$$

where $\sqrt{\widehat{\text{Var}}(\hat{\beta}_1)}$ denotes the estimated standard error of $\hat{\beta}_1$. Econometric software programs use $\tilde{\sigma}^2$, and therefore report critical values, and *p-values* for the relevant t-distribution.

Without the normality (i.e., Gaussian) assumption, the inference methods apply in an approximate manner, for large n. To improve the approximation, modern econometrics packages typically report robust standard errors, which correct for departures from the normality assumption.

Another pair of results that we will refer to later is

$$\text{Cov}(\hat{\alpha}, \hat{\beta}_1) = 0, \tag{2.46}$$

but

$$\text{Cov}(\hat{\beta}_0, \hat{\beta}_1) = \bar{X}\frac{\sigma^2}{n\hat{\sigma}_X^2} \neq 0, \tag{2.47}$$

where $\hat{\sigma}_X^2 = n^{-1}\sum_{i=1}^{n}(X_i - \bar{X})^2$. The estimators of the constant term and the slope coefficient are correlated in the original parametrization of the regression model, while they are uncorrelated (orthogonal) in the reparametrized model equation; see Bårdsen and Nymoen (2011, Section 5.3) for a detailed derivation.

Box 2.3. Inference when there are departures from normality

When the assumption about Gaussian (normal) distribution does not hold exactly, the above estimation and testing theory continue to hold approximately. This is the case for the econometric regression model that we specified above; a result that follows from asymptotic statistical theory.

When there are departures from the assumptions, for example in the form of heteroskedasticity, which is implied if X and Y are bivariate t-distributed, rather than normal, there may be reason to change the estimation method, to generalized least squares (GLS, see below), or to use robust standard errors.

However, also in this case, the seriousness of the departure from normality can be mitigated by having a relatively large sample. For example, when the degrees of freedom of the t-distribution is larger than 20, the conditional variance of Y given X becomes as good as constant (see Spanos, 1999, p. 344). In Section 2.8, some standard tests of residual misspecification are reviewed.

2.4.5. Method of moment estimation

Due to the independence assumption, all of the pairs (Y_i, X_i) are mutually independent, and the assumption about the moments of ϵ_i also holds unconditionally, in particular:

$$E(\epsilon_i) = 0, \tag{2.48}$$

and

$$\text{Cov}(\epsilon_i, X_i) = E\left[(\varepsilon_i - E(\epsilon_i))(X_i - E(X_i))\right] = 0. \tag{2.49}$$

The estimation principle, *method of moments* (*MM*), restricts the sample (i.e., empirical) moments in accordance with the assumed properties of the theoretical moments. The empirical counterparts to (2.48) and (2.49) are

$$\frac{1}{n}\sum_{i=1}^{n} \hat{\epsilon}_i = 0, \tag{2.50}$$

$$\frac{1}{n}\sum_{i=1}^{n} \hat{\epsilon}_i(X_i - \bar{X}) = 0, \tag{2.51}$$

as we estimate the expectation of the disturbance by the average of the residuals, and the covariance by the empirical covariance between the residual and the regressor.

Hence, it follows that, for the simple regression model specified above, the three estimation principles, OLS, ML and MM, give the same estimators for β_0 and β_1 (and α); cf. Exercise 2.9.

The MM estimator of σ^2 is, by direct reasoning, $\frac{1}{n}\sum_{i=1}^{n} \hat{\epsilon}_i^2$, i.e., the same estimator as the ML estimator.

2.4.6. Inference about nonlinear combinations of parameters

When we estimate a linear-in-parameter conditional expectation function, one purpose can be to test hypotheses about (derived) parameters that are nonlinear combinations of the regression coefficients. The *Delta method* gives an asymptotically valid estimate of the variance of such parameters.

The Delta method, as the name suggests, can be derived by the use of a Taylor expansions (linearization), under relatively weak assumptions (see Sydsæter *et al.*, 2016, Section 7.4). We only give the results needed for practical use of the method here, see Box 2.4 for references to other books.

Assume the simple regression model above, estimated by OLS,

$$Y_i = \beta_0 + \beta_1 X_i + \epsilon_i$$

and that we are interested in the derived parameter, denoted θ:

$$\theta = \frac{\beta_0}{\beta_1}. \tag{2.52}$$

We choose the ratio as our example of nonlinearity, because this will be directly applicable several times later in the book. A natural choice of estimator of θ is the ratio of the two OLS estimators $\hat{\beta}_0$ and $\hat{\beta}_1$:

$$\hat{\theta} = \frac{\hat{\beta}_0}{\hat{\beta}_1}. \tag{2.53}$$

It can be shown, specifically under the assumptions of the regression model, that

$$E(\hat{\theta}) = E\left(\frac{\hat{\beta}_0}{\hat{\beta}_1}\right) \approx \theta, \tag{2.54}$$

and that the variance $\text{Var}(\hat{\theta})$ is well approximated by the estimator $\widehat{\text{Var}(\hat{\theta})}$, given by

$$\widehat{\text{Var}(\hat{\theta})} = \left(\frac{1}{\hat{\beta}_1}\right)^2 \left[\widehat{\text{Var}(\hat{\beta}_0)} + \hat{\theta}^2 \widehat{\text{Var}(\hat{\beta}_1)} - 2\hat{\theta}\,\widehat{\text{Cov}(\hat{\beta}_0, \hat{\beta}_1)}\right], \tag{2.55}$$

when the sample size n is reasonably large.

As we shall see below, we will often use (2.55) to test hypotheses about long-run coefficients of dynamic models. However, there are many other applications as well. Estimation of the so-called natural rate of unemployment is a well-known macroeconomic example, which we will review briefly.[2]

In order to estimate the natural rate, we must specify a model where it is a parameter (explicitly or implicitly). As an example, we consider a price Phillips curve model (PCM) of the simplest type found in macroeconomic textbooks:

$$\text{INF}_i = \beta_0 + \beta_1 U_t + \epsilon_i, \tag{2.56}$$

[2]Another macroeconomic example is the empirical construction of an Monetary Conditions Index (see Eika *et al.*, 1996).

where INF_i is the annual inflation percentage in year i and U_i is the unemployment percentage. Later in the book, we will consider dynamic versions of the price PCM.

The natural rate of unemployment can be defined in such a way that it becomes a parameter in (2.56). Rewrite the PCM as

$$\begin{aligned}\text{INF}_i &= \beta_1\left(U_t - \frac{-\beta_0}{\beta_1}\right) + \epsilon_i \\ &= \beta_1(U_t - U^{\text{nat}}) + \epsilon_i, \end{aligned} \tag{2.57}$$

and define

$$U^{\text{nat}} \underset{\text{def}}{=} \frac{-\beta_0}{\beta_1},$$

as the natural rate of unemployment. U^{nat} is a parameter in both (2.56) and (2.57), although implicit in (2.56).

Equation (2.57) is however nonlinear in parameters. To estimate U^{nat} from (2.57) requires nonlinear least squares (NLS). However, with the aid of the Delta method, we can make inference about U^{nat} by estimating the linear-in-parameter model (2.56).

Assume that we have estimated the empirical PCM:

$$\text{INF}_i = \underset{(1.639)}{10.5088} - \underset{(0.4613)}{1.83147}U_i,$$

where the conventional standard errors of the OLS estimates are reported below the estimates. The estimate of the natural rate of unemployment becomes

$$\hat{U}^{\text{nat}} = \frac{10.5088}{1.83147} = 5.7379.$$

Assume that the estimated covariance $\text{Cov}(\hat{\beta}_0, \hat{\beta}_1)$ is -0.71525. Using (2.55), we obtain

$$\begin{aligned}\text{Var}(\hat{U}^{\text{nat}}) \approx& \left(\frac{1}{-1.83147}\right)^2 \\ &\times [2.6851 + ((5.7379)^2) \times 0.21277 \\ &- 2 \times (-5.7379) \times (-0.71525)] \\ =& \left(\frac{1}{-1.83147}\right)^2 \times 1.4822 \\ =& \ 0.44188.\end{aligned}$$

Note that in the third term, -5.7379 corresponds to $\hat{\theta}$ in (2.55). Hence, we have to "plug in" the negative of the estimated natural rate, to use the formula correctly. An approximate 95% confidence interval for U^{nat} is therefore:

$$5.7379 \pm 2\sqrt{0.44188} = 5.7379 \pm 2 \cdot 0.66474$$

or, with one decimal:

$$[4.4\%; \ 7.1\%].$$

If you solve Exercise 2.11, you can check these results by solving a practical computer exercise.

As pointed out by Ericsson *et al.* (1999), if β_1 is precisely estimated, the above method is usually quite satisfactory. However, if β_1 is imprecisely estimated (i.e., not very significant statistically), the approach can be misleading. Specifically, the method (and this problem also applies to estimation by NLS) ignores how $\frac{\hat{\beta}_0}{\hat{\beta}_1}$ behaves for values of $\hat{\beta}_1$ relatively close to zero, where "relatively" reflects the uncertainty in the estimation of $\hat{\beta}_1$. In such cases, a likelihood ratio-based confidence interval is usually more correct than what the Delta method gives.

Box 2.4. The Delta method in textbooks

The method is covered in modern elementary books, for example, Hill, Griffiths and Lim (2012, Sections 5B.4 and 5B.5). In Bårdsen and Nymoen (2011), the Delta method is presented in Section 4.4.5. In the advanced book by Davidson and MacKinnon (2004), it is presented in Section 5.6.

2.5. Estimation of a Structural Equation Between Two Variables by IV

Although our research questions can often be answered by focusing on the conditional distribution of one variable given the others(s), at least in order to get a reasonably good (first) approximation to the relationship we are interested in, we are just as often led in the direction of modelling other aspects of the joint distribution, and sometimes even the complete joint distribution. We can maybe think of "aspects of the joint distribution" as corresponding to *single equation structural modelling*, and a complete representation of the joint distribution as *multiple equation structural modelling*.[3]

2.5.1. Model specification

In order to define a single equation structural model, we can refer to the linear relationship (2.20), namely:

$$Y_i = \beta_0 + \beta_1 X_i + \epsilon_i, \quad i = 1, 2, \ldots, n, \tag{2.58}$$

with the important remark that we now assume that ϵ_i and the explanatory variable X_i are correlated.

$\text{Cov}(X_i, \varepsilon_i) \neq 0$ has the implication that the OLS estimator $\hat{\beta}_1$ is *inconsistent*; it is biased even as $n \to \infty$. In order to have a logical possibility of finding a consistent estimator, call it $\hat{\beta}_1^c$, we obviously need to find a way of breaking the correlation between X and ϵ_i, so that as the sample size increases, the correlation is reduced towards zero. In that case, we may hope to find an estimator $\hat{\beta}_1^c$ which has an asymptotic distribution that is "degenerate" around β_1 (it has no variance):

$$\underset{n\to\infty}{\text{plim}}\,(\hat{\beta}_1^c) = \beta_1$$

even though $\text{plim}_{n\to\infty}(\hat{\beta}_1) \neq \beta_1$, in the case of the OLS estimator. As many readers will know, plim denotes *probability limit*, and often we write it without $n \to \infty$ in the label below plim.

Box 2.5. Properties of probability limits

Probability limits have certain properties, not satisfied by the algebra of expectations, which enable us to discuss consistency in certain situations where unbiasedness in finite samples does not hold (or cannot be proven). In particular, if g is some continuous function, and Q_n a random variable, then $\text{plim}\, g(Q_n) = g(\text{plim}\, Q_n)$. More generally, the probability limit of a function of several variables is equal to the function

[3]This does not mean that systems of variables cannot be studied by regression methods though. For example, the reduced form equations of simultaneous equation model can be well estimated by OLS on each equation, although a genuine system estimator like seemingly unrelated regression (SUR) estimation will be more efficient in many instances (cf. Hendry and Nielsen, 2007, p. 212).

Box 2.5 (*Continued*)

evaluated at the probability limits of the random variables. Three specific useful applications of this result are:

(i) $\text{plim}(Q_{1n} + Q_{2n}) = \text{plim}\, Q_{1n} + \text{plim}\, Q_{2n}$,
(ii) $\text{plim}(Q_{1n}Q_{2n}) = \text{plim}\, Q_{1n}\, \text{plim}\, Q_{2n}$,
(iii) $\text{plim}(Q_{1n}/Q_{2n}) = \text{plim}\, Q_{1n}/\text{plim}\, Q_{2n}$,

where Q_{1n} and Q_{2n} are random variables. In general, $\text{plim}\, Q_{1n}$ and $\text{plim}\, Q_{2n}$ are random variables, but if they are constants, properties (i)–(iii) continue to hold, and can often be used to investigate whether an estimator converges to the true coefficient as the sample size n increases. The discussion of the consistency of $\hat{\beta}_1^{\text{IV}}$ is an example.

How can we obtain the estimator $\hat{\beta}_1^c$? First of all, we note that it does not always exist, in which case β_1 is an *unidentified* parameter. However, if β_1 is identified, at least one consistent estimator exists. Identification is a property of the theoretical statistical model, in other words, of the population distribution.

Hence, in order to "break the correlation", we need to assume that the underlying population distribution function includes a third variable, which we denote by Z. Hence, we now assume that we have n independent triplets:

$$(X_1, Y_1, Z_1), (X_2, Y_2, Z_2), \ldots, (X_n, Y_n, Z_n),$$

where there are correlation within the triplets, but not between them (they are mutually independent). Hence, the ordering of the triplets does not matter and we can write the sample as $\{Y_1, Y_2, \ldots, Y_n, X_1, X_2, \ldots, X_n, Z_1, Z_2, \ldots, X_n\}$, as long as we remember that only variables with the identical subscripts may be correlated.

Since the model equation (2.58) only involves the X_i and Y_i variables, not Z_i, we may utilize that the joint pdf of all the n-triplets can be factorized in terms of a "smaller" joint distribution for $\{(X_1, Y_1), (X_2, Y_2), \ldots, (X_n, Y_n)\}$ conditional on the $(Z_1, Z_2, \ldots, Z_n)$:

$$\begin{aligned} &f(Y_1, Y_2, \ldots, Y_n, X_1, X_2, \ldots, X_n, Z_1, Z_2, \ldots, Z_n) \\ &\quad \equiv f(Y_1, X_1, Y_2, X_2 \ldots, Y_n, X_n \mid Z_1, Z_2, \ldots, Z_n) f(Z_1, Z_2, \ldots, Z_n) \\ &\quad \equiv f(Y_1, Y_2, \ldots, Y_n, X_1, X_2, \ldots, X_n \mid Z_1, Z_2, \ldots, Z_n) f(Z_1, Z_2, \ldots, Z_n). \end{aligned}$$

The assumptions now refer to the "joint (but conditional)" distribution of X and Y given the Z_s, instead of the conditional distribution of Y given X that characterized the regression model.

The model equation is (2.58) and the assumptions are:

a′ $E(\epsilon_i \mid Z_j) = 0$, $\forall i$ and j,
b′ $\text{Var}(\epsilon_i \mid Z_i) = \sigma^2$, $\forall i$,
c′ $\text{Cov}(\epsilon_i, \epsilon_j \mid Z_i, Z_j) = 0$, $\forall i \neq j$,
d′ $\text{Cov}(X_i, Z_i) \neq 0$, $\forall i$
e′ β_0, β_1 and σ^2 are constant parameters.

We see that **a–c** in the first list of assumption above have been replaced by assumptions that are conditional on the variable Z, which is known as an *instrumental variable*, and it is indeed instrumental in the possibility of formulating the consistent estimator $\hat{\beta}_1^c$. The assumption **d′** restates what we have assumed above, namely that there is correlation within triplets, but not between triplets.

Note also that **a′** implies that $\text{Cov}(\epsilon_i, Z_i) = 0$. Together with **d′**, it defines the properties of IV *validity* and IV *relevance*:

$$\text{Cov}(\epsilon_i, Z_i) = 0, \quad \text{Instrument validity,} \tag{2.59}$$

$$\text{Cov}(X_i, Z_i) \neq 0, \quad \text{Instrument relevance.} \tag{2.60}$$

When (2.58) is the model equation and **e′** holds, it is implied that $\text{Cov}(X_i, Z_i) \neq 0$ as well. The availability of the IV gives rise to the *instrumental variable* (IV) estimator. The IV estimator is an MM estimator, and can be derived by multiplying the orthogonalized model equation (2.58):

$$Y_i = \alpha + \beta_1(X_i - \bar{X}) + \epsilon_i,$$

by the instrument variable $(Z_i - \bar{Z})$, giving:

$$Y_i(Z_i - \bar{Z}) = \alpha(Z_i - \bar{Z}) + \beta_1(X_i - \bar{X})(Z_i - \bar{Z}) + \epsilon_i(Z_i - \bar{Z}),$$

and

$$\sum_{i=1}^{n} Y_i(Z_i - \bar{Z}) = \beta_1 \sum_{i=1}^{n}(X_i - \bar{X})(Z_i - \bar{Z}) + \sum_{i=1}^{n} \epsilon_i(Z_i - \bar{Z}),$$

after summation on both sides of the equation. We can now introduce $\hat{\beta}_1^{\text{IV}}$ as notation for the IV estimator:

$$\sum_{i=1}^{n} Y_i(Z_i - \bar{Z}) = \hat{\beta}_1^{\text{IV}} \sum_{i=1}^{n}(X_i - \bar{X})(Z_i - \bar{Z}) + \sum_{i=1}^{n} \hat{\epsilon}_i(Z_i - \bar{Z}),$$

where $\hat{\epsilon}_i$ denotes the IV-residuals (and not the OLS residuals). According to the MM principle, we set

$$\frac{1}{n}\sum_{i=1}^{n}\hat{\epsilon}_i(Z_i - \bar{Z}) = 0,$$

which can be solved for $\hat{\beta}_1^{\mathrm{IV}}$:

$$\hat{\beta}_1^{\mathrm{IV}} = \frac{\sum_{i=1}^{n} Y_i(Z_i - \bar{Z})}{\sum_{i=1}^{n}(X_i - \bar{X})(Z_i - \bar{Z})}, \tag{2.61}$$

which is the expression for the IV estimator for the slope coefficient of the model relationship (2.58).

By insertion from (2.58), we can express the IV estimator as equal to the true coefficient plus a bias term:

$$\hat{\beta}_1^{\mathrm{IV}} = \beta_1 + \frac{\frac{1}{n}\sum_{i=1}^{n} \epsilon_i(Z_i - \bar{Z})}{\frac{1}{n}\sum_{i=1}^{n}(X_i - \bar{X})(Z_i - \bar{Z})}.$$

With reference to the assumptions of the statistical model, and the properties of probability limits, we obtain

$$\text{plim}(\hat{\beta}_1^{\mathrm{IV}}) = \beta_1 + \frac{\text{plim}(\frac{1}{n}\sum_{i=1}^{n} \epsilon_i(Z_i - \bar{Z}))}{\text{plim}\left(\frac{1}{n}\sum_{i=1}^{n}(X_i - \bar{X})(Z_i - \bar{Z})\right)}.$$

We have that $\text{plim}(\beta_1) = \beta_1$, $\text{plim}(\frac{1}{n}\sum_{i=1}^{n} \epsilon_i(Z_i - \bar{Z})) = \text{Cov}(\epsilon_i, Z_i) = 0$, and $\text{plim}(\frac{1}{n}\sum_{i=1}^{n}(X_i - \bar{X})(Z_i - \bar{Z})) = \text{Cov}(X_i, Z_i) \neq 0$, hence

$$\text{plim}(\hat{\beta}_1^{\mathrm{IV}}) = \beta_1, \tag{2.62}$$

which shows that the IV estimator is a consistent estimator of β_1.

As we shall see below, the two central conditions (2.59) and (2.60) can be stated, more generally, as asymptotic uncorrelatedness between the model equation error and the IV, and asymptotic correlatedness between the model's explanatory variable and the instrument. This makes IV estimation applicable to a wider class of models than the independence of sampling model that we have considered here. In this book, the most important member of that wider class is of course dynamic models.

2.5.2. The importance of IV strength

In principle, we can regard that the requirements of instrumental validity and relevance are theoretical properties of a specified econometric model.

This is because the structural equation logically speaking must be part of a larger system of equations, and if we specify that system as a multiple equation model, that specification will make clear where the IV Z resides in the system, and why it is both valid and relevant (as defined by (2.59) and (2.60)). This view is closely linked to the classical discussion of identification of simultaneous equations models, which we present in Chapter 7.

However, quite often IV estimation is used in situations where the specification of the larger system that has Y, X and Z as variables is unclear or incomplete. In practice, the sample which is available for estimation can also be relatively small. Hence, it is important to establish an understanding of how large the correlation between endogenous and instrument needs to be for the IV method to work well in such practical situations.

Even though there is no reason to use IV estimation in cases where the assumptions of the regression model hold, that case can nevertheless aid the understanding of the properties of IV estimation in small samples. Assume therefore that we have a regression model equation, and for simplicity, assume that regressor is a deterministic variable. The variance of (2.61) is then:

$$\mathrm{Var}(\hat{\beta}^{\mathrm{IV}}) = \sigma^2 \frac{\sum_{i=1}^{n}(Z_i - \bar{Z})^2}{\left\{\sum_i (X_i - \bar{X})Z_i\right\}^2},$$

while the variance of the OLS estimator is

$$\mathrm{Var}(\hat{\beta}_1) = \sigma^2 \frac{1}{\sum_{i=1}^{n}(X_i - \bar{X})^2}.$$

The expression for relative efficiency of the two estimators is therefore:

$$\frac{\mathrm{Var}(\hat{\beta}_1)}{\mathrm{Var}(\hat{\beta}^{\mathrm{IV}})} = r_{ZX}^2,$$

where r_{ZX}^2 denotes the squared empirical correlation coefficient between Z and X.

We see that if r_{ZX}^2 is high, IV estimation is efficiently relative to OLS. Conversely, if r_{WX}^2 is close to zero, the high variance of the IV estimator can become just a large practical problem as the bias of the OLS estimator, in particular if the known direction of the OLS bias can take it into account when we interpret the estimation results.

This simple result is quite important because it generalizes to all structural model equations (i.e., where one or more right-hand side variables are correlated with the error-term). In principle, IV estimation should be employed for such model equations. However, if the IV set (see Section 2.6.8) "as a whole" is weakly correlated with the endogenous variables, the results of IV estimation can become unreliable. This problem has become known as the *weak instruments* problem.

Box 2.6. Testing IV strength

A much used test uses the regression between the endogenous right-hand variable and the whole set IVs. It has been shown that a value of the F-test above 10 gives rejection of the hypothesis of weak instruments (see Stock and Watson, 2012, Section 12.5).

It has turned out to be difficult to generalize the test to cover model equations with two or more endogenous right-hand side variables. However, the lack of a formal test does not reduce the importance of investigating the set of IVs for signs of low correlation with the endogenous variables (i.e., weak instrument relevance), for example by estimation of reduced form model equations, and careful inspection of the variables' significance.

2.6. Multivariate Regression and Structural Equations

In applied econometrics, we deal with complex relationships and systems. In practical modelling, regression equations and structural equations are therefore typically multivariate. The statistical interpretation of regression equations and structural models that we have reviewed above is unaffected by the increase in number of variables in the models. What changes is the economic interpretation of the coefficients, which in multivariate models becomes partial derivatives or elasticities (or a semi-elasticity, depending on variable transformations).

2.6.1. Multivariate regression with scalar notation

Several aspects of multivariate modelling can be illustrated by only increasing the number of variables by one, and this paragraph therefore begins with that case.

Models with two explanatory variables can be formulated with scalar notation. The regression model equation is

$$Y_i = \beta_0 + \beta_1 X_{1i} + \beta_2 X_{2i} + \epsilon_i, \tag{2.63}$$

where β_1 and β_2 are partial derivatives (elasticities if the variables are measured in logs). The econometric specification of the model with respect to the conditional distribution of ϵ_i is given by the $2n$ X-variables. The correlation coefficient ρ_{12} of X_1 and X_2,

$$\rho_{12} \underset{\text{def}}{=} \frac{\sigma_{X_1X_2}}{\sigma_{X_1}\sigma_{X_2}}, \tag{2.64}$$

is between -1 and 1, i.e.,

$$-1 < \rho_{12} < 1. \tag{2.65}$$

In (2.64), $\sigma_{X_i} = \sqrt{\sigma^2_{Xi}}$ $(i = 1, 2)$ is the standard deviation, and $\sigma_{X_1X_2}$ denotes the covariance $\text{Cov}(X_{1i}, X_{2i})$.

Condition (2.65) is the assumption about absence of perfect multicollinearity in the population distribution of X_1 and X_2. The OLS estimators of the two slope coefficients of the model are

$$\hat{\beta}_1 = \frac{\hat{\sigma}^2_{X_2}\hat{\sigma}_{YX_1} - \hat{\sigma}_{YX_2}\hat{\sigma}_{X_1X_2}}{\hat{\sigma}^2_{X_1}\hat{\sigma}^2_{X_2} - \hat{\sigma}^2_{X_1X_2}}, \tag{2.66}$$

$$\hat{\beta}_2 = \frac{\hat{\sigma}^2_{X_1}\hat{\sigma}_{YX_2} - \hat{\sigma}_{YX_1}\hat{\sigma}_{X_1X_2}}{\hat{\sigma}^2_{X_1}\hat{\sigma}^2_{X_2} - \hat{\sigma}^2_{X_1X_2}}, \tag{2.67}$$

where $\hat{\sigma}^2_{X_k}, \hat{\sigma}_{Y,X_k}$ $(k = 1, 2)$ and $\hat{\sigma}_{X_1,X_2}$ denote empirical second-order moments (variances and covariances):

$$\hat{\sigma}_{YX_k} = \frac{1}{n}\sum_{i=1}^{n} Y_i(X_{ki} - \bar{X}_k), \quad k = 1, 2,$$

$$\hat{\sigma}^2_{X_k} = \frac{1}{n}\sum_{i=1}^{n}(X_{ki} - \bar{X}_k)^2, \quad k = 1, 2,$$

$$\hat{\sigma}_{X_1X_2} = \frac{1}{n}\sum_{i=1}^{n} X_{1i}(X_{2i} - \bar{X}_k).$$

We can rewrite the expressions for $\hat{\beta}_1$ and $\hat{\beta}_2$ in order to bring the empirical correlation coefficient of the two regressors into the picture. For $\hat{\beta}_1$:

$$\hat{\beta}_1 = \frac{\hat{\sigma}^2_{X_2}\hat{\sigma}_{YX_1} - \hat{\sigma}_{YX_2}\hat{\sigma}_{X_1X_2}}{\hat{\sigma}^2_{X_1}\hat{\sigma}^2_{X_2}(1 - r^2_{12})},$$

where r_{12} denotes the empirical correlation coefficient,

$$r_{12} \underset{\text{def}}{=} \frac{\hat{\sigma}_{X_1X_2}}{\hat{\sigma}_{X_1}\hat{\sigma}_{X_2}}. \tag{2.68}$$

In some textbooks, $-1 < r_{12} < 1$ is stated as an assumption of the regression model. This is imprecise, because model assumptions are about population moments and parameters, and specifically (2.65) above, not about sample moments. However, even if $-1 < \rho_{12} < 1$ is valid, we could be unlucky and experience perfect multicollinearity in a given sample. If $r_{12} = 1$, estimation is impossible due to zero in the denominator in the expressions for $\hat{\beta}_1$ and $\hat{\beta}_2$.

As many readers will have experienced, perfect sample multicollinearity is usually something that happens by mistake. For example, if we have $n = 100$ and specify X_1 and X_2 as two step-dummies: X_{1i} equal to 1 for $i = 1, 2, \ldots, 20$ and zero elsewhere, and X_{2i} equal to 1 for $i = 21, 22, \ldots, 100$ and zero elsewhere, the computer program will produce an error-message about "perfect collinearity" (or maybe "unable to invert matrix"). The reason is that the two step-dummies are perfectly correlated with the constant term in the model equation.[4]

Mistakes aside, the practical problem is therefore high, but not perfect multicollinearity. The regression coefficients will be calculated, but the estimated standard errors of the coefficients may become large, as the variances of the two estimated coefficients are given by

$$\text{Var}(\hat{\beta}_k) = \frac{\tilde{\sigma}^2}{n\hat{\sigma}^2_{Xk}(1 - r^2_{12})}, \quad k = 1, 2, \tag{2.69}$$

where most programs will use $\tilde{\sigma}^2 = \frac{1}{n-3}\sum_{i=1}^{n}\hat{\epsilon}_i^2$, as a generalization of the unbiased estimate of the regression-error variance in (2.44) above.

[4]For example, PcGive will issue: *** Warning: regressors are linearly dependent (numerically or exact — some coefficients set to zero). Stata will also drop a variable, and report the estimation result for the degenerate model.

Due to the independence of sampling assumption, the empirical second-order moments will be consistent estimators of the corresponding population moments, hence

$$\text{plim}(\hat{\beta}_1) = \frac{\sigma^2_{X_2}\sigma_{YX_1} - \sigma_{YX_2}\sigma_{X_1X_2}}{\sigma^2_{X_1}\sigma^2_{X_2}(1-\rho^2_{12})} = \beta_1,$$

and likewise for $\hat{\beta}_1$ and $\hat{\beta}_0$ (or $\hat{\alpha}$ if that parameterization is used).

The testing of hypotheses about the coefficients can be done in the same way as in the simple regression case. The degrees of freedom of the Student t-distribution (and the F-distribution) that we take critical values from will have one degree of freedom less, since the model contains one more parameter. Hence, if the t-value in (2.45) referred to (2.63), the degrees of freedom will be the number of observations minus 3 (one intercept and two other regressors), while in the simple regression the degree of freedom will be number of observations minus 2.

2.6.2. Regression with matrix notation

For $k > 2$, scalar notation becomes impractical. Let $\mathbf{X}$ be an $n \times k$ matrix with the regressors, and write the model equation as

$$\mathbf{y} = \mathbf{X}\boldsymbol{\beta} + \boldsymbol{\epsilon}, \tag{2.70}$$

where $\mathbf{y}$ is an $n \times 1$ vector holding the n random Y-variables, $\boldsymbol{\epsilon}$ is the $n \times 1$ vector with disturbances (error terms). The coefficient vector is $\boldsymbol{\beta}$. $\mathbf{X}$ is the matrix that holds the regressors. Looking back at (2.63), to match that model equation, the $\boldsymbol{\beta}$ vector must be 3×1 and the matrix $\mathbf{X}$ must have dimension $n \times 3$. Hence, the number of rows in $\boldsymbol{\beta}$, and the number of columns of $\mathbf{X}$, is equal to the number of X-variables plus one.

In the general case, with k indicating the number of X-variables, the structure of the matrix equation is

$$\begin{bmatrix} Y_1 \\ Y_2 \\ \vdots \\ Y_n \end{bmatrix} = \underbrace{\begin{bmatrix} X_{01} & X_{11} & \dots & X_{k1} \\ X_{02} & X_{12} & \dots & X_{k2} \\ \vdots & \vdots & & \vdots \\ X_{0n} & X_{1n} & \dots & X_{kn} \end{bmatrix}}_{n\times(k+1)} \underbrace{\begin{bmatrix} \beta_0 \\ \beta_1 \\ \vdots \\ \beta_k \end{bmatrix}}_{(k+1)\times 1} + \begin{bmatrix} \epsilon_1 \\ \epsilon_2 \\ \vdots \\ \epsilon_n \end{bmatrix}, \tag{2.71}$$

where the first column of $\mathbf{X}$ holds 1 in every cell: $X_{0i} = 1$, $\forall i$. If we let $\mathbf{x}_i$ denote the ith row in $\mathbf{X}$, (a $1 \times (k+1)$ matrix), we can write "row i" in equation (2.70) as

$$Y_i = \mathbf{x}_i\boldsymbol{\beta} + \varepsilon_i = \sum_{j=0}^{k} \beta_j X_{ji} + \epsilon_i, \quad i = 1, 2, \ldots, n, \tag{2.72}$$

and (2.63) is a special case, with $k = 2$.

The assumption about constant and identical disturbance variance is written as

$$\mathrm{Var}(\boldsymbol{\epsilon} \mid \mathbf{X}) = \sigma^2\mathbf{I}, \tag{2.73}$$

where $\mathbf{I}$ is the *identity matrix* $(n \times n)$.

When we write the regression equation as in (2.71), we think of the constant term as "explanatory variable number zero" and define k as the *number of regressors with genuine variation* (they do not take a constant value). But there are other conventions, and other textbooks refer to k as the total number of Xs, including the constant. In this case, $\mathbf{X}\boldsymbol{\beta}$ in (2.70) is written:

$$\begin{bmatrix} X_{11} & X_{21} & \ldots & X_{k1} \\ X_{11} & X_{22} & \ldots & X_{k2} \\ \vdots & \vdots & & \vdots \\ X_{1n} & X_{2n} & \ldots & X_{kn} \end{bmatrix}_{n\times k} \begin{bmatrix} \beta_1 \\ \beta_2 \\ \vdots \\ \beta_k \end{bmatrix}_{k\times 1}$$

as the constant term is counted as "variable 1", and k now refers to the number of regressors *including the constant.*

Of course, it does not matter for the statistical theory how we number the columns in $\mathbf{X}$. But in practice it is important to remember whether k includes the constant or not, because it affects the degrees of freedom of the test statistics.

There is a straightforward way of obtaining the matrix notation expression for the OLS estimator of the coefficient vector $\boldsymbol{\beta}$ in (2.70). Note first that the difference between simple regression and multiple regression is dimensionality: we condition on several Xs, not just one. With that in mind, the econometric specification of the model is the same as in the simple regression case, and this means that the result about equivalence of MM estimation and OLS estimation also holds in the multivariate regression case. The generalization of the MM condition (2.51) is

$$\mathbf{X}'\hat{\boldsymbol{\epsilon}} = \mathbf{0}, \tag{2.74}$$

where **0** in the $n \times 1$ matrix with zeros, $\mathbf{X}'$ denotes the *transpose* **X** matrix, and $\hat{\boldsymbol{\epsilon}}$ is the vector with residuals:

$$\hat{\boldsymbol{\epsilon}} = \mathbf{y} - \mathbf{X}\hat{\boldsymbol{\beta}}. \tag{2.75}$$

Substitution in (2.74) gives

$$\mathbf{X}'(\mathbf{y} - \mathbf{X}\hat{\boldsymbol{\beta}}) = \mathbf{0}, \tag{2.76}$$

and multiplication by $\mathbf{X}'$ gives:

$$\mathbf{X}'\mathbf{y} - (\mathbf{X}'\mathbf{X})\hat{\boldsymbol{\beta}} = \mathbf{0} \quad \Leftrightarrow \quad (\mathbf{X}'\mathbf{X})\hat{\boldsymbol{\beta}} = \mathbf{X}'\mathbf{y}. \tag{2.77}$$

In order to isolate $\hat{\boldsymbol{\beta}}$ on the left-hand side, we multiply (from the left) by the inverse matrix $(\mathbf{X}'\mathbf{X})^{-1}$, which gives

$$\hat{\boldsymbol{\beta}} = (\mathbf{X}'\mathbf{X})^{-1}\mathbf{X}'\mathbf{y} \tag{2.78}$$

as the expression for the MM estimator and the OLS estimator. Moreover, and in direct parallel to simple regression, if the conditional distribution of ϵ_i given the X-variables is Gaussian normal, (2.78) also represents the maximum likelihood estimator (MLE) of $\hat{\boldsymbol{\beta}}$, which generalizes the result for the simple Gaussian regression model above.

Note that it is essential that the matrix $(\mathbf{X}'\mathbf{X})$ is invertible. If **X** is not invertible, the estimator $\hat{\boldsymbol{\beta}}$ cannot be calculated. Mathematically $(\mathbf{X}'\mathbf{X})$ is invertible if it has *full rank*. Hence, if we count the intercept as the zero-column in **X**, $\text{rank}(\mathbf{X}'\mathbf{X}) = k + 1$ is the necessary and sufficient condition for invertibility of $(\mathbf{X}'\mathbf{X})$. Full rank means that there is no linear combination of variables (individual columns) of **X** that are perfectly correlated with any of the variables. Hence, the full-rank (invertibility) condition is the same as the *absence of perfect multicollinearity condition* that we discussed above. A third term, that is often used to express this property, is that $(\mathbf{X}'\mathbf{X})$ is a *non-singular* matrix.

In one of the exercises in the appendix, you are invited to derive the OLS estimator from "first principles", with matrix notation.

If we want to make the distinction between the constant term and the other regressors explicit, we can rewrite **X** as the *partitioned* matrix (see Section 2.6.5):

$$\mathbf{X} = [\boldsymbol{\iota} \quad \mathbf{X}_2],$$

where

$$\boldsymbol{\iota} = \begin{bmatrix} 1 \\ 1 \\ \vdots \\ 1 \end{bmatrix}_{n\times 1},$$

$$\mathbf{X}_2 = \begin{bmatrix} X_{11} & \dots & X_{k1} \\ X_{12} & \dots & X_{k2} \\ \vdots & & \vdots \\ X_{1n} & \dots & X_{kn} \end{bmatrix}_{n\times k},$$

and partitioning $\boldsymbol{\beta}$ conformingly as

$$\boldsymbol{\beta} = \begin{bmatrix} \beta_0 \\ \boldsymbol{\beta}_2 \end{bmatrix}.$$

By solving another of the exercises at the end of the chapter (Exercise 2.17), you can show that $\hat{\boldsymbol{\beta}}' = (\hat{\beta}_1 \quad \hat{\boldsymbol{\beta}}_2')$, and that the estimator of $\hat{\boldsymbol{\beta}}_2$ can be expressed as

$$\hat{\boldsymbol{\beta}}_2 = [(\mathbf{X}_2 - \overline{\mathbf{X}}_2)'(\mathbf{X}_2 - \overline{\mathbf{X}}_2)]^{-1}(\mathbf{X}_2 - \overline{\mathbf{X}}_2)'\mathbf{y}. \tag{2.79}$$

In $\overline{\mathbf{X}}_2$, the typical row is $\boldsymbol{\iota}\bar{X}_i, i = 2, \dots, k$. Hence, (2.79) gives a matrix notation counterpart to the OLS estimator of the slope coefficient in the simple regression model.

As in the case with intercept and a single explanatory variable, the ML estimator of the regression-error variance is the average of the squared residuals, which we can write as

$$\hat{\sigma}^2 = \frac{1}{n}\hat{\boldsymbol{\epsilon}}'\hat{\boldsymbol{\epsilon}}, \tag{2.80}$$

but where we usually will prefer the unbiased estimator:

$$\tilde{\sigma}^2 = \frac{1}{n-(k+1)}\hat{\boldsymbol{\epsilon}}'\hat{\boldsymbol{\epsilon}}. \tag{2.81}$$

2.6.3. Projection matrices

The matrix

$$\mathbf{M} = \mathbf{I} - \mathbf{X}(\mathbf{X}'\mathbf{X})^{-1}\mathbf{X}' \tag{2.82}$$

is often called the "residual maker". That nickname is apt, since

$$\begin{aligned}\mathbf{My} &= (\mathbf{I} - \mathbf{X}(\mathbf{X}'\mathbf{X})^{-1}\mathbf{X}')\mathbf{y} \\ &= \mathbf{y} - \mathbf{X}(\mathbf{X}'\mathbf{X})^{-1}\mathbf{X}'\mathbf{y} \\ &= \mathbf{y} - \mathbf{X}\hat{\boldsymbol{\beta}} \equiv \hat{\boldsymbol{\epsilon}}.\end{aligned}$$

M plays a central role in many derivations. The following properties are worth noting:

$$\mathbf{M} = \mathbf{M}' \quad \text{symmetric matrix,} \tag{2.83}$$

$$\mathbf{M}^2 = \mathbf{M} \quad \text{idempotent matrix,} \tag{2.84}$$

$$\mathbf{MX} = \mathbf{0} \quad \text{regression of X on X gives a perfect fit.} \tag{2.85}$$

Another way of interpreting $\mathbf{MX} = \mathbf{0}$ is that since **M** produces the OLS residuals, **M** is orthogonal to **X**.

M does not affect the residuals:

$$\mathbf{M}\hat{\boldsymbol{\varepsilon}} = \mathbf{M}(\mathbf{y} - \mathbf{X}\hat{\boldsymbol{\beta}}) = \mathbf{My} - \mathbf{MX}\hat{\boldsymbol{\beta}} = \hat{\boldsymbol{\epsilon}}. \tag{2.86}$$

Since $\mathbf{y} = \mathbf{X}\boldsymbol{\beta} + \boldsymbol{\epsilon}$, we also have

$$\mathbf{M}\boldsymbol{\epsilon} = \mathbf{M}(\mathbf{y} - \mathbf{X}\boldsymbol{\beta}) = \hat{\boldsymbol{\epsilon}}. \tag{2.87}$$

Note that this gives

$$\hat{\boldsymbol{\epsilon}}'\hat{\boldsymbol{\epsilon}} = \boldsymbol{\epsilon}'\mathbf{M}\boldsymbol{\epsilon}, \tag{2.88}$$

which shows that *RSS* is a *quadratic form* in the theoretical disturbances.

A second important matrix in regression analysis is

$$\mathbf{P} = \mathbf{X}(\mathbf{X}'\mathbf{X})^{-1}\mathbf{X}', \tag{2.89}$$

which is called the "prediction maker", or "hat matrix", since:

$$\hat{\mathbf{y}} = \mathbf{X}\hat{\boldsymbol{\beta}} = \mathbf{X}(\mathbf{X}'\mathbf{X})^{-1}\mathbf{X}'\mathbf{y} = \mathbf{Py}. \tag{2.90}$$

$\mathbf{P}$ is also symmetric and idempotent. In linear algebra, $\mathbf{M}$ and $\mathbf{P}$ are both known as projection matrices.

$\mathbf{M}$ and $\mathbf{P}$ are orthogonal:

$$\mathbf{MP} = \mathbf{PM} = \mathbf{0}. \tag{2.91}$$

Since

$$\mathbf{M} = \mathbf{I} - \mathbf{P},$$

$\mathbf{M}$ and $\mathbf{P}$ are also complementary projections:

$$\mathbf{M} + \mathbf{P} = \mathbf{I}, \tag{2.92}$$

which gives

$$(\mathbf{M} + \mathbf{P})\mathbf{y} = \mathbf{I}\mathbf{y},$$

and therefore:

$$\mathbf{y} = \hat{\mathbf{y}} + \hat{\boldsymbol{\epsilon}} = \mathbf{Py} + \mathbf{My} = \hat{\mathbf{y}} + \hat{\boldsymbol{\epsilon}}. \tag{2.93}$$

The above properties are consequences of choosing the estimator in (2.78), with reference to the principle of MM. We can also turn the argument around, by asking which estimate $\hat{\boldsymbol{\beta}}$ we would choose if we require that it should deliver a vector $(\mathbf{y} - \tilde{\mathbf{y}})$ which is orthogonal to all the columns of $\mathbf{X}$. In other words:

$$\mathbf{X}'(\mathbf{y} - \tilde{\mathbf{y}}) = \mathbf{0}. \tag{2.94}$$

The vector $\tilde{\mathbf{y}}$ which satisfies (2.94) is called the orthogonal projection of $\mathbf{y}$ (cf. Lay, 2003, Section 6.5; Sydsæter *et al.*, 2016, Section 8). We have seen that by choosing $\hat{\boldsymbol{\beta}}$ so that:

$$\tilde{\mathbf{y}} \equiv \hat{\mathbf{y}} = \mathbf{Py},$$

we have our orthogonal projection given as $\mathbf{Py}$. Hence, the normal equations in (2.77) can be motivated by the intuitive idea that we want a value of $\boldsymbol{\beta}$ that leaves none of the information in $\mathbf{X}$ unused for the prediction of the dependent variable.

2.6.4. TSS, RSS and R^2

The scalar product $\mathbf{y}'\mathbf{y}$ becomes

$$\begin{aligned}\mathbf{y}'\mathbf{y} &= (\mathbf{y}'\mathbf{P} + \mathbf{y}'\mathbf{M})(\mathbf{Py} + \mathbf{My}) \\ &= \hat{\mathbf{y}}'\hat{\mathbf{y}} + \hat{\boldsymbol{\epsilon}}'\hat{\boldsymbol{\epsilon}}.\end{aligned}$$

Written out, this is

$$\underbrace{\sum_{i=1}^{n} Y_i^{\,2}}_{\text{TSS}} = \underbrace{\sum_{i=1}^{n} \hat{Y}_i^{\,2}}_{\text{ESS}} + \underbrace{\sum_{i=1}^{n} \hat{\epsilon}_i^2}_{\text{RSS}}, \tag{2.95}$$

where the reader is reminded of the customary abbreviations: TSS (total sum of squares), ESS (explained sum of squares) and RSS (residual sum of squares). You may be more familiar with writing this famous decomposition as

$$\underbrace{\sum_{i=1}^{n}(Y_i - \bar{Y})^2}_{\text{TSS}} = \underbrace{\sum_{i=1}^{n}(\hat{Y}_i - \overline{\hat{Y}})^2}_{\text{ESS}} + \underbrace{\sum_{i=1}^{n} \hat{\epsilon}_i^2}_{\text{RSS}}, \tag{2.96}$$

where the Y_is and $\hat{Y}_i$s have been "de-meaned" or "centred". As long as there is a constant in the model, there is no contradiction between (2.95) and (2.96). First, note that:

$$\mathbf{X}'\hat{\boldsymbol{\epsilon}} = \mathbf{X}'(\mathbf{y} - \mathbf{X}\hat{\boldsymbol{\beta}}) = \mathbf{0}, \tag{2.97}$$

and with $\mathbf{X}$ partitioned as

$$\mathbf{X} = [\,\boldsymbol{\iota} \quad \mathbf{X}_2\,],$$

equation (2.97) gives

$$\boldsymbol{\iota}'\hat{\boldsymbol{\epsilon}} = \sum_{i=1}^{n} \hat{\epsilon}_i = 0, \tag{2.98}$$

in the first row of $\mathbf{X}'\hat{\boldsymbol{\epsilon}} = \mathbf{0}$, and therefore:

$$\bar{Y} = \overline{\hat{Y}}. \tag{2.99}$$

Using this (well-known) property, you can show that (2.96) can be written as (2.95).

There are also other ways of writing RSS that sometimes come in handy. Using the "residual maker":

$$\hat{\boldsymbol{\epsilon}}'\hat{\boldsymbol{\epsilon}} = (\mathbf{y}'\mathbf{M}')\mathbf{M}\mathbf{y} = \mathbf{y}'\mathbf{M}\mathbf{y} = \mathbf{y}'\hat{\boldsymbol{\epsilon}} = \hat{\boldsymbol{\epsilon}}'\mathbf{y}, \tag{2.100}$$

and using the prediction matrix:

$$\begin{aligned}\hat{\boldsymbol{\epsilon}}'\hat{\boldsymbol{\epsilon}} &= \mathbf{y}'\mathbf{y} - \mathbf{y}'\mathbf{P}'\mathbf{P}\mathbf{y} = \mathbf{y}'\mathbf{y} - \mathbf{y}'[\mathbf{X}(\mathbf{X}'\mathbf{X})^{-1}\mathbf{X}'][\mathbf{X}(\mathbf{X}'\mathbf{X})^{-1}\mathbf{X}']\mathbf{y} \\ &= \mathbf{y}'\mathbf{y} - \mathbf{y}'\mathbf{X}(\mathbf{X}'\mathbf{X})^{-1}\mathbf{X}'\mathbf{y} = \mathbf{y}'\mathbf{y} - \mathbf{y}'X\hat{\boldsymbol{\beta}} = \mathbf{y}'\mathbf{y} - \hat{\boldsymbol{\beta}}'\mathbf{X}'\mathbf{y}. \end{aligned} \tag{2.101}$$

The multiple correlation coefficient R^2 can also be expressed with the use of the decompositions above:

$$\begin{aligned} R^2 &= 1 - \frac{\hat{\boldsymbol{\epsilon}}'\hat{\boldsymbol{\epsilon}}}{\sum_{i=1}^{n}(Y_i - \bar{Y})^2} \\ &= 1 - \frac{\hat{\boldsymbol{\epsilon}}'\hat{\boldsymbol{\epsilon}}}{(\mathbf{M}_\iota\mathbf{y})'(\mathbf{M}_\iota\mathbf{y})}, \end{aligned}$$

where we have used the so-called *centring matrix* $\mathbf{M}_\iota$:

$$\mathbf{M}_\iota = \mathbf{I} - \frac{1}{n}\boldsymbol{\iota}\boldsymbol{\iota}'. \tag{2.102}$$

$\mathbf{M}_\iota$ has the property that when we premultiply an n-dimensional vector with $\mathbf{M}_\iota$, we get a vector where the mean is subtracted, which is the same as the residual from regressing a variable on a constant. Therefore, the centring matrix is a special particular version of the "residual maker".

2.6.5. Partitioned regression

Above, we have referred to partitioning of vectors and matrices on a couple of occasions. In this section, we give a few more useful results for partitioned regression.

We write $\boldsymbol{\beta} = [\,\hat{\boldsymbol{\beta}}_1 \quad \hat{\boldsymbol{\beta}}_2\,]'$ where $\boldsymbol{\beta}_1$ contains $k_1 + 1$ parameters (including the intercept), and $\boldsymbol{\beta}_2$ contains k_2 coefficients. We include the intercept in k_1, so that $(k_1 + 1) + k_2 = k + 1$ (the number of regressors with genuine variation is k, consistent with the above notation).

The corresponding partitioning of $\mathbf{X}$ is $\mathbf{X} = [\underset{n\times(k_1+1)}{\mathbf{X}_1} \; \underset{n\times k_2}{\mathbf{X}_2}]$ with the constant term placed in $\mathbf{X}_1$. In this notation, the OLS estimated model becomes:

$$\mathbf{y} = \mathbf{X_1}\hat{\boldsymbol{\beta}}_1 + \mathbf{X_2}\hat{\boldsymbol{\beta}}_2 + \hat{\boldsymbol{\epsilon}}, \tag{2.103}$$

with $\hat{\boldsymbol{\epsilon}}$ given by

$$\hat{\boldsymbol{\epsilon}} = \mathbf{M}\mathbf{y}.$$

We begin by rewriting the normal equations:

$$(\mathbf{X}'\mathbf{X})\hat{\boldsymbol{\beta}} = \mathbf{X}'\mathbf{y},$$

in terms of the partitioning:

$$\begin{pmatrix} \mathbf{X}_1'\mathbf{X}_1 & \mathbf{X}_1'\mathbf{X}_2 \\ \mathbf{X}_2'\mathbf{X}_1 & \mathbf{X}_2'\mathbf{X}_2 \end{pmatrix} \begin{pmatrix} \hat{\boldsymbol{\beta}}_1 \\ \hat{\boldsymbol{\beta}}_2 \end{pmatrix} = \begin{pmatrix} \mathbf{X}_1'\mathbf{y} \\ \mathbf{X}_2'\mathbf{y} \end{pmatrix}, \tag{2.104}$$

where we have used:

$$\mathbf{X}'\mathbf{X} = \begin{bmatrix} \mathbf{X}_1' \\ \mathbf{X}_2' \end{bmatrix} [\mathbf{X}_1 \quad \mathbf{X}_2] \tag{2.105}$$

(see, e.g., Davidson and MacKinnon, 2004, Section 1.4). The vector of OLS estimators can therefore be expressed as

$$\begin{pmatrix} \hat{\boldsymbol{\beta}}_1 \\ \hat{\boldsymbol{\beta}}_2 \end{pmatrix} = \begin{pmatrix} \mathbf{X}_1'\mathbf{X}_1 & \mathbf{X}_1'\mathbf{X}_2 \\ \mathbf{X}_2'\mathbf{X}_1 & \mathbf{X}_2'\mathbf{X}_2 \end{pmatrix}^{-1} \begin{pmatrix} \mathbf{X}_1'\mathbf{y} \\ \mathbf{X}_2'\mathbf{y} \end{pmatrix}. \tag{2.106}$$

We finally need a result for the inverse of a partitioned matrix. There are several versions depending on which of the submatrices are invertible (see Sydsæter *et al.*, 2005). We assume that both $\mathbf{X}_1$ and $\mathbf{X}_2$ have full rank, and from Hansen (2017) we have the useful result:

$$\mathbf{A}^{-1} = \begin{pmatrix} \mathbf{A}_{11} & \mathbf{A}_{12} \\ \mathbf{A}_{21} & \mathbf{A}_{22} \end{pmatrix}^{-1} = \begin{pmatrix} \mathbf{A}_{11\cdot 2}^{-1} & -\mathbf{A}_{11\cdot 2}^{-1}\mathbf{A}_{12}\mathbf{A}_{22}^{-1} \\ -\mathbf{A}_{22\cdot 1}^{-1}\mathbf{A}_{21}\mathbf{A}_{11}^{-1} & \mathbf{A}_{22\cdot 1}^{-1} \end{pmatrix}, \tag{2.107}$$

where

$$\mathbf{A}_{11\cdot 2} = \mathbf{A}_{11} - \mathbf{A}_{12}\mathbf{A}_{22}^{-1}\mathbf{A}_{21}, \tag{2.108}$$

$$\mathbf{A}_{22\cdot 1} = \mathbf{A}_{22} - \mathbf{A}_{21}\mathbf{A}_{11}^{-1}\mathbf{A}_{12}. \tag{2.109}$$

With the aid of (2.107)–(2.109), it can be shown that

$$\begin{pmatrix} \hat{\boldsymbol{\beta}}_1 \\ \hat{\boldsymbol{\beta}}_2 \end{pmatrix} = \begin{pmatrix} (\mathbf{X}_1'\mathbf{M}_2\mathbf{X}_1)^{-1}\mathbf{X}_1'\mathbf{M}_2\mathbf{y} \\ (\mathbf{X}_2'\mathbf{M}_1\mathbf{X}_2)^{-1}\mathbf{X}_2'\mathbf{M}_1\mathbf{y} \end{pmatrix}, \tag{2.110}$$

where $\mathbf{M}_1$ and $\mathbf{M}_2$ are the two residual-makers:

$$\mathbf{M}_1 = \mathbf{I} - \mathbf{X}_1(\mathbf{X}_1'\mathbf{X}_1)^{-1}\mathbf{X}_1', \tag{2.111}$$

$$\mathbf{M}_2 = \mathbf{I} - \mathbf{X}_2(\mathbf{X}_2'\mathbf{X}_2)^{-1}\mathbf{X}_2'. \tag{2.112}$$

As an exercise in the use of the different matrices above, commence with

$$\mathbf{X} = [\boldsymbol{X}_1 \quad \mathbf{X}_2] = [\boldsymbol{\iota} \quad \mathbf{X}_2],$$

where (as an example of the set-up with the intercept as variable number one):

$$\boldsymbol{\iota} = \begin{bmatrix} 1 \\ 1 \\ \vdots \\ 1 \end{bmatrix}_{n\times 1},$$

$$\mathbf{X}_2 = \begin{bmatrix} X_{12} & \dots & X_{1k} \\ X_{22} & \dots & X_{2k} \\ \vdots & & \vdots \\ X_{n2} & \dots & X_{nk} \end{bmatrix},$$

$$\mathbf{M}_1 = \mathbf{I} - \boldsymbol{\iota}\left(\boldsymbol{\iota}'\boldsymbol{\iota}\right)^{-1}\boldsymbol{\iota}',$$

$\boldsymbol{\iota}'\boldsymbol{\iota} = n$, so

$$\mathbf{M}_1 = \mathbf{I} - \frac{1}{n}\boldsymbol{\iota}\boldsymbol{\iota}' \equiv \mathbf{M}_\iota,$$

which is the centring matrix. Show that it is

$$\mathbf{M}_\iota = \begin{bmatrix} 1-\frac{1}{n} & -\frac{1}{n} & \dots & -\frac{1}{n} \\ -\frac{1}{n} & 1-\frac{1}{n} & \dots & \vdots \\ \vdots & \vdots & \vdots & \vdots \\ -\frac{1}{n} & -\frac{1}{n} & \dots & 1-\frac{1}{n} \end{bmatrix}_{n\times n}.$$

By using the general formula for partitioned regression above, we get

$$\begin{aligned} \hat{\boldsymbol{\beta}}_2 &= \left(\mathbf{X}_2'\mathbf{M}_1\mathbf{X}_2\right)^{-1}\mathbf{X}_2'\mathbf{M}_1\mathbf{y} \\ &= ([\mathbf{M}_\iota\mathbf{X}_2]'[\mathbf{M}_\iota\mathbf{X}_2])^{-1}[\mathbf{M}_\iota\mathbf{X}_2]'\mathbf{y} \\ &= [(\mathbf{X}_2 - \bar{\mathbf{X}}_2)'(\mathbf{X}_2 - \bar{\mathbf{X}}_2)]^{-1}(\mathbf{X}_2 - \bar{\mathbf{X}}_2)'\mathbf{y}, \end{aligned} \tag{2.113}$$

where $\bar{\mathbf{X}}_2$ is the $n \times k$ matrix with the variable means in the k columns.

Above you were invited to show the same result more directly, without the use of the results from partitioned regression, by rewriting the regression model (and for the set-up of the regression model where the intercept has coefficient β_0).

2.6.6. Frisch–Waugh theorem

The expression for $\hat{\boldsymbol{\beta}}_2$ in (2.110) suggests that there is another simple method for finding $\hat{\boldsymbol{\beta}}_2$ by using $\mathbf{M}_1$: We premultiply the model (2.103), first with $\mathbf{M}_1$ and then with $\mathbf{X}_2'$:

$$\mathbf{M}_1\mathbf{y} = \mathbf{M}_1\mathbf{X}_2\hat{\boldsymbol{\beta}}_2 + \hat{\boldsymbol{\epsilon}}, \tag{2.114}$$

$$\mathbf{X}_2'\mathbf{M}_1\mathbf{y} = \mathbf{X}_2'\mathbf{M}_1\mathbf{X}_2\hat{\boldsymbol{\beta}}_2, \tag{2.115}$$

where we have used $\mathbf{M}_1\boldsymbol{X}_1 = \mathbf{0}$ and $\mathbf{M}_1\hat{\boldsymbol{\epsilon}} = \hat{\boldsymbol{\epsilon}}$ in (2.114) and $\mathbf{X}_2'\hat{\boldsymbol{\epsilon}} = \mathbf{0}$ in (2.115). We can solve this last equation for $\hat{\boldsymbol{\beta}}_2$:

$$\hat{\boldsymbol{\beta}}_2 = (\mathbf{X}_2'\mathbf{M}_1\mathbf{X}_2)^{-1}\mathbf{X}_2'\mathbf{M}_1\mathbf{y}. \tag{2.116}$$

It can be shown that the covariance matrix is

$$\widehat{\text{Cov}(\hat{\boldsymbol{\beta}}_2)} = \hat{\sigma}^2\left(\mathbf{X}_2'\mathbf{M}_1\mathbf{X}_2\right)^{-1}.$$

where we let $\hat{\sigma}^2$ denote the unbiased estimator of the variance of the disturbances:

$$\hat{\sigma}^2 = \frac{\hat{\boldsymbol{\epsilon}}'\hat{\boldsymbol{\epsilon}}}{n-k-1}.$$

The corresponding expressions for $\hat{\boldsymbol{\beta}}_1$ are

$$\hat{\boldsymbol{\beta}}_1 = \left(\mathbf{X}_1'\mathbf{M}_2\mathbf{X}_1\right)^{-1}\mathbf{X}_1'\mathbf{M}_2\mathbf{y},$$

$$\widehat{\text{Cov}(\hat{\boldsymbol{\beta}}_1)} = \hat{\sigma}^2\left(\mathbf{X}_1'\mathbf{M}_2\mathbf{X}_1\right)^{-1}. \tag{2.117}$$

We now give an interpretation of (2.116): Use symmetry and idempotency of $\mathbf{M}_1$:

$$\hat{\boldsymbol{\beta}}_2 = \left((\mathbf{M}_1\mathbf{X}_2)'(\mathbf{M}_1\mathbf{X}_2)\right)^{-1}(\mathbf{M}_1\mathbf{X}_2)'\mathbf{M}_1\mathbf{y}.$$

In this expression, $\mathbf{M}_1\mathbf{y}$ is the residual vector $\hat{\boldsymbol{\epsilon}}_{y|X_1}$ and $\mathbf{M}_1\mathbf{X}_2$ is the matrix with k_2 residuals obtained from regressing each variable in $\mathbf{X}_2$ on $\mathbf{X}_1$,

$\hat{\varepsilon}_{X_2|X_1}$. But this means that $\hat{\boldsymbol{\beta}}_2$ can be obtained by first running these two auxiliary regressions, saving the residuals in $\hat{\varepsilon}_{Y|X_1}$ and $\hat{\varepsilon}_{X_2|X_1}$, and then running a second regression with $\hat{\varepsilon}_{Y|X_1}$ as regressand, and with $\hat{\varepsilon}_{X_2|X_1}$ as the matrix with regressors:

$$\hat{\boldsymbol{\beta}}_2 = \left(\underbrace{(\mathbf{M}_1\mathbf{X}_2)'}_{\hat{\varepsilon}_{X_2|X_1}} \underbrace{(\mathbf{M}_1\mathbf{X}_2)}_{\hat{\varepsilon}_{X_2|X_1}} \right)^{-1} \underbrace{(\mathbf{M}_1\mathbf{X}_1)'}_{\hat{\varepsilon}_{X_2|X_1}} \underbrace{(\mathbf{M}_1\mathbf{y}_2)}_{\hat{\varepsilon}_{Y|X_1}}. \tag{2.118}$$

We have shown the Frisch–Waugh theorem (Frisch and Waugh, 1933). This famous theorem says that, if we want to estimate the partial effects on Y of changes in the variables in $\mathbf{X}_2$ (i.e., controlled for the influence of $\mathbf{X}_1$), we can do that in two ways: either by estimating the full multivariate model:

$$\mathbf{y} = \mathbf{X}_1\hat{\boldsymbol{\beta}}_1 + \mathbf{X}_2\hat{\boldsymbol{\beta}}_2 + \hat{\boldsymbol{\epsilon}},$$

or, by following the above two-step procedure of obtaining residuals with $\mathbf{X}_1$ as regressor and then obtaining $\hat{\boldsymbol{\beta}}_2$ from (2.118).

This theorem has many applications, some of them that we will make use of later in the book, for example, trend correction, seasonal adjustment by seasonal dummy variables; see Davidson and MacKinnon (2004, Section 2.4), Bårdsen and Nymoen (2011, Section 7.2), Bårdsen and Nymoen (2014, Section 2.6) among others.

2.6.7. Generalized least squares

In the same way as in the single regressor case, these estimators are optimal when the homoskedasticity assumption (2.73) in the regression model specification holds. The generalization of the weighted least squares estimator which takes account of heteroskedasticity is the generalized least squares (GLS) estimator:

$$\hat{\boldsymbol{\beta}}^{\text{GLS}} = (\mathbf{X}'\hat{\boldsymbol{\Omega}}^{-1}\mathbf{X})^{-1}\mathbf{X}'\hat{\boldsymbol{\Omega}}^{-1}\mathbf{y}, \tag{2.119}$$

where $\hat{\boldsymbol{\Omega}}$ is a consistent estimator of the $\boldsymbol{\Omega}$ matrix in the model assumption:

$$\text{Var}(\boldsymbol{\epsilon} \mid \mathbf{X}) = \sigma^2\boldsymbol{\Omega}, \tag{2.120}$$

which replaces $\text{Var}(\boldsymbol{\epsilon} \mid \mathbf{X}) = \sigma^2\mathbf{I}$ in the classical regression model. $\boldsymbol{\Omega}$ is a square $n \times n$ matrix. It is *symmetric* by definition, and *positive definite* by assumption. Positive definite means that all quadratic forms that can be formed with the use of $\mathbf{\Omega}$ are strictly positive:

$$\underbrace{\mathbf{v}'\mathbf{\Omega}\mathbf{v}}_{\text{quadratic form in } n \text{ variables}} > 0 \quad \text{for all } \mathbf{v} \neq \mathbf{0}, \tag{2.121}$$

where $\mathbf{v}'$ denotes a row vector of variables: $\mathbf{v}' = (V_1, V_2, \ldots, V_n)$. The positive definite property plays an important role in the derivation of the expression in (2.119) For the positive definite matrix $\mathbf{\Omega}$, there exists an $n \times n$ matrix $\mathbf{\Psi}$ which is invertible, i.e., *non-singular*, with properties:

$$\mathbf{\Psi}\mathbf{\Sigma}\mathbf{\Psi}' = \mathbf{I}, \tag{2.122}$$

$$\mathbf{\Psi}'\mathbf{\Psi} = \mathbf{\Omega}^{-1} \Leftrightarrow \mathbf{\Psi}\mathbf{\Psi}' = \mathbf{\Omega}^{-1} \text{ (due to symmetry of } \mathbf{\Omega}). \tag{2.123}$$

$\mathbf{\Psi}$ can be interpreted as matrix with weights that have the property that they "reinstall" homoskedasticty property of the classical regression model.

Multiplication from the left in (2.70) by $\mathbf{\Psi}'$ gives

$$\underbrace{\mathbf{\Psi}'\mathbf{y}}_{\mathbf{y}_*} = \underbrace{\mathbf{\Psi}'\mathbf{X}}_{\mathbf{X}_*}\boldsymbol{\beta} + \underbrace{\mathbf{\Psi}'\boldsymbol{\epsilon}}_{\boldsymbol{\epsilon}_*}. \tag{2.124}$$

The variance of the transformed regression-error $\boldsymbol{\epsilon}_*$ becomes

$$\begin{aligned}
\text{Var}(\boldsymbol{\epsilon}_* \mid \mathbf{X}_*) &= E\left[\boldsymbol{\epsilon}_*\boldsymbol{\epsilon}_*' \mid \mathbf{X}_*\right] = E[(\mathbf{\Psi}'\boldsymbol{\epsilon})(\boldsymbol{\epsilon}'\mathbf{\Psi})' \mid \mathbf{X}_*] \\
&= E[\mathbf{\Psi}'(\boldsymbol{\epsilon}\boldsymbol{\epsilon}')\mathbf{\Psi}' \mid \mathbf{X}_*] \\
&= \sigma^2 E[\mathbf{\Psi}'(\mathbf{\Omega})\mathbf{\Psi}' \mid \mathbf{X}_*] = \sigma^2\mathbf{I},
\end{aligned}$$

showing the point about homoskedasticity of the weighted regression equation (2.124). In fact, using the notation in labels below (2.124), and applying the OLS estimation principle gives

$$\begin{aligned}
\hat{\boldsymbol{\beta}} &= (\mathbf{X}_*'\mathbf{X}_*)^{-1}\mathbf{X}_*'\mathbf{y}_* = (\mathbf{X}'\mathbf{\Psi}\mathbf{\Psi}'\mathbf{X})\mathbf{X}'\mathbf{\Psi}\mathbf{\Psi}'\mathbf{y} \\
&= (\mathbf{X}'\mathbf{\Omega}^{-1}\mathbf{X})\mathbf{X}'\mathbf{\Omega}^{-1}\mathbf{y},
\end{aligned}$$

showing that $\hat{\boldsymbol{\beta}}^{\text{GLS}}$ is a feasible version of this estimator, in that GLS replaces $\mathbf{\Omega}$ by the estimate $\hat{\mathbf{\Omega}}$.

In the literature, the GLS estimator is also known as the *Aitken*-estimator, after the statistician Aitken (1935). Of course, the estimation of $\mathbf{\Omega}$ is not always trivial, but modern econometric software programs include good estimation routines (using numerical iteration). Sometimes, however, we can have prior knowledge, or at least well-founded ideas, about the exact form of heteroskedasticity, and sometimes no estimation is required. Returning to the simple regression case $Y_i = \beta_0 + \beta_1 X_i + \epsilon_i$, a common example is that the variance of the error term ϵ_i is proportional to X_i:

$$\text{Var}(\epsilon_i \mid X_i) = \sigma^2 X_i \quad \forall i, \tag{2.125}$$

while all the covariances between ϵ_i and ϵ_h ($h \neq i$) are zero. We may express this assumption as

$$\text{Var}(\boldsymbol{\varepsilon}) = \sigma^2 \boldsymbol{\Omega} = \sigma^2 \begin{pmatrix} X_1 & 0 & \cdots & 0 \\ 0 & X_2 & \cdots & 0 \\ \vdots & \vdots & \ddots & \vdots \\ 0 & 0 & \cdots & X_n \end{pmatrix}, \tag{2.126}$$

and in one of the exercises you are asked to specify $\boldsymbol{\Psi}'$ and the corresponding homoskedastic disturbance $\boldsymbol{\epsilon}_*$.

2.6.8. Multivariate structural equations

In Section 2.5, we defined a structural model as a model equation $Y_i = \beta_0 + \beta_1 X_i + \epsilon_i$ where $\text{Cov}(X_i, \epsilon_i) \neq 0$. We also made the point that β_0 and β_1 cannot be estimated consistently from the conditional distribution of Y given X. They are instead coefficients related to the parameters of the joint (simultaneous) probability distribution of Y and X.

To be able to estimate β_0 and β_1, that joint distribution must however in its turn be conditional on a variable Z, called the IV, for which we defined the requirements of IV validity and relevance, see (2.59) and (2.60).

In a multivariate setting, it is natural to assume that the structural equation contains some explanatory variables that are correlated with the disturbance, as well as other variables that are uncorrelated with the error term of the model equation. It is custom to refer to the first category as endogenous right-hand side variables, and the other category as exogenous (or predetermined) variables. In line with this, we partition the $\mathbf{X}$ matrix in (2.70) as

$$\mathbf{X} = \Big[\underset{\text{exogenous}}{\mathbf{X}_X} \quad \underset{\text{endogenous}}{\mathbf{X}_Y} \Big]_{n \times (k+1)}, \tag{2.127}$$

where $\mathbf{X}_X$ is an $n \times (k_1 + 1)$ matrix, with exogenous or predetermined variables, and $\mathbf{X}_Y$ is an $n \times k_2$ matrix with endogenous variables. Clearly

$k_1 + k_2 = k + 1$, as the constant term (and any other deterministic variable for that matter) is counted as a variable in $\mathbf{X}_X$.

The model in Section 2.5 corresponds to $\mathbf{X}_{n\times 2} = [\boldsymbol{\iota} \quad \mathbf{X}_Y]$ since the structural equation had an intercept, and a single explanatory variable that was endogenous.

Another change from Section 2.5 is that we now will use the weaker form of asymptotic dependence and independence that we hinted to at the end of that section, because it is this form that will be most useful later in the book. Hence, we define independence and dependence between the variables in $\mathbf{X}$ and the disturbance as

$$\text{plim}\left(\frac{1}{n}\mathbf{X}'_X\boldsymbol{\epsilon}\right) = \mathbf{0},$$

$$\text{plim}\left(\frac{1}{n}\mathbf{X}'_Y\boldsymbol{\epsilon}\right) \neq \mathbf{0},$$

where $\mathbf{0}$ is the matrix with zeros in all cells. Therefore, for $\mathbf{X}$ as a whole:

$$\text{plim}\left(\frac{1}{n}\mathbf{X}'\boldsymbol{\epsilon}\right) \neq \mathbf{0}, \tag{2.128}$$

which is contrary to the regression model assumption (2.74), and which implies that the OLS estimator (and GLS for that matter) will be inconsistent for $\boldsymbol{\beta}$.

However, if we can establish a matrix $\mathbf{Z}$ consisting of variables that are both valid and relevant as instruments, the *method of moments* estimator will yield consistent estimation of $\boldsymbol{\beta}$, by an argument which is a direct generalization from Section 2.5.

To construct the $\mathbf{Z}$ matrix, we first use $\mathbf{X}_X$ since those variables are (asymptotically) independent of the disturbance and they are perfectly correlated with themselves (i.e., perfect instruments). Next, we need to replace $\mathbf{X}_Y$ by a matrix with k_2 columns (and with full rank to avoid multicollinear IVs) that satisfies the validity and relevance assumptions:

$$\text{plim}\left(\frac{1}{n}\mathbf{X}'_Z\boldsymbol{\epsilon}\right) = \mathbf{0}, \tag{2.129}$$

$$\text{plim}\left(\frac{1}{n}\mathbf{X}'_Z\mathbf{X}_Y\right) \neq \mathbf{0}. \tag{2.130}$$

Hence our matrix counterpart to the single IV Z in Section 2.5 becomes

$$\mathbf{Z} = \Big[\underset{\text{exogenous}}{\mathbf{X}_X} \quad \underset{\text{instruments}}{\mathbf{X}_Z}\Big]_{n\times k+1},$$

with properties

$$\operatorname{plim}\left(\frac{1}{n}\mathbf{Z}'\boldsymbol{\epsilon}\right) = \mathbf{0}, \text{ instrument validity,} \tag{2.131}$$

$$\operatorname{plim}\left(\frac{1}{n}\mathbf{Z}'\boldsymbol{X}\right) = \mathbf{S}_{ZX}, \text{ instrument relevance,} \tag{2.132}$$

as well as invertibility of $\mathbf{S}_{ZX}$.

Multiplication of the structural equation $\mathbf{y} = \mathbf{X}\boldsymbol{\beta} + \boldsymbol{\epsilon}$ from the left gives

$$\mathbf{Z}'\mathbf{y} - \mathbf{Z}'\mathbf{X}\boldsymbol{\beta} = \mathbf{Z}'\boldsymbol{\epsilon}.$$

Applying the IV relevance as if it holds in the actual sample, we obtain the normal equations for the MM estimator of $\boldsymbol{\beta}$ as

$$\mathbf{Z}'(\mathbf{y} - \mathbf{X}\hat{\boldsymbol{\beta}}_{\text{IV}}) = \mathbf{0}, \tag{2.133}$$

where the estimator has been labelled IV:

$$\hat{\boldsymbol{\beta}}^{\text{IV}} = (\mathbf{Z}'\mathbf{X})^{-1}\mathbf{Z}'\mathbf{y}. \tag{2.134}$$

Clearly, to be able to obtain IV estimates in any given sample, we need $\mathbf{Z}'\mathbf{X}$ to be invertible, and this is the counterpart to absence of perfect sample multicollinearity among the regressors of a regression model.

It is easy to confirm that $\hat{\boldsymbol{\beta}}_{\text{IV}}$ is consistent by the assumptions above. First substitute $\mathbf{y}$ in the expression by $\mathbf{X}\boldsymbol{\beta} + \boldsymbol{\epsilon}$:

$$\hat{\boldsymbol{\beta}}^{\text{IV}} = (\mathbf{Z}'\mathbf{X})^{-1}\mathbf{Z}'\mathbf{X}\boldsymbol{\beta} + (\mathbf{Z}'\mathbf{X})^{-1}\mathbf{Z}'\boldsymbol{\epsilon},$$

and then take plim on both sides:

$$\operatorname{plim}(\hat{\boldsymbol{\beta}}^{\text{IV}}) = \boldsymbol{\beta} + \operatorname{plim}((\mathbf{Z}'\mathbf{X})^{-1})\operatorname{plim}(\mathbf{Z}'\boldsymbol{\epsilon}) = \boldsymbol{\beta}. \tag{2.135}$$

Since $\hat{\boldsymbol{\beta}}^{\text{IV}}$ is a consistent estimator of $\boldsymbol{\beta}$, the coefficient vector is also identified, as noted earlier in the chapter. However, if the $\mathbf{X}_Z$ matrix that we can formulate contains more instruments than there are included endogenous variables in the structural model equation, we find ourselves in the situation where there are two or maybe more IV estimators that are identified, which is the case of over identification of $\boldsymbol{\beta}$.

Unlike "under identification", meaning that no consistent estimator exists, over identification is a luxury problem and is solved by the use of the generalized IV estimator (GIVE), which is also known as 2-*stage least squares* (2*SLS*).

We define another IV matrix $\widehat{\mathbf{Z}}$, which has dimension $n \times k+1$:

$$\widehat{\mathbf{Z}} = (\mathbf{X}_X \quad \widehat{\mathbf{X}}_Y), \tag{2.136}$$

where $\widehat{\mathbf{X}}_Y$ is $n \times k_2$ and is made up of the best linear predictors of the k_2 endogenous variables in the structural equation:

$$\widehat{\mathbf{X}}_Y = (\widehat{\mathbf{x}}_{y1}\ \widehat{\mathbf{x}}_{y2}\ \dots)_{n \times k_2}. \tag{2.137}$$

Where does the optimal predictors come from? Logically, they are the fitted values from k_2 regressions between the included endogenous variables and the full set of IVs, namely:

$$\hat{\mathbf{x}}_{Yj} = \mathbf{X}_Z \widehat{\boldsymbol{\pi}}_j, \quad j = 1, 2, \dots, k_2, \tag{2.138}$$

where $\widehat{\boldsymbol{\pi}}_j$ is the OLS estimator for the included endogenous variable number j, i.e.,

$$\widehat{\boldsymbol{\pi}}_j = (\mathbf{X}_Z'\mathbf{X}_Z)^{-1}\mathbf{X}_Z'\mathbf{x}_{Yj}, \quad j = 1, 2, \dots, k_2. \tag{2.139}$$

The generalized IV (GIV) estimator can be written as

$$\hat{\boldsymbol{\beta}}^{\text{GIV}} = (\widehat{\mathbf{Z}}'\mathbf{X})^{-1}\widehat{\mathbf{Z}}'\mathbf{y}.$$

We can write $\widehat{\mathbf{X}}_Y$ as

$$\widehat{\mathbf{X}}_Y = (\mathbf{Z}(\mathbf{Z}'\mathbf{Z})^{-1}\mathbf{Z}'\mathbf{x}_{Y1} \dots \mathbf{Z}(\mathbf{Z}'\mathbf{Z})^{-1}\mathbf{Z}'\mathbf{x}_{Yk_2} \quad), \tag{2.140}$$

and more compactly:

$$\widehat{\mathbf{X}}_Y = \mathbf{Z}(\mathbf{Z}'\mathbf{Z})^{-1}\mathbf{Z}'\mathbf{X}_Y = \mathbf{P}_Z\mathbf{X}_Y. \tag{2.141}$$

$\mathbf{P}_Z$ is another example of a projection matrix, i.e., of the "the prediction maker", namely:

$$\mathbf{P}_Z = \mathbf{Z}(\mathbf{Z}'\mathbf{Z})^{-1}\mathbf{Z}'. \tag{2.142}$$

It can be shown (using matrix partitioning) that $\hat{\boldsymbol{\beta}}^{\text{GIV}}$ is identical to the 2-stage least square estimator $\hat{\boldsymbol{\beta}}^{\text{2SLS}}$ that uses $\widehat{\mathbf{X}}_Y$ as a regressor in the regression:

$$\mathbf{y} = \mathbf{X}_X\boldsymbol{\beta}_1 + \hat{\mathbf{X}}_Y\boldsymbol{\beta}_2 + \text{disturbance}. \tag{2.143}$$

Hence,

$$\hat{\boldsymbol{\beta}}_{\text{GIV}} = \begin{pmatrix} \hat{\boldsymbol{\beta}}_1^{\text{GIV}} \\ \hat{\boldsymbol{\beta}}_2^{\text{GIV}} \end{pmatrix} \equiv \begin{pmatrix} \hat{\boldsymbol{\beta}}_1^{\text{2SLS}} \\ \hat{\boldsymbol{\beta}}_2^{\text{2SLS}} \end{pmatrix}, \tag{2.144}$$

where $\hat{\boldsymbol{\beta}}_1^{\text{2SLS}}$ and $\hat{\boldsymbol{\beta}}_1^{\text{2SLS}}$ are the OLS estimators obtained by estimation of (2.143). 2SLS and its relationship to IV and the MM are discussed in greater detail in Section 7.9, where the context is estimation of a structural equation in a multiple equation model.

However, we note that when there are more instruments than included endogenous variables, the GIV/2SLS estimator is algebraically different from any of the IV estimators that can be constructed from the available instrument set.

It is perhaps worth mentioning that the remarks made above (in Section 2.5.2), about the dangers of weak instruments, also apply to the general linear-in-parameters structural equation. If the instruments are weak, both the consistency and asymptotic normality of estimators and t-values may not hold.

Moreover, in large samples, GIV/2SLS is the MM estimator with best asymptotic properties (Davidson, 2000, p. 184). Intuitively this must be correct since $\mathbf{P}_Z\mathbf{X}_Y$ is the best predictor of the included endogenous variables in the structural equation.

However, the efficiency of GIV/2SLS only holds when structural equations are homoskedastic. If the model equation is specified to allow for heteroskastic or correlated disturbances, we can write

$$\text{Var}(\boldsymbol{\epsilon}) = \sigma^2\boldsymbol{\Omega}, \tag{2.145}$$

with $\boldsymbol{\Omega} = \boldsymbol{I}$ as the special case where GIVE/2SLS is the asymptotically efficient estimation method. In the general case of $\boldsymbol{\Omega} \neq \boldsymbol{I}$, the generalized method of moments (GMM) estimator, is asymptotically efficient (see, e.g., Davidson and MacKinnon, 2004, Chapter 9). GMM also allows for nonlinear-in-parameters structural equations.

Heuristically, GMM does to GIV estimation, what GLS does to OLS estimation: It reinstalls the homoskedasticity property by a weighting method. For a full discussion of GMM, we refer to Davidson and MacKinnon (2004, Chapter 9).

On the other hand, unless the heteroskedasticity that is corrected by GLS and GMM is specified as part of the model in the first place, it may be that these estimation methods effectively patch-up a misspecified econometric model. One reason for nevertheless using them, may be that they make the estimates and t-values of the parameters of main interest, $\boldsymbol{\beta}$ robust to residual misspecification. The problem with that argument is that, in practice, GMM is not always robust to changes in the (details) of how it is operationalized, (see e.g., Bårdsen *et al.*, 2004).

Below we will follow the methodological principle of congruent modelling, meaning that the properties of the assumed statistical model have observable counterparts in the properties of the empirical model.

If a congruent model has been achieved, OLS will often at least approximately give the ML estimator, for conditional models, and GIV will be asymptotically efficient for a single structural equation. As we shall see in the next chapters, the principle of ML can also be applied to dynamic models, and to systems of equations. With good software, it is also easy to use in practical modelling work. Hence, while GMM became popular in single equation modelling (where the wider equation and system properties are often not made explicit), its usefulness in applied system modelling may be more limited.

Another situation in which 2SLS/GIV is asymptotically inefficient is when the structural equation is one equation in a multipleequation simultaneous equations model where the disturbances are contemporaneously correlated. In that context, the Aitken-estimator has played an important role in the history of econometrics, under the name of 3-stage least squares estimator (3SLS); see Section 7.9.

2.7. Model Equations with Time Series Variables

A common assumption for the different models that we have reviewed above is the mutual independence between the pairs $(X_1, Y_1), (X_2, Y_2), \ldots, (X_n, Y_n)$. As a consequence of the independence, the ordering of the pairs (which of them comes first, which comes second, and so on) is arbitrary and up to us. With time series data the ordering is no longer arbitrary. Time flows from the past (history) to the present, and away from us into the future. Hence, if we have n pairs of time series variables (X_t, Y_t) where t is used to denote time period (as in Chapter 1) the ordering is that (X_1, Y_1) is the first variable pair, (X_2, Y_2) is the second, and (X_n, Y_n) is the last pair of variables. To mark this important change we replace n by T when we discuss models of an ordered series of time series data:

$$\underbrace{(X_1, Y_1), (X_2, Y_2), \ldots, (X_T, Y_T)}_{T \text{ pairs, from past (left) to present (right)}}.$$

It is possible that the pairs of variables (with the given ordering of time) are mutually independent. In that case the fixed ordering forced on us by time would be a mere formality and the results that we have reviewed above would apply also to time series data. However, independence is not really realistic for observable time series variables which are typically autocorrelated, in the way that we saw in the introductory chapter.

An important (and old, see Yule (1926) and Haavelmo (1943b)) question is therefore how suited the estimation and testing methods that we have reviewed above are if they are applied to time series data? For example, the direct counterpart to (2.20) would be the model equation:

$$Y_t = \beta_0 + \beta_1 X_t + \epsilon_t, \quad t = 1, 2, \ldots, T, \tag{2.146}$$

and where we can complete the econometric specification by listing a set of assumptions about the conditional distribution of ϵ_t given X_t. Among the properties **a**–**d** in the specification in Section 2.4.1, there are a few that may be realistic also for (2.146). For example, **d** (parameter constancy) is a possible assumption, and one that can be easily tested with time series data, exactly because the ordering for data variables is unique. Homoskedastcity, **b** is another example of an assumption that may hold quite often.

However, due to the typical autocorrelation in time series, assumption **c**, which would imply:

$$\text{Cov}(\epsilon_t, \epsilon_{t-j} \mid X_t, X_{t-1}) = 0,$$

cannot be a valid assumption, except in extremely rare cases.

Hence, the *IID-model of econometrics* reviewed above, does not cover time series variables, as the model equation (2.146) will typically be characterized by $\text{Cov}(\epsilon_t, \epsilon_{t-j} \mid X_t, X_{t-j}) \neq 0$, which many readers will recognize as *autocorrelated regression errors.*

Readers may also know from introductory econometrics, that the OLS estimator of $\hat{\beta}_1$ can be unbiased and consistent also in the case of autocorrelated errors. However, it will not be identical to the ML estimator of β_1, since the expression for the log-likelihood will be different from the one we analyzed above (with independent pairs of variables).

The main point is that, as long as there is a certain limitation on the temporal dependence between observation pairs, the estimators we have reviewed can be used, but their statistical properties will be affected by the changed nature of the data (i.e., away from the independence assumption).

In the next chapters, we will state precisely the requested limitation on the degree of autocorrelation. Dynamic versions of the regression model, and of the structural equation model, can be established by conditioning on the history of time series variables. In the simplest case, (X_t, Y_t) can become independent of (X_{t-2}, Y_{t-2}) once we have conditioned on (X_{t-1}, Y_{t-1}), and in that case the conditional distribution:

$$f(X_t, Y_t \mid X_{t-1}, Y_{t-1}), \tag{2.147}$$

represents a basis for models that are of interest to us as econometricians.

For example, the econometric theory that we will work our way through, tells us when the estimation of the final form equation that we defined above is well founded, and when it is not. The theory will also provide the basis for building dynamic regression models (for which OLS is feasible ML), dynamic structural equations (IV or ML), and for systems that consists of these equation types.

A well-known dynamic regression model is the *Autoregressive Distributed Lag* model, which is usually referred to as ADL model, or ARDL model:

$$Y_t = \phi_0 + \phi_1 Y_{t-1} + \beta_0 X_t + \beta_1 X_{t-1} + \epsilon_t, \quad t = 1, 2, \ldots, T, \tag{2.148}$$

where $E(\epsilon_t \mid X_t, X_{t-1}, Y_{t-1}) = 0$. The autoregressive part of this model equation is $\phi_1 Y_{t-1}$, and the distributed lag part is $\beta_0 X_t + \beta_1 X_{t-1}$. The distributed lag part does what the name suggest: it distributes the effects of a change in X over two periods. This clearly opens up for flexibility in the modelling of the relationship between X and Y.

Note 2.1. Notation for regression coefficients

When discussing both cross-sections and time series, it is almost impossible to avoid some change in notation. Hence, while the symbol β_0 has represented the constant term (before reparameterization and centring of X_i) so far in the chapter, it symbolizes the slope coefficient of X_t in (2.148). That change allows us to let β_1 denote the coefficient of X_{t-1}, which brings the notation used for the distributed lag in line with the autoregressive part, where ϕ_1 denotes the coefficient of the lag-variable Y_{t-1}. This notation will also be used in later chapters, and with ϕ_0 denoting the constant term in the model equation.

In the following chapters, we will define the precise solution of a dynamic model, but intuitively, since (2.148) is an equation that must hold not only for period t, but for period $t-1$ as well:

$$Y_{t-1} = \phi_0 + \phi_1 Y_{t-2} + \beta_0 X_{t-1} + \beta_1 X_{t-2} + \epsilon_{t-1}, \tag{2.149}$$

we can obtain

$$\begin{aligned} Y_t = {} & \phi_0(1+\phi_1) + \phi_1^2 Y_{t-2} + \beta_0 X_t + (\beta_1 + \phi_1\beta_0)X_{t-1} \\ & + \phi_1\beta_1 X_{t-2} + \epsilon_t + \phi_1\epsilon_{t-2} \end{aligned}$$

by substituting Y_{t-1} in (2.149) by the right-hand side of (2.149). Continuing this line of thought, by repeated substitution (or insertion) until we reach the start of the time series, we get for Y_t:

$$Y_t = \phi_0 \sum_{j=0}^{t-1} \phi_1^j + \phi_1^t Y_0 + \sum_{j=0}^{t} \omega_j X_{t-j} + \sum_{j=0}^{t-1} \phi_1^j \epsilon_{t-j}, \tag{2.150}$$

where the coefficients w_j are called *lag weights* or *dynamic multipliers* of Y_t with respect to X_{t-j}.

We see directly that $w_0 = \beta_0$ and $w_1 = (\beta_1 + \phi_1\beta_0)$. The higher order multipliers are however more complicated, and we leave the derivation of the general expressions for dynamic multipliers to a later chapter. The main point here is to show that although there are only two distributed lag variables in (2.148), the principle of obtaining the solution for Y_T by repeated substitution shows that Y_T depends on the whole time series $(X_T, X_{T-1}, \ldots, X_1)$. Clearly, the appeal of estimating this relationship in terms of the relatively simple model equation (2.148) is quite large.

Which brings us back to the question about the properties of, for example, OLS estimators of the coefficients of a dynamic regression model like (2.148). A first thing to note is that $E(\epsilon_t \mid X_t, X_{t-1}, Y_{t-1}) = 0$ does not imply that the regressors in (2.148) are independent of the disturbances. In fact, as long as $\phi_1 \neq 0$, the opposite must be the case. This is seen by applying (2.150) to Y_{t-1} for example:

$$Y_{t-1} = \phi_0 \sum_{j=0}^{t-2} \phi_1^j + \phi_1^{t-1} Y_0 + \sum_{j=0}^{t-1} w_j X_{t-1-j} + \sum_{j=0}^{t-1} \phi_1^j \epsilon_{t-1-j} \tag{2.151}$$

showing that Y_{t-1} is correlated with all the past disturbances (when $\phi_1 \neq 0$). On the other hand, it also shows that Y_{t-1} is independent of ϵ_t and all future disturbances.

This precisely defines the concept of a *predetermined* variable which was introduced in Chapter 1. As we shall see below, in the case of $-1 < \phi_1 < 1$, predeterminedness represents the limitation of the degree of temporal dependence that we mentioned above, and which is the essential requirement for applying OLS (and more generally MLE and IV methods) to time series data.

As many readers will know, the OLS estimators of $(\phi_0, \phi_1, \beta_0, \beta_1)$ are consistent if the error terms are not autocorrelated. There are finite sample biases in the OLS estimators, but they will be small for well-specified models, and for moderate sample lengths for stationary time series. In order to give a self-contained exposition of the theory that underlies this important result, as well as generalizations of it, we give a review of difference equations in Chapter 3 and of statistical theory of stationary time series in Chapter 4.

2.8. Misspecification Testing

When we apply the estimation principles and inference theory reviewed above to observational data, care must be taken to test the validity of the assumptions underlying the statistical model. Observational data, where the researcher in principle plays no active role in the generation of the data, are different from experimental data, interpreted widely as including sample survey data (Spanos, 1999, Chapter 11).

In modelling experimental data, the problem of choosing a statistical model (the specification stage) may be relatively simple, and often there is no explicit discussion of it in statistical textbooks. With observational data, which cannot be viewed as generated from a nearly isolated system (i.e., the laboratory ideal), but from collecting data taken from the real-world economy, the situation is very different. Specification of a satisfactory model is a difficult task, and the possibility of misspecification of the statistical model should not be neglected. If one or more of the assumptions of the model are invalid, the statistical inference theory reviewed above will, in general, be invalid; see Spanos (1999, Chapters 1, 11, 15), Hendry and Nielsen (2007, Chapters 9, 11, 13), Bårdsen and Nymoen (2011, Chapter 8) among others.

2.8.1. Why misspecification testing of econometric models?

As econometricians, we must relate to the fact that the DGP, which has produced the data, is not the same as the econometric model that we have specified and estimated; see Granger (1999), Kennedy (2008, Chapter 5), Hendry (2009) among others. The two exceptions to this rule that come to mind are: (i) when the data have been computer-generated in a program (i.e., script) that simulate the precise DGP, and (ii) when the data are from a laboratory experiment.

The first exception is when we do Monte Carlo simulation to learn about the properties of statistical estimators and test statistics under the assumptions of the precise DGP that is simulated when the program is executed. Monte Carlo simulation plays an important role in support for analytical results. For example, while the large sample properties of the IV estimator is known from asymptotic theory, Monte Carlo simulation can be used to learn about the sign and size of the IV estimator bias in small (realistic) samples. Hence, Monte Carlo simulations (also called Monte Carlo experiments) can aid the understanding of statistical and econometric theory. Below we will use several Monte Carlo experiments with this pedagogical purpose in mind (Section 4.6.4 is the first example of this).

The second exception from the rule that the DGP is unknown is the case of a classical laboratory experiment. Since the lab experiment has been devised and supervised by the researchers themselves, the DGP can in principle be assumed to be known (departures from the assumptions can however occur as a result of "bad experimental design").

Hence, the situation that an experimental researcher is in can be thought of as

$$\underset{\text{result}}{Y_i} = \underset{\text{input}}{g(X_i)} + \underset{\text{shock}}{v_i} \tag{2.152}$$

(see Hendry, 1995a, Section 1.11). The variable Y_i is the result of the experiment, while the X_i is the imputed input variable which is decided by the researcher. $g(X_i)$ is a deterministic function. The variable v_i is a shock which leads to some separate variation in Y_i for the chosen X_i. The aim of the experiment is to find the effect that X has as a causal variable on Y. If the $g(X_i)$-function is linear, this causal relationship can be investigated with the use of OLS estimation.

Box 2.7. Data Generating Process

The term data generating process (DGP) takes a double meaning. The first meaning is that DGP denotes the complicated and high-dimensional DGP of an economy (or of the part, sector or "subset" of the economy that an empirical modelling project focuses on). The second meaning is that DGP refers to Monte Carlo experiments (simulations).

Box 2.7 (*Continued*)

It is the precise process generating the experimental data used to simulate the properties of econometric estimation methods and tests.

The use of experimental data is increasing in economics, but the brunt of applied econometric analysis will continue to make use of non-experimental data. Economic data are usually collected for purposes than research (although the data are often "refined" in important ways by statistical agencies), and the data reflect the real-life decisions made by a vast number of heterogeneous agents. Hence, the starting point of an econometric modelling project is usually fundamentally different from the experimental situation. In order to maintain (2.152) as a "model of econometrics" for observable data, one would have to appeal to the *axiom of correct specification*, meaning that we know the DGP *before* the analysis is made, which is clearly unrealistic (see Leamer, 1983). If we want to avoid the axiom of correct specification, we instead face the consequence that based on our model of the unknown DGP that has generated the observations, the disturbance is a derived variable, namely:

$$\underset{\text{observed}}{Y_i} = \underset{\text{explained}}{f(X_i)} + \underset{\text{remainder}}{\varepsilon_i}, \tag{2.153}$$

where Y_i are the observations of the dependent variable which we seek to explain by the use of economic theory and our knowledge of the subject matter. Our explanation is given by the function $f(X_i)$ which (in the regression case, the conditional expectation function), and the result of a range of decisions, including variable selection (Hendry, 2018). The non-experimental Y_i is not determined or caused by $f(X_i)$, it is determined by a DGP that is unknown for us, and all variation in Y_i that we do not account for, must therefore "end up" in the remainder ε_i. Unlike (2.152), where v_i represents free and independent variation to Y_i, ε_i in (2.153) is an *implied* variable which gets its properties from the DGP and the explanation, in effect from the model $f(X_i)$. Hence in econometrics, we should write:

$$\varepsilon_i = Y_i - f(X_i) \tag{2.154}$$

to describe that whatever we do on the right-hand side of (2.154) by way of changing the specification of $f(X_i)$ or by changing the measurement of Y_i, the left-hand side is derived as a result.

This analysis poses at least two important questions. The first is related to causation: Although we can make $f(X_i)$ precise, as a conditional expectation function, we cannot claim that X_i is a causal variable. Again this is different from the randomized laboratory experiment case. However, as we shall see, we can often combine economic theory and further econometric analysis of the *system* that contains Y_i and X_i as endogenous variable, to reach a meaningful interpretation of the joint evidence in favour of one-way causality, or two-way causality. Recently, there has also been a surge in microdatasets based on large registers, which has opened up a new approach to causal modelling using data from so-called natural experiments and the *Differences-in-Differences* estimator.[5]

The second major issue has to do with mis-specification, how to discover mis-specification when it occurs, and the advisable response to revealed mis-specification; see, e.g., Pagan (1984) and Spanos (1995), and Box 2.8. Residual mis-specification, in particular, can be defined relatively to a regression model equation or to a structural model equation. Hence we say that there is residual mis-specification if the residual from the model behaves significantly differently from what we would expect to see if the true disturbances of the model adhered to the classical assumptions about homoskedasticity, non-autocorrelation, or no cross-sectional dependence.

Clearly, if the axiom of correct specification holds, we would see little evidence of residual misspecification. However, even the smallest experience of applied econometrics will show that misspecification frequently occurs. As we know from elementary econometrics, the consequences of misspecification for the properties of estimators and tests are sometimes not very serious. For example, non-normality entails that we do not know the exact distribution of the t-values in small sample sizes, but standard asymptotic theory implies that the normal distribution holds in large samples.

Other forms of misspecification give more serious problems: Autocorrelated disturbances in a dynamic model may for example lead to coefficient estimators being biased, even in very large samples (i.e., they are inconsistent).

Table 2.1 gives an overview and can serve as a reminder of what we know from elementary econometrics.

---

[5]Stewart and Wallis (1981) book is an early textbook presentation of the basic form of this estimator (see pp. 180–184), but without the label *Differences-in-Differences*, which is more recent terminology.

Table 2.1. Consequences of residual misspecification.

	Disturbances ε_i are:			
	heteroskedastic		autocorrelated	
X_i	$\hat{\beta}_0$	$\widehat{\text{Var}}(\hat{\beta}_0)$	$\hat{\beta}_0$	$\widehat{\text{Var}}(\hat{\beta}_0)$
exogenous	biased consistent	wrong	unbiased consistent	wrong
predetermined	biased consistent	wrong	biased inconsistent	wrong

Table 2.1 has been made with the simple regression model in mind:

$$Y_i = \phi_0 + \beta_0 X_i + \varepsilon_i, \tag{2.155}$$

and that $\hat{\beta}_0$ is the OLS estimator for the slope coefficient β_0 and $\widehat{\text{Var}}(\hat{\beta}_0)$ is the standard error of the estimator. The entry "wrong" in the table indicates that this estimator of the variance of $\hat{\beta}_0$ is not the correct estimator to use, it can overestimate or underestimate the uncertainty.

We assume that we estimate by OLS because we are interested in β_0 as a parameter in the conditional expectation function. This means that we can regard X_i as exogenous in the sense that all the disturbances are uncorrelated with X_i. As just noted, when we have time series data and X_t is the lag of Y_t, X_i in the table cannot be strictly exogenous, but it may be predetermined in the absence of residual autocorrelation.

Although Table 2.1 refers to a regression model, the same qualitative consequences of departures from the assumptions apply to a structural model. Basically, residual misspecification invalidates the statistical inference that a researcher wants to use the model for.

Because of its importance in the assessment of the quality of econometric models, most econometric programs contain a battery of misspecification test. The rest of this paragraph gives brief explanations of the misspecification tests that we will assume some familiarity with below.

Box 2.8. Tackling misspecification

If the tests indicate significant departures from the assumptions about the disturbances, we should always consider changing the model equation, or at least to change the estimation of the standard errors of the estimated coefficients. This is because the validity of all inference

Box 2.8 (*Continued*)

that we make requires that the assumptions are approximately correct.

Note that a change from OLS to weighted least squares and GLS estimation, can be regarded as a model change: the functional form is changed, e.g., from being linear both in variables and in parameters, to being nonlinear in variables but maintaining linearity in parameters.

Quite often, misspecification can only be tackled by undertaking more fundamental respecification. At the other end of the spectrum, the widespread use of robust standard errors can be seen as a pragmatic response to mild forms of misspecification, that a researcher has reason to believe will not induce damaging bias in estimation of the coefficients of interest.

2.8.2. A review of some standard diagnostic tests

Examples of textbooks with chapters about diagnostic testing are Hendry and Nielsen (2007, Chapters 9 and 13), Kennedy (2008, Chapter 5) and Bårdsen and Nymoen (2011, Chapter 8).[6]

Normality test

The normality assumption for the disturbances is important for the exact statistical distribution of OLS estimators and the associated test statistics. It is decisive for which p-values to use for t-tests and F-tests and for confidence intervals and prediction intervals.

If the normality assumption holds, it is correct inference to use the t-distribution to test a hypothesis about single parameters of the models, and the F-distribution to test a joint hypothesis.

If the normality assumption cannot be maintained, inference with the t- and F-distributions is no longer exact, but it can still be a good approximation. And it get increasingly better with increasing sample size.

The normality test is based on the two moments $\hat{\kappa}_3^2 = \sum \hat{\varepsilon}_i^3/\hat{\sigma}^3$ (skewness) and $\hat{\kappa}_4^2 = \sum \hat{\varepsilon}_i^4/\hat{\sigma}^4 - 3$ (kurtosis) where $\hat{\varepsilon}_i$ denotes a *residual* from

[6]Doornik and Hendry (2013a, c) contain details about how the tests have been implemented and reported in PcGive, as well as tutorials. Coverage is also given in the documentation of other leading software products.

the estimated model. Skewness refers to how symmetric the residuals are around zero. Kurtosis refers to the "peakedness" of the distribution. For a normal distribution, the kurtosis value is 3. These two moments are used to construct the test statistics

$$\chi^2_{\text{skew}} = n\frac{\hat{\kappa}_3^2}{6}\ \chi^2_{\text{kurt}} = n\frac{\hat{\kappa}_4^2}{24} \text{ and, jointly: } \chi^2_{\text{norm}} = \chi^2_{\text{skew}} + \chi^2_{\text{kurt}},$$

with degrees of freedom 1, 1 and 2 under the null hypothesis of normality of ε_i. The χ^2_{norm}-statistics is often referred to as the *Jarque–Bera*-test due to Jarque and Bera (1980).

Heteroskedasticity tests (White test)

Formal tests of the homoskedasticity assumption were proposed by White (1980), and these tests are often referred to as White tests. In the simplest case, the test is based on a so-called auxiliary regression:

$$\hat{\varepsilon}_i^2 = a_0 + a_1 X_i + a_2 X_i^2, \quad i = 1, 2, \ldots, n, \tag{2.156}$$

where the $\hat{\varepsilon}_i$s are the OLS residuals from the model. Under the null hypothesis of homoskedasticity, we have

$$H_0\colon a_1 = a_2 = 0,$$

which can be tested by the usual F-test on (2.156). This statistic, which we will refer to by the symbol F_{het}, is then F-distributed with 2 and $n-3$ degrees of freedom under the H_0. n denotes the number of observations.

There is also a Chi-square distributed version of White's test which is distributed $\chi^2(2)$ in the present example. It is calculated as nR^2_{het}, where R^2_{het} is the multiple correlation coefficient from (2.156). From elementary econometrics, we know that the F-distributed statistic can be written as

$$F_{\text{het}} = \frac{R^2_{\text{het}}}{(1 - R^2_{\text{het}})}\frac{n-3}{2},$$

confirming that the two versions of the test use the same basic information, and that the difference is that the F-version "adjusts for" degrees of freedom. The F-version is recommended to use when the sample is small because Monte Carlo simulations have shown that F_{het} has better small sample properties. Specifically, the actual Type-I error probability is usually closer to the significance level we have chosen when the F-version is used, compared to using the Chi-squared version.

With two or more explanatory variables, there is an extended version of White's test that includes product (i.e., squares) and cross-products of the regressors in the auxiliary regression. For example, if we include a second regressor in the model, F_{het} becomes F-distributed with 5 and $n-6$ degrees of freedom under the null hypothesis. This is because the auxiliary regression contains $X_{1i}, X_{2i}, X_{1i}^2, X_{2i}^2$ and $X_{1i} \times X_{2i}$.

Regression specification error test

A popular form of the regression specification error test (RESET) is based on the auxiliary regression:

$$Y_i = a_0 + a_1 X_i + a_2 \hat{Y}_i^2 + a_3 \hat{Y}_i^3 + v_i, \quad i = 1, 2, \ldots, n, \tag{2.157}$$

where $\hat{Y}_i$ denotes the fitted values. In this case, there are both a squared and a cubic term in (2.157) so that the joint null hypothesis is: $a_2 = a_3 = 0$ and the natural test statistic to use is again F-distributed with a degree of freedom that reflects the restrictions under the null hypothesis.

As the name suggests, the RESET is sometimes interpreted as a test of the correctness of the model, the functional form in particular. However, modern textbooks stress that the RESET is non-constructive: by itself, "it gives no indication what the researcher should do next if the null model is rejected"(see Greene, 2012, p. 177). Hence, the modern consensus is to interpret the RESET as a general misspecification test.

The above misspecification tests are just as relevant for cross-section data, as for models that use time series data. But there are also misspecification issues that are special for time series data. This is due to the fundamental autocorrelation of the observable data, which, if left unaccounted for by the econometric model, will lead to residual autocorrelation, or to time dependency in the residual variance.

Some dimensions of misspecification are special to time series. To describe briefly a selection of test, we focus on the same simple model equation as (2.155), but we change subscript from i to t to signal time series data:

$$Y_t = \phi_0 + \beta_0 X_t + \varepsilon_t. \tag{2.158}$$

Residual autocorrelation

Historically, the most important test of residual autocorrelation is perhaps the Durbin–Watson (DW) test. However, the DW test has several limitations (notably when used for dynamic regressions), and the modern approach is instead to make use of the procedure with an auxiliary regression.

For example, if the purpose is to test the joint hypothesis of absence of (up to) second-order autocorrelation, we use of the auxiliary regression:

$$\hat{\varepsilon}_t = a_0 + a_1\hat{\varepsilon}_{t-1} + a_2\hat{\varepsilon}_{t-2} + a_3X_t + v_t, \tag{2.159}$$

and the null hypothesis that can be tested by an F-distributed statistic is

$$H_0 : a_1 = a_2 = 0,$$

and the first degree of freedom will therefore be two. Several researchers have contributed to this test for residual autocorrelation, notably Godfrey (1978) and Harvey (1981).

As with many of the other tests, the underlying theory is asymptotic, and leads to the χ^2-distributed test statistics with degrees of freedom identical to the order of residual autocorrelation tested for (i.e., 2 in this example). Many textbooks refer to this test (rather technically) as the Lagrange multiplier test. But then one should add "for autocorrelation" since also the heteroskedasticity test is derived as a Lagrange multiplier test. In any case, a recommendation which has become common is to use the F-distributed version of the test in small samples to achieve actual Type-I error probability close to the chosen significance level (see Harvey, 1990, pp. 174 and p. 278; Kiviet, 1986).

This test procedure is flexible. If you have reason to believe that the likely form of autocorrelation is of the first order, it is efficient to base the test on an auxiliary regression with only a single lag. Conversely, extension to higher order autocorrelation is also straightforward. Below we will denote this general misspecification test $F_{ar(i-j)}$ where $i \leq j$.

Autoregressive conditional heteroskedasticity

With time series data, it is possible that the variance of ε_t depends on time. If the variance follows an autoregressive model of the first order, this type of heteroskedasticity is represented as

$$\text{Var}(\varepsilon_t \,|\varepsilon_{t-1}) = a_0 + \alpha_1\varepsilon_{t-1}^2.$$

The null hypothesis of constant variance can be tested by using the auxiliary regression:

$$\hat{\varepsilon}_t^2 = \sigma^2 + \delta\hat{\varepsilon}_{t-1}^2 + v_t, \tag{2.160}$$

where $\hat{\varepsilon}_t^2$ $(t = 1, 2, \ldots, T)$ are squared residuals. The coefficient of determination R^2_{arch} from (2.160) is used to calculate $\text{TR}^2_{\text{arch}}$ which is $\chi^2(1)$ under the null hypothesis. In the same way as we have seen above, it widely accepted that the F-form of the test is preferable (i.e., with reference to Type-I errors probability). Extensions to higher order residual autoregressive conditional heteroskedasticity (ARCH) is therefore also straightforward by use of a larger auxiliary regressions.

We have introduced the ARCH model as a misspecification test, but this class of models has become widely used for modelling volatile time series, especially in finance. The ARCH model was introduced by Engle (1982) as a way of modelling volatility in economic and financial time series. In Section 6.8, we give an introduction to the use of ARCH in the specification of the econometric relationship (rather than as a test of misspecification).

2.8.3. System versions of tests

Generalization of the above tests are available for multiple equation models (see Doornik and Hendry, 2013c, Chapters 15 and 17). For example, the multivariate test of normality $(\chi^{2,v}_{\text{norm}}(2n))$ developed by Doornik and Hansen (2008). System versions of the F-test for residual autocorrelation $F^v_{ar(1-j)}$, where j indicates the order of autocorrelation, and F^v_{het} generalizing White (1980), are also available, and examples of their use are given in later chapters of this book.

2.8.4. Recursive estimation and parameter stability tests

When the data are time series, so that there is a natural ordering of the observations, a direct way of investigating the degree of stability of a model equation's parameters is by the use of recursive estimation. We start by fitting the model equation (2.158) to an initial sample $t = 1, 2, \ldots, T_1$ and then fit the equation to samples of $T_1 + 1$, $T_1 + 2$ up to T observations. This is called *recursive estimation* and is done in a trice with the use of modern computer software.

The output can be used to graph coefficients $\hat{\beta}_0$, $\hat{\sigma}$ etc. over the sample, which gives a powerful way to study parameter constancy of the empirical model (not least when it is absent). This type of graph is called *recursive graph* and is often easiest to inspect if the initial sample is not too short, since otherwise the changes brought about by each additional observation may be large even if the underlying DGP has stable parameters.

A main test for parameter constancy of the conditional expectation function is the Chow (1960) test. One version of the test is given as

$$F_{\text{Chow}} = \frac{\text{RSS}_T - \text{RSS}_{T_{\text{break}}}}{\text{RSS}_{T_{\text{break}}}} \frac{(T_{\text{break}} - (k+1))}{(T - T_{\text{break}})}, \tag{2.161}$$

for the general case of $k+1$ regressors (i.e., including the constant). In this expression, RSS_T refers to the residual sum of squares for the complete sample, while $\text{RSS}_{T_{\text{break}}}$ is the residual sum of squares after fitting the model to the T_{break} first observations. Clearly, $T_{\text{break}} > k+1$.

Note that for a given break date, we can define $h = T - T_{\text{break}}$ where h is the *number of post-break sample periods.* If the break period is known *a priori*, we often speak of the test as the known break point version of the test. Critical values for this test are of the F-distribution with $(T - T_{\text{break}})$ and $(T_{\text{break}} - (k+1))$ degrees of freedom.[7]

In practice, the hypothesized break point are often not known. It is therefore convenient to calculate and plot the whole sequence of (recursive) Chow tests, and conclude that the break occurred in the period for which the largest Chow test value in the sequence is significant. This can be done in several ways. We can calculate and plot all 1-step Chow statistics (i.e., $h = 1$), and we can inspect plots of h-increasing, and h-decreasing Chow tests.

However, since we are making use of many test, it is good practice to choose a tight significance level, for example 1%, to avoid unintended large Type-I error probability. The h-increasing Chow test (variously called the Forecast Chow test) can for example be plotted against a line representing the one-off critical value (see Doornik and Hendry, 2013a, Chapter 7). A formal test, for which correct critical vales are available, is the *Quandt Likelihood Ratio* (QLR) *test* (see Quandt, 1960; Andrews, 1993, 2003).

If the tendency is that the model equation fits better towards the end of the sample, the h-increasing Chow tests will often have little chance of detecting a break point. Hence, it is well worth considering the sequence of h-decreasing Chow tests. In this version, the first test value is for the longest forecast period $h = T - T_1$, the second is the test value obtained

[7]If the known break point is such that we have two samples with enough observations to allow relatively precise estimation of the model equation, F_{Chow} may not be optimal, and the two-sample version of the Chow test can be used instead (Stewart and Wallis, 1981, p. 200).

after adding one observation to the initial sample (hence $T_{\text{break}} = T_1 + 1$)), and so on. Again, as there are many individual Chow tests in the sequence, the overall significance level can be controlled by comparing the highest test values in the sequence, for example, with the e.g., 1% percent critical value for a single (one-off) test.

2.9. Recommended Textbooks in Econometrics and Mathematics for Economists

The material in this chapter will be covered by courses in statistics and introductory course in econometrics, and so it will be familiar to many readers. As mentioned, this chapter is not intended as a substitute for such a course, and readers who find the chapter (and the exercises) almost overtly difficult would benefit from consulting a textbook.

Introductory and intermediate econometrics

David F. Hendry and Bent Nielsen, *Econometric Modelling. A Likelihood Approach*, Princeton (2007).

We refer frequently to this textbook among other things because of the perspective that econometric models can be interpreted as probability distributions "put on" model equation form, a view that we have adopted. The book is subtitled *A Likelihood Approach*, and it is an introduction to econometrics from that perspective. The presentation of the statical theory is systematic and holds a high level of precision for an introductory book. Chapter 11 is also without counterparts among introductory books, it explains why empirical models are essentially different from theoretical models, including econometric ones, as they are inevitably the result of a specification process. The book has chapters that cover both forecasting and automatic model selection.

Peter Kennedy, *A Guide to Econometrics*, 6th edition, Blackwell (2008).

Perhaps the most accessible introduction econometrics currently in print, because of its non-technical style. Chapters 1–4 cover the basic estimation and inference theory for regression models. Chapter 5 is well worth reading since it contains a balanced review of competing methodologies for applied econometrics, a controversy that we also comment on in Chapter 11. Methods of moments (MM) is presented in Chapter 9 in Kennedy's book.

James Stock and Mark M. Watson, *Introduction to Econometrics*, 3rd edition, Pearsons (2012).

Chapters 2 and 3 of this popular textbook contain the probability theory and review the statistics that we assume you are familiar with. Chapters 4–9 contain the fundamentals of regression analysis, but for the level of this book, the more concise presentations of the theory of linear regression in Chapters 17 and 18, are also necessary background. If you only need to refresh your knowledge, these two chapters may be what you need to review. Matrix notation is used in Chapter 18. Chapter 12 contains the book's introduction to IVs estimation, albeit under the confusing label of "instrumental variables regression". Chapter 18 contains a theoretical exposition of IV estimation, including Generalized method of moments.

R. Carter Hill, William Griffiths and Guay C. Lim, *Principles of Econometric*, 4th edition, Wiley (2012).

The unnumbered "Probability primer" appendix to Chapter 1 is essential, but the numbered appendices at the end of the book B, C and C provides a complete review. Chapters 2–8 and 10 in the main text cover the level of econometrics that we assume in this book.

Mathematics

The level of mathematics necessary to read this book is represented by:

Knut Sydsæter, Peter Hammond, Arne Strøm and Andrés Cravajal, *Essential Mathematics for Economic Analysis*, 5th edition, Pearson (2016) (or earlier editions).

Note that matrices and determinants are found in the last chapters of the book. We will in particular make use of eigenvalues of matrices, and which can be found in Chapter 1 of: Knut Sydsæter, Peter Hammond, Atle Seierstad and Arne Strøm, *Further Mathematics for Economic Analysis*, 2nd edition, FT Prentice-Hall (2008). This book also covers the mathematics that we introduce as we develop the theory of dynamic econometric modelling. Chapter 11 covers difference equations and Appendix B trigonometric functions.

Alternatively, one of the many excellent books on linear algebra can be used (see, e.g., Lay, 2003). The results for differentiation of vector and matrices that we use (though few) are often found in advanced books in multivariate statistics and econometrics. However, the convenient source is often a formula collection, for example, Sydsæter *et al.* (2005), which we refer to in the text.

2.10. Exercises

Exercise 2.1. Give examples of theoretical and empirical first- and second-order moments of statistical distributions.

Exercise 2.2. Show that $\text{Var}(X)$ can be written as

$$\text{Var}(X) = E(X^2) - \mu_X^2.$$

This seems to imply that $\text{Var}(X)$ can be negative if μ_X^2 is large enough. Is that correct?

Exercise 2.3. Is a location shift of a distribution caused by a change in a first-order moment, or in a second-order moment?

Exercise 2.4. Explain why the simple regression model is a model with two regressors.

Exercise 2.5. Show that assumption **b** in the specification of the regression model can equivalently be written as

$$\text{Var}(Y_i \mid X_i) = \sigma^2_{Y_i|X_i}.$$

Exercise 2.6. Assume that X and Y are jointly normally distributed. What are the first- and second-order moments of the marginal distribution of Y? And of the conditional distribution of Y?

Exercise 2.7. Derive the expressions for $\hat{\beta}_0$ and $\hat{\beta}_1$ using RSS $= \sum_{i=1}^{n}(Y_i - \beta_0 - \beta_1 X_i)^2$, i.e., with the original parametrization of the regression model equation.

Exercise 2.8. Explain why, based on the regression model assumptions, the ML estimator $\hat{\sigma}^2$ is biased.

Exercise 2.9. Use (2.50) and (2.51) to show that the MM estimators of β_1, β_0 and α in the regression model are identical to the OLS and ML estimators of these coefficients.

Exercise 2.10. Show that under the assumptions of the regression model,

$$\hat{\theta} = \frac{\hat{\beta}_0}{\hat{\beta}_1}$$

is a consistent estimator of $\theta \underset{\text{def}}{=} \beta_0/\beta_1$.

Exercise 2.11. The internet pages with data and code to the book contain a file NORPCMa.zip with the data used in the example of the use of the Delta method in the construction of a confidence interval for the PCM natural rate of unemployment. The zip file contains two data bank formats: the PcGive format (consisting of the two files with extensions .in7 and .bn7) and the Stata format (the single file with extension .dta). The PcGive databank format is directly usable in Eviews. The zip file also contains the data in MS-Excel format.

The dataset contains only two variables, labelled INF (inflation in Norway) and U (the unemployment rate). Both series are measured in percent. The sample available for estimation of model equation (2.56) is 1973–2012. However, we used the subsample 1981–2005 to obtain the reported results.

Use your statistical software to replicate the estimation results for (2.56), and check the calculations for the U^{nat}. What is the standard error of U^{nat} when you estimate by NLS ?

Exercise 2.12. With reference to Section 2.8, comment on the residual misspecification tests for the estimated PCM in Exercise 2.11.

Exercise 2.13. The natural rate of unemployment $\hat{U}^{\mathrm{nat}}$ above follows custom in that it is defined for the hypothetical state of zero inflation. While the implied price level stability may be achievable, the operation inflation target that several countries opted for during the 1990s and later allowed for an inflation in the range of 2.0% and 2.5%.

In Norway, the inflation target was set to 2.5% in 2001. How can you calculate the corresponding "inflation target rate of unemployment", $\hat{U}^{it}$ using the numbers in Section 2.4.6?

Exercise 2.14. Derive (2.78) as the OLS estimator of $\boldsymbol{\beta}$ of (2.70) starting from the expression of the sum of squared disturbances.

Exercise 2.15. Show that the elements in $n^{-1}\mathbf{X}'\mathbf{X}$ and $n^{-1}\mathbf{X}'\mathbf{y}$ are (uncentred) second-order empirical moments.

Exercise 2.16. Assume that the first column in $\mathbf{X}$ has the number 1 in each position. Partition $\mathbf{X}$ as $\mathbf{X} = [\boldsymbol{\iota} : \mathbf{X}_2]$ where $\boldsymbol{\iota}$ is the $n \times 1$ column vector with ones and $\mathbf{X}_2$ is the $n \times k$ matrix with the variables $X_1, \ldots X_k$. Partition $\boldsymbol{\beta}$ accordingly as $\boldsymbol{\beta}' = (\beta_1 : \boldsymbol{\beta}_2')$ where β_1 is a scalar and $\boldsymbol{\beta}_2$ is

$k \times 1$. Show that you can write:

$$\mathbf{y} = \mathbf{X}\boldsymbol{\beta} + \boldsymbol{\varepsilon} = \boldsymbol{\iota}\alpha + (\mathbf{X}_2 - \bar{\mathbf{X}}_2)\boldsymbol{\beta}_2 + \boldsymbol{\epsilon},$$

where $\bar{\mathbf{X}}_2$ is the $n \times k$ matrix with the means of each variable in each column and

$$\alpha = \beta_1 + \bar{\mathbf{x}}_2'\boldsymbol{\beta}_2,$$

where $\bar{\mathbf{x}}_2$ is the $k \times 1$ vector with the means of each of the k variables $X_1, \ldots X_k$.

Exercise 2.17. Explain why the OLS estimator $\hat{\boldsymbol{\beta}}_2$ is found as

$$\hat{\boldsymbol{\beta}}_2 = [(\mathbf{X}_2 - \bar{\mathbf{X}}_2)'(\mathbf{X}_2 - \bar{\mathbf{X}}_2)]^{-1}(\mathbf{X}_2 - \bar{\mathbf{X}}_2)'\mathbf{y} \tag{2.162}$$

and why the OLS estimator of α becomes

$$\hat{\alpha} = (\boldsymbol{\iota}'\boldsymbol{\iota})^{-1}\boldsymbol{\iota}'\mathbf{y} = \bar{Y}, \tag{2.163}$$

where $\bar{Y}$ is the mean of the variables $\{Y_i;\ i = 1, 2, \ldots, n\}$ in the vector $\mathbf{y}$.

Exercise 2.18. Show that in the simple regression case $Y_i = \beta_0 + \beta_1 X_i + \epsilon_i$, with

$$\text{Var}(\epsilon_i \mid X_i) = \sigma^2 X_i \quad \forall i, \tag{2.164}$$

and all covariances between ϵ_i and ϵ_h $(h \neq i)$ equal to zero, a homoskedastic model is achieved by weighting the observations by $\sqrt{X_i}$ and that OLS on the homoskedastic model is identical to the GLS estimator.

Chapter 3

Review of Difference Equations

The statistical theory that underlies time series analysis and dynamic econometric modelling builds on the mathematical theory of difference equations. This chapter contains a review of the theory of difference equations that will be useful for us. We begin with the deterministic form, which is the discrete version of differential equations that many readers will know from growth models, and other models of economic dynamics. The main topic of this chapter is, however, stochastic difference equations, which represent the mathematical basis for statistical and econometric modelling of time series data.

3.1. Introduction

In Chapter 1, it was pointed out that instantaneous and full adjustments to changes are rare in economic systems. Adjustments that take place over several periods are the rule rather than the exception, and these dynamic processes are also the objective of macroeconometric modelling. Dynamics imply that time series data are typically autocorrelated, which means that the independence (between observations) assumption of the IID model of econometrics cannot be used as a basis for dynamic econometrics. A more general statistical theory is needed.

On the other hand, Chapter 1 also included examples of very small estimation errors, when OLS was used to estimate dynamic models, using computer simulated autocorrelated data. Admittedly, the models used as examples were simple, but the results nevertheless indicate that at least some of the estimation methodology from the IID model can be used also to estimate dynamic econometric models.

To improve our understanding of estimation methods for dynamic models, we need to familiarize ourselves with the statistical theory of time series. In this chapter, we present the mathematical basis for dynamic econometrics, which is the theory of linear stochastic difference equations.

3.2. Deterministic Difference Equations

Readers may be familiar with *differential equations* for continuous time as it is used in economic theory (e.g., Solow's model of economic growth). The discrete time counterpart to differential equations is called *difference equations*. We begin with a review of deterministic difference equations, and continue with the stochastic version, which will be our main mathematical tool in the following.

A general difference equation of order p can be written as

$$x_t = f(t, x_{t-1}, x_{t-2}, \ldots, x_{t-p}), \tag{3.1}$$

where the $f(\cdot)$-function is defined for all admissible values of the variables $\{x_t;\, t = 0, \pm 1, \pm 2, \ldots\}$. If we require that

$$x_{t-1}, x_{t-2}, \ldots, x_{t-p}$$

are given numbers, we will refer to this as the case of known *initial conditions*, an insertion method leads to the conclusion that the solution to (3.1) exists and is unique: Start by setting $t = 0$, which implies that x_0 is determined. Next, set $t = 1$, which implies that also x_1 is uniquely determined, and so on.

Existence and uniqueness of solutions to *linear* difference equation follow from this general insight. Note that the only assumption is that the initial conditions are given, meaning that they are known and fixed numbers. However, existence and uniqueness of solution tell us nothing about other features of a solution that we are interested in. For example: is the solution oscillating or monotonous? Does it follow a stable path, or is the time path of the solution explosive? In mathematics, the answers to these questions have been shown to lie in the solution to another problem, which is to find a sequence of real numbers $\{x_t;\, t = 0, \pm 1, \pm 2, \ldots\}$ that satisfies the *homogeneous linear difference equation*:

$$a_0 x_t + a_1 x_{t-1} + \cdots + a_p x_{t-p} = 0. \tag{3.2}$$

Note that, in general, the coefficients a_i can be (known) functions of time, $a_i(t)$, but to simplify the notation, we concentrate on the case where they are constants.

The *characteristic polynomial* associated with (3.2) is defined as

$$p(x) = a_0 x^p + a_1 x^{p-1} + \cdots + a_p. \tag{3.3}$$

Let λ denote a root (i.e., a solution) of the *characteristic equation* $p(\lambda) = 0$. Then, $x_t = C\lambda^t$ is a solution of (3.2). C denotes an arbitrary constant. We can confirm that $x_t = C\lambda^t$ is a solution directly:

$$\begin{aligned} a_0 x_t + a_1 x_{t-1} + \cdots + a_p x_{t-p} &= C(a_0\lambda^t + a_1\lambda^{t-1} + \cdots + a_p\lambda^{t-p}) \\ &= C\lambda^{t-p}(a_0\lambda^p + a_1\lambda^{p-1} + \cdots + a_p) = 0. \end{aligned}$$

This shows the form of a single solution of equation (3.2), and it also suggests that the general solution will have a similar, though more complicated form, which we for completeness give in Theorem 3.1.

Theorem 3.1 (General solution). *The general solution to* (3.2) *is*

$$x_t^h = \sum_{l=1}^{k} \sum_{j=1}^{m_l} C_{lj}\, t^{j-1} \lambda_l^t, \tag{3.4}$$

where C_{lj} are arbitrary constants. The parameters λ_l ($l = 1, 2, \ldots, k$) are the distinct roots of the characteristic equation $p(\lambda) = 0$ associated with (3.3), *hence,*

$$p(x) = a_0(x - \lambda_1)^{m_1}(x - \lambda_2)^{m_2} \cdots (x - \lambda_k)^{m_k},$$

where we have used the fundamental theorem of algebra (see Appendix 3.A). The multiplicities m_j sum to the number of roots, i.e., p.

Proofs of this theorem are found in advanced books in time series analysis (see Brockwell and Davies, 1991, Section 3.6).

Note that m_l denotes the number of repetitions of a distinct root λ_l, hence $m_1 + m_2 + \cdots + m_k = p$.

If we let $k = p$ and $m_l = 1$, for all l, we have the case where no roots are identical to each other (they are distinct). In this case, the expression for the solution takes the simpler form:

$$x_t^h = \sum_{l=1}^{p} \sum_{j=1}^{1} C_{lj}\, t^{j-1}\, \lambda_l^t = \sum_{l=1}^{p} C_{l1}\, \lambda_l^t, \tag{3.5}$$

which is the general solution of the homogeneous equation in the case of p distinct roots. In this case, we can further simplify the notation, and express the solution as

$$x_t^h = C_1\lambda_1^t + C_2\lambda_2^t + \cdots + C_p\lambda_p^t. \tag{3.6}$$

Having reviewed the form of the solution of the homogeneous difference equation, we might ask: How practical is this solution for applied work? It is all very well that we can obtain the roots λ_l by solving the characteristic equation $p(\lambda) = 0$. Computer programs will do that for us for cases of $p > 2$ which are unmanageable manually. But what about the arbitrary constants C_l? If the constants really are arbitrary, it is difficult to see that the solution is of much help in determining x_t in practice. However, in many cases, the arbitrariness is removed by the purpose (or motivation) that we had for studying the solution.

For example, we often want to use the mathematical solution to determine x, starting "today", $t = 0$, and for future time periods, under the assumption that we know the history of x. Hence, we seek to determine a sequence of numbers $\{x_t^h;\, t = 0, 1, 2, \ldots\}$ under the assumption that we know the historical number sequence: $\{x_t;\, t = -1, -2, -3, \ldots\}$.

This is the same as known initial values, or known initial conditions, that we mentioned above. Since equation (3.2) holds in every period, we can use that equation and the initial condition to determine the C_l constants. For example, if we set $p = 2$ and we assume that the roots are distinct, the two constants C_1 and C_2 in

$$x_t^h = C_1\lambda_1^t + C_2\lambda_2^t,$$

are determined by solving the two equations:

$$x_{-1} = C_1\lambda_1^{-1} + C_2\lambda_2^{-1},$$
$$x_{-2} = C_1\lambda_1^{-2} + C_2\lambda_2^{-2},$$

for C_1 and C_2.

We next turn to the *inhomogeneous* linear difference equation:

$$a_0x_t + a_1x_{t-1} + \cdots + a_px_{t-p} = b_t, \tag{3.7}$$

which is defined for $x_t;\, t = 0, \pm1, \pm2, \ldots$. The augmentation of the homogeneous equation by the term b_t, which also represents a sequence of numbers, is important for applied modelling, as we shall see. Already the introductory chapter contained a couple of examples in the form of the permanent shift of the demand schedule in the cobweb model, and the autonomous expenditure component J_t in the macromodel. The solution of the inhomogeneous equation is

$$x_t = x_t^h + x_t^s, \tag{3.8}$$

where x_t^s is a *special* solution of (3.7) and x_t^h is the solution of the homogeneous equation. We include the proof.

Proof. Let x_t^s denote a special solution of (3.7) and let x_t denote another, arbitrary, solution of the same equation. By insertion of $x_t - x_t^s$ in (3.2), we see that $x_t - x_t^s$ is one solution of the homogeneous equation. But then Theorem 3.1 implies:

$$x_t - x_t^s = \sum_{l=1}^{k}\sum_{j=1}^{m_l} C_{lj}\, t^{j-1}\, r_l^t = x_t^h$$

and (3.8) is the solution of the inhomogeneous equation. □

3.3. Stochastic Difference Equations with Constant Coefficients

A stochastic difference equation of order p with constant coefficients is given by:

$$Y_t = \phi_0 + \phi_1 Y_{t-1} + \phi_2 Y_{t-2} + \cdots + \phi_p Y_{t-p} + \varepsilon_t \tag{3.9}$$

where Y_{t-i}, $i = 0, 1, \ldots, p$ and ε_t are random variables and where ϕ_i are constants.

In this section, we first show how the theorem about the solution of a deterministic difference equation can be applied to the stochastic version. In this context, the specification of the distribution function of ε_t is not important. However, the stochastic properties of Y_t, which we shall derive by using the solution to (3.9), will depend on the assumptions about ε_t. Since it is relevant for many of the cases we will be interested in, we assume from the start that $\varepsilon_1, \varepsilon_2, \ldots, \varepsilon_T$ are independent and identically distributed variables with expectation 0 and variance σ_ε^2. In line with the notation in Chapter 2, we write it as

$$\varepsilon_t \sim \text{IID}(0, \sigma_\varepsilon^2), \quad \forall t. \tag{3.10}$$

3.3.1. Solution

Mathematically speaking, (3.9) has the same properties as the inhomogeneous difference equation (3.7). We see this by defining $x_t = Y_t$, $b_t = \phi_0 + \varepsilon_t$, $a_0 = 1$ and $a_i = -\phi_1$ $(i = 1, 2, \ldots, p)$, and then use these definitions in the resulting equation:

$$a_0 x_t + a_1 x_{t-1} + \cdots + a_p x_{t-p} = b_t.$$

As a consequence, we can use the same method as above to find a formal mathematical solution of (3.9). In particular, we can define the characteristic polynomial associated with the homogeneous part of (3.9) as

$$p(y) = y^p - \phi_1 y^{p-1} - \cdots - \phi_p, \tag{3.11}$$

for an arbitrary number y. We also define λ as a root in the associated *characteristic equation* $p(\lambda) = 0$:

$$\lambda^p - \phi_1 \lambda^{p-1} - \cdots - \phi_p = 0. \tag{3.12}$$

Another name for these characteristic roots is *eigenvalues*. We will use both terms in the following.

By direct analogy to the deterministic case, it also follows that $Y_t^h = C\lambda^t$, for an arbitrary C, is a solution of the homogeneous part of (3.9). We can confirm this directly:

$$\begin{aligned} Y_t^h - \phi_1 Y_{t-1}^h - \cdots - \phi_p Y_{t-p}^h &= C(\lambda^t - \phi_1 \lambda^{t-1} - \cdots - \phi_p \lambda^{t-p}) \\ &= C\lambda^{t-p}(\lambda^p - \phi_1 \lambda^{p-1} - \cdots - \phi_p) = 0. \end{aligned}$$

The general solution Y_t is also analogous to the deterministic case above:

$$Y_t = Y_t^h + Y_t^s,$$

where Y_t^s represents one particular (special), solution of (3.9).

3.3.2. Solution in the case of first-order dynamics

We now apply the general solution to the case of first-order dynamics, $p = 1$, meaning that equation (3.9) takes the simple form:

$$Y_t = \phi_0 + \phi_1 Y_{t-1} + \varepsilon_t. \tag{3.13}$$

In Chapter 1, we looked at two examples of theoretical models that implied final form equations with first-order dynamics. The cobweb model implied negative values of the autoregressive coefficient ϕ_1, while the Keynesian macro model implied positive values. We referred to this as negative and positive autocorrelation. In the introduction, we also discussed solutions of those dynamic models by appealing to the economic interpretation of the models. In this chapter, we go through the mathematical solution in a relatively detailed manner.

The homogeneous equation is

$$Y_t - \phi_1 Y_{t-1} = 0,$$

with associated characteristic equation:

$$\lambda - \phi_1 = 0,$$

which gives a single characteristic root:

$$\lambda = \phi_1.$$

The general solution of the homogeneous equation is therefore

$$Y_t^h = C\phi_1^t, \tag{3.14}$$

for an arbitrary constant C. In the same way as in the deterministic case, two issues must be settled before we have a complete solution. First, the arbitrariness of C needs to be removed. Second, we need a particular solution Y_t^s.

We start by solving the second problem. A much used particular solution is based on the additional requirement that the solution (if it exists) is globally asymptotically stable, meaning that any solution Y_t reaches a stationary state (or more generally, a steady state) as $t \to \infty$ (see Definition 3.1, which covers the case of higher order dynamics).

Theorem 3.2 shows that this requirement implies the condition that the absolute value of the coefficient ϕ_1 is less than one, $|\phi_1| < 1$.

In order to see what this implies for Y_t^s, we insert repeatedly on the right-hand side of (3.13). First, for Y_{t-1}:

$$Y_t = \phi_0(1 + \phi_1) + \phi_1^2 Y_{t-2} + \varepsilon_t + \phi_1 \varepsilon_{t-1},$$

then for Y_{t-2}, and so on, up to and including Y_{t-j}. This method gives

$$Y_t = \phi_0 \sum_{i=0}^{j} \phi_1^i + \phi_1^{j+1} Y_{t-1-j} + \sum_{i=0}^{j} \phi_1^i \varepsilon_{t-i}. \tag{3.15}$$

Note that $|\phi_1| < 1$ implies that $\phi_1^{(j+1)} Y_{t-j-1} \to 0$ as $j \to \infty$. By choosing to consider a stable solution, we can therefore use

$$Y_t^s = \phi_0 \sum_{i=0}^{\infty} \phi_1^i + \sum_{i=0}^{\infty} \phi_1^i \varepsilon_{t-i} = \frac{\phi_0}{1-\phi_1} + \sum_{i=0}^{\infty} \phi_1^i \varepsilon_{t-i}, \tag{3.16}$$

as a particular solution.[1]

When Y_t^h, from (3.14), and Y_t^s given by (3.16), are added together, we obtain the full solution as

$$\begin{aligned} Y_t &= Y_t^h + Y_t^s \\ &= C\phi_1^t + \frac{\phi_0}{1-\phi_1} + \sum_{i=0}^{\infty} \phi_1^i \varepsilon_{t-i}. \end{aligned} \tag{3.17}$$

Again, we can confirm that this is indeed a solution of (3.13) by inserting (3.17) on both sides of (3.13):

$$\begin{aligned} C\phi_1^t &+ \frac{\phi_0}{1-\phi_1} + \sum_{i=0}^{\infty} \phi_1^i \varepsilon_{t-i} \\ &= \phi_0 + \phi_1 \left(C\phi_1^{t-1} + \frac{\phi_0}{1-\phi_1} + \sum_{i=0}^{\infty} \phi_1^i \varepsilon_{t-i-1} \right) + \varepsilon_t \\ &= C\phi_1^t + \frac{\phi_0}{1-\phi_1} + \sum_{i=0}^{\infty} \phi_1^i \varepsilon_{t-i} = Y_t. \end{aligned}$$

We next turn to the other (i.e., the first) problem, namely, how to resolve the arbitrariness of the solution by finding a distinct value for C in the solution. Since (3.17) holds for each and every period, we can use it to express Y_0 as

$$Y_0 = C + \frac{\phi_0}{1-\phi_1} + \sum_{i=0}^{\infty} \phi_1^i \varepsilon_{-i}. \tag{3.18}$$

By conditioning on the known history of the time series, which in this case is simply Y_0, equation (3.18) can be used to determine C:

$$C = Y_0 - \frac{\phi_0}{1-\phi_1} - \sum_{i=0}^{\infty} \phi_1^i \varepsilon_{-i}, \quad |\phi_1| < 1. \tag{3.19}$$

[1] Using sums from $i = 0$ as above, and in several other equations below, is efficient in terms of notation, but can lead to a question about how 0^0 is to be understood, since the expressions clearly should "hold for" $\phi_1 = 0$. The convention we use is to define $0^0 = 1$ (while $0^i = 0$ for $i = 1, 2, \ldots$), thus extending $\phi_1^0 = 1$ from the cases where $\phi_1 \neq 0$.

We now have a non-arbitrary, and therefore relevant, solution: Since C is given by (3.19), equation (3.17) gives the solutions for Y_t for all periods $(t = 1, 2, 3, \ldots)$.

This completes the solution by the use of the general result that the solution of the inhomogeneous equation is the general solution of the homogeneous equation, and a particular solution of the inhomogeneous equation.

But what about the expression in (3.15)? It was obtained by repeated insertion backwards in time, which is both intuitive and reasonable, and without any use of the mathematical theory of difference equations. If that expression also represents a solution for Y_t, must it not be identical to the solutions gives by (3.19) and (3.17)? The answer is "yes, for the stable case", and we can show that for the sake of completeness.

We begin by changing the index in (3.15) by substituting j by $t-1$. The expression is therefore changed to

$$Y_t = \phi_0 \sum_{i=0}^{t-1} \phi_1^i + \phi_1^t Y_0 + \sum_{i=0}^{t-1} \phi_1^i \varepsilon_{t-i}. \tag{3.20}$$

Often, it is this way of writing the solution, as obtained by backward iteration, that is the most convenient form of the solution to use.

Next, we show that (3.19) and (3.17) give (3.20) as an implication. Replace C in (3.17) by the right-hand side of (3.19):

$$\begin{aligned} Y_t &= \left(Y_0 - \frac{\phi_0}{1-\phi_1} - \sum_{i=0}^{\infty} \phi_1^i \varepsilon_{-i} \right) \phi_1^t + \frac{\phi_0}{1-\phi_1} + \sum_{i=0}^{\infty} \phi_1^i \varepsilon_{t-i} \\ &= \frac{\phi_0}{1-\phi_1} + \left(Y_0 - \frac{\phi_0}{1-\phi_1} \right) \phi_1^t - \phi_1^t \sum_{i=0}^{\infty} \phi_1^i \varepsilon_{-i} + \sum_{i=0}^{\infty} \phi_1^i \varepsilon_{t-i}. \end{aligned}$$

The two last elements in this expression can be written as

$$\begin{aligned} &- \phi_1^t \sum_{i=0}^{\infty} \phi_1^i \varepsilon_{-i} + \sum_{i=0}^{\infty} \phi_1^i \varepsilon_{t-i} \\ &\quad = -\phi_1^t \left(\phi_1^0 \varepsilon_{-0} + \phi_1^1 \varepsilon_{-1} + \cdots \right) \\ &\qquad + \phi_1^0 \varepsilon_t + \phi_1 \varepsilon_{t-1} + \cdots + \phi_1^t \varepsilon_{-0} + \phi_1^{t+1} \varepsilon_{-1} + \cdots \\ &\quad = \phi_1^0 \varepsilon_t + \phi_1 \varepsilon_{t-1} + \cdots + \phi_1^{t-1} \varepsilon_1 = \sum_{i=0}^{t-1} \phi_1^i \varepsilon_{t-i}, \end{aligned}$$

which gives

$$Y_t = \frac{\phi_0}{1-\phi_1} + \left(Y_0 - \frac{\phi_0}{1-\phi_1}\right)\phi_1^t + \sum_{i=0}^{t-1}\phi_1^i\varepsilon_{t-i}. \tag{3.21}$$

Finally, we note that if we are able to show the identity

$$\frac{\phi_0}{1-\phi_1} + \left(Y_0 - \frac{\phi_0}{1-\phi_1}\right)\phi_1^t \equiv \phi_0\sum_{i=0}^{t-1}\phi_1^i + \phi_1^t Y_0, \tag{3.22}$$

we will have shown that (3.21) is the same solution as (3.20). In order to show the identity, we make use of the result about the sum of the t first elements in a geometric progression:

$$\phi_0\sum_{i=0}^{t-1}\phi_1^i = \phi_0\frac{1-\phi_1^t}{1-\phi_1}, \quad \text{for } |\phi_1| < 1.$$

The right-hand side of (3.22) can therefore be written as:

$$\begin{aligned}\phi_0\sum_{i=0}^{t-1}\phi_1^i + \phi_1^t Y_0 &= \phi_0\frac{1-\phi_1^t}{1-\phi_1} + \phi_1^t Y_0 = \frac{\phi_0}{1-\phi_1} - \phi_0\frac{\phi_1^t}{1-\phi_1} + \phi_1^t Y_0 \\ &= \frac{\phi_0}{1-\phi_1} + \left(Y_0 - \frac{\phi_0}{1-\phi_1}\right)\phi_1^t\end{aligned}$$

showing the identity in (3.22).

It is worth noting that the implication is *from* the solution given by (3.17) and (3.19) *to* the solution in (3.20). The converse implication does not hold. This may seem as a paradox, but the explanation is simple enough: Mathematically speaking, (3.20) is more general than the stable solution given by (3.19) and (3.17). Hence, it is when we add $|\phi_1| < 1$, as an assumption, that (3.20) implies the stable solution.

When we use equations with simple dynamics, the method of repeated substitution, or iteration, is often all we need to obtain a solution that is useful for the research purpose we have. In that light, the point of the detailed review of the solution of (3.13) is to bring out that the "direct and intuitive" solution consists of a solution of the homogeneous equations, and a particular solution, in accordance with the mathematical theory of difference equations. We will, however, often work with equations for higher order dynamics, ($p \geq 2$). Repeated insertion then becomes impractical, showing the importance of learning more about the general solution principles.

The solution we have established for first-order dynamics is nevertheless an important reference, also for more general models. It is an example of what time series statisticians call a *causal* solution, since it is conditional on the past and the stability of the solution requires $|\phi_1| < 1$, (see, e.g., Brockwell and Davies, 1991, Chapter 3; Schumway and Stoffer, 2000, Chapter 2). Economists more frequently refer to the solutions above as a backward-looking solution. In mathematical analysis, $|\phi_1| < 1$ is known as the condition for *global asymptotic stability* (see Sydsæter *et al.*, 2008, p. 393). It is not always that a solution of this type exists. In economics, an important example is models with rational expectations, since these models will imply $|\phi_1| > 1$. There is a stable solution for Y_t also for this case. However, such a solution cannot be conditional on given initial conditions (history), which has to be replaced by other assumptions, e.g., known terminal conditions. Bårdsen *et al.* (2005, Chapter 7) includes an introduction to the so-called forward-looking solutions of dynamic equations. Another solution category, which will be central in the later chapters is the case of instable solution, corresponding to $|\phi_1| = 1$. Why instability is a good label for this case is seen already from the solution of the equation, which now becomes $Y_t^h = Ct$. With $C \neq 0$, this solution will imply that Y_t increases, or declines, monotonically as a function of time.

3.3.3. Stable and unstable solutions

As we have seen, the question of stability or instability of solutions is a matter of considerable importance. In this section, we therefore review the main result about the conditions for stability of the solution of the general difference equation (3.9). We have already mentioned that the stochastic properties of the disturbances ε_t are unimportant for the question of stability (or not) of the solution. We can therefore, in this section, proceed *as if* the ε_t's are known numbers, and interpret (3.9) as a deterministic equation. With this interpretation of (3.9) in mind, the following definition of stability can be used:

Definition 3.1 (Global asymptotic stability). Equation (3.9) is called globally asymptotically stable if any solution of the homogeneous equation:

$$Y_t^h - \phi_1 Y_{t-1}^h - \phi_2 Y_{t-2}^h - \cdots - \phi_p Y_{t-p}^h = 0.$$

approaches 0 as $t \to \infty$.

If Y_t^s, as above denotes one particular (special) solution of (3.9), it follows that

$$Y_t \to Y_t^s \quad \text{as } t \to \infty, \tag{3.23}$$

when (3.9) is a stable equation. A popular, and often relevant, choice of Y_t^s in economics is a solution the type $Y_t^s - Y_{t-1}^s = \text{a constant}$. If the constant is zero, we speak of a stationary or static long-run solution. If the constant change in Y_t^s is positive, the solution will be with *steady-state* growth (usually, a constant growth rate and the measurement unit of Y_t is then natural logarithm).

Above, we saw in detail that the condition for (global asymptotic) stability of the first-order difference equation was that its associated characteristic root was less than one. In the following, we generalize that condition. The solution of the homogeneous equation is, with reference to (3.4):

$$Y_t^h = \sum_{l=1}^{k} \sum_{j=1}^{m_l} C_{lj}\, t^{j-1}\, \lambda_l^t. \tag{3.24}$$

We can commence by assuming that all characteristic roots are distinct. It simplifies the notation, we lose nothing in terms of understanding, and we can write the expression for Y^h in the same way we did in (3.6) above:

$$Y_t^h = C_1\lambda_1^t + C_2\lambda_2^t + \cdots + C_p\lambda_p^t. \tag{3.25}$$

Assume first that all the roots are real numbers. Direct inspection shows that $Y_t^h \longrightarrow 0$ as $t \to \infty$ if all roots are less than 1 in absolute value. In other words, $|\lambda_l| < 1, \forall l$ is a sufficient condition for stability of the solution. It is also necessary that all the roots are less than one in magnitude. Inspection of (3.24) shows that a single root equal to 1 (one so-called unit-root) is enough to imply $Y_t^h \nrightarrow 0$ as $t \longrightarrow \infty$.

More generally, two, four (or more) roots can make out the so-called *complex pairs*. In order to relate to that possibility, we may need a reminder (or brief introduction to) complex numbers. Appendix 3.A is a self-contained exposition of what we need to know about complex numbers. We will refer to this appendix. However, in the following few paragraphs, we extract from Appendix 3.A what is needed conceptually to complete our exposition of the solution of difference equations, in particular the characterization of solutions as stable, unstable or explosive.

A short review of complex numbers

Let z denote a complex number. The following definition is standard.

Definition 3.2 (Complex number). The complex number z is defined by the following equation:

$$z = a + ib, \tag{3.26}$$

where a and b are real numbers, and $i = \sqrt{-1}$ is an imaginary "number" that satisfies $i^2 = -1$.

We often write

$$\text{Re}(z) = a,$$

for the *real part* of z and

$$\text{Im}(z) = b,$$

for the *imaginary part* of z. A real number like a can be interpreted as a special complex number by writing it as $a + i \cdot 0$. Similarly, one way of writing i is $0 + i \cdot 1$.

A complex number $(a + ib)$ can be shown graphically in a diagram with the real part (a) along the horizontal axis, and the imaginary part (b) along the vertical axis (see Figure 3.1). Note that "i" is the unit of measurement on the vertical axis.

Definition 3.3 (Addition and multiplication of complex numbers). We have the following definitions for addition and multiplication of complex numbers:

$$\begin{aligned} z_1 + z_2 &= (a_1 + ib_1) + (a_2 + ib_2) \stackrel{\text{def}}{=} (a_1 + a_2) + i(b_1 + b_2), \\ z_1 z_2 &= (a_1 + ib_1)(a_2 + ib_2) \quad \stackrel{\text{def}}{=} (a_1 a_2 - b_1 b_2) + i(a_1 b_2 + a_2 b_1). \end{aligned}$$

From these definitions follow several properties of complex numbers that makes it possible to work algebraically with complex numbers, as if they were real numbers (except for inequalities), Appendix 3.A contains more details.

The absolute value of $z = a + ib$, the norm (also called modulus) of z, is written as $|z|$ and is defined as the distance from the number to the origin in a graph with the real part (a) along the horizontal axis, and the imaginary part (b) along the vertical axis, as illustrated by the dashed line in Figure 3.1.

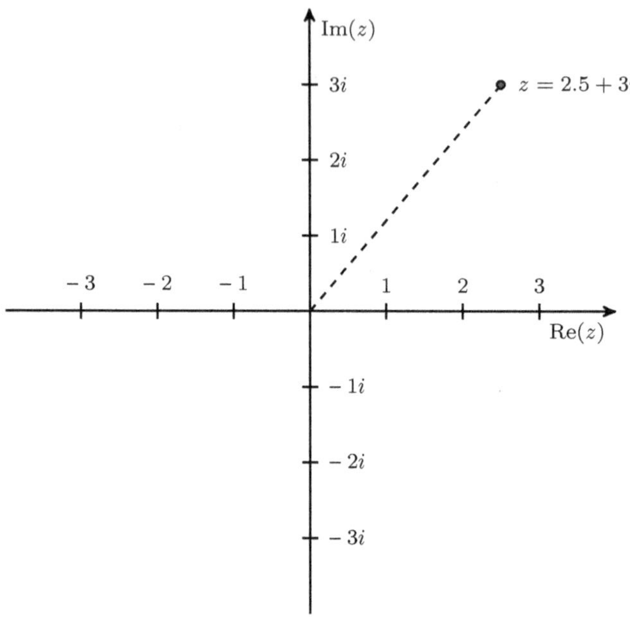

Figure 3.1. The complex number $z = 2.5 + 3i$ plotted as the vector $(2.5, 3)$. The dashed line from the origin to the number represents the *modulus* (*norm*). The angle between the dashed line (modulus) and the horizontal axis is called the *argument* of the complex number.

Definition 3.4 (Modulus (norm)). The distance from $z = a + ib$ to the origin is the *modulus* of z:

$$|z| = \sqrt{a^2 + b^2}.$$

Modulus and norm are synonyms.

The use of *norm* in connection with complex number is analogous to the definition of the norm of a vector in linear algebra. Modulus, in the context of complex numbers, is a generalization of the absolute value (magnitude) of a real number. As noted, since we can write a real number (a) as $a + i \cdot 0$, the absolute value of this real number is of course $\sqrt{a^2}$. In the following, we will occasionally use the term absolute value, or magnitude, also in the wide sense that covers the norm for a complex number (typically in the context of discussion of characteristic roots).

Definition 3.5 (Conjugate and complex pair). The complex conjugate to $z = a + ib$ is

$$\overline{z} = a - ib,$$

z and $\overline{z}$ are called a complex pair.

Using these definitions, we have, for example, $\overline{i+1} = 1 - i$, $\overline{i} = -i$ and $\overline{2} = 2$. It is worth noting that z and $\overline{z}$ have the same modulus (norm):

$$|\overline{z}| = |a + i(-b)| = \sqrt{a^2 + (-b)^2} = |z|.$$

Addition and multiplication of a complex pair take the following form (use the above rules and definitions to show):

$$z + \overline{z} = a + a + i(b - b) = 2a,$$
$$z \cdot \overline{z} = (a^2 + b^2) + i(-ab + ab_2) = (a^2 + b^2).$$

By comparing with (3.4), we see that the modulus of a complex pair can be interpreted as the square root of the product of the number and its conjugate:

$$|a + ib| = \sqrt{(a + ib)(a - ib)}.$$

As noted above, Appendix 3.A reviews more of the theory of complex numbers.

We can now use the modulus of a complex number to generalize the result about characteristic root less than one as necessary and sufficient condition for stability of the solution for Y_t.

Theorem 3.2 (Condition for global asymptotic stability). *Equation* (3.9) *is globally asymptotically stable if and only if all the roots of the associated characteristic equation* (3.12) *have moduli less than* 1.

For completeness, we also include the theorem for the instability of the solution.

Theorem 3.3 (Instability of solution). *The solution of a difference equation with constant coefficients is dynamically unstable if at least one root of the associated characteristic equation has modulus (norm) equal to* 1.

Assume first that all the characteristic roots are real numbers. We can understand the relevance of the two theorems by inspecting (3.25) because it is clear that it is the largest root that will dominate the properties of the solution. No matter how many roots there are in the expression for the solution, it is the root with absolute value 1 that will dominate as t grows towards infinity. Hence, there is no way that we can get $Y_t^h \longrightarrow 0$

as $t \longrightarrow \infty$ in the case of (even) a single unit-root. That can only happen when all roots are less than one in magnitude.

What then about the case of complex roots? We will again consider (3.25), and restrict ourselves to the case of second-order dynamics, and assume that the two roots are a complex pair.

$$Y_t^h = C_1 \lambda_1^t + C_2 \overline{\lambda}_1^t.$$

By the using the *trigonometric representation* of complex numbers (see Appendix 3.A), we can write the homogeneous solution as

$$Y_t^h = |\lambda_1|^t S_t, \tag{3.27}$$

where S_t represents a sequence of numbers that oscillates as a function of time (a cosine wave), see equation (3.A.16) in Appendix 3.A.6. We see by direct inspection that the solution is stable if the modulus is less than 1, and that it is unstable if the modulus is identical to 1.

It is also straightforward to see that the theorem also covers higher order dynamics, where some roots may be real, and others may be complex pairs. Assume, for example, $p = 3$, with one real root (λ_1), and one complex pair (λ_2 and $\overline{\lambda}_2$). The only possibility for stability of the solution is that $|\lambda_1| < 1$ and $|\lambda_2| < 1$.

Following these main results, we can also formulate a theorem for explosive solution:

Theorem 3.4 (Explosive solution). *The solution of a difference equation with constant coefficients, when we consider the case of given initial conditions, is explosive if at least one root of the characteristic equation has modulus larger than* 1.

As noted above, the reason for including "given initial conditions" is that there may be cases where we want to use a solution which is conditioned on a future, the so-called terminal condition. In such cases, modulus larger than unity does not imply an explosive solution, but the opposite, a stable solution. Processes of this kind have been dismissed as "useless" by statisticians because they require us to know the future (rather than to know the initial conditions) in order to predict the future (see Schumway and Stoffer, 2000, p. 94). However, as the reader may have noted, processes that are future-dependent, and not causal, play an important role in macroeconomic models that make use of the rational expectation assumption. Section 7.11

contains an introduction to the solution of future-dependent models, in the context of estimation methods for that model class.

Box 3.1. Unit-root

A characteristic root, or eigenvalue, with modulus equal to 1 is often referred to as a unit-root, a terminology that we adopt. The unit-root that we encounter most frequently is the real number 1. However, for equation (3.9), there are several other possible unit-roots. In the cobweb model above, the relevant unit root was -1. Other unit-roots must be complex numbers with modulus 1 (see Section 3.3.4). Such unit-roots can be relevant for the modelling of business-cycles and seasonality.

We can now apply the general theorems for the case with first-order dynamics. Hence, we reconsider (3.20), which was

$$Y_t = \phi_0 \sum_{i=0}^{t-1} \phi_1^i + \phi_1^t Y_0 + \sum_{i=0}^{t-1} \phi_1^i \varepsilon_{t-i}.$$

The single characteristic root in the homogeneous equation associated with (3.13) is $\lambda = \phi_1$. If $|\phi_1| < 1$, it means that the equation is stable. The "impact" or weight of the initial condition Y_0 for the solution is reduced as the distance in time between t and $t = 0$ is increased. This is a typical trait of globally asymptotically stable equations. In the case of unstable solution, either $\phi_1 = 1$ or $\phi_1 = -1$, the initial condition carries full weight no matter how long the distance becomes between the solution period and the initial period. Finally, if ϕ_1 is larger than 1 in absolute value, the solution is explosive. As t grows toward infinity, Y_t moves away from the initial value Y_0. In the cobweb model case, the "explosive path" becomes oscillating due to (long-run) supply being more elastic than demand.

There are many economic and natural phenomena that can be modelled as by explosive time paths. Nuclear chain reactions are characterized by a "reproduction factor" larger than one, corresponding to $\phi_1 > 1$ in our notation. Such reactions have to be carefully controlled to avoid meltdown and catastrophic damage (see Rhodes, 1986, Chapter 13). A hyperinflation is difficult to control, and the objects of meltdown are private financial savings, the purchasing power of money wages salaries and, eventually, the nation's monetary system.

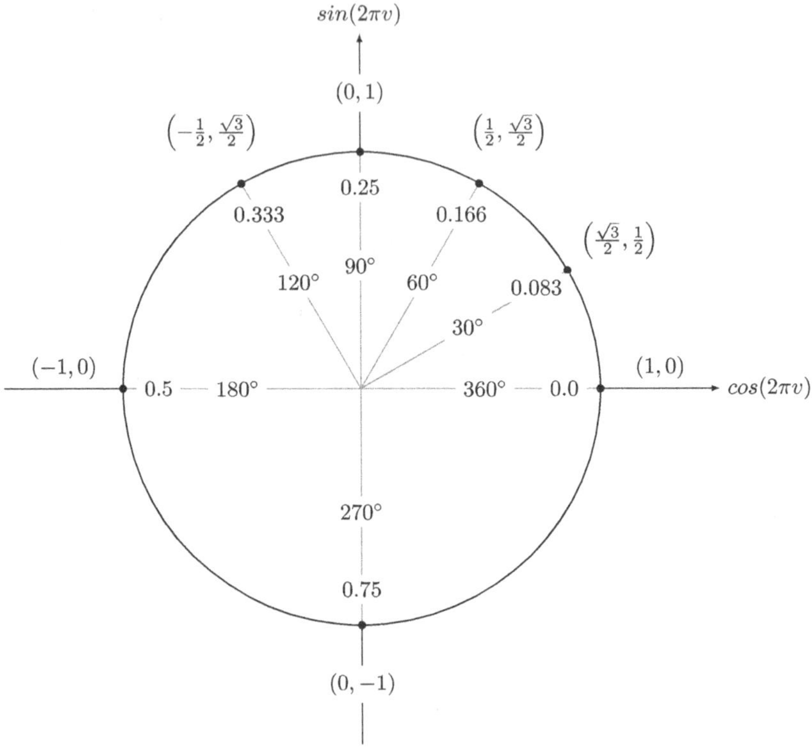

Figure 3.2. The unit-circle.

3.3.4. Stability conditions and the complex unit-circle

One common way of expressing the conditions for (asymptotic global) stability is that all the characteristic roots associated with the general difference equation (3.9) must be located inside the complex unit-circle. Figure 3.2 shows a picture of the unit-circle for the case when we have utilized that all the p roots, both real and complex, can be written as complex numbers. Again, with reference to Appendix 3.A, we can write the complex number z as

$$z = |z| \left(\cos(\vartheta) + i \sin(\vartheta)\right), \tag{3.28}$$

and define the argument ϑ in this expression as

$$\vartheta = 2\pi v, \tag{3.29}$$

where π is the number $\pi = 3.14159$ and the variable v, $0 \leq v \leq 1$, is the *frequency* measured as the number of cycles per unit of time.

In Figure 3.2, the values of $\cos(2\pi v)$ are on the horizontal axis, and $\sin(2\pi v)$ is on the vertical axis. Each point on the circle gives the coordinates of the z-numbers that are characterized by modulus 1, hence the name *unit-circle.* A "unit-complex number" can therefore be expressed as

$$z = (\cos(2\pi v) + i \sin(2\pi v)). \tag{3.30}$$

The point on the unit-circle corresponding to $v = 0$, which in turn can be translated to the 360 degree angle, has coordinates $(1, 0)$, since $\cos(2\pi 0) = 1$ and $\sin(2\pi 0) = 0$. Hence, modules of this root have the real number 1, and it is standard to refer to such a root as a *zero-frequency root*, implying that the period is infinite. Moving counter-clockwise along the unit-circle, the frequency corresponding to the 30 degrees line is $v = 0.083$ (with three decimals). The number with modulus 1 along that line has coordinates $(\sqrt{3}/2, 1/2)$, as shown in Figure 3.2. In the same way, we have given the coordinates of some other frequencies (angles). We can, for example, note $v = 1/4$ (coordinates (0,1)) which corresponds to a *period* (wavelength) or four periods. With quarterly data, it means that there are four quarters between one peak and the next, and therefore the $v = 1/4$ frequency is called the seasonal frequency, and a root at that frequency is termed as a *seasonal unit-root.* Appendix B presents the theory of unit-roots at different frequencies in more detail.

We can now return to the formulation that an equation is (asymptotically globally) stable if and only if all its characteristic roots associated are inside the (complex) unit-circle. Hence, they are located in any of the four quadrants in Figure 3.2, but always inside the unit-circle, and that entails that their moduli are less than one. Hence, the formulation "inside the unit-circle" has exactly the same meaning as our earlier formulation about moduli being less than one, as necessary and sufficient for stability. In the stable case, all the p roots of the general difference equation can be expressed as

$$\lambda = |\lambda| (\cos(2\pi v) + i \sin(2\pi v)), \quad |\lambda| < 1. \tag{3.31}$$

It also follows that unstable solutions are characterized by at least one root that has modulus equal to one:

$$\lambda = (\cos(2\pi v) + i \sin(2\pi v)), \quad |\lambda| = 1, \tag{3.32}$$

and finally, the unstable roots, are those for which

$$\lambda = |\lambda| \left(\cos(2\pi v) + i \sin(2\pi v)\right), \quad |\lambda| > 1. \tag{3.33}$$

is true.

In the econometrics literature, an alternative formulation of the stability condition, namely equation (3.9), is stable if and only if all the characteristic roots are located *outside* the unit-circle. This may seem the direct opposite of what we have just said, but the explanation is quite simple: If we multiply the characteristic equation (3.12) by λ^{-p}, we obtain

$$1 - \phi_1 \lambda^{-1} - \cdots - \phi_p \lambda^{-p} = 0.$$

If we define $r = \lambda^{-1}$, and write

$$1 - \phi_1 r - \cdots - \phi_p r^p = 0, \tag{3.34}$$

we have p roots that are the reciprocals for the p λ-roots. Hence, the formulation of the stability condition as "no roots inside the unit-circle", refers to the alternative form of the characteristic equation, namely (3.34).

3.3.5. An example of a cyclical solution

Assume a second-order equation with coefficients $\phi_0 = 0$, $\phi_1 = 1.6$, $\phi_2 = -0.9$:

$$Y_t = 1.6Y_{t-1} - 0.9Y_{t-2} + \varepsilon_t, \tag{3.35}$$

where $\varepsilon_t \sim \text{IID}(0, \sigma_\varepsilon^2)$. The equation implies that Y_t $(t = 1, 2, \ldots, T)$ are T random variables. Since we have second-order dynamics, the solution is conditional on Y_0 and Y_{-1}, which are assumed to be known numbers.

The characteristic equation which is associated with the homogeneous difference equation

$$Y_t - 1.6Y_{t-1} + 0.9Y_{t-1} = 0,$$

is

$$\lambda^2 - 1.6\lambda + 0.9 = 0. \tag{3.36}$$

The characteristic roots are the complex pair $\lambda_1 = 0.8 + i0.5099$ and $\lambda_2 = 0.8 - i0.5099$. From the properties of complex numbers, the modulus

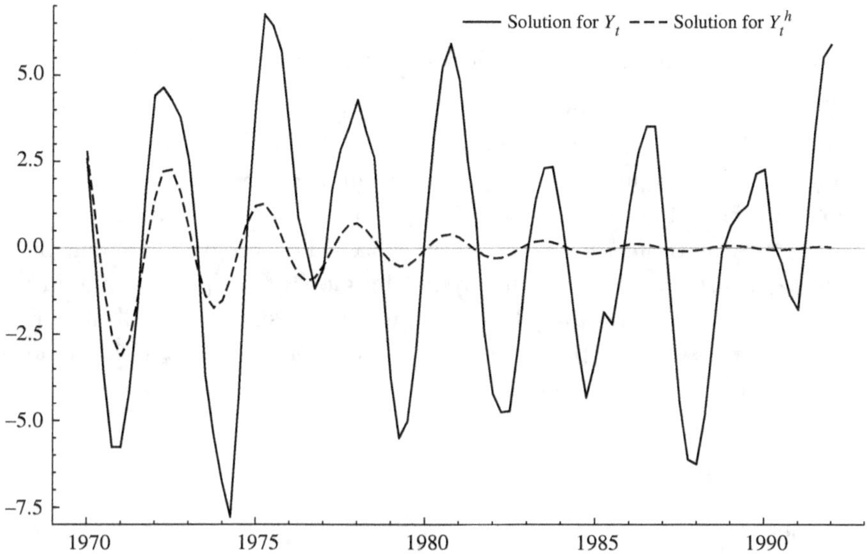

Figure 3.3. Homogeneous (dashed line) and full solution of equation (3.35), obtained by simulation.

of λ_1 is

$$|\lambda_1| = |0.8 + i(0.5099)| = \sqrt{0.8^2 + 0.5099^2} = 0.94868.$$

The modulus of λ_2 is also 0.94868, since λ_2 is the conjugate number. Since the moduli are less than one, equation (3.35) is stable, and in particular we have: $Y_t^h \longrightarrow 0$ as $t \longrightarrow \infty$. The complex roots imply that both the homogeneous solution Y_t^h and the full solution Y_t contain cycles, which are apparent in the two graphs in Figure 3.3. We have labelled the data so that the first solution period is given as the first quarter of 1970, 1970q1, while the last solution period is the 1990q1. Due to the moduli being less than one, the cyclical swings are dampened as we move away from the initial condition of 1969q4 and 1969q3. This is easy to see in the graph of the homogeneous solution. The graph of the full solution is influenced by the new disturbances in each period in the form of realizations of the random variables ε_t.

The graph for the homogeneous solution shows that there are approximately 10–12 quarters between one peak (or through) and the next. It illustrates equation (3.27), where S_t is a sinus-function of time, and shows that the period or wavelength in this solution is roughly 3 years, alternatively, that the frequency is 0.3 cycles per year.

Box 3.2. Finding the solution by simulation

When the coefficients of the difference equation have been quantified, by choosing some example numbers as in (3.35) or after estimation, the solution of the equation can be easily found by computer simulation. The graphs in Figure 3.3 were produced by simulation by using a built in feature of *Oxmetrics* (see Exercise 3.1). The program implements the backward-solution, without requiring global asymptotical stability so both explosive and unstable solutions can be simulated. All modern econometric software programs offer simulation, but how it is implemented differs between the different packages.

3.3.6. Equilibrium correction

Consider the equation with first-order dynamics. Assume that we specify the particular solution Y_t^s to be the deterministic stationary solution Y^*:

$$Y_t^p = Y^* = \frac{\phi_0}{1-\phi_1} \quad \text{for } t = 1, 2, \ldots. \tag{3.37}$$

This particular equilibrium solution fits in (3.13) when we set $\varepsilon_t = 0$ for $t = 1, 2, \ldots$

$$\phi_0 + \phi_1 Y^* = \phi_0 + \phi_1 \frac{\phi_0}{1-\phi_1} + \varepsilon_t = Y^*,$$

and we therefore have

$$Y_t \longrightarrow Y^* \quad \text{as } t \longrightarrow \infty, \quad \text{when } \varepsilon_t = 0 \text{ for } t = 1, 2, \ldots. \tag{3.38}$$

It is a general property of the stable solution that it approaches the stationary solution in the case of $\varepsilon_t = 0$ for $t = 1, 2, \ldots$. Y^* which therefore represents the *equilibrium* of the process, where it "comes to rest" if it is allowed to run out its course from a given initial condition without any interventions or (random) disturbances. In the case of first-order dynamics, equilibrium correction is already embedded in equation (3.21). If we set: $\varepsilon_t = 0$ for $t = 1, 2, \ldots$, and use the definition of Y^* above, (3.21) gives

$$Y_t = Y^* + (Y_0 - Y^*)\phi_1^t, \quad \text{for } t = 1, 2, \ldots.$$

In the case of a positive characteristic root, $0 < \phi_1 < 1$, the equilibrium correction dynamics will be monotonous. Y_t declines smoothly towards Y^*

when $Y_0 > Y^*$, and grows monotonously towards Y^* when $Y_0 < Y^*$. With a negative, stable root, $-1 < \phi_1 < 0$, the solution path will be oscillating, but nevertheless equilibrium correcting.

Higher order equations that are asymptotically globally stable also have solutions that are characterized by equilibrium correction. However, the correction is not necessarily monotonous, or sharply oscillating. If the roots of the associated characteristic equation contain complex pairs, the solution will contain periodic fluctuations (cycles), as demonstrated by the graphs in Figure 3.3.

Box 3.3. Equilibrium correction and stability

In Chapter 1, we showed that both the cobweb model (when it was stable) and the Keynesian macromodel implied that the change in the endogenous variable equilibrium corrected deviations from the stationary equilibrium in the previous period. We will meet equilibrium correction several times in the book, e.g., in Section 6.4, as it is a general property of models that have a stable solution.

3.4. The Companion Form

In order to analyze difference equations with general dynamics of order $p > 1$, we need to enlarge our tool-kit. We present two approaches, which are used in dynamic econometrics and in time series analysis. The first method is known as companion from analysis, the second uses lag-operator notation.

The first approach is to reexpress (3.9)

$$Y_t = \phi_0 + \phi_1 Y_{t-1} + \phi_2 Y_{t-2} + \cdots + \phi_p Y_{t-p}, + \varepsilon_t$$

as a first-order difference equation for the $p \times 1$-vector $\mathbf{y}_t$:

$$\underbrace{\begin{pmatrix} Y_t \\ Y_{t-1} \\ \vdots \\ Y_{t-p+1} \end{pmatrix}}_{\mathbf{y}_t} = \underbrace{\begin{pmatrix} \phi_1 & \phi_2 & \cdots & \phi_{p-1} & \phi_p \\ 1 & 0 & 0 & \cdots & 0 \\ 0 & 1 & 0 & \cdots & 0 \\ \vdots & \vdots & \vdots & \vdots & \vdots \\ 0 & 0 & 0 & 1 & 0 \end{pmatrix}}_{\mathbf{B}} \underbrace{\begin{pmatrix} Y_{t-1} \\ Y_{t-2} \\ \vdots \\ Y_{t-p} \end{pmatrix}}_{\mathbf{y}_{t-1}} + \underbrace{\begin{pmatrix} \phi_0 + \varepsilon_t \\ 0 \\ \vdots \\ 0 \end{pmatrix}}_{\mathbf{e}_t}, \quad (3.39)$$

and, using the symbols for the matrix and vectors indicated in (3.39):

$$\mathbf{y}_t = \mathbf{B}\mathbf{y}_{t-1} + \mathbf{e}_t. \tag{3.40}$$

By performing the multiplication in (3.40), we see that the first row contains the difference equation (3.9), while the other rows consist of the identities:

$$Y_{t-j} \equiv Y_{t-j} \quad j = 1, 2, \ldots, p-1.$$

Matrix $\mathbf{B}$ is known as the *companion matrix*. It is common to refer to expression (3.40) as the *companion form* of the difference equation (cf. Hendry, 1995b, Chapter 8).

The classical textbook by Hamilton (1994) uses the companion matrix to derive general results for the solution of difference equations, as well as for the properties of dynamic multipliers/impulse responses, without using the name companion matrix though. The following exposition (in Sections 3.4 and 3.6) draws on Chapters 2 and 3 in Hamilton's book. Readers who are interested in a more technically detailed exposition, and proofs, should consult these chapters in Hamilton's book.

Since (3.40) has first-order dynamics, it lies close at hand to find the solution by repeated insertion, backwards, in the same manner as we have done above. Following this approach, we get

$$\mathbf{y}_t = \mathbf{B}^t\mathbf{y}_0 + \mathbf{B}^{t-1}\mathbf{e}_1 + \mathbf{B}^{t-2}\mathbf{e}_2 + \cdots + \mathbf{B}\mathbf{e}_{t-1} + \mathbf{e}_t, \tag{3.41}$$

as the solution for $\mathbf{y}_t$. In the same way as before, we note that the solution is conditional on the history of the series, as it is summarized in $\mathbf{y}_0$. By performing the multiplications on the right-hand side of (3.41), we can express the solution of Y_t as

$$\begin{aligned} Y_t &= b_{11}^{(t)}Y_0 + b_{12}^{(t)}Y_{-1} + \cdots + b_{1p}^{(t)}Y_{-(p-1)} \\ &\quad + \phi_0(b_{11}^{(t-1)} + b_{11}^{(t-2)} + \cdots + b_{11}^{(1)} + 1) \\ &\quad + b_{11}^{(t-1)}\varepsilon_1 + b_{11}^{(t-2)}\varepsilon_2 + \cdots + b_{11}^{(1)}\varepsilon_{t-1} + \varepsilon_t \end{aligned} \tag{3.42}$$

where $b_{11}^{(t)}$ represents element $(1,1)$ in the matrix $\mathbf{B}^t$, $b_{12}^{(t)}$ is element $(1,2)$ in the matrix $\mathbf{B}^t$, and so on. Hence, (3.42) gives the solution for Y_t as a function of the p initial conditions and the history of ε_t, from period 1 to t.

An eigenvalue of the matrix $\mathbf{B}$ is a scalar ι that satisfies the characteristic equation:

$$|\mathbf{B} - \iota\mathbf{I}| = 0, \tag{3.43}$$

where **I** is the identity matrix. It can be shown that (3.43) can be expressed as

$$\iota^p - \phi_1 \iota^{p-1} - \phi_2 \iota^{p-2} - \cdots - \phi_{p-1}\iota - \phi_p = 0. \tag{3.44}$$

Apart from the change in notation, namely, that ι denotes an eigenvalue (root), this is the same characteristic equation which is associated with the difference equation (3.9).[2] It may be added that this result is not surprising when we remember the uniqueness property of the solution.

To avoid doubling of notation, we use λ as the symbol for a characteristic root. We therefore have

$$|\mathbf{B} - \lambda \mathbf{I}| = 0 \Longleftrightarrow \lambda^p - \phi_1 \lambda^{p-1} - \cdots - \phi_p = 0. \tag{3.45}$$

Assume that **B** has p distinct eigenvalues (not all of them necessarily real), implying that it can be diagonalized in the following way:

$$\mathbf{B} = \mathbf{D}\Lambda\mathbf{D}^{-1}, \tag{3.46}$$

where $\mathbf{\Lambda}$ is a $(p \times p)$ diagonal matrix with the p characteristic roots along the main diagonal. **D** is the corresponding $(p \times p)$-matrix made up of the linearly independent *eigenvectors* as columns.[3] If **B** is multiplied with itself, diagonalization is preserved in an interesting way as follows:

$$\mathbf{B}^2 = (\mathbf{D\Lambda D}^{-1})(\mathbf{D\Lambda D}^{-1}) \tag{3.47}$$

$$= (\mathbf{D\Lambda})(\mathbf{D}^{-1}\mathbf{D})(\mathbf{\Lambda D}^{-1}) \tag{3.48}$$

$$= (\mathbf{D\Lambda})\mathbf{I}_p(\mathbf{\Lambda D}^{-1}) = \mathbf{D\Lambda}^2\mathbf{D}^{-1}. \tag{3.49}$$

The diagonal structure of $\mathbf{\Lambda}$ also implies that also $\mathbf{\Lambda}^2$ is diagonal with the squared eigenvalues as elements along the main diagonal. In general, we can characterize the matrix $\mathbf{B}^t$ in (3.41) in terms of powers of eigenvalues:

$$\mathbf{B}^t = \mathbf{D\Lambda}^t\mathbf{D}^{-1}, \tag{3.50}$$

where a typical diagonal element in $\mathbf{\Lambda}^t$ is λ_i^t $(i = 1, 2, \ldots, p)$.

---

[2]See Hamilton (1994, Appendix 1.A) for a proof.

[3]In the case where some of the eigenvalues are identical, the diagonalization is achieved by the use of the Jordan decomposition (see Hamilton, 1994, pp. 18–19).

In the following, let d_{ij} denote the element in row i, column j of $\mathbf{D}$, and let d^{ij} denote the corresponding element in the inverse matrix of eigenvectors, $\mathbf{D}^{-1}$. By inspecting the results of the multiplication on the right-hand side of (3.50), we see that the expression for $b_{11}^{(t)}$, which is central in (3.42), becomes

$$b_{11}^{(t)} = \{d_{11}d^{11}\}\lambda_1^t + \{d_{12}d^{21}\}\lambda_2^t + \cdots + \{d_{1p}d^{p1}\}\lambda_p^t. \tag{3.51}$$

Note that the sum of the constants $d_{1i}d^{i1}$ is one:

$$\sum_{i=1}^{p} d_{1i}d^{i1} = 1, \tag{3.52}$$

since this sum is element $(1,1)$ in $\mathbf{DD}^{-1}$ which is the $(p \times p)$ identity matrix.

The terms $b_{1j}^{(t)}$ $(j = 2, \ldots, p)$ in (3.42), can be expressed as

$$b_{1j}^{(t)} = \{d_{11}d^{1j}\}\lambda_1^t + \{d_{12}d^{2j}\}\lambda_2^t + \cdots + \{d_{1p}d^{pj}\}\lambda_p^t, \tag{3.53}$$

with

$$\sum_{i=1}^{p} d_{1i}d^{ij} = 0, \quad j \geq 2. \tag{3.54}$$

Let us consider the solution for Y_t in (3.42) in the light of these expressions. Then it becomes clear that the first line in (3.42) approaches zero as $t \to \infty$:

$$(b_{11}^{(t)}Y_0 + b_{12}^{(t)}Y_{-1} + \cdots + b_{1p}^{(t)}Y_{-(p-1)}) \underset{t\to\infty}{\to} 0, \tag{3.55}$$

if and only if all the characteristic roots are less than 1 in magnitude. This is logically consistent with the general stability condition above, namely, that the equation is stable if and only if the solution of the homogeneous equation approaches zero as $t \to \infty$.

All roots inside the unit-circle is also necessary and sufficient for convergence of $(b_{11}^{(t-1)} + b_{11}^{(t-2)} + \cdots + b_{11}^{(1)} + 1)$ in the second line of (3.42):

$$\lim_{t\to\infty}\left(\sum_{j=1}^{t-1} b_{11}^{(j)} + 1\right) = \frac{1}{(1 - \phi_1 - \phi_2 - \cdots - \phi_p)} \tag{3.56}$$

(see Exercise 3.2). Hence, in the special case where all the disturbances are set to zero, we have that Y_t approaches the equilibrium value Y^*, given by

$$Y_t \underset{t\to\infty}{\to} Y^* = \frac{\phi_0}{(1 - \phi_1 - \phi_2 - \cdots - \phi_p)}, \quad \text{when } \varepsilon_t = 0 \text{ for } t = 1, 2, \ldots. \tag{3.57}$$

We now reconsider the case with second-order dynamics, $p = 2$:

$$Y_t = \phi_0 + \phi_1 Y_{t-1} + \phi_2 Y_{t-2} + \varepsilon_t.$$

Using (3.42), the solution can be written as

$$\begin{aligned} Y_t &= b_{11}^{(t)} Y_0 + b_{12}^{(t)} Y_{-1} \\ &\quad + \phi_0 (b_{11}^{(t-1)} + b_{11}^{(t-2)} + \cdots + b_{11} + 1) \\ &\quad + b_{11}^{(t-1)} \varepsilon_1 + b_{11}^{(t-2)} \varepsilon_2 + \cdots + b_{11} \varepsilon_{t-1} + \varepsilon_t, \end{aligned} \tag{3.58}$$

where

$$b_{11}^{(t)} = \{d_{11} d^{11}\} \lambda_1^t + \{d_{12} d^{21}\} \lambda_2^t,$$

$$b_{12}^{(t)} = \{d_{11} d^{12}\} \lambda_1^t + \{d_{12} d^{22}\} \lambda_2^t.$$

For $p = 2$, there can either be two real roots, or λ_1 is a complex number and λ_2 is the conjugate, $\lambda_2 = \bar{\lambda}_1$. At first sight, it seems that the solution with complex roots implies complex numbers for Y_t, which of course would be an irrelevant solution. However, the mathematical relationships between the roots and the weights of the roots (i.e., $d_{ij} d^{ji}$) secure that no inconsistency occur. For example, it is possible to show that[4]

$$d_{11} d^{11} = \frac{\lambda_1}{\lambda_1 - \lambda_2}. \tag{3.59}$$

Since $d_{11} d^{11} + d_{12} d^{21} = 1$, as indicated in (3.52), we also have that:

$$d_{12} d^{21} = \frac{-\lambda_2}{\lambda_1 - \lambda_2}, \tag{3.60}$$

which gives some idea why the "problem" induced by assuming that λ_1 and λ_2 are a complex pair can be removed by similar properties in the associated weights. For those interested, a formal argument which involves the use of the trigonometric representation is given in Appendix 3.A.6.

3.5. Difference Equations and Lag Operator Notation

In this section, we review the theory of difference equations when they are expressed in terms of the lag operator, L. Since the solution of the homo-

[4]See Hamilton (1994, Proposition 1.2, p. 12). The result is derived for the case of distinct eigenvalues.

geneous difference equation is unique, given that we condition on known initial conditions, we will not discover any "new" solutions by switching to lag operator notation. Lag operator notation is nevertheless very useful to us. First, using the lag operator notation gives a more direct route to the solution of a difference equation, and sheds new light on the properties of the solution. Second, the use of lag operator notation bridges the gap to econometric time series models, the topic of the following chapters because the lag operator notation is popular in the econometric literature.

3.5.1. The lag and difference operators

Put simply, the *lag operator*, denoted L, shifts the dating of a variable one period back in time.[5] Hence, writing LY_t is equivalent to writing Y_{t-1}:

$$LY_t \equiv Y_{t-1}. \tag{3.61}$$

Applying the lag operator twice, written as L^2, shifts Y_t two periods back:

$$LLY_t = L^2 Y_t = LY_{t-1} = Y_{t-2}. \tag{3.62}$$

And, in general, for L^p, $p = 0, 1, 2, \dots$

$$L^p Y_t = Y_{t-p}. \tag{3.63}$$

Consistent with the last property, we also have, for the case of $p = 0$,

$$L^0 = 1, \tag{3.64}$$

$$L^0 Y_t = Y_t. \tag{3.65}$$

Finally, we note two useful properties:

$$L^p L^s = L^p L^k = L^{(p+s)}, \tag{3.66}$$

and

$$(aL^p + bL^s) Y_t = aL^p Y_t + bL^s Y_t = aY_{t-p} + bY_{t-s}, \tag{3.67}$$

where a and b denote constants.

We see that the lag operator follows the same rules as multiplication does in ordinary algebra. Therefore, we will sometimes write "multiply by L" instead of the more technically correct "operate L on the time series Y_t".

[5] A detailed introduction of the lag operator is in Hamilton (1994, Chapter 2).

For some purposes, we will also find it useful to work with a *lead operator*. This can be defined by allowing the "power" p in L^p to be a negative number. In particular, L^{-1} operates on Y_t so that $L^{-1}Y_t = Y_{t+1}$. In general,

$$L^{-s} = Y_{t+s}. \tag{3.68}$$

Constants can be thought of as a series of numbers that are the same in each time period, t. The convention is therefore that if we multiply a constant, for example, a by the lag operator, the result is the same sequence of constants, hence,

$$La = a. \tag{3.69}$$

We often want to perform the operation of differencing, by subtracting the lagged time series from the current dated time series. For that purpose, the *difference operator* is defined as

$$\Delta \stackrel{\text{def}}{=} 1 - L. \tag{3.70}$$

From the rules of the lag operator polynomial, we have

$$\Delta Y_t = (1 - L)Y_t = Y_t - Y_{t-1}, \tag{3.71}$$

showing that ΔY_t performs the differencing operation. Δ^2 operates on Y_t to give the second difference:

$$\Delta^2 Y_t = (1 - L)^2 Y_t = ((1 - L) - (L - L^2))Y_t = \Delta Y_t - \Delta Y_{t-1}. \tag{3.72}$$

In many situations, it is also useful to use the multi-period difference operator, Δ_h, as

$$\Delta_h \stackrel{\text{def}}{=} 1 - L^h, h = 1, 2, \ldots. \tag{3.73}$$

Setting $h = 1$ gives back the single period difference operator (3.70), while $h = 4$ for quarterly data gives the time series of annual changes:

$$\Delta_4 Y_t \equiv Y_t - Y_{t-4}. \tag{3.74}$$

3.5.2. Lag polynomial and difference equations

An expression like $(\phi_1 L + \phi_2 L^2)$ is referred to as a polynomial in the lag operator L, or more simply as a *lag polynomial*. It is algebraically similar to an ordinary polynomial in a scalar z, $(\phi_1 z + \phi_2 z^2)$. As just shown, the lag operator in the polynomial operates linearly on the variables, hence:

$$(\phi_1 L + \phi_2 L^2)Y_t = \phi_1 Y_{t-1} + \phi_2 Y_{t-2}.$$

By introducing the general lag polynomial of order p:

$$\pi(L) = 1 - \phi_1 L - \phi_2 L^2 - \cdots - \phi_p L^p, \tag{3.75}$$

we can write the difference equation (3.9) compactly as

$$\pi(L)Y_t = \phi_0 + \varepsilon_t. \tag{3.76}$$

In the same way that L operates on Y_t and transforms it to Y_{t-1}, we can say that the lag polynomial $\pi(L)$ operates on Y_t and transforms this variable to $\phi_0 + \varepsilon_t$.

Below, it will be convenient to define the $\pi(L)$-polynomial as

$$\pi(L) \underset{\text{def}}{=} 1 - \phi(L) \tag{3.77}$$

where $\phi(L)$ is defined as

$$\phi(L) \underset{\text{def}}{=} \sum_{i=1}^{p} \phi_i L^i \equiv \sum_{i=0}^{p} \phi_{i+1} L^i. \tag{3.78}$$

The motivation for including the two equivalent expressions for $\phi(L)$ is that sometimes we want to write $\sum_{i=1}^{p} \phi_i Y_{t-1}$ as $\phi(L)Y_t$ (the first expression), while in other situations $\phi(L)Y_{t-1}$ (the second) is easier to use.

For later use, we note that by setting $L = 1$ (even if strictly speaking L is not a number) in the expression for the polynomial, we define $\phi(1)$ as the sum of the coefficients of the polynomial.

$$\pi(1) \underset{\text{def}}{=} 1 - \phi(1) = 1 - \sum_{i=1}^{p} \phi_i, \text{ for } L = 1. \tag{3.79}$$

With the aid of these definitions, the sum of all the lag coefficients, from 1 to p, can be written as $1 - \pi(1)$, and the sum of the lag coefficients minus one is given by $-\pi(1)$. Both relationships will be used several times below.

3.5.3. Factorization of the lag polynomial

It will prove to be useful to be able to factorize the lag polynomial $\pi(L)$. We first consider the case of second-order dynamics, $p = 2$. A first step is to write $\pi(L)$ as

$$\pi(L) = L^2(L^{-2} - \phi_1 L^{-1} - \phi_2). \tag{3.80}$$

Let us again, for a minute, use L as if it was a scalar. By setting $x = L^{-1}$, we can write the right-hand side of (3.80) as $x^{-2}p(x)$, where

$$p(x) = (x^2 - \phi_1 x - \phi_2).$$

With reference to the fundamental theorem of algebra, $p(x)$ can be factorized as

$$p(x) = (x - \lambda_1)(x - \lambda_2),$$

where λ_1 and λ_2 are two distinct roots in the characteristic equation $p(\lambda) = 0$:

$$\lambda^2 - \phi_1\lambda - \phi_2 = 0.$$

$x^{-2}p(x)$ can be expressed as

$$\begin{aligned} x^{-2}p(x) &= x^{-2}(x - \lambda_1)(x - \lambda_2) \\ &= x^{-1}(1 - \lambda_1 x^{-1})(x - \lambda_2) \\ &= (1 - \lambda_1 x^{-1})(1 - \lambda_2 x^{-1}). \end{aligned}$$

By introducing $x = L^{-1}$, one more time, we get

$$L^2(L^{-2} - \phi_1 L^{-1} - \phi_2) = (1 - \lambda_1 L)(1 - \lambda_2 L),$$

which gives the factorization of $\pi(L)$ that we are looking for:

$$\pi(L) = (1 - \lambda_1 L)(1 - \lambda_2 L). \tag{3.81}$$

In the general case, the factorization of (3.75) is

$$\pi(L) = (1 - \lambda_1 L)(1 - \lambda_2 L) \cdots (1 - \lambda_p L), \tag{3.82}$$

when we assume (to simplify) that there are p distinct roots of the characteristic equation $p(\lambda) = 0$:

$$\lambda^p - \phi_1\lambda^{p-1} - \cdots - \phi_p = 0.$$

We can also note the following expression for the characteristic polynomial:

$$p(\lambda) = |\mathbf{B} - \lambda\mathbf{I}| = \begin{vmatrix} \phi_1 - \lambda & \phi_2 \\ 1 & -\lambda \end{vmatrix}$$

where $\mathbf{B}$ is the companion matrix in the case of second-order dynamics. Hence, we can achieve the factorization in (3.81) by finding λ_1 and λ_2 as the eigenvalues of the $\mathbf{B}$-matrix.

3.5.4. The stable solution expressed by the use of the lag operator

Assume that the lag polynomial $\pi(L)$ has an inverse $\pi(L)^{-1}$, so that $\pi(L)\pi(L)^{-1} = 1$. In this case, we can write a solution of (3.76) as

$$Y_t = \pi(L)^{-1}(\phi_0 + \varepsilon_t). \tag{3.83}$$

By using the above factorization, we can write the solution as

$$Y_t = (1 - \lambda_1 L)^{-1}(1 - \lambda_2 L)^{-1} \cdots (1 - \lambda_p L)^{-1}(\phi_0 + \varepsilon_t). \tag{3.84}$$

We have a closer look at the case with second-order dynamics:

$$\begin{aligned} Y_t &= (1 - \phi_1 L - \phi_2 L)^{-1}(\phi_0 + \varepsilon_t) \\ &= (1 - \phi_1 L - \phi_2 L)^{-1}\phi_0 + (1 - \phi_1 L - \phi_2 L)^{-1}\varepsilon_t. \end{aligned} \tag{3.85}$$

We can first write

$$(1 - \phi_1 L - \phi_2 L)^{-1}\phi_0 \; = \phi_0(1 - \phi_1 - \phi_2)^{-1} \text{ for } L = 1, \tag{3.86}$$

because we know that, no matter which form the lag polynomial $(1-\phi_1 L - \phi_2 L)^{-1}$ takes, it does not operate on the constant ϕ_0. However, to make $(1 - \phi_1 - \phi_2)^{-1}$ meaningful, we require

$$1 - \phi_1 - \phi_2 \neq 0. \tag{3.87}$$

Using (3.85) and (3.86), the solution can be written as

$$Y_t = \frac{\phi_0}{\pi(1)} + \frac{\varepsilon_t}{\pi(L)}, \tag{3.88}$$

given condition (3.87).

We next inspect the second term on the right-hand side of the equation. First, the factorization of the polynomial implies that

$$\frac{\varepsilon_t}{\pi(L)} = (1 - \phi_1 L - \phi_2 L)^{-1}\varepsilon_t = \frac{1}{(1 - \lambda_1 L)}\frac{1}{(1 - \lambda_2 L)}\varepsilon_t.$$

Second, we are interested in the (globally asymptotic) stable solution with both roots inside the unit-circle:

$$|\lambda_1| < 1 \quad \text{and} \quad |\lambda_2| < 1 \tag{3.89}$$

implying that

$$(1 - \lambda_i L)^{-1} = \sum_{j=0}^{\infty}(\lambda_i^j L^j), \tag{3.90}$$

where we have used the result for the sum of an infinite geometric progression. The next step is to make use of a result that holds under the stability conditions (see Sargent, 1987, p. 184):

$$(\lambda_1 - \lambda_2)^{-1}\left(\frac{\lambda_1}{1-\lambda_1 L} - \frac{\lambda_2}{1-\lambda_2 L}\right) = \frac{1}{(1-\lambda_1 L)} \cdot \frac{1}{(1-\lambda_2 L)}. \tag{3.91}$$

By the use of (3.91), we can write:

$$\begin{aligned}
&\frac{1}{(1-\lambda_1 L)}\frac{1}{(1-\lambda_2 L)}\varepsilon_t \\
&\quad = (\lambda_1 - \lambda_2)^{-1}\left(\frac{\lambda_1}{1-\lambda_1 L} - \frac{\lambda_2}{1-\lambda_2 L}\right)\varepsilon_t \\
&\quad = (\lambda_1 - \lambda_2)^{-1}\left(\lambda_1 \sum_{j=0}^{\infty} \lambda_1^j L^j - \lambda_2 \sum_{j=0}^{\infty} \lambda_2^j L^j\right)\varepsilon_t \\
&\quad = (c_1 + c_2)\varepsilon_t + (c_1\lambda_1 + c_2\lambda_2)\varepsilon_{t-1} \\
&\qquad + (c_1\lambda_1^2 + c_2\lambda_2^2)\varepsilon_{t-2} + (c_1\lambda_1^3 + c_2\lambda_2^3)\varepsilon_{t-3} + \cdots,
\end{aligned}$$

where we have made use of the notation:

$$c_1 = \frac{\lambda_1}{\lambda_1 - \lambda_2} \quad \text{and} \quad c_2 = \frac{-\lambda_2}{\lambda_1 - \lambda_2}.$$

By insertion of these results in (3.88), you can see that the solution found by "direct" use of the lag polynomial, namely (3.83), can be written as:

$$Y_t = \frac{\phi_0}{1-\phi_1-\phi_2} + \sum_{j=0}^{\infty}(c_1\lambda_1^j + c_2\lambda_2^j)\varepsilon_{t-j}, \quad \text{for } |\lambda_j| < 1,\ j = 1, 2. \tag{3.92}$$

We can now compare this solution with the expression for the solution in (3.58) above, for the case of second-order dynamics, $p = 2$ in (3.58). It is not immediately clear that they are equivalent. We start by looking at the third line of (3.58). First, we change notation in that line by setting $c_1 = d_{11}d^{11}$ and $c_2 = g_{12}g^{21}$. If we next continue the summation back to infinity, and not (only) to the two initialization periods (cf. Y_0 and Y_{-1} in the first line), we see that we could have written the third line of (3.58) as

$$\sum_{j=0}^{\infty}(c_1\lambda_1^j + c_2\lambda_2^j)\varepsilon_{t-i}$$

which is identical to the second term on the right-hand side of (3.92). The first term in (3.92), $\phi_0(1-\phi_1-\phi_2)^{-1}$, corresponds to the second line in

(3.58) because the second row of (3.58) converges to $\phi_0(1-\phi_1-\phi_2)^{-1}$ as $t \to \infty$. Finally, the initial condition in the first line of (3.58) disappears asymptotically as $t \to \infty$.

This conclusion can be generalized to dynamics of order p, and shows that (3.83) represents a direct way of obtaining the particular solution that does not condition on initial values.

We end this section with a remark about (3.87), which we used in the expression for the solution in (3.88). In the general case with dynamics of order p, using the definitions in Section 3.5.2, the corresponding condition is

$$\pi(1) \neq 0 \Leftrightarrow 1 - \sum_{i=1}^{p} \phi_i \neq 0 \Leftrightarrow \phi(1) \neq 1 \Leftrightarrow \sum_{i=1}^{p} \phi_i \neq 1, \tag{3.93}$$

and is a necessary, but not sufficient, condition for characteristics roots inside the unit-circle. It is, however, necessary and sufficient for the exclusion of 1 (the positive real number) as one unit-root.

3.6. Impulse-Responses and Dynamic Multipliers

One purpose of dynamic econometric modelling is to estimate the dynamic responses in the model's endogenous variables to changes in any of the non-modelled variables. At one level, this type of analysis is answering the same questions as comparative statics in economics do, only that the partial derivatives are functions of the number of periods since the increase in the non-modelled variable.

When the model is defined by (3.9) and (3.10), the only non-modelled variables are the random disturbance terms ε_t $(t = 1, 2, \ldots, T)$. At first, it may seem difficult to give economic interpretation to responses to a shock in a non-observable variable. However, such interpretability is exactly what macroeconomic models promise to deliver. Hence, the analysis gives important mathematical background of the dynamic response functions that are popular in modern macroeconomics. Another reason for "digging into" the mathematics of the impulse responses of (3.9) is that the same algebra applies to endogenous responses to exogenous changes in an *observable* economic variable.

In order to distinguish the two versions of comparative dynamics, we will use the term *impulse-responses* when we have in mind the responses with respect to changes in a disturbance term, and *dynamic multipliers* when we have in mind the responses to a change in a measured exogenous variable. The analysis of dynamic multipliers is found in Section 6.3, and the impulse-responses will also appear when we present structural VAR models in Section 7.8.

When we analyze the impulse-responses, we do not necessarily require stability of the difference equation from the outset. We therefore take the solution in (3.42) as our starting point, since that solution is valid independently of whether the characteristic roots are located inside the unit-circle or not. The solution is also general in the sense that it holds for Y_{t+j}, $j = 0, 1, 2, \ldots, 0$ conditional on $Y_{t-1}, \ldots, Y_{t-p}$, we just need to change the notation accordingly. Hence, the expression for Y_{t+j} is

$$\begin{aligned} Y_{t+j} &= b_{11}^{(j+1)} Y_{t-1} + b_{12}^{(j+1)} Y_{t-2} + \cdots + b_{1p}^{(j+1)} Y_{t-p} \\ &\quad + \phi_0 (b_{11}^{(j)} + b_{11}^{(j-1)} + \cdots + b_{11}^{(1)} + 1) \\ &\quad + b_{11}^{(j)} \varepsilon_t + b_{11}^{(j-1)} \varepsilon_{t+1} + \cdots + b_{11}^{(1)} \varepsilon_{t+j-1} + \varepsilon_{t+j}. \end{aligned} \tag{3.94}$$

We let δ_j denote the effect on Y_{t+j} of a marginal increase in ε_t. Mathematically speaking, this is the partial derivative of Y_{t+j} with respect to ε_t. Using (3.94), the response δ_j is therefore

$$\delta_j = \frac{\partial Y_{t+j}}{\partial \varepsilon_t} = b_{11}^{(j)}, \quad j = 0, 1, 2, \ldots, \quad b_{11}^{(0)} = 1. \tag{3.95}$$

Hence, the whole sequence of dynamic responses δ_j $(j = 0, 1, 2, \ldots)$ is indeed a function of j, the number of time periods since the shock and the response in Y_{t+j}, hence, the term *impulse-response function*.

As established above, $b_{11}^{(j)}$ denotes element (1,1) in the matrix $\mathbf{B}^j$, and the expression for $b_{11}^{(j)}$ in (3.51) can be written more compactly as

$$b_{11}^{(j)} = c_1 \lambda_1^j + c_2 \lambda_2^j + \cdots + c_p \lambda_p^j, \quad j = 0, 1, 2, \ldots, \tag{3.96}$$

with the use of the definition:

$$c_i = d_{1i} d^{i1}, \quad i = 1, 2, \ldots, p. \tag{3.97}$$

Hence, we have

$$\sum_{i=1}^{p} c_i = 1, \tag{3.98}$$

in accordance with (3.52).

For the case of first-order dynamics, $p = 1$, this implies that we find δ_j as

$$\delta_j = c_1\lambda_1^j = \phi_1^j, \quad j = 0, 1, 2, \ldots, \tag{3.99}$$

since $c_1 = 1$ and the single characteristic root is ϕ_1.

With second-order dynamics, ($p = 2$), the dynamic multipliers are given by

$$\delta_j = c_1\lambda_1^j + (1 - c_1)\lambda_2^j, \quad j = 0, 1, 2, \ldots \tag{3.100}$$

where

$$c_1 = \frac{\lambda_1}{\lambda_1 - \lambda_2},$$

as shown in (3.59) above (recall also $c_1 = d_{11}d^{11}$).

The general expression for the impulse-response function becomes

$$\delta_j = \sum_{i=1}^{p} c_i\lambda_i^j, \quad j = 0, 1, 2, \ldots, \tag{3.101}$$

where the coefficients c_i sum to 1 in accordance with (3.98). The general expression for c_i is

$$c_i = \frac{\lambda_i^{p-1}}{\prod_{\substack{k=1 \\ k \neq i}}^{p}(\lambda_i - \lambda_k)}, \tag{3.102}$$

as shown in Hamilton (1994, p. 12).

These results bring out that the impulse response function, in the same manner as the solution for Y_{t+j}, depends fundamentally on the characteristic roots. In particular, we see that the function will be periodic, with cycles, if some of the roots are complex pairs. Another property is that the absolute values of the responses decline if and only if all the characteristic roots are located inside the unit-circle.

Theorem 3.5 (Asymptotic behaviour of impulse response functions). *Let δ_j denote the value of the impulse-response function with argument, j of a difference equation with constant coefficients. The necessary and sufficient condition for*

$$\delta_j \longrightarrow 0 \quad \text{as } j \longrightarrow \infty, \tag{3.103}$$

is that all the characteristic roots associated with the difference equation are less than one in magnitude (moduli less that one, all roots are located inside the unit-circle).

Hence, another property of asymptotically stable difference equations is that the effect of a shock (an increase that lasts for only one period) to the non-homogeneous part of the equations eventually dies out, as the number of periods after the shock increases. The "decay function" is not necessarily monotonous. It can be cyclical, due to characteristic roots that are complex numbers.

The opposite is true for unstable equations. The effect of a shock (of one period duration) never goes away. Explosive solutions imply that the response to a shock increases (in absolute value) with the number of periods that has gone by since the shock occurred.

In the case of globally asymptotic stable equations, we can derive the expressions for the multipliers by the use of the lag operator. We start by considering (3.83), which we reproduce here:

$$Y_t = \pi(L)^{-1}(\phi_0 + \varepsilon_t).$$

The solution in unique, and therefore, we can write $\pi(L)^{-1}$ as the infinite lag polynomial with the dynamic multipliers as coefficients:

$$\pi(L)^{-1} = \delta_0 + \delta_1 L + \delta_2 L^2 + \cdots .$$

The responses can be found from

$$\pi(L)(\delta_0 + \delta_1 L + \delta_2 L^2 + \cdots) = 1 + 0L + 0L^2 + \cdots$$

by multiplication on the left-hand side, and collecting terms that have the same power of the lag operator, L^j:

$$\begin{aligned}
&L^0 : 1 \cdot \delta_0 = 1 && \Rightarrow \delta_0 = 1, \\
&L^1 : (-\phi_1\delta_0 + \delta_1)\, L = 0 && \Rightarrow \delta_1 = \phi_1\delta_0, \\
&L^2 : (-\phi_2\delta_0 - \delta_1\phi_1 + \delta_2)\, L^2 = 0 && \Rightarrow \delta_2 = \phi_2\delta_0 + \delta_1\phi_1, \\
&\quad\vdots && \quad\vdots
\end{aligned} \tag{3.104}$$

This approach shows how to derive the impulse responses without the use of the characteristic roots. Even in the general case of dynamics of order p, we can find the response function by the recursive method: first δ_0, then δ_1 and the other higher order responses, as given by the result on the right-hand side of (3.104). Often we are interested in the effects of a change in an exogenous variable that lasts for more than one period. These responses are called interim multipliers or cumulated dynamic multipliers. A "permanent shock" to a disturbance term should not be interpreted literally (since it would entail a change in the mean of the disturbance). However, as we noted above, the algebra applies to models with non-modelled, observable variables. For exogenous variables, it does make good sense to speak of permanent changes. The effect of a shock that lasts in three periods is found in a straightforward manner:

$$\delta_0 + \delta_1 + \delta_2.$$

The cumulated multiplier that we come across most frequently may be the *long-run multiplier*, which gives the effect of a permanent increase in an exogenous variable. In other words, the long-run multiplier, per definition, gives the effect of a shock to the stationary solution Y^*. We write Y^* as

$$Y^* = \pi(1)^{-1}(\varepsilon^*), \tag{3.105}$$

where we omit the intercept for simplicity, but where we have introduced ε^* as variables that we can take the derivative of Y^* with respect to. The long-run response becomes

$$\frac{\partial Y^*}{\partial \varepsilon^*} = \frac{1}{1 - \phi_1 - \phi_2 - \cdots - \phi_p} \tag{3.106}$$

It is only defined for the case of a stable difference equation.

Finally in this section, we note that we obtain the same expressions for the dynamic responses if we, instead of the solution for Y_{t+j}, use the expression for the solution of Y_t:

$$Y_t = b_{11}^{(t)} Y_0 + b_{12}^{(t)} Y_{-1} + \cdots + b_{1p}^{(t)} Y_{-(p-1)} + \sum_{j=0}^{t-1} b_{11}^{(j)} \varepsilon_{t-j},$$

We define the response of Y_t of a partial change in ε_t as

$$\frac{\partial Y_t}{\partial \varepsilon_{t-j}} = b_{11}^{(j)}, \quad j = 0, 1, 2, \ldots, t-1, \tag{3.107}$$

and by comparison with the expressions above, we find that

$$\frac{\partial Y_t}{\partial \varepsilon_{t-j}} = \delta_j = b_{11}^{(j)}, \quad j = 0, 1, 2, \ldots, t-1.$$

3.7. Final Equation Form of a Multiple Equation System

As noted above, we will often be interested in systems of stochastic difference equations. The simplest system, with two endogenous variables X_t and Y_t, can be written as

$$\begin{pmatrix} Y_t \\ X_t \end{pmatrix} = \begin{pmatrix} a_{11} & a_{12} \\ a_{21} & a_{22} \end{pmatrix} \begin{pmatrix} Y_{t-1} \\ X_{t-1} \end{pmatrix} + \begin{pmatrix} \varepsilon_{yt} \\ \varepsilon_{xt} \end{pmatrix}, \tag{3.108}$$

where a_{ij} denotes a constant coefficient and $\varepsilon_{y,t}$ and $\varepsilon_{x,t}$ are two random variables, which in general are correlated (but as noted we can wait until later with the detailed specification of the random disturbances to the equations). In order to save notation, we have omitted two intercepts (constant terms). Non-zero intercepts are important for the particular solution, but they play no role for the dynamic stability of the system.

We first write the system more compactly, so that we can apply the results that we have already established for single equations for the system. We start by solving the equation in the first row for X_{t-1}:

$$X_{t-1} = (1/a_{12})Y_t - (a_{11}/a_{12})Y_{t-1} - (1/a_{12})\varepsilon_{yt}. \tag{3.109}$$

Insertion in the second equation in (3.108) gives

$$X_t = \frac{a_{22}}{a_{12}}Y_t + \left(a_{21} - a_{22}\frac{a_{11}}{a_{12}}\right)Y_{t-1} - \frac{a_{22}}{a_{12}}\varepsilon_{yt} + \varepsilon_{xt},\ a_{12} \neq 0. \tag{3.110}$$

Finally, we substitute t by $t+1$ in the first equation in (3.108), and substitute X_t by the right-hand side of (3.110):

$$Y_{t+1} = a_{11}Y_t + a_{12}\left(\frac{a_{22}}{a_{12}}Y_t + \left(a_{21} - a_{22}\frac{a_{11}}{a_{12}}\right)Y_{t-1} - \frac{a_{22}}{a_{12}}\varepsilon_{yt} + \varepsilon_{xt}\right)$$
$$+ \varepsilon_{yt+1}.$$

By collecting terms that involve Y_t and Y_{t-1}, we see that the system (3.108) implies that Y_{t+1} is given by the second-order difference equation:

$$Y_{t+1} = (a_{11} + a_{22})Y_t + (a_{12}a_{21} - a_{22}a_{11})Y_{t-1} + \varepsilon_{yt+1} - a_{22}\varepsilon_{yt} + a_{12}\varepsilon_{xt}.$$

Since the equation must hold for all periods, we can just as well write

$$Y_t = \phi_1 Y_{t-1} + \phi_2 Y_{t-2} + e_{yt}, \tag{3.111}$$

where the constants ϕ_1 and ϕ_2 are given by the coefficients of the two-equation system (3.108)

$$\phi_1 = (a_{11} + a_{22}), \tag{3.112}$$

$$\phi_2 = a_{12}a_{21} - a_{22}a_{11}, \tag{3.113}$$

and the random variable e_{yt} is a linear combination of the two random disturbances in (3.108):

$$e_{yt} = \varepsilon_{y,t} - a_{22}\varepsilon_{y,t-1} + a_{12}\varepsilon_{x,t-1}. \tag{3.114}$$

By the use of lag operator notation, $\phi(L)$, (3.111) can be expressed as

$$\phi(L)Y_t = e_{yt}, \quad \text{where } \phi(L) = 1 - \phi_1 L - \phi_2 L^2. \tag{3.115}$$

The associated characteristic polynomial is

$$p(\lambda) = 0 \Longleftrightarrow \lambda^2 - \phi_1\lambda - \phi_2 = 0. \tag{3.116}$$

Equation (3.111) is a linear difference equation, and therefore all the results above hold equally for this equation. For example, we have that the condition for a (globally asymptotically) stable solution of Y_t is that both characteristic roots have moduli that are less than 1.

A difference equations that has been derived in this manner, from a system of dynamic equations, has earned its own name in econometrics. It is called a *final from equation* for an endogenous variable in a dynamic equation system (see Haavelmo, 1940; Wallis, 1977). In Chapter 1, we introduced final form equations for the models that were used as introductory examples of dynamics (the cobweb model and the Keynesian model).

System (3.108) is made up of equations that are reduced-form equations, since the right-hand side of the equations only contain predetermined variables and no contemporaneous endogenous variables. Another name for such systems of variables is *vector autoregressive* model, with the well-known acronym VAR.

More generally, reduced-form equations can contain observable variables that are determined outside the specified equation systems, i.e., open systems, or VAR-EX system, where "EX" indicates that when we use this model, the assumption is that the non-modelled variables are exogenous, and do not depend on the endogenous variables of the VAR. Both (closed) VAR and VAR-EX (variously called Open VAR) are central models in the following chapters. The concept of final equation also allows for open systems. In general, a final equation denotes an equation which has been derived from a system of equations and which only includes lags of itself and exogenous variables in the system of equations.

The characteristic equation associated with (3.111) is all we need to characterize the solution for Y_t as stable or not even though Y_t is determined by the equation system (3.108). But what about the solution for the other variable in the system, namely, X_t? Intuitively, because X_t is jointly determined with Y_t, the same characteristic equation must also determine the stability properties of X_t. You can show that this is true by deriving the final equation for X_t. This shows that the stability condition that the two roots of (3.116) have moduli less than one is really a condition about the stability of the solution for the vector variable (Y_t, X_t).

For the vector to be stable, both X_t and Y_t must have stable solutions. Of course, it is possible to imagine systems where, for example X_t has an unstable solution, while Y_t is stable. However, for this to be possible, we must have $a_{12} = a_{21} = 0$, and in that case there is not much point in formulating X_t and Y_t as a system in the first place. We can just as well say that X_t is determined by an unstable first-order process ($a_{22} = \pm 1$), while Y_t is determined by a stable first-order equation ($(-1 < a_{11} < 1)$) — at least if the disturbances $\varepsilon_{y,t}$ and $\varepsilon_{x,t}$ are uncorrelated. If they are correlated, there may still be a point in formulating ΔX_t and Y_t as endogenous variables in a system, since they are only "seemingly" uncorrelated, but in fact related by the correlated equation disturbances (note the use of the difference operator Δ that we introduced in Section 3.5.1).

3.8. Companion Form Representation of a System

For systems with more than two equations, or for systems where the equations have higher order dynamics, it is impractical to obtain the final equation by substitution. However, the companion form, which we introduced in Section 3.4 above, can be generalized to systems.

We begin by writing (3.108) in companion form. Define

$$\mathbf{y}_t = [Y_t, X_t]' \quad \text{and} \quad \boldsymbol{\varepsilon}_t = [\varepsilon_{y,t}, \varepsilon_{x,t}]',$$

in such a way that (3.108) can be written as

$$\mathbf{y}_t = \mathbf{B}\mathbf{y}_{t-1} + \boldsymbol{\varepsilon}_t, \tag{3.117}$$

where $\mathbf{B}$ is the matrix with coefficients:

$$\mathbf{B} = \begin{pmatrix} a_{11} & a_{12} \\ a_{21} & a_{22} \end{pmatrix}.$$

From Section 3.4, we have that the characteristic polynomial associated with $\mathbf{B}$ is

$$|\mathbf{B} - \lambda\mathbf{I}| = \begin{vmatrix} a_{11} - \lambda & a_{12} \\ a_{21} & a_{22} - \lambda \end{vmatrix},$$

where λ is an eigenvalue of $\mathbf{B}$ that satisfies the characteristic equation:

$$|\mathbf{B} - \lambda\mathbf{I}| = 0. \tag{3.118}$$

If λ is a root in (3.118), it is also a root in the characteristic equation of the final equation (3.111), i.e.,

$$\lambda^2 - \phi_1\lambda - \phi_2 = 0,$$

with $\phi_1 = (a_{11} + a_{22})$ and $\phi_2 = a_{12}a_{21} - a_{11}a_{22}$. It follows that the vector-variable $(X_t, Y_t)'$ has a (globally asymptotic) stable solution if and only if all the eigenvalues of the matrix $\mathbf{B}$ have moduli less than 1.

Finally, we establish the companion form for the general case of n equations and dynamics of degree p. We define $\mathbf{y}_t$ as the $n \times 1$-vector:

$$\mathbf{y}_t = [Y_{1t}, Y_{2t}, \ldots, Y_{nt}]',$$

and write the system with dynamics of order p as

$$\mathbf{y}_t = \mathbf{\Phi}_1\mathbf{y}_{t-1} + \mathbf{\Phi}_2\mathbf{y}_{t-2} + \cdots + \mathbf{\Phi}_p\mathbf{y}_{t-p} + \boldsymbol{\varepsilon}_t, \tag{3.119}$$

where $\mathbf{\Phi}_i$ denotes an $n \times n$-matrix with autoregressive coefficients for lag i, and $\boldsymbol{\varepsilon}_t$ is an $n \times 1$ vector of random variables. Formulated by the use of the companion form, the system takes the form

$$\underbrace{\begin{pmatrix} \mathbf{y}_t \\ \mathbf{y}_{t-1} \\ \vdots \\ \mathbf{y}_{t-p+1} \end{pmatrix}}_{\mathbf{Y}_t} = \underbrace{\begin{pmatrix} \mathbf{\Phi}_1 & \mathbf{\Phi}_2 & \cdots & \mathbf{\Phi}_{p-1} & \mathbf{\Phi}_p \\ \mathbf{I} & \mathbf{0} & \mathbf{0} & \cdots & \mathbf{0} \\ \mathbf{0} & \mathbf{I} & \mathbf{0} & \cdots & \mathbf{0} \\ \vdots & \vdots & \vdots & \vdots & \vdots \\ \mathbf{0} & \mathbf{0} & \mathbf{0} & \mathbf{I} & \mathbf{0} \end{pmatrix}}_{\mathbf{B}} \underbrace{\begin{pmatrix} \mathbf{y}_{t-1} \\ \mathbf{y}_{t-2} \\ \vdots \\ \mathbf{y}_{t-p} \end{pmatrix}}_{\mathbf{Y}_{t-1}} + \underbrace{\begin{pmatrix} \boldsymbol{\varepsilon}_t \\ \mathbf{0} \\ \vdots \\ \mathbf{0} \end{pmatrix}}_{\mathbf{e}_t}, \tag{3.120}$$

where the dimensions of the identity and null matrices in $\mathbf{B}$ are $n \times n$, while each $\mathbf{0}$, in the last column denotes an $n \times 1$ vector with zeros. The companion form of the system can be written compactly using the notation indicated by the labels below (3.120):

$$\underset{(np\times 1)}{\mathbf{Y}_t} = \underset{(np\times np)}{\mathbf{B}} \mathbf{Y}_{t-1} + \underset{(np\times 1)}{\mathbf{e}_t}. \tag{3.121}$$

The vector variable $\mathbf{Y}_t$ has a (globally asymptotically) stable solution if and only if all the eigenvalues of $\mathbf{B}$ found as solutions of

$$|\mathbf{B} - \lambda\mathbf{I}| = 0,$$

have moduli less than one. Said with different words: they are inside the unit-circle.

3.9. Summary and Looking Ahead

The theory of linear difference equations represents the common ground, and foundation, of a broad range of methods in time series analysis and in dynamic econometrics. This includes all methods that build on the assumption of linearity in parameters, including models of rational expectations and rational learning. Nonlinear econometric models also have a strong connection to the theory of linear dynamics, at least as a reference point, but influential authors also make a stronger point that a nonlinear model should in most cases be an extension of a econometrically well-specified linear relationship (see Granger and Teräsvirta, 1993).

In the Chapter 4, we use the theory of difference equations to define the important concept of a stationarity of a time series variable, and of systems of time series variables. Difference equations are important references for working with econometric time series model, both the stationary class, and even the models for non-stationary time series that we will present later in this book.

3.10. Exercises

Exercise 3.1. From the book's webpage, you can download the file SimdataAR2.fl with OxMetrics code that was used to produce the solution of the second-order difference equation (3.35). Reproduce the solution and experiment with parameter values that give (a) globally asymptotically solution without cycles, (b) an explosive solution, and (c) an unstable solution.

Exercise 3.2. Show the asymptotic result in (3.56).

Exercise 3.3. Show that (3.108) implies a final equation for X_t which has the same characteristic equation as in (3.116), but that the error term of the final equation for X_t is different from e_{yt} in 3.114.

Exercise 3.4. Set $n = 2$ and $p = 3$, and write the expression of the VAR by starting from (3.121).

The following exercises may require reading the chapter appendix.

Exercise 3.5. Factorize the polynomial

$$p(x) = 4 + (x-1)^2.$$

Exercise 3.6. Show equation (3.A.2).

Exercise 3.7. Show equation (3.A.3).

Appendix 3.A. Some Results for Complex Numbers

This appendix collects the definitions and theorems related to complex numbers that we have referred to above, and that will be useful below.

3.A.1. Definition and representations

We introduce the symbol i which is interpreted as a "number" that satisfies $i = \sqrt{-1}$ and which we call *imaginary*. It can be shown that ordinary algebra can be used for i without any inconsistencies, for example,

$$\frac{1}{i} = \frac{i}{ii} = \frac{i}{-1} = -i.$$

More generally, all complex numbers can be expressed as

$$z = a + ib, \tag{3.A.1}$$

where a, b are real numbers. We can write

$$\mathrm{Re}(z) = a,$$

for the *real part* of z, and

$$\mathrm{Im}(z) = b,$$

for the *imaginary part* of z. If we want, a real number like a can be interpreted as a special complex number by writing it as $a + i \cdot 0$. Similarly, i can be expressed as $0 + i \cdot 1$.

Definition 3.6 (Addition and multiplication). We have the following definitions for addition and multiplication of complex numbers:

$$\begin{aligned} z_1 + z_2 &= (a_1 + ib_1) + (a_2 + ib_2) \overset{\text{def}}{=} (a_1 + a_2) + i(b_1 + b_2), \\ z_1 z_2 &= (a_1 + ib_1)(a_2 + ib_2) \overset{\text{def}}{=} (a_1 a_2 - b_1 b_2) + i(a_1 b_2 + a_2 b_1). \end{aligned}$$

Several useful algebraic properties follow from the above definitions: Let z_1,z_2, z_3 denote arbitrary complex numbers, we then have

$$\begin{aligned}
&\text{(i)} \quad z_1 + z_2 = z_2 + z_1,\\
&\text{(ii)} \quad z_1 z_2 = z_2 z_1,\\
&\text{(iii)} \quad (z_1 + z_2) + z_3 = z_1 + (z_2 + z_3),\\
&\text{(iv)} \quad (z_1 z_2) z_3 = z_1(z_2 z_3),\\
&\text{(v)} \quad z_1(z_2 + z_3) = z_1 z_2 + z_1 z_3.
\end{aligned}$$

(vi) Equation $z_1 + x = z_2$ has a unique solution which we write as

$$x = z_2 - z_1.$$

(vii) If $z_1 \neq 0$, then the equation $z_1 x = z_2$ has a unique solution which we write as

$$x = z_2.$$

From these properties, it follows that all the algebraic rules that we use for real numbers, apply to complex numbers as well (the exception is inequalities). Example are as follows:

$$\frac{z_1 z_3}{z_2 z_3} = \frac{z_1}{z_2}, \quad \frac{z_1}{z_2} = z_1 \frac{1}{z_2} \quad \frac{1}{z_1} + \frac{1}{z_2} = \frac{z_1 + z_2}{z_1 z_2}$$

$$1 + z + z^2 + \cdots + z^n = \frac{1 + z^{n+1}}{1 - z}.$$

As noted in the main text above, a complex number $(a + ib)$ can be shown graphically in a diagram with the real part (a) along the horizontal axis, and the imaginary part (b) along the vertical axis (see Figure 3.1).

Definition 3.7 (Modulus (norm)). The distance from $z = a + ib$ to origo is the *norm* of z:

$$|z| = \sqrt{a^2 + b^2}.$$

Norm and modulus are synonyms.

A real number $a = a + i \cdot 0 = (a, 0)$ (note the vector notation after the second equality) is a special complex number with modulus $|a| = \sqrt{a^2 + i \cdot 0} = a^2$, i.e., the usual absolute value.

The modulus (norm) satisfies

$$|z_1 z_2| = |z_1|\,|z_2| \tag{3.A.2}$$

(see Exercise 3.6). Specifically, we get: $\left|z^2\right| = |zz| = |z|\,|z| = |z|^2$, and more generally, $\left|z^j\right| = |z|^j$ for $j = 1, 2, \ldots$.

Moreover, $|1/z| = 1/|z|$, since $1 = |1| = |z \cdot 1/z| = |z|\,|1/z|$.

Finally, we note the property that

$$z^j \longrightarrow 0, \text{ as } j \longrightarrow \infty, \text{ if } |z| < 1 \tag{3.A.3}$$

(see Exercise 3.7).

Definition 3.8 (Conjugate). The complex conjugate to $z = a + ib$ is

$$\overline{z} = a - ib.$$

Using these definitions, we have, for example, $\overline{i+1} = 1 - i$, $\overline{i} = -i$ and $\overline{2} = 2$.

Definition 3.9 (Trigonometric form). The trigonometric representation of the complex number z is

$$z = a + ib = |z| \cos\vartheta + i\,|z| \sin\vartheta = |z|\,(\cos\vartheta + i\sin\vartheta),$$

where ϑ, called the argument, is given by

$$\sin\vartheta = \frac{b}{\sqrt{a^2+b^2}} = \frac{b}{|z|}, \tag{3.A.4}$$

$$\cos\vartheta = \frac{a}{\sqrt{a^2+b^2}} = \frac{a}{|z|}. \tag{3.A.5}$$

The representation is often referred to as the polar-coordinate form.

Note that the argument ϑ is not uniquely defined: If ϑ fits in (3.A.4) and (3.A.5), then $\vartheta + 2k\pi$, $k = \pm1, \pm2, \ldots$ also fit. A convention is to choose ϑ to be in region $-\pi < \vartheta \leq \pi$. If $-\pi/2 < \vartheta < \pi/2$, we find ϑ as

$$\vartheta = \arctan\left(\frac{b}{a}\right),$$

since $\tan(\vartheta) = \sin(\vartheta)/\cos(\vartheta) = b/a$ from the properties of trigonometric functions.

3.A.2. Frequency and period

In the time series analysis, it is practical to measure the *frequency* in *cycles per unit of time*, which we denote by v. If the unit of time is 1 year, the frequencies could be, for example, 1/8, 1/4, 1 or maybe 2 cycles per year. Hence, in this application, the relevant argument in the trigonometric function is positive. In the classical harmonic analysis, the frequency is measured in terms of radians *per unit of time*, and we have the equation:

$$\vartheta = 2\pi v,$$

relating the frequency in cycles per unit of time to radians per unit of time. From the properties of the cosine function we have for example: $v = 0 \Rightarrow \cos(2\pi 0) = 1$, $v = 1/4 \Rightarrow \cos(\pi/2) = 0$, $v = 3/4 \Rightarrow \cos(3\pi/2) = 0$, $v = 1 \Rightarrow \cos(2\pi) = 1$.

In line with this convention, v is defined as *cycles per unit of time*, we therefore determine the argument of the trigonometric form by solving (3.A.5)

$$\cos(2\pi v) = \frac{a}{|z|}$$

$$\Rightarrow 2\pi v = \cos^{-1}\left(\frac{a}{|z|}\right) \equiv \arccos\left(\frac{a}{|z|}\right).$$

The *period* is defined as the length in time of one full cycle:

$$period = \frac{2\pi}{\vartheta} - \frac{0}{\vartheta} = \frac{2\pi}{\vartheta}.$$

If *period* = 2 years, the number of cycles per year is 1/2. With quarterly data, a two-year cycle means that the number of cycles per quarter is $1/8 = 0.125$.

We see that *period* is equivalent with the inverse of the frequency:

$$period \equiv \frac{1}{v},$$

and it gives the number of periods between two peaks. Hence, a frequency of 1/2 corresponds to a *period* of 2 time periods, as just noted.

As an example, consider the complex pair $z = 0.25 \pm 0.86i$. Hence $|z| = 0.9$, $2\pi v = 1.29$ and $v = 1.29/(2 \cdot 3.14159) = 0.20531$. Hence, the period is

$$period = \frac{1}{0.20531} = 4.8707.$$

As we have seen above, characteristic roots (eigenvalues) are important drivers of the solutions of dynamic equations. For example, if the pair $z = 0.25 \pm 0.86i$ is the root in the solution of model with second-order dynamics, the solution will be cyclical (with dampened cycles) and there will be approximately five periods between two peaks. Hence, about 1/5 of a cycle is completed within each time period (e.g., one year).

Formally, the definition of *period* requires $v > 0$. However, in practice, it creates no misunderstanding to say that the "zero frequency corresponds to an "infinite *period*". In fact, many economic time series variables are characterized by low frequency roots, and it has become the custom in time series analysis to speak of *low frequency data* and *long-memory processes* as typical features in economics. Among econometricians, such time series are known as unit-roots series, or integrated series. The theory of this important class of time series is presented in Chapters 9 and 10.

3.A.3. The exponential function

A function of a complex number is referred to as a *complex function of a complex variable.*

Definition 3.10 (The exponential function). If z is a complex number

$$z = x + iy,$$

we have

$$\exp(z) \stackrel{\text{def}}{=} \exp(x)(\cos y + i \sin y),$$

which is the definition of the (the natural) exponential function for complex values of z.

In most cases, the complex exponential function has the same properties as the real version of the function. For example, we have

$$\exp(z_1)\exp(z_2) = \exp(z_1 + z_2), \tag{3.A.6}$$

since,

$$\begin{aligned}&\exp(x_1)\{\cos(y_1) + i\sin(y_1)\} \cdot \exp(x_2)\{\cos(y_2) + i\sin(y_2)\}\\ &\quad = \exp(x_1 + x_1)\{\cos(y_1 + y_2) + i\sin(y_1 + y_2)\} = \exp(z_1 + z_2).\end{aligned}$$

The complex exponential function also has certain unique properties, for example,

$$\overline{\exp(z)} = \exp(\overline{z}), \tag{3.A.7}$$

and

$$\exp(z + ik2\pi) = \exp(z), \quad k = 0, \pm 1, \pm 2, \ldots. \tag{3.A.8}$$

Equation (3.A.8) follows from (3.A.6), and:

$$\exp(ik2\pi) = \cos(k2\pi) + i\sin(k2\pi) = 1, \tag{3.A.9}$$

since sin and cos have the same *period*, namely 2π.

Definition 3.11 (Exponential form). From the trigonometric representation, we have that

$$z = a + ib = |z|\,(\cos\vartheta + i\sin\vartheta).$$

From the definition of the exponential function, we see that

$$(\cos\vartheta + i\sin\vartheta) = \exp(i\vartheta)$$

implying that another way of writing the complex number z is

$$z = a + ib = |z|\exp(i\vartheta). \tag{3.A.10}$$

The following rules are useful:

$$\begin{aligned} \exp(ix) &= \cos(x) + i\sin(x), \\ \exp(-x) &= \cos(x) - i\sin(x), \\ \cos(x) &= \{\exp(ix) + \exp(-ix)\}/2, \\ \sin(x) &= \{\exp(ix) - \exp(-ix)\}/2i. \end{aligned} \tag{3.A.11}$$

3.A.4. The unit-circle

The unit-circle shown in Figure 3.2 can be defined with the use of the above representations.

Definition 3.12. The complex unit-circle is defined as the set of complex numbers that have norm (or modulus) equal to one 1.

We say that $z = a + ib = |z|\exp(i\vartheta)$ is on the unit-circle when $|z| = 1$. z is inside the unit-circle when $|z| < 1$, and that z is outside the unit-circle when $|z| > 1$.

The complex number given by

$$z = \exp(iy) = \cos(y) + i\sin(y), \tag{3.A.12}$$

defines the unit-circle when $0 \leq y \leq 2\pi$, since $|\exp(iy)| = \sqrt{\cos(y)^2 + \sin(y)^2} = 1$, from the properties of *sin* and *cos*, or directly:

$$|\exp(iy)| = \sqrt{|\exp(iy)|^2} = \sqrt{\exp(-iy)\exp(iy)} = \sqrt{\exp(0)} = 1.$$

Above, we defined the variable $0 \leq v \leq 1$ as the *frequency* measured as the number of cycles per unit of time. With reference to (3.A.12), we set $y = 2\pi v$. This gives the following listing of the relationship between frequency and points on the unit-circle:

	$\cos(2\pi v)$	$\sin(2\pi v)$	z	$\|z\|$
$v = 0$	1	0	1	1
$v = 1/4$	0	1	i	1
$v = 1/2$	-1	0	-1	1
$v = 3/4$	0	-1	$-i$	1

3.A.5. The fundamental theorem of algebra

We have the following theorem, for example, from Sydsæter and Hammond (2002, p. 114).

Theorem 3.6 (The Fundamental Theorem of Algebra). *Any polynomial of degree p can be factorized into factors of degree 1:*

$$p(x) = a_0 x^n + a_1 x^{n-1} + \cdots + a_{p-1} x + a_p \tag{3.A.13}$$

$$= a_0 (x - r_1)^{m_1} (x - r_2)^{m_2} \cdots (x - r_l)^{m_2} \tag{3.A.14}$$

where multiplicities m_j satisfy

$$m_1 + m_2 + \cdots + m_l = p.$$

$r_1, r_2, \ldots, r_l$ are roots of the homogeneous nth-order equation:

$$a_0 x^p + a_1 x^{p-1} + \cdots + a_{p-1} x + a_p = 0.$$

In general, the roots are (or can be written as) complex numbers. If each r_l is counted m_j times, it follows that at any equation of degree p has n roots.

Theorem 3.7 (Complex pairs). *If r is a root in an pth-order equation with real coefficients a_i, it follows that the conjugate, $\bar{r}$, also is a root. This implies that complex roots always come in pairs.*

Complex pairs. From the rules for complex numbers:

$$a_0 r^p + a_1 r^{n-1} + \cdots + a_{p-1} r + a_p = 0$$

$$\Rightarrow \overline{a_0 r^p + a_1 r^{p-1} + \cdots + a_{p-1} r + a_p} = \overline{0} = 0$$

$$\Rightarrow a_0 \bar{r}^p + a_1 \bar{r}^{p-1} + \cdots + a_{p-1} \bar{r} + a_p = 0$$

□

it follows that if p is an odd number, there must be at least one real root.

In particular, we have that the pth-order equation

$$X^p = c, \tag{3.A.15}$$

has p roots: We first express c with the use of the exponential form $c = |c|\exp(i(\vartheta + k2\pi))$, $k = 0, \pm 1, \pm 2, \ldots$, where we have used that $\exp(k2\pi i) = 1$. We can then write (3.A.15) as

$$X = \sqrt[n]{|c|}\exp\left(i\frac{(\vartheta + k2\pi)}{n}\right),$$

and the solution is found by choosing k such that $0 \leq (\vartheta + k2\pi)/n < 2\pi$. Specifically, we have that

$$X^3 = 1 \Rightarrow X = \exp\left(i\frac{k2\pi}{3}\right)$$

which gives the roots:

$$X = \exp(i \cdot 0) = 1,$$

$$X = \exp\left(i\frac{2\pi}{3}\right) = \cos\left(\frac{\pi}{6}\right) + i\sin\left(\frac{\pi}{6}\right) = -\frac{1}{2} + i\frac{\sqrt{3}}{2},$$

$$X = \exp\left(i\frac{4\pi}{3}\right) = \cos\left(\frac{2\pi}{6}\right) + i\sin\left(\frac{2\pi}{6}\right) = -\frac{1}{2} - i\frac{\sqrt{3}}{2},$$

where we have used the trigonometric form, and that complex roots always come in pairs.

3.A.6. Complex roots in the solution of difference equations

As the main text already shows, complex roots play an important role in the solution of difference equations with higher order dynamics, and such equations are common in macroeconomics. If, for example, the roots of a second-order equation are given by $\lambda = 0.25 \pm 0.86i$, the homogeneous solution Y_t^h is a periodic function of time. From the given initial conditions, the time function will show oscillations that become dampened over time, and there will be approximately five periods between each top (or between each trough). As just noted, in this example, $1/5$ of a full cycle will be completed in each of the time periods. This homogeneous solution of the second order equation is therefore

$$Y_t^h = C_1\lambda_1^t + C_1\lambda_2^t,$$

where the roots (λ_1, λ_2) form a complex pair. By the use of the exponential and trigonometric forms, we can write the roots as

$$\lambda_1 = |\lambda_1|\exp(i\vartheta) = |\lambda_1|\left(\cos(\vartheta) + i\sin(\vartheta)\right),$$
$$\lambda_2 = |\lambda_2|\exp(-i\vartheta) = |\lambda_2|\left(\cos(\vartheta) - i\sin(\vartheta)\right),$$

where

$$|\lambda| \stackrel{\text{def}}{=} |\lambda_1| = |\lambda_2| = \sqrt{\left(\frac{\phi_1}{2}\right)^2 - \frac{(\phi_1^2 + 4\phi_2)}{4}} = \sqrt{\phi_2},$$

since we by definition have $\lambda_1 = a + bi$, with $a = \phi_1/2$ and $b = 1/2\sqrt{-\phi_1^2 - 4\phi_2}$. By the use of the rules given above, we obtain

$$\lambda_1^t = |\lambda|^t \exp(i\vartheta t) = |\lambda|^t \left(\cos(t\vartheta) + i\sin(t\vartheta)\right),$$
$$\lambda_2^t = |\lambda|^t \exp(-i\vartheta t) = |\lambda|^t \left(\cos(t\vartheta) - i\sin(t\vartheta)\right),$$

and

$$Y_t^h = (C_1 + C_2)\,|\lambda|^t\cos(t\vartheta) + i(C_1 - C_2)\,|\lambda|^t\sin(t\vartheta).$$

At first sight, we may think that the solution is imaginary because of the appearance of i in the expressions. However, if the roots are complex numbers, C_1 and C_2 are also conjugates and can be expressed as

$$C_1 = \alpha + \beta i,$$
$$C_2 = \alpha - \beta i,$$

and

$$C_1 + C_2 = \alpha,$$
$$C_1 - C_2 = i2\beta.$$

By the use of these results, we can write the homogeneous solution as

$$\begin{aligned} Y_t^h &= 2\alpha\,|\lambda|^t\cos(t\vartheta) + i^2 2\beta\,|\lambda|^t\sin(t\vartheta) \\ &= 2\alpha\,|\lambda|^t\cos(t\vartheta) - 2\beta\,|\lambda|^t\sin(t\vartheta) \\ &= |\lambda|^t\, 2\left[\alpha\cos(t\vartheta) - \beta\sin(t\vartheta)\right], \end{aligned} \qquad (3.A.16)$$

which is the same as (3.27) when we set $S_t = 2\left[\alpha\cos(t\vartheta) - \beta\sin(t\vartheta)\right]$ in that equation, see, e.g., Sydsæter *et al.* (2008, Section 11.4) or Sydsæter *et al.* (2004, Section 9.4) for a concise mathematical expositions. Two other references, from the macroeconomic and time series literature, are Sargent (1987, p. 186) and Hamilton (1994, pp. 14–16).

In Section 3.6, we showed that the dynamic multipliers δ_j ($j = 0, 1, 2, \ldots$) are driven by the same eigenvalues that appear in the expression for the homogeneous solution Y_t^h. Using the notation above, the response function δ_j can be therefore be expressed as

$$\delta_j = 2\alpha\,|\lambda|^j \cos(\vartheta j) - 2\beta\,|\lambda|^j \sin(j\vartheta), \quad j = 0, 1, 2, \ldots. \tag{3.A.17}$$

The responses will follow the same cosine wave as Y_t itself. The amplitude will be declining when the roots are located inside the unit-circle, it will be constant if there are roots on the unit-circle, and it will increase at the rate λ_1^j if the modulus is larger than one.

3.A.7. Complex functions of a real variable

$f(x)$ is a complex function of a real variable x if $f(x)$ can be written as

$$f(x) = u(x) + iv(x),$$

where u and v are usual real functions. Derivation and integration are defined in a natural way:

Definition 3.13 (Derivation and integration).

$$f'(x) \stackrel{\text{def}}{=} u'(x) + iv'(x),$$

$$\int_a^b f(x)dx \stackrel{\text{def}}{=} \int_a^b u(x)dx + i\int_a^b v(x)dx.$$

The usual rules for derivations and integration can be used, here are some examples:

$$\begin{aligned}
(f+g)' &= f' + g', \\
(fg)' &= f'g + g'f, \\
\left(\frac{f}{g}\right)' &= \frac{f'g - g'f}{g^2}, \\
\int (f+g)dx &= \int f\,dx + \int g\,dx, \\
\textstyle\int_a^b f'dx &= f(b) - f(a).
\end{aligned}$$

Since $\exp(ix) = \cos(x) + i\sin(x)$, we have

$$\begin{aligned} f'(x) &= -\sin(x) + i\cos(x) \\ &= i\left[\frac{-1}{i}\sin(x) + \cos(x)\right] \\ &= i\left[-(-i)\sin(x) + \cos(x)\right] \\ &= i\exp(ix), \end{aligned}$$

where we use $\cos'(x) = -\sin(x)$ and $\sin'(x) = \cos(x)$ and $1/i = -i$ and the rules in (3.A.11).

Chapter 4

Stationary Time Series

Sequences of random variables, stochastic processes, represent the main objects of time series analysis, and of dynamic econometrics. The chapter explains how time series processes can be formulated by the use of stochastic difference equations. The concepts of stationary, ergodicity and invertibility of time series are explained. Several important stationary processes are defined: white noise, autoregressive (AR) and mixed autoregressive and moving average (ARMA). The theoretical autocorrelation functions (ACFs) of these processes are introduced. Maximum likelihood (ML) estimation of the parameters of stationary processes from a given sample is discussed for the first-order autoregressive process, AR(1). Although it is simple, the properties of the ML estimator of AR(1) hold a lot of generality: about consistency of estimators and about the typical size of finite sample biases, and why classical testing based on standard t-values and F-statistics can be used for well-specified AR models. The chapter ends with a generalization to multivariate stationary processes, with the vector AR process (VAR), as an important system class, that will play a prominent role in later chapters.

4.1. Introduction

The theory of stationary time series represents the statistical foundation of econometric modelling of time series data. From Chapter 3, the reader may suspect that there is a close relationship between the stationary time series and the mathematics of stochastic difference equations. Such a suspicion will be confirmed in this chapter.

We will proceed in steps: The concepts of time series and stationarity of a time series are presented in Sections 4.2 and 4.3, while Section 4.5 gives a relatively broad introduction to stationary variables that are given by linear difference equations. We progress from simple processes (white noise and AR(1)) to general *autoregressive moving average (ARMA) processes.* Sections 4.6 and 4.8 cover the estimation of AR and ARMA models, and give the maximum likelihood interpretation of the OLS estimation that we motivated on intuitive grounds in Chapter 1. In the last section of the chapter, the multiple equation autoregressive (AR) model, namely VAR, is introduced.

4.2. Time Series, Stochastic Processes and Difference Equations

In Chapter 3, the focus was on difference equations, and the mathematical properties of the solutions of difference equations. Since stochastic difference equations consist of a deterministic part and a random part, it is intuitive to interpret the solution of a stochastic difference equation as an ordered sequence of random variables. The ordering is by a time index t, leading to the notion of a *time series*, as opposed to a cross-section, where there is no natural ordering of the random variables.

At an intuitive level, a random variable is defined as a real variable that can assume different values with different probabilities. This definition leaves something to be desired from a mathematical viewpoint. For example, the simplistic view of a random variable suppresses the theoretical point that probabilities are defined for a set of outcomes (cf. coin tossing). Hence, it is more correct to regard a random variable as a function from a set of outcomes to the real line, attaching numbers to outcomes. However, for our purposes, the simpler view of is good enough, and we identify the notion of a random variable with its range of values, hence the term *variable*.

A *stochastic process* is a collection of random variables defined on the same *probability space* (see Spanos, 1999, Section 8.2). With time series, the collection is ordered by the time index t. Without going into too much detail, we can see that a stochastic process can be regarded as a function with two arguments: the time index set (T) and the outcomes set (S).

Hence, a precise notation for a stochastic process is

$$\{Y(t, s); t \in \mathrm{T}, s \in S\}.$$

The index set T can, for example, be: $\{0, \pm 1, \pm 2, \ldots\}$, $\{1, 2, 3, \ldots\}$, $[0, \infty\}$, or $(-\infty, \infty)$. In turn, this means that we can regard stochastic processes from two angles, or perspectives:

The random variable perspective: For a given $t = \bar{t}$, $Y(\bar{t}, s)$ is an ordinary random variable with its own distribution and density function. For a given subset of T, say $t_1, t_2, \ldots, t_T$, $T \in \mathrm{T}$, we obtain the ordered sequence of T random variables which is fully described by a *joint distribution function.*

The realization perspective: For a given $s = \bar{s}$, $Y(t, \bar{s})$ is a function with t as the (deterministic) argument and values of Y as outcomes. We call this a realization, or the sample path, because it is the feature of the stochastic process that we associate with the observed data.

From introductory statistics, we are used to the idea of using the empirical moments (means and variances) from a data sample to make inference about the population parameters of the random variables. In a similar way, for the time series, we develop an empirical model of a time series (the realization perspective) with the aim to learn about the properties of the underlying stochastic process that has generated the data (the random variable perspective), through estimation, and by generalization from the specific sample to the population (theoretical) parameters.

But when we look closer, the situation with time series data is very different from the case with independent and identically distributed (IID) random variables. In the IID case, each pair (or vector) or variables are independent from the $n - 1$ other pairs, and each observation contributes with genuinely new information that can be used for estimation of dependence. From the random variables perspective on stochastic processes, we are reminded that all we can say is that the (random) time series are characterized by a *joint distribution.* The typical case is that the joint distribution will be characterized by correlation, so that the random variables in the stochastic process are dependent, not independent. This is the feature of autocorrelation (positive or negative) that we have already encountered in the first chapter.

Imagine that autocorrelation is so strong that each random variable in the process, say Y_{t_j}, can be made almost perfectly predictable by conditioning on its neighbour in the process, $Y_{t_{j-1}}$. But then $Y_{t_{j-1}}$ can also be made highly predictable by knowing $Y_{t_{j-2}}$ and so on. Hence, in this (extreme) case, there is as good as no independent information in the time series that can be used for estimation of the population parameters. Hence, a necessary requirement for inference based on time series data is that the dependence between neighbouring random variables is limited, and that each variable in the stochastic process contain an element of "news" compared to the earlier (and later) variables.

In this book, we will study stochastic processes that are defined by stochastic difference equations, and for those processes the necessary condition for meaningful inference is generally fulfilled. If not for the original process, then for the process which we obtain by applying the difference operator Δ to the random variables of process.

In the following, the perspective we take on the stochastic process will usually be clear from the context, and we therefore use the simpler notation:

$$\{Y_t; t \in \mathrm{T}\},$$

which suppresses the outcome set, but which on the other hand puts the time index as a subscript to serve as a reminder that we consider discrete time processes. Other variations may be to include the time index set explicitly, for example, $\{Y_t; t = 0, \pm 1, \pm 2, \ldots\}$, or $\{Y_t; t = 0, 1, 2, 3, \ldots\}$.

Box 4.1. Vector time series process and final equations

The notion of a stochastic time series process, and its definition, can easily be extended to an $(n \times 1)$ vector of random variables. Intuitively, this is because a vector process can always be written as a single process with reference to the final form equation, see Section 3.7. Hence, a process defined by a second-order difference equation can both be a stochastic process "in its own right", or it can be derived from a vector system, cf. (3.108), and can then be a *final equation*, which was the point we made in Section 3.7.

Like in Chapter 3, the difference equations that define the stochastic process will be assumed to be linear in the parameters. The variables of the analysis can be nonlinear transformations of the original data, meaning that nonlinear relationships between variables can be done within the framework of linear-in-parameter difference equations. For example, this is similar to the "choice of functional form stage" in the specification of a regression model.

Even if the relevance of linear-in-parameter models can be extended considerably by variable transformations, linearity in parameters does represent a limitation on the type of nonlinear behaviour that we can hope to represent in model form. Hence, at some point, extensions to nonlinear models become desirable, see e.g., Granger and Teräsvirta (1993) and Castle and Hendry (2014b).

As noted above, we often use the term *time series* both to denote an observed data series, and to denote the process that it is a realization of. This simplification will not create confusion when we take care to (re)introduce the distinction in the cases where it is essential.

An example of a stochastic process (time series) which is defined by a stochastic difference equation is

$$Y_t = \phi_0 + \phi_1 Y_{t-1} + \phi_2 Y_{t-2} + \cdots + \phi_p Y_{t-p} + \varepsilon_t,$$

where

$$\varepsilon_t \sim \text{IID}(0, \sigma_\varepsilon^2) \ \ \forall t, \tag{4.1}$$

exactly as in (3.9) and (3.10) in Chapter 3.

The appropriate methods for modelling depend on whether the stochastic process is stationary or non-stationary. The process is called *weakly stationary* if the expectation and covariances are constant parameters (independent of time). The process is non-stationary if the expectation or variance depends on time. For example, the stochastic process

$$Y_t = t + \varepsilon_t, \quad \varepsilon_t \sim \text{IID}(0, \sigma_\varepsilon^2), \tag{4.2}$$

is non-stationary, while

$$\Delta Y_t = 1 + \Delta\varepsilon_t, \tag{4.3}$$

gives a stochastic process $\{\Delta Y_t; t \in T\}$ which is stationary. Note the use of the difference operator, Δ, which was defined by the use of the lag operator in Section 3.5.1.

Stationarity is a relevant modelling assumption mainly because several economic time series variables have stationary-like features, at least after some initial treatment. In particular, after controlling for deterministic terms, such as regular seasonal variation, a deterministic trend, and temporary structural breaks, it is often possible to imagine that the variable is associated with an inhomogeneous difference equation that has a stationary solution. The rate of unemployment, capacity utilization rate, price changes, and interest rates are examples of such variables.

Nevertheless, there are other time series, macroeconomic ones in particular, that show manifest signs of non-stationarity. Such variables have means and variances that depend on time in a way that are not well captured by including a linear trend and dummies in the deterministic part of the equation. But also for such variables the stationary framework becomes relevant for modelling. This is because systems of non-stationary variables can be "reduced to" stationary ones by giving econometric treatment to the unit-roots that are the source of non-stationarity. This is a main point in the econometrics of co-integrated systems in Chapter 10.

4.3. Stationarity

Let $\{Y_t;\ t = 0, \pm 1, \pm 2, \pm 3, \ldots\}$ denote a time series process. Stationarity is a characteristic of the linear properties of the process, namely expectation, variance and (auto)covariance.

For the time series Y_t, we define the *autocovariances* $\gamma_{j,t}$ as

$$\gamma_{j,t} = E[(Y_t - \mu_t)(Y_{t-j} - \mu_t)], \quad j = 0, 1, 2, \ldots, \tag{4.4}$$

where the expectation μ_t is defined in the standard way:

$$\mu_t = E(Y_t) = \int_{-\infty}^{\infty} Y_t f_{Y_t}(Y_t) dY_t,$$

for a density function $f_{Y_t}(Y_t)$.

Definition 4.1 (Weak stationarity). If $E(|Y_t|^2) < \infty$, $\forall t$, and if neither μ nor γ_j, depend on t, the Y_t-process $\{Y_t;\ t = 0, \pm 1, \pm 2, \pm 3, \ldots\}$ is covariance stationary, or weakly stationary:

$$E(Y_t) = \mu, \quad \forall t,$$

and

$$E[(Y_t - \mu)(Y_{t-j} - \mu)] = \gamma_j, \quad \forall t,\ j.$$

See Brockwell and Davies (1991, Section 3.1).

The terms covariance stationarity and weak stationarity suggest that there is another definition of stationarity in the literature, and this is *strong (strict) stationarity*. This definition is in terms of the simultaneous distribution function of the time series. However, the most important concept for us is weak stationarity, and we use the term in that meaning in the following.[1]

By setting $j = 0$, we see that γ_0 is the variance of Y_t: $\text{Var}(Y_t) = \gamma_0$, which is constant (does not depend on time) if Y_t is a stationary time series.

Note that if Y_t is stationary, we get $\gamma_j = \gamma_{-j}$, and the covariance between Y_t and the lagged variable Y_{t-j} is the same as the covariance between Y_t and the leading variable Y_{t+j}. From the autocovariances, we can define the *theoretical autocorrelation function* $\{\zeta_{t1}, \zeta_{t2}, \ldots\}$ as

$$\zeta_{j,t} = \frac{\text{Cov}(Y_t, Y_{t-j})}{\text{Var}(Y_t)} = \frac{\gamma_{j,t}}{\gamma_{0,t}}. \tag{4.5}$$

Often in the following, we will denote the autocorrelation function by the acronym *ACF*. We see that $\zeta_j = \zeta_{-j}$ in the case of stationarity.

For an actual (observed) time series realization $\{Y_t;\, t = 1, 2, 3, \ldots, T\}$, the *empirical autocovariances* are used:

$$\hat{\gamma}_j = \frac{1}{T} \sum_{t=j+1}^{T} (Y_t - \bar{Y})(Y_{t-j} - \bar{Y}), \quad j = 0, 1, 2, \ldots, T-1, \tag{4.6}$$

where $\bar{Y} = 1/T \sum_{t=1}^{T} Y_t$. Note that $\hat{\gamma}_j$ is often calculated using $T-1$ instead of T. Using $T-1$ for the variance $\hat{\gamma}_j$ is consistent with using one degree of freedom to estimate the mean of the process (i.e., unbiased estimate when regressing on a constant only). Using T gives the maximum likelihood estimate. Of course, for reasonable sample lengths, the difference is not large.

Correspondingly, the empirical *ACF* becomes

$$\hat{\zeta}_j = \frac{\hat{\gamma}_j}{\hat{\gamma}_0}. \tag{4.7}$$

Box 4.2. Estimation of autocorrelations

Among the many important results in statistical theory that we build on is the following: If $\{Y_t;\, t = 0, \pm 1, \pm 2, \pm 3, \ldots\}$ is a stationary process, $\hat{\zeta}_j$ $(j = 0, 1, 2, \ldots)$ are consistent estimators of the theoretical autocorrelations, see Schumway and Stoffer (2000, Section 1.6). A rough test

[1]Stationarity and its implications for modelling is a concern in other disciplines than economics, see e.g., Myers (1989) for usage in the field of geostatistics.

Box 4.2 (*Continued*)

of whether peaks in $\hat{\zeta}_j$ are significant can be based on the interval $0 \pm z_{\alpha/2}/\sqrt{T}$, where $z_{\alpha/2}$ is the (critical) value of the standard normal variable z with $P(|z|) > z_{\alpha/2} = \alpha$. Figure 4.1 shows an application of this test (in the case where the theoretical autocorrelations are zero).

4.4. Ergodicity

Stationarity is related to, but different from, the concept of *ergodicity*.[2] When we consider expectation or variance, the concepts can either refer to the moments calculated for number of M *ensembles* at a given point in time, for example $Y_{t_j}^m$, $m = 1, 2, \ldots, M$ or the moments can refer to a sample of length T of a time series Y_t; $t = 0, 1, 2, 3, \ldots, T$, cf. the realization perspective above.

The mean of the ensemble (in time period t_j) is *one* estimator of the expectation of the process. It is not a given thing that the average of the T observations of a single process equals the ensemble average (at a given point in time). However, if the process is ergodic, this is what we will observe, as T becomes sufficiently large.

When we do Monte Carlo simulations, we let the computer generate as many realizations (replications) of a process as we like, and from experience we know that the mean of, say 1000, replications, usually gives a precise estimate of expectation parameters. For the ergodic process, we can obtain precise estimates from a single realization, if the sample length is long. Intuitively, ergodicity can therefore be reexpressed as the requirement that the realizations in an observed time series must be "sufficiently" similar, otherwise getting more observations will not help us pin down the same (time series-based) average as the ensemble average.

On the other hand, there should not be too high dependency between Y_t and Y_{t+j}. Because with too high correlation, getting more observations

[2]Most advanced textbooks include explanations of ergodicity with some differences in emphasis and in the level of formalism. A small sample of references are: Harvey (1993, p. 11), Hamilton (1994, p. 46–47), Hendry (1995a, Section 3.3), Davidson (2000, Section 4.4.3), and Spanos (1999, Section 8.4.4). A radical sceptic Taleb (2004) challenges the econometricians by taking the view that processes that generate time series data cannot be ergodic.

(larger T) will not give more information that we can use to estimate the expectation. In other words, time series observations that are sufficiently far apart should be as good as uncorrelated. At the level of precision that we use, this property can be said to be inherent in the time series processes that we will study in the following section. All the stationary processes that we cover in this chapter are ergodic.

4.5. Stationary Time Series Variables

In this section, we first define a *white noise* process, which many readers will know from the econometric specification of regression models. The notion of linear filtering proves to be a powerful concept, which together with white noise processes allows us to define a class of stationary processes known as ARMA.

4.5.1. White noise

A process $\{\varepsilon_t;\, t = 0, \pm 1, \pm 2, \pm 3, \ldots\}$ is called *white noise* if:

$$E(\varepsilon_t) = 0, \tag{4.8}$$

$$\mathrm{Var}(\varepsilon_t) = E(\varepsilon_t^2) = \sigma_\varepsilon^2, \tag{4.9}$$

$$\mathrm{Cov}(\varepsilon_t, \varepsilon_{t-j}) = \gamma_j = 0, \quad \text{for } j \neq 0. \tag{4.10}$$

It is also common to denote $\varepsilon_t \sim \mathrm{IID}\left(0, \sigma_\varepsilon^2\right)$ in (4.1) as white noise. In most cases, the choice of wording is not important, but strictly speaking, $\varepsilon_t \sim \mathrm{IID}\left(0, \sigma_\varepsilon^2\right)$ implies white noise in the sense defined by (4.8)–(4.10). The two formulations are equivalent if ε_t is a process of independent variables with a common normal distribution:

$$\varepsilon_t \sim \mathrm{IIN}(0, \sigma_\varepsilon^2) \quad \text{for all } t.$$

When the normality assumption is made explicit, it is common to denote ε_t as *Gaussian white noise*, or (shorter) as a *Gaussian process.*

As an application of the rough test mentioned in Box 4.2, Figure 4.1 shows empirical autocorrelations for a computer-generated white noise series with 100 observations, with $\pm 2/\sqrt{100} = \pm 0.20$ indicated as the bounds of the approximate 95% confidence interval. There are 12 autocorrelations shown as bars in the figure, hence the argument j in the empirical ACF takes the values $j = 1, 2, \ldots, 12$. In the theoretical ACF, all correlations are zero, and consistent with this all the empirical autocorrelations are

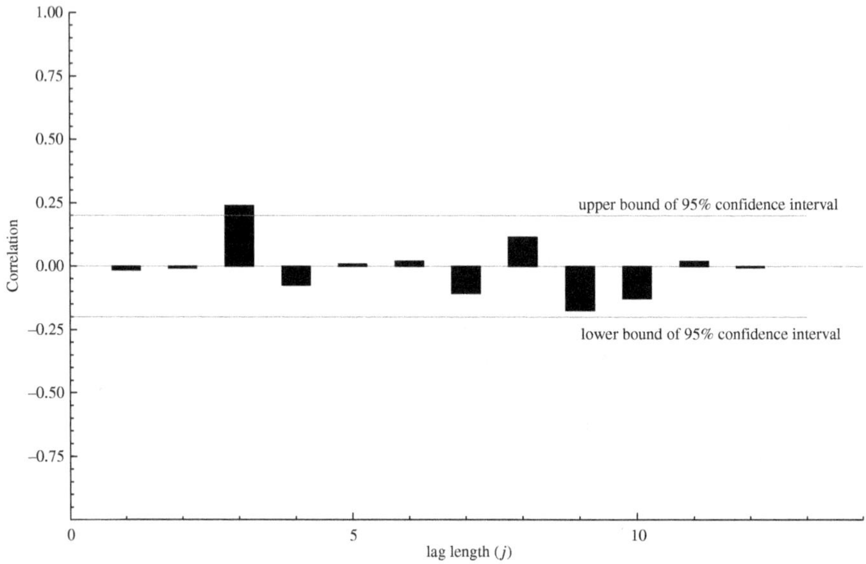

Figure 4.1. Empirical *ACF*, see Box 4.2, of a white noise series. The estimation is based on computer-generated data with $\sigma_\varepsilon^2 = 1$ and $t = 1, 2, \ldots, 100$.

small in magnitude, and there are switching signs with no significant sign patters. The only exception is the $j = 3$ autocorrelation which is outside the indicated confidence interval. As we know the data generation process (DGP) in this case, it is a *false positive* indicating a significant third-order autocorrelation when in fact the null hypothesis is true.

4.5.2. Preservation of stationarity by use of well-behaved linear filters

We define a *linear filter* as a linear combination of L^k, $k = 0, \pm 1, \pm 2, \pm 3, \ldots$. An example of a linear filter is

$$Y_t = \frac{1}{3}(\varepsilon_{t+1} + \varepsilon_t + \varepsilon_{t-1}), \text{ i.e., } a(L) = \frac{1}{3}L^{-1} + \frac{1}{3}L^0 + \frac{1}{3}L^1,$$

which gives Y_t as a moving average of three white noise variables. Differences of time series variables can also be written with the aid of a filter:

$$Y_t = \Delta\varepsilon_t = (\varepsilon_t - \varepsilon_{t-1}), \text{i.e., } a(L) = 1 - L \equiv \Delta.$$

If two linear filters are multiplied, the result is a new linear filter. For example, the two linear filters $a(L)$ and $b(L)$, and a time series X_t, can give a new time series Y_t as

$$Y_t = a(L)b(L)X_t = c(L)X_t,$$

where the multiplication

$$c(L) = a(L)b(L),$$

is carried through as if the lag operator L is a number. A linear filter can be infinite, as in

$$\psi(L) = \sum_{j=-\infty}^{\infty} \psi_j L^j, \tag{4.11}$$

which is a *two-sided filter*, also called a *symmetric filter*. Often, we will use a *one-sided filter*, and in particular

$$\psi(L) = \sum_{j=0}^{\infty} \psi_j L^j. \tag{4.12}$$

As the reader will have recognized, a one-sided filter in L^k, $k = 0, 1, 2, 3, \ldots,$ is the same as a lag-polynomial that we introduced above.

Theorem 4.1 (Preservation of stationarity (short version)). *If $\sum_{j=-\infty}^{\infty} |\psi_j| < \infty$, a linear filtering of a stationary process by $\psi(L)$ will give a new stationary process.*

We see that the theorem specifies that a stationarity preserving filter should satisfy: $\sum_{j=-\infty}^{\infty} |\psi_j| < \infty$, or alternatively, $\sum_{j=-\infty}^{\infty} \psi_j^2 < \infty$. Such a filter is sometimes referred to in statistical theory as a *well-behaved filter*, although "well behaved" is often dropped when it is clear from the context what kind of linear filter one has in mind.

Appendix 4.A contains a more detailed version of this theorem together with a proof.

4.5.3. First-order autoregressive model

The first-order autoregressive process, AR(1), illustrates several general properties of stationary time series.

The time series $\{Y_t;\ t = 0, \pm 1, \pm 2, \pm 3, \ldots\}$ has first-order dynamics when it is defined by the difference equation:

$$Y_t = \phi_0 + \phi_1 Y_{t-1} + \varepsilon_t, \tag{4.13}$$

where ϕ_0 and ϕ_1 are constant parameters, and ε_t is white noise with variance σ_ε^2, as defined in Section 4.5.1. In terms of mathematics, (4.13) is an inhomogeneous first-order difference equation. It is a special case of the general equation of order p, i.e., (3.9) in Chapter 3, where we found that the solution was

$$\begin{aligned} Y_t &= \phi_0 \sum_{j=0}^{t-1} \phi_1^j + \phi_1^t Y_0 + \sum_{j=0}^{t-1} \phi_1^j \varepsilon_{t-j} \\ &\equiv \phi_0 \sum_{j=0}^{t-1} \lambda_1^j + \lambda_1^t Y_0 + \sum_{j=0}^{t-1} \lambda_1^j \varepsilon_{t-j}, \end{aligned}$$

where Y_0 is the initial condition, and λ_1 is the root of the associated characteristic equation:

$$\lambda - \phi_1 = 0.$$

The conditional expectation of Y_t, given Y_0, is (cf. Exercise 4.2)

$$E(Y_t \mid Y_0) = \frac{\phi_0(1-\phi_1^t)}{(1-\phi_1)} + \phi_1^t Y_0, \tag{4.14}$$

which is a function of t. The unconditional (marginal) expectation, denoted μ_t, is obtained from the stable solution for Y_t. We remember from Section 3.3.2 that this solution is based on the condition $-1 < \phi_1 < 1$. It is

$$Y_t = \frac{\phi_0}{1-\phi_1} + \sum_{i=0}^{\infty} \phi_1^i \varepsilon_{t-i} \quad \text{for } |\phi_1| < 1, \tag{4.15}$$

which gives

$$E(Y_t) = \frac{\phi_0}{(1-\phi_1)} = \mu, \tag{4.16}$$

since

$$E\left(\sum_{i=0}^{\infty} \phi_1^i \varepsilon_{t-i}\right) = \sum_{i=0}^{\infty} \phi_1^i E(\varepsilon_{t-i}) = 0.$$

The conditional variance of Y_t, given Y_0, is (cf. Exercise 4.2)

$$\mathrm{Var}(Y_t \mid Y_0) = \frac{\sigma_\varepsilon^2(1-\phi_1^{2t})}{(1-\phi_1^2)}, \tag{4.17}$$

while the unconditional variance, which is found from the stable solution in (4.15), is

$$\mathrm{Var}(Y_t) = \frac{\sigma_\varepsilon^2}{(1-\phi_1^2)}, \quad |\phi_1| < 1, \tag{4.18}$$

using

$$\mathrm{Var}\left(\sum_{i=0}^{\infty} \phi_1^i \varepsilon_{t-i}\right) = \sum_{i=0}^{\infty} (\phi_1^2)^i \,\mathrm{Var}(\varepsilon_{t-i}) = \sigma_\varepsilon^2 \sum_{i=0}^{\infty} (\phi_1^2)^i.$$

Note that the expectation and the variance of the Y_t process are independent of the time index t, if and only if the stability condition $-1 < \phi_1 < 1$ is fulfilled. This bodes well for our guess that Y_t given by (4.13) is a stationary time series, exactly in the case where the difference equation has a (globally asymptotically) stable solution. However, we also need to confirm that the autocovariances are independent of t. To do that, we can first subtract the expectation on both sides of the equality sign (4.13):

$$\begin{aligned} Y_t - \mu &= \phi_0 + \phi_1 Y_{t-1} + \varepsilon_t - \mu \\ &= \phi_0 + \phi_1 Y_{t-1} - \phi_1\mu + \phi_1\mu + \varepsilon_t - \mu \\ &= \phi_0 + \phi_1(Y_{t-1} - \mu) - \mu(1-\phi_1) + \varepsilon_t \\ &= \mu(1-\phi_1) + \phi_1(Y_{t-1} - \mu) - \mu(1-\phi_1) + \varepsilon_t \\ &= \phi_1(Y_{t-1} - \mu) + \varepsilon_t, \end{aligned}$$

where we have used that (4.16) implies the following relationship between the parameters:

$$\phi_0 = (1-\phi_1)\mu.$$

The autocovariance between Y_t and Y_{t-j} becomes

$$\begin{aligned} \mathrm{Cov}(Y_t, Y_{t-j}) &= E[(Y_t - \mu)(Y_{t-j} - \mu)] \\ &= \phi_1 E[(Y_{t-1} - \mu)(Y_{t-j} - \mu)] + E[\varepsilon_t(Y_{t-j} - \mu)]. \end{aligned}$$

Since

$$E[\varepsilon_t(Y_{t-j} - \mu)] = 0 \quad \text{for } j \geq 1,$$

the expression for the autocovariance function simplifies to

$$E[(Y_t - \mu)(Y_{t-j} - \mu)] = \phi_1 E[(Y_{t-1} - \mu)(Y_{t-j} - \mu)], \tag{4.19}$$

or

$$\gamma_j = \phi_1 \gamma_{j-1}, \tag{4.20}$$

when we use the notation that we introduced above. Hence, we have that also the autocovariances are independent of the time index when they are calculated from the stable solution for Y_t.

This means that, at least for the case of first-order dynamics, the condition for stationarity is the same condition as the condition for global asymptotic stability, namely $|\phi_1| < 1$.

The autocorrelation function (ACF) of the AR(1) process becomes

$$\zeta_j = \frac{\mathrm{Cov}(Y_t, Y_{t-j})}{\mathrm{Cov}(Y_t)} = \phi_1 \frac{\gamma_{j-1}}{\mathrm{Var}(Y_t)} \equiv \phi_1 \zeta_{j-1}, \quad j = 1, 2, \ldots, \tag{4.21}$$

which shows that the ACF of an AR(1) process follows the same homogeneous difference equation as Y_t does.

For $0 < \phi_1 < 1$, all the autocorrelation coefficients are positive, and decline exponentially to zero as j increases towards infinity. Also, in the case of $-1 < \phi_1 < 0$, the ACF is declining in absolute value, but with oscillations around zero. The cobweb model in Chapter 1 gave an economic example of this kind of dominant negative autocorrelation. The Keynesian model in the introductory chapter provides an example of positive autocorrelation as a property of the solution of that macroeconomic model.

Box 4.3. Empirical ACF of an AR(1) process

As noted above, see Box 4.2, the empirical autocorrelations of an observed time series can be used to estimate the ACF. Section 4.5.4 contains a plot of an empirical ACF of an AR(1)-process together with an empirical ACF of a first-order autoregressive moving average process, ARMA(1, 1).

Another way of looking at the relationship between stationarity and stability is to make use of the theorem about preservation of stationarity by linear filtering. Since the intercept ϕ_0 in (4.13) does not come into the stability condition, we can set $\phi_0 = 0$, which simplifies the solution for Y_t to

$$Y_t = \sum_{j=0}^{\infty} \phi_1^j \varepsilon_{t-j},$$

which we can express as a linear filtering of the white noise process ε_t:

$$Y_t = \sum_{j=-\infty}^{\infty} \psi_j \varepsilon_{t-j},$$

where

$$\psi_j = 0 \quad \text{for } j = -1, -2, \ldots, -\infty,$$
$$\psi_j = \phi_1^j \quad \text{for } j = 0, 1, 2, \ldots, \infty.$$

This filter is well behaved if and only if (4.13) has a (global asymptotic) stable solution:

$$\sum_{j=-\infty}^{\infty} |\psi_j| < \infty \text{ if and only if } |\phi_1| < 1,$$

and then the stationarity of Y_t follows from the theorem about preservation of stationarity by means of filtering.

4.5.4. First-order autoregressive moving average model

In the time series analysis, and also in econometric applications, it is popular to use a mixed process which is a combination of an AR process and a moving average of a white noise process. A mixed process of this type is known as the autoregressive moving average (ARMA) process. The simplest case, with first-order dynamics in both the AR and MA parts, is referred to as ARMA$(1,1)$:

$$Y_t = \phi_0 + \phi_1 Y_{t-1} + \varepsilon_t + \theta_1 \varepsilon_{t-1}, \quad t = 1, 1, 2, \ldots, T, \tag{4.22}$$

where ϕ_0, ϕ_1 and θ_1 are constant parameters and ε_t is white noise with variance σ_ε^2.[3]

We now consider the conditions under which the mixed process defines a stationary time series. In order to simplify the notation, for this purpose,

[3]Strictly speaking the term ARMA$(1,1)$ should perhaps be reserved for the stationary version of the model. However, we allow ourselves to use ARMA$(1,1)$ (and below also ARMA(p,q)), more widely as acronyms that efficiently indicate the orders of the AR and moving average polynomials in the model equations.

we set $\phi_0 = 0$. Repeated backward insertion to period $t - J$ gives

$$\begin{aligned} Y_t = {} & \phi_1^J Y_{t-J} + \varepsilon_t + (\phi_1 + \theta_1)\varepsilon_{t-1} + (\phi_1^2 + \phi_1\theta_1)\varepsilon_{t-2} \\ & + \cdots + (\phi_1^{J-1} + \phi_1^{J-2}\theta_1)\varepsilon_{t-(J-1)} + (\phi_1^{J-1}\theta_1)\varepsilon_{t-J}. \end{aligned} \tag{4.23}$$

If we allow J to grow towards infinity, we see that Y_t can be expressed as a one-sided filter of the white noise process $\{\varepsilon_{t-j};\, j = 0, 1, 2, 3, \ldots\}$

$$Y_t = \sum_{j=0}^{\infty} \psi_j \varepsilon_{t-j}, \tag{4.24}$$

where

$$\begin{aligned} &\psi_0 = 1, \quad j = 0 \\ &\psi_j = (\phi_1^{j-1}\theta_1 + \phi_1^j) = \phi_1^{j-1}(\theta_1 + \phi_1), \quad j = 1, 2, \ldots. \end{aligned}$$

Note that $\sum_{j=0}^{\infty} |\psi_j| < \infty$ if and only if $|\phi_1| < 1$. It follows that Y_t given in model (4.22) is a stationary time series if the difference equation (4.22) has a stable solution. The stability (or not) only depends on the roots of the characteristic equation associated with the homogeneous part of (4.22), i.e., the solution of $\lambda - \phi_1 = 0$. Hence, we have that the stationarity condition must be $|\phi_1| < 1$, the same condition that we found for the AR(1)-process. The MA parameter θ_1 is of no consequence for the stationarity of the model equation (4.22). From before, we know that the intercept in the process, which was set to zero above, plays no role in the stability/stationary condition (it just fixes the expectation of a stationary series to zero, hence $Y^* = 0$ in the notation used for stationary (equilibrium) value in Chapter 3).

The autocovariances of ARMA(1, 1) can be calculated directly if we assume stationarity. It is practical to write the process in "deviation from mean" form:

$$Y_t - \mu = \phi_1(Y_{t-1} - \mu) + \varepsilon_t + \theta_1\varepsilon_{t-1}, \tag{4.25}$$

where $\mu = \phi_0/(1 - \phi_1)$ as above. We multiply by $(Y_{t-j} - \mu)$ on both sides of the equality sign, and then take the expectation:

$$\begin{aligned} E\left[(Y_t - \mu)(Y_{t-j} - \mu)\right] = {} & \phi_1 E\left[(Y_{t-1} - \mu)(Y_{t-j} - \mu)\right] + E\left[\varepsilon_t(Y_{t-j} - \mu)\right] \\ & + \theta_1 E\left[\varepsilon_{t-1}(Y_{t-j} - \mu)\right]. \end{aligned} \tag{4.26}$$

The first term on the right-hand side is the autocovariance γ_j. The second term is zero when $j > 0$, and the third is zero for $j > 1$. For $j = 0$ we obtain

$$\gamma_0 = \phi_1\gamma_1 + \sigma_\varepsilon^2 + \theta_1\phi_1\sigma_\varepsilon^2 + \theta_1^2\sigma_\varepsilon^2. \tag{4.27}$$

For $j = 1$ we obtain

$$\gamma_1 = \phi_1\gamma_0 + \theta_1\sigma_\varepsilon^2, \tag{4.28}$$

and for $j > 1$

$$\gamma_j = \phi_1\gamma_{j-1}. \tag{4.29}$$

By replacing γ_1 in (4.27) by the right-hand side of (4.28), we obtain

$$\gamma_0 = \phi_1(\phi_1\gamma_0 + \theta_1\sigma_\varepsilon^2) + \sigma_\varepsilon^2 + \theta_1\phi_1\sigma_\varepsilon^2 + \theta_1^2\sigma_\varepsilon^2,$$

which can be solved for γ_0, i.e., the variance of the process

$$\gamma_0 = \frac{1 + 2\phi_1\theta_1 + \theta_1^2}{1 - \phi_1^2}\sigma_\varepsilon^2. \tag{4.30}$$

Inserting from (4.30) for γ_0 in (4.28), the first autocovariance can alternatively be expressed as

$$\begin{aligned}\gamma_1 &= \phi_1\frac{1 + 2\phi_1\theta_1 + \theta_1^2}{1 - \phi_1^2}\sigma_\varepsilon^2 + \theta_1\sigma_\varepsilon^2 \\ &= \frac{\phi_1(1 + 2\phi_1\theta_1 + \theta_1^2) + (1 - \phi_1^2)\theta_1}{1 - \phi_1^2}\sigma_\varepsilon^2 \\ &= \frac{(1 + \phi_1\theta_1)(\phi_1 + \theta_1)}{1 - \phi_1^2}\sigma_\varepsilon^2. \end{aligned} \tag{4.31}$$

Hence, we conclude that the ACF for $Y_t \sim \text{ARMA}(1, 1)$ can be expressed as

$$\zeta_1 = \frac{(1 + \phi_1\theta_1)(\phi_1 + \theta_1)}{1 + 2\phi_1\theta_1 + \theta_1^2}, \tag{4.32}$$

$$\zeta_j = \phi_1\zeta_{j-1}, \quad j = 2, 3, \ldots. \tag{4.33}$$

This shows that the MA part of the mixed process affects the first autocorrelation, but also that the ACF is dominated by the AR part of the process. With the exception of $j = 1$, the ACF is governed by the difference equation

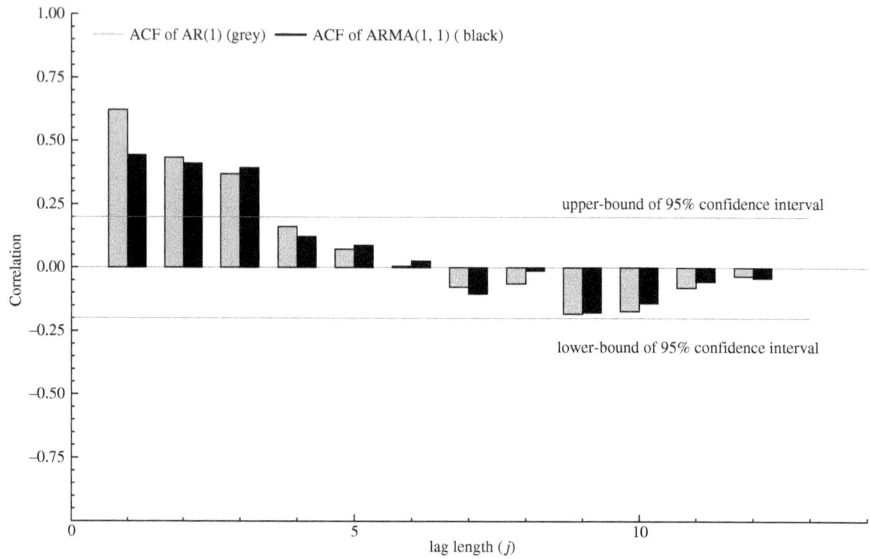

Figure 4.2. Empirical ACF of an AR(1) process ($\phi_1 = 0.6$), and of an ARMA(1, 1), ($\phi_1 = 0.6$, $\theta_1 = -0.3$). The estimation is based on computer-generated data, $t = 1, 2, \ldots, 100$, with $\sigma_\varepsilon^2 = 1$, for both processes.

(4.33). As a consequence, the autocorrelations will decay exponentially, but with oscillations in the case of negative ϕ_1.

For example, for coefficient values $\phi_1 = 0.6$ and $\theta_1 = -0.3$, the theoretical correlation for $j = 1$, ζ_1 becomes 0.34 for ARMA(1, 1) and 0.6 for AR(1). For ζ_2, we obtain 0.20 in the case of ARMA(1, 1) and 0.36 for AR(1), hence the two autocorrelations are already quite close for $j = 2$. The convergence of the autocorrelations is also noticeable in the empirical ACF in Figure 4.2 although those autocorrelations are affected by sampling variation. Theoretically, the third autocorrelation of this ARMA(1, 1) becomes 0.12, and appears to be overestimated by the empirical ACF. However, the fourth correlation is estimated to be lower than the upper 95% confidence interval, reflecting that the true (theoretical) fourth autocorrelation is also quite small, 0.07, for ARMA(1, 1), with the chosen of coefficient values.

In practice, if we are interested in determining empirically whether a time series has been generated by an AR(1) or ARMA(1, 1) process, it will be difficult to reach a conclusion by only looking at the empirical ACF. However, the partial autocorrelation function, denoted PACF, may give additional information that can be used to discriminate empirically between

AR(1) and ARMA(1, 1). In general, a *partial correlation coefficient* between two variables measures the degree of correlation that remains after the removal of the correlation that is due to indirect correlation, see e.g., Hendry and Nielsen (2007, Section 7.3), Bårdsen and Nymoen (2011, Section 7.4). Indirect correlation typically occurs because two variables are correlated with a third variable, as in the case of "spurious correlation" illustrated in Figure 1.7.[4]

In the time series analysis, partial correlations are relevant since they can be useful to eliminate the indirect correlation that is due to the AR part of a mixed process like ARMA(1, 1). The partial autocorrelation between Y_t and Y_{t-j} eliminates the influence of the intervening values Y_{t-1} through $Y_{t-(j-1)}$. In the case of AR(1), the whole correlation between Y_t and Y_{t-2} is due to their common covariance with Y_{t-1}. Hence, abstracting from sampling variation, the PACF of an AR(1) should be equal to the first ordinary autocorrelation (say, $\xi_{1|1} = \xi_1$), but zero for $j \geq 2$. For ARMA(1, 1), there will be an element of autocorrelation left in the process also after the removal of the indirect dependency on Y_{t-1}. This is due to the moving average coefficient θ_1, and the PACF of ARMA(1, 1) will typically be non-zero for $j = 2$. However, the function will be decaying as j grows. The decay is direct in the case of $\phi_1 < 0$, and it will be oscillating in the case of $\phi_1 > 0$.

At least, those are the theoretical properties of the PACF of the AR(1) and ARMA(1, 1) processes (see, e.g., Enders, 2010, Section 2.6). In practice, the empirical PACFs will be affected by sampling variability. Figure 4.3 shows empirical partial autocorrelations for the same two computer-generated series that Figure 4.2 shows the ACFs for.

We see that the estimated partial correlations pick up the reduction in correlation after the first lag ($j \geq 2$) which is characteristic of AR(1). For the higher order autocorrelation, there are two falsely significant correlations, if we consider the indicated confidence interval. The estimated PACF for the ARMA(1, 1) data captures the oscillating behaviour that we expect from theory, but not perfectly, as neighbouring correlations tend to have the same sign before switching. Possibly, the MA coefficient of -0.3 is not negative enough, compared to the variance of the white noise input process and the AR-coefficient, to leave a clear footprint in the data.

[4] "Third variable" should be interpreted widely, as it can often refer to a group of variables, not necessarily a single variable.

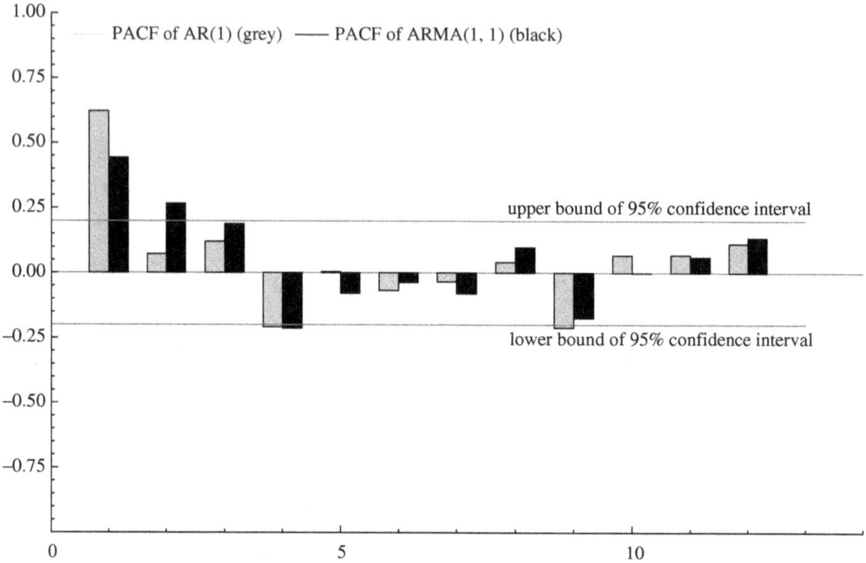

Figure 4.3. Empirical PACF of an AR(1) process ($\phi_1 = 0.6$), and of an ARMA(1, 1), ($\phi_1 = 0.6$, $\theta_1 = -0.3$). The estimation is based on computer-generated data, $t = 1, 2, \ldots, 100$, with $\sigma_\varepsilon^2 = 1$, for both processes.

The empirical identification of ARMA processes is a main step in univariate time series analysis. For that purpose, the theoretical properties of different special cases are well documented in textbooks in time series analysis. See Enders (2010, Chapter 2) for more details about partial correlations and their estimation, but still at the same technical level as in this book, and Schumway and Stoffer (2000, Chapter 2) for a more advanced statistical text.

4.5.5. Invertibility

Invertibility is a concept that applies to moving average processes and mixed processes. The property of invertibility, or lack thereof, can be most easily explained for the case of a first-order moving average process:

$$Y_t = \varepsilon_t + \theta_1 \varepsilon_{t-1}. \tag{4.34}$$

For period $t - 1$ the equation is

$$Y_{t-1} = \varepsilon_{t-1} + \theta_1 \varepsilon_{t-2}.$$

If we solve this equation for the lagged white noise disturbance ε_{t-1} and substitute in (4.34), we obtain

$$Y_t = \varepsilon_t + \theta_1 Y_{t-1} - \theta_1^2 \varepsilon_{t-2}. \tag{4.35}$$

The homogeneous part of this equation is the same as the homogeneous part of an AR(1) process. That AR(1) will be stationary if $-1 < \theta_1 < 1$.

Hence, the invertibility condition $-1 < \theta_1 < 1$ implies that the MA(1) process can be written as ("inverted to become") a stationary AR process.

A similar analysis applies to ARMA(1, 1) in (4.22). Invertibility represents a less fundamental property of time series than stationarity. Nevertheless, it is custom in time series analysis to require that mixed processes are invertible mainly because of technical estimation problems for non-invertible processes, see, for example, Harvey (1993, Section 3.5) for details.

4.5.6. The properties of ΔY_t when Y_t is stationary AR(1)

In econometrics, we are often interested in the changes in a time series variable, for example, ΔY_t. Recall that the difference operator Δ, and the lag operator L were both explained in Section 3.5.1. The properties of ΔY_t follow from the stochastic difference equation of Y_t. We can first write (4.13) as

$$\Delta Y_t = (\phi_1 - 1)Y_{t-1} + \varepsilon_t.$$

In order to find the difference equation for ΔY_t we use that

$$\Delta Y_t = (\phi_1 - 1)\{\phi_1 Y_{t-2} + \varepsilon_{t-1}\} + \varepsilon_t,$$

and

$$\Delta Y_{t-1} = (\phi_1 - 1)Y_{t-2} + \varepsilon_{t-1}.$$

By substituting Y_{t-2} we get

$$\Delta Y_t = \phi_1 \Delta Y_{t-1} + (1 - L)\varepsilon_t. \tag{4.36}$$

We can now consider ΔY_t as a time series which is of interest in its own right, and which is generated by the difference equation (4.36). This process is ARMA(1, 1) since the difference equation includes both an AR term and a moving average process in the white noise variable ε_t. The (theoretical)

ACF of ΔY_t is

$$\zeta_1 = \frac{-(1-\phi_1)^2}{2(1-\phi_1)} = -\frac{1}{2}(1-\phi_1)$$
$$\zeta_j = \phi_1 \zeta_{j-1} \quad \text{for } j = 2, 3, \ldots.$$

Note the following:

1. The MA parameter ($\theta_1 = -1$) only affects ζ_1 directly. For $j > 1$, ζ_j is given by the same difference equation as in the case of a pure AR(1)-process.
2. The MA part affects ζ_j, $j > 1$, indirectly, hence the ACF of the differenced series will be different from the AR(1)-case also for $j > 1$.

We could have derived (4.36) by using the linear filter $a(L) = 1 - L$ on both sides of (4.13), which reminds us that a linear filtering preserves stationarity, but that the ACF is affected by the filtering.

A final point is that ΔY_t given by (4.36) is an example of a series which is stationary but not invertible, because the MA coefficient is $\theta_1 = -1$. Such series are often called *over-differenced* series (see Harvey, 1993, p. 117).

4.5.7. General AR moving average

It is important to note the central role of the stationary solution of the difference equation (4.15) in the argument for (covariance) stationarity of the first-order Y_t process in (4.13). The stationary solution applies because we have assumed that $|\phi_1| < 1$. If instead, $\phi_1 = 1$, no stationary solution exists, and Y_t is not a (covariance) stationary time series variable. With $\phi_1 = 1$, Y_t is instead a *random-walk process*, and will be studied in Chapter 9.

This point also applies to the general case of p AR-terms and q MA-terms. We include a definition of the general ARMA model equation.

Definition 4.2 (ARMA). Let $\{Y_t; t = 0, \pm 1, \pm 2, \pm 3, \ldots\}$ denote a time series, and let $\{\varepsilon_t\}$ denote a white noise process as defined in Section 4.5.1. We define the ARMA model equation as

$$\pi(L) Y_t = \phi_0 + \theta(L)\varepsilon_t, \tag{4.37}$$

where $\pi(L) = 1 - \phi_1 L - \cdots - \phi_p L^p$ and $\theta(L) = 1 + \theta_1 L + \cdots + \theta_q L^q$.

The AR lag polynomial $\pi(L)$ was defined in (3.77) in Section 3.5.2. This "AR part" of the model equation (4.37) can be expressed as $\pi(L) = 1 - \phi(L)$ with reference to the definition of $\phi(L)$ given in (3.78).

Mathematically speaking, (4.37) is a difference equation. Hence, we can use the concept of stationary solution also for a time series generated by (4.37). This is stated in a concise manner in the following theorem which we include for completeness of exposition, and without proof:

Theorem 4.2 (Stationary solution of ARMA). *Consider the polynomial associated with the AR part of* (4.37):

$$\pi(z) = 1 - \phi_1 z - \cdots - \phi_p z^p.$$

(A) *If* $\pi(z) = 0$ *does not have any characteristic roots on the unit-circle,* (4.37) *has a unique stationary solution:*

$$Y_t - \mu = \psi(L)\varepsilon_t = \sum_{j=-\infty}^{\infty} \psi_j \varepsilon_{t-j}, \tag{4.38}$$

where the expectation $E(Y_t)$ *is denoted* μ *and is given by*

$$\mu = \frac{\phi_0}{\pi(1)} = \frac{\phi_0}{1 - \phi(1)}, \tag{4.39}$$

and where $\psi(L)$ *is determined by*

$$\pi(L)\psi(L) = \theta(L). \tag{4.40}$$

The solution may also be written as

$$Y_t - \mu = \psi(L)\varepsilon_t = \theta(L)\pi(L)^{-1}\varepsilon_t.$$

(B) *If* $\pi(z) = 0$ *has at least one characteristic root on the unit-circle,* (4.37) *has no stationary solution.*

Note that the roots of the AR part are the reciprocals of the roots of the characteristic equation as defined in Chapter 3. We have the following relationship:

$$z^{-p}\pi(z) = p(\lambda), \quad \text{when } z = 1/\lambda, \tag{4.41}$$

where $p(\lambda)$ is the characteristic polynomial of a difference equation of order p with constant coefficients:

$$p(\lambda) = \lambda^p - \phi_1 \lambda^{p-1} - \cdots - \phi_p. \tag{4.42}$$

Hence, we have that if z_i is a root of $\pi(z) = 0$, $\lambda_i = 1/z_i$ is a root of $p(\lambda) = 0$, and vice versa.

Note also how little in terms of restrictions that stationarity of the solution implies for the characteristic roots. "Anything goes", except roots that are exactly one in magnitude. Stationary solutions of a general ARMA process are therefore compatible with λ-roots that are outside the unit-circle. There is a correspondence at this point with the remarks at the end of Section 3.3.2 about global asymptotic stability (the backward-looking solution) and the possibility that also a "forward-looking" solution can be stable.

This is also seen by noting that the stationary solution (4.38) is given in terms of the two-sided filter $\sum_{j=-\infty}^{\infty} \psi_j \varepsilon_{t-j}$. The future part of the two-sided filter means that stationarity, in general, allows for roots that are larger than one in magnitude.

In the statistical time series literature, attention is often confined to stationarity that corresponds to global asymptotical stability of difference equations. A variable that has a stationary solution in this stricter sense is called a *causal processes* (see Brockwell and Davies, 1991, Chapter 3; Schumway and Stoffer, 2000, Chapter 2). Conversely, when the stationary solution is in terms of the two-sided filter, the process is future-dependent, i.e., non-causal. We include the definition of a causal process, and the corresponding special case of Theorem 4.2.

Definition 4.3 (Causal ARMA). If the stationary solution of model equation (4.37) is a one-sided filter of the form:

$$Y_t - \mu = \psi(L)\varepsilon_t = \sum_{j=0}^{\infty} \psi_j \varepsilon_{t-j}, \tag{4.43}$$

the ARMA(p,q)-process is referred to as a causal process.

Theorem 4.3 (Causal ARMA). $Y_t \sim$ ARMA(p,q) *is causal if and only if the characteristic roots of* $p(\lambda) = 0$ *are inside the unit-circle.*

In the rest of this chapter, we focus on causal ARMA processes. Although this class is useful for a wide range of purposes, it is restricted in the sense that it excludes economic models where rational expectation behaviour is assumed. This follows from the fact that those models imply stochastic difference equations with at least one characteristic root larger than one in magnitude (outside the unit-circle).

However, even if we are interested in exactly those rational expectations models, it is not wasted time to have a grounding in causal processes. One reason is that the solution of forward-looking models can be expressed in terms of a causal process (see Bårdsen *et al.*, 2005, Chapter 7). We return to this point in Section 7.11.

By using Theorem 4.2, we can prove the Causal ARMA theorem. We find the one-sided filter: $\psi(L) = \sum_{j=0}^{\infty} \psi_j L^j$. From (4.40), we have

$$(1 - \phi_1 L - \cdots - \phi_p L^p)(1 + \psi_1 L + \cdots) = (1 + \theta_1 L + \cdots + \theta_q L^q).$$

We carry out the multiplication and then identify the coefficients on each side of the equality signs:

$$\begin{aligned} \psi_1 - \phi_1 &= \theta_1 \\ \psi_2 - \phi_1\psi_1 - \phi_2 &= \theta_2 \\ \vdots \quad \vdots \quad &\vdots \\ \psi_q - \phi_1\psi_{q-1} - \cdots - \phi_p\psi_{q-p} &= \theta_q \\ \psi_s - \phi_1\psi_{s-1} - \cdots - \phi_p\psi_{s-p} &= 0, \quad \text{for } s > q. \end{aligned} \tag{4.44}$$

The equation in the last row is a homogeneous difference equation. The associated characteristic polynomial is

$$p(\lambda) = \lambda^p - \phi_1\lambda^{p-1} - \cdots - \phi_p,$$

i.e., the characteristic polynomial (4.42). From the theory of linear difference equations, we know that ψ_s is given as

$$\psi_s = C_1\lambda_1^s + C_2\lambda_2^s + \cdots + C_p\lambda_p^s$$

when we assume (as above) that there are p distinct characteristic roots. The C_is are determined by the q first equations in (4.44). It follows that

$$\sum_{j=0}^{\infty} |\psi_j| < \infty$$

as required of a linear filter, if and only if $|\lambda_i| < 1$, $\forall i$. Hence, a stationary solution exists if and only if $|\lambda_i| < 1$, $\forall i$, which proves Theorem 4.3.

We also see that in the discussion of AR(1) and ARMA(1, 1) above, it was the causal interpretation of the process that was used (although it was implicit there).

In the same way as in the first-order case, covariance (or weak) stationarity of a time series given by ARMA(p, q) is equivalent to the existence of a stationary solution.

Theorem 4.4 (Covariance stationarity of ARMA(p, q)). *The time series $\{Y_t; t = 0, \pm 1, \pm 2, \pm 3, \dots\}$ given by (4.37) in Definition 4.2 is covariance stationary if and only if it has a stationary solution.*

A stable and causal ARMA(p, q)-process defines Y_t as a linear filtering of the white noise process ε_t, hence:

$$Y_t - \mu = \psi(L)\varepsilon_t = \sum_{j=0}^{\infty} \psi_j \varepsilon_{t-j},$$

where $\sum_{j=0}^{\infty} |\psi_j| < \infty$. But in that case, we also have $\sum_{j=-\infty}^{\infty} |\psi_j| < \infty$, and the theorem follows from the property of well-behaved linear filters (see Appendix 4.A).

As an application of the above theorems, we obtain the ACF of the AR(p)-process:

$$Y_t - \phi_1 Y_{t-1} - \cdots - \phi_p Y_{t-p} = \phi_0 + \varepsilon_t$$

where the parameter ϕ_0 is given by

$$\phi_0 = \mu(1 - \phi_1 - \cdots - \phi_p),$$

and where μ denotes $E(Y_t)$. We start by writing the process in terms of variables that are measured as deviation from mean, i.e., from the expectation μ:

$$(Y_t - \mu) - \phi_1(Y_{t-1} - \mu) - \cdots - \phi_p(Y_{t-p} - \mu) = \varepsilon_t.$$

When we multiply by $(Y_{t-j} - \mu)$ on both sides of the equality sign, we obtain

$$(Y_t - \mu)(Y_{t-j} - \mu) - \phi_1(Y_{t-1} - \mu)(Y_{t-j} - \mu) - \cdots - \phi_p(Y_{t-p} - \mu)(Y_{t-j} - \mu)$$
$$= \varepsilon_t(Y_{t-j} - \mu).$$

We first consider $j > 0$, and note that the causality of the process implies $E(\varepsilon_t(Y_{t-j} - \mu)) = 0$. By applying the expectation operator to both sides of the equality sign, and keeping in mind that $\gamma_j = E(Y_t - \mu)(Y_{t-j} - \mu)$ is autocovariance number j, we obtain

$$\gamma_j - \phi_1\gamma_{j-1} - \cdots - \phi_p\gamma_{j-p} = 0 \quad \text{for } j > 0.$$

For the case of $j = 0$

$$\gamma_0 - \phi_1\gamma_{-1} - \cdots - \phi_p\gamma_{-p} = \sigma_\varepsilon^2.$$

Hence, γ_j can be expressed by the characteristic roots of the polynomial,

$$p(\lambda) = \lambda^p - \phi_1 \lambda^{p-1} - \cdots - \phi_p, \quad j \geq 0,$$

that is to say,

$$\gamma_j = C_1 \lambda_1^j + C_2 \lambda_2^j + \cdots + C_p \lambda_p^j, \tag{4.45}$$

where (again) the C_is denote the given numbers in the expression for the solution of the difference equation. Note that $\sum_{i=1}^{p} C_i = \gamma_0 = \text{Var}(Y_t)$.

4.5.8. The importance of initial values

In practice, we will not know the infinite history of white noise variables, and will instead base the solution on a set of initial values of Y_t. In Chapter 3, we showed that for a difference equation of order p (and setting $\phi_0 = 0$ to save notation), the solution for Y_{t+j} can be expressed as

$$\begin{aligned} Y_{t+j} = {} & b_{11}^{(j+1)} Y_{t-1} + b_{12}^{(j+1)} Y_{t-2} + \cdots + b_{1p}^{(j+1)} Y_{t-p} \\ & + b_{11}^{(j)} \varepsilon_t + b_{11}^{(j-1)} \varepsilon_{t+1} + b_{11}^{(j-2)} \varepsilon_{t+2} + \cdots + b_{11} \varepsilon_{t+j-1} + \varepsilon_{t+j}, \end{aligned} \tag{4.46}$$

where

$$b_{11}^{(j)} = c_1 \lambda_1^j + c_2 \lambda_2^j + \cdots + c_p \lambda_p^j,$$

and where the c_is are numbers (see, e.g., Section 3.6). The initial values in this case are $Y_{t-1}, \ldots, Y_{t-p}$, with weights $b_{1i}^{(j+1)}$ for $i = 1, 2, \ldots, p$. Also, these weights are linear combinations of the characteristic roots λ_i (cf. (3.53)).

Assume that $E(\varepsilon_{t+j}) = 0$, $j = 0, 1, 2, \ldots$, we obtain

$$E(Y_{t+j}) = b_{11}^{(j+1)} Y_{t-1} + b_{12}^{(j+1)} Y_{t-2} + \cdots + b_{1p}^{(j+1)} Y_{t-p}. \tag{4.47}$$

With reference to the expression for $b_{1j}^{(j+1)}$ in (3.53), we see from (4.47) that, for example, the first starting value Y_{t-1} declines in magnitude as a consequence of roots inside the unit-circle (less than one in magnitude). And the same is true for the other initial conditions. Hence, we have that $E(Y_{t+j}) \to 0$ as $j \to \infty$ if and only if all the roots are located inside the complex unit-circle.

A typical property of stationarity is therefore that the importance of the initial conditions (starting values) declines as we "move the process forward in time". A stationary process does not depend fundamentally on its starting values.

Box 4.4. The Wold decomposition

Note that (4.43) shows that Y_t can be written as a sum of a deterministic component (μ), and a random (stochastic) part $\sum_{j=0}^{\infty} \psi_j \varepsilon_{t-j}$:

$$Y_t = \mu + \sum_{j=0}^{\infty} \psi_j \varepsilon_{t-j},$$

where $\sum_{j=0}^{\infty} |\psi_j| < \infty$. We found this decomposition by starting from the assumption that Y_t is generated by an ARMA(p, q)-process, but the result is directly related to a famous theorem due to Wold (1938). Wold's theorem states that the non-deterministic part of a time series can be represented by an infinite moving average of the one-period ahead prediction errors obtained by predicting linearly Y_t from known values of $Y_{t-1}, Y_{t-2}, \ldots$, and is much cited in the literature, see e.g., Sargent (1987, pp. 297–290) and Lütkepohl (2007, pp. 25–26).

4.6. ML and OLS Estimation of the AR(1) Model

In Chapter 1, we estimated final equations of the two example models by OLS. Since the data were computer-generated, we could also observe that the OLS-estimated AR coefficients were close to the parameter values that had been used in the data generation. But was that just good luck or is OLS a sound estimation principle to use with the AR model? In this section, we give the theoretical motivation for the use of OLS to estimate the parameter of an AR(1)-process.

For reference, we give the econometric specification of the AR(1) model in compact form:

$$Y_t = \phi_0 + \phi_1 Y_{t-1} + \varepsilon_t, \quad |\phi_1| < 1, \, \varepsilon_t \sim \text{IIN}(0, \sigma_\varepsilon^2) \quad \forall t. \tag{4.48}$$

IIN is the acronym for identically and independently normally distributed. The assumption about normal (Gaussian) distribution is used to derive a log-likelihood function, and based on that, the ML estimators for the coefficients of the model in (4.48) are derived. However, the estimators have unchanged asymptotic properties if we replace the normality assumption by IID (identically and independently distributed): $\varepsilon_t \sim \text{IID}\left(0, \sigma_\varepsilon^2\right), \, \forall t$.

4.6.1. Joint probability density for AR(1)

We start by establishing the joint probability density function for the process:

$$Y_T, Y_{T-1}, \ldots, Y_1,$$

when the model is (4.48), and the initial condition Y_0 is a fixed number that we can condition the density function on. At the end of the section, we consider the consequences for the likelihood of not conditioning on a known initial condition.

The first random variable in the sample, Y_1, has a normal density, conditional on the fixed Y_0:

$$f_{Y_1|Y_0}(y_1 \mid y_0) = \frac{1}{\sqrt{2\pi}\sqrt{\sigma^2}} \exp\left(\frac{-(y_1 - \phi_0 - \phi_1 y_0)^2}{2\sigma^2}\right), \tag{4.49}$$

since

$$(Y_1 \mid Y_0 = y_0) \sim N(\phi_0 + \phi_1 y_0, \sigma^2).$$

The probability density of Y_2 and Y_1 can, as always, be written as the product of a conditional and marginal density, in our case

$$f_{Y_2,Y_1}(y_2, y_1) = f_{Y_2|Y_1}(y_2 \mid y_1) \cdot f_{Y_1|Y_0}(y_1 \mid y_0),$$

and, if we consider the three first variables in the process

$$\begin{aligned} f_{Y_3,Y_2,Y_1}(y_3, y_2, y_1) &= f_{Y_3|Y_2}(y_3 \mid y_2) \cdot f_{Y_2,Y_1}(y_2, y_1) \\ &= f_{Y_3|Y_2}(y_3 \mid y_2) \cdot f_{Y_2|Y_1}(y_2 \mid y_1) \cdot f_{Y_1|Y_0}(y_1 \mid y_0), \end{aligned}$$

where the three densities in the product are all normal densities. The same reasoning can be applied to the whole process $\{Y_T, Y_{T-1}, \ldots, Y_1\}$, and the joint probability density function can therefore be written as

$$f_{Y_T,Y_{T-1},\ldots,Y_1}(y_T, y_{T-1}, \ldots, Y_1) = \prod_{t=1}^{T} f_{Y_t|Y_{t-1}}(y_t \mid y_{t-1}),$$

and, after insertion of the expression for the normal densities:

$$f_{Y_T,Y_{T-1},\ldots,Y_1}(y_T, y_{T-1}, \ldots, y_1) = \prod_{t=1}^{T} \frac{1}{\sqrt{2\pi\sigma^2}} \exp\left(\frac{-(y_t - \phi_0 - \phi_1 y_{t-1})^2}{2\sigma^2}\right). \tag{4.50}$$

4.6.2. The log-likelihood function for AR(1)

In expression (4.50), the numbers $\pi = 3.14159$ and T are known. If we, in addition, know the values of the two coefficients in the model equation, ϕ_0 and ϕ_1, and the variance σ^2, the joint density for any outcome of the process $\{Y_T, Y_{T-1}, \dots, Y_1\}$ can be calculated, conditional on Y_0.

In practice, and because we are now considering using (4.50) for estimation, the premises are turned around: We take the realization view on the process, and regard $\{y_T, y_{T-1}, \dots, y_1\}$ as given and known, and consider the parameter vector $\boldsymbol{\theta} = (\phi_0, \phi_1, \sigma^2)'$ as unknown. In this interpretation, $\boldsymbol{\theta}$ becomes the argument in the function, and we can imagine calculating the likelihood of our particular realization of a time series for different values of the argument $\boldsymbol{\theta}$, hence the notion of a *likelihood function*. The *maximum likelihood* estimation principle states that we choose as our estimate of $\boldsymbol{\theta}$ the $\widehat{\boldsymbol{\theta}}$ which is most likely for the given sample realization. In practice, we do ML estimation after applying the logarithmic transformation to the likelihood function. The natural logarithm is a (strictly) monotonous transformation, and a value of $\boldsymbol{\theta}$ that maximizes the likelihood function will also maximize the log-likelihood function.[5]

In order to simplify the notation, we will use the symbol $\mathcal{L}$ to denote the log-likelihood function. Sometimes, we will write it with explicit arguments, $\mathcal{L}(\phi_0, \phi_1, \sigma^2)$ in the case of the AR(1) model. With the use of the new symbol, we can express the log-likelihood function based on (4.50) as

$$\mathcal{L}(\phi_0, \phi_1, \sigma^2 \mid y_0) = -\frac{T}{2}(\ln(2\pi/\sigma^2)) - \sum_{t=1}^{T} \frac{(y_t - \phi_0 - \phi_1 y_{t-1})^2}{2\sigma^2}, \quad (4.51)$$

see Exercise 4.4. Strictly speaking, this is a conditional likelihood, as we have indicated by the notation $\mid y_0$.

Note also that when we write the summation on the right-hand side as starting from $t = 1$ and ending with $t = T$, we are assuming that Y_0 is available for the calculation of the likelihood. This gives convenient notation, however, in practice one observation at the start of the sample will be lost due to the lagged variable (Y_{t-1}) in the model.

---

[5]The technical requirement of only positive arguments in the natural logarithm function is taken care of by the properties of the density functions.

4.6.3. ML estimators of AR(1) parameters

The ML estimates of the parameters $(\phi_0, \phi_1, \sigma^2)$ are determined as the values that give the maximum value of $\mathcal{L}$. However, the ML estimation principle would not be much of a principle of estimation if it was to be used only for a particular sample realization. The idea is of course to use it for any realization in the outcome set. With that in mind, the likelihood function is often expressed in term of the random variables, in our case:

$$\mathcal{L}(\phi_0, \phi_1, \sigma^2 \mid Y_0) = -\frac{T}{2}(\ln(2\pi/\sigma^2)) - \sum_{t=1}^{T} \frac{(Y_t - \phi_0 - \phi_1 Y_{t-1})^2}{2\sigma^2}. \tag{4.52}$$

By inspection of the expression, we see that the log-likelihood function is maximized for $\hat{\phi}_0$ and $\hat{\phi}_1$ that minimize the residual sum of squares (RSS):

$$\min_{\hat{\phi}_0, \phi_1} \left\{ \sum_{t=1}^{T} (Y_t - \hat{\phi}_0 - \hat{\phi}_1 Y_{t-1})^2 \right\}.$$

Hence, the OLS estimators of ϕ_0 and ϕ_1 are also the ML estimators. For reference, we give the expressions of the estimators as

$$\hat{\phi}_1 = \frac{\sum_{t=1}^{T} Y_t (Y_{t-1} - \bar{Y}_{(-)})}{\sum_{s=1}^{T} (Y_{s-1} - \bar{Y}_{(-)})^2}, \tag{4.53}$$

where $\bar{Y}_{(-)} = T^{-1} \sum_{t=1}^{T} Y_{t-1}$ and

$$\hat{\phi}_0 = \bar{Y} - \hat{\phi}_1 \bar{Y}_{(-)}, \tag{4.54}$$

see Exercise 4.5. The notation used in (4.53) and (4.54) is deliberately detailed in order to bring out explicitly that the mean in the numerator is the mean of the regressor, Y_{t-1}, and that the sum of squares in the denominator is also for the regressor Y_{t-1}. However, since it does not usually create any misunderstanding, we will often use the simpler notation

$$\hat{\phi}_1 = \frac{\sum_{t=1}^{T} Y_t (Y_{t-1} - \bar{Y})}{\sum_{t=1}^{T} (Y_{t-1} - \bar{Y})^2}, \tag{4.55}$$

and

$$\hat{\phi}_0 = \bar{Y} - \hat{\phi}_1 \bar{Y}, \tag{4.56}$$

where it is understood that $\bar{Y}$ is the mean of the lagged process $\{Y_{T-1}, Y_{T-2}, \dots, Y_0\}$.

We find the ML estimator of the variance σ^2 by maximization of the so-called concentrated log-likelihood function:

$$\mathcal{L}(\hat{\phi}_0, \hat{\phi}_1, \sigma^2 \mid Y_0) = -\frac{T}{2}(\ln(2\pi/\sigma^2)) - \frac{1}{2\sigma^2}\text{RSS}(\hat{\phi}_0, \hat{\phi}_1) \tag{4.57}$$

with respect to σ^2. $\text{RSS}(\hat{\phi}_0, \hat{\phi}_1)$ is treated as a known number in (4.57), and is defined in the usual way as

$$\text{RSS}(\hat{\phi}_0, \hat{\phi}_1) \underset{\text{def}}{=} \sum_{t=1}^{T} \hat{\varepsilon}_t^2 = \sum_{t=1}^{T}(Y_t - \phi_0 - \phi_1 Y_{t-1})^2.$$

You can solve Exercise 4.6 to show that the ML estimator of σ^2 is given by

$$\hat{\sigma}^2 = T^{-1}\sum_{t=1}^{T} \hat{\varepsilon}_t^2 = T^{-1}\sum_{t=1}^{T}\underbrace{(Y_t - \hat{\phi}_0 - \hat{\phi}_1 Y_{t-1})}_{\hat{\varepsilon}_t}]^2. \tag{4.58}$$

Before we turn to the properties of the estimators given by (4.55), (4.56) and (4.58), we will briefly consider the consequence of the alternative of *not* assuming that Y_0 is a fixed number. In that case, we cannot "start with" the conditional density of Y_1. Instead, we use the marginal density, which is also normal since Y_1 can be written as a well-behaved linear filter of $\varepsilon_1, \varepsilon_0, \dots, \varepsilon_{-\infty}$. The expectation and variance of Y_0 are

$$E(Y_1) = \frac{\phi_0}{(1-\phi_1)} = \mu,$$

$$\text{Var}(Y_1) = \frac{\sigma_\varepsilon^2}{(1-\phi_1^2)},$$

and the density function is therefore

$$f_{Y_1}(y_1) = \frac{1}{\sqrt{2\pi}\sqrt{\sigma^2/(1-\phi_1^2)}} \exp\left(\frac{-(y_1 - \phi_0/(1-\phi_1))^2}{2\sigma^2/(1-\phi_1^2)}\right). \tag{4.59}$$

The density of the sample in this case is

$$f_{Y_T, Y_{T-1}, \dots, Y_1}(y_T, y_{T-1}, \dots, Y_1) = f_{Y_1}(y_1) \times \prod_{t=2}^{T} f_{Y_t \mid Y_{t-1}}(y_t \mid y_{t-1}).$$

When we insert expressions for all the conditional densities $f_{Y_t|Y_{t-1}}(y_t \mid y_{t-1})$, we obtain

$$\begin{aligned} &f_{Y_T,Y_{T-1},\ldots,Y_1}(y_T, y_{T-1},\ldots,y_1) \\ &\quad = \frac{1}{\sqrt{2\pi}\sqrt{\sigma^2/(1-\phi_1^2)}} \exp\left(\frac{-(y_1-\phi_0/(1-\phi_1))^2}{2\sigma^2/(1-\phi_1^2)}\right) \\ &\quad \times \prod_{t=2}^{T} \frac{1}{\sqrt{2\pi\sigma^2}} \exp\left(\frac{-(y_t-\phi_0-\phi_1 y_{t-1})^2}{2\sigma^2}\right) \end{aligned} \tag{4.60}$$

and the "full" log-likelihood function:

$$\mathcal{L}(\phi_0,\phi_1,\sigma^2) = \ln(f_{Y_1}(Y_1)) - \frac{T}{2}(\ln(2\pi/\sigma^2)) - \sum_{t=2}^{T} \frac{(Y_t-\phi_0-\phi_1 Y_{t-1})^2}{2\sigma^2}. \tag{4.61}$$

The parameters ϕ_0 and ϕ_1 enter into $\ln(f_{Y_1}(Y_1))$ in a non-trivial manner. Maximization of this version of the log-likelihood function is therefore computationally more demanding than the two-step procedure that we used for the case where we regarded Y_0 as fixed. On the other hand, it is also clear that the contribution of $\ln(f_{Y_1}(Y_1))$ to the total likelihood becomes small even for a moderately large sample size T. Asymptotically, it plays no role. Hence, it is custom to simply say that the estimators that we have derived above *are* the ML estimators.

4.6.4. Monte Carlo simulation of the properties of estimators, AR(1)

We start by considering the bias of the estimator of the AR parameter $\hat{\phi}_1$. It is useful to express $\hat{\phi}_1$ as

$$\hat{\phi}_1 = \phi_1 + \frac{\sum_{t=1}^{T} \varepsilon_t (Y_{t-1} - \bar{Y}_{(-)})}{\sum_{s=1}^{T} (Y_{s-1} - \bar{Y}_{(-)})^2}, \tag{4.62}$$

see Exercise 4.7. The expectation of the difference between the ML estimator $\hat{\phi}_1$ and the AR coefficient is therefore

$$E(\hat{\phi}_1 - \phi_1) = E\left[\frac{\sum_{t=1}^{T} \varepsilon_t (Y_{t-1} - \bar{Y}_{(-)})}{\sum_{s=1}^{T} (Y_{s-1} - \bar{Y}_{(-)})^2}\right]. \tag{4.63}$$

Since the expectation operator is linear, and the bias term is a ratio of random variables, there is no simple way of finding a closed form expression for the finite sample bias. However, due to Y_{t-1}, the numerator will contain (well-behaved) filters of the disturbances as "typical elements". These random variables will be relatively smooth if $0 < \phi_1 < 1$, and since they are multiplied by single disturbances, it is possible that there is a tendency of negative correlation in the numerator. This turns out to be correct. For the case of $\phi_0 = 0$, it has been shown that an approximate expression of the finite sample bias is

$$E(\hat{\phi}_1 - \phi_1) \approx \frac{-2\phi_1}{T}. \tag{4.64}$$

This approximation is due to Hurwicz (1950), and it is therefore often referred to as the *Hurwicz bias*.[6] Equation (4.64) confirms that the ML estimator of ϕ_1 is biased in finite samples. The bias is negative for $0 < \phi_1 < 1$, so the AR coefficient tends to be underestimated. But the approximation also shows that the bias is reduced (in absolute value) as the sample size increases.

The size and "behaviour" of the finite sample bias can be illustrated for more general processes with the aid of Monte Carlo simulation, which we will now give a first example of.

The aim of Monte Carlo simulation is to give a numerical assessment of an estimator (the OLS estimator of ϕ_1, for example), or of a test statistic (the standard 't-value' used to test the hypothesis that $\phi_1 = 0$, for example) under known properties about the stochastic process. Hence, to do a Monte Carlo analysis we need to specify a time series process, called the Data Generation Process (DGP), as mentioned above, see Box 2.7.

In our first Monte Carlo analysis, we specify the DGP as

$$Y_t = 0.5 + 0.8Y_{t-1} + \varepsilon_t, \quad \varepsilon_t \sim \text{IIN}\,(0, 1)\,. \tag{4.65}$$

The estimator bias that we want to assess is (4.63) above. It is for the OLS estimator $\hat{\phi}_1$, estimated by the use of correctly specified regression model, namely a model equation which includes an intercept (constant) and the correct regressor (the first lag Y_{t-1}). In other applications, the purpose may be to assess the properties (e.g., bias) of an estimator of an econometric model, which is misspecified relative to the DGP. However, we first assess

[6] A slightly better approximation, based in a so-called response surface in Hendry (1984), is

$$E(\hat{\phi}_1 - \phi_1) \approx \frac{-1.8\phi_1}{(T+2)}.$$

the OLS estimator of ϕ_1 in the most favourable situation, when the model we estimate conforms with the DGP.

To do the simulation, we used the Monte Carlo package in OxMetrics, which is called PcNaive (Doornik and Hendry, 2013b). The code we have specified generates 1000 time series, each with 96 observations $t = 1, 2, \ldots, 96$. We first collect and store the mean of 1000 estimations using an initial sample with very few observations, e.g., $T = T_{\text{min}}$. We next do 1000 estimations with one more observation included in the sample, $T = T_{\text{min}} + 1$, and so on until we reach the maximum sample length, $T_{\text{max}} = 95$ (note that one observation is lost due to the lag). By plotting the averages (of the 1000 estimates) against the sample length (T), we obtain a visualization of how the bias develops as a function of the sample size:

$$\hat{E}(\widehat{\phi}_{1,T} - \phi_1) = \frac{1}{1000}\sum_{i=1}^{1000}(\widehat{\phi}_{1,T,i} - 0.8), \quad T = T_{\text{min}}, \ldots, T_{\text{max}} = 95. \tag{4.66}$$

The "hat" in $\hat{E}$ is used to denote that this is the Monte Carlo estimate of the true bias of the AR parameter in the case where the true value of $\phi_1 = 0.8$ (and the process in other respects is given as in (4.65)). The idea is of course that for 1000 ensembles and estimations, the estimated bias becomes a good approximation to the true bias.

We make the same assessment of the bias of the estimation of the intercept:

$$\hat{E}(\widehat{\phi}_{0,T} - \phi_0) = \frac{1}{1000}\sum_{i=1}^{1000}(\widehat{\phi}_{0,T,i} - 0.5), \quad T = T_{\text{min}}, \ldots, T_{\text{max}} = 95.$$

The result of the Monte Carlo simulation is shown in Figure 4.4, panels (a) and (b). The biases in panel (a) are negative, and quite large in magnitude for sample lengths shorter than 20 periods. The underestimation of the AR coefficient confirms both our intuitive reasoning and the expression for the *Hurwicz bias* above (although strictly speaking, that expression is for the case of no constant term in the DGP and model). The size of the bias is reduced markedly for sample length 60 for example, and continues to fall in magnitude as the sample size in increased. The monotonous reduction of the bias makes it possible to believe in the theory saying that the coefficient would become perfectly estimated in an infinitely large sample (consistency of the OLS estimator).

Panel (b) shows the same development of the bias in the estimator of the constant term ϕ_0 as the sample length is increased. Note the differences

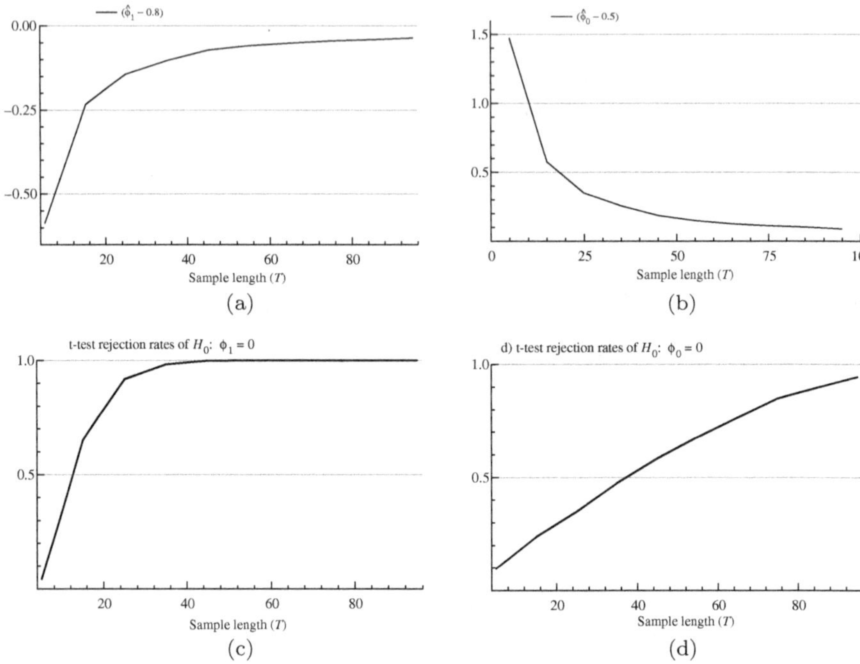

Figure 4.4. Results of Monte Carlo simulation of the OLS estimators of ϕ_0 and ϕ_1 when the DGP is (4.65). The bias of the estimated AR term (panel (a)) and the constant term (panel (b)). Panels (c) and (d) show rejection frequencies based on conventional t-values, using 5% critical values, for the null hypotheses of $\phi_1 = 0$ (panel c)) and $\phi_0 = 0$ (panel d)).

in scale on the two y-axes, indicating that for small and moderate size it is actually more difficult to estimate the constant term than it is to estimate the AR coefficient. This result has important implications for forecasting, a point that we will develop in a later chapter.

In addition to finite sample coefficient biases, Monte Carlo simulation can be used to assess test statistics, for example, t-values for individual coefficients. For the AR coefficient, the t-value is

$$t\text{-value} = \frac{\hat{\phi}_1}{\sqrt{\text{Var}(\hat{\phi}_1)}}.$$

Panels (c) and (d) show rejection ratios for the t-values used to test the two null hypotheses of $\phi_1 = 0$ and $\phi_0 = 0$, respectively. The rejection rates are based on 5% critical values. We see that the rejection frequencies increase quite rapidly to unity (1000 rejections out of 1000 tests performed) for the AR coefficient, and more slowly for the intercept (even if the estimated constant is overestimated in moderate samples). Despite the finite sample coefficient biases, the probability of Type-II error is very low for moderate samples, in particular for the hypothesis that $\phi_1 = 0$ when the true value is $\phi_1 = 0.8$.

In order to check the probability of Type-I error, we re-ran the Monte Carlo experiment with $\phi_1 = 0$. In this case, the rejection rates for $\phi_1 = 0$ came close to the nominal significance level of 5% and 10%, also for the moderate sample size like 30. Hence, the standard inference procedure seems to give Type-I error probabilities that are very close to the formal significance level (the test appears to be "correctly sized").

These simple experiments illustrate that the standard t-value can be used for statistical inference for the AR(1) model. Hence, inference is not much affected by the *Hurwicz biases* in the coefficient estimates. This is because $\sqrt{\text{Var}(\hat{\phi}_1)}$ is also affected, and in a way that cancels the bias in the numerator of the "t-value".

In fact, the good news is more general: For correctly specified dynamic econometric models, the standard econometric inference procedures, based on t-values, F-statistics (for joint hypotheses) and Chi-squared distributed likelihood-ratio test-statistics, continue to hold. This indicates that the main challenge for modelling of stationary time series is not to invent a new inference theory, tailormade for time series so to speak. The challenge is instead to be able to formulate, or discover, relationships that are close enough approximations to the data generating process (DGP) to be treated as not misspecified econometric models.

4.7. ML Estimation of the AR(p) Model

The estimation methodology for the AR(1) model equation extends to models with higher order AR dynamics, i.e., with p-lags.

If the error term is Gaussian white noise, the OLS estimators of $\phi_0, \phi_1, \ldots, \phi_p$ are (conditional) ML estimators. The OLS estimators are consistent. They are affected by biases of the Hurwicz type in small samples. However, conventional t-values (and Chi-square or F-distributed tests for composite null hypotheses) give reliable inference.

4.8. ML Estimation of ARMA Processes

In the same spirit as for the AR(1) process, a conditional likelihood function can be formulated for ARMA(1, 1). But unlike the AR(1), the conditional likelihood function is nonlinear both for MA and mixed processes like ARMA(1, 1). However, modern statistical and econometric computer software allows fast and reliable maximization of the conditional likelihood (e.g., based on setting $\varepsilon_0 = 0$). Exact maximum likelihood estimation requires specifying the distribution for the initial observations and disturbances, see e.g., Harvey (1993). In practice, the approximate ML estimators are obtained by nonlinear least squares (NLS).

We can illustrate the estimation by using the simulated ARMA(1, 1) time series that we showed the ACF of in Figure 4.2 and the PACF of in Figure 4.3. Since we use a single realization of the time series, not of a large number of replication, it is not a genuine Monte Carlo analysis. It can nevertheless be of interest to see how close the NLS comes to the true parameters in a "one-off Monte Carlo". Using NLS and the time series underlying the ARMA(1, 1) parts of Figures 4.2 and 4.3, we obtain

$$\hat{Y}_t = \underset{(0.118)}{0.755} Y_{t-1} - \underset{(0.167)}{0.376}\ \varepsilon_{t-1},$$

for 100 observations. Both parameters become overestimated in absolute value, as the true AR coefficient is 0.60 and the true MA coefficient is −0.3. Although this is only a particular case, it may also be seen as a signal of the more general difficulties associated with estimating models that contain both AR and moving average terms. Intuitively, this reflects the tendency of the AR part to become dominant in ACF, as we saw analytically above.

4.9. Multiple Equation Processes

For a dynamic multivariate and multiple equation system to be dubbed stationary, we require that all the endogenous processes of the system have globally asymptotically stable solutions. Not surprisingly, a corresponding requirement on the characteristic roots of the system as we have for a single process does exist, as the Chapter 5 will show. Moreover, the estimation theory that we have introduced above carries over to dynamic systems. For example, subject to approximate normality of disturbances, OLS gives conditional maximum likelihood estimators also for the class of dynamic systems known as *Vector Autoregressive Systems*, usually referred to by the acronym VAR. The estimation of VAR models is the topic of Chapter 5.

To round-off this chapter, we draw the line back to Chapter 3, and establish the equivalence between the multivariate AR process, i.e., VAR, and the systems of difference equations that we considered in that chapter.

The simplest example is a system with two-time series variables, no intercepts, and with first-order dynamics:

$$\begin{pmatrix} Y_t \\ X_t \end{pmatrix} = \begin{pmatrix} \phi_{11} & \phi_{12} \\ \phi_{21} & \phi_{22} \end{pmatrix} \begin{pmatrix} Y_{t-1} \\ X_{t-1} \end{pmatrix} + \begin{pmatrix} \varepsilon_{yt} \\ \varepsilon_{xt} \end{pmatrix}, \tag{4.67}$$

where $\varepsilon_{y,t}$ and $\varepsilon_{x,t}$ are two white noise processes, which are in general correlated.

Although it is possible to specify multivariate and multiple equation ARMA processes, we will not follow that line of modelling in this book. The reason is that a mildly over-specified AR system will approximate a vector ARMA process relatively well at the same time as it will be much easier to estimate. By "over-specified", we mean that the order of autoregression may be a little higher than the "p" in an exact vector ARMA(p, q) with $q > 0$. In many applications, this seems to be a "low price to pay" for feasibility (robustness and ease) of estimation.

With reference to Chapter 3, we see that the bivariate system (4.67) has exactly the same form as the system of difference equations in (3.108). Hence, with reference to the final equation that we introduced in Section 3.7, we can write Y_t in terms of Y_{t-1}, Y_{t-2} and a disturbance.

With the use the lag-polynomial:

$$\pi(L) = 1 - \phi_1 L - \phi_2 L^2,$$

where the coefficients are given by $\phi_1 = (\phi_{11} + \phi_{22})$ and $\phi_2 = (\phi_{12}\phi_{21} - \phi_{22}\phi_{11})$, the final equation for Y_t becomes

$$\pi(L)Y_t = \varepsilon_t,$$

where ε_t is given by

$$\varepsilon_t = \varepsilon_{yt} - \phi_{22}\varepsilon_{yt-1} + \phi_{12}\varepsilon_{xt-1}.$$

The associated characteristic polynomial is

$$p(\lambda) = \lambda^2 - \phi_1\lambda - \phi_2. \tag{4.68}$$

From Theorem 4.2, we know that Y_t has a stationary solution if the roots of $p(\lambda) = 0$ are less than one in magnitude (modulus less than one). We also know that subject to the same condition, Y_t is a stationary process, and that the stationary solution can be expressed as a well-defined filter of ε_t. From Chapter 3, we also have that the same final equation applies to X_t. Hence for Y_t and X_t to be jointly stationary, none of the characteristic roots (of their common final equation) can be equal to one in magnitude. For causal vector processes to be stationary, this means in particular that all roots must be located inside the complex unit-circle.

The stationarity conditions of more general VARs can also be formulated in terms of the eigenvalues of the companion matrix of Section 3.8. Let $\mathbf{Y}_t$ denote the vector containing n time series variables, each of them following a difference equation of order p. The n-dimensional VAR-process of order p can be written as in (3.119), (3.120) and (3.121) in Section 3.8. The matrix $\mathbf{B}$, defined in equation (3.120), is the companion matrix of the VAR. The VAR defines a multivariate covariance stationary process if and only if all the roots of

$$|\mathbf{B} - \lambda\mathbf{I}| = 0$$

have modulus less than one. Again, it can be added that this applies to causal processes. In general, no eigenvalue can be located on the unit-circle.

The VAR with first-order dynamics, VAR(1), two variables ($n = 2$), and with constant terms included, is

$$\begin{pmatrix} Y_t \\ X_t \end{pmatrix} = \begin{pmatrix} \phi_{10} \\ \phi_{20} \end{pmatrix} + \begin{pmatrix} \phi_{11} & \phi_{12} \\ \phi_{21} & \phi_{22} \end{pmatrix} \begin{pmatrix} Y_{t-1} \\ X_{t-1} \end{pmatrix} + \begin{pmatrix} \varepsilon_{yt} \\ \varepsilon_{xt} \end{pmatrix}. \tag{4.69}$$

This two-equation dynamic system is a generalization of (4.67), as the constant terms ϕ_{10}, ϕ_{20} were set to zero in that system.

Inclusion of non-zero intercepts in the VAR has no implications for the question about stationarity or not, since ϕ_{10}, ϕ_{20} will belong to the non-homogeneous part of the difference equation we have introduced as the final equation. Correspondingly, the companion matrix will always be constructed from the matrices with the AR coefficients. However, in the stationary case, the inclusion of the non-zero constant terms implies that the unconditional expectations $E(X_t) = \mu_x$ and $E(Y_t) = \mu_y$ are also non-zero parameters, which is important in applications.

4.10. Summary and Looking Ahead

Taken together, Chapters 3 and 4 represent a grounding in difference equations and time series processes. The concept of stationary of time series is fundamental for both statistical time series analysis and for dynamic econometric modelling. This is true even when we leave the realm of stationarity and venture into the modelling of non-stationary time series. Because, without a clear understanding of stationarity, how can we hope to identify (and give appropriate treatment to) non-stationarities in economic time series?

This chapter ends with a generalization from a single stationary variable to a vector autoregressive process, VAR. We confirmed that there is a duality between the notion of a vector stationary process and the stationarity of one of the variables that are endogenous in the dynamic system. For example, the conditions for stationarity can either be checked from the eigenvalues of the companion matrix or from the characteristic roots of the final form equation for one of the endogenous variables.

The VAR will play a prominent role in the following chapters. In Chapter 5, where the topic is econometric modelling of stationary variables, the VAR is the main statistical model. However, although the VAR may be of interest in its own right, for example, for forecasting, in many other cases there are other models that we want to formulate and estimate. Such models may be conditional regression models or systems of simultaneous equations, as well as recursive equations. We will see that it can be tested whether the models preserve the statistical information of the VAR, at the same time as they may have a clearer economic interpretation. As we shall see, a coherent methodology can be developed on the basis of the chapters that we have been through.

4.11. Exercises

Exercise 4.1. Let

$$Y_t = a + \varepsilon_t,$$

where ε_t is white noise, and a is a constant. Is Y_t a stationary time series variable?

Exercise 4.2. Show (4.14) and (4.17).

Exercise 4.3. Explain how the ACF of an AR(1)-process can be written:

$$\zeta_1 = \phi_1 \zeta_0 = \phi_1$$

$$\zeta_2 = \phi_1 \zeta_1 = \phi_1^2$$

$$\vdots$$

$$\zeta_j = \phi_1 \zeta_{j-1} = \phi_1^j,$$

and sketch the graphs of two functions for $\phi_1 = 0.5$ and $\phi_1 = -0.5$.

Exercise 4.4. Derive the log-likelihood expression in equation (4.51).

Exercise 4.5. Derive the expressions for the ML estimators of ϕ_0 and ϕ_1 in the Gaussian AR(1) model.

Exercise 4.6. Derive the expressions for the ML estimator of σ_ε^2 in the Gaussian AR(1) model.

Exercise 4.7. Derive the decomposition of the expression of $\hat{\phi}_1$ given in equation (4.62).

Exercise 4.8. Estimate AR(2) models for the variables *price* and *qty* in the fish market dataset in Exercise 1.7, and comment on the results.

Exercise 4.9. Extend the two AR(2) models in Section 4.8 with the two dummy variables *stormy* and *hol*. How does the extension affect the results?

Appendix 4.A. Preservation of Stationarity by Linear Filtering

A fundamental result in time series analysis is that by applying a well-defined linear filter to a stationary times series, another stationary process is produced.

Theorem 4.A.1 (Preservation of stationarity). *Assume that*

$$X_t; \{t = \ldots - 2, -1, 0, 1, 2, \ldots\}$$

is a covariance stationary time series with ACF $\gamma_x(h)$, $h = 0, \pm 1, \pm 2 \ldots$, *and let*

$$\psi(L) = \sum_{j=-\infty}^{\infty} \psi_j L^j$$

represent a linear filter with $\sum_{j=-\infty}^{\infty} |\psi_j| < 0$. *Then,*

$$Y_t = \psi(L)X_t = \sum_{j=-\infty}^{\infty} \psi_j X_{t-j}$$

is a stationary series with ACF:

$$\gamma_y(h) = \sum_{j=-\infty}^{\infty} \sum_{k=-\infty}^{\infty} \psi_j \psi_k \gamma_x(h - j + k).$$

The proof of this result makes use of the *norm of a random variable* and of *convergence in expected (mean) squared deviation.*

Definition 4.A.1 (Norm of a random variable). The norm of a random variable Z is defined as

$$\|Z\| = \sqrt{E(Z^2)}.$$

Note the similarity between this concept and the modulus (or norm) of a complex number that we defined above. The *distance* between two random variables Z and Y can be defined as the norm of $Z - Y$:

$$\|Z - Y\| = \sqrt{E(Z - Y)^2}.$$

Definition 4.A.2 (Convergence in expected (mean) squared deviation). Let $X_n = X_1, X_2, \ldots$ represent a sequence of random variables. X_n converges to X in expected (mean) squared deviations (ms),

$$X_n \overset{ms}{\to} X,$$

if $\|X_n - X\| \underset{n\to\infty}{\to} 0$.

Hence, convergence in expected (mean) squared deviations can be expressed as $\|X_n - X\| \underset{n\to\infty}{\to} 0$, or equivalently, as $E\left[(X_n - X)^2\right] \underset{n\to\infty}{\to} 0$, which can also be written as $\lim_{n\to\infty} E\left[(X_n - X)^2\right] = 0$.

A notation which is used frequently is $\underset{n\to\infty}{\text{l.i.m.}} X_n = 0$, where "l.i.m." is short for "limit in the mean". Note also that convergence in expected squared deviation is stronger than limit in probability. We have

$$X_n \overset{ms}{\to} X \Rightarrow \text{plim}\{X_n\} = X,$$

which follows from the inequality:[7]

$$P(|X_n - X| > \varepsilon) \leq \frac{(X_n - X)}{\varepsilon^2}.$$

We note that convergence in expected (mean) squared deviations is transferred to the moments.

Theorem 4.A.2 (Convergence of moments). *If $X_n \overset{ms}{\to} X$ and $Y_n \overset{ms}{\to} Y$, then*

$$E(X_n) \overset{ms}{\to} E(X)$$
$$\mathrm{Var}(X_n) \overset{ms}{\to} \mathrm{Var}(X)$$
$$\mathrm{Cov}(X_n, Y_n) \overset{ms}{\to} \mathrm{Cov}(X, Y).$$

In order to show convergence in expected (mean) squared deviations, the following theorem is also useful.

Theorem 4.A.3 (Cauchy's convergence criterium). *Let $X_1, X_2, \ldots$ be a sequence of random variables with finite variance, so that the following condition holds:*

$$\|X_n - X_m\| \underset{n,m\to\infty}{\to} 0$$

where n and m both can grow towards infinity, and independently of each other. In this case, a unique random variable X, with finite variance, exists, so that $X_n \overset{ms}{\to} X$ as $n \to \infty$.

The benefit of this theorem is that it makes it possible to assert the existence of the variable X also in cases where we are unable to find an explicit expression for X or its distribution function.[8]

To sketch a proof of Theorem 4.A.1, we first note that the infinite sequence $Y_t = \sum_{j=-\infty}^{\infty} \psi_j X_{t-j}$ converges in ms. The existence of Y_t follows from Cauchy's convergence criterium: Let us focus on one side of the

[7]Markov's inequality: If $Z \geq 0$ is an arbitrary random variable which cannot take negative values, we have $P(Z > \varepsilon) \leq \mathsf{E}[Z^2]/\varepsilon^2$.

[8]Hamilton (1994) refers to Cauchy's convergence criterium on several occasions, for example in Chapter 3 of his book.

filter $\sum_{j=0}^{\infty} \psi_j X_{t-j}$. We note that, due to stationarity, $E(X_t) = \mu_x$ independently of t, and $|\gamma_x(h)| \leq \gamma_x(0)$. Define the variable S_n as

$$S_n = \sum_{j=0}^{n} \psi_j X_{t-j}.$$

Remember that $E(X\,Y) = \text{Cov}(X, Y) + E(X)E(Y)$. Let $n > m$, then

$$\begin{aligned}
\|S_n - S_m\|^2 &= E\left[\left(\sum_{j=m+1}^{n} \psi_j X_{t-j}\right)^2\right] \\
&= \sum_{k=m+1}^{n} \sum_{j=m+1}^{n} \psi_j \psi_k \left[\text{Cov}\left(X_{t-j}, X_{t-k}\right) + E\left(X_{t-j}\right) E\left(X_{t-k}\right)\right] \\
&\leq \sum_{k=m+1}^{n} \sum_{j=m+1}^{n} |\psi_j|\,|\psi_k| \left[|\gamma_x(k-j)| + \mu_x^2\right] \\
&\leq \sum_{k=m+1}^{n} \sum_{j=m+1}^{n} |\psi_j|\,|\psi_k| \left[\gamma_x(0) + \mu_x^2\right] \\
&= \left[\gamma_x(0) + \mu_x^2\right] \sum_{k=m+1}^{n} \sum_{j=m+1}^{n} |\psi_j|\,|\psi_k| \\
&= \left[\gamma_x(0) + \mu_x^2\right] \left(\sum_{j=m+1}^{n} |\psi_j|\right)^2 \\
&\leq \left[\gamma_x(0) + \mu_x^2\right] \left(\sum_{j=m+1}^{\infty} |\psi_j|\right)^2 \underset{m\to\infty}{\to} 0.
\end{aligned}$$

from the definition of convergence of $\sum_{j=0}^{\infty} |\psi_j|$. This shows that $\|S_n - S_m\| \underset{n,m\to\infty}{\to} 0$. A symmetric argument holds for the other side of the filter, and secures the existence of Y_t as

$$Y_t = \underset{n\to\infty}{\text{l.i.m.}} \sum_{j=-n}^{n} \psi_j X_{t-j}.$$

The ACF follows from Theorem 4.A.2.

Chapter 5

The VAR

The multivariate counterpart to the ARMA process of Chapter 4 is the vector-ARMA process, which can generally be well approximated by a vector autoregressive (VAR) process. In this chapter, we review an important theorem about maximum likelihood estimation of VARs. The theorem gives a basis for valid statistical inference not only for VARs, but also for the different econometric models related to the VAR that we discuss in the following chapters. We give examples of VAR estimation, and the chapter ends with a section about the use of VARs for the purpose of forecasting.

5.1. Introduction

The estimation of stationary time series represents the backbone of dynamic econometrics. This is true, even though the real-world data that we want to build empirical models for are typically wide-sense non-stationary. The theory of estimation of stationary time series (ARMA) is based on assumptions that are in general too strong to be tenable in practice. How can we then claim that the study of the stationary framework is essential? Why not "move directly to" the non-stationary case?

There are two main reasons. The first is that a good understanding of the stationary case gives the best background for understanding the challenges to time series econometrics that non-stationarity represents, and to the solutions and tools that statisticians and econometricians have come up with. The second is related, but more linked to practical modelling methodology: Often, the variable set chosen for modelling can be analyzed in a stationary framework after initial treatment of non-stationarities. That stage of an applied modelling project can involve removal of unit roots either by differencing or by cointegration restrictions (Chapter 10). It can also entail the inclusion of a deterministic trend and seasonal dummies. Finally, location shifts in the distribution of an endogenous variable may need to be captured by indicator variables (also known as dummies).

Of course, the second type of treatment is so common in econometrics that we often do not even think of it as a non-stationary aspect of our model. But conceptually it is, and the OLS estimators of the trend coefficient may, for example, have properties that are different from the distributions the coefficients of the random time series variables in our model. The third treatment also has a long tradition in econometric modelling, but it is only recently that the status of dummies has changed from a sort of "patching-up" device to a method for achieving robust estimators of parameters of interest in a wide-sense non-stationary world; see Hendry and Doornik (2014) for a comprehensive exposition.

We return to the different aspects of non-stationarity in Chapter 9. As noted, the importance of those issues will hopefully be easier to appreciate against the background of this chapter on the modelling of stationary data.

In this chapter, we review an important theorem about maximum likelihood estimation of the coefficients of VAR, which in many ways represents the foundation for valid statistical inference not only for VARs but also for the different econometric models of the VAR that we discuss in the following chapters.

5.2. Estimation of the VAR

Chapter 4 established ARMA(p, q) as a general class of stationary processes, and we ended the chapter by noting the close link between a univariate ARMA model and the final equation of a system of difference equations. As noted, such systems are known as vector autoregressions, or vector autoregressive systems or models, best known by its acronym VAR.

In Chapter 4, we also looked at the properties of the OLS estimator of the coefficient of the simplest VAR, namely, the AR(1) model,

$$Y_t = \phi_0 + \phi_1 Y_{t-1} + \varepsilon_t, \quad |\phi_1| < 1, \, t = 1, \ldots, T, \tag{5.1}$$

where $\varepsilon_1, \varepsilon_2, \ldots, \varepsilon_T$ represent a white noise process, $\varepsilon_t \sim \text{IID}\left(0, \sigma_\varepsilon^2\right)$, $\forall t$. The main conclusion was that the OLS estimator $\hat{\phi}_1$ is consistent, but that it is biased in finite samples. That finite sample bias is known as Hurwicz bias. It is an inevitable consequence of dynamics since Y_{t-1} is a predetermined variable, not a strictly exogenous variable.

However, in most cases, the magnitude of the Hurwicz bias of $\hat{\phi}_1$ is not large, and it will decline quite rapidly toward zero as T increases. $\hat{\phi}_1$ is asymptotically normally distributed, and the conventional t-statistic can be used to test hypotheses because the t-statistic has a standard normal distribution under the null hypothesis $\phi_1 = 0$.

As noted, (5.1) is the simplest VAR we can imagine: A VAR of dimension one, and with first-order dynamics. A very important result for time series econometrics is therefore that the properties of the OLS estimators of the simplest model can be generalized to a high-dimensional VAR with higher order dynamics. We give that result in Theorem 5.1.

The simplest example of a genuine dynamic system of variables is the bivariate VAR(1) in (4.69), which we reproduce for completeness:

$$\begin{pmatrix} Y_t \\ X_t \end{pmatrix} = \begin{pmatrix} \phi_{10} \\ \phi_{20} \end{pmatrix} + \begin{pmatrix} \phi_{11} & \phi_{12} \\ \phi_{21} & \phi_{22} \end{pmatrix} \begin{pmatrix} Y_{t-1} \\ X_{t-1} \end{pmatrix} + \begin{pmatrix} \varepsilon_{yt} \\ \varepsilon_{xt} \end{pmatrix}. \tag{5.2}$$

Here, and for general VAR below, we regard the *initial* values as given numbers. In this case, the initial values are held in a single vector $(Y_0, X_0)'$. When the assumption of independent and identically Gaussian disturbances is explicit:

$$\begin{pmatrix} \varepsilon_{yt} \\ \varepsilon_{xt} \end{pmatrix} \sim \text{IIN}\left(\begin{pmatrix} 0 \\ 0 \end{pmatrix}, \underbrace{\begin{pmatrix} \sigma_x^2 & \sigma_{xy} \\ \sigma_{xy} & \sigma_y^2 \end{pmatrix}}_{\boldsymbol{\Sigma}} \right), \quad t = 1, \ldots, T. \tag{5.3}$$

it is the custom to refer to (5.2) as a Gaussian VAR.

The T variable pairs $(\varepsilon_{yt}, \varepsilon_{xt})$ are mutually independent with identical bivariate normal distributions. The matrix with variances and the covariance will be denoted by $\boldsymbol{\Sigma}$ as indicated in (5.3). It represents the instantaneous covariance matrix of $(\varepsilon_{yt}, \varepsilon_{xt})'$.

In the general case, we collect the Y_{it}, $i = 1, 2, \ldots, n$, endogenous variables in the vector

$$\underset{(n\times 1)}{\mathbf{y}_t} = (Y_{1t}, Y_{2t}, \ldots, Y_{nt})',$$

and express the n-dimensional VAR(p) as:

$$\mathbf{y}_t = \mathbf{\Phi}_1 \mathbf{y}_{t-1} + \mathbf{\Phi}_2 \mathbf{y}_{t-2} + \cdots + \mathbf{\Phi}_p \mathbf{y}_{t-p} + \mathbf{\Upsilon}\mathbf{D}_t + \boldsymbol{\varepsilon}_t \quad (5.4)$$

where $\mathbf{\Phi}_i$ $(i = 1, 2, \ldots, p)$ are $(n \times n)$ matrices holding the coefficients of the lagged variables, and $\boldsymbol{\varepsilon}_t$ is Gaussian multivariate white noise:

$$\boldsymbol{\varepsilon}_t \sim \text{IIN}(\mathbf{0}, \mathbf{\Sigma}), \quad (5.5)$$

where the elements in the covariance matrix $\mathbf{\Sigma}$ are σ_i^2 $(i = 1, 2, \ldots, n)$ and σ_{ij}, $i \neq j$. To simplify the notation, we have suppressed the conditioning on history.

In (5.4), we have also generalized the notation for the deterministic part of the equation by including the matrix $\mathbf{D}_t$. The corresponding matrix with coefficients is denoted as $\mathbf{\Upsilon}$. In the simplest case, $\mathbf{D}_t$ is a single column vector which takes the value of one for all t, i.e., there is a constant term (intercept) in each equation. For quarterly and monthly data, it is common to allow seasonal variation in the intercepts, which is achieved by the use of seasonal dummies. A deterministic trend can also be included in $\mathbf{D}_t$, as well as impulse indicators variables (i.e., dummies) which take the value of +1 in a single time period and zero in all other periods. Step indicators (step dummies) are also useful variables in empirical models. Step indicators can be constructed as sums of impulse indicators, as a step dummy is the sum of indicators for every observations from T_1 to T, where $T_1 < T$ denotes a subsample.

We can note that although the deterministic terms in $\mathbf{D_t}$ imply that the expectations of the variables in $\mathbf{y}_t$ depend on time, we may still interpret the variables in $\mathbf{y}_t$ as covariance stationary. This is reasonable since, as we have seen above, stationarity depends on the eigenvalues of the companion matrix that we construct from the matrices $\mathbf{\Phi}_i$ with autoregressive coefficients. In other words, stationarity (or not) depends on the magnitudes of the characteristic roots associated with the homogeneous difference equation that the variables have in common. $\mathbf{D_t}$ is not a part of the homogeneous equations. The role of the deterministic variables (constant terms, dummies and trends) is another, and that is to affect the particular solution.

Hence, the wide-sense non-stationarity that is represented by inclusion of deterministic terms $\mathbf{D_t}$ in the model, can be thought of as something that we can "keep inside" the stationarity modelling framework by conditioning on those terms. Perhaps, for that reason, one terminology which is quite common for the case where $\mathbf{D}_t$ includes trends is that $\mathbf{y}_t$ is *trend-stationary* around a (deterministic) trend.

Box 5.1. Location-shift and Frisch–Waugh theorem

The interpretation of the deterministic trends in VARs is also related to the Frisch–Waugh theorem (see Section 2.6.6). If we regress $\mathbf{y_t}$ on $\mathbf{D_t}$, calculate the n residual time series and estimate a VAR(p) with the use of those residuals, we obtain the same estimates of $\mathbf{\Phi}_i$ $(i = 1, 2, \ldots, p)$ as we do if we estimate (5.4) directly (in one step). Hence, if the VAR variables are subject to location-shifts, which can be represented by deterministic terms, it does not matter for the results whether we "regress-out" the location-shifts before estimation of the VAR or include the deterministic terms as regressors.

Theorem 5.1 gives an important formal basis for estimation of VAR systems.

Theorem 5.1 (Maximum likelihood estimation of VAR by OLS). *If* $\mathbf{y}_t$ *is covariance stationary, and given by* (5.4) *and* (5.5), *and there are no restrictions on the parameters* $\mathbf{\Phi}_i$ $(i = 1, 2, \ldots, p)$, $\mathbf{\Upsilon}$ *and* $\mathbf{\Sigma}$, *the OLS estimators of* $\mathbf{\Phi}_i$ $(i = 1, 2, \ldots, p)$, $\mathbf{\Upsilon}$, *are approximate maximum likelihood estimators (MLEs). The MLE of* $\mathbf{\Sigma}$ *is given by the means of the sums of squared OLS residuals, i.e.,* $1/n \sum_{t=1}^{n} \hat{\varepsilon}_{it}\hat{\varepsilon}_{jt}$, *for all* i *and* j.

Proofs of Theorem 5.1 are available in textbooks in multivariate time series analysis; see Johansen (1995, Chapter 2) Hamilton (1994, Chapter 11 and Section 16.3), Harvey (1993, Section 5.7), among others.

Intuitively, the result follows because maximization of the conditional log-likelihood function of the multivariate time series $\mathbf{y}_t$, made analytically tractable by the normality assumption (5.5), is achieved by minimization of the sum of squared residuals. As the attentive reader will already have noted, this is a generalization of the argument that we presented in Sections 4.6.1–4.6.3, for $Y_t \sim \text{AR}(1)$.

In the same way as for the AR(1) case, the word "approximate" in the theorem reminds us that the likelihood function we maximize is conditional on the fixed initial conditions, $\mathbf{y}_0, \mathbf{y}_{-1}, \ldots, \mathbf{y}_{-p+1}$. The unconditional log-likelihood function is nonlinear in the VAR case, as it was for the AR(1) model. However, for moderately large samples, it is custom to regard the conditional log-likelihood function as a sufficiently good approximation to the exact likelihood.

Since the right-hand side variables in the VAR are lags of the endogenous variables, they are not strictly exogenous regressors. Under the assumption of the Gaussian VAR they are however predetermined variables. It follows that the ML estimators of $\mathbf{\Phi}_i$ $(i = 1, 2, \ldots, p)$ are biased in small samples (cf. Hurwicz-bias). However, they are consistent estimators.

The practical importance of the theorem is that we obtain ML estimators of the parameters by using OLS on each row (line) in the VAR, as if they were separate regression equations. Due to the normality assumption, as a generalization of (4.51), the conditional likelihood function of the VAR is a linear function of the n sums of squared OLS residuals. We can use the subscript U to denote results from *unrestricted* estimation, hence RSS_U^* denotes the minimum value of the unrestricted residual sum of squares. The maximum of the likelihood function, $\mathcal{L}_U^*$, is a function of RSS_U^*.

Often, we want to test hypotheses about the validity of restrictions on the parameters $\mathbf{\Phi}_i$ $(i = 1, 2, \ldots, p)$, $\mathbf{\Upsilon}$ of the VAR. A null hypotheses can apply within equations, as well as between equations, often referred to as cross-equation restrictions. With the aid of modern econometric software packages, the estimation of a *restricted* VAR, with the parameter restrictions implied by the null hypothesis under test, does not represent any practical problem. We refer to the restricted minimized sum of squared residuals as RSS_R^* and the corresponding restricted maximum of the log-likelihood function as $\mathcal{L}_R^*$.

For ease of reference, we collect the points in the above paragraphs in Box 5.2.

Box 5.2. Consistency of estimators and hypothesis testing in the VAR

(1) The MLE estimators of $\mathbf{\Phi}_i$ $(i = 1, 2, \ldots, p)$ and $\mathbf{\Upsilon}$ mentioned in Theorem 5.1 are consistent estimators.
(2) If $\mathbf{\Sigma}$ is estimated by a consistent estimator, for example, the MLE mentioned in Theorem 5.1, the t-values of the estimated $\mathbf{\Phi}_i$ $(i = 1, 2, \ldots, p)$ and $\mathbf{\Upsilon}$ can be used to test hypotheses about individual coefficients.

Box 5.2 (*Continued*)

(3) The relevant asymptotic critical values are percentiles of the standard normal distribution.

(4) In small samples, in order to control Type-I error probability at the chosen significance level, critical values of the Student t-distribution can be used instead of normal critical values.

(5) In the case of a joint null hypothesis, involving r parameter restrictions, the likelihood ratio (LR) test statistic can be calculated as $-2(\mathcal{L}_R^* - \mathcal{L}_U^*)$. Under the null hypothesis that the r restrictions on the coefficients of the VAR are jointly valid, this LR-statistic has an asymptotic χ^2 distribution with r degrees of freedom.

Note again the importance of the assumption about Gaussian disturbance terms. If this assumption is very difficult to defend in a practical situation (due to, for example, significant residual autocorrelation or clear heteroskedasticity), the relevance of the theorems is reduced. The standard statistical inference (using normal, Chi-square and Student's t- and F-distributions) may become unreliable. In such a case, respecification of the VAR may be necessary. Another possibility is to seek to robustify the inference, which can work for some forms of misspecification. A usual choice many practitioners make is to apply robust standard errors to the estimated coefficients, which is an option which most modern econometric software packages provide.

5.3. A VAR Example (Cobweb Model Data)

In this subchapter, we illustrate the use of the theory above. In order to keep the example simple, we use an artificial dataset consisting of the price (P_t) and quantity (Q_t) time series of the cobweb model in Section 1.5. The reduced form of the cobweb model is a first-order VAR. We first estimate the unrestricted VAR, and then estimate a restricted VAR according to the expressions for the reduced form in equation (1.15) and (1.16).

In Section 1.5, we graphed 60 observations of the price and quantity time series, see, e.g., Figure 1.3. But, since this is a computer-generated dataset, we actually have longer time series available for estimation. We choose a sample from period 5 to 100, so the sample size is 95, which we denote by $T = 95$.[1] We first look at the estimation results in the matrix-equation form of (5.4) for the case of a first-order VAR, i.e., $p = 1$:

$$\underbrace{\begin{pmatrix} P_t \\ Q_t \end{pmatrix}}_{\boldsymbol{y}_t} = \underbrace{\begin{pmatrix} \underset{(0.04)}{-0.72} & \underset{(0.03)}{0.02} \\ \underset{(0.05)}{0.94} & \underset{(0.04)}{-0.03} \end{pmatrix}}_{\widehat{\boldsymbol{\Phi}}_1} \underbrace{\begin{pmatrix} P_{t-1} \\ Q_{t-1} \end{pmatrix}}_{\boldsymbol{y}_{t-1}} + \underbrace{\begin{pmatrix} \underset{(0.12)}{4.09} & \underset{(0.03)}{0.72} \\ \underset{(0.15)}{-0.83} & \underset{(0.04)}{0.06} \end{pmatrix}}_{\widehat{\boldsymbol{\Upsilon}}} \underbrace{\begin{pmatrix} 1_t \\ S11_t \end{pmatrix}}_{\boldsymbol{D}_t} + \underbrace{\begin{pmatrix} \hat{\varepsilon}_{1t} \\ \hat{\varepsilon}_{2t} \end{pmatrix}}_{\widehat{\boldsymbol{\varepsilon}}_t}. \tag{5.6}$$

The OLS estimate of the coefficient of P_{t-1} in the first row ($\phi_{1,11}$) of the VAR is -0.72, hence $\hat{\phi}_{1,11} = -0.72$. The number in brackets below is the estimated standard error of $\hat{\phi}_{1,11}$. The other coefficient estimates are also reported with their respective standard errors. The vector with deterministic terms, $\boldsymbol{D}_t$, contains a constant term, written as 1_t since it is a variable which is 1 in every observation period. The second variable in $\boldsymbol{D}_t$, denoted $S11_t$, is the demand-shift variable that we introduced in Section 1.6. It is zero for $t = 5, 6, \ldots, 10$, and 1 in all other periods ($t \geq 11$). Finally, the residual vector, $\widehat{\boldsymbol{\varepsilon}}_t$, holds the two residuals obtained by OLS estimation of the two rows of the VAR.

Table 5.1 shows the VAR results in table format. The estimated elements, $\hat{\phi}_{1,ij}$, are reported in the two columns marked Coeff. and the corresponding estimated standard errors in the columns marked St.error.

Below the coefficient estimates, the table reports the estimation method (OLS on each row in the VAR), the Sample dates, the number of observations (T) and the number of parameters. The number of parameters is 6, since we follow convention in most statistical packages and only count the elements in the autoregressive matrix (4) and the coefficients of the other regressors (2). However, another convention could have been to also count the elements of the covariance matrix of the VAR disturbances, since they also are parameters in the statistical model. That would bring the number of parameters up to 9. When we later consider econometric modelling of the VAR with the aid of conditional and marginal models, how we count the number of parameters is actually important in order to get model comparisons logically correct.

[1] We have followed custom by excluding the first four observations to avoid any excessive influence of initial conditions.

Table 5.1. OLS estimation results, and summary statistics for the unrestricted reduced form (URF) of the cobweb model.

	P_t		Q_t	
	Coeff.	St. error	Coeff.	St. error
P_{t-1}	−0.716	0.039	0.935	0.049
Q_{t-1}	0.021	0.032	−0.029	0.040
1_t	4.094	0.123	−0.834	0.154
$S11_t$	0.723	0.029	0.062	0.036

OLS, Sample 5–100, $T = 96$ no. of parameters = 8
$\mathcal{L}_U = 523.805$ $\frac{T}{2}\ln\left|\hat{\mathbf{\Sigma}}_U\right| = 796.242$

Residual correlations: $\hat{\sigma}_P = 0.0270$ $\hat{\sigma}_Q = 0.0338$
$\hat{\sigma}_{PQ} = -0.958$

Information criteria: AIC = −16.421 HQ = −16.34 SC = −16.208

The second line of summary statistics shows the maximized likelihood, denoted as $\mathcal{L}_U$.[2] It is the highest attainable likelihood value for this VAR, and hence is the statistical baseline against which simplifications can be tested.

It is quite common to refer to an unrestricted VAR, as an *Unrestricted Reduced Form* (URF), which reminds us that an interpretation which also fits our case is that the VAR is the reduced form of a structural model. It can be shown that $\mathcal{L}_U$ (given the assumption of Gaussian disturbances) can be expressed as

$$\mathcal{L}_U^* = -\frac{T}{2}\ln|\hat{\mathbf{\Sigma}}_U| - \frac{Tn}{2}(1 + \ln 2\pi), \tag{5.7}$$

where $\hat{\mathbf{\Sigma}}_U$ denotes the estimated covariance matrix of the OLS residuals, where we have added U for "unrestricted estimation". We also report $-\frac{T}{2}\ln|\hat{\mathbf{\Sigma}}_U|$ as a summary statistic in the table.

Finally, at the bottom of the table, the estimated residual standard deviation $\hat{\sigma}_P, \hat{\sigma}_Q$, and the residual correlation coefficient $\hat{\sigma}_{PQ}$ are reported. The two standard deviations are natural measures of goodness-of-fit, for example when calculated as percent of the means of P_t and Q_t respectively.

[2]We could add the superscript * as above. However, when the log-likelihood appears in a table with estimation results, it is understood that it is the maximized value that is being reported.

Note that the correlation between the residuals is negative in this case. Information criteria are often seen as a tie-breaker between model specifications, see for example Hill *et al.* (2012, Chapter 6) Hendry and Doornik (2014, Section 5.7), and we include three of the most used criteria on the table because of their relationship to the log-likelihood. They are the Akaike Information Criterion (AIC), Hannan–Quinn criterion (HQ) and the Schwarz Criterion (SC), also known as the Bayesian information criterion (the acronym is then BIC). They are defined as:

$$\begin{aligned} \text{AIC} &= \ln|\hat{\boldsymbol{\Sigma}}| + 2k/T, \\ \text{HQ} &= \ln|\hat{\boldsymbol{\Sigma}}| + 2k\ln(\ln(T))/T, \\ \text{SC} &= \ln|\hat{\boldsymbol{\Sigma}}| + k\ln(T)/T, \end{aligned} \tag{5.8}$$

where k is the number of parameters in the model ($k = 6$ in this example as we have seen) and we have dropped the U subscript of $\hat{\boldsymbol{\Sigma}}$ since it is understood that the criteria can be calculated for both unrestricted and restricted system. All three criteria penalize the number of estimated parameters. For example, SC penalizes extra variables more heavily than AIC. We see that in Table 5.1, the SC takes a higher (less negative) value than the AIC (and also the HQ). Hence, the Bayesian information criterion gives most positive weight to the six estimated parameters.

Some readers will know these information criteria from regression models with a single-dependent variable. In that case, $\ln|\hat{\boldsymbol{\Sigma}}|$ is replaced by $\ln(\hat{\sigma}^2)$ where $\hat{\sigma}^2$ is the MLE estimate of the variance of the single regression disturbance. Hence, the generalization in (5.8) should be clear enough. Another thing to note is that to connect the criteria to the log-likelihood function, you need to add the constant $\frac{Tn}{2}(1 + \ln 2\pi)$ to the right-hand sides of (5.8). It is useful to be aware of this fact in case the software package you use reports the more general version (PcGive reports both for VARs). However, although it obviously changes the criterion values, adding a constant does not change the choice of variables that minimize the criteria.

In this case, since the data have been computer-generated, we know that the assumption about Gaussian disturbances holds. Hence, we can do formal statistical inference about the individual parameters by computing the "t-values" from Table 5.1, or equation (5.6), and comparing them with critical values of the standard normal, or (for better finite sample properties) of a t-distribution. However, with real-world data, a close correspondence

Table 5.2. Residual misspecification tests for the VAR estimated in equation (5.6), and Table 5.1.

	P_t	Q_t	System
$F_{ar(1-2)}(2, 90)$	1.15[0.32]	1.12[0.33]	
$\chi^2_{\text{norm}}(2)$	0.47[0.79]	2.80[0.25]	
$F_{\text{het}}(5, 90)$	0.47[0.79]	1.88[0.11]	
$F_{\text{arch}(1-1)}(1, 94)$	0.037[0.85]	0.00006[0.99]	
$F^v_{ar(1-2)}(8, 174)$			0.58[0.80]
$\chi^{2,v}_{\text{norm}}(4)$			3.50[0.48]
$F^v_{\text{het}}(15, 243)$			1.21[0.27]

between DGP and model cannot be taken for granted. Therefore, it is necessary to test whether assumptions about Gaussian white noise disturbances can be defended. A battery of residual misspecification tests is therefore a useful tool (cf. Section 2.8).

Table 5.2 contains test values and the corresponding p-values in hard-brackets. $F_{ar(1-2)}$ denotes the F-form of the Lagrange-multiplier test for second-order residual autocorrelation (see Harvey, 1990, Chapter 8). The degrees of freedom, under the null of absence of autocorrelation, are 2 and 90, and the reported p-values of 0.32 (for no autocorrelation in the ε_{P_t} series) and 0.33 (for the ε_{Q_t} series) are therefore taken from the F-distribution with 2 and 90 degrees of freedom. χ^2_{norm} tests the null hypothesis of Gaussian disturbances against the joint alternative of skewness and excess kurtosis ("fat tails"). The test is due to Doornik and Hansen (1994) and has a Chi-square distribution with two degrees of freedom under the null hypothesis. Finally, we include two tests of heteroskedasticity in the disturbance processes. White's test is denoted F_{het}, while $F_{\text{arch}(1-1)}$ denotes the test of first-order Autoregressive Conditional Heteroskedasticity (ARCH) in the residuals.

As noted, since the data are generated in accordance to the null hypotheses of the different tests, it is not surprising that none of the diagnostic tests in the P_t-and Q_t-columns have p-values that suggest significant misspecification. White's heteroskedasticity test comes quite close as it would be significant at the 11 percent significance level. This illustrates that also when the null hypothesis is correct, there is a probability of it being rejected by a formally correct test (Type-I error).

As noted above, there are vector (or system) versions of the tests of residual autocorrelation, heteroskedasticity and non-normality (see, e.g., Doornik and Hendry, 2013c, Chapter 15). The tests are reported in the three last rows of the table, with v for "vector" superscript, with values entered in the System-column of the table. Again, they do not indicate misspecification.

As an illustration of the type of inference that might be of interest in a case like this, we can test the validity of the *restricted reduced form* (RRF), represented by equations (1.15) and (1.16) in Chapter 1. They imply the joint null-hypothesis

$$H_0\colon \phi_{1,12} = \phi_{1,22} = 0,$$

which can be tested by the use of the likelihood ratio test (LR) mentioned in Box 5.2. In order to calculate the test, we impose the two-parameter restrictions and estimate the RRF, with the results shown in (5.9):

$$\begin{pmatrix} P_t \\ Q_t \end{pmatrix} = \begin{pmatrix} \underset{(0.03)}{-0.73} & 0 \\ \underset{(0.04)}{0.95} & 0 \end{pmatrix} \begin{pmatrix} P_{t-1} \\ Q_{t-1} \end{pmatrix} + \begin{pmatrix} \underset{(0.09)}{4.16} & \underset{(0.02)}{0.74} \\ \underset{(0.10)}{-0.91} & \underset{(0.024)}{0.04} \end{pmatrix} \begin{pmatrix} 1_t \\ S11_t \end{pmatrix} + \begin{pmatrix} \hat{\varepsilon}^R_{1t} \\ \hat{\varepsilon}^R_{2t} \end{pmatrix},$$

$$\mathcal{L}_R = 523.533, \quad \frac{T}{2}\ln|\hat{\boldsymbol{\Sigma}}_R| = 795.969, \quad T = 95. \tag{5.9}$$

The two VARs, the URF and the RRF, have been estimated on the same sample of 96 observations, hence the unrestricted ($\mathcal{L}_U$) and restricted ($\mathcal{L}_R$) log-likelihoods are comparable. The LR test static for H_0 above therefore becomes

$$-2 \cdot (523.533 - 523.805) = 0.544,$$

which has a p-value of 0.76 when the χ^2-distribution with two degrees of freedom is used. Hence, the null hypothesis is not rejected at any of the conventional significance levels, like 1 percent, 5 percent or 10 percent.

Before we leave this example, there are a couple of additional remarks that can be made. First, the correlation matrix of the restricted VAR disturbances is almost unchanged from the unrestricted estimation:

$$\begin{array}{rr} 0.0270 & -0.958 \\ -0.958 & 0.0338 \end{array}$$

which may also be seen as proof of the validity of the two restrictions on the reduced form.

The second point can be put as a question: Are there additional restrictions that the cobweb model implies for the VAR? Give it a thought, and try to solve Exercise 5.2.

5.4. VAR Impulse-Response Functions

One of the main usages of VAR models is to compute impulse-responses. Above, we have seen that a VAR inherits the mathematical properties of a system of stochastic difference equations. In particular, we have seen that the final equations for the endogenous variables in the VAR not only have the same associated characteristic equation but also that there are differences in the non-homogeneous parts of the final equations for the different variables. Therefore, the responses to shocks (impulses) will also differ between the endogenous variables of the VAR.

With reference to Section 3.7, we have for the bivariate variable VAR(1) obtained by setting $n = 2$ and $p = 1$ in (5.4), the two final equations:

$$Y_{1t} = \gamma_1 + \phi_1 Y_{1t-1} + \phi_2 Y_{1t-2} + e_{1t}, \tag{5.10}$$

$$Y_{2t} = \gamma_2 + \phi_1 Y_{2t-1} + \phi_2 Y_{2t-2} + e_{2t}, \tag{5.11}$$

where the autoregressive coefficients are

$$\phi_1 = (\phi_{1,11} + \phi_{1,22}), \tag{5.12}$$

$$\phi_2 = \phi_{1,12}\phi_{1,21} - \phi_{1,22}\phi_{1,11}, \tag{5.13}$$

and the specific disturbances and intercepts are

$$e_{1t} = \varepsilon_{1t} - \phi_{1,22}\varepsilon_{1t-1} + \phi_{1,12}\varepsilon_{2t} \tag{5.14}$$

$$e_{2t} = \varepsilon_{2t} - \phi_{1,11}\varepsilon_{2t-1} + \phi_{1,21}\varepsilon_{1t}, \tag{5.15}$$

$$\gamma_1 = (1 - \phi_{1,22})\phi_{10} + \phi_{1,12}\phi_{20}, \tag{5.16}$$

$$\gamma_2 = (1 - \phi_{1,22})\phi_{20} + \phi_{1,12}\phi_{10}. \tag{5.17}$$

Because the only difference between (5.10) and an AR(2) model equation for Y_{1t}, is the definition of the disturbance e_{1t}, as a weighted sum of VAR disturbances, we can use the results for the companion form in Section 3.4 to find the impulse-response function. With reference to expression (3.94), we can write the solution for Y_{1t+j} as

$$\begin{aligned} Y_{1t+j} = {} & b_{11}^{(j+1)} Y_{1t-1} + b_{12}^{(j+1)} Y_{1t-2} \\ & + \gamma_1 (b_{11}^{(j)} + b_{11}^{(j-1)} + \cdots + b_{11}^{(1)} + 1) \\ & + b_{11}^{(j)} e_{1t} + b_{11}^{(j-1)} e_{1t+1} + \cdots + b_{11}^{(1)} e_{1t+j-1} + b_{11}^{(0)} e_{1t+j}, \end{aligned} \tag{5.18}$$

where γ_1 has taken the place of ϕ_0 in (3.94) as the notation for the constant term in the equation.

We remind the reader that $b_{11}^{(j)}$ is element (1, 1) in the matrix $\mathbf{B}^j$ ($j = 1, 2, \ldots$), where $\mathbf{B}$ is the companion matrix

$$\mathbf{B} = \begin{pmatrix} \phi_1 & \phi_2 \\ 1 & 0 \end{pmatrix}$$

for the second-order process that we have here. $b_{12}^{(j)}$ is element (1,2) in $\mathbf{B}^j$. Finally, in the same way as above, $b_{11}^{(0)} = 1$ for $j = 0$. It follows that

$$\frac{\partial Y_{1t+j}}{\partial e_{1t}} = b_{11}^{(j)}, \text{ for } j = 0, 1, 2, \ldots; \quad b_{11}^{(0)} = 1.$$

and, taking account of how e_{1t} is defined above

$$\frac{\partial Y_{1t+j}}{\partial \varepsilon_{1t}} = b_{11}^{(j)} - b_{11}^{(j-1)} \phi_{1,22}, \tag{5.19}$$

$$\frac{\partial Y_{1t+j}}{\partial \varepsilon_{2t}} = b_{11}^{(j)} \phi_{1,12}, \quad \text{for } j = 0, 1, 2, \ldots \tag{5.20}$$

showing that the impulse-response functions of Y_{1t} are different with respect to the two "shocks" represented by ε_{1t} and ε_{2t}. A similar result exists for the two impulse response functions of Y_{2t}. Impulse-responses are subject to identification issues that we will discuss below. Nevertheless, many researchers and consumers of econometric result regard impulse-responses as important statistics in their own right: they provide the empirical regularities that can substantiate theoretical models of the economy.

Jordà (2005) proposed to calculate impulse-responses by so-called *local projections* that utilize the structure of solution in (5.18), but which does not rely on estimating the underlying VAR. Instead, a sequence of local-projection is estimated as indicated by

$$\begin{aligned} Y_{1t+j} &= b_{11}^{(j+1)} Y_{1t-1} + b_{12}^{(j+1)} Y_{1t-2} + \alpha_1^{(j)} + \text{disturbance}, \\ Y_{2t+j} &= b_{11}^{(j+1)} Y_{2t-1} + b_{12}^{(j+1)} Y_{2t-2} + \alpha_2^{(j)} + \text{disturbance}, \; j = 0, 1, 2, \ldots, J, \end{aligned}$$

where $b_{11}^{(j+1)}$, $b_{12}^{(j+1)}$, $\alpha_1^{(j)}$, $\alpha_2^{(j)}$ are regarded as coefficients to be estimated. An example of this approach is found in OECD (2017).

Box 5.3. "Imaginary shocks" critique of modern macroeconomics

Macroeconomics is a controversial field, and an interesting debate was rekindled by Paul Romer's (World Bank Chief Economist) critique of the dominance of impulse-responses in modern macro, see Romer (2016), which he dubbed as responses to imaginary shocks. One underlying issue is identification of VAR shocks, which will be discussed in Chapter 7.

5.5. Forecasting from VARs

One main objective of VAR modelling is macroeconomic forecasting. Historically, during the 1970s and 1980s, the rise in popularity of VARs was in part related to the weaknesses of the macroeconometric models of that epoch in the same department. For reasons that can be understood, given the macroeconomic stability that characterized the first post-war decades in many western economies, model developers (and users) became interested in operating large systems of economic relationships that were static, and paid much less attention to dynamic specification. As pointed out by Granger and Newbold (1986), many theory driven macromodels largely ignored dynamics and temporal properties of the data, so it should not come as surprise that they produced suboptimal forecasts, and were outperformed by (what was regarded as) simpler models that put dynamics in the foreground. VARs belonged to the class of dynamic forecasting tools.

The use of VARs in forecasting has theoretical basis in an important theorem saying that if the VAR corresponds to a stationary DGP, forecasts calculated as the conditional expectation are unbiased, and no other predictor conditional on $\mathbf{y}_{t-1}$(i.e., setting $p = 1$ for simplicity) has a smaller Mean Squared Forecast Error (MSFE), see Clements and Hendry (1998, Chapter 2). In Chapter 12, forecasting from VARs is discussed together with other methods. However, given how central VARs have become in macroeconomic forecasting, we point out in this section the close connection between the solution concepts developed above, and the forecasts from VARs.

We denote a forecast for a variable by the subscript $T + h$, where T denotes the period that we condition the forecast on, and $T + h$ is the period being forecasted based on information available in period T. Finally, we let H denote the forecast horizon, hence $h = 1, 2, \ldots, H$. Setting $H = 1$

corresponds to a one-step forecast, which is also called a static forecast. For $H > 1$, we speak of dynamic forecasts.

Consider the bivariate VAR with first-order dynamics, i.e., $n = 2$ and $p = 1$. Assuming that the VAR is identical to the DGP in the forecast period, the solution for Y_{1T+h} can be written as

$$\begin{aligned} Y_{1T+h} = {} & b_{11}^{(h)} Y_{1T} + b_{12}^{(h)} Y_{1T-1} \\ & + \gamma_1 (b_{11}^{(h-1)} + b_{11}^{(h-2)} + \cdots + 1) \\ & + b_{11}^{(h-1)} e_{1T+1} + \cdots + b_{11}^{(1)} e_{1T+h-1} + e_{T+h}, \quad h = 1, 2, \ldots, H \end{aligned} \tag{5.21}$$

by using (5.18), and adopting the notation for forecasting. In practice, the VAR will be estimated using data up to and including period T before a forecast can be produced, but for simplicity we can for the time being assume that $b_{11}^{(h)}$, $b_{12}^{(h)}$ are known numbers. The conditional expectation of Y_{1T+h} is therefore

$$\begin{aligned} E(Y_{1T+h} \mid \mathcal{I}_T) = {} & b_{11}^{(h)} Y_{1T} + b_{12}^{(h)} Y_{1T-1} \\ & + \gamma_1 (b_{11}^{(h-1)} + b_{11}^{(h-2)} + \cdots + 1) \end{aligned} \tag{5.22}$$

since all the future shocks (disturbances) have expectation zero. $\mathcal{I}_T$ denotes the information set used for the forecast, a concept that we will discuss in Chapter 12.

Choosing $E(Y_{1T+h} \mid \mathcal{I}_T)$ as our forecasting function, it follows that the forecast errors $(Y_{1T+h} - E(Y_{1T+h}))$ will be random variables, each with expectation zero, but with variances that are functions of h. We return to the analysis of the properties of the forecast function (5.22), and the associated forecast errors, in Chapter 12.

Meanwhile, as an illustration, Figure 5.1 shows dynamic forecasts for $H = 8$ for the two endogenous variables in the cobweb model. In the figure, panel (a) shows the price time series for the historical period ($t = 89, \ldots, 100$), and the price forecasts (for $T + h = 101, \ldots, 108$) in a *fan chart.* Panel (b) shows the same for the quantity variable. In the middle of the fans lies the sequence of dynamic point forecasts that are values of forecasting functions similar to (5.22). Those forecasts also have interpretations as the medians (50th percentile) in the distributions of forecasts generated by drawing future disturbances from the assumed (Gaussian) distribution of the VAR errors. Hence, fan charts are a method of visualizing a distribution of economic forecasts. In Figure 5.1, the upper edge of the fans represents 97.5 percentiles, and the lower edge represents 2.5 percentiles corresponding to a confidence interval for the forecasts of 95%.

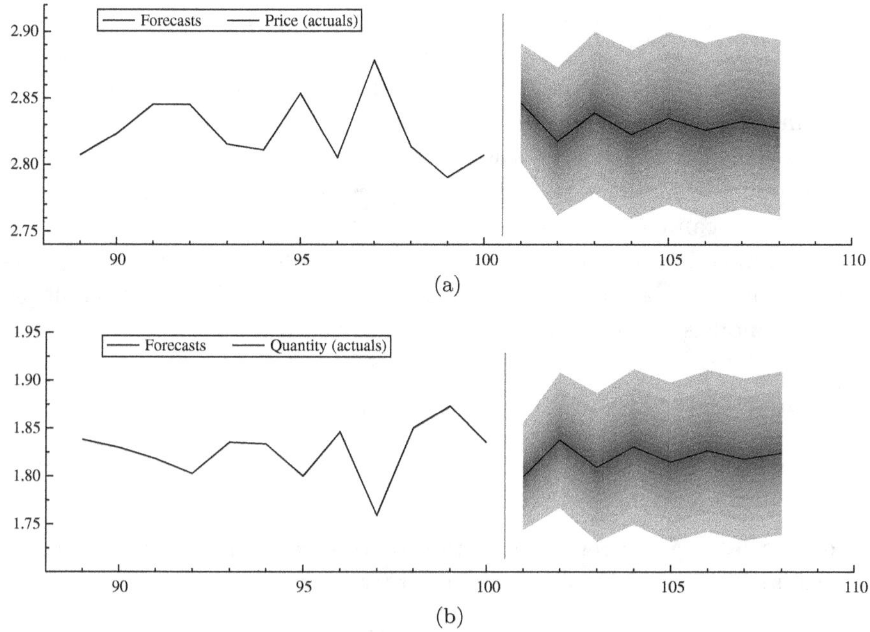

Figure 5.1. Actual values shown as line graphs, and forecasts as fan charts for price (panel (a)) and quantity (panel (b)) for the cobweb VAR estimated in Table 5.1. In this example, the forecasts are conditional on period $T = 100$, and the forecast periods are $T + h = 101, \ldots, 108$, i.e., $H = 8$.

Looking at the fan charts, we are reminded that a perfect forecast is extremely unlikely, and that a point forecast, while optimal in the MSFE sense as noted above, is a very unlikely future event. Other ways of illustrating the forecast uncertainty, are forecast error bars (with length representing the size of the forecast interval at a given confidence level), and lines representing upper and lower bounds of the forecast intervals.

5.6. Modelling Beyond the VAR

The VAR is one of the main statistical models of empirical macroeconomic modelling. Nevertheless, in applied dynamic econometrics, we often make use of other models and systems as well. A main reason for this has to with modelling (or research) purpose. Often, the parameters that we focus on in a particular study are not directly represented in the VAR. Assume, for example, that you are interested in estimating the slope coefficient of the demand curve in the cobweb model, the parameter a in (1.13) of Section 1.5.

In the VAR, a is not an estimated parameter. As (1.16) shows, the second line of the VAR (5.9) gives an estimate of c and not of a, and the first line gives the estimate of the ratio c/a. Of course, it is possible to "back-out" an estimate of a, but it would be more practical to be able to estimate a directly. To achieve the estimation of parameters of interest, other econometric models than the VAR are often required (or they are more practical). Such models can consist of a single equation or of multiple equations. We cover the most important classes of models in the following chapters, starting with single-equation models (Chapter 6), and then move on to multiple equation models (Chapter 7).

5.7. Exercises

Exercise 5.1. Calculate the value of AIC in Table 5.1 by using the likelihood information in the table.

Exercise 5.2. With reference to the cobweb model in Chapter 1, and in particular (1.15) and (1.16), are there other hypotheses than

$$H_0\colon \phi_{1,12} = \phi_{1,22} = 0$$

that can be formulated and tested within the VAR of Section 5.3?

Exercise 5.3. Replicate the results of the analysis of the cobweb model in Section 5.3, using the dataset *dgp_determandstoch* which can be downloaded from the internet pages of the book. The data is provided in both OxMetrics/PcGive format, and in MS-Excel format for easy import to other software packages that you may want to use. Use P_STOCH as the price variable, and Q_STOCH as the quantity variable. The step indicator variable is STEP11, the same name as in the text.

Exercise 5.4. Show the expressions in (5.19) and (5.20).

Exercise 5.5. Extend the analysis of the cobweb model in Exercise 5.3 by calculating impulse-responses of price and quantity with respect to a shock to ε_{1t}. Use the estimated VAR model in Table 5.1 and set the shock to $+1$ for ε_{1t}.

Exercise 5.6. Formulate and estimate a VAR which is consistent with the two AR(2) models in Exercise 4.9. What are the eigenvalues of the companion matrix? Are they supportive of stationarity? Test if an extension of the system by the indicator variable *mixed* gets support if you use an LR-test.

Chapter 6

Single Equation Models

In econometrics, the interest is often to specify a model of the VAR that has economic interpretation. The econometric model can be intended as a partial representation of the relationship generated by a VAR or it can be an attempt to model all the statistical relationships in an economically interpretable way. A conditional model (i.e., regression model) represents a partial model of the full dynamic system, and another example is a single structural econometric equation (which has one or more endogenous explanatory variables). At the other end of the spectrum, we find multiple equation models intended as a full representation of the VAR. These models come in several variants as well: recursive models, simultaneous equations models and structural VARs. In this chapter, the topic is the single equation model, and the emphasis is on conditional models.

6.1. Introduction

Often the purpose of an econometric analysis is not to represent all the relationships of a system, but instead to analyze a part of it. The class of model equations for this type of analysis is known as *autoregressive distributed lag* (ADL) model. The exact statistical interpretation of an ADL model equation can be one of the two: as a conditional regression model or as a structural equation (the distinction is the same as in Chapter 2). In Section 6.2, we present the two interpretations of an ADL model equation, and we also give examples of estimation by OLS (conditional model) and by instrumental variables (IV). Section 6.3 discusses dynamic multipliers (responses) in the context of conditional ADL model equations. In Section 6.4, the equilibrium correction interpretation of ADL models is established, and Section 6.5 presents a typology of special cases of ADL models. An alternative to single equation ADL models are distributed lag models with the so-called rational lag distributions. Section 6.6 gives a brief introduction to this alternative. The two last sections show examples of modelling of interest rate transmission with the aid of conditional ADL models without and with volatility components in the model equation.

6.2. ADL Model Equations

A dynamic regression model with one explanatory variable and first-order dynamics can be written as

$$Y_t = \phi_0 + \phi_1 Y_{t-1} + \beta_0 X_t + \beta_1 X_{t-1} + \epsilon_t, \quad t = 1, 2, \ldots, T, \tag{6.1}$$

where ϵ_t is a random disturbance, which is white noise and unpredictable by conditioning on X_t, X_{t-1}, Y_{t-1} or any longer lags of the two variables. Hence, $E(\varepsilon_t \mid Y_{t-1}, X_t, X_{t-1}) = 0$.

Equation (6.1) is seen to be the same model equation as we indicated in Section 2.7 as an extension of the classical regression model for independent and identically distributed pairs of random variables. As noted there, we refer to it as an autoregressive distributed lag (ADL) model because it contains both an autoregressive term and two terms that distribute the impact effect of a change in X over two periods. In the same way as we indicate an AR process with first-order dynamics by writing AR(p), it is sometimes seen that equation (6.1) is referred to as ADL$(1, 1)$ to indicate that both lag polynomials are of the first order.

6.2.1. ADL as a conditional model of the VAR

We can obtain a more precise statistical characterization of the ADL model by starting from the bivariate first-order VAR(1) with two intercepts as deterministic components. Hence, with reference to (5.4), we set $n = 2$ and $p = 1$, and we define $\mathbf{\Upsilon D}_t$ in such a way that there is a constant in each row: $\mathbf{\Upsilon D}_t = (\phi_{10}, \phi_{20})'$. Finally, we redefine the variables so that they conform with (6.1) and the bivariate VAR (5.2) of Chapter 5: $Y_{1t} = Y_t$, $Y_{2t} = X_t$ and $\varepsilon_{1t} = \varepsilon_{yt}$ and $\varepsilon_{2t} = \varepsilon_{xt}$.

The normal (Gaussian) distribution of the disturbance vector $\boldsymbol{\epsilon}_t = (\varepsilon_{yt}, \varepsilon_{xt})'$ of the VAR is conditional on the history of the observable variables. In the first-order case that we consider now, the conditioning is on X_{t-1} and Y_{t-1}:

$$\begin{pmatrix} \varepsilon_{yt} \\ \varepsilon_{xt} \end{pmatrix} \sim \text{IIN}\left(\mathbf{0}, \begin{pmatrix} \sigma_y^2 & \sigma_{xy} \\ \sigma_{xy} & \sigma_x^2 \end{pmatrix} \middle| Y_{t-1}, X_{t-1}\right). \tag{6.2}$$

We can now write the VAR in terms of its two rows:

$$Y_t = \mu_{y,t-1} + \varepsilon_{yt}, \tag{6.3}$$

$$X_t = \mu_{x,t-1} + \varepsilon_{xt}, \tag{6.4}$$

where $\mu_{y,t-1}$ and $\mu_{x,t-1}$ denote the expectations of Y_t and X_t with respect to their history, hence $\mu_{y,t-1} = E(Y_t \mid Y_{t-1}, X_{t-1})$ and $\mu_{x,t-1} = E(X_t \mid Y_{t-1}, X_{t-1})$ are given by

$$\mu_{y,t-1} = \phi_{10} + \phi_{11} Y_{t-1} + \phi_{12} X_{t-1}, \tag{6.5}$$

$$\mu_{x,t-1} = \phi_{20} + \phi_{21} Y_{t-1} + \phi_{22} X_{t-1}. \tag{6.6}$$

The Gaussian VAR of (X_t, Y_t) can therefore be interpreted as the joint probability density function $f(X_t, Y_t \mid X_{t-1}, Y_{t-1})$, see (2.147), written in the model equation form. From the properties of the bivariate normal distribution, it follows that the conditional distribution of Y_t given X_t is normal, with expectation:

$$\begin{aligned} E(Y_t \mid X_t, X_{t-1}, Y_{t-1}) &= \mu_{y,t-1} - \rho_{xy}\frac{\sigma_y}{\sigma_x}\mu_{x,t-1} + \rho_{xy}\frac{\sigma_y}{\sigma_x}X_t \\ &= \phi_{10} - \frac{\sigma_{xy}}{\sigma_x^2}\phi_{20} + \frac{\sigma_{xy}}{\sigma_x^2}X_t + \left(\phi_{12} - \frac{\sigma_{xy}}{\sigma_x^2}\phi_{22}\right)X_{t-1} \\ &\quad + \left(\phi_{11} - \frac{\sigma_{xy}}{\sigma_x^2}\phi_{21}\right)Y_{t-1}, \end{aligned} \tag{6.7}$$

where ρ_{xy}, as earlier in the book, is the correlation coefficient between ε_{xt} and ε_{yt}:

$$\rho_{xy} = \frac{\sigma_{xy}}{\sigma_x \sigma_y}.$$

We can now define the model equation's parameters as follows:

$$\phi_0 = \phi_{10} - \frac{\sigma_{xy}}{\sigma_x^2}\phi_{20},$$

$$\phi_1 = \phi_{11} - \frac{\sigma_{xy}}{\sigma_x^2}\phi_{21},$$

$$\beta_0 = \frac{\sigma_{xy}}{\sigma_x^2},$$

$$\beta_1 = \phi_{12} - \frac{\sigma_{xy}}{\sigma_x^2}\phi_{22},$$

and write the conditional expectation as

$$E(Y_t \mid X_t, X_{t-1}, Y_{t-1}) = \phi_0 + \phi_1 Y_{t-1} + \beta_0 X_t + \beta_1 X_{t-1}. \tag{6.8}$$

Finally, define the disturbance term of the model equation as

$$\epsilon_t = Y_t - E(Y_t \mid X_t, X_{t-1}, Y_{t-1}). \tag{6.9}$$

A final rearrangement gives the conditional model of Y_t given X_t, namely

$$Y_t = \phi_0 + \phi_1 Y_{t-1} + \beta_0 X_t + \beta_1 X_{t-1} + \epsilon_t, \tag{6.10}$$

which is the same model equation as the ADL in (6.1).

In Exercise 6.1, you are invited to show that the disturbance ε_t in (6.9) can be expressed as

$$\epsilon_t = \varepsilon_{yt} - \frac{\sigma_{xy}}{\sigma_x^2}\varepsilon_{xt}. \tag{6.11}$$

Remember that the starting point is that the simultaneous distribution of ε_{yt} and ε_{xt} is conditional on X_{t-1} and Y_{t-1} (cf. (6.2)). Hence, it follows that the error term of the ADL model equation is uncorrelated with the conditioning variables of the VAR:

$$E(\epsilon_t \mid X_{t-1}, Y_{t-1}) = 0.$$

We also have, again with reference to the normal distribution (although the result holds more generally),

$$E(\epsilon_t \mid \varepsilon_{xt}) = 0, \tag{6.12}$$

the error term of the conditional model is uncorrelated with the disturbance in (6.4), the equation for X_t in the VAR. In this context, we refer to it as the *marginal model equation* for X_t, i.e., relative to the conditional model equation for Y_t that we have just derived. Moreover, since this random variable is defined by $\varepsilon_{xt} = X_t - E(X_t \mid X_{t-1}, Y_{t-1})$, (6.12) can be expressed as

$$E(\epsilon_t \mid X_t, X_{t-1}, Y_{t-1}) = 0, \tag{6.13}$$

implying that the ADL disturbance ϵ_t is uncorrelated with *all* the model's explanatory variables. This is the same kind of orthogonality that is typical of regression theory (as reviewed in Chapter 2).

It also follows from the model assumptions above that ε_t is normally distributed:

$$\varepsilon_t \sim N(0, \sigma^2 \mid X_t, X_{t-1}, Y_{t-1}), \tag{6.14}$$

where the variance can be expressed as

$$\sigma^2 = \sigma_y^2(1 - \rho_{xy}^2), \tag{6.15}$$

see Exercise 6.2 at the end of the chapter.

Box 6.1. ADL as partial model of the VAR

In summary, we have the following: If we start from a stationary VAR of Y_t and X_t, with first-order dynamics and a Gaussian disturbance vector, the conditional model of Y_t given X_t is an ADL model with first-order dynamics. The disturbance term of the conditional model (ε_t) is normally distributed, with expectation zero, variance (6.15), and it is uncorrelated with X_t, Y_{t-1}, X_{t-1}, and with the disturbance of the marginal model equation for X_t.

6.2.2. ADL estimation and inference

One important consequence of the ADL as a model of the Gaussian VAR is that the results about maximum likelihood (ML) estimation of the parameters of the VAR carry over to the estimation of the parameters of the ADL model (6.10): The ML estimators of $(\phi_0, \phi_1\ \beta_0, \beta_1)'$ are given by the OLS estimators of these coefficients.

The conditional likelihood function can be constructed in the same manner as for the AR(1) model by the use of the conditional densities $f_{Y_t|Y_{t-1},X_t,X_{t-1}}(y_t \mid y_{t-1}, x_t, x_{t-1})$. Hence, while the log-likelihood function of the AR(1) process is (4.52), the expression in the ADL model becomes

$$\begin{aligned}
&\mathcal{L}(\phi_0, \phi_1, \beta_0, \beta_1, \sigma^2 \mid Y_0, X_0) \\
&\quad = -\frac{T}{2}(\ln(2\pi/\sigma^2)) \\
&\qquad - \sum_{t=1}^{T} \frac{(Y_t - \phi_0 - \phi_1 Y_{t-1} - \beta_0 X_t - \beta_1 X_{t-1})^2}{2\sigma^2}.
\end{aligned} \tag{6.16}$$

Finding the minimum of the residual sum of squares is a multivariate regression problem. We can write expressions for the OLS estimators by using the matrix notation that we reviewed in Chapter 2 for the model equation:

$$\boldsymbol{y} = \boldsymbol{X\beta} + \boldsymbol{\epsilon}, \tag{6.17}$$

where $\mathbf{y} = (Y_T, Y_{T-1}, \ldots, Y_2)'$ and $\boldsymbol{X}$ is the $(T-1) \times 4$ matrix with right-hand side variables (including the constant). The number of rows is $(T-1)$, not T, since we lose one observation at the start of the sample due to the lags Y_{t-1} and X_{t-1}. If we partition the matrix $\mathbf{X}$ as

$$\mathbf{X} = [\boldsymbol{\iota} \quad \mathbf{X}_2],$$

where $\boldsymbol{\iota}$ is a column vector of 1s, and $\mathbf{X}_2$ has the observations of Y_{t-1}, X_t and X_{t-1} as columns, and partition $\boldsymbol{\beta}$ conformingly as

$$\boldsymbol{\beta} = \begin{bmatrix} \phi_0 \\ \boldsymbol{\beta}_2 \end{bmatrix},$$

we have from Section 2.6.2, that the ML estimator of the vector $\boldsymbol{\beta}_2 = (\phi_1, \beta_0, \beta_1)'$ is

$$\hat{\boldsymbol{\beta}}_2 = [(\mathbf{X}_2 - \overline{\mathbf{X}}_2)'(\mathbf{X}_2 - \overline{\mathbf{X}}_2)]^{-1} (\mathbf{X}_2 - \overline{\mathbf{X}}_2)'\mathbf{y}. \tag{6.18}$$

In the same way as in the other cases we have considered, the ML estimator of the regression-error variance is the average of the squared residuals, which we can write as

$$\hat{\sigma}^2 = \frac{1}{(T-1)} \hat{\boldsymbol{\epsilon}}'\hat{\boldsymbol{\epsilon}}, \tag{6.19}$$

for the ADL model with first-order dynamics. As in the other cases we have considered, the difference between the MLE estimator and the unbiased estimator,

$$\tilde{\sigma}^2 = \frac{1}{(T-1)-(k+1)} \hat{\boldsymbol{\epsilon}}'\hat{\boldsymbol{\epsilon}}, \tag{6.20}$$

will hardly be noticeable when T is reasonably large (k denotes the number of right-hand side variables excluding the constant term).

Under the assumption that the ADL disturbances are independent (not autocorrelated) and identically distributed, the OLS estimators of the coefficients are consistent but biased in finite samples. The finite sample estimation bias is of the Hurwicz bias type, since the regressors are predetermined, and not strictly exogenous. This is obviously the case for Y_{t-1}, which logically must be correlated with past ADL disturbances in the same way as for the AR(1) model. However, also X_t and X_{t-1} will in general be predetermined due to feedback from Y_{t-1} to X_t in the VAR. For X_t to be a strictly exogenous variable, the restriction $\phi_{21} = 0$ needs to hold in the VAR (4.67).

Above, we have derived the ADL model for Y_t given X_t from the first-order VAR with constant terms; cf. $\mathbf{\Upsilon D}_t = (\phi_{10}, \phi_{20})'$. As already noted, we will usually want to include other forms of deterministic variables, for example,

- Dummies that capture regular seasonal variation, and more generally impulse dummies and combinations of them.
- Step dummies, that take non-zero values over two or more periods, and are zero elsewhere.
- Deterministic trend. A linear trend is $\text{Trend}_t = t$ where $t = 1, 2, \ldots, T$. Sometimes, a quadratic trend t^2 is relevant.

The properties of the OLS estimators extend to ADL models that include one or more of these types of deterministic terms. The same is the case for the inference based on t-values and LR-tests, which have standard normal and Chi-square distributions asymptotically under the null hypotheses of the tests. In practice, the critical values of the Student t-distribution and F-distributions can be used. The reason is the same as mentioned earlier, namely that these tests, which are adjusted for the number of estimated parameters (i.e., degrees of freedom), can have better properties in moderately large samples.

6.2.3. Two examples of ADL estimation

We can illustrate the estimation of ADL$(1, 1)$ equations by the using the two computer-generated datasets that we introduced in Chapter 1.

Example of ADL, the cobweb model data

As a first example of an ADL, we again consider the computer-generated cobweb model data that we used to estimate the VAR in Section 5.3. The economic theory of this model suggests that because of inelastic supply in the short run, the market price P_t can be modelled conditionally on the predetermined quantity Q_t. This implies the following ADL model (compare

Table 5.1):

$$P_t = \phi_0 + \phi_1 P_{t-1} + \beta_0 Q_t + \beta_1 Q_{t-1} + \gamma_1 S11_t + \epsilon_t, \quad t = 5, 6, \ldots, 100. \tag{6.21}$$

The estimation results, using OLS, are:

$$\begin{aligned} P_t = &\underset{(0.0406)}{3.457} - \underset{(0.0251)}{0.001558}\, P_{t-1} - \underset{(0.0239)}{0.7641}\, Q_t \\ &- \underset{(0.00928)}{0.0006913}\, Q_{t-1} + \underset{(0.00849)}{0.7708}\, S11_t \\ &\mathcal{L}_{P\text{-}ADL,U} = 332.861, \quad T = 95, \end{aligned} \tag{6.22}$$

where the standard errors of the estimates are reported in parentheses below each estimate. By calculating t-values, it is seen that the variables that are significant in this model are Q_t and $S11_t$. This is as it should be, as the demand shock represented by $S11_t$ can only be reconciled with the predetermined supply by increasing the product price. In the DGP, the true parameter of Q_t was set as 0.77, hence the estimated coefficient 0.76 in (6.22) is very precise on this example dataset.

As the model in (6.22) is the equation form of the conditional density of P_t consistent with the URF-VAR in Table 5.1, we have labelled the log-likelihood value $\mathcal{L}_{P\text{-}ADL,U}$, with U for "unrestricted". We can complete the model representation of the VAR by estimating the marginal model for Q_t. But this is simply the second row of the VAR-URF (5.6). For completeness, we repeat it here as a single equation model:

$$\begin{aligned} Q_t = &- \underset{(0.15)}{0.83} + \underset{(0.05)}{0.94}\, P_{t-1} - \underset{(0.04)}{0.03}\, Q_{t-1} \\ &+ \underset{(0.04)}{0.06}\, S11_t, \\ &\mathcal{L}_{Q\text{-}ADL,U} = 190.944, \quad T = 95. \end{aligned} \tag{6.23}$$

To check that (6.22) and (6.23) represent a reparametrization of the VAR, in the form of one conditional model and one marginal model, we can calculate the sum of the conditional and marginal likelihoods: $\mathcal{L}_{P\text{-}ADL,U} + \mathcal{L}_{Q\text{-}ADL,U}$. This gives $332.861 + 190.944 = 523.805$, which is identical to the unrestricted log-likelihood $\mathcal{L}_U$ in Table 5.1. Hence no statistical information has been lost by representing the VAR as an econometric model consisting of one conditional model, i.e., (6.22), and one marginal model, namely (6.23).

Note 6.1. Number of parameters in VAR and ADL

In connection with Table 5.1, we mentioned that most statistical packages report the number of parameters estimated in the VAR without including the correlations between the disturbances. This can create confusion when we compare VAR estimation results with results for models of the VAR that consist of conditional models and marginal model equations. In Table 5.1, there are eight parameters, but there are nine coefficients in the econometric model consisting of (6.21) and (6.23). As the derivation in Section 6.2.1 showed, the solution of this paradox is that the correlation coefficient of the VAR disturbances becomes parametrized in the conditional ADL model, in fact, it is one-to-one with the coefficient of X_t in the ADL.

A structural equation on ADL form, the Keynes model data

As a second example, we consider the macromodel in Section 1.7. The consumption function of the model is seen to be a dynamic equation on the ADL form, with C_t in the role of Y_t, and GDP_t in the role of X_t. With the notation used in Section 1.7, we have

$$C_t = a + b\,\text{GDP}_t + cC_{t-1} + \epsilon_{Ct}, \tag{6.24}$$

and the distributed lag of the equation is seen to be of the simplest possible kind, since it only included the current GDP, not the lag.

However, care must be taken. Given the specification of the macromodel, there is no way that (6.24) can be a valid conditional model of C_t given the disposable income GDP_t. This is due to the simultaneous determination of C_t and GDP_t in the model, which implies that GDP_t is correlated with the error term ϵ_{Ct}. GDP_t cannot be a predetermined variable in equation (6.24), since ϵ_{Ct} and GDP_t must logically be correlated. The role that the general budget equation (1.23) plays in this model (making GDP_t "demand determined"), means that GDP_t is an endogenous variable in (6.24). Hence, econometrically speaking, (6.24) is a structural equation.

If we nevertheless use OLS for estimation of (6.24), the results are as follows:

$$\begin{aligned} C_t = &- \underset{(0.948)}{0.92} + \underset{(0.005)}{0.251}\,\text{GDP}_t + \underset{(0.011)}{0.647}\,C_{t-1}, \\ &\text{OLS} \quad T = 100. \end{aligned} \tag{6.25}$$

As noted above, the true values of b (marginal propensity to consume) and c (habit formation) in the DGP that we used to generate the dataset are 0.25 and 0.65, respectively. Hence, despite the inevitable correlation between GDP_t and ϵ_{Ct}, those two coefficients are very precisely estimated by OLS in this case. This illustrates that estimation biases may not be detrimental, as long as the model equation corresponds to the DGP in all other respects. In Section 7.9, we analyze the theoretical *simultaneity bias* closely. We will then see which property of the DGP explains the negligible biases in (6.25), and we will look at another DGP, another dataset, where the biases become much larger.

However, to complete this section, we note that the macromodel (1.22)–(1.24) also implies that J_t is a valid instrumental variable: it is correlated with GDP_t, but uncorrelated with ϵ_t if ϵ_{Jt} is uncorrelated with ϵ_{Ct} and ϵ_{St} (which is what we assumed in the data generation).

Estimating (6.24) by IV gives

$$\begin{aligned} C_t &= \underset{(0.950)}{-\,0.731} + \underset{(0.005)}{0.248}\ \text{GDP}_t + \underset{(0.011)}{0.650}\ C_{t-1}, \\ &\text{IVE } T = 100. \end{aligned} \tag{6.26}$$

showing that IV estimation, which uses estimators that are consistent, gives coefficient estimates of GDP_t and C_{t-1} that in practice are the same as the OLS estimates in this case. As noted, in Section 7.9, we revisit the estimation of the consumption function of this macromodel, and analyze another (artificial dataset) where the difference between the IV and OLS estimation results become much larger.

6.2.4. General ADL

The ADL$(1, 1)$ model equation can be extended to several explanatory variables, and to higher lag orders (denoted by p).

When a higher order ADL is a conditional model, the conditioning is on X_t in the same manner as above, and we obtain the ADL(p_Y, p_X):

$$\begin{aligned} Y_t - \phi_1 Y_{t-1} - \cdots - \phi_{p_Y} Y_{t-p} \\ = \phi_0 + \beta_0 X_t + \beta_1 X_{t-1} + \cdots + \beta_{p_X} X_{t-p} + \epsilon_t. \end{aligned} \tag{6.27}$$

The econometric specification of the model will be the same as above, the only formal change is that the conditional distribution of ϵ_t is conditional on a longer history of X and Y. Empirically, the lag lengths of different variables in the model can often be different, hence we may have $p_Y \neq p_X$.

Formally, this can be interpreted as a consequence of starting from a VAR where the rows contain lag polynomials with different lag lengths. However, to simplify the notation, we will often assume in the following that $p_Y = p_X = p$.

Extension to any number of X_t distributed lag polynomials is also straightforward. The underlying distribution function is then multivariate: We start with the n dimensional VAR with dynamics of order p (for simplicity of notation), and number the explanatory variables X_{1t}, $X_{2t}, \ldots, X_{(n-1)t}$. The conditional ADL equation can therefore be written as

$$Y_t = \phi_0 + \sum_{i=1}^{p} \phi_i Y_{t-i} + \sum_{j=1}^{n-1} \sum_{i=0}^{p} \beta_{ji} X_{j(t-i)} + \epsilon_t. \tag{6.28}$$

As noted above, in connection with the estimation of the Keynesian consumption function, it is not always the "ADL-like" dynamic equations can be interpreted as conditional econometric models, it depends on the system properties of the DGP. Specifically, an "ADL-like" equation may be a structural econometric equation of an simultaneous equation model. To draw the distinction between conditional and structural ADL model equations, one often has to think in terms of the larger system even though the research purpose focuses on a single equation relationship. Hence, system thinking is needed, also when the objective is to capture only a (small) part of the system with an econometric relationship.

6.3. Dynamic Multipliers of ADL Model Equations

In Sections 3.6 and 5.4, we defined the dynamic multipliers as the changes in Y_{t+j} that result after a temporary change in ε_t. In the ADL model, we can do the same with respect to a change in ϵ. However, one very attractive feature of ADL models is that they allow us to study the effects of changes in any of the observed explanatory variables. We refer to these effects as dynamic multipliers. Without loss of generality, we can first consider the bivariate case ($n = 2$). We can write the ADL model (6.27) with the aid of the lag-polynomials $\pi(L)$ and $\beta(L)$

$$\pi(L) = 1 - \phi_1 L - \phi_2 L^2 - \cdots - \phi_p L^p, \tag{6.29}$$

$$\beta(L) = \beta_0 + \beta_1 L + \cdots + \beta_p L^p. \tag{6.30}$$

Equation (6.29) is equivalent to (3.75) in Chapter 3. Hence we can write the ADL model equation (6.28) as

$$\pi(L)\,Y_t = \phi_0 + \beta(L)X_t + \epsilon_t. \tag{6.31}$$

Due to stationarity, the lag polynomial $\pi(L)$ has an inverse $\pi(L)^{-1}$:

$$\pi(L)\pi(L)^{-1} = 1,$$

and hence the ADL model can be expressed as

$$Y_t = \pi(L)^{-1}(\phi_0 + \beta(L)X_t + \epsilon_t), \tag{6.32}$$

or

$$Y_t = \frac{\phi_0}{\pi(1)} + \frac{\beta(L)}{\pi(L)}X_t + \frac{1}{\pi(L)}\epsilon_t. \tag{6.33}$$

In Section 3.6, we established that

$$\pi(L)^{-1} \equiv \delta(L) = \delta_0 + \delta_1 L + \delta_2 L^2 + \cdots ,$$

and hence the dynamic multipliers with respect to the disturbance term are given by

$$\frac{\partial Y_t}{\partial \epsilon_{t-j}} = \delta_j, \quad j = 1, 2, \ldots .$$

These dynamic multipliers are sometimes referred to as the *impulse distribution*, as they represent the dynamic effects of a change to the impulse variable ϵ, which is different from the effects of a change in the observable variable X. This impulse distribution is fully described by the eigenvalues of the autoregressive lag polynomial $\phi(L)$, as shown in Section 3.6.

If X_t is independent of the lagged Y-variables, $Y_{t-j}\ \forall j$, (later, we shall refer to this as the case of strong exogeneity of X_t), the dynamic multiplier with respect to X is obtained from $\delta(L)\beta(L)X_t$.

By solving Exercise 6.3, you can show that the multipliers may be expressed as

$$\frac{\partial Y_t}{\partial X_{t-j}} \equiv w_j = \begin{cases} \delta_0\beta_0, & j = 0, \\ \delta_0\beta_1 + \delta_1\beta_0, & j = 1, \\ \delta_{j-2}\beta_2 + \delta_{j-1}\beta_1 + \delta_j\beta_0, & j = 2, 3, \ldots \end{cases} \tag{6.34}$$

for an ADL with second-order dynamics $p = 2$. Remember that $\delta_0 = 1$ in these expressions. This example shows that it is only the impact effect of a change in X that can be read-off directly from the $\beta(L)$-polynomial, i.e., $w_0 = \beta_0$. Already the first dynamic multiplier, w_1, is influenced by the autoregressive part, through δ_1, and so on for the higher order dynamic multipliers. The long-run multiplier gives the effect of a permanent change in X on the stationary solution of Y. In the same way as above, we let Y^* denote the stationary solution, and we choose the particular deterministic solution defined by setting $\epsilon_t = 0$, $\forall t$:

$$Y^* = \frac{\phi_0}{\pi(1)} + \frac{\beta(1)}{\pi(1)} X^*, \tag{6.35}$$

and let X^* denote a constant value of X. This expression is similar to (3.105) above. The only difference is that X^* takes the place of ε^* in (3.105). This is, however, important for the interpretation of the results, since it is easier to imagine a permanent change (a location shift) in an observable conditioning variable X_t than in a random disturbance term. The long-run multiplier with respect to a permanent increase in X, symbolized by β_*, is therefore

$$\frac{\partial Y^*}{\partial X^*} = \frac{\beta(1)}{\pi(1)} \equiv \beta_*.$$

In Chapter 3, we showed that the long-run multiplier is identical to the sum of dynamic multipliers. This also holds for ADL model equations, and the result is easy to establish for the case of second order dynamics $p = 2$. By taking the sum of the multipliers (6.34) and collecting terms, we obtain

$$\begin{aligned}
\sum_{j=0}^{\infty} w_j &= \beta_0\delta_0 + \delta_0\beta_1 + \delta_0\beta_1 + \delta_1\beta_0 + \delta_1\beta_1 + \delta_1\beta_2 + \cdots \\
&= (\beta_0 + \beta_1 + \beta_2) \sum_{j=1}^{\infty} \delta_j \\
&= \frac{(\beta_0 + \beta_1 + \beta_2)}{\pi(1)} = \frac{\partial Y^*}{\partial X^*} \equiv \beta_*.
\end{aligned}$$

Box 6.2. Stationary state and steady state

The long-run relationship (6.35) was defined for the hypothetical stationary case of $X_t = X_{t-1} = X^*$. For economic data, a more relevant hypothetical situation is the *steady state*, where the change in X is

Box 6.2 (*Continued*)

a constant $g_X \neq 0$. By solving Exercise 6.4, you can show that the relationship

$$Y_t^* = S_0 + \beta_* X_t^*$$

holds in the steady state when S_0 is defined in accordance with the ADL model equation. Hence, the long-run multiplier is the same in the more general steady state situation, as it is in the special case of a completely stationary long-run.

It is also possible to take the sum of a finite number of periods. The cumulated effect of a permanent change in X after J periods is

$$w_J^* = \sum_{j=0}^{J} w_j, \quad J = 0, 1, 2, \ldots,$$

where w_j^* is often, and fittingly, referred to as the J-period *interim multiplier*.

Both the dynamic multipliers and the interim multipliers are sometimes presented in a standardized form. The standardized interim multipliers are defined by

$$\bar{w}_J^* = \frac{w_J^*}{\beta_*}, \tag{6.36}$$

which gives the share of the long-run effect achieved J periods after the change in X.

In order to demonstrate the use of these formulas, and the earlier results in Chapter 3, we consider an example where the two lag polynomials are

$$\begin{aligned} \pi(L) &= 1 - 1.1L + 0.4L^2, \\ \beta(L) &= 0.4 + 0.8L + 1.1L^2. \end{aligned} \tag{6.37}$$

The characteristic root associated with $p(\lambda) = \lambda^2 - 1.1\lambda + 0.40$ (cf. (4.42)) is the complex pair $\lambda_1 = 0.55 - 0.31225i$ and $\lambda_2 = 0.55 - 31225i$, with modulus

$$|\lambda| = \sqrt{0.55^2 + (0.31225)^2} = 0.63246.$$

By using equation (3.100)

$$\delta_j \equiv \frac{\partial Y_t}{\partial \varepsilon_{t-j}} = c_1 \lambda_1^j + (1 - c_1)\lambda_2^j, \qquad j = 0, 1, 2, \ldots,$$

and

$$c_1 = \frac{\lambda_1}{\lambda_1 - \lambda_2}, \qquad j = 0, 1, 2, \ldots,$$

we can calculate the first values of the impulse distribution δ_0, δ_1, δ_2, δ_3, δ_4, and a selection of higher order values as well: δ_{10} and δ_{50}. Insertion of the values of the roots gives the value of c_1' that we use in the calculations of δ_j:

$$c_1 = \frac{0.55 + 0.31225i}{0.55 + 0.31225i - (0.55 - 0.31225i)}.$$

For the values of impulse distribution that we have singled out, we obtain

$$\begin{aligned}
\delta_0 &= 1, \\
\delta_1 &= c_1(0.55 + 0.31225i) + (1 - c_1)(0.55 - 0.31225i) = 1.1, \\
\delta_2 &= c_1(0.55 + 0.31225i)^2 + (1 - c_1)(0.55 - 0.31225i)^2 = 0.81, \\
\delta_3 &= c_1(0.55 + 0.31225i)^3 + (1 - c_1)(0.55 - 0.31225i)^3 = 0.451, \\
\delta_4 &= c_1(0.55 + 0.31225i)^4 + (1 - c_1)(0.55 - 0.31225i)^4 = 0.1721, \\
\delta_{10} &= c_1(0.55 + 0.31225i)^{10} + (1 - c_1)(0.55 - 0.31225i)^{10} = -0.011768, \\
\delta_{50} &= c_1(0.55 + 0.31225i)^{50} + (1 - c_1)(0.55 - 0.31225i)^{50} = 0.0000021265.
\end{aligned}$$

As δ_{10} is a small number, and as δ_{50} is practically zero, we infer from (6.34) that the dynamic multiplier numbers 10 and 50 will also be small and negligible. We therefore concentrate on the first four multipliers, which by the use of (6.34) become

$$\begin{aligned}
w_0 &= 0.4, \\
w_1 &= 0.8 + 1.1 \times 0.4 = 1.24, \\
w_2 &= 1.1 + 1.1 \times 0.8 + 0.81 \times 0.4 = 2.3, \\
w_3 &= 1.1 \times 1,1 + 0.81 \times 0.8 + 0.451 \times 0.4 = 2.4, \\
w_4 &= 0.1721 \times 1.1 + 1.1 \times 0.8 + 0.81 \times 0.4 = 1.39.
\end{aligned}$$

This method requires several calculations, and rounding errors are inevitable. It is more practical to calculate the multipliers recursively, and without the use of complex number. The ADL equation corresponding to our example is

$$Y_t = 1.1Y_{t-1} - 0.4Y_{t-2} + 0.4X_t + 0.8X_{t-1} + 1.1X_{t-2} + \epsilon_t, \tag{6.38}$$

and we can find the partial derivatives directly:

$$w_0 = \frac{\partial Y_t}{\partial X_t} = 0.4,$$

$$w_1 = 1.1\frac{\partial Y_{t-1}}{\partial X_{t-1}} + 0.8 = 1.1 \times 0.4 + 0.8 = 1.24,$$

$$w_2 = 1.1\frac{\partial Y_{t-1}}{\partial X_{t-2}} - 0.4\frac{\partial Y_{t-2}}{\partial X_{t-2}} + 1.1 = 1.1 \times 1.24 - 0.4 \times 0.4 + 1.1 = 2.304,$$

$$w_3 = 1.1\frac{\partial Y_{t-1}}{\partial X_{t-3}} - 0.4\frac{\partial Y_{t-2}}{\partial X_{t-3}} = 1.1 \times 2.304 - 0.4 \times 1.24 = 2.0384,$$

$$w_4 = 1.1\frac{\partial Y_{t-1}}{\partial X_{t-4}} - 0.4\frac{\partial Y_{t-2}}{\partial X_{t-4}} = 1.1 \times 2.0384 - 0.4 \times 2.304 = 1.3206.$$

These results confirm the multipliers that we have found above, and also show that rounding errors can affect the decimal values.

Using (6.35) the long-run multiplier is 7.67 in this example. The sum of the five dynamic multipliers is 7.31, hence the fifth interim multiplier is 95% of the long-run effect.

When modern software packages are used to estimate ADL model equations, the different multipliers will be available from the output. Figure 6.1 is based on *PcGive* and plots the dynamic multipliers in panel (a) and the interim multipliers in panel (b).

Box 6.3. Different names for dynamic multipliers

As we have seen above, the mathematics of the dynamic multipliers is closely linked to the impulse response functions of Section 3.6. The convention we use is that impulse responses refer to the dynamic responses with respect to a change in an unobservable disturbance, while dynamic multipliers refer to the responses with respect to a change in an observable, non-modelled explanatory variable. We have also

Box 6.3 (*Continued*)

introduced interim multipliers, the cumulated sum of dynamic multipliers. Finally, long-run multipliers, dynamic and interim multipliers can be standardized (by division with the long-run multiplier).

However, there is no generally accepted terminology. For example, dynamic multipliers are referred to as lag weights in some books and programs, and interim multipliers are sometimes called cumulated lag weights, and also cumulated multipliers.

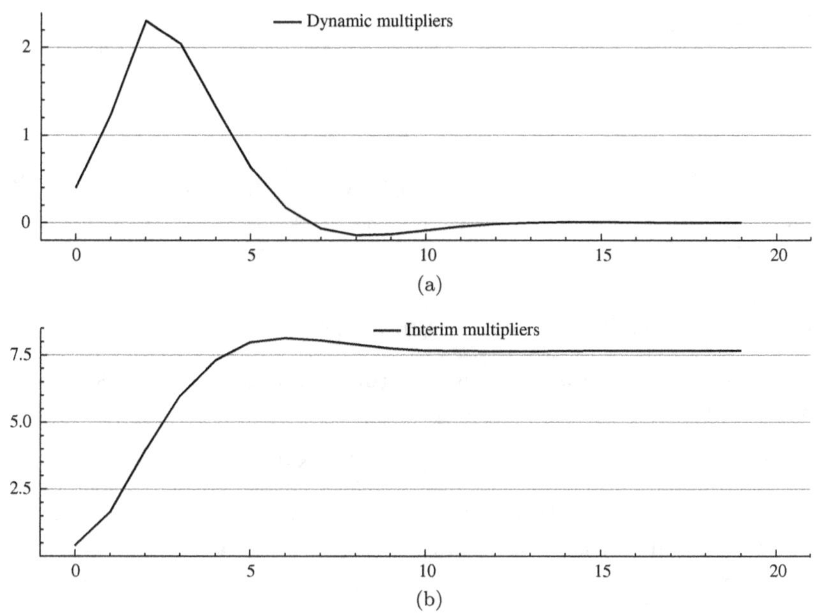

Figure 6.1. Dynamic multipliers and interim multipliers of the ADL equation (6.38).

We have derived the multiplier expressions of the ADL with a single economic explanatory variable. The same mathematics applies for ADL model equations with two or more explanatory variables. In multivariate ADLs, there will be more than one distributed lag in the model equation. Within the framework where the ADL model equation has been derived as a conditional model of a n-dimensional VAR, we have

$$\pi(L)Y_t = \beta_1(L)X_{1t} + \beta_2(L)X_{2t} + \cdots + \beta_{n-1}(L)X_{n-1\ t} + \epsilon_t, \qquad (6.39)$$

where ϵ_t is defined correspondingly to (6.13) and ϵ_t is therefore uncorrelated with $X_{1t}, X_{2t}, \ldots, X_{n-1t}$. The analysis above can be used to find the dynamic multipliers of each distributed lag variable in (6.39), which re-expresses the model equation (6.28) above with the use of lag-polynomial notation.

The estimation of the long-run multipliers $\beta_{*j} = \beta_j(1)/\pi(1)$, $j = 1, 2, \ldots, n-1$, is often of particular interest because of the correspondence to comparative statics that economists are used to work with. Hypothesis testing of long-run multipliers can be done with the aid of the Delta method that we reviewed in Section 2.4.6. How the Delta method can be used for long-run multipliers is explained in Section 6.4, where we focus on the ECM form of the ADL.

6.4. Equilibrium Correction Model

The equilibrium correction model (ECM), is a reparametrization of the ADL which has many applications. In this section we first show the ECM version of the ADL(1, 1) in (6.1), and then discuss generalizations for the ADL's with longer lags and with several explanatory variables.

6.4.1. ECM with first-order dynamics

By subtracting Y_{t-1} on each side of (6.1), and adding and subtracting $\beta_0 X_{t-1}$ on the right-hand side, we obtain

$$\Delta Y_t = \phi_0 + \beta_0 \Delta X_t + (\phi_1 - 1)Y_{t-1} + (\beta_0 + \beta_1)X_{t-1} + \epsilon_t \tag{6.40}$$

which is called an equilibrium correction model although the name error correction model is also in use. However, equilibrium correction is the most precise name of the model since, subject to $-1 < \phi_1 < 1$, we can re-express the model equation with last period's deviation from equilibrium as an explicit variable in the model:

$$\begin{aligned}\Delta Y_t &= \beta_0 \Delta X_t \\ &\quad + (\phi_1 - 1)\left\{Y_{t-1} - \frac{\phi_0}{(1-\phi_1)} - \frac{(\beta_0 + \beta_1)}{(1-\phi_1)}X_{t-1}\right\} + \epsilon_t, \quad -1 < \phi_1 < 1.\end{aligned} \tag{6.41}$$

We can next define $\mu^*_{Y_t|X_t}$ as the conditional equilibrium of Y_t given X_t

$$\mu^*_{Y_t|X_t} = \frac{\phi_0}{(1-\phi_1)} + \frac{(\beta_0 + \beta_1)}{(1-\phi_1)}X_t, \quad -1 < \phi_1 < 1, \tag{6.42}$$

which is a generalization of (6.35), as we obtain

$$\mu^*_{Y_t|X_t} = Y^*,$$

in the stationary case with $X_t = X_{t-1} = X^*$. Hence, (6.41) can be written as

$$\Delta Y_t = \beta_0 \Delta X_t + (\phi_1 - 1)\{Y_{t-1} - \mu^*_{Y_{t-1}|X_{t-1}}\} + \epsilon_t, -1 < \phi_1 < 1. \quad (6.43)$$

The equilibrium correction interpretation is most obvious for the case of $0 < \phi_1 < 1$. In this case, $(\phi_1 - 1)$ is negative, but larger than -1, implying that ΔY_t partly corrects last period's deviation between Y and the conditional equilibrium value $\mu^*_{Y_{t-1}|X_{t-1}}$. In this case, an economic interpretation is also close at hand: $\mu^*_{Y_{t-1}|X_{t-1}}$ can be interpreted as a target variable, and adjustment towards the target is gradual (due to, e.g., costs or information lags). The ECM form of the dynamic equation also covers the case $-1 < \phi_1 < 0$, which is logical, since stationarity also allows the cobweb-style dynamics that we have come across several times in earlier chapters. As we have seen, in this case, the correction is so forceful that a negative deviation from equilibrium in one period is changed to a positive deviation in the next period, and so on.

It is also useful to write the model equation in terms of the two lag-polynomials $\pi(L)$ and $\beta(L)$ above, evaluated at $L = 1$:

$$\Delta Y_t = \phi_0 + \beta_0 \Delta X_t - \pi(1) Y_{t-1} + \beta(1) X_{t-1} + \epsilon_t. \quad (6.44)$$

Note that $\pi(1)$ is the parameter $\pi(1) = 1 - \phi_1$ and $0 < \pi(1) < 2$, as $-1 < \phi_1 < 1$. $\beta(1)$ is also a parameter. Under the same assumptions that OLS gives MLE of the ADL coefficients $(\phi_0, \phi_1, \beta_0, \beta_1)$, the OLS estimation of (6.44) gives MLE of the parameter $(\phi_0, \beta_0, \pi(1), \beta(1))$. Hence, the impact multiplier β_0 can be directly estimated from (6.44). As above, the long-run multiplier is defined for the steady state $X_t = X_{t-1} = X^*$ which implies $\Delta X_t = 0$ in (6.44). Taking the expectation on both sides of (6.44) gives

$$E(\Delta Y_t) = \phi_0 - \pi(1) E(Y_{t-1}) + \beta(1) X^* \quad (6.45)$$

and noting that $E(\Delta Y_t) = 0$ in a stationary state with $\Delta X_t = 0$, we obtain $E(Y_{t-1}) = E(Y_t)$, and we have

$$E(Y_t) \equiv \mu_{Y_t|X^*} \equiv Y^* = \frac{\phi_0}{\pi(1)} + \frac{\beta(1)}{\pi(1)} X^*, \quad (6.46)$$

hence the same long-run relationship as in (6.35) above. The long-run multiplier β_* can therefore be estimated as

$$\widehat{\beta_*} = \frac{\widehat{\beta(1)}}{\widehat{\pi(1)}}. \tag{6.47}$$

Moreover, we can use the Delta-method formula (2.55) above to obtain an estimate of the variance of $\widehat{\beta_*}$. With the notation we use for ECMs, the variance of the long-run multiplier becomes

$$\widehat{\text{Var}}\,(\hat{\beta}_*) \approx \left(\frac{1}{\widehat{\pi(1)}}\right)^2 [\widehat{\text{Var}}\,(\widehat{\beta(1)}) + (\hat{\beta}_*)^2\,\widehat{\text{Var}}\,(\widehat{\pi(1)}) - 2\hat{\beta}_*\widehat{\text{Cov}}\,(\widehat{\beta(1)}, \widehat{\pi(1)})]. \tag{6.48}$$

Box 6.4. ECM and near orthogonalization

As noted above, a high degree of autocorrelation is typical of many macroeconomic time series. Hence, X_t and X_{t-1} are typically highly correlated and as a consequence it may be difficult to make well-founded decisions about the inclusion of the current variable or the lag in an empirical model. One advantage of the ECM reparametrization is that the model equation is in terms of variables that are mutually more orthogonal than the ADL model equation. Specifically, if the correlation between X_t and X_{t-1} is positive and large, the correlation between ΔX_t and X_{t-1} can be near zero. As a result, the estimation of the coefficient β_0 and $\beta(1)$ can be quite precise.

In Section 2.4.6, we used the estimation of a textbook price Phillips curve model (PCM), and the natural rate of unemployment, as an example of the use of the Delta method. As an extension of that model, we assume the following augmented PCM equation:

$$\text{INF}_t = \phi_0 + \phi_1 \text{INF}_{t-1} + \beta_0 U_t + \epsilon_t. \tag{6.49}$$

where INF_t is the annual inflation percentage in period t, and U_t is the unemployment percentage. In ECM form, this equation becomes

$$\Delta\text{INF}_t = \phi_0 - \phi(1)\text{INF}_{t-1} + \beta(1)U_t + \epsilon_t. \tag{6.50}$$

Assume that we are interested in the slope parameter of the long-run PCM, defined by assuming a constant rate of unemployment $U_t = U_{t-1} = U$, and taking the expectation on both sides of (6.50):

$$E(\Delta \text{INF}_t) = \phi_0 + E(-\phi(1)\text{INF}_{t-1} + \beta(1)U). \tag{6.51}$$

Logical consistency implies that the expected rate of inflation is constant, $E(\Delta \text{INF}_t) = 0$, and solving for that constant rate gives the expression for the long-run PCM:

$$\text{INF} = \frac{\phi_0}{\phi(1)} + \underbrace{\frac{\beta(1)}{\phi(1)}}_{\beta_*}U, \tag{6.52}$$

hence the slope parameter that we are interested in estimating is the long-run multiplier β_*. Assume that we estimate β_* as

$$\hat{\beta}_* = \frac{-0.657243}{-(-0.251924)} = -2.608893 \tag{6.53}$$

and that the estimated variances are 0.069692, for $\beta(1)$, and 0.0075731, for $\phi(1)$. Finally, $\widehat{\text{Cov}}(\widehat{\beta(1)}, -\widehat{\phi(1)}) = -0.011887$. Insertion of these numbers in the Delta-method formula (6.48) gives

$$\begin{aligned}\text{Var}(\hat{\beta}_*) &\approx \left(\frac{1}{-0.251924}\right)^2 \times [0.069692 + ((-2.608893)^2) \times 0.0075731 \\ &\quad - 2 \times (-2.60883) \times (-0.011887)] \\ &= \left(\frac{1}{-0.251924}\right)^2 \times 5.9215 \times 10^{-2} = 0.93302.\end{aligned}$$

Hence,

$$\text{Standard error of } \hat{\beta}_* \approx \sqrt{0.93302} = 0.96593.$$

By solving Exercise 6.10, you can compare these results with the results from direct estimation of the long-run PCM slope parameter by nonlinear least squares (NLS). That exercise will also show a third practical way of obtaining the estimated standard errors of long-run multipliers.

Box 6.5. AR(1) is also an ECM

Above we made the point the AR(1) can be interpreted as a special case of ADL(1, 1). However, remember that (unlike the model in differences) the AR(1) is a special case which retains the equilibrium correction interpretation. This is because as long as $-1 < \phi_1 < 1$ the AR(1) defines a stationary time series Y_t, and equilibrium correction is inherent for stationary processes, see Section 3.3.6.

6.4.2. Generalization of the ECM form of ADL

In the (common) case where the ADL model equation contains higher order dynamics, there are more than one ways of writing a valid ECM version of the model equation.

We can use the case with $p = 4$ (ADL(4,4)) as an example to illustrate the point:

$$Y_t - \sum_{i=1}^{4} \phi_i Y_{t-i} = \phi_0 + \sum_{i=0}^{4} \beta_i X_{t-i} + \epsilon_t. \tag{6.54}$$

With lag order four, one possibility is to express the equilibrium correction in terms of Y_{t-4} and X_{t-4}:

$$\begin{aligned} \Delta Y_t = \phi_0 + \sum_{i=1}^{3} \phi_i^{\dagger} \Delta Y_{t-i} + \sum_{i=0}^{3} \beta_i^{\dagger} \Delta X_{t-i} \\ - \pi(1) Y_{t-4} + \beta(1) X_{t-4} + \epsilon_t, \end{aligned} \tag{6.55}$$

where

$$\phi_i^{\dagger} = \sum_{j=1}^{i} \phi_j - 1, \quad i = 1, 2, 3,$$

$$\beta_i^{\dagger} = \sum_{j=0}^{i} \beta_j, \quad i = 1, 2, 3,$$

and $\pi(1)$ and $\beta(1)$ are given by (6.29) and (6.30) by setting $L = 1$ as before. Another possibility is to use Y_{t-1} and X_{t-1} as we did for the simplest ADL with one lag, which gives

$$\begin{aligned} \Delta Y_t = \phi_0 + \sum_{i=1}^{3} \phi_i^{\ddagger} \Delta Y_{t-i} + \sum_{i=0}^{3} \beta_i^{\ddagger} \Delta X_{t-i} \\ - \pi(1) Y_{t-1} + \beta(1) X_{t-1} + \epsilon_t, \end{aligned} \tag{6.56}$$

where

$$\phi_i^{\ddagger} = - \sum_{j=i+1}^{4} \phi_j, \quad i = 1, 2, 3, \tag{6.57}$$

$$\beta_0^{\ddagger} = \beta_0, \tag{6.58}$$

$$\beta_i^{\ddagger} = - \sum_{j=i+1}^{4} \beta_j, \quad i = 1, 2, 3. \tag{6.59}$$

In both (6.55) and (6.55), the long-run multiplier is $\beta^* = \beta(1)/\pi(1)$. The impact multipliers of the two representations are also identical, namely,

$$\beta_0^\dagger = \beta_0^\ddagger = \beta_0,$$

but the remaining coefficients of the ECM model equations are different:

$$\phi_i^\dagger \neq \phi_i^\ddagger, \quad i = 1, 2, 3,$$
$$\beta_i^\dagger \neq \beta_i^\ddagger, \quad i = 1, 2, 3$$

(see Bårdsen, 1989).

Hence, (6.55) and (6.56) have the same statistical interpretation as re-parametrizations of the ADL(4,4). The difference lies in the interpretation of the lag polynomial coefficient of the changes ΔX_t and ΔY_t. The same is true for different hybrid ECMs that we can think of. One such will be where the level part of the equation is $-\phi(1)Y_{t-1} + \beta(1)X_{t-4}$. In practice, it will be properties of the dataset chosen for the modelling purpose that will decide which re-parametrization that will be most easy to work with.

There is also a straightforward extension of the ECM formulation to ADLs with two or more distributed lags, as in model equation (6.39). Without loss of generality, we set $n = 3$ so that we have two conditioning variables (X_{1t} and X_{2t}) and their associated distributed lags:

$$\pi(L)Y_t = \phi_0 + \beta_1(L)X_{1t} + \beta_2(L)X_{2t} + \epsilon_t.$$

If we choose to collect the levels variables on the first lag, we obtain

$$\begin{aligned}\Delta Y_t = \phi_0 + \phi^\ddagger(L)\Delta Y_{t-i} + \beta_1^\ddagger(L)\Delta X_{1t} + \beta_2^\ddagger(L)\Delta X_{2t}\\ - \pi(1)Y_{t-1} + \beta_1(1)X_{1t-1} + \beta_2(1)X_{2t-1} + \varepsilon_t,\end{aligned}$$

where the three lag-polynomials $\phi^\ddagger(L)$, $\beta_1^\ddagger(L)$ and $\beta_2^\ddagger(L)$ are defined in accordance with (6.57)–(6.59).

The two long-run multipliers $\beta_{*1} = \beta_1(1)/\pi(1)$ and $\beta_{*2} = \beta_2(1)/\pi(1)$ can be estimated by the use of the Delta method in the same way as we have seen for only a single distributed lag. In order to obtain estimates of the variances $\widehat{\text{Var}}(\hat{\beta}_{*1})$ and $\widehat{\text{Var}}(\hat{\beta}_{*2})$ we therefore use formula (6.48).

6.5. Special Cases of the ADL Model

As we have seen, the ECM is a one-to-one reparametrization of the ADL model. There is however, a typology of models that can be seen as special cases of the ADL model. For simplicity of notation, we consider the case with first-order dynamics, as the extension to higher order dynamics suggests itself for these models.

6.5.1. Static model

If the joint hypothesis $\phi_1 = \beta_1 = 0$ is true, (6.1) simplifies to

$$Y_t = \phi_0 + \beta_0 X_t + \epsilon_t, \tag{6.60}$$

without affecting the statistical properties of ϵ_t. In this case, the static regression is a valid reduction or simplification of the ADL$(1, 1)$. As already explained, we expect this to be a rare finding for real-life economic time series data because non-trivial adjustment lags represent the normal case.

If the joint hypothesis $\phi_1 = \beta_1 = 0$ does not hold, the disturbance of the static regression between Y_t and X_t cannot logically be independent of the information set Y_{t-1}, X_t and X_{t-1}, even if it is uncorrelated with X_t alone. Hence, the estimation of β_0 will be biased due to omitted variables. In general, the error terms will also be autocorrelated.

The test of the joint hypothesis is of the likelihood ratio type using either the critical values of the Chi-square distribution with 2 degrees of freedom (asymptotic test) or the Student t-distribution for better finite sample properties.

The estimation results in (6.21) indicate that the coefficients of P_{t-1} and Q_{t-1} can be restricted to zero, which would be an example of $\phi_1 = \beta_1 = 0$ holding (of course, looking back at the data construction in the DGP shows that this is not surprising). By solving Exercise 6.5, you can conclude on the basis of a formal test. On the other hand, (6.23) may not be reducible to a static model, see Exercise 6.6.

6.5.2. Common factor model

In order to show a special case of (6.1) called as the *common factor model*, we start by writing the ADL$(1, 1)$ equation by the use of the lag-operator

$$(1 - \phi_1 L)Y_t = \phi_0 + (\beta_0 + \beta_1 L)X_t + \epsilon_t,$$

and then factorizing the two lag-polynomials

$$(1 - \phi_1 L) = \phi^*(L)\phi^{**}(L),$$

$$(\beta_0 + \beta_1 L) = \beta^*(L)\beta^{**}(L),$$

where $\phi^*(L) = 1$, $\phi^{**}(L) = 1-\phi_1 L$, $\beta^*(L) = \beta_0$ and $\beta^{**}(L) = 1+(\beta_1/\beta_0)\,L$. If the restriction

$$\phi^{**}(L) = \beta^{**}(L),$$

holds, the two polynomials have a common factor

$$(1-\phi_1 L) = \left(1+\frac{\beta_1}{\beta_0}L\right),$$

or

$$(\beta_0 + \beta_1 L) = (1-\phi_1 L)\beta_0. \tag{6.61}$$

In this case, a simplification of (6.1) becomes

$$Y_t = \frac{1}{1-\phi_1 L}\phi_0 + \beta_0 X_t + \frac{1}{1-\phi_1 L}\epsilon_t,$$

or

$$Y_t = \eta + \beta_0 X_t + u_t, \qquad u_t = \phi_1 u_{t-1} + \epsilon_t \tag{6.62}$$

where $\eta = \phi_0/(1-\phi_1)$ and the error term u_t therefore follows a first-order autoregressive process: $u_t \sim \text{AR}(1)$.

Hence, in the case restriction (6.61) holds, the dynamics of the ADL(1, 1) model have been "packaged into" an autocorrelated regression error term of an otherwise static equation. Note that the common-factor model has the same strong implication as the static equation, namely that the impact multiplier is identical to the long-term multiplier. The first dynamic multiplier is also zero; see Exercise 6.7. Hence, the common-factor model (6.62) is only suitable in cases where it is realistic that the adjustment period may be very short, so that a static model is good approximation in the first place.

In the case of higher order dynamics, its relevance is perhaps greater, as a modification of lag length truncation (see Hendry and Mizon, 1978). On the other hand, estimation of a static model equation together with observation of serially correlated residuals do not constitute valid evidence that the common factor restriction holds, even if the serial correlation appears to be well modelled by an AR(1) process. What needs to be tested statistically is (6.61), which needs to be validated empirically.

In the first-order case, the Comfac-restriction (6.61) is equivalent with $\beta_1 = -\phi_1\beta_0$, which is a nonlinear restriction between the parameters. This complicates the statistical tests, which is, however, shown to be Chi-square with one degree of freedom distributed under the null hypothesis that the restriction is true. The test is available in PcGive, which also has the capability of testing generalizations of (6.61) within the framework of general ADL model equations (with $n-1$ explanatory variables, and lag order p; cf. Doornik and Hendry (2013a, Section 18.3.4)).

6.5.3. Distributed lag

If the joint hypothesis $\phi_1 = 0$ is true, (6.1) simplifies to

$$Y_t = \phi_0 + \beta_0 X_t + \beta_1 X_{t-1} + \epsilon_t. \tag{6.63}$$

Unlike the static model (obviously) and the Common factor model, model equation (6.63) represents a genuine dynamic relationship between X and Y, as the impact multiplier is β_0 while the long-run multiplier is $\beta_0 + \beta_1$. Nevertheless, the property that the multipliers are uniquely determined by the distributed lag (DL) coefficient is a serious limitation in many applications.

However, it would leave a wrong impression to only present the DL model as a special case of the ADL. Models with relatively long distributed lags, and perhaps in combination with a rational lag distribution hypothesis (see Section 6.6), can be seen as an *alternative* to the ADL approach. In statistical modelling in particular, that approach is known as the estimation of transfer functions (see Harvey, 1990, Chapter 7).

6.5.4. Model in differences

If the hypothesis

$$\phi_1 = 1 \quad \text{and} \quad \beta_1 = -\beta_0, \tag{6.64}$$

is true, (6.1) simplifies to

$$\Delta Y_t = \phi_0 + \beta_0 \Delta X_t + \epsilon_t. \tag{6.65}$$

Equation (6.65) is a static model for the change in Y_t. If, for example, Y is the natural logarithm of the price level, the left-hand side variable of (6.65) is approximately equal to the inflation rate, and $\Delta Y_t \times 100$ is the approximate inflation rate in percent. The β_0 coefficient measures the response of the inflation rate to a small change in ΔX_t, an increase in the rate of wage growth for example.

At the same time, (6.65) implies a dynamic model equation for Y_t. However, that difference equation does not have a globally asymptotically stable solution (see Exercise 6.8). Hence, model equation (6.65) cannot be used to estimate a long-run relationship between X and Y. Unlike in the static model equation case, β_0 has the interpretation of a short-term multiplier. It says nothing about a long-run response because a long-run relationship has been "ruled out" by the model specification (6.65).

In the opposite case, where either $\phi_1 = 1$ or $\beta_1 = -\beta_0$ are invalid restrictions on the ADL$(1,1)$ model equation, (6.65) becomes an example of what we have referred to as over-differentiation, cf. Section 4.5.6, and in that case the properties of the error term of the model in differences cannot have the same (classical) properties as assumed for the ADL model equation. If we, for example, consider $-1 < \phi_1 < 1$ and $\beta_1 = -\beta_0$, the correct model equation becomes

$$\Delta Y_t = \phi_1 \Delta Y_{t-1} + \beta_0 \Delta^2 X_t + \Delta \epsilon_t, \tag{6.66}$$

which is different from (6.65), and where in particular the error term is a non-invertible MA process in the same way as in equation (4.36) above.

However, if the purpose is to estimate a restricted version of the original ADL relationship (6.1), it is unnecessarily complicated to estimate (6.66). Instead, we can simply estimate

$$Y_t = \phi_0 + \phi_1 Y_{t-1} + \beta_0 \Delta X_t + \epsilon_t,$$

as the disturbance term of this relationship is the same as in the ADL (under the null hypothesis that restriction $\beta_1 = -\beta_0$ holds).

6.5.5. AR(1)

The AR(1) is the simplest example a stochastic difference equation (Chapter 3) and we discussed the estimation of the AR(1) as a stationary econometric model in Section 4.6.

The joint zero restriction $\beta_0 = \beta_1 = 0$, and the stationarity condition $-1 < \phi_1 < 1$ gives the AR(1) as a special case of the ADL (6.1).

6.5.6. The null model

A null model has no explanatory variables apart from the intercept, Agresti (2015, p. 41). Another name that statisticians sometimes use is the location model, since the only estimated coefficients are the location parameter ϕ_0, and the scale parameter σ^2, Hendry and Nielsen (2007, p. 32). In the context of the ADL$(1,1)$ it is the special case that corresponds to not being able to reject the joint null hypothesis: $\phi_1 = \beta_0 = \beta_1 = 0$.

6.6. Geometric Lag Distribution

As pointed out above, one attractive feature of ECM model equations is the reduction of multicollinearity by the combination of differenced data with lagged levels of variables (cf. Box 6.4). Historically, there have been other attempts to reduce the degree of multicollinearity by imposing some *a priori* structure on the form of the lag. Two important contributions were Koyck (1954) and Almon (1965). The first of these has given rise to the Koyck-transformation and is an example of a so-called rational distributed lag (see Harvey, 1990, Section 7.1). The starting point of that method was the model equation

$$Y_t = \phi_0 + \sum_{i=0}^{p} \beta_i X_{t-i} + \epsilon_t, \tag{6.67}$$

which is known as a distributed lag equation. Due to autocorrelation, a practical problem with this class of dynamic model has been multicollinearity "within the distributed lag". If p is a relatively large number, a big reduction in the number of parameters to be estimated is achieved by assuming the *geometric lag distribution*

$$\beta_i = \beta_0 \alpha^i, \quad i = 0, 1, 2 \ldots, p, \quad \text{and} \quad 0 < \alpha < 1 \tag{6.68}$$

which is a special case of *rational lag distribution.* Analytically, it is convenient to assume an infinite distributed lag

$$Y_t = \phi_0 + \beta_0 \sum_{i=0}^{\infty} \alpha^i X_{t-i} + \epsilon_t. \tag{6.69}$$

Writing this equation for period $t-1$ and multiplying both sides by α gives

$$\alpha Y_{t-1} = \alpha\phi_0 + \beta_0 \sum_{i=0}^{\infty} \alpha^{i+1} X_{t-i-1} + \alpha\epsilon_{t-1}.$$

Subtraction of the lagged equation from the first gives

$$Y_t = (1-\alpha)\phi_0 + \alpha Y_{t-1} + \beta_0 X_t + \epsilon_t + \alpha\epsilon_{t-1}. \tag{6.70}$$

The simple form of the observable part of this equation is appealing, but note that the simplicity is, to some extent, illusory. If the disturbance term in the distributed lag model equation (6.67) is Gaussian white noise, equation (6.70) is not an ADL, but an ARMA, augmented with the regressor X_t. Due to the residual autocorrelation, OLS needs to be replaced by a maximum likelihood estimation method (feasible GLS).

However, the above transformation has proven to be useful in other applications, such as in the derivation of the GARCH model below, see Section 6.8.

Finally, we note an interesting duality between the dynamic multipliers of ADL models and the geometric lag distribution. As we saw in Section 6.3, the dynamic multipliers after a while (for relatively low j numbers) become dominated by the impulse distribution (δ_j), which are determined by the eigenvalues of the autoregressive lag polynomial. If the largest eigenvalue is real, positive (but less than one, as stationarity requires), the middle and upper parts of the multiplier distribution will be similar to a general geometric decay.

6.7. Empirical ADL Modelling of Interest Rate Transmission

The two examples of ADL estimation above, a conditional model (cobweb), and a structural equation that was estimated by IV (Keynes model,) were using computer-generated data. We also took care to specify the ADL model equations in accordance with the DGP used to simulate the experimental time series data. Hence, there was no danger of misspecifying the ADL model equations.

As noted above, in Section 2.8, when we model real-world observable data, the specification issue moves to the forefront. Any real-world DGP is unknown to us as econometricians, and is likely to be complex even when the purpose is to model only a couple of variables for which we have good measurements.

As the reader will be aware, there are many sources and consequences of misspecification. There may be nonlinearities hidden in the data that are not represented by a linear in parameter model, and can result in, for example, heteroskedasticity. Outliers, due to structural breaks, are typical in real-world data, and will produce residuals that are extremely unlikely as realization of a normal distribution.

The most consequential misspecification may be omitted variables. However, variables that only play a minor effect in the DGP, or which are orthogonal to the included variables, do not produce large biases in the estimated ADL coefficients, so there are negligible costs of omitting such variables. But already that conclusion implies that the researcher has given a good deal of thought to the DGP, and how it can approximated by a model.

In practice, orthogonality is hard to achieve with respect to all the parameters of interest, and the cost of thinking wrong about the system may be large even if the research purpose is to model only a part of the system, as we have indicated above. For example, if the VAR that represents the true DGP has three correlated endogenous variables, X_t, Y_t and Z_t, the coefficients of a two-variable ADL will be biased relative to the true conditional model coefficients even if we manage to get the dynamic specification right.

We will discuss strategies for model specification in Chapter 11, and for the present example, we refer to the specification algorithm known as General-to-specific (Gets), which starts from an initial specification that is likely to contain the DGP as a special case.

Often, real-world applications require that we give econometric treatment to non-stationarity in the form of unit-roots. That step is explained in detail in a later chapter. Meanwhile, we can choose to model a relationship that goes clear of at least the most blatant non-stationarity issues. The relationship between the monetary policy instrument and a representative interest rate on bank loans is a possible candidate, and has considerable economic interest. The existence and robustness of such a relationship is an important part of the transmission mechanism from the policy determined interest rate to the macroeconomy (see Bårdsen *et al.* (2003) for a complete econometric treatment of transmission in the context of the changed monetary policy regime).

Figure 6.2 shows the time plots of quarterly data of the interest rate *RNB* set by the Norwegian monetary policy authority, Norges Bank, and the average interest rate on bank loan, RL. The graphs are clearly in support of a relationship, which also appears to have become stronger from the mid-1990s and onwards. This is not surprising since the 1990s was a period of transition, away from a policy of nominal exchange rate control, and towards inflation targeting. The formal introduction of inflation targeting came in March 2001, but in practise the policy may have been geared in that direction during the last half of the 1990s. We therefore attempt to model a relationship on a sample which starts in 1994(1) and ends in 2016(3).

With quarterly data, a lag length of two is relevant for this relationship due to the relatively fast transmission through credit markets. As a control variable, we included a foreign money market interest rate, hence with reference to (6.28) we have $p = 2$ and $(n - 1) = 2$. The final specification produced by the Gets algorithm that was used, see Chapter 11, retained single lags of each variable, but specifies two impulse dummies in addition

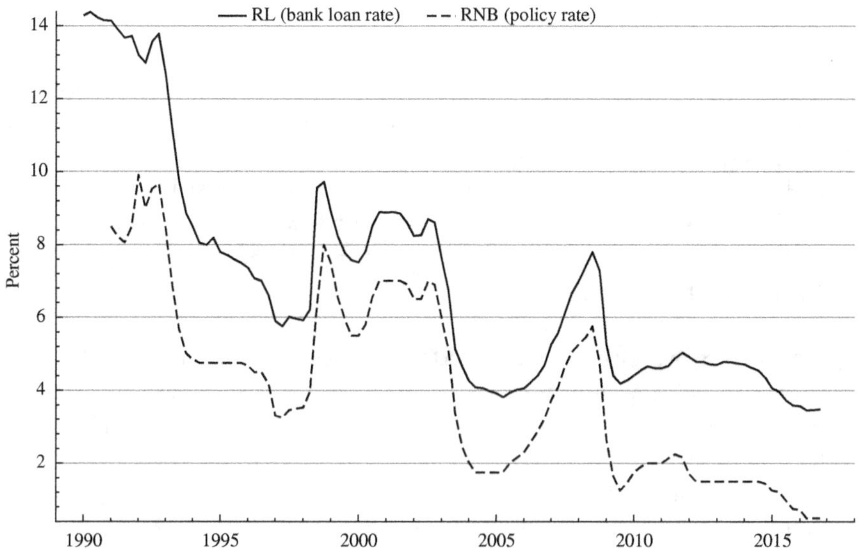

Figure 6.2. Bank loan interest rate (RL) and Norges Bank's policy interest rate (RNB). *Source:* Database of NAM (Norwegian Aggregate Model).

to the constant term: $I_{1998(3),t}$ is an indicator variable which is 1 in 1998(3) and zero elsewhere. $I_{1998(4),t}$ is 1 in 1998(4) and zero elsewhere.

$$\begin{aligned}\text{RL} = \underset{(0.08)}{0.26} + \underset{(0.026)}{0.91}\ \text{RL}_{t-1} + \underset{(0.03)}{0.86}\ \text{RNB}_t - \underset{(0.04)}{0.79}\ \text{RNB}_{t-1} \\ + \underset{(0.15)}{1.31}\ I_{1998(3),t} - \underset{(0.14)}{1.14}\ I_{1998(4),t}, \end{aligned} \tag{6.71}$$

$$\text{OLS}\quad \mathcal{L} = 63.602,\ \hat{\sigma} = 0.1244,\ T = 91, [1994(1) - 2016(3)],$$

$$\begin{aligned} F_{ar(1-5)}(5,80) &= 1.24[0.30] \\ \chi^2_{\text{norm}}(2) &= 5.91[0.05] \\ F_{\text{het}}(6,82) &= 2.83[0.02] \\ F_{\text{arch}(1-4)}(4,83) &= 2.30[0.07] \end{aligned}$$

Note that since the coefficients of the two dummies are comparable in size, but have different signs, they can be replaced by a single variable $\Delta I_{1998(3),t} = I_{1998(3),t} - I_{1998(4),t}$, i.e., +1 followed by −1 and zero elsewhere without much loss of explanatory power.

In the battery of misspecification test, only the test of heteroskedasticty due to squares of regressor is significant at the 2.5% level. Hence, the estimated coefficient standard error could have been replaced by heteroskedastic consistent ones, but in this case the impression of clear significance in (6.71) of the retained coefficients is not changed. The coefficients also have the expected signs, that also include the negative coefficient of the lagged policy interest rate. As long as the coefficient is less in absolute value than the coefficient of RNB_t, (6.71) is consistent with positive transmission of an increase in RNB on to RL. We return to this point below.

6.8. Volatility Modelling

In Section 2.8, we introduced the ARCH process in the context of testing the linear model's assumption about constant and time invariant variance (σ^2) of the model equation's error term. However, ARCH has also represented the start of financial econometrics because it represents an operational model for modelling the volatility of yields or returns in financial markets. To illustrate this, we can use the simple model location model of a Gaussian time series Y_t:

$$Y_t = \phi_0 + \varepsilon_t, \tag{6.72}$$

$$\varepsilon_t \sim N(0, \sigma_{\varepsilon t}^2 \mid \mathcal{I}_{t-1}), \tag{6.73}$$

where the interpretation of (6.72) is that the variance of ε_t is itself a random variable conditional on information available in period $t-1$. To make progress, we need to specify a time series model for $\sigma_{\varepsilon t}^2$. One of the most successful specifications is known as Generalized ARCH (GARCH), and is due to Bollerslev (1986). The basic GARCH model, and the one most used in practice, is

$$\sigma_{\varepsilon t}^2 = \sigma^2 + \tau\varepsilon_{t-1}^2 + \varsigma\sigma_{\varepsilon t-1}^2, \quad \tau \geq 0, \varsigma > 0. \tag{6.74}$$

By solving Exercise 6.12, you can see that (6.74) can be derived from the infinite ARCH process:

$$\sigma_{\varepsilon t}^2 = \varkappa^2 + \sum_{j=1}^{\infty} \varrho_j \varepsilon_{t-j}^2,$$

by imposing a geometric lag distribution in the same way as in Section 6.6. We note that the restriction $\tau + \varsigma < 1$ is required for the stationarity of the GARCH process, and hence for internal consistency with overall stationarity of Y_t. $\tau > 0$ together with $\varsigma = 0$ is seen to give a first-order ARCH, which is usually regarded as a too restrictive model of the variability of financial returns.

As we have just seen, the GARCH model (6.74) is motivated as parsimonious in parameter approximation of higher order ARCH processes. A significant value of ς in particular implies a smoothly, and potentially slowly, decaying autocorrelation function for $\sigma^2_{\varepsilon t}$. The higher ς is, the more manifest is the phenomenon of *volatility clustering*, which refers to the observation that large changes in returns tend to be followed by large changes of either sign (hence the squared return gets large) and small changes tend to be followed by small changes (see Mandelbrot, 1963).

Modern econometric software packages allows easy estimation of volatility models. Re-estimating the model equation for RL with the use of the GARCH model category in PcGive gives the estimation results in (6.75).

$$\begin{aligned}
\mathrm{RL} = {} & \underset{(0.06)}{0.37} + \underset{(0.019)}{0.88}\ \mathrm{RL}_{t-1} + \underset{(0.02)}{0.86}\ \mathrm{RNB}_t - \underset{(0.03)}{0.77}\ \mathrm{RNB}_{t-1} \\
& + \underset{(0.09)}{1.25}\ I_{1998(3),t} - \underset{(0.09)}{1.22}\ I_{1998(4),t}, \\
& \mathcal{L} = 71.10,\ T = 91, [1994(1) - 2016(3)], \\
& \mathrm{GARCH}(1,1): \\
& \qquad \tau = 0.79[0.25], \\
& \qquad \varsigma = 0.07[0.12].
\end{aligned} \tag{6.75}$$

We see that there is empirical support for first-order ARCH effect, as the τ parameter is estimated to 0.79 with a t-value of 3.3. This is not entirely surprising when we consider the test for residual fourth-order ARCH effects in (6.71), which has a p-value of 0.07. There is little evidence of volatility clustering in the residuals of the RL model equation, as the estimate of ς is close to zero and statistically insignificant. The estimates of the derivative coefficients of the conditional expectation function change very little, the most noticeable change from (6.71) is that all the estimated standard errors become lower in (6.75).

6.9. Exercises

Exercise 6.1. Show that the error term ϵ_t in the ADL model (6.10) can be written as

$$\epsilon_t = \varepsilon_{yt} - \frac{\sigma_{xy}}{\sigma_x^2}\varepsilon_{xt},$$

where $(\varepsilon_{yt}, \varepsilon_{xt})'$ is normally distributed (cf. (6.2)).

Exercise 6.2. Show the result in equation (6.15).

Exercise 6.3. Show the result in equation (6.34).

Exercise 6.4. Consider an ADL$(1,1)$ model with Y_t as the endogenous variable, and X_t as the exogenous variable. Assume that X_t evolves around a deterministic growth path, so that

$$\Delta X_t^* = g_X,$$

where g_X is a constant. Determine the coefficients S_0 and S_1 in the long-run equation:

$$Y_t^* = S_0 + S_1 X_t^*,$$

so that ΔY_t^* is consistent with the ADL.

Exercise 6.5. Use the (computer-generated) data for the cobweb model to test whether (6.22) can be simplified to a static model equation based on a valid statistical test.

Exercise 6.6. Use the (computer-generated) data for the cobweb model to test whether (6.23) can be simplified to a static model equation based on a valid statistical test.

Exercise 6.7. Show for the Comfac version of the ADL$(1,1)$ equation, the impact multiplier is β_0, and that all the dynamic multipliers are zero.

Exercise 6.8. Show that the model equation in difference (6.65) implies that there is no globally stable solution of Y_t.

Exercise 6.9. Consider the ADL$(1,1)$ in (6.1) with Gaussian properties of the disturbance ϵ_t. Assume $-1 < \phi_1 < 1$ and $\beta_0 = -\beta_1$. Show that the implied (correct) difference equation of ΔY_t is given by (6.66).

Exercise 6.10. Use one of the formats of the datasets in NORPCMb.zip to replicate the result for $\hat{\beta}_*$ and $\mathrm{Var}(\hat{\beta}_*)$ above, where β_* are the slope coefficients of the long-run PCM as defined in the main text of this chapter.

There are three data series in NORPCMb. INF and U are the same variables as in the dataset called NORPCMa set, which we used for estimation of a price Phillips curve model for Norway in Section 2.4.6, and the associated natural rate of unemployment, see also Exercise 2.11. The third variable is $D80$. It is an indicator variable for the year 1980: It is 1 in 1980 and zero elsewhere. The interpretation is that price-and-wage freezes were a part of active income policies during the 1960s and 1970s (this was common in western European countries). In Norway, there was a prize freeze in

1979 which was lifted in 1980. Hence, if there was a price *catch-up* after the end of the freeze-period, we expect $D80$ to have a positive and significant coefficient when included in the model.

In order to replicate the results, you need to include $D80$ in the model, and choose the sample period 1980–2005.

Exercise 6.11. What are the expressions for the ECM lag polynomials if (6.54) is rewritten with $\pi(1)Y_{t-1}$ and $\beta(1)X_{t-4}$?

Exercise 6.12. Assume a geometric lag distribution, and show that the GARCH process (6.74) can be derived by the use of the same transformation as in Section 6.6.

Chapter 7

Multiple Equation Models

A multiple equation econometric model can consist of conditional and marginal equations or it can be a simultaneous equation model (SEM). Both types of models can be formulated as reparametrizations of the vector autoregressive (VAR) models, and they also can be further specified in ways that imply testable restrictions on the VAR. The restrictions can represent economic theoretical hypotheses or they may represent institutional and historical knowledge. Other types of multiple equations models are recursive models, and structural VARs. This chapter presents the different models within a common framework. SEMs, in particular, require careful analysis of identification, and of choice of estimators that not subject to the simultaneous equation bias.

7.1. Introduction

Multiple equation models in econometrics can be viewed as attempts to give economic interpretation to the system of variables in the vector autoregressive (VAR) model. As noted above, it may also be that a single equation project leads us to giving econometric treatment to a larger system. For example, the validity of estimated dynamic multipliers rests on exogeneity assumptions about the regressors in the autoregressive distributed lag (ADL) model. Testing those assumptions can only be done in a multiple equation model.

We commence by extending the closed VAR of Chapter 6 with non-modelled variables. The open VAR is also known as the VAR-EX. We show that a model that consists of both conditional and marginal equations can represent the same statistical information as the VAR, and that restrictions can be imposed (after testing) to give economic interpretability to the relationships between the variables. Another "one-to-one" reparametrization of the VAR is an exactly identified simultaneous equations model (SEM). An over-identified SEM represents an economically interpretable model that encompasses the VAR. Other types of multiple equations models are *recursive models*, and *structural VARs*. This chapter presents different models within a common framework. SEM, in particular, requires careful analysis of identification prior to estimation. In order to have consistently estimated coefficients, identified SEM equations require estimation methods that avoid the simultaneous equation bias of ordinary least square (OLS) estimation. Instrumental variable (IV), generalized IV (GIV) and 2-stage least square (2SLS) estimations were reviewed in Chapter 2, and these methods are used in this chapter in the context of dynamic simultaneous equations.

7.2. Extending the System: VAR-EX

We start by augmenting the VAR in (5.4) with a vector of m non-modelled (exogenous) time series:

$$\underset{(m\times 1)}{\mathbf{x}_t} = (X_{1t}, X_{2t}, \ldots, X_{mt})',$$

in addition to the n endogenous variables $\underset{(n\times 1)}{\mathbf{y}_t} = (Y_{1t}, Y_{2t}, \ldots, Y_{nt})'$, and write the VAR as

$$\mathbf{y}_t = \sum_{i=1}^{p} \mathbf{\Phi}_i \mathbf{y}_{t-i} + \sum_{i=0}^{q} \mathbf{\Gamma}_i \mathbf{x}_{t-i} + \mathbf{\Upsilon D}_t + \varepsilon_t, \tag{7.1}$$

$$\varepsilon_t \sim \text{IIN}(\mathbf{0}, \mathbf{\Sigma}), \tag{7.2}$$

where $\mathbf{\Gamma}_i$ $(i = 1, 2, \ldots, q)$ are $(m \times m)$ matrices holding the coefficients of the non-modelled variables. The other notation is defined in the same way as for (5.4).

Equations (7.1) and (7.2) are called Open-VAR or VAR-EX, since there are non-modelled (exogenous) variables in the system.

In principle, it is possible to interpret (7.1) as a derived system obtained by conditioning the first n endogenous variables (the Ys) on the last m variables (the Xs) of an even larger VAR with $n + m$ endogenous variables. In that interpretation, (7.1) is a (big) conditional VAR, and we can think of $\mathbf{x}_t$ as given by a "marginal VAR".

7.3. Modelling the VAR by Conditional and Marginal Equations

In Section 6.2.1 of Chapter 6, we showed how a first-order VAR with two endogenous variables ($n = 2$), and with only constant terms ($\boldsymbol{\Upsilon}\mathbf{D}_t = (\phi_{10}, \phi_{20})'$), can be reparametrized in terms of two econometric equations. The first equation was the conditional model of Y_t given the other endogenous variable in the VAR (X_t in that chapter). The second equation was simply the second row of the VAR, the marginal model for the second endogenous variable in the VAR; see the summary in Box 6.1. For reference, we repeat the equations of the *conditional plus marginal model* of the bivariate VAR(1) as

$$Y_t = \phi_0 + \phi_1 Y_{t-1} + \beta_0 X_t + \beta_1 X_{t-1} + \epsilon_t, \tag{7.3}$$

$$X_t = \phi_{20} + \phi_{21} Y_{t-1} + \phi_{22} X_{t-1} + \varepsilon_{xt}, \tag{7.4}$$

where $(\epsilon_t, \varepsilon_{xt})$, $t = 1, 2, \ldots, T$, are independent and identically distributed variable pairs $\mathrm{Cov}(\epsilon_t, \varepsilon_{xt}) = 0$, $\mathrm{Var}(\epsilon_t) \equiv \sigma^2 = \sigma_y^2(1 - \rho_{xy}^2)$ and $\mathrm{Var}(\varepsilon_{2t}) = \sigma_x^2$.

We illustrated this point by using the cobweb model dataset by showing that the sum of the maximized log-likelihoods of the conditional model of P_t given Q_t, and of the marginal model of Q_t, become identical to the maximized likelihood of the VAR. This proves, by example, that we can represent the statistical information in the VAR by using multiple equation models that consist of conditional model equations, and of marginal equations.

As another example, we look at the VAR-EX with $n = 3$, $m = 1$, $p = 1, q = 0$. In this case, the statistical information of the VAR cannot be represented by a single conditional model and one (or two) completely marginal model equations. Instead, we formulate a multiple equation model that consists of structured conditional models. For example, if we choose Y_{1t} as our focus variable, the multiple equation model of the VAR can be written as

$$\begin{aligned} Y_{1t} &= \phi_{0|2,3} + \phi_{11|2,3} Y_{1t-1} + \beta_{10|2,3} Y_{2t} + \beta_{11|2,3} Y_{2t-1} \\ &\quad + \beta_{20|2,3} Y_{3t} + \beta_{21|2,3} Y_{3t-1} + \beta_{40|2,3} X_{1t} + \epsilon_{1|2,3\,t}, \end{aligned} \tag{7.5}$$

$$\begin{aligned} Y_{2t} &= \phi_{0|3} + \phi_{21|3} Y_{1t-1} + \phi_{22|3} Y_{2t-1} + \beta_{20|3} Y_{3t} \\ &\quad + \beta_{21|3} Y_{3t-1} + \beta_{40|3} X_{1t} + \epsilon_{2|3\,t}, \end{aligned} \tag{7.6}$$

$$Y_{3t} = \phi_{30} + \phi_{31} Y_{1t-1} + \phi_{32} Y_{2t-1} + \phi_{33} Y_{3t-1} + \gamma_{30} X_{1t} + \varepsilon_{3t}, \tag{7.7}$$

where the notation for the coefficients is chosen in order to highlight the conditioning.

Hence, in (7.5), $\phi_{0|2,3}$ denotes the intercept in the ADL model equation for Y_{1t} that conditions on both Y_{2t} and Y_{3t}. $\phi_{11|2,3}$ is the autoregressive coefficients in that model equation. $\beta_{10|2,3}$ and $\beta_{20|2,3}$ are the impact coefficients of Y_{2t} and Y_{3t} in that conditional model, and so on. The notation used for the disturbance, $\epsilon_{1|2,3\ t}$, is also chosen to highlight that it is the error term in an ADL equation for the first variable in the VAR, conditional on variable numbers 2 and 3 in the VAR.

In equation (7.6), the conditioning is on Y_{3t}. $\beta_{20|3}$ is therefore the impact coefficient of Y_{3t} in that conditional model of Y_{2t}. $\epsilon_{2|3t}$ is the disturbance of this particular conditional model equation. Finally, in equation (7.7), there is no conditioning. This equation is identical to the last row in the VAR-EX, i.e., it is the marginal model equation for Y_{3t}.

By solving Exercise 7.1, you can, in an example, show that the estimation of (7.5)–(7.7) by OLS for each equation gives exactly the same log-likelihood as the estimation of the unrestricted VAR.

A model like (7.5)–(7.7) can be particularly useful when the purpose is to estimate the dynamic multipliers of Y_{1t} with respect to a change in X_{1t}. If the estimation of the dynamic multipliers is done as a single equation analysis, i.e., (7.5) as an ADL for Y_{1t}, we will miss the indirect effects that a change in X_1 may have on Y_1. By inspecting (7.5)–(7.7), we see that indirect effects can be due to $\beta_{40|3} \neq 0$ and/or $\gamma_{30} \neq 0$. Clearly, by estimation of the three equation model, we can not only test the two hypotheses that would validate the single equation analysis, but also calculate the multipliers based on the multiple equation model.

As this approach is general, we have summarized it in Box 7.1.

Box 7.1. Conditional equations model of the VAR

The statistical information of a VAR, or VAR-EX, with n endogenous variables can be represented by a n-equation model, where the first equation is the conditional model of one of the variables given the $n-1$ other endogenous variables of the VAR. The second model equation conditions on the remaining $n-2$ variables, and so on. The last equation of the multiple equation model is identical to the last row of the VAR (no conditioning).

Box 7.1 (*Continued*)

The error terms of the model equations are contemporaneously uncorrelated and the estimation is by OLS on each of the model's equations.

The sum of the maximized log-likelihoods of the conditional equations model is identical to the maximized likelihood of the VAR.

7.4. Simultaneous Equation Model

A famous model type can be defined by premultiplying (7.1) by a nonsingular matrix $\mathbf{A}$:

$$\mathbf{A}\mathbf{y}_t = \sum_{i=1}^{p} \mathbf{A}\boldsymbol{\Phi}_i \mathbf{y}_{t-i} + \sum_{i=0}^{q} \mathbf{A}\boldsymbol{\Gamma}_i \mathbf{x}_{t-i} + \mathbf{A}\boldsymbol{\Upsilon}\mathbf{D}_t + \mathbf{A}\boldsymbol{\varepsilon}_t. \tag{7.8}$$

Due to normalization (on one endogenous variable in each equation), all elements in the main diagonal of $\mathbf{A}$ are 1. Clearly, if $\mathbf{A}$ is the identity matrix, (7.8) is identical to (7.1), hence we are interested in $\mathbf{A}$ matrices with nonzero elements outside the main diagonal. This means that in the multiple equation model (7.1), at least one equation (usually several) contains at least one contemporaneous endogenous variable with unknown coefficient. A multiple equation model of this type is known as a simultaneous equation model (SEM).

The contemporaneous covariance matrix of the SEM disturbances $\boldsymbol{\epsilon}_t = \mathbf{A}\boldsymbol{\varepsilon}_t$ is denoted by $\boldsymbol{\Omega}$:

$$\boldsymbol{\Omega} = \text{Var}(\boldsymbol{\epsilon}_t) = E(\boldsymbol{\epsilon}_t \boldsymbol{\epsilon}_t'). \tag{7.9}$$

The relationship between the SEM and VAR disturbance covariance matrices is

$$\boldsymbol{\Omega} = \text{Var}(\boldsymbol{\epsilon}_t) = \text{Var}(\mathbf{A}\boldsymbol{\varepsilon}_t) = \mathbf{A}\boldsymbol{\Sigma}\mathbf{A}'. \tag{7.10}$$

When we discuss the identification of SEMs, we start by assuming that there are no restrictions on the $\boldsymbol{\Omega}$ matrix. By this, we mean that no covariances are "set to zero", for example, or that none of the variances are known numbers (that does not require estimation). We mention this since we will see below that it can matter for identification whether $\boldsymbol{\Omega}$ is assumed to be diagonal for example. Diagonal $\boldsymbol{\Omega}$ means that the SEM disturbances are contemporaneously uncorrelated.

7.5. Identification

Identification is a large field of research in econometrics, and there is a plethora of concepts (see Lewbel, 2017). In this book, we stick to the idea that the identification issue (or "problem") is about the logical possibility of consistent estimation of the model's parameters. Hence, we can investigate identification by assuming that a "perfect sample" that annihilates all estimation uncertainty is at our disposal. Put differently, identification is a logical property of the model, it is not an issue about the sample.

Assuming a perfect sample, a relevant and operational definition of identification is that a parameter of a model is identified if at least one consistent estimator of the parameter exists. We can then see that for the model equations we have considered so far, identification is the rule, not the exception, as long as they are well-specified econometric models (hence the importance of mis-specification testing). The coefficients of well-specified ADL/ECM model equations are identified parameters. The coefficients of VARs can be consistently estimated, hence VARs are identified dynamic models. Nevertheless, derived parameters like the impulse responses of VARs are not generally identified (we return to this point when we introduce the SVAR below). Multiple equation models that consist of conditional model equations are identified, since OLS gives consistent estimation of the coefficients, including the dynamic multipliers. Hence, we can add "the equations of the model are identified", to the properties listed in Box 7.1.

However, the coefficients of the equations in SEMs are not always identified. We can show this by considering an example of a SEM where no consistent estimator exists, and hence the parameters of the simultaneous model cannot be identified. Consider (7.1)–(7.2) in the simplest possible case where $n = 2$, $m = 0$, and $p = q = 0$. To aid intuition, we can think of a partial equilibrium model of the market for a product, and define Y_1 as quantity, Q, and Y_2 as price, P.

In matrix notation this model can be written as

$$\underbrace{\begin{pmatrix} 1 & a_{12} \\ a_{21} & 1 \end{pmatrix}}_{\mathbf{A}} \underbrace{\begin{pmatrix} Q_t \\ P_t \end{pmatrix}}_{\boldsymbol{y}_t} = \underbrace{\begin{pmatrix} a_{10} \\ a_{20} \end{pmatrix}}_{\mathbf{A}\boldsymbol{\Upsilon}\mathbf{D}_t} + \underbrace{\begin{pmatrix} \epsilon_{1t} \\ \epsilon_{2t} \end{pmatrix}}_{\boldsymbol{\epsilon}_t},$$

while written in the model equation form, the SEM is

$$Q_t + a_{12}P_t = a_{10} + \epsilon_{1t} \quad \text{(demand, } a_{12} > 0\text{)}, \tag{7.11}$$

$$a_{21}Q_t + P_t = a_{20} + \epsilon_{2t} \quad \text{(supply, } \quad a_{21} < 0\text{)}. \tag{7.12}$$

Remember that we do not assume that ϵ_{1t} are ϵ_{2t} are independent ($\boldsymbol{\Omega}$ is unrestricted). Solving the two simultaneous equations (7.11)–(7.12), we obtain the reduced form of (Q_t, P_t), as a VAR with only constant terms:

$$Q_t = \underbrace{\frac{a_{10} - a_{12}a_{20}}{1 - a_{12}a_{21}}}_{\phi_{10}} + \underbrace{\frac{\epsilon_{1t} - a_{12}\epsilon_{2t}}{1 - a_{12}a_{21}}}_{\varepsilon_{1t}}, \tag{7.13}$$

$$P_t = \underbrace{\frac{a_{20} - a_{21}a_{10}}{1 - a_{12}a_{21}}}_{\phi_{20}} + \underbrace{\frac{\epsilon_{2t} - a_{21}\epsilon_{1t}}{1 - a_{12}a_{21}}}_{\varepsilon_{2t}}, \tag{7.14}$$

i.e., the reduced form model consists of the null models (location models). The identification issue (or problem) is whether the structural parameters $(a_{10}, a_{12}, a_{20}, a_{21})$ can be determined from (perfect) knowledge of the reduced-form parameters.

So, what do we know about the reduced form? First, we know ϕ_{10} and ϕ_{20}. In addition, we know the three parameters in the covariance matrix $\boldsymbol{\Sigma}$. However, these three parameters do not help us determine $a_{10}, a_{12}, a_{20}, a_{21}$, since there are also three unknown parameters in the covariance matrix $\boldsymbol{\Omega}$ for the structural disturbances. Hence, the information we have available can be summarized by two equations:

$$\phi_{10} = \frac{a_{10} - a_{12}a_{20}}{1 - a_{12}a_{21}}, \tag{7.15}$$

$$\phi_{20} = \frac{a_{20} - a_{21}a_{10}}{1 - a_{12}a_{21}}, \tag{7.16}$$

with the known reduced-form parameters on the left-hand sides of the equations. Hence, (7.15)–(7.16) are two equations in four unknowns. The equation system is underdetermined. Hence, there is no way that we can learn about the relationships (7.11) and (7.12) even if we know the reduced form parameters to perfection (the population values). None of the parameters are identified, so neither of the relationships are identified, and the structure of the SEM as a whole is therefore unidentified.

Luckily, not all SEMs are unidentified. For example, for a partial equilibrium model, a relevant theory might specify dynamics and non-modelled variables that shift demand, X_{1t} say, and supply, X_{2t}:

$$Q_t + a_{12}P_t = a_{10} + \gamma_{11}X_{1t} + \epsilon_{1t},\ a_{12} > 0, \quad \gamma_{11} \neq 0, \tag{7.17}$$

$$a_{21}Q_t + P_t = a_{20} + \gamma_{22}X_{2t} + \epsilon_{2t},\ a_{21} < 0, \quad \gamma_{22} \neq 0, \tag{7.18}$$

where γ_{11} and γ_{22} have been used to denote the coefficients of the two exogenous variables of the SEM.

In this structure, there are six unknown parameters: $a_{10}, a_{12}, \gamma_{11}, a_{20}, a_{21}$ and γ_{22}. The reduced form of (7.17)–(7.18) contains six parameters that we can consider as known: Two constant terms and the four reduced-form parameters of X_{1t} and X_{2t}. We can therefore formulate a determined equation system for the six unknown $a_{10}, a_{12}, \gamma_{11}, a_{20}, a_{21}, \gamma_{22}$ parameters and the six known parameters of the reduced form. Since a unique solution exits given the assumption of the theory ($a_{12} < 0$, $\gamma_{11} \neq 0, a_{21} < 0$, $\gamma_{22} \neq 0$), equations (7.17)–(7.18) are two identified equations, and the SEM (as a whole) is therefore identified.

We can get some intuition about the difference between the unidentifiable model and the identified model in this case. The point is that the theoretical formulation in (7.17)–(7.18) specifies variables that helps us "trace out" the supply and demand curves as separate relationships. When X_{1t} changes, there will be shifts in demand, and such shifts will trace out the supply relationship. Likewise, when X_{2t} is increased or reduced, there will be shifts in supply which help us identify the demand function.

7.6. Order and Rank Conditions

Our approach to identification generalizes to all linear in parameter SEMs, and there are rules that we can use to investigate the identification of relationships of a SEM. This is practical because it is often that we are interested in learning about one of the identified relationships of the model, even though there are other relationships in the system of equations which are unidentified. The first general rule is the *order condition* for identifiability:

Box 7.2. Order condition for identification

In a SEM model of n linear equations, and with no restrictions on the covariance matrix of the disturbances, to be identified, an equation must exclude at least $n-1$ of the variables appearing in the equations of the model.

The excluded variables mentioned in the order condition can be both endogenous or exogenous. In the context of identification, both non-modelled variables (the Xs in the VAR) and lags of the endogenous variables count as exogenous (because they are predetermined). Note also that the deterministic variables (e.g., intercept, indicators for structural breaks) are counted as exogenous variables.

We typically distinguish between a *just-identified* equation, from which exactly $n-1$ variables are excluded, and an *over-identified* equation which excludes more than $n-1$ variables.

The order condition is often presented as a necessary condition for identification, since, for example, excluding X_{2t} from the first equation does not contribute to its identification if the coefficient of X_{2t} is zero in the other equation. The way we presented model (7.17)–(7.18) above, that possibility was ruled out by including $\gamma_{22} \neq 0$ in the model specification (and vice versa for the second equation). Hence, the order condition cannot fail for that model or for other models where the relevance of excluded variables elsewhere in the system has been clearly stated in the theoretical assumptions.

However, a *rank condition* of identification has been formulated as a necessary and sufficient condition.

Box 7.3. Rank condition for identification

In a SEM model of n linear equations, and with no restrictions on the covariance matrix of the disturbances, an equation is identified if and only if at least one non-zero $(n-1) \times (n-1)$ determinant is contained in the array of coefficients with which those variables excluded from the equation in question appear in the other equations.

If the rank condition is satisfied, the order condition is automatically satisfied.

Note that "array of coefficients" is synonymous with matrix. Recall that the rank of a matrix is given by the order of the largest non-zero determinant that it contains. In model (7.17)–(7.18), for the first equation, the relevant array of coefficients is the scalar $[\gamma_{22}]$ which is non-zero by assumption. Hence, in this case, the rank condition merely underlines the order condition, and the same will be the case when the relevance of the excluded variables is stated as part of the model, as just noted. Nevertheless, since the rank condition lends itself to computer treatment, and because it is sufficient, modern software usually report the result of a check of the rank condition, before it will estimate a SEM, so it is important to understand the condition to interpret that type of program message.

As noted, the order condition made no mention of the distinction between endogenous and exogenous/predetermied variables in the equation under investigation for identification. However, we can separate the two variable categories, and obtain an equivalent formulation which is often used. Without loss of generality, write the equation we are interested in as the first equation in the SEM. We can also use notation that comes as close as possible to the notation that we used for multivariate structural equations in Section 2.6.8.[1] Hence, we write the first (structural) equation of a SEM as

$$\mathbf{y}_1 = \mathbf{X}_{1X}\boldsymbol{\beta}_{11} + \mathbf{X}_{1Y}\boldsymbol{\beta}_{21} + \boldsymbol{\epsilon}_1, \tag{7.19}$$

where

- $\mathbf{y}_1$ is the $T \times 1$ vector with observations of the Y-variable that the first equation in the SEM is normalized on;
- $\mathbf{X}_{1X}$ is the $T \times k_{1X}$ matrix with observations of the k_{1X} included predetermined or exogenous variables (including the constant term);
- $\mathbf{X}_{1Y}$ is the $T \times k_{1Y}$ matrix that holds observations of the k_{1Y} included endogenous variables, minus one.

Note that since the intercept of the equation is counted as an exogenous variable, the total number of variables in the equation is therefore: $k_{1X} + k_{1Y} = k_1 + 1$, when k_1 is defined as the total number of variables *less* the constant term. (This is also in line with the notation used in Equation (2.127)).

Care must also be taken in noting that k_{1Y} is defined as the number of endogenous "right-hand" side variables in the equation, which is equal to the total number of included endogenous variables less one. The endogenous variable not included in $\mathbf{X}_{1Y}$ is of course the "dependent" variable (i.e., the endogenous variable on which the first equation has been normalized).

[1]The obvious change in notation is that n symbolizes the number of observations in Section 2.6.8, since the exposition referred to a sample with n independent variable vectors, while we in later chapters have used n to denote the number of endogenous variables in VARs and other multiple equation models.

Let k_X denote the total number of exogenous variables in the SEM. In terms of this notation, the order condition can be expressed as

$$\underbrace{(k_X - (k_{1X} + 1))}_{\text{excluded exogenous}} + \underbrace{(n - k_{1Y})}_{\text{excluded endogenous}} \geq n - 1. \tag{7.20}$$

We can eliminate n and -1 from this expression and obtain the equivalent formulation of the order condition:

$$k_X - k_{1X} \geq k_{1Y}. \tag{7.21}$$

Said with other words:

> To be an identified equation, the number of excluded exogenous and predetermined variables from the equation must be not less than the number of included right-hand side endogenous variables in the equation.

So far, we have considered the identification obtained by excluding variables from an equation, that is, by working through the consequences of theoretically motivated "zero restrictions" on the coefficient of the SEM equations. But as we know, zero restrictions are only one way of incorporating theoretical information. They are special cases of homogeneous linear restrictions among the parameters. $a_{12} = a$ and $a_{12} - c\gamma_{11} = a$ (where a and c are known numbers) are examples in the notation of the market equilibrium model.

The first formulation of the order condition can be extended as follows:

> In an n-equation linear model, a necessary condition for the identification of a single equation is that there is at least $n - 1$ independent linear homogeneous equations on the parameters of the equation.

The new form of the order condition is frequently required when identities have been substituted into an equation system. However, in general, it is easier to investigate the identification of an equation by simply treating the identities as ordinary equations of the model. Identities themselves of course do not need to be investigated for identifiability, but they need to be taken into account when assessing the identification of the other relationships of the model (i.e., the econometric model equations). Hence when there are identities in the SEM, the n linear equations mentioned in the order condition in Box 7.2 are including the identities of the model.

7.7. Recursive Model

As mentioned, the order and rank conditions cover models where the contemporaneous covariance matrix $\mathbf{\Omega}$, in (7.9), of the multiple equation model is unrestricted. If there are restrictions on $\mathbf{\Omega}$, the structural model may be identifiable even if the rank and order conditions fail.

To see how the identification can be affected by restricting $\mathbf{\Omega}$, we consider the simple market equilibrium model and find the expressions for the first- and second-order moments of the observable variables Q_t and P_t, i.e., $E(Q_t) \equiv \mu_1$, $E(P_t) \equiv \mu_2$, $\text{Var}(Q_t) \equiv \sigma_1$, $\text{Var}(P_t) \equiv \sigma_2$, $\text{Cov}(P_t, Q_t) \equiv \sigma_{12}$.

From (7.13)–(7.14), we obtain the first and second moments:

$$\mu_1 = \frac{a_{10} - a_{12}a_{20}}{1 - a_{12}a_{21}}, \tag{7.22}$$

$$\mu_2 = \frac{a_{20} - a_{21}a_{10}}{1 - a_{12}a_{21}}, \tag{7.23}$$

$$\sigma_1^2 = \frac{\omega_1^2 + a_{12}^2\omega_2^2 - 2a_{12}\omega_{12}}{(1 - a_{12}a_{21})^2}, \tag{7.24}$$

$$\sigma_2^2 = \frac{\omega_2^2 + a_{21}^2\omega_1^2 - 2a_{21}\omega_{12}}{(1 - a_{12}a_{21})^2}, \tag{7.25}$$

$$\sigma_{12} = \frac{\omega_{12}(1 + a_{12}a_{21}) - a_{12}\omega_2^2 - a_{21}\omega_1^2}{(1 - a_{12}a_{21})^2}, \tag{7.26}$$

where (7.22)–(7.26) are five independent equations. Again, assuming a perfect sample, we can consider $\mu_1, \mu_2, \sigma_1^2, \sigma_1^2, \sigma_{12}$ as five known parameters, but there are seven unknowns, namely, $a_{12}, a_{21}, a_{10}, a_{20}, \omega_1^2, \omega_2^2, \omega_{12}$. Hence, the equation system is underdetermined, there is no solution for the unknown structural parameters. Hence, the rank and order conditions' conclusion about unidentifiability is confirmed.

If the structural model specifies $a_{21} = 0$ as a restriction, the number of unknowns is reduced by one, but still the model is unidentified. However, if in addition, $\omega_{12} = 0$ is part of the specification of the SEM, equations (7.22)–(7.26) become a determined system, since we then have five equations and five unknowns. The solution for a_{12} is

$$a_{12} = -\frac{\sigma_{12}}{\sigma_2^2}, \tag{7.27}$$

which is the negative of the population regression coefficient of Q_t on P_t.

The expression for the intercept a_{10} is

$$a_{10} = \mu_1 + a_{12}a_{20} = \mu_1 + \left(-\frac{\sigma_{12}}{\sigma_2^2}\right)\mu_2, \tag{7.28}$$

since a_{20} in the second equation is given by μ_2. We see that if the structural model is specified with a contemporaneous (instantaneous) coefficient matrix, which is *lower triangular* ($a_{21} = 0$) and with a diagonal $\mathbf{\Omega}$ matrix, the structural model is identified. Another structure, with *upper triangular* contemporaneous coefficient matrix, is also identified.

Box 7.4. Triangular coefficient matrix

In the context of multiple equation models, upper/lower triangular of the contemporaneous (instantaneous) coefficient matrix only reflects how the equations of the SEM have been ordered. The two terms refer to the same type of multiple equation model: the recursive model.

Despite the simplicity of this model example, the result holds in general: A multiple equation model with upper/lower triangular coefficient matrix $\mathbf{A}$ and diagonal $\mathbf{\Omega}$ matrix is identified. Such a model is called a (contemporaneously) *recursive* model. Recursiveness in this context refers to the interpretation that one variable is "determined first" (in period t), the second endogenous variable is determined given the first one, and so on. Historically, recursive models have also been called "causal chains", and have sometimes been seen as an alternative to the SEMs of Haavelmo (1943a); see, for example, Wold and Juréen (1953) as explained in Hendry (1995a, p. 333).

The identifiability of recursive models extends to dynamic multiple equation models. Without loss of generality, we can consider the market model with first-order dynamics:

$$\begin{pmatrix} 1 & a_{12,0} \\ a_{21,0} & 1 \end{pmatrix} \begin{pmatrix} Q_t \\ P_t \end{pmatrix} = \begin{pmatrix} a_{10} \\ a_{20} \end{pmatrix} + \begin{pmatrix} a_{11,1} & a_{12,1} \\ a_{21,1} & a_{22,1} \end{pmatrix} \begin{pmatrix} Q_{t-1} \\ P_{t-1} \end{pmatrix} + \begin{pmatrix} \epsilon_{1t} \\ \epsilon_{2t} \end{pmatrix}, \tag{7.29}$$

where the notation for the coefficient has been elaborated a little to distinguish between the contemporaneous coefficient matrix and the matrix with lagged coefficients.

The structural coefficients of this model are identified subject to $\omega_{12} = 0$ (diagonal $\mathbf{\Omega}$) if either $a_{12,1} = 0$, or $a_{21,1} = 0$. Note that models with triangular contemporaneous coefficient matrices and orthogonal error terms are formally equivalent to multiple equation models consisting of conditional (and marginal) model equations (cf. the models in Section 7.3).

Identification of the structural coefficients does not require a diagonal coefficient matrix for the lagged variables. However, multiple equation models can also be recursive in a stricter sense: the solution of one endogenous variable can be found without taking the rest of the system into account (and that solution can be inserted in the other equation(s) to find the solution of the other variables). Recursiveness of (7.29) in this stricter sense requires also the matrix with the lagged coefficients triangular (either $a_{21,1} = 0$ or $a_{12,1} = 0$). Restrictions of this type can be tested empirically after first estimating the exactly identified model.

7.8. Structural VAR

So far we have addressed identification of the coefficients of the observable variables of VARs, SEMs, and recursive models. As we have seen, given the assumption of the statistical model, all VAR coefficients and the elements of the instantaneous matrix $\boldsymbol{\Sigma}$ are identified. Structural models may or may not be identified. They may also be partially identified in the meaning that some of the relationships in the multiple equation model are identifiable, but not every structural equation of the model.

However, another class of parameters that we are often interested in, namely, the impulse responses that we reviewed mathematically in Section 3.6, is not identified in the VAR. This is seen by noting that the instantaneous shocks to a standard VAR are generally correlated, as the covariance matrix $\boldsymbol{\Sigma}$ has non-zero elements outside the main diagonal. Conversely, if we start from a SEM with uncorrelated error terms, for example (7.29), with $\omega_{12} = 0$, or more generally, (7.8) with $\boldsymbol{\Omega}$ as a diagonal matrix, the $\boldsymbol{\Sigma}$ matrix of the reduced form (i.e., the VAR) will have non-zero elements outside the main diagonal. Because a VAR can be viewed as the reduced form of a SEM, the implied reduced-form VAR disturbances are necessarily composites of the simultaneous equation disturbances.

The point is also clearly illustrated by the model of partial market equilibrium above; the reduced-form expressions (7.13) and (7.14) show that the VAR disturbances are given by

$$\varepsilon_{1t} = \underbrace{\frac{\epsilon_{1t} - a_{12}\epsilon_{2t}}{1 - a_{12}\beta_{21}}}_{\varepsilon_{1t}}, \tag{7.30}$$

$$\varepsilon_{2t} = \underbrace{\frac{\epsilon_{2t} - a_{21}\epsilon_{1t}}{1 - a_{12}a_{21}}}_{\varepsilon_{2t}}. \tag{7.31}$$

Hence, without making further assumptions, there is no way of telling whether a change (a random impulse) to ε_{1t} is due to a demand impulse, ϵ_{1t}, or to a supply shock, ϵ_{2t}. Put differently, while we can do the algebra of impulse responses in a standard VAR, first with respect to, for example, ε_{1t}, and then with respect to ε_{2t}, there is no way of knowing to what extent we are looking at the endogenous responses to an imaginary demand shock (if that was the intention), or to a supply shock. The impulse responses are not identified in the standard VAR.

Structural VARs, often called SVARs, are models that secure identification of impulse responses by imposing restrictions on the VAR (Sims, 1980; 1986). The best known identification method is called the *Cholesky decomposition* of $\mathbf{\Sigma}$ (see, for example, Hamilton, 1994, pp. 320 and 327–330; Lütkepohl, 2007, Sections 2.3 and 9.1; Bjørnland and Thorsrud, 2015, Chapter 8).[2]

Using the Cholesky decomposition to obtain unique impulse response functions is, however, equivalent to choosing a recursive model specification, Lütkepohl (2007, Chapter 9, Section 1). Hence, in the bivariate VAR case ($n = 2$), the identification of shocks, and therefore of impulse responses, is achieved by formulating a model of the VAR consisting of one conditional equation (for Q_t given P_t), and one marginal equation (for P_t), and estimating the model equation-by-equation by OLS. The conditioning forces the triangularization of the contemporaneous coefficient matrix, and the estimation by OLS ensures that the $\mathbf{\Omega}$ matrix is diagonalized.

The duality between SVARs and recursive models can be generalized. For an n-dimensional VAR, the impulse responses are identified if the theoretical model specifies $(n^2 - n)/2$ zero restrictions to give a recursive contemporaneous coefficient matrix $\mathbf{A}$ above. In principle, there could be other zero restrictions (or in general homogeneous linear restrictions) on $\mathbf{A}$, see Bernanke (1986) and Blanchard and Watson (1986). In the SVAR literature, the triangular form has perhaps been the most common case, for example, Christiano *et al.* (1996).

Indeed, with reference to the definition of identification, there is no reason why other identification schemes cannot be used for SVARs. After all, identification is a logical property of an economic theory (formulated as equation systems). Hence, the issue is whether the theory in question implies enough restrictions on the VAR in order for the impulse responses

[2]In PcGive, the Cholesky decomposition is found as *orthogonalized residuals*, as an option under the impulse responses part of the program.

to be identifiable. In macroeconomic applications, identification has been formulated not only in the form of recursiveness but also as restriction on the long-run multipliers (see for example, Blanchard and Quah, 1989). Chapter 5 in the textbook by Enders (2010, Sections 5.10–5.13) and Chapter 8 in Bjørnland and Thorsrud (2015) contain insightful discussions of identification schemes for SVARs.

7.9. Estimation Methods for Structural Models

Estimation of multiple equation models with identified parameter does not represent a problem nowadays, as we have access to good econometric software. As already noted, the unrestricted VAR can be estimated by OLS on each equation, and with Gaussian disturbances, the OLS estimators of the coefficients are interpretable as maximum likelihood (ML) estimators.

Multiple equation models that take the form of recursive models can also be estimated efficiently using equation-by-equation OLS (also known as 1-stage least squares (1SLS)).

Finally, identified simultaneous model equations can be estimated consistently. In the following, we therefore focus on identified cases of the structural equation (7.19) above.

7.9.1. Simultaneity bias of OLS

When (7.19) represents an identified model equation, at least one consistent estimator exists for the coefficients of the model. However, the OLS estimator is not the consistent estimator. Instead, the OLS estimator contains a bias that does not diminish as the sample size is increased towards infinity. This is known as the *simultaneity bias*. We saw one example in Section 6.2.3, where we applied OLS to the consumption function in our simple closed economy Keynesian macromodel.

In that example, the OLS estimated coefficients turned out to be very close to the true parameter values, which illustrates that the simultaneity bias may not always be large in practice. We now review the relevant econometric theory which will help us understand that result, and we will consider another example where the simultaneity bias is indeed substantial.

We can write (7.19) more compactly as

$$\mathbf{y}_1 = \mathbf{X}_1\boldsymbol{\beta}_1 + \boldsymbol{\epsilon}_1, \tag{7.32}$$

where

$$\mathbf{X}_1 = (\mathbf{X}_{11} \quad \mathbf{X}_{1Y}), \tag{7.33}$$

$$\boldsymbol{\beta}_1 = (\boldsymbol{\beta}_{11} \quad \boldsymbol{\beta}_{21})'. \tag{7.34}$$

The covariance matrix of the structural disturbances is typically assumed to be

$$\text{Var}(\boldsymbol{\epsilon}_1) = E(\boldsymbol{\epsilon}_1\boldsymbol{\epsilon}_t') = \sigma_1^2\boldsymbol{\Omega}_1$$

with $\boldsymbol{\Omega}_1 = \boldsymbol{I}$, giving

$$\text{Var}(\boldsymbol{\epsilon}_1) = \sigma_1^2\boldsymbol{I},$$

as an important special case. Equation (7.32) may look like a standard regression equation at first sight, but as it is the first equation in a SEM we have

$$\text{plim}\left(\frac{1}{n}\mathbf{X}_1'\epsilon_1\right) \neq \mathbf{0}, \tag{7.35}$$

since $\mathbf{X}_1$ includes k_{1Y} endogenous variables. Hence, the OLS estimator $\widehat{\boldsymbol{\beta}}_1$ will be inconsistent, and this is known as the simultaneous equation bias (or simultaneity bias). All the coefficient estimates will, in principle, be affected, not only those in $\widehat{\boldsymbol{\beta}}_{21}$.

The Keynesian macromodel that we have used earlier in the book provides the classical example of the bias as analyzed by Haavelmo (1943a). In fact, we can make the point by using a static version of the model (the source of the bias we now study is simultaneity, not predeterminedness). Assume that our parameter of interest is b, the marginal propensity to consume, and that the SEM is

$$C_t = a + b(\text{GDP}_t) + \epsilon_{Ct}, \quad 0 < b < 1, \tag{7.36}$$

$$\text{GDP}_t = C_t + J_t, \tag{7.37}$$

$$J_t = J^* + \epsilon_{Jt}, \tag{7.38}$$

with the notation used above. To complete the specification, we make the following assumptions about the structural disturbances:

$$E(\epsilon_{Ct} \mid J_t) = 0, \quad \text{Var}(\epsilon_{Ct} \mid J_t) = \sigma_C^2, \tag{7.39}$$

$$E(\epsilon_{Jt}) = 0, \quad \text{Var}(\epsilon_{Ct}) = \sigma_J^2, \tag{7.40}$$

$$\text{Cov}(\epsilon_{Ct}, \epsilon_{Jt}) = 0. \tag{7.41}$$

Note that since $\text{Cov}(\epsilon_{Ct}, \epsilon_{Jt}) = 0$, we can think of the multiple equation model as consisting of a block of the two simultaneous equations (7.36) and (7.37), and a recursive block consisting of the single equation (7.38). In the simultaneous block, we can regard J_t as exogenous, and the consumption function is therefore identified on the order and rank conditions.

The OLS estimator of b is

$$\widehat{b}_{\text{OLS}} = \frac{\sum_{t=1}^{T}(\text{GDP}_t - \overline{\text{GDP}})C_t}{\sum_{t=1}^{T}(\text{GDP}_t - \overline{\text{GDP}})^2} = b + \frac{\sum_{t=1}^{T}\text{GDP}_t(\epsilon_{Ct} - \bar{\epsilon}_C)}{\sum_{t=1}^{T}(\text{GDP}_t - \overline{\text{GDP}})^2}.$$

To assess the probability limit of the bias term, we use the reduced form

$$\text{GDP}_t = \frac{a + J^*}{1 - b} + \frac{\epsilon_{Ct} + \epsilon_{Jt}}{1 - b}, \tag{7.42}$$

$$C_t = \frac{(a + bJ^*)}{1 - b} + \frac{\epsilon_{Ct} + b\epsilon_{Jt}}{1 - b}, \tag{7.43}$$

which together with the assumptions (7.39)–(7.39) define the properties of the two random variables GDP_t and C_t. We obtain

$$\text{plim}(\widehat{b}_{\text{OLS}} - b) = \text{plim}\frac{\sum_{t=1}^{T}\text{GDP}_t(\epsilon_{Ct} - \bar{\epsilon}_C)}{\sum_{t=1}^{T}(\text{GDP}_t - \overline{\text{GDP}})^2},$$

$$\text{plim}(\widehat{b}_{\text{OLS}} - b) = \text{plim}\frac{\sum_{t=1}^{T}\left(\frac{a+J^*}{1-b} + \frac{\epsilon_{Ct}}{1-b} + \frac{\epsilon_{It}}{1-b}\right)(\epsilon_{Ct} - \bar{\epsilon}_C)}{\sum_{t=1}^{T}\left(\frac{\epsilon_{Ct}-\bar{\epsilon}_C}{1-b} + \frac{\epsilon_{It}-\bar{\epsilon}_I}{1-b}\right)^2},$$

and finally

$$\text{plim}(\widehat{b}_{\text{OLS}} - b) = (1 - b)\left(\frac{\sigma_C^2}{\sigma_C^2 + \sigma_I^2}\right) > 0. \tag{7.44}$$

Hence, OLS is overestimating the structural parameter b in the model given by (7.36)–(7.38) even with a perfect sample. This bias is generic to simultaneous structural equations. The size of the bias will depend on the specification of the econometric model in question, though.

Using (7.44) as our guideline, we can now reconsider the estimation result in (6.25), which showed practically zero biases in the estimation of the short-run propensity to consume parameter (true value 0.25) and habit parameter (true value 0.65). In fact, in the data generation of the time series, the parameter σ_C^2 was 0.25, and σ_J^2 was 50, hence the theoretical result in (7.44) predicts that with those variance values, the simultaneity bias will be almost zero.

Conversely, if we construct another dataset, with $\sigma_C^2 = 25$, the simultaneity bias should become more visible in the results. Estimating the consumption function on that dataset with OLS gives

$$\begin{aligned} C_t &= -\underset{(4.462)}{11.84} + \underset{(0.037)}{0.478}\,\mathrm{GDP}_t + \underset{(0.04787)}{0.439}\,C_{t-1} \\ &\quad \text{OLS } T = 100, \end{aligned} \tag{7.45}$$

which shows substantial simultaneous equation biases: $0.478 - 0.25 = 0.228$ for propensity to consume, and $0.439 - 0.65 = -0.21$ for habit-formation. Note also that the sign of the bias for the propensity to consume coefficient has the sign that theory predicts: It is positive (the propensity to consume is overestimated).

Although the clarification of the simultaneity bias problem (and its solution, as we shall soon see) was achieved many decades ago, it still seems to represent a pitfall to modern day econometricians. As pointed out by Reed (2015), one approach that has been employed to avoid problems associated with simultaneity is to replace the "suspect" explanatory variables with its lagged value. It follows from the above theory that such a procedure is tantamount to estimating a different equation (namely, a reduced form type equation), and not the structural equation that we started out with.

We now turn to the long established estimation procedures that can give consistent estimators for identified equations in SEMs.

7.9.2. Indirect least squares

According to the rank and order conditions, the consumption function (7.36) is exactly identified. Hence, there is one consistent estimator "to be found", and that estimator should be pretty basic given the simplicity of the model. Hence we can consider the reduced form, and see which reduced form parameters contain the information needed to obtain a solution for b. Intuitively, the covariances between C_t and J_t, and between GDP_t and J_t, hold some promise. Using (7.42), (7.43), and (7.38), we write the population covariances as

$$\mathrm{Cov}(C_t, J_t) = \frac{b\sigma_J^2}{1-b},$$

$$\mathrm{Cov}(\mathrm{GDP}_t, J_t) = \frac{\sigma_J^2}{1-b},$$

and the structural parameter b can be found as

$$b = \frac{\mathrm{Cov}(C_t, J_t)}{\mathrm{Cov}(\mathrm{GDP}_t, J_t)}, \tag{7.46}$$

confirming its identification. The two covariances are consistently estimated by their empirical counterpart, hence the method of moments (MM) estimator

$$\widehat{b}_{\mathrm{MM}} = \frac{T^{-1}\sum_{t=1}^{T} C_t(J_t - \overline{J})}{T^{-1}\sum_{t=1}^{T} \mathrm{GDP}_t(J_t - \overline{J})}, \tag{7.47}$$

is a consistent estimator of the marginal propensity to consume in the model (7.36)–(7.41).

However, it is more practical to work with regression coefficients than covariances. Note that the two first equations of the macromodel, (7.36), and (7.37), can be solved with J_t as an observable exogenous variable. Let γ_{11} denote the coefficient of J_t in the first reduced-form equation (with GDP_t) and dependent variable, and let γ_{21} denote the coefficient of J_t in the other reduced-form equation (for C_t). The OLS estimators $\widehat{\gamma}_{11}$ and $\widehat{\gamma}_{21}$ have plim:

$$\begin{aligned}
\mathrm{plim}\ \widehat{\gamma}_{11} &= \frac{\mathrm{Cov}(\mathrm{GDP}_t, J_t)}{\mathrm{Var}(J_t)}, \\
\mathrm{plim}\ \widehat{\gamma}_{21} &= \frac{\mathrm{Cov}(C_t, J_t)}{\mathrm{Var}(J_t)}.
\end{aligned}$$

Hence, we have that

$$\widehat{b}_{\mathrm{ILS}} = \frac{\widehat{\gamma}_{21}}{\widehat{\gamma}_{11}} \tag{7.48}$$

is a consistent estimator of b. It is known as the indirect least squares (ILS) estimator, since it utilizes the OLS estimates of the reduced-form coefficients to "back-out" an estimate of b.

Clearly, $\widehat{b}_{\mathrm{MM}}$ and $\widehat{b}_{\mathrm{ILS}}$ are identical, so these expressions do not contradict the result about exact identification. On the other hand, since another name for the MM estimator is the instrumental variable (IV) estimator, we conclude that ILS estimation is equivalent with IV estimation.

ILS has mainly interest for pedagogical and historical reasons. In practice, it has been replaced by IV estimation.

7.9.3. IV and 2SLS

We first consider the matrix of instrumental variables (IVs) for the case where the structural equation (7.19) is exactly identified. Hence;

$$k_X - k_{1X} = k_{1Y},$$

as there are exactly as many exogenous and predetermined variables in the $n-1$ other equations of the system, and which are not included in the equation, as there are included endogenous variables on the right-hand side in the first equation. We collect these variables in the $T \times k_{1Y}$ matrix $\mathbf{X}_{(n-1)X}$, and define the IV matrix as

$$\mathbf{Z}_1 = (\mathbf{X}_{1X}\mathbf{X}_{(n-1)X})_{T\times(k_{1X}+k_{1Y})}. \tag{7.49}$$

The IV estimator of $\boldsymbol{\beta}_1$ in the structural equation (7.32) is therefore

$$\widehat{\boldsymbol{\beta}}_{1,\mathrm{IV}} = (\mathbf{Z}_1'\mathbf{X}_1)^{-1}\mathbf{Z}_1'\mathbf{y}_1, \tag{7.50}$$

where the IVs are defined by the system of equations, which also secures the instrument validity and relevance (see Section 2.6.8). As a consequence, $\boldsymbol{Z}_1 \equiv \boldsymbol{X}_{1m}$ in this exactly identified case, where $\boldsymbol{X}_{1m}$ is the $T \times k_{1X} + (k_X - k_{1X})$ matrix with the observations of all the exogenous and predetermined variables of the model. In $\boldsymbol{X}_{1m}$, the k_{1X} columns with the included exogenous and predetermined variables come first, then the $(k_X - k_{1X})$ columns with the exogenous and predetermined variables that are excluded from the equation. Hence,

$$\widehat{\boldsymbol{\beta}}_{1,\mathrm{IV}} = (\mathbf{X}_{1m}'\mathbf{X}_1)^{-1}\boldsymbol{X}_{1m}'\mathbf{y}_1, \tag{7.51}$$

is the IV estimator in the context of the multiple equation SEM.

In the case of over-identification, $\mathbf{Z}_1$ is $T \times k_X$ where $k_X > k_{1X} + k_{1Y}$, hence $\mathbf{Z}_1'\mathbf{X}_1$ is no longer quadratic. Alternatively, we can say that there is more that one matrix with IVs (based on $\mathbf{Z}_1'\mathbf{X}_1$) that are quadratic and invertible. Each one of these matrices represents a consistent IV-estimator of $\boldsymbol{\beta}_1$. To solve this "luxury problem", we can define another IV-matrix $\widehat{\mathbf{Z}}_1$ that has the right dimension $T \times (k_{1X} + k_{1Y})$:

$$\widehat{\mathbf{Z}}_1 = (\mathbf{X}_{1X} \quad \widehat{\mathbf{X}}_{1Y}), \tag{7.52}$$

where $\widehat{\mathbf{X}}_{1Y}$ has dimension $T \times k_{1Y}$, and is made up of the best linear predictors of the k_{1Y} endogenous variables included in the first equation:

$$\widehat{\mathbf{X}}_{1Y} = (\widehat{\mathbf{y}}_2 \quad \widehat{\mathbf{y}}_3 \quad \ldots)_{T\times k_{1Y}}. \tag{7.53}$$

Where does the best predictors come from? Since we are looking at a single equation in a system-of-equations, they must come from the reduced-form equations for the endogenous variables:

$$\widehat{\mathbf{y}}_j = \mathbf{X}_{1m}\widehat{\boldsymbol{\pi}}_j, \quad j = 2, \ldots, k_{1Y} + 1, \tag{7.54}$$

where

$$\widehat{\boldsymbol{\pi}}_j = (\mathbf{X}'_{1m}\mathbf{X}_{1m})^{-1}\mathbf{X}'_{1m}\mathbf{y}_j \tag{7.55}$$

are the OLS estimators of the regression coefficients in the conditional expectation function for each included endogenous variables in the first equation. That conditional expectation conditions on the full set of predetermined variables in the multiple equation model. We can write $\widehat{\mathbf{X}}_{1Y}$ in (7.53):

$$\widehat{\mathbf{X}}_{1Y} = (\mathbf{X}_{1m}(\mathbf{X}'_{1m}\mathbf{X}_{1m})^{-1}\mathbf{X}'_{1m}\mathbf{y}_2 \ldots \mathbf{X}_{1m}(\mathbf{X}'_{1m}\mathbf{X}_{1m})^{-1}\mathbf{X}'_{1m}\mathbf{y}_{(k_{1Y}+1)}).$$

and more compactly

$$\widehat{\mathbf{X}}_{1Y} = \mathbf{X}_{1m}(\mathbf{X}'_{1m}\mathbf{X}_{1m})^{-1}\mathbf{X}'_{1m}\mathbf{X}_{1Y} = \mathbf{P}_{X_{1m}}\mathbf{X}_{1Y},$$

where we have used the prediction-maker matrix

$$\mathbf{P}_{X_{1m}} = \mathbf{X}_{1m}(\mathbf{X}'_{1m}\mathbf{X}_{1m})^{-1}\mathbf{X}'_{1m}. \tag{7.56}$$

We define the Generalized IV (GIV), estimator, as

$$\widehat{\boldsymbol{\beta}}_{1,\mathrm{GIV}} = (\widehat{\mathbf{Z}}'_1\mathbf{X}_1)^{-1}\widehat{\mathbf{Z}}'_1\mathbf{y}_1, \tag{7.57}$$

where $\widehat{\mathbf{Z}}_1$ is defined, in (7.52). It consists of (a) the exogenous variables in the equation, and (b) the best predictors of the endogenous variables included on the right-hand side of the equation. The best predictors are obtained from the conditional expectation of each of these endogenous variables conditional on the full set of exogenous and predetermined variables of the model. $\widehat{\boldsymbol{\beta}}_{1,\mathrm{GIV}}$ is also known as the 2-*stage least square* (2SLS) estimator of $\boldsymbol{\beta}_1$ in (7.32). This name indicates to a first stage, where OLS is used to estimate the $k_{1Y} \times k_X$ weights of each of the exogenous variables that are used as IVs. It is less intuitive that the estimator (7.57), that makes use of the first stage to form the optimal combination of instruments, can be written as a least squares estimator. However, it can be shown that

$$\widehat{\boldsymbol{\beta}}_{1,\mathrm{GIV}} = \begin{pmatrix} \widehat{\boldsymbol{\beta}}_{11,\mathrm{GIV}} \\ \widehat{\boldsymbol{\beta}}_{21,\mathrm{GIV}} \end{pmatrix}$$

$$= \begin{pmatrix} \mathbf{X}'_{1X}\mathbf{X}_{1X} & \mathbf{X}'_{1X}\widehat{\mathbf{X}}_{1Y} \\ \widehat{\mathbf{X}}'_{1Y}\mathbf{X}_{1X} & \widehat{\mathbf{X}}'_{1Y}\widehat{\mathbf{X}}_{1Y} \end{pmatrix}^{-1} \begin{pmatrix} \mathbf{X}'_{1X}\mathbf{y}_1 \\ \widehat{\mathbf{X}}'_{1Y}\mathbf{y}_1 \end{pmatrix}. \tag{7.58}$$

An appendix to this chapter contains the details. Next, consider using OLS on the structural equation (7.19), after substitution of $\mathbf{X}_{1Y}$ by $\widehat{\mathbf{X}}_{1Y}$:

$$\mathbf{y}_1 = \mathbf{X}_{1X}\boldsymbol{\beta}_{11} + \widehat{\mathbf{X}}_{1Y}\boldsymbol{\beta}_{21} + \text{disturbance}$$

$$= (\mathbf{X}_{1X} \quad \widehat{\mathbf{X}}_{1Y}) \begin{pmatrix} \boldsymbol{\beta}_{11} \\ \boldsymbol{\beta}_{21} \end{pmatrix} + \text{disturbance}.$$

Call the OLS estimator from this second least-square estimation, the 2-stage least square (2SLS) estimator:

$$\widehat{\boldsymbol{\beta}}_{1,\mathrm{2SLS}} = \begin{pmatrix} \widehat{\boldsymbol{\beta}}_{11,\mathrm{2SLS}} \\ \widehat{\boldsymbol{\beta}}_{21,\mathrm{2SLS}} \end{pmatrix} = [(\mathbf{X}_{1X} \quad \widehat{\mathbf{X}}_{1Y})'(\mathbf{X}_{1X} \quad \widehat{\mathbf{X}}_{1Y})]^{-1} \begin{pmatrix} \mathbf{X}'_{1X} \\ \widehat{\mathbf{X}}'_{1Y} \end{pmatrix} \mathbf{y}_1$$

$$= \begin{pmatrix} \mathbf{X}'_{1X}\mathbf{X}_{1X} & \mathbf{X}'_{1X}\widehat{\mathbf{X}}_{1Y} \\ \widehat{\mathbf{X}}'_{1Y}\mathbf{X}_{1X} & \widehat{\mathbf{X}}'_{1Y}\widehat{\mathbf{X}}_{1Y} \end{pmatrix}^{-1} \begin{pmatrix} \mathbf{X}'_{1X}\mathbf{y}_1 \\ \widehat{\mathbf{X}}'_{1Y}\mathbf{y}_1 \end{pmatrix}, \tag{7.59}$$

which is identical to (7.58). This shows the equivalence of the GIV estimators and 2SLS in the over-identified case:

$$\begin{pmatrix} \widehat{\boldsymbol{\beta}}_{11,\mathrm{GIV}} \\ \widehat{\boldsymbol{\beta}}_{21,\mathrm{GIV}} \end{pmatrix} \equiv \begin{pmatrix} \widehat{\boldsymbol{\beta}}_{11,\mathrm{2SLS}} \\ \widehat{\boldsymbol{\beta}}_{21,\mathrm{2SLS}} \end{pmatrix}. \tag{7.60}$$

The "problem" of selecting appropriate instruments has therefore been solved not by throwing some IVs away, but by taking k_{1Y} optimal linear combinations of all the k_X predetermined variables of the multiple equation model.

It should come as no surprise that if 2SLS is applied to a just identified equation, the resulting estimates are the same as those given by IV and ILS.

We now move on to review the properties of 2SLS/GIV. The main property is consistency, which is secured (logically, given that the assumptions of the model holds) by the asymptotic independence between the variables in $\widehat{\mathbf{Z}_1}$ and the structural disturbances in $\boldsymbol{\epsilon}_1$. For the first component in $\widehat{\mathbf{Z}_1}$, the independence can be directly stated as

$$\operatorname{plim}\left(\frac{1}{T}\mathbf{X}'_{1X}\boldsymbol{\epsilon}_1\right) = \mathbf{0}.$$

For the second component, a moment's reflection makes us see that we have likewise

$$\operatorname{plim}\left(\frac{1}{T}\widehat{\mathbf{X}}'_{1Y}\boldsymbol{\epsilon}_1\right) = \mathbf{0},$$

because the predicted endogenous variables are linear combinations of all the exogenous and predetermined variables of the model, i.e.,

$$\operatorname{plim}\left(\frac{1}{T}\mathbf{X}'_{1m}\boldsymbol{\epsilon}_1\right) = \mathbf{0} \Longrightarrow \operatorname{plim}\left(\frac{1}{T}\widehat{\mathbf{X}}'_{1Y}\boldsymbol{\epsilon}_1\right) = \mathbf{0}.$$

Thus, the 2SLS estimators are consistent. As usual, in structural equation estimation, one cannot prove unbiasedness, and in dynamic equations there is, in any case, the Hurwicz bias in small samples.

Without going into details, econometric software programs compute approximate covariance matrices for 2SLS estimated coefficients, which can be used to carry out tests of hypotheses, and are used in the calculation of the standard errors of the estimated coefficients that the programs report (see e.g., (Doornik and Hendry, 2013c, Chapters 13 and 17). As always with IVs estimators, these properties can be undermined by the *weak instruments problem* (see Section 2.5.2). However, unlike IV estimation of a more loosely specified model, where the list of potential IVs is sometimes very long, the discussion of identifiability of a structural equation of a SEM may also clarify the weak instrument problem. As we have seen, if a model equation is identified on the rank condition, the IVs available for estimation are, in principle, relevant and not weak.

The 2SLS/GIV estimators of $\boldsymbol{\beta}_1$ are asymptotically efficient under the maintained assumption that the contemporaneous covariance matrix $\boldsymbol{\Omega}$ of the SEM is diagonal. If there are off-diagonal elements that are non-zero, full information ML (FIML) and 3-stage least squares (3SLS) are more efficient. These estimation methods, which take the wider system into consideration, are briefly described in Section 7.9.6.

However, we first present an alternative expression for the GIV estimator, and an important test of over-identifying restrictions.

7.9.4. The IV criterion function

An alternative expression for the GIV estimator (we consider $k_X > k_{1X} + k_{1Y}$) is obtained by post-multiplying $\mathbf{X}_{1m}$ by a matrix $\mathbf{J}_1$ so that $\mathbf{X}_{1m}\mathbf{J}_1$ is an IV matrix of dimension $T \times (k_{1X} + k_{1Y})$

If we choose

$$\mathbf{X}_{1m}\mathbf{J}_1 = \mathbf{P}_{X_{1m}}\mathbf{X}_1, \tag{7.61}$$

as the IV matrix (recall $\mathbf{P}_{X_{1m}} = \mathbf{X}_{1m}(\mathbf{X}'_{1m}\mathbf{X}_{1m})^{-1}\mathbf{X}'_{1m}$), we can determine $\mathbf{J}_1$ as

$$\mathbf{J}_1 = (\mathbf{X}'_{1m}\mathbf{X}_{1m})^{-1}\mathbf{X}'_{1m}\mathbf{X}_1. \tag{7.62}$$

Let us, for the time being, denote the estimator that uses $\mathbf{X}_{1m}\mathbf{J}_1$ as IV matrix by $\widehat{\boldsymbol{\beta}}_{1,\text{JGIV}}$:

$$\begin{aligned}\widehat{\boldsymbol{\beta}}_{1,\text{JGIV}} &= ((\mathbf{X}_{1m}\mathbf{J}_1)'\mathbf{X}_1)^{-1}(\mathbf{X}_{1m}\mathbf{J}_1)'\mathbf{y}_1\\ &= ((\mathbf{P}_{X_{1m}}\mathbf{X}_1)'\mathbf{X}_1)^{-1}(\mathbf{P}_{X_{1m}}\mathbf{X}_1)'\mathbf{y}_1\\ &= (\mathbf{X}'_1\mathbf{P}_{X_{1m}}\mathbf{X}_1)^{-1}\mathbf{X}'_1\mathbf{P}_{X_{1m}}\mathbf{y}_1,\end{aligned} \tag{7.63}$$

which is the expression for the GIV estimator preferred in some books, e.g., equation (8.29) in Davidson and MacKinnon (2004, p. 321). Above, in (7.57), we have the expression for the GIV-estimator:

$$\widehat{\boldsymbol{\beta}}_{1,\text{GIV}} = (\widehat{\mathbf{Z}}'_1\mathbf{X}_1)^{-1}\widehat{\mathbf{Z}}'_1\mathbf{y}_1,$$

which we can show is equivalent to the expression for $\widehat{\boldsymbol{\beta}}_{1,\text{JGIV}}$. First, we can express $\widehat{\mathbf{Z}}_1$ as

$$\widehat{\mathbf{Z}}_1 = (\mathbf{X}_{1X} : \widehat{\mathbf{X}}_{1Y}) = (\mathbf{P}_{X_{1m}}\mathbf{X}_{1X} : \mathbf{P}_{X_{1m}}\mathbf{X}_{1Y}) = \mathbf{P}_{X_{1m}}\mathbf{X}_1.$$

We next replace $\widehat{\mathbf{Z}}_1$ in $\widehat{\boldsymbol{\beta}}_{1,\text{GIV}}$ by $\mathbf{P}_{X_{1m}}\mathbf{X}_1$ to obtain

$$\begin{aligned}\widehat{\boldsymbol{\beta}}_{1,\text{GIV}} &= (\widehat{\mathbf{Z}}'_1\mathbf{X}_1)^{-1}\widehat{\mathbf{Z}}'_1\mathbf{y}_1\\ &= (\mathbf{X}_1\mathbf{P}_{X_{1m}}\mathbf{X}_1)^{-1}\mathbf{X}'_1\mathbf{P}_{X_{1m}}\mathbf{y}_1\\ &\equiv \widehat{\boldsymbol{\beta}}_{1,\text{JGIV}}\end{aligned}$$

showing the equivalence.

The projection matrix $\mathbf{P}_{X_{1m}}$ also plays a role in the definition of the *IV criterion function* $Q(\boldsymbol{\beta}_1, \mathbf{y}_1)$:

$$Q(\boldsymbol{\beta}_1, \mathbf{y}_1) = (\mathbf{y}_1 - \mathbf{X}_1\boldsymbol{\beta}_1)'\mathbf{P}_{X_{1m}}(\mathbf{y}_1 - \mathbf{X}_1\boldsymbol{\beta}_1), \tag{7.64}$$

note the close relationship to the sum of squared residuals.

Minimization of $Q(\boldsymbol{\beta}_1, \mathbf{y}_1)$ with respect to $\boldsymbol{\beta}_1$ gives the first-order condition:

$$\mathbf{X}_1'\mathbf{P}_{X_{1m}}(\mathbf{y}_1 - \mathbf{X}_1\widehat{\boldsymbol{\beta}}_{1,\mathrm{GIV}}) = \mathbf{0}, \tag{7.65}$$

which gives $\widehat{\boldsymbol{\beta}}_{1,\mathrm{GIV}}$ as the solution:

$$\widehat{\boldsymbol{\beta}}_{1,\mathrm{GIV}} = (\mathbf{X}_1'\mathbf{P}_{X_{1m}}\mathbf{X}_1)^{-1}\mathbf{X}_1'\mathbf{P}_{X_{1m}}\mathbf{y}_1.$$

Note that from (7.61)

$$\mathbf{X}_1'\mathbf{P}_{X_{1m}} = \mathbf{J}_1'\mathbf{X}_{1m}',$$

we can reexpress (7.65) as

$$\mathbf{J}_1'\mathbf{X}_{1m}'(\mathbf{y}_1 - \mathbf{X}_1\widehat{\boldsymbol{\beta}}_{1,\mathrm{GIV}}) = \mathbf{0}. \tag{7.66}$$

We can now represent the just identified case by assuming that $\mathbf{J}_1$ is a non-singular $(k_{1X} + k_{1Y}) \times (k_{1X} + k_{1Y})$ matrix. Premultiplication in (7.66) by $(\mathbf{J}_1')^{-1}$ gives

$$\mathbf{X}_{1m}'(\mathbf{y}_1 - \mathbf{X}_1\widehat{\boldsymbol{\beta}}_{1,\mathrm{GIV}}) = \mathbf{0},$$

confirming that in the just identified case, $\widehat{\boldsymbol{\beta}}_{1,\mathrm{GIV}} = \widehat{\boldsymbol{\beta}}_{1,\mathrm{IV}}$.

7.9.5. Over-identifying restrictions and a specification-test

In the just identified case, the minimized value of the IV criterion function is zero:

$$\begin{aligned} Q(\widehat{\boldsymbol{\beta}}_{1,\mathrm{IV}}, \mathbf{y}_1) &= (\mathbf{y}_1 - \mathbf{X}_1\widehat{\boldsymbol{\beta}}_{1,\mathrm{IV}})'\mathbf{P}_{X_{1m}}(\mathbf{y}_1 - \mathbf{X}_1\widehat{\boldsymbol{\beta}}_{1,\mathrm{IV}}) \\ &= \widehat{\boldsymbol{\epsilon}}'_{\mathrm{IV},1}\left[\mathbf{X}_{1m}(\mathbf{X}_{1m}'\mathbf{X}_{1m})^{-1}\mathbf{X}_{1m}'\right]\widehat{\epsilon}_{\mathrm{IV},1} \\ &= \widehat{\boldsymbol{\epsilon}}'_{\mathrm{IV},1}X_{1m}(\mathbf{X}_{1m}'\mathbf{X}_{1m})^{-1}\left[\mathbf{X}_{1m}'\widehat{\epsilon}_{\mathrm{IV},1}\right] = 0, \end{aligned} \tag{7.67}$$

from the orthogonality between instrumental variables and IV residuals.

However, if $k_X - k_{1X} > k_{1Y}$, the validity of the over-identifying instruments can be tested. The basic intuition is the following: If the instruments are valid, they should have no significant explanatory power in an (auxiliary) regression that has the GIV residual (in $\widehat{\epsilon}_{\mathrm{GIV},1}$) as regressand. Conversely, an invalid instrument may be significant when added to that auxiliary regression.

We consider the simplest case with a single endogenous explanatory variable in the first structural equation. The regression of $\widehat{\epsilon}_{\mathrm{GIV},1}$ on the instruments and a constant produces an R^2 that we can call R^2_{GIVres}. Heuristically, R^2_{GIVres} is close to zero when the instrumental variables indeed only play of role for Y_{1t} through the endogenous variables that they are used as instruments for. A formal statistical test can be based on the Chi-square distribution. We follow the custom and refer to it as the *Specification test*:

$$\text{Specification test} = TR^2_{\text{GIVres}} \underset{a}{\sim} \chi^2(k_X - k_{1X}), \tag{7.68}$$

where the asymptotic distribution holds under the H_0 that the IVs are asymptotically independent from the error of the structural equation. We recognize the degrees of freedom as the number of over-identifying instruments available in the multiple equation model.

This *Specification test* is often called a *Sargan test* because of the contribution of the British econometrician Denis Sargan who worked on IV estimation theory during the 1950s and 1960s (see Sargan, 1958; 1964).

Sargan's specification test can be computed elegantly by the use of the IV criterion function. As noted, in the over-identified case, $Q(\widehat{\boldsymbol{\beta}}_{1,\text{GIV}}, \mathbf{y}_1) > 0$ since the GIV residuals are uncorrelated with the optimal instruments, but not each individual variable. We can therefore imagine constructing an exactly identified equation by adding the over-identifying exogenous and predetermined variables to the structural equation. The minimized value of the criterion function of this hypothetical exactly identified equation is zero, as shown above.

Hence, when we observe that the minimized value of the criterion function for the actual over-identified equation is non-zero, $Q(\widehat{\boldsymbol{\beta}}_{1,\text{GIV}}, \mathbf{y}_1) > 0$, the interpretation is that the over-identified restrictions represent loss of information in the estimation of $\boldsymbol{\beta}_1$. That there is some loss is inevitable, and may be a small price to pay for theoretical content, economic interpretability and relevance of the estimation results. The important question is whether the loss is statistically significant or not. Therefore, a test of the validity of the degree of over-identification can be based on

$$Q(\widehat{\boldsymbol{\beta}}_{1,\text{GIV}}, \mathbf{y}_1) - 0,$$

where the zero represents the value function when all instruments are used to obtain exact identification), hence

$$\text{Specification test} = \frac{Q(\widehat{\boldsymbol{\beta}}_{1,\text{GIV}}, \mathbf{y}_1)}{\widehat{\sigma}_1^2} \underset{a}{\sim} \chi^2(k_X - k_{1X}), \tag{7.69}$$

where $\widehat{\sigma}_1^2$ is the usual consistent estimator for σ_1^2. The two ways of computing the Sargan *Specification test* are numerically identical. Many econometric software packages report the *J-test* or the *Hansen test* for instrument validity, Hansen (1982). This test statistic uses the F-statistic from the auxiliary regression instead of R^2_{GIVres}:

$$J\text{-}test = l_1 F^2_{\text{GIVres}} \underset{a}{\sim} \chi^2(k_X - k_{1X}). \tag{7.70}$$

A significant value of an IV specification test is always subject to further interpretation because there are two distinct situations in which a rejection of the statistical null hypothesis can be expected. The first is when the structural equation is indeed correctly specified, but one or more of the IVs are correlated with the structural error term. In this case, the logical response seems to be to remove the invalid IVs from the system, and replace them with variables that are valid instruments. The second possibility is that the test of instrumental variable validity becomes significant because one, or several, instruments have predictive power for the GIV residuals as a result of invalid exclusion from the structural equation. In this case, dropping the "invalid instruments" from the system is a bad decision. Instead, we should reconsider the specification of the structural equation.

In this perspective, we see that the name Specification test, instead of just "IV validity" test, is appropriate. A significant test outcome is a sign of specification error either of the structural equation or of the system which we import instrumental variables from. Or, maybe both equation and system need careful reconsideration.

Even if it may be difficult to know how to interpret a significant value of the over-identification test statistic, it is always important to compute it, and to consider the possibilities. If it is significantly larger than it should be under the null hypothesis, care should be taken before one presents the empirical structural equation as reliable, because it is quite likely that the model is specified incorrectly.

7.9.6. Estimation methods for systems

As noted above, 2SLS is a way of implementing GIV. 2SLS is optimal when the variance–covariance matrix of the disturbances of the equation being estimated is homoskedastic, while in the more general case of heteroskedasticity, GMM is asymptotically more efficient (cf. Section 2.6.8). Moreover, 2SLS can also lose efficiency when the disturbances of the equation being estimated are correlated with the disturbances of other structural equations of the multiple equation model. In the case of off-diagonal elements in the $\boldsymbol{\Omega}$ matrix, 2SLS/GIV is not the most efficient estimator even under the maintained assumption that $\boldsymbol{\Omega}_1$ is homoskedastic. This can be regarded as a cost of applying an estimator of $\boldsymbol{\Omega}$ which is inconsistent in general (since it assumes that the disturbances of the equations are uncorrelated).

As we have discussed identification without imposing any restrictions on $\boldsymbol{\Omega}$, it is also logically appealing to base the estimation on a consistent estimator of $\boldsymbol{\Omega}$. A consistent estimator of $\boldsymbol{\Omega}$ does indeed exist. It is simply the "sample" covariance matrix of the 2SLS residuals of the system (see Dhrymes, 1974, Chapter 4, Section 6).

The use of that estimator in a third step of OLS estimation gives the 3SLS estimator with the following intuitive interpretation: In the first stage, we purge from the explanatory current endogenous variables their stochastic components by replacing them by the predicted values obtained from the reduced form. In the second stage, we obtain the consistent (2SLS/GIV) estimators of the equation coefficients. The third stage we form that consistent estimator $\widehat{\boldsymbol{\Omega}}$ by the use the second stage residuals, and obtain the GLS estimator for all the coefficients in the model equations. 3SLS is therefore the system version of the Aitken estimator mentioned in Section 2.6.8. Historically, 3SLS has played an important role, at a time when FIML was complicated to be applied with the existing computers. However, that situation changed decades ago, and, for example, PcGive will compute both unrestricted and constrained (restricted) FIML estimates of all coefficients of an identified SEM. As a consequence, it has become straightforward to compute Likelihood Ratio (LR) tests for identified systems of equations. For readers who want to get a better analytical grip on 3SLS and FIML estimation of SEMs, two good references are Davidson (2000, Chapter 13) and Martin *et al.* (2012, Chapter 5 and Appendix C).

Before we end this section, we present the 2SLS estimates of the consumption function of the Keynesian macromodel for a closed economy. Above, we saw in equation (7.45) that when there is a sizable variance in the consumption function disturbance relative to the disturbance of investments, the simultaneous equation biases of the OLS estimates become quite large, and with the expected signs. Estimation by 2SLS gives

$$\begin{aligned} C_t &= \underset{(5.91)}{6.40} + \underset{(0.056)}{0.218}\,\mathrm{GDP}_t + \underset{(0.062)}{0.610}\,C_{t-1} \\ &\quad \text{2SLS } T = 100 \end{aligned} \tag{7.71}$$

showing that the 2SLS estimates are very accurate for this dataset.

Estimation by 3SLS or FIML will give exactly the same point estimates for this model because the 3SLS estimator exactly coincides with 2SLS in the case where every equation in the system is exactly identified (Dhrymes, 1974, p. 219). Of course, that only reflects what exact identification means: that there exists only one consistent estimator.

7.10. Model Equations with Rational Expectations

So far in this chapter, the term structural equation has been synonymous with simultaneous equations. There is a large class of models which are of interest in macroeconomics because they are based on the hypothesis of rational expectations. These model equations have some properties in common with simultaneous equations that are worth pointing out.

We can consider the following example of a rational expectation model (specified without intercepts without loss of generality):

$$Y_t = b_0 E(X_{t+1} \mid \mathcal{I}_{t-1}) + \epsilon_t, \tag{7.72}$$

$$X_t = \phi_{22} X_{t-1} + \varepsilon_{xt}, \quad -1 < \phi_{22} < 1, \tag{7.73}$$

$$\epsilon_t \sim \text{IID}(0, \sigma^2), \tag{7.74}$$

$$\varepsilon_{xt} \sim \text{IID}(0, \sigma_x^2), \tag{7.75}$$

$$\text{Cov}(\epsilon_t, \varepsilon_{xs}) = 0 \text{ for all } t \text{ and } s. \tag{7.76}$$

Equation (7.72) is the structural equation, and b_0 is the parameter of interest in this model. b_0 measures by how much Y is adjusted in period t when the expectation about X in period $t+1$ is changed based on the information that the agents have available in period $t-1$. Hence, the agents are forward-looking in this model, but they still need to build on history in order to formulate their expectations about the future X. The information set used by the agents to form expectations is denoted by $\mathcal{I}_{t-1}$ in (7.72).

7.10.1. Bias of OLS estimators for rational expectations models

A first candidate for estimation is to replace $E(X_{t+1} \mid \mathcal{I}_{t-1})$ by the observable X_{t+1}, and estimate the equation

$$Y_t = b_0 X_{t+1} + u_t \tag{7.77}$$

by OLS, giving

$$\widehat{b}_0 = \frac{\sum_{t=1}^{T-1} X_{t+1}Y_t}{\sum_{t=1}^{T-1} X_{t+1}^2}. \tag{7.78}$$

We want to investigate the difference $(\widehat{b}_0 - b_0)$ to see if the estimator is at least asymptotically unbiased. We start by writing $\widehat{b}_0$ in the usual way

$$\widehat{b}_0 = b_0 + \frac{\sum_{t=1}^{T-1} X_{t+1}u_t}{\sum_{t=1}^{T-1} X_{t+1}^2}, \tag{7.79}$$

so that we can work with the bias-expression

$$(\widehat{b}_0 - b_0) = \frac{\sum_{t=1}^{T-1} X_{t+1}u_t}{\sum_{t=1}^{T-1} X_{t+1}^2}. \tag{7.80}$$

In order to make progress, we need to find expressions for X_{t+1} and u_t. For X_{t+1}, that means the solution for X_{t+1} is conditional on X_{t-1} (which is in the information set):

$$X_{t+1} = \phi_{22}^2 X_{t-1} + \phi_{22}\varepsilon_{xt} + \varepsilon_{xt+1}. \tag{7.81}$$

Because the estimation equation (7.77) is obtained by substitution of $E(X_{t+1} \mid \mathcal{I}_{t-1})$ by X_{t+1}, the error term u_t in the estimation equation is given by

$$u_t = \epsilon_t - b_0(X_{t+1} - E(X_{t+1} \mid \mathcal{I}_{t-1})) = \epsilon_t - b_0(\varepsilon_{xt+1} + \phi_{22}\varepsilon_{xt}). \tag{7.82}$$

We can now calculate the probability limit of the right-hand side of (7.80) as

$$\begin{aligned}
&\text{plim}\left(\frac{\sum_t X_{t+1}u_t}{\sum_t X_{t+1}^2}\right) \\
&\quad = \frac{1}{\text{Var}(X_t)}\text{plim}\left(\frac{1}{T}\sum_t (X_{t+1})(\epsilon_t - b_0\varepsilon_{xt+1} - b_0\phi_{22}\varepsilon_{xt})\right).
\end{aligned}$$

The disturbances ε_t and ϵ_{xt} are independent of each other, as stated in assumption (7.76), and they have classical properties conditional on the agents' information set $\mathcal{I}_{t-1}$. These assumptions are used to find the asymptotic association between X_{t+1} and the disturbances ϵ_t, ε_{xt+1} and ε_{xt}:

$$\begin{aligned}
&\operatorname{plim}\left(\frac{1}{T}\sum_t (X_{t+1})(\epsilon_t - b_0\varepsilon_{xt+1} - b_0\phi_{22}\varepsilon_{xt})\right)\\
&= \operatorname{plim}\left(\frac{1}{T}\sum_t (\phi_{22}^2 X_{t-1} + \phi_{22}\varepsilon_{xt} + \varepsilon_{xt+1})\right.\\
&\qquad \left.\times(\epsilon_t - b_0\varepsilon_{xt+1} - b_0\phi_{22}\varepsilon_{xt})\right)\\
&= -\, b_0\phi_{22}^2\sigma_x^2 - b_0\sigma_x^2.
\end{aligned}$$

Collecting results, we have

$$\operatorname{plim}(\widehat{b}_0 - b_0) = \frac{-b_0\sigma_x^2(\phi_{22}^2 + 1)}{\operatorname{Var}(X_t)}.$$

By the stationarity of X_t, $\operatorname{Var}(X_t)$ is given by

$$\operatorname{Var}(X_t) = \frac{\sigma_x^2}{1 - \phi_{22}^2},$$

giving a compact expression for the asymptotic bias as

$$\begin{aligned}
\operatorname{plim}(\widehat{b}_0 - b_0) &= \frac{-b_0\sigma_x^2(\phi_{22}^2 + 1)}{\operatorname{Var}(X_t)} = -b_0(\phi_{22}^2 + 1)(1 - \phi_{22}^2)\\
&= -b_0(1 - \phi_{22}^4) < 0. \qquad (7.83)
\end{aligned}$$

The conclusion is that the OLS estimator of the parameter of interest b_0 is inconsistent. If b_0 is a positive parameter, it is underestimated by OLS. It is the assumption about how expectations are formed that are of importance for the qualitative result about biased OLS estimation, not how near or far into the future that the agents form expectations about X. For example, by solving Exercise 7.5, you can show that if we change the model equation (7.72) to

$$Y_t = b_0 E(X_t \mid \mathcal{I}_{t-1}) + \epsilon_t,$$

so that the agents base their decisions on a nowcasted variable, there is a similar but not identical expression for $\operatorname{plim}(\widehat{b}_0 - b_0)$.

7.10.2. Relationship to measurement errors equations

The source of the OLS bias is that we "contaminate" the disturbance term by the forecast error for X_{t+1} (or X_t, depending on the specification of (7.72)). Therefore, the bias is a special case of the *errors-in-variables* bias. Another famous example is the *measurement-error* bias. The measurement-error bias is usually presented using the model for cross-section data

$$Y_i = \beta_0 + \beta_1 X_i^* + \epsilon_i^*, \quad i = 1, 2, \ldots, n, \tag{7.84}$$

where $\mathrm{Cov}(\varepsilon_i^*, X_i^*) = 0$, and ε_i^* have the other classical properties as well. We assume that X_i^* is an unobservable random variable which is replaced by the observable X_i in the estimation of (7.84). The difference between X_i and X_i^* is random as follows:

$$e_i = X_i - X_i^*.$$

Even if all e_i and ε_i^* are independent, OLS on

$$Y_i = \beta_0 + \beta_1 X_i + \epsilon_i, \quad i = 1, 2, \ldots, n, \tag{7.85}$$

will produce an inconsistent estimator of β_1, because $\mathrm{Cov}(\varepsilon_i, X_i) \neq 0$ as a consequence of

$$\epsilon_i = \epsilon_i^* - \beta_1 e_i.$$

As usual, the probability limit of $\widehat{\beta}_0 - \beta_0$ is

$$\mathrm{plim}(\widehat{\beta}_1 - \beta_1) = \mathrm{plim}\frac{\frac{1}{n}\sum_{i=1}^{n}(X_i - \bar{X})\epsilon_i}{\frac{1}{n}\sum_{i=1}^{n}(X_i - \bar{X})^2}. \tag{7.86}$$

The denominator of (7.86) is equal to the theoretical variance of X, which is the sum of the variance of X^*, $\sigma_{X^*}^2$, and the measurement-error variance, σ_e^2:

$$\mathrm{Var}(X) = \sigma_{X^*}^2 + \sigma_e^2. \tag{7.87}$$

The numerator is

$$\begin{aligned}
&\mathrm{plim}\left[\frac{1}{n}\sum_{i=1}^{n}(X_i - \bar{X})\epsilon_i\right] \\
&= \mathrm{plim}\left[\frac{1}{n}\sum_{i=1}^{n}(X_i^* - \bar{X}^* + e_i - \bar{e})(\epsilon_i^* - \beta_1 e_i)\right] \\
&= -\beta_1 \mathrm{Var}(e) = -\beta_1 \sigma_e^2,
\end{aligned}$$

since the probability limit of all the other terms is zero by the assumptions of the model. Collecting results, we have the compact expressions:

$$\text{plim}(\widehat{\beta}_1 - \beta_1) = \frac{-\beta_1\sigma_e^2}{\text{Var}(X)} = \frac{-\beta_1\sigma_e^2}{\sigma_{X^*}^2 + \sigma_e^2}, \tag{7.88}$$

for the asymptotic bias of the OLS estimator in the measurement-error model.

To see the errors-in-variables interpretation of the bias of the OLS estimator (7.83) in the model (7.72)–(7.76), set

$$\sigma_e^2 \equiv \text{Var}(u_t) = \text{Var}(\varepsilon_{xt+1} + \phi_{22}\varepsilon_{xt}) = \sigma_x^2 + \phi_{22}^2\sigma_x^2,$$

$$\text{Var}(X_t) \equiv \frac{\sigma_x^2}{1-\phi_{22}^2},$$

and insert in (7.88)

$$\begin{aligned}\text{plim}(\widehat{\beta}_1 - \beta_1) &= \frac{-\beta_1\sigma_e^2}{\text{Var}(X)} = \frac{-\beta_1(\sigma_x^2 + \phi_{22}^2\sigma_x^2)}{\frac{\sigma_x^2}{1-\phi_{22}^2}} \\ &= -\beta_1(1+\phi_{22}^2)(1-\phi_{22}^2) \\ &= -\beta_1(1-\phi_{22}^4),\end{aligned} \tag{7.89}$$

which (allowing the obvious change in notation) is the same expression as in (7.83) above.

7.10.3. Identification and estimation by IV

Since we have found that OLS is *not* a consistent estimator, there is a possibility that an underlying problem is lack of identification. However, in our example model, that is not the case. We can see this by rewriting (7.72)–(7.76) as a simultaneous equation system, for example,

$$Y_t = b_0 X_{t+1} + u_t,$$

$$X_{t+1} = \phi_{22}^2 X_{t-1} + \xi_t,$$

where we have used ξ_t to denote the forecast error for X_{t+1}. Simply regarding this as a two-equation SEM, with no restrictions on the covariance between u_t and ξ_t, we have that the first equation is exactly identified on the order condition. Under the assumptions of the model, $\phi_{22} \neq 0$, and hence X_{t-1} is a relevant instrumental variable.

The IV estimator is

$$\widehat{b}_{0,IV} = \frac{\sum_{t=1}^{T} X_{t-1}Y_t}{\sum_{t=1}^{T} X_{t+1}X_{t-1}},$$

with the probability limit

$$\text{plim}(\widehat{b}_{0,IV}) = \frac{\text{Cov}(X_{t-1}, Y_t)}{\text{Cov}(X_{t+1}, X_{t-1})}.$$

The denominator is the second autocovariance of the X_t process, $\phi_{22}^2\sigma_x^2$. The numerator is

$$\text{Cov}(X_{t-1}, b_0(\phi_{22}^2 X_{t-1} + \xi_t) + \epsilon_t) = b_0\phi_{22}^2\sigma_x^2,$$

as X_{t-1} is uncorrelated with ξ_t and ϵ_t. Hence the estimator has the probability limit

$$\text{plim}(\widehat{b}_{0,IV}) = b_0,$$

and IV therefore gives a consistent estimator.

Note, however, that to avoid spurious instruments, care must be taken in specification of the forecasting equations. In our example model, the only forecasting equation is the marginal equation for X_t, and since that equation is an AR(1) process, the single available instrument is X_{t-1}.

7.11. Future-Dependent Models

So far we have discussed the modelling of causal stationary processes, following Definition 4.3 and Theorem 4.3 above. However, as we remember, stationarity is a more general property, and allows that some roots are located outside the complex unit-circle. In this section, we first illustrate the main challenge represented by non-causal models for the case of first-order dynamics. We next illustrate how the formal problems can be resolved for a New Keynesian Phillips curve, which is a forward-looking model of inflation dynamics. The non-causal version of the first-order autoregressive process is conspicuously similar to the usual causal model:

$$Y_t = \phi_0 + \phi_1 Y_{t-1} + \varepsilon_t, \quad |\phi_1| > 1, \tag{7.90}$$

where ε_t $(t = 0, \pm 1, \pm 1, \ldots)$ is a Gaussian white noise process. It is the assumption $|\phi_1| > 1$ which makes this Y_t process non-causal. Without loss of generality, we consider the case of root larger than one, i.e., $\phi_1 > 1$.

First, and for completeness, it is clear that if we consider the usual (causal) solution with repeated substitution from a given initial condition, the solution will not be stationary: the importance of the initial conditions for example will grow exponentially with time, instead of declining. Such solutions are called explosive for obvious reasons. Explosive solutions are very relevant in economics, and maybe more so when they have some form of check imposed or built into the process, i.e., a mechanism that stops the explosive process, at least for a period.

However, for the time being, we are interested in whether there can be a stationary solution of (7.90). There is a positive answer to that question, and it is achieved by considering the solution that is forward dependent. To see why, we can renormalize (7.90), so that Y_t depends on the lead-variable Y_{t+1} instead of the lag:

$$Y_t = \frac{-\phi_0}{\phi_1} + \frac{1}{\phi_1} Y_{t+1} + \frac{1}{\phi_1} \varepsilon_t$$

and consider repeated forward insertion on the right-hand side in this process, giving

$$Y_t = \frac{-\phi_0}{\phi_1} \sum_{i=0}^{H-1} \left(\frac{1}{\phi_1}\right)^i + \left(\frac{1}{\phi_1}\right)^H Y_{t+H} + \frac{1}{\phi_1} \sum_{i=0}^{H-1} \left(\frac{1}{\phi_1}\right)^i \varepsilon_{t+i} \tag{7.91}$$

after $H-1$ substitutions. Clearly, since $0 < \phi_1^{-1} < 1$, this solution implies that the unconditional expectation, the variance and the ACF are independent of time. Hence, the time series generated by (7.90), with Gaussian disturbances in particular, is indeed a stationary process, exactly as the theorems of Section 4.5.7 stated.

The challenge represented by (7.91) is instead one of relevance. The future dependence of the solution seems to make it necessary to know the whole sequence of future shocks, and for a finite horizon H, also the terminal condition Y_{T+H}. In many disciplines, these requirements simply seem unrealistic or unattainable, and the non-causal solution is therefore often dismissed as unpractical or "unnatural", Brockwell and Davies (1991, p. 81).

Economics is different in this respect, and non-causal models play a large role, in particular in modern macroeconomics. In fact, the expectation model in Section 7.10, where Y_t depended on the conditional expectation of X_{t+1}, already illustrated future dependence due to expectation formation for an explanatory variable.

However, for that model the focus was on the estimation, rather than on finding one (or many) solutions for the case of characteristic roots outside the unit-circle. In the following, we therefore show an example of how the challenge of finding a solution with explosive roots can be resolved. Also in this case, we shall see, the hypothesis of rational expectations is essential, to be able to work around the problems posed by future dependency problem for the existence of stationarity solutions (see Blanchard and Kahn, 1980).

The hybrid New Keynesian Phillips curve, NKPC is well established in modern macroeconomic theory. We write the NKPC as

$$\Delta p_t = \underset{\geq 0}{a^f} E_t[\Delta p_{t+1}] + \underset{\geq 0}{a^b} \Delta p_{t-1} + \underset{>0}{b} s_t + \varepsilon_{\pi t}, \tag{7.92}$$

where Δp_t is the rate of inflation, $E_t\left[\Delta p_{t+1}\right]$ is the expected rate of inflation in period $t+1$, given the information available for forecasting at the end of period t. The intercept of the equation has been omitted for simplicity. The variable s_t denotes the logarithm of firms' real marginal costs and $\varepsilon_{\pi t}$ is a disturbance term.

In many applications, notably Galí and Gertler (1999), the disturbance term is omitted, which suggests a stronger interpretation which is often referred to as the NKPC holding in "exact form". The theory's consistent signs are given below the parameters. The so-called "pure" NKPC is specified without the lagged inflation term (i.e., $a^b = 0$). Regarding the sum of the inflation coefficients, it is the custom to specify $a^f + a^b \leq 1$ as a restriction, which rules out an explosive solution in the purely backward-looking case.

In the following, the third variable in (7.92), s_t, is taken to be the logarithm of the wage share, which is the common operational definition of firms' marginal cost of production in the NKPC literature. The coefficient b is assumed to be strictly positive, and there are no other economic explanatory variables in this model of inflation dynamics for the closed economy case.

In order to derive the solution for Δp_t , we need to make assumptions about the process of the explanatory variable. We follow Galí and Gertler (1999), who base their solution on the assumption that s_t is a variable that Granger-causes Δp_t.[3]

[3]Sbordone (2002) makes use of the definition $s_t = \text{ulc}_t - p_t$, where ulc_t is the logarithm of nominal unit labour costs and p_t is the logarithm of the price level, to derive a rational expectations solution that is separate from the Gali and Gertler's solution. In Sbordone's solution, unit labour costs, not the wage share, take the role of forcing variable in the solution. Sbordone takes the pure NKPC with $a^b = 0$, as her starting point, but the closed-form solution for inflation nevertheless contains Δp_{t-1} on the right-hand side.

Hence, we consider the closed-form rational expectations solution when s_t follows an autoregressive process of order k:

$$s_t = c_{s1}s_{t-1} + \cdots + c_{sk}s_{t-k} + \varepsilon_{s,t}. \tag{7.93}$$

Equations (7.92) and (7.93) define the NKPC model. For simplicity, we assume that the two disturbances $\varepsilon_{\pi t}$ and ε_{st} are independently normally distributed variables. The two equations define a model of one-way causality between s_t and π_t, hence the term *forcing variable* for s_t is often used.

It can be shown that the solution for Δp_t can be written as

$$\Delta p_t = r_1 \Delta p_{t-1} + \frac{b}{a^f r_2} \sum_{i=0}^{\infty} \left(\frac{1}{r_2}\right)^i E_t s_{t+i} + \frac{1}{a^f r_2}\varepsilon_{\pi t}, \tag{7.94}$$

where r_1 and r_2 are the two roots of $r^2 - (1/a^f)r + (a^b/a^f) = 0$; cf. Bårdsen *et al.* (2005, Appendix A) who build on Pesaran (1987, pp. 108–109). $E_t s_{t+i}$ denotes the rational expectation of s_{t+i}, conditional on (7.93) and information available in period t. We follow the custom and find a solution by imposing the so-called transversality condition

$$\left(\frac{1}{r_2}\right)^i E_t s_{t+i} \to 0 \text{ as } i \to \infty. \tag{7.95}$$

The closed-form solution is discussed in detail in Nymoen *et al.* (2012). It is

$$\Delta p_t = r_1 \pi_{t-1} + \frac{b}{a^f r_2} K_{s1} s_t + \cdots + \frac{b}{a^f r_2} K_{sk} s_{t-k+1} + \frac{1}{a^f r_2}\varepsilon_{\pi t}, \tag{7.96}$$

where $r_1 \leq 1$ and it is assumed that

$$\left|\frac{r_{sj}}{r_2}\right| < 1 \quad \text{for } j = 1, 2, \ldots, k, \tag{7.97}$$

where r_{sj} are the roots $r_s^k - c_{s1}r_s^{k-1} - c_{sk-1}r_s - c_{sk} = 0$, the characteristic equation associated with the process of the forcing variable s_t. When (7.97) holds, the transversality condition is satisfied, and the coefficients K_{sj} in the solution (7.96) exist (cf. Nymoen *et al.*, 2012). For concreteness, consider the case of $k = 2$ with the closed-form solution:

$$\Delta p_t = r_1 \Delta p_{t-1} + \frac{b}{a^f r_2} K_{s1} s_t + \frac{b}{a^f r_2} K_{s2} s_{t-1} + \frac{1}{a^f r_2}\varepsilon_{\pi t}, \tag{7.98}$$

where s_t is stationary, and logical consistency therefore requires that $r_1 < 1$, which makes sure that Δp_t also is stationary when we regard (7.93) and (7.98) as the two-equation model.

Although the notation is somewhat cluttered, we can recognize (7.98) as an ADL model equation for inflation. Hence, despite the future-dependency in the structural model equation representation (7.92), the solution with rational expectations produces an ADL model equation for inflation which is causal and conditional on s_t. In principle, (7.98) can be estimated by OLS, and the results compared with competing models of inflation. This appears to give a direct approach that can supplement the tests of the NKPC that use IV or GMM estimation of the theoretical model equation (7.92), see Bårdsen *et al.* (2005, Chapter 7) and Castle *et al.* (2014), among others. However, so far, little has been done empirically to follow up the "direct route". Can it be that researchers think that it takes the rational expectations solution too seriously?

7.12. Exercises

Exercise 7.1. Use the dataset in *pcnaive_VARbyCond_d.zip* to estimate a VAR-EX model for the three endogenous time series Ya, Yb, Yc. If you want, you can rename the three series as $Y1, Y2$ and $Y3$. Include the variable Za as a regressor in the VAR, you can rename it as $X1$ to match the text. Include a constant term in the VAR as well. After estimating the VAR, estimate the multiple equation model (7.5)–(7.7), and compare the likelihoods.

Exercise 7.2. Start from (1.15)–(1.16) and obtain the structural form of the cobweb model by multiplication with a suitable matrix (e.g., $\mathbf{A}$ in the text).

Exercise 7.3. In the main text, we discuss the identification of a simple structural model

$$Q_t + a_{12}P_t = a_{10} + \epsilon_{1t} \text{ (demand)},$$

$$a_{21}Q_t + P_t = a_{20} + \epsilon_{2t} \text{ (supply)},$$

under different assumptions about the coefficients a_{12} and a_{21} and about the structural disturbance covariance matrix $\mathbf{\Omega}$. Show the expressions for the first- and second-order moments of the observable variables of a model, where $a_{12} = \omega_{12} = 0$. What are the expressions for the identified structural coefficients?

Exercise 7.4 (Exam 2015 ECON4160 UiO). Note: This exercise could also have been placed in Chapter 2, in particular the first two questions. However, since the main part of the exercise is about a system (though static) we place it here.

(1) Assume that the conditional expectation of Y grows linearly with X. Consider the n variable pairs $(Y_1, X_1), \ldots, (Y_n, X_n)$, and assume that the variable pairs are mutually independent and have identical normal distributions. In this case, what are the expressions for the ML of the two parameters

$$\frac{\partial}{\partial X_i} E(Y_i \mid X_i) \quad \text{and} \quad \text{Var}(\varepsilon_i \mid X_i) = \sigma^2?$$

(2) How can you estimate the parameter $\frac{\partial}{\partial X_i} E(Y_i \mid X_i)$ efficiently, if the assumption $\text{Var}(\varepsilon_i \mid X_i) = \sigma^2$ is changed to $\text{Var}(\varepsilon_i \mid X_i) = \sigma^2 X_i^2$?

(3) Assume that the relationship

$$Y_i = \beta_1 + \beta_2 X_i + \varepsilon_{1i} \tag{7.99}$$

is an equation in a model consisting of two equations. Discuss identification and estimation of the parameter β_2 in the following three cases: (We denote parameters in the second equation by γ_j in all three cases, and that the only unobservable variables are disturbances.)

(a) The second equation is

$$Z_i = \gamma_0 + \gamma_1 X_i + \varepsilon_{2i}, \tag{7.100}$$

and we assume $\text{Cov}(\varepsilon_{1i}, \varepsilon_{2i}) = \omega_{12} \neq 0$, and that X_i is uncorrelated with both disturbances.

(b) The second equation is

$$X_i = \gamma_0 + \varepsilon_{2i} \tag{7.101}$$

and we assume $\omega_{12} = 0$.

(c) The second equation is

$$X_i = \gamma_0 + \gamma_1 Y_i + \gamma_2 Z_{1i} + \gamma_3 Z_{2i} + \varepsilon_{2i} \tag{7.102}$$

and we assume $\omega_{12} \neq 0$.

(4) In case of 3(b) and 3(c), is the second equation of the model identified?

Exercise 7.5. Assume that (7.72) is replaced by

$$Y_t = b_0 E(X_t \mid \mathcal{I}_{t-1}) + \epsilon_t$$

but that the model (7.72)–(7.76) is unchanged in all other respects. Show that the bias becomes

$$\text{plim}(\widehat{b_0} - b_0) = -b_0(1 - \phi_{22}^2) < 0. \tag{7.103}$$

Exercise 7.6.

(1) Use the datasets in *SEMbias_data.zip* to reproduce the results with small and large simultaneity bias in equations (6.25) and (7.45). The dataset with $\sigma_C^2 = 0.25$ is named *Keynes_closed_notax_nobreakA*. The large-bias dataset has the same name, but with the letter B in the place of the letter A.
(2) Explain why the consumption function can be regarded as identified.
(3) Use the large-bias dataset to estimate the consumption function by IV, 2SLS, 3SLS and FIML. Why are the point estimates of the parameters of the consumption function identical for all four estimation methods?

Exercise 7.7. With reference to the Fulton fish market data in the earlier chapters, for example, Exercise 5.6, investigate whether a SEM of the VAR that you estimated in the answer to Exercise 5.6 can be established.

The theoretical model (structure) that we want to estimate assumes that the demand does not depend on *stormy* and *mixed*, since these two variables are indicators of weather at sea. Hence, with reference to the order condition, the demand equation is over-identified in this theory. Next, the theory states that the supply of fish is largely determined by catch-capacity (which can be regarded as fixed, since we have daily data over a short historical time period) and weather, therefore the supply is independent of the lags of both *price* and *quantity*. Hence, the supply equation also is over-identified in the theory under investigation.

Appendix 7.A. Algebra Showing 2SLS and GIV Equivalence

This appendix fills in a couple of steps in the algebra showing that the GIV estimator of $\boldsymbol{\beta}_1$ in the structural equation (7.19) is identical to the 2SLS estimator of the same coefficient vector.

We start with the expression for the GIV estimator:

$$\widehat{\boldsymbol{\beta}}_{1,\text{GIV}} = (\widehat{\mathbf{Z}}_1'\mathbf{X}_1)^{-1}\widehat{\mathbf{Z}}_1'\mathbf{y}_1, \tag{7.A.1}$$

where

$$\widehat{\mathbf{Z}}_1 = (\mathbf{X}_{1X} \quad \widehat{\mathbf{X}}_{1Y}), \tag{7.A.2}$$

$$\mathbf{X}_1 = (\mathbf{X}_{1X} \quad \mathbf{X}_{1Y}) \tag{7.A.3}$$

and

$$\widehat{\mathbf{X}}_{1Y} = \mathbf{P}_{X_{1m}}\mathbf{X}_{1Y}. \tag{7.A.4}$$

The matrices are defined in the main text, in particular

$$\mathbf{P}_{X_{1m}} = \mathbf{X}_{1m}(\mathbf{X}'_{1m}\mathbf{X}_{1m})^{-1}\mathbf{X}'_{1m}. \tag{7.A.5}$$

Using the partitioning, the product $\widehat{\mathbf{Z}}'_1\mathbf{X}_1$ becomes

$$\begin{aligned}\widehat{\mathbf{Z}}'_1\mathbf{X}_1 &= (\mathbf{X}_{1X} : \widehat{\mathbf{X}}_{1Y})' \times (\mathbf{X}_{1X} : \mathbf{X}_{1Y}) \\ &= \begin{pmatrix}\mathbf{X}'_{1X} \\ \widehat{\mathbf{X}}'_{1Y}\end{pmatrix}(\mathbf{X}_{1X} : \mathbf{X}_{1Y}) = \begin{pmatrix}\mathbf{X}'_{1X}\mathbf{X}_{1X} & \mathbf{X}'_{1X}\mathbf{X}_{1Y} \\ \widehat{\mathbf{X}}'_{1Y}\mathbf{X}_{1X} & \widehat{\mathbf{X}}'_{1Y}\mathbf{X}_{1Y}\end{pmatrix}\end{aligned}$$

so

$$\widehat{\boldsymbol{\beta}}_{1,\text{GIV}} = \begin{pmatrix}\mathbf{X}'_{1X}\mathbf{X}_{1X} & \mathbf{X}'_{1X}\mathbf{X}_{1Y} \\ \widehat{\mathbf{X}}'_{1Y}\mathbf{X}_{1X} & \widehat{\mathbf{X}}'_{1Y}\mathbf{X}_{1Y}\end{pmatrix}^{-1}\begin{pmatrix}\mathbf{X}'_{1X}\mathbf{y}_{1} \\ \widehat{\mathbf{X}}'_{1Y}\mathbf{y}_1\end{pmatrix}_t. \tag{7.A.6}$$

We now focus on $\mathbf{X}'_{1X}\mathbf{X}_{1Y}$ and $\widehat{\mathbf{X}}'_{1Y}\mathbf{X}_{1Y}$, and begin with the second

$$\widehat{\mathbf{X}}'_{1Y}\mathbf{X}_{1Y} = (\mathbf{P}_{X_{1m}}\mathbf{X}_{1Y})'\mathbf{X}_{1Y}.$$

The reduced-form residual $\mathbf{e}_1$ matrix is given by

$$\mathbf{e}_1 \equiv \mathbf{X}_{1Y} - \underbrace{\mathbf{P}_{X_{1m}}\mathbf{X}_{1Y}}_{\widehat{\mathbf{X}}_{1Y}} = \mathbf{M}_{X_{1m}}\mathbf{X}_{1Y},$$

where

$$\mathbf{M}_{X_{1m}} = \mathbf{I} - \mathbf{P}_{X_{1m}}.$$

Collecting results we have

$$\begin{aligned}\widehat{\mathbf{X}}'_{1Y}\mathbf{X}_{1Y} &= (\mathbf{P}_{X_{1m}}\mathbf{X}_{1Y})'\mathbf{X}_{1Y} \\ &= (\mathbf{P}_{X_{1m}}\mathbf{X}_{1Y})'(\widehat{\mathbf{X}}_{1Y} + \mathbf{e}_1) \\ &= \mathbf{X}'_{1Y}\mathbf{P}'_{X_{1m}}\widehat{\mathbf{X}}_{1Y} = \widehat{\mathbf{X}}'_{1Y}\widehat{\mathbf{X}}_{1Y},\end{aligned} \tag{7.A.7}$$

where the last line of the equation has made use of: $(\mathbf{P}_{X_{1m}}\mathbf{X}_{1Y})'\mathbf{e}_1 = \mathbf{X}'_{1m}\mathbf{P}'_{X_{1m}}(\mathbf{I} - \mathbf{P}_{X_{1m}})\mathbf{X}_{1Y} = \mathbf{0}$.[4] Next, we consider $\mathbf{X}'_{1X}\mathbf{X}_{1Y}$. We want to show that $\mathbf{X}'_{1X}\mathbf{X}_{1Y} = \mathbf{X}'_{1X}\widehat{\mathbf{X}}_{1Y}$. This is achieved by writing $\mathbf{X}'_{1X}\widehat{\mathbf{X}}_{1Y}$ as

$$\mathbf{X}'_{1X}\widehat{\mathbf{X}}_{1Y} = \mathbf{X}'_{1X}(\mathbf{X}_{1Y} - \mathbf{e}_1) = \mathbf{X}'_{1X}\mathbf{X}_{1Y} - \mathbf{X}'_{1X}\mathbf{e}_1,$$

[4]Recall the properties of the prediction maker matrix:

$$\begin{aligned}\mathbf{P}'_{X_{1m}} &= \mathbf{P}_{X_{1m}} \text{(symmetry)}, \\ \mathbf{P}'_{X_{1m}}\mathbf{P}_{X_{1m}} &= [\mathbf{X}_{1m}(\mathbf{X}'_{1m}\mathbf{X}_{1m})^{-1}\mathbf{X}'_{1m}]'[\mathbf{X}_{1m}(\mathbf{X}'_{1m}\mathbf{X}_{1m})^{-1}\mathbf{X}'_{1m}] \\ &= \mathbf{P}_{X_{1m}} \text{(idempotency)}.\end{aligned}$$

and noting that $\mathbf{X}'_{1X}\mathbf{e}_1 = (\mathbf{e}'_1\mathbf{X}_{1X})' = \mathbf{0}$, since the effect of the exogenous $\mathbf{X}_{1X}$ has been regressed out. Hence,

$$\mathbf{X}'_{1X}\mathbf{X}_{1Y} = \mathbf{X}'_{1X}\widehat{\mathbf{X}}_{1Y}, \tag{7.A.8}$$

which is what we wanted to show. Replacing $\mathbf{X}'_{1X}\mathbf{X}_{1Y}$ by $\mathbf{X}'_{1X}\widehat{\mathbf{X}}_{1Y}$, and $\widehat{\mathbf{X}}'_{1Y}\mathbf{X}_{1Y}$ by $\widehat{\mathbf{X}}'_{1Y}\widehat{\mathbf{X}}_{1Y}$ in (7.A.6), we obtain

$$\widehat{\boldsymbol{\beta}}_{1,\mathrm{GIV}} = \begin{pmatrix} \mathbf{X}'_{1X}\mathbf{X}_{1X} & \mathbf{X}'_{1X}\widehat{\mathbf{X}}_{1Y} \\ \widehat{\mathbf{X}}'_{1Y}\mathbf{X}_{1X} & \widehat{\mathbf{X}}'_{1Y}\widehat{\mathbf{X}}_{1Y} \end{pmatrix}^{-1} \begin{pmatrix} \mathbf{X}'_{1X}\mathbf{y}_1 \\ \widehat{\mathbf{X}}'_{1Y}\mathbf{y}_1 \end{pmatrix} \tag{7.A.9}$$

which is identical to the expression for $\widehat{\boldsymbol{\beta}}_{1,2\mathrm{SLS}}$ in (7.59).

Chapter 8

Exogeneity

Exogeneity is a fundamental concept in both theoretical and empirical model specifications in economics. In theoretical models, any variable which is not determined by the specified equation system is exogenous. In econometric model specifications, several exogeneity concepts are in use, and they have relevance for different modelling purposes. Weak exogeneity may be said to be the fundamental concept, since without it, consistent estimation of parameters of interest is impossible. However, other concepts (strong and super exogeneity) become important when the research purpose is to use an empirical model for forecasting and policy analysis. This chapter also reviews the testing of exogeneity.

8.1. Introduction

Above, the term exogenous variable has been used in two main meanings. First, as an explanatory variable that is uncorrelated with all the disturbances in the model equation. Second, as an explanatory variable that is correlated with past disturbances in a dynamic model equation, but which is uncorrelated with future disturbances. The first meaning of the term corresponds to the concept of *strict exogeneity*, while the second is the concept of *predeterminedness*. These two concepts show that exogeneity is important for estimation: In the IID-regression model, the OLS estimators are unbiased and have other desirable properties due to the strict exogeneity of the regressors. In the context of a dynamic model equation, the OLS estimators are biased in finite samples due to the lack of strict exogeneity, but they are consistent as long as the explanatory variables are predetermined.

Exogeneity is also a model property that exists (or not) relative to the DGP. For a model for cross-section data, strict exogeneity may be lost if the statistical conditioning underlying the specification of the model equation is invalid. With observable data, omitted variables (not enough system thinking) are probably the most usual cause. In the case of dynamic models, predeterminedness is lost if the model's disturbances are autocorrelated. Hence, even though we speak about exogenous and predetermined variables, exogeneity is a model property more than a property of variables *per se*. This point is well illustrated by the distinction made above between conditional model equations and structural model equations. In the example of macroeconometric system of Chapter 7, a valid conditional model for consumption exists, but that conditional model equation does not correspond to the consumption function of the model even though both model equations include GDP as an explanatory variable.

This ambiguity in "exogeneity status" of an explanatory variable in an econometric model equation can be resolved if the term exogeneity is more clearly related to the research purpose, and to the concept of parameter of interest, which we have used on several occasions above.

8.2. Weak Exogeneity

Weak exogeneity is a concept that sets requirements for the necessary relation between the *estimand* (the parameter of interest to be estimated), and the variables used to form the estimator. The desired quality of the relationship is that it should secure efficient estimation. We do not need to be precise about finite or asymptotic efficiency. The point is, in any case, that a variable is said to be weakly exogenous for the parameter of interest if we not forego any useful information about that estimand by conditioning on the variable, and not taking into the account the process whereby the variable is generated. Hence, weak exogeneity is about being able to estimate a parameter of interest by using a conditional approach that does not rely on specifying the part of the economic system where the conditioning variable is determined or generated. It is immediately clear that weak exogeneity is a relevant concept for single equation models where the right-hand side variables are determined in the wider economic system. They can be regressor variables, but not only that. Weak exogeneity applies to instrumental variables as well, and in that context weak exogeneity might be seen as closely related to the joint property of instrument relevance and instrument validity. Hence, exogeneity may be seen as a fundamental concept for the possibility of estimation.

Despite the considerable generality of concept, it is often clarifying to discuss weak exogeneity using a system-representation consisting of a marginal and a conditional model equation. Hence, we assume the bivariate first-order Gaussian VAR, and the ADL model equation defined in Section 6.2.1.

Let $\boldsymbol{\theta}$ denote the parameters of VAR, and let $\boldsymbol{\theta}_1$ and $\boldsymbol{\theta}_2$ denote the parameters of the conditional model equation and the marginal model equation:

$$\boldsymbol{\theta} = [\phi_{10}, \phi_{11}, \ldots, \phi_{22}, \sigma_y^2, \sigma_x^2, \sigma_{xy}]', \tag{8.1}$$

$$\boldsymbol{\theta}_1 = [\phi_0, \phi_1, \beta_0, \beta_1, \sigma^2]' \tag{8.2}$$

$$\boldsymbol{\theta}_2 = [\phi_{20}, \phi_{21}, \phi_{22}, \sigma_x^2]'. \tag{8.3}$$

Weak exogeneity is defined as the situation where statistically efficient estimation of the parameters of interest can be achieved by only considering the conditional model and not taking the rest of the system into account. This implies that there is no direct or indirect (in the form of cross-restrictions) dependency between the parameters in the two vectors $\boldsymbol{\theta}_1$ and $\boldsymbol{\theta}_2$. If there are such restrictions, the maximized log-likelihood of the VAR does not factorize as

$$\mathcal{L}_{\hat{\boldsymbol{\theta}}} = \mathcal{L}_{\hat{\boldsymbol{\theta}}_1} + \mathcal{L}_{\hat{\boldsymbol{\theta}}_2},$$

where $\mathcal{L}_{\hat{\boldsymbol{\theta}}_1}$ denotes the maximized conditional log-likelihood (unrestricted), and $\mathcal{L}_{\hat{\boldsymbol{\theta}}_2}$ represents the marginal log-likelihood, X_t in the conditional model would not be weakly exogenous for the parameter vector $\boldsymbol{\theta}_1$.

The hallmark of weak exogeneity is that there is no loss of information by abstracting from the marginal model when the purpose is to estimate the parameters of interest of the conditional model. As noted above, weak exogeneity is defined relative to the parameters of interest. The parameter of interest can be $\boldsymbol{\theta}$ or a subset. For example, if the parameter of interest is β_0 in the ADL model equation, X_t is weakly exogenous for that parameter of interest. However, if the parameters of interest are the eigenvalues of the companion matrix of, for example, the bivariate VAR in Section 6.2.1, X_t is not weakly exogenous as λ_1 and λ_2 depend on ϕ_{12} and ϕ_{22} which belong to $\boldsymbol{\theta}_2$. Valid and reliable estimation of the eigenvalues in general require that econometric treatment is given to the system.

8.3. Granger Causality and Strong Exogeneity

If the purpose is to forecast a time series variable in a valid and efficient way by the use of a single equation model (ADL or ECM form), weak exogeneity is a necessary but not a sufficient condition. A fundamental concept in this context is Granger-causality, and its converse: Granger non-causality. In a paper that was path breaking when it was published, Granger (1969b) proposed a definition that linked causality to how events evolve in the time dimension, and to the principle that the future cannot cause the past; see Cartwright (2009) and Hoover (2001) among others. Granger's definition of causality is that an event A causes event B if predictions that make use of knowledge about the history of both A and B are better than predictions that only condition on the history of B events. Granger's definition is directly applicable to VARs. For the simplest case we considered for weak exogeneity ($n = 2$, $p = 1$, $m = 0$ and with Section 6.2.1 as our reference), the VAR implies that Y *Granger causes* X, but also that X Granger causes Y. This constellation is an example of joint or mutual Granger causality. Exogeneity is related to one-way *Granger non-causality,* which in the bivariate VAR(1) means either that $\phi_{12} = 0$ (X does not Granger cause Y) or $\phi_{21} = 0$ (Y does not Granger cause X).

Assume that the purpose is forecasting of Y_{T+h} ($h = 1, 2, \ldots, H$) conditional on period T information, as set out in Section 5.5. Again, with weak exogeneity of X_t alone, Y_T influences X_{T+1} if $\phi_{21} \neq 0$ in which case X_{T+1} cannot be treated as "fixed" when using the conditional model (6.10) for forecasting Y_{T+1}. For the same reason, X_{T+h} and X_{T+h-1} cannot be treated as fixed in dynamic forecasts. The requisite additional restriction is that $\phi_{21} = 0$, which implies Granger non-causality from Y to X.

Weak exogeneity plus Granger non-causality generate *strong exogeneity.* Strong exogeneity permits dynamic, multi-step, forecasting of Y from the ADL model equation (6.10) conditional on predictions of X generated from the marginal model equation (the second row in the VAR,) with $\phi_{21} = 0$ imposed. With $\phi_{21} \neq 0$, valid forecasting of Y must account for the feedback of Y onto X, violating the exogeneity of X for the purpose of forecasting.

More generally, Granger non-causality means that no lags of the variable that we are interested in forecasting enter into any of the rows of the VAR from which the conditional model equation for the variable has been derived. Since it is easy to imagine that joint dynamic dependencies are common in economics, Granger non-casuality can be regarded as a strong requirement, hence the name strong exogeneity seems to be appropriate.

8.4. Parameter Invariance and Super Exogeneity

As mentioned above, structural breaks are frequent in economics. A structural break is a change in the system's parameter vector $\boldsymbol{\theta}$, and hence can be due to changes in $\boldsymbol{\theta}_1$ and/or $\boldsymbol{\theta}_2$. In the context of exogeneity, we are interested in breaks in $\boldsymbol{\theta}_2$ that do not affect $\boldsymbol{\theta}_1$, in which case we say that $\boldsymbol{\theta}_1$ is *invariant* or *autonomous* with respect to the changes in $\boldsymbol{\theta}_2$.

For example, $\boldsymbol{\theta}_2$ can be constant over one time period, corresponding to one "regime", and then change to a new level, temporarily or more permanently. The change can be fast or slow. Hence, there are several possible types or forms of structural breaks in the marginal model. X_t is *super exogenous* in the conditional model if X_t is weakly exogenous and the parameters $(\phi_1, \beta_0, \beta_1, \sigma^2)$ are invariant with respect to structural breaks in the marginal model. This definition can be generalized to invariance of the parameters of a given conditional model with respect to structural breaks elsewhere in the economy (as represented by a set of marginal model equations). Note also that while super exogeneity is a property that conditional model equations may or may not have, invariance is a concept that also applies to the structural model equations of the previous chapter.

In the simplest case, with a static regression model (i.e., $\phi_1 = \beta_1 = 0$ in the conditional ADL) we have

$$\sigma_{XY} = \beta_0 \sigma_X^2, \tag{8.4}$$

and super exogeneity of X_t is seen to require that σ_{XY} changes proportionally to a break in the marginal model's variance σ_X^2 (an intervention in the marginal model).

While there is nothing hindering that a condition like (8.4) may hold, there is also nothing that makes it hold either. Hence, both super exogeneity and its converse (lack of invariance) represent possible properties of conditional model equations. This balanced perspective has more in common with the discussion in Haavelmo (1944) than with the Lucas-critique about the inherent lack of invariance of conditional models due to misrepresentation of rational expectations (see Lucas, 1976). As noted above, in his 1944 monograph, Haavelmo also wrote about the degree of autonomy of econometric relationships, which in the modern terminology translates to degree of invariance (Aldrich, 1989). Relationships that maintain parameter constancy with respect to a wide range of different breaks and shocks elsewhere in the economy have a high degree of autonomy compared to relationships that break down more easily. Hence, autonomy, invariance and super exogeneity are relative concepts: A conditional model can have parameters that are super exogenous with respect to certain interventions (structural breaks), but not to all. As other products of civilization, all empirical models are doomed to break down, sooner or later! However, in the course of their lifetime, good models can aid in understanding policy judgement and even forecasting.

The structural change that we have in mind can be a result of a policy change, sometimes called an intervention. For valid analysis of the effect of the policy change on the endogenous variable in a conditional model, invariance is the requisite property. Hence, super exogeneity as a concept is linked to the purpose of valid policy analysis from conditional models. Super exogeneity does not require Granger noncausality, and submodels characterized by joint Granger causality can therefore be well suited for policy analysis.

Figure 8.1 illustrates the basic concepts (weak exogeneity, Granger noncausality and invariance), see Ericsson (1992), and Figure 8.2 shows how the different exogeneity concepts correspond to different intersection areas in the diagram.

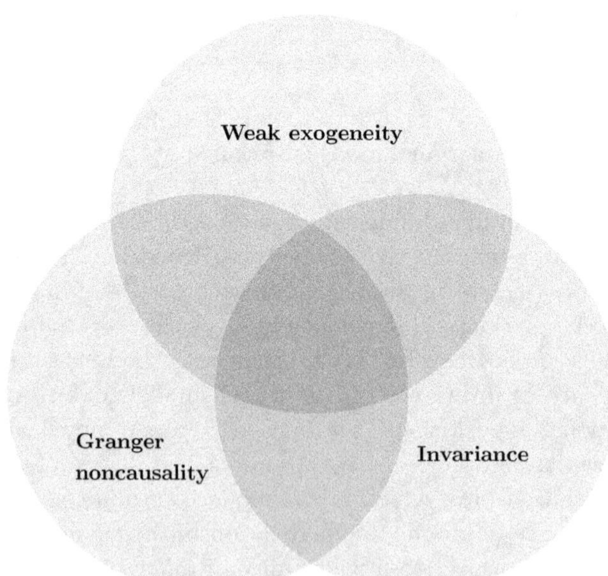

Figure 8.1. Exogeneity: Basic concepts.

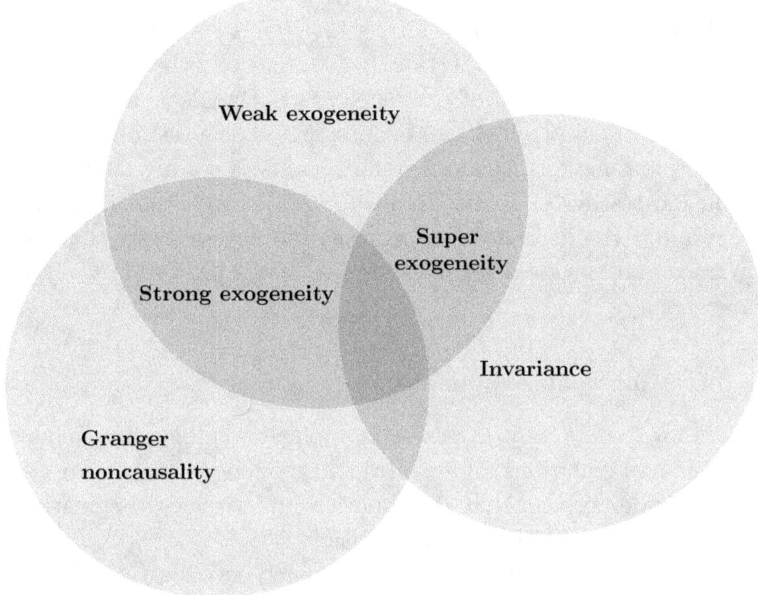

Figure 8.2. Exogeneity: All concepts, Ericsson (1992).

It is also possible to summarize the concepts by three questions and answers:

1. Can we estimate our parameters of interest efficiently without specifying the process that generated X_t?

   If the answer is "yes", then X_t is weakly exogenous.
2. Can we forecast Y efficiently by conditioning on a forecast for X that does not involve the forecasted Y values?

   If the answer is "yes", and the answer to 1 is also "yes", then X_t is strongly exogenous.
3. Can we do valid policy analysis based on the conditional model?

   If the answer is "yes", and the answer to 1 is also "yes", then X_t is super exogenous.

8.5. Exogeneity Tests

It is beyond the scope of this chapter to give a comprehensive overview of the literature on exogeneity testing. However, it is possible to sketch some of the tests and procedures that have shown to been useful in applied work. We start with the test referred to as the Hausman test of endogeneity, see Hill *et al.* (2012, Section 104.1), and by others as the Durbin–Wu–Hausman (DWH) test of exogeneity, see Davidson and MacKinnon (2004, Section 8.7), and which can be interpreted as a test of weak exogeneity in conditional models. Granger non-causality is readily testable by variable exclusion testing in VARs. Hendry (1988), Engle and Hendry (1993) and Favero and Hendry (1992) have proposed several tests that are tests of invariance and weak exogeneity, and are hence interpretable as tests of super exogeneity.

8.5.1. Testing weak exogeneity

As noted above, there may, in practical applications, be a fine line between structural model equations and conditional model equations. For example, because the wider system that the equation under study "belongs" to may be difficult to specify with enough precision.

Hence, the focus may become the difference between two estimators of the coefficient vector $\boldsymbol{\beta}$ in

$$\mathbf{y} = \mathbf{X}\boldsymbol{\beta} + \boldsymbol{\varepsilon}, \tag{8.5}$$

where one is the OLS estimator $\hat{\boldsymbol{\beta}}_{\text{OLS}}$, and another is consistent both with exogeneity and without it, i.e., the IV estimator, $\hat{\boldsymbol{\beta}}_{\text{IV}}$. The test situation can be written as

$$H_0 : \text{plim}(\hat{\boldsymbol{\beta}}_{\text{IV}} - \hat{\boldsymbol{\beta}}_{\text{OLS}}) = 0 \text{ against } H_1 : \text{plim}(\hat{\boldsymbol{\beta}}_{\text{IV}} - \hat{\boldsymbol{\beta}}_{\text{OLS}}) \neq 0.$$

But where should any significant difference between $\hat{\boldsymbol{\beta}}_{\text{OLS}}$ and $\hat{\boldsymbol{\beta}}_{\text{IV}}$ come from? The answer must be: From the rest of the system, and from the marginal models of the variables in $\mathbf{X}$ in (8.5). This interpretation means that we can perform the test without actually doing IV estimation, which of course is a convenient simplification.

To be precise, we assume that the parameters are constant both in the marginal model and in the conditional model equation. If weak exogeneity holds, there is no information contained in the marginal model that can increase the efficiency of estimation of the parameters of the conditional model.

We can therefore test H_0 by estimating the marginal models for $\mathbf{X}$ by OLS, calculate residuals from the set of marginal models and then test if those residuals are significant when added to the original model (estimated by OLS) as regressors, see Davidson and MacKinnon (2004, Section 8.7), who refer to the test as the Durbin–Wu–Hausman (DWH) test.

An equivalent way of implementing the test is to add the fitted values from the marginal models to the regression and test if they are significant. In both versions, the interpretation of a significant test outcome is that the marginal model contains information about $\boldsymbol{\beta}$, meaning that weak exogeneity is rejected. In practice, the test is an OLS-based F-test where the first degree of freedom is the number of "suspected" endogenous explanatory variables in (8.5).

As an example of the DWH test, we make use of the dataset for annual inflation that we analyzed in Exercise 6.10. To simplify the notation, we drop the 1980 observation and obtain the empirical relationship for inflation (INF) conditional on one lag, and on the contemporaneous unemployment percent (U_t):

$$\begin{aligned}
\text{INF}_t &= \underset{(0.26)}{3.02} + \underset{(0.087)}{0.75}\,\text{INF}_{t-1} - \underset{(0.264)}{0.66}\,U_t, \\
&\text{OLS } \mathcal{L} = -40.3834,\ \hat{\sigma} = 1.297,\ T = 25\ [1981\text{–}2005], \\
&\mathsf{F}_{\mathsf{AR}(1-2)}(2,20) = 0.30\,[0.74], \\
&\chi^2_{\mathsf{normality}}(2) = 3.86\,[0.15], \\
&\mathsf{F}_{\mathsf{HET}x^2}(4,20) = 1.05\,[0.41], \\
&\mathsf{F}_{\mathsf{ARCH}(1-1)}(1,23) = 0.60\,[0.45],
\end{aligned} \tag{8.6}$$

which can be compared to the equation estimated in the answer to Exercise 6.10.

A simple marginal model equation for U_t gives the residual series:

$$\hat{\varepsilon}_{Ut} = U_t - 0.12 - 0.05\text{INF}_{t-1} - 0.91U_{t-1},$$

which, when added to (8.6), gets a t-value of $-0.88[0.39]$. Hence, weak exogeneity of U_t with respect to the parameters of the conditional PCM is not rejected (at conventional significance levels).

Note that it is important that (8.6) does not include U_{t-1}, which is part of the implicit VAR for INF_t and U_t and which therefore is included in the marginal equation that we estimated for U_t. If U_{t-1} was in the PCM, adding the residual would have resulted in perfect multicollinearity.

An alternative interpretation of the insignificant DWU test is therefore that U_{t-1} is an irrelevant explanatory variable in the conditional ADL model for INF_t. A significant DWH test would also have been subject to further interpretation. Is the correct interpretation that U_t is endogenous? Or is it that the ADL is misspecified, due to the omission of U_{t-1}? Hence, it is often necessary to support the chosen interpretation of the test outcome with arguments from the economic theory or from factual knowledge about the subsystem which is the focus of the study.

The situation is similar to the one we commented on in connection with the over-identification test statistic in Section 7.9.5. The point there was the ambiguity of interpretation of a significant value of the test statistic (i.e., the Sargan test). It may be that the variables used as instruments are invalid because they are correlated with the error term in a correctly specified structural equation. But another interpretation is that the structural equation is specified incorrectly relative to the system. The same can be said for the DWH test: It is a test of the possible misspecification of the conditional ADL model. Either because the parameters of interest are not correctly represented in the conditional expectation function (weak exogeneity fails) or because relevant variables (in the VAR) have been dropped from the model equation (invalid conditioning).

8.5.2. Testing strong exogeneity

As noted above, strong exogeneity requires both weak exogeneity and Granger noncausality. This means that strong exogeneity can be tested by supplementing, for example, the DWU test with the Granger non-causality tests as indicated in Section 8.3. For example, if X_t is weakly exogenous in the conditional model for Y_t in the bivariate VAR(1), X_t is strongly exogenous if $\phi_{21} = 0$ is not rejected by an exclusion test for the marginal model equation. Testing of Granger non-causality in multivariate VAR(p) systems can be done by using the conventional LR test for linear restrictions in Box 5.2. In a VAR with three of more variables, it is easy to imagine that a subset of the variables can be found to be Granger non-caused by other variables, which we may call finding evidence of partial strong exogeneity.

8.5.3. Testing super exogeneity

According to the definition above, X_t is super exogenous in the conditional model if it is weakly exogenous and $\boldsymbol{\theta}_1$ is invariant to changes in the marginal model parameter vector $\boldsymbol{\theta}_2$. A practical method to investigate super exogeneity is therefore to first test if there is evidence of one or several structural breaks in the marginal model equation, and next investigate the degree of invariance of $\boldsymbol{\theta}_1$ with respect to those breaks.

An appealing, though informal, test is to compare recursive coefficient estimates of the marginal and conditional models. Recursive plots that show that $\hat{\beta}_0$ changes significantly in the sample period, where the plots of the marginal coefficient estimates show signs of breaks, represent evidence that X_t cannot be regarded as super exogenous. To build a formal test, indicator variables can be used to represent significant breaks in the marginal model. The conditional model is invariant to these breaks if the indicator variables are insignificant when they are added to the conditional model. Based on this logic, tests of the Lucas critique, and of super exogeneity in general, have been developed, see e.g., Favero and Hendry (1992) and Engle and Hendry (1993).

As a simple example of testing based on indicators for breaks in the marginal model, we investigate the stability of the marginal model for the Norwegian unemployment percentage above. The Norwegian economy experienced a huge housing and banking crises that started in the late 1980s, see e.g., Bårdsen *et al.* (2005, Section 4.6). It is therefore reasonable to expect that an indicator variable which is 1 in 1989 and 0 elsewhere is significant when it is introduced in the marginal model equation for U_t. The estimated equation becomes

$$U_t = \underset{(0.45)}{0.52} - \underset{(0.64)}{0.05}\ \Delta \ln P_{t-1} + \underset{(0.10)}{0.86}\ U_{t-1} + \underset{(0.57)}{1.33}\ I_{89t}, \tag{8.7}$$

where the indicator variable I_{89t} has p-value 0.03. However, when the conditional model (8.6) is tested for omission of I_{89t}, that p-value becomes 0.44, and the evidence therefore supports super exogeneity with respect to that (large) break in the unemployment percentage. This test methodology can be generalized and also semi-automatized, as we will discuss in Chapter 11.

Testing of super exogeneity can also be done with reference to non-invertibility of stable conditional models under regime shifts. For example, in the bivariate case, we denote the regression coefficient when Y is the regressand by the usual symbol β_0, and the slope coefficients in the inverted model which has X as regressand by β_0'. The two regression coefficients can be written as

$$\beta_0 = \beta_0' \frac{\sigma_y^2}{\sigma_x^2}, \tag{8.8}$$

showing that if there is a structural break in σ_x^2, and β_0 is constant, β_0' cannot be constant. And vice versa, if β_0' is stable, β_0 cannot be invariant to the break in the X-process.

This argument demonstrates a more general non-invertibility property of conditional models when super exogeneity holds: If the marginal models exhibit enough change at least one of the "directions of regression" can be ruled out on non-constancy grounds. Hence, if only one of the regression directions provides evidence of stability and invariance, we have empirical support for the hypothesis that causality also runs in that direction (say from X to Y, because β_0 is constant and β_0' changes), and not the opposite. Natural test statistics to look at are the sequences of recursively estimated coefficients $\hat{\beta}_0$ $\hat{\beta}_0'$, as well as recursively estimated standard errors and Chow tests (see Section 2.8.4).

8.5.4. Testing expectations (feed-forward) models

The logic of non-invertibility of conditional models when there is sufficient change in the marginal models can also be used to test expectation models against models where the subjective expectations are not identical to the mathematical conditional expectation functions. The reference point is the Lucas critique interpreted as an encompassing implication for conditional models, namely, that a conditional model's parameters will change when there is a large enough change in the marginal processes of the conditioning variables. Specifically, expressions (7.83) and (7.89) showed that under the assumption of rational expectations, the OLS estimator for the parameter of interest (it was denoted β_1) will change in the period where there is a break in the marginal equation. To test this encompassing implication, Hendry (1988) showed that when both the IV estimated rational expectations model and the conditional model are constant, but the marginal process is not, then the conditional (feed-back) model cannot be derived from any rational expectations (feed-forward) structural model. The forecasting implications of the feed-forward model fail in that constellation of evidence, which also refutes the relevance of the Lucas critique.

Tests that utilize addition of indicators for breaks in the marginal processes to the structural model equation under investigation can also be used to test the hypothesis that parameters of structural models have high degrees of autonomy and invariance. The logic is that significant and substantial changes in the marginal parts of the system are "taken care of" by the expectations part of the model equation, and break indicators should therefore be statistically insignificant when added to the (exactly identified) structural equation. Castle *et al.* (2014) developed the theory of this test method, and applied it to the New Keynesian Phillips Curve that we presented in Section 7.11.

8.6. Exercises

Exercise 8.1. Use the data in NORPCMb.zip to replicate the result of the DWH test for the Norwegian inflation model equation in Section 8.5.1.

Exercise 8.2. Show empirically that the OLS estimates you get when (8.6) is extended with the residual from the marginal model equation for U_t are identical to the coefficient estimates obtained by applying IV to the price Phillips curve model. What is the explanation?

Chapter 9

Non-stationarity

In this chapter, and the next, we extend the theory to non-stationary time series. There are two broad forms of non-stationarity, deterministic trends and non-stationarity due to unit-roots. Deterministic non-stationarity covers, in addition to the linear time trend t, t^2, impulse indicator variables and step-indicator variables. Non-stationarity due to unit-roots means that the characteristic polynomial, which is associated with the stochastic difference equation of the process, has one or more roots that are one in magnitude. Hence, deterministic non-stationarity is a matter of the specification of the inhomogeneous part of the difference equation, while unit-root non-stationarity represents a restriction on the homogeneous part of the difference equation. In developing empirical models for macroeconomic time series, we need to consider both types of non-stationarity.

9.1. Introduction

Although the previous chapters have been about stationary dynamics, the attentive reader will have noted that, strictly speaking, we have ventured outside the realm of weak stationarity on several occasions already. In each of the cases, where we have included an indicator variable (dummy) for a structural break for example, the implication is that the expectation of the time series depends on time. However, this type of non-stationarity, which we, for lack of a better word, will refer to as deterministic trend non-stationarity, is covered by the inference theory for stationary time series.

The reason is that a deterministic trend can be treated as any other control variable: either it can be "regressed out" from the time series prior to the estimation of a relationship or can be included in the econometric model as a regressor. This is a case of the Frisch–Waugh theorem mentioned in Chapter 2.

Deterministic non-stationarity represents ways of extending (i.e., augmenting) the inhomogeneous part of the time series process. Hence, deterministic non-stationarity can be thought of as a model extension. Unit-root non-stationarity is different. It is a restriction on the time series process. More specifically, a unit-root is a restriction on the characteristic polynomial of the associated homogeneous difference equation of the process.

We start with a short review of the most popular forms of deterministic non-stationarity that we can use to augment stationary models. The rest of this chapter is an introduction to unit-root non-stationarity, which represents an important new category of econometric models.

As we shall see, variables with unit-roots evolve along well-defined trends, but the trend is random instead of deterministic. As a reflection of that property, another name for a variable which is unit-root non-stationary is that it is a *stochastic trend*. Yet another term used is *local trend*, reflecting that, unlike the slope of a deterministic trend, the slope of the trend can change. As we shall see, the stochastic trend interpretation is due to summation (i.e., integration), of constant terms into trends, and white noise disturbances into random walks. A fourth name for a time series with unit-roots is therefore *integrated variable.*

Unit-root variables can be combined with other unit-root variables in a macroeconomic model, as well as with stationarity variables. However, that step requires non-trivial econometric treatment of the integrated time series. Variables can be made stationary after differencing, giving rise to a yet another name (the fifth): *difference stationarity*. If X_t is an integrated time series, while ΔX_t is weakly stationary, X_t is said to be integrated of order one, which it is the custom to write as $X_t \sim I(1)$. In this notation, stationary variables (with or without a deterministic trend) are denoted by writing $X_t \sim I(0)$. Some time series need to be differentiated more than once to become weakly stationary. We write $X_t \sim I(d)$, to denote integration of order d, for the case where $\Delta^d X_t \sim I(0)$. There are tests for the order of integration, and we review an important class of tests called Dickey–Fuller tests below. Variables that are integrated of the same order can be *cointegrated*, meaning that a linear combination of variables is stationary $I(0)$. For example, if X_t and Y_t are two $I(1)$ variables, they are cointegrated if the time series $Z_t = b_0 + X_t + b_1 Y_t$ is an $I(0)$-variable. Cointegration represents an important extension of equilibrium correction models, as Chapter 10 shows.

9.2. Deterministic Trend

The time series $\{Y_t;\ t = 1, 2, 3, \ldots, T\}$ is said to be a *deterministic trend* (DT) if the data generating process is

$$Y_t = \phi_0 + \delta t + \varepsilon_t, \quad \delta \neq 0, \tag{9.1}$$

where δ denotes the slope parameter of the trend, and where $\{\varepsilon_t;\ t = 1, 2, 3, \ldots, T\}$ denotes a white noise time series with variance σ_ε^2. The expectation of Y_t is a function of time

$$E(Y_t) = \phi_0 + \delta t,$$

meaning that Y_t is a non-stationary time series. However, the variance of Y_t is constant, and therefore independent of time:

$$\text{Var}(Y_t) = \sigma_\varepsilon^2,$$

and hence the non-stationarity only affects the expectation of the series. The same holds for processes that include impulse indicators or step indicator dummies, as long as ε_t is a white noise series. We will refer to such variables as wide-sense deterministic trends.

As long as the non-stationarity only "resides" in the expectation of a process, the departure from covariance stationarity is mainly a matter of definition. We understand intuitively, and with reference to the Frisch–Waugh theorem mentioned above (see Section 2.6), that models of this type can be "brought back" into the stationary realm by purging the deterministic part from the series by the use of regression. Therefore, the inference theory for stationary models will, with a few remarks, also hold for time series models that include wide-sense deterministic trends.

9.2.1. Weak stationarity of series with deterministic trend

The separation between expectation and variance can be used to "bring the time series back" to stationary form". In the simplest case, this can be done with the aid of a new variable

$$Y_t^s = Y_t - \delta t.$$

Y_t^s has the same properties as Y_t, with the exception of the expectation, which is

$$E(Y_t^s) = \phi_0.$$

Y_t^s is covariance stationary, and the stationarity is established by subtracting the linear trend from Y_t in (9.1). Y_t has therefore often been called a *trend-stationary* process. The name has stuck despite being a little misleading. "Trend-non-stationary" would have been a more descriptive name, as the mathematical expectation of Y_t depends on time due to the deterministic trend. We get a more general trend-stationary process if the AR(1) is augmented by a deterministic trend

$$Y_t = \phi_0 + \phi_1 Y_{t-1} + \delta t + \varepsilon_t, \quad |\phi_1| < 1,\, \delta \neq 0. \tag{9.2}$$

Repeated substitution back to Y_0, in the same manner as we have done several times above gives

$$\begin{aligned} Y_t = {} & \phi_0 \sum_{j=0}^{t-1} \phi_1^j - \delta \sum_{j=1}^{t-1} (\phi_1^j) \cdot j \\ & + \phi_1^t Y_0 + \delta \left(\sum_{j=0}^{t-1} \phi_1^j \right) \cdot t + \sum_{j=0}^{t-1} \phi_1^j \varepsilon_{t-j}. \end{aligned} \tag{9.3}$$

The two first terms converge to finite numbers as $t \to \infty$:

$$\phi_0 \lim_{t \longrightarrow \infty} \sum_{j=0}^{t-1} \phi_1^j \rightarrow \frac{\phi_0}{(1-\phi_1)},$$

$$\delta \lim_{t \longrightarrow \infty} \sum_{j=1}^{t-1} (\phi_1^j) \cdot j \rightarrow \delta \frac{\phi_1}{(1-\phi_1)^2}.$$

The first convergence result is well known (sum of an infinite geometric progression), but the second may not be known, (see Exercise 9.5). The third term in (9.3) is well known from stationary solutions and is asymptotically zero. The fourth term in (9.3) contains the deterministic trend-component. If we define the trend corrected variable

$$Y_t^s = Y_t - \delta \left(\sum_{j=1}^{t} \phi_1^{j-1} \right) t,$$

we obtain its expectation and variance as

$$E(Y_t^s) = \frac{\phi_0}{(1-\phi_1)} - \delta\frac{\phi_1}{(1-\phi_1)^2} + \delta\left(\sum_{j=0}^{\infty}\phi_1^j\right)t - \delta\left(\sum_{j=1}^{\infty}\phi_1^{j-1}\right)t$$

$$= \frac{\phi_0}{(1-\phi_1)} - \delta\frac{\phi_1}{(1-\phi_1)^2}, \tag{9.4}$$

$$\text{Var}(Y_t^s) = \frac{\sigma_\varepsilon^2}{(1-\phi_1^2)}, \tag{9.5}$$

which confirm that the trend corrected variable is covariance stationary.

These results are as expected from our knowledge of stationary time series. After all, the conditions for stationarity apply to the roots of characteristic equation associated with the homogeneous part of the stochastic difference equation. Therefore, covariance stationarity is not lost by inclusion of deterministic functions of time in the model equation.

9.2.2. Estimation and inference theory for trend-stationary variables

If the value of the parameter δ in (9.2) is known, and only ϕ_0 and ϕ_1 need to be estimated, we are in exactly the same situation as before. The question therefore boils down to whether the estimation of δ leads to any changes in the estimation theory in the earlier chapters. The short answer is that there are no changes. In the same vein as Davidson and MacKinnon (2004, Section 2.4), we can make an appeal to the Frisch–Waugh theorem. By first regressing Y_t on a deterministic trend and then estimating an AR(1) model for the residuals (trend-corrected Y_t), will result in the same maximum likelihood estimators for ϕ_0 and ϕ_1 as in the AR(1) model *without* the deterministic trend, and, by the Frisch–Waugh theorem, the OLS estimators for the AR(1) model for trend-corrected Y_t are the same estimators that we obtain by estimating (9.2) directly. Hence, as far as intuition goes, deterministic trend variables do not represent any new problems for estimation and inference. This turns out to be correct. The only exception is the simplest model (9.1). Hamilton (1994, Chapter 13, p. 460) shows that for

$$Y_t = \phi_0 + \delta\, t + \varepsilon_t, \quad t = 1, 2, \ldots$$

(assuming $\text{Var}(\varepsilon_t) = \sigma^2$ and $E(\varepsilon_t^4) < \infty$), the OLS estimators $\hat{\phi}_0$ and $\hat{\delta}$ have the asymptotic distribution

$$\begin{pmatrix} T^{1/2}(\hat{\phi}_0 - \phi_0) \\ T^{3/2}(\hat{\delta} - \delta) \end{pmatrix} \xrightarrow{d} N\left(\begin{pmatrix} 0 \\ 0 \end{pmatrix}, \sigma_\varepsilon^2 \begin{pmatrix} 1 & \frac{1}{2} \\ \frac{1}{2} & \frac{1}{3} \end{pmatrix}^{-1}\right),$$

which means that the rate (or speed of) convergence of $\hat{\delta}$ is $T^{3/2}$, while the usual speed of convergence is $T^{1/2}$. The speed of convergence is often referred as *order in probability*, which in this case will be denoted by $O_p(T^{-3/2})$ for the estimator for the trend coefficient ($\hat{\delta}$), and $O_p(T^{-1/2})$ for the estimator for the intercept $\hat{\phi}_0$.

$\hat{\phi}_0$ is seen to be consistent and its speed of convergence generalizes to all estimators for coefficients of random variables in VARs and in models of VARs. $\hat{\delta}_T$ is said to be *super-consistent* because the speed of convergence is faster than normal. However, the OLS-based estimator for the variance of $\hat{\delta}$ has the same convergence properties, meaning that the standard t-distributions can be used for statistical inference about δ; see Hamilton (1994, Section 16.2) and Davidson (2000, Section 7.2.2).

The consistency results hold for stationary processes more generally, such as AR(p) augmented by trend, and ADL models with trend in the deterministic part of the model. In these models, all OLS coefficient estimators are characterized by being $O_p(T^{-1/2})$. The reason $\hat{\delta}$ is not super-consistent in, for example, ADL(p, p) with a *trend* is that this estimator is a linear combination of moments that converge with different speeds, and in such cases it is the slowest rate of adjustment that will dominate (see Hamilton, 1994, Section 16.3).

The reader may already have noticed that these important properties of OLS estimators are covered by the theorems in Chapter 5, namely Theorem 5.1 and Box 5.2, when we interpret the VAR models as containing wide-sense deterministic trends.

9.3. Integrated Series

As usual, the innovations $\{\varepsilon_t;\, t = 1, 2, 3, \ldots, T\}$ are assumed to be white noise with variance σ_ε^2. The process

$$Y_t = \phi_0 + Y_{t-1} + \varepsilon_t \tag{9.6}$$

is known as a *random walk*. The intercept ϕ_0 is often referred to as the drift term of the Y_t, process. By conditioning on Y_0, the solution for Y_t is found by repeated substitution to be

$$Y_t = \phi_0 t + Y_0 + \sum_{j=0}^{t-1} \varepsilon_{t-j}, \tag{9.7}$$

showing that the solution for Y_t in model (9.6) contains both the deterministic trend ($\phi_0 t$), and the term $\sum_{j=0}^{t-1} \varepsilon_{t-j}$, which is called a *stochastic trend.* We can define a new variable which is the deviation between Y_t and the deterministic trend. But the trend-corrected variable $Y_t - \delta t$ will not be weakly stationary because the variance is a function of t:

$$\text{Var}(Y_t - \phi_0 t) = \sigma_\varepsilon^2 t. \tag{9.8}$$

The same applies to $\text{Var}(Y_t)$:

$$\text{Var}(Y_t) = \sigma_\varepsilon^2 t,$$

and we therefore conclude that neither Y_t, nor $Y_t - \delta t$, are covariance stationary variables.

The interpretation that we will follow is that (9.6) is a special case of the first-order difference equation:

$$Y_t = \phi_0 + \phi_1 Y_{t-1} + \varepsilon_t,$$

namely, that (9.6) is the result of imposing the restriction $\phi_1 = 1$ in the difference equation which is equivalent to the single root of the associated characteristic equation being $\lambda = 1$. This interpretation motivates the name *unit-root process* for Y_t when the generating process is (9.6) with white noise innovations. A third name which is also often used is to denote Y_t as a *difference stationary* time series: By subtracting Y_{t-1} from both sides of the equality sign, we get

$$Y_t - Y_{t-1} = \phi_0 + \varepsilon_t,$$

giving the stationary variable ΔY_t as

$$\Delta Y_t = \phi_0 + \varepsilon_t,$$

which clearly is stationary as ε_t is white noise by assumption.[1]

---

[1]Care must be taken when applying the difference operator. Consider the case when the Y_t process includes a deterministic trend. Also, this series can be "made stationary" by differencing. The deterministic trend is eliminated from the expectation of ΔY_t, but the equation for ΔY_t will have a disturbance term which is a non-invertible MA-process. Hence, if Y_t is trend stationary with white noise disturbances, applying the difference operator leads to what we referred to as over-differencing in Section 4.5.6.

When we consider the solution (9.7) more closely, we can see that it is different from the stationary AR(1) process in that $\sum_{j=0}^{t-1}\varepsilon_{t-j}$ is not a well-defined linear filter of the white noise process ε_t (see Section 4.5). This is a consequence of the unit-root $\phi_1 = 1$, and it follows from Theorems 4.2 and 4.4 that the process (9.6) cannot generate a stationary time series.

We have drawn the line between deterministic and stochastic trends with the aid of first-order dynamics, but the generalization is straightforward. A time series that meets the conditions for a stationary solution (Theorem 4.2 and 4.4) is covariance stationary. This applies also for series that include wide-sense deterministic trend variables. Conversely, a time series associated with a homogeneous difference equation with at least one root on the unit-circle is a non-stationary variable with a stochastic trend, an integrated series. This is true also for processes which do not include any deterministic trends. The best known example is the random walk without the drift term:

$$Y_t = Y_{t-1} + \varepsilon_t, \tag{9.9}$$

obtained by setting $\phi_0 = 0$ in (9.6).

In order to make the generalization explicit, we can start from the AR(p)-process:

$$\pi(L)Y_t = \phi_0 + \varepsilon_t, \tag{9.10}$$

where

$$\begin{aligned}\pi(L) &= 1 - \phi(L) = 1 - \sum_{i=1}^{p}\phi_i L^i \\ &= 1 - \phi_1 L - \phi_2 L^2 - \cdots - \phi_p L^p,\end{aligned} \tag{9.11}$$

in the same way as in Chapters 3 and 4. By reparametrizing in the same way as above, we obtain

$$\Delta Y_t = \phi_0 + \phi^{\ddagger}(L)\Delta Y_{t-1} - \pi(1)Y_{t-1} + \varepsilon_t, \tag{9.12}$$

where the coefficients $\phi_i^{\ddagger}$ $(i = 1, 2, \ldots, p-1)$ in the lag-polynomial:

$$\phi^{\ddagger}(L) = \phi_1^{\ddagger}L + \phi_2^{\ddagger}L^2 + \cdots + \phi_{p-1}^{\ddagger}L^{p-1},$$

are known expressions of the coefficients ϕ_i $(i = 1, 2, \ldots, p)$ in $\phi(L)$.

There exists no stationary solution for Y_t if at least one of the characteristic roots

$$\pi(z) = 1 - \phi_1 z - \cdots - \phi_p z^p = 0,$$

are located on the unit-circle. The real number 1 is of course on the unit-circle, and $z = 1$ is equivalent with $\pi(1) = 0$, meaning that (9.12) is reduced to

$$\Delta Y_t = \phi_0 + \phi^{\ddagger}(L)\Delta Y_{t-1} + \varepsilon_t, \tag{9.13}$$

which has a stationary solution for ΔY_t, but not for Y_t.

Time series that are characterized by stochastic trends have solutions that include an unweighted summation of white noise variables, $\sum_{j=0}^{t-1} \varepsilon_{t-j}$, corresponding to integration in continuous time. Hence, the name integrated series is quite fitting for this class of time series processes.

Definition 9.1 (Integrated series). If Y_t is given by (9.10), where ε_t is white noise, Y_t is integrated of order one, $Y_t \sim I(1)$, if the associated characteristic equation $\pi(z) = 0$ has a root equal to $+1$.

As noted above, it is common to denote a stationary time series by $I(0)$. Hence, if $Y_t \sim I(1)$, we have $\Delta Y_t \sim I(0)$ to denote that a series which is integrated of order 1 is a difference stationary series.

A remark worth noting at this point is that the characteristic equation associated with $Y_t \sim \text{AR}(p)$ can have other unit-roots than the real root of $+1$. For example, if Y_t is generated by

$$Y_t = \phi_0 + Y_{t-4} + \varepsilon_t,$$

the associated characteristic polynomial has one characteristic root equal to $+1$, and three other characteristic roots with modulus (norm) equal to one (see Exercise 9.6). The motivation for the focus on the real root of one is about relevance. As Appendix B about spectral analysis shows, the real root of 1 is a so-called *zero frequency root*, and this implies that $Y_t \sim I(1)$ has what Clive Granger (1966) dubbed a *typical spectral shape*, which we show in Figure 9.1.

The limitation of the above definition is therefore that we abstract from unit-roots that are located at the seasonal and business cycle frequencies. Hence, we rule out that "summer can become winter", or that there can be perpetual business cycle fluctuations. Appendix B contains some technical clarifications.

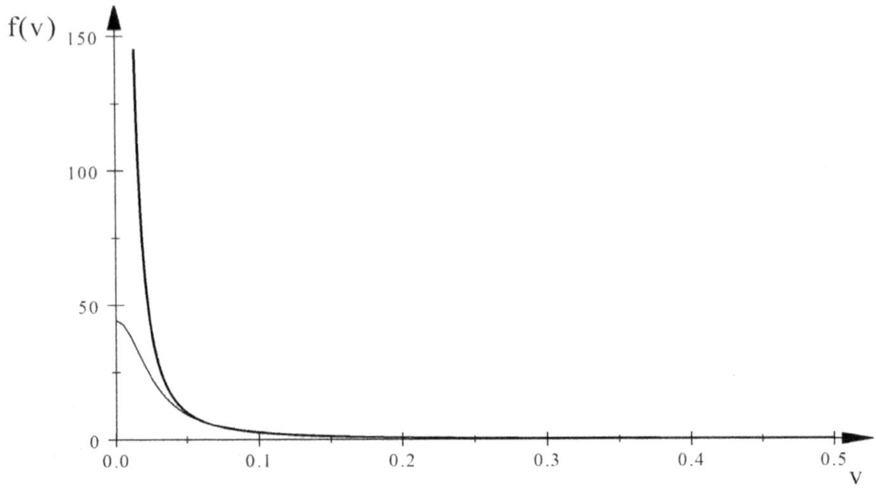

Figure 9.1. Graph of theoretical PSD function $f(v)$ for a random walk process, and the AR(1) process with $\phi_1 = 0.85$, both with $\sigma_\varepsilon^2 = 1$.

Models with variables that are integrated of order 2 can also be considered (see Juselius, 2007). We denote such a series $Y_t \sim I(2)$, and $\Delta^2 Y_t \sim I(0)$, where $\Delta^2 = (1-L)^2$. In the $I(2)$-case, there is a unit-root in the characteristic polynomial associated with (9.13):

$$p(\lambda) = \lambda^{p-1} - \phi_1^{\ddagger}\lambda^{p-2} - \cdots - \phi_{p-1}^{\ddagger}.$$

9.4. Contrasting Stationary and Integrated Series

As we have seen, the expectation of a $I(0)$-series is independent of the initial condition Y_0. The expectation of an $I(1)$-series on the other hand depends fundamentally on the initialization value. For the random walk with drift, the solution is (9.7), and we obtain

$$E(Y_t \mid Y_0) = Y_0 + \delta t.$$

If the drift parameter δ is zero, there is no deterministic trend in the solution for Y_t, but the expectation nevertheless depends on history via the initial condition. As noted, the expression for the variance of Y_t in (9.8) illustrates the general property of an $I(1)$-variable: the variance grows toward infinity (as a function of time).

The autocovariances of $I(1)$-variables also behave differently from the autocovariances of $I(0)$-variables. For the random walk process, we have

$$\begin{aligned}\text{Cov}(Y_t, Y_{t-k}) &= E\left(\sum_{j=0}^{t-1} \varepsilon_{t-j} \sum_{j=0}^{t-k-1} \varepsilon_{t-k-j}\right) \\ &= 2E\left(\sum_{j=0}^{t-k-1} \varepsilon_{t-k-j}^2\right) = 2(t-k)\sigma_\varepsilon^2,\end{aligned}$$

and the theoretical autocorrelation function (ACF), denoted by ζ in Chapter 4:

$$\begin{aligned}\zeta_k &= \frac{(t-k)\sigma_\varepsilon^2}{\sqrt{\sigma^2 t}\sqrt{\sigma_\varepsilon^2(t-k)}} \\ &= \frac{(t-k)}{\sqrt{t}\sqrt{(t-k)}} = \frac{\sqrt{(t-k)}}{\sqrt{t}}, \quad \text{for } k = 1, 2, \ldots. \end{aligned} \tag{9.14}$$

The importance of this expression is that it shows that the autocorrelations are close to 1 for all lag lengths as long as t is large compared to k. As we have seen above, the estimation of the autocorrelogram requires that the sample is sizeable, hence the empirical autocorrelation functions ($\hat{\zeta}_k$) for $I(1)$ series will typically be close to 1 for all values of the argument k. The typical shape of the autocorrelogram of a $I(1)$ series will therefore be a horizontal line at the value 1. We will not see the monotone or oscillating pattern which is typical of stationary ARMA processes.

The above differences between $I(0)$ and $I(1)$ series are sometimes referred to as differences in the *time domain*. There are corresponding differences in the *frequency domain*, where a key concept is the power spectral density (PSD) function (see Appendix B). The theoretical PSD shows how the different frequencies (for example defined as number of cycles per time period) contribute to the total variance of the time series. In the case of a white noise series, the graph of the PSD is a horizontal line, showing that all frequencies contribute equally to the overall variance. It is easy to draw the analogy to white light, where all colours in the spectrum are present. Since sound is also composed of waves with different periods (wavelengths), this also suggests the original motivation for labelling a time series with constant variance as white noise.

As the appendix shows, the PSD function of stationary ARMA processes can take many interesting forms, including peaks at the seasonal and business cycle frequencies, but the value of the function is finite at all frequencies. Time series that have a unit-root is associated with a PSD function which is infinite at the frequency where the unit-root is located.

For the random walk process, where the unit root is located at the zero frequency, there is a single, completely dominating peak very close to the zero frequency, the long-run frequency. The value of the function declines sharply with increasing frequency. This means that all the information in the series is located at the low frequencies — the series is dominated by long waves. Figure 9.1 shows a plot of the function together with the graph for the stationary AR(1) process for comparison.

As Appendix B explains, empirical PSD functions can be estimated in the spectral domain. It is common to find that, before differencing, many economic time series have a marked peak at the zero frequency and maybe smaller peaks located at, for example, the seasonal frequencies. This shape is referred to as Granger's *typical spectral shape*, and is taken as a clear indication of unit-root non-stationarity, and therefore difference stationarity of many economic time series.

Figure 9.2 shows empirical power spectral density functions for the log of private consumption expenditure in Norway, and of the first difference of that series. The graphs are strongly indicating a near unit-root close to the zero frequency. The seasonality of the level series is hardly noticeable in the PDF for $\ln(CP_t)$, but it is more clearly visible in the graphed PSD for the differenced series $\Delta \ln(CP_t)$. Table 9.1 summarizes the points above, and a couple of additional ones. Properties 1–3 summarize the consequence of covariance (non-)stationarity. The same can be said about the impulse-responses in number 4 (see Exercise 9.2). The typical spectral shape (i.e., number 5) has been commented above, while the forecasting properties listed as 6a and 6b follow directly from the expression for the solution (before requiring stationarity) (see Exercise 9.3). Moreover, we will return to the properties of dynamic forecasts in Chapter 12.

Line 7 in the table has to do with the appropriate statistical inference theory for use in the integrated time series. We now turn to that issue starting with the important phenomenon of *spurious regression*.

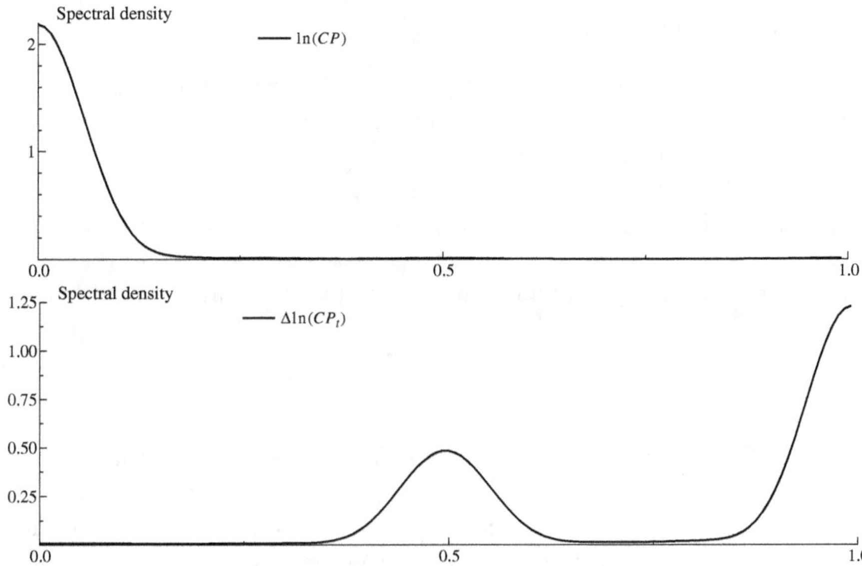

Figure 9.2. Estimated PSD functions for log of private consumption, $\ln(CP_t)$, and $\Delta \ln(CP_t)$. CP_t is measured in million kroner. Fixed 2015 prices. The data are quarterly and the samples are 1971(1)–2017(2). Note that the number 0.5 on the horizontal axes corresponds to a frequency of 1/4 and 1 corresponds to the 3/4 frequency (see Appendix B).

Table 9.1. Typical differences between integrated and stationary series.

Property	I(1)	I(0)
1. $E(Y_t)$	depends on Y_0	Constant
2. $\text{Var}(Y_t)$	$\underset{t\to\infty}{\to} \infty$	Constant
3. $\text{ACF}(Y_t, Y_{t-j})$	$\approx 1\ \forall j$	$\underset{j\to\infty}{\to} 0$
4. Impulse-responses	Do not "die out"	$\to 0$
5. PSD	Peak at $v = 0$	Finite at all v
6a. Forecasting Y_{T+h}	$E(Y_{T+h\|T})$ depends on $Y_T\ \forall h$	$\underset{h\to\infty}{\to} E(Y_t)$
6b. Forecasting Y_{T+h}	Var of forecast errors $\to \infty$	$\underset{h\to\infty}{\to} \text{Var}(Y_t)$
7. Inference theory	Non-standard theory	Standard theory

Box 9.1. ARIMA and ARFIMA

The special case of non-stationary processes that we focus on is known as ARIMA models in the time series literature, where the "I" refers to integrated. The generalization to the ARFIMA model allows for likelihood ratio and Wald tests for the null of short-memory stationarity ($d = 0$), as well as for the null of unit-root non-stationarity ($d = 1$) against long memory and intermediate memory alternatives ($0 < d < 1$) that are referred to as fractionally integrated series (see Doornik *et al.*, 2013).

9.5. Spurious Regression

In 1974, Clive Granger and Gary Newbold published a paper that became very influential (see Granger and Newbold, 1974). The authors noticed that while observable time series variables featured strong signs of being integrated, of order one or higher, the inference method used by econometricians assumed that the time series were covariance stationary. The question they posed was whether this discrepancy was a mere academic detail or a serious matter that could lead to many false positives in the form of seemingly significant regression relationships. In this, they resounded the analysis of Yule (1926), who had shown that integrated processes created "nonsense correlations" between independent time series (see Castle and Hendry, 2017).

Granger and Newbold used Monte Carlo simulation in their article, and it can be instructive to look at a simple simulation that reproduces their main result.

Example 9.1 (Spurious regression). We let YA_t and YB_t be generated by

$$\begin{aligned}\text{YA}_t &= \phi_{A1}\text{YA}_{t-1} + \varepsilon_{A,t},\\ \text{YB}_t &= \phi_{A2}\text{YB}_{t-1} + \varepsilon_{B,t},\end{aligned}$$

where

$$\begin{pmatrix}\varepsilon_{A,t}\\ \varepsilon_{B,t}\end{pmatrix} \sim N\left(\begin{pmatrix}0\\0\end{pmatrix}, \begin{pmatrix}\sigma_A^2 & 0\\ 0 & \sigma_B^2\end{pmatrix}\right).$$

We see that the DGP has first-order dynamics and specify two independent variables YA_t and YB_t. In the first simulation, the DGP is assumed to stationary, with $\phi_{A1} = \phi_{B1} = 0.5$. In the second simulation, YA_t and YB_t are independent random walks, hence $\phi_{A1} = \phi_{B1} = 1$. In both experiments, $\sigma_A^2 = \sigma_B^2 = 0.01$ and the regression model is

$$\text{YA}_t = \phi_0 + \beta_0 \text{YB}_t + \epsilon_t,$$

and the tested hypothesis is H_0: $\beta_0 = 0$ against H_0: $\beta_0 \neq 0$ In the experiment, $T = 200$, and the number of replications was 1000.

In Figure 9.3, the rejection frequencies are plotted against the sample size when the t-values of H_0: $\beta = 0$ is used with 5% critical values from the Student t-distribution. The lower graph shows the rejection frequencies in the stationary, $I(0)$, case. For all sample sizes larger than 20, the rejection occurs in more that 10% of the tests, while the nominal significance level is 5%. A minute's thought reminds us that the over-rejection is due to the autocorrelation in the regression disturbances, see Section 2.8.2, and it is therefore an understandable result.

The upper graph shows the Type-I inference errors when the two series are $I(1)$. The problem of false rejection (false positive) is now massive: The rejection frequency increases sharply with the sample sizes in the

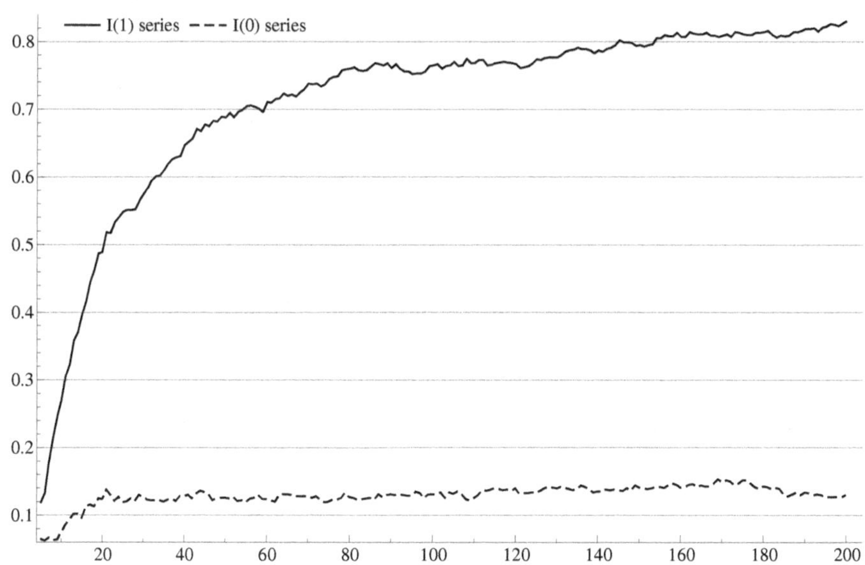

Figure 9.3. Rejection frequencies in the Monte Carlo in Example 9.1. H_0: $\beta_0 = 0$ in the model $\text{YA}_t = \phi_0 + \beta_0 \text{YB}_t + \epsilon_t$ when ϵ_t is I(0) (lower line), and I(1) (upper). 5% nominal level.

$T = (50, 80)$, interval, and continues to grow also for larger samples still. For $T = 200$, 8 of 10 tests reject that there is no relationship between the two series. This is the phenomenon called spurious regression that Granger and Newbold identified. One critique of Granger's and Newbold's study was that the disturbance term ϵ_t in the regression is autocorrelated both under the null hypothesis and under the alternative hypothesis. Since the model equation is misspecified, is it really surprising that the inference became misleading? In order to investigate this possibility, we can redo the experiment, but instead of a static model equation, we estimated a dynamic model on the ECM form

$$\Delta \mathrm{YA}_t = \phi_0 + \underbrace{(\phi_1 - 1)}_{-\pi(1)}\mathrm{YA}_{t-1} + \beta_0 \Delta \mathrm{YB}_t + \underbrace{(\beta_0 + \beta_1)}_{\beta(1)}\mathrm{YB}_{t-1} + \epsilon_t, \tag{9.15}$$

where the disturbance ϵ_t is white noise under H_0: $-\pi(1) = 0$, as well as under the alternative H_1: $\pi(1) < 1$. The rejection frequencies for the t-values for $-\pi(1) = 0$ are shown in the graph in panel (a) of Figure 9.4, and can be compared with the graphs for the $I(1)$-series in Figure 9.3. We see that although over-rejection has been reduced in this test, the false

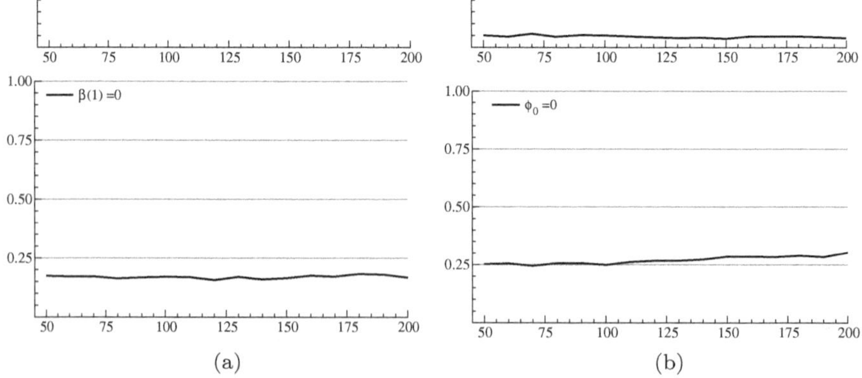

Figure 9.4. Rejection frequencies when the DGP is the same as in the Monte Carlo in Example 9.1, but the estimated model equation is the ECM (9.15). 5% nominal level.

rejection rate is still almost 10 times larger than indicated by the 5% nominal significance level. The rejection frequencies in panel (b) of Figure 9.4 show that the test of no short-run relationship ($\beta_0 = 0$ in (9.15)) is much more well behaved, with rejection close to the 5% nominal level. However, the two last panels again show clear indication that the standard inference theory does not apply.

The results indicate that the phenomenon of spurious regression is a more fundamental problem than the residual autocorrelation problem due to dynamic mis-specification. This turns out to be true. In particular, the t-value of the ECM-coefficient $\pi(1)$ in (9.15)

$$t\text{-value} = \frac{\widehat{\pi_1(1)}}{\sqrt{\text{Var}(\widehat{\pi(1)})}}$$

does not have an asymptotic normal distribution under H_0: $(\phi_1 - 1) = 0$. Instead, it is has a Dickey–Fuller distribution, and it is the percentiles of this distribution that are the correct ones to use as critical values when we do statistical inference in models with integrated variables. In Section 9.6, we therefore look briefly at this (for us) new distribution, and how it can be applied.

9.6. The Dickey–Fuller Distribution

In Section 4.6, we studied the properties of the OLS estimator $\hat{\phi}_1$ of the autoregressive coefficient in

$$Y_t = \phi_1 Y_{t-1} + \epsilon_t, \tag{9.16}$$

in the case where $-1 < \phi_1 < 1$ and where ϵ_t was Gaussian white noise. We found that there was a finite sample bias in $\hat{\phi}_1$ (Hurwicz bias). However, the bias cancelled for the t-values, so the hypothesis testing was practically unaffected compared to the IID case, and completely unaffected in large samples. But what are the properties of the OLS estimator $\hat{\phi}_1$ if the DGP is not stationary, but instead the random walk:

$$Y_t = Y_{t-1} + \varepsilon_{yt},\ \varepsilon_{yt} \sim N(0, \sigma^2)? \tag{9.17}$$

First, we note that since the model equation can be written as

$$\Delta Y_t = \underbrace{(\phi_1 - 1)}_{-\pi(1)} Y_{t-1} + \epsilon_t, \tag{9.18}$$

it follows that the OLS estimator $\widehat{\pi(1)}$ is consistent at zero, i.e., $\text{plim}(\widehat{\pi(1)}) = 0$. The intuitive explanation is that since the regressand $\Delta Y_t \sim I(0)$ has finite variance, while the regressor $Y_{t-1} \sim I(1)$ has infinite variance, the two variables must be asymptotically independent. For the random walk DGP, (9.18) is an example of a so-called *unbalanced* model equation (see Box 9.2). The consistency of the estimator (at zero) does however not secure that

$$\sqrt{T} \cdot (\hat{\phi}_1 - 1)$$

is asymptotically normally distributed when $\phi_1 = 1$ in the DGP. In fact, $\sqrt{T} \cdot (\hat{\phi}_1 - 1)$ has a degenerate asymptotic distribution, because $\hat{\phi}_1$ approaches 1 with speed faster than that indicated by $\sqrt{T}$. To compensate for the super consistency, we change from $\sqrt{T}$ to T. Advanced text books show that

$$T \cdot (\hat{\phi}_1 - 1) \underset{T \to \infty}{\overset{D}{\longrightarrow}} \frac{(B(1)^2 - 1)}{2 \int_0^1 [B(r)]^2 \, dr}, \tag{9.19}$$

where the distribution on the right-hand side of (9.19) is called a Dickey–Fuller (D–F) distribution; cf. Banerjee *et al.* (1993, Chapter 3), Davidson (2000, Chapter 14), Hamilton (1994, Chapter 17) among others. In the denominator, $B(r)$ represents a Brownian Motion process. It defines stochastic variables for any r in the interval $(0, 1]$. Realization of Brownian motions has the interesting property of exhibiting local trends: As any point on the $(0, 1]$ line, the curve with realizations rises or falls with the same probability. Hence, a Brownian motion is sometimes likened to a continuous random walk process.

Box 9.2. Balanced and unbalanced equations

Because of the fundamental differences between $I(0)$ and $I(1)$ variables, model equations that combine the two types are sometimes referred to as unbalanced equations. An $I(1)$ variable cannot explain an $I(0)$ variable, and hence (9.18) is unbalanced under the null hypothesis of a unit-root, and therefore $\text{plim}(\widehat{\pi(1)}) = 0$, as noted. An equation with $I(1)$ variables on both sides is balanced, but it does only represent a genuine relationship if the variables are cointegrated (see Chapter 10). A model equation on the ECM form is a balanced equation if the $I(1)$ variables on the left-hand side are cointegrated.

The denominator in the expression for the asymptotic distribution in (9.19) is positive. In the numerator, where the argument r is seen to be 1, we can use a property of Brownian motion processes, namely, that $B(1) \sim N(0,1)$. Hence, since $B(1)^2 \sim \chi^2(1)$, Chi-square distributed with one degree of freedom, values of $B(1)^2$ close to 0 are therefore quite probable due to that distribution being skewed towards zero. For example, only 32% of the probability mass is located to the right of 1.

Under the null hypothesis of $\phi_1 = 1$, also the t-value, which we will denote by t_{DF}, has a Dickey–Fuller distribution:

$$t_{\mathrm{DF}} \underset{T\to\infty}{\overset{D}{\longrightarrow}} \frac{(B(1)^2 - 1)}{2\sqrt{\int_0^1 [B(r)]^2\, dr}}. \tag{9.20}$$

where again there is 0.68 probability of negative values in the numerator. Both (9.19) and (9.20) are non-standard distributions that need to be tabulated by the use of Monte Carlo simulations, and this work was done by Dickey and Fuller in the early 1970s (see Fuller, 1976).

9.7. Testing the Null Hypothesis of a Unit-Root

As noted, the critical values of the distribution of t_{DF} in (9.20) can be used to do valid inference of the unit-root hypotheses given that the DGP under the null hypothesis is (9.17) and the estimated Dickey–Fuller regression is (9.16). However, there is another more practical side of the non-standard distribution theory to note, namely that there is not one single table with Dickey–Fuller critical values, there are several.

The reason is that the "order of deterministic trends", both of the DGP, and of the Dickey–Fuller regression, plays a role for the distribution of t_{DF}. At first sight, this may seem to make unit-root testing unmanageable in practice, but fortunately the statisticians have come up with the following rule that we use: Always include in the Dickey–Fuller regression the order of deterministic trends necessary to account for the trend behaviour of the series both under the null of a unit-root, and under the alternative hypothesis of stationarity (see Patterson, 2011, Section 6.3).

As an example of a test situation, consider the case where the graph of (the realizations of) the time series under inspection shows a manifest positive trend. This is often the case with macroeconomic variables. Under the null hypothesis of a unit-root (the series is $I(1)$), this feature is accounted for by inclusion of an intercept in the Dickey–Fuller regression. However, under the alternative hypothesis of stationarity, a deterministic trend is part of the DGP. In order to cover both possibilities, we therefore use the Dickey–Fuller regression:

$$\Delta Y_t = \phi_0 - \pi(1)Y_{t-1} + \delta t + \epsilon_t, \tag{9.21}$$

and test H_0: $\pi(1) = 0$ by comparing the t-value of $\hat{\pi}(1)$, and call it $t_{\mathrm{DF},c+t}$ (for constant plus trend) with the critical values from the appropriate Dickey–Fuller distribution. These critical values are used automatically when we test for unit-roots using PcGive and other modern software: However, a very useful literature reference is nevertheless Ericsson and MacKinnon (2002). Among other things, the tables in that paper can be used also when we get to the testing for spurious regression, as we shall see below.

In practical testing of unit-roots, it is also necessary to tackle higher order dynamics. This is a smaller issue than the decision about deterministic trends. We simply estimate the augmented Dickey–Fuller regression

$$\Delta Y_t = \phi_0 + \sum_{i=1}^{p-1} \phi_i^{\dagger} \Delta Y_{t-i} + \delta t - \pi(1)Y_{t-1} + \epsilon_t, \tag{9.22}$$

which we see is the ECM-version of the AR(p) with constant term and trend.

The t-values of OLS estimates of $\phi_i^{\dagger}$ are t-distributed both under H_0: $\pi(1) = 0$ and under the stationary alternative. A good approach in practice is therefore to choose a lag length $p - 1$ that secures that there is no significant residual autocorrelation in the DF-regression. From that general model or from a more parsimonious DF-regression with valid restrictions on the lag polynomial in the differences, the test of H_0: $\pi(1) = 0$ is based on the t-value $t_{\mathrm{DF},c+t}$.

The reason for paying attention to the lag specification of the augmented Dickey–Fuller regression is that the level of the Dickey–Fuller test (i.e., Type-I error probability) is robustified by avoiding residual autocorrelation. On the other hand, a too large estimation model can make the power of the test become unnecessary low. Since we in general will use Dickey–Fuller regressions with one of more lags (ΔY_{t-i}) on the right-hand side, the test is often referred to as ADF-test of a unit-root, where the "A" represents the augmentation of the Dickey–Fuller regression, i.e., the lags. There is a range of other tests for unit-root non-stationarity, which can be used together with or instead of the Dickey–Fuller test. Some of these tests have stationarity as the null hypothesis, and unit-root as the alternative hypothesis. A comprehensive exposition of the different approaches is Patterson (2011).

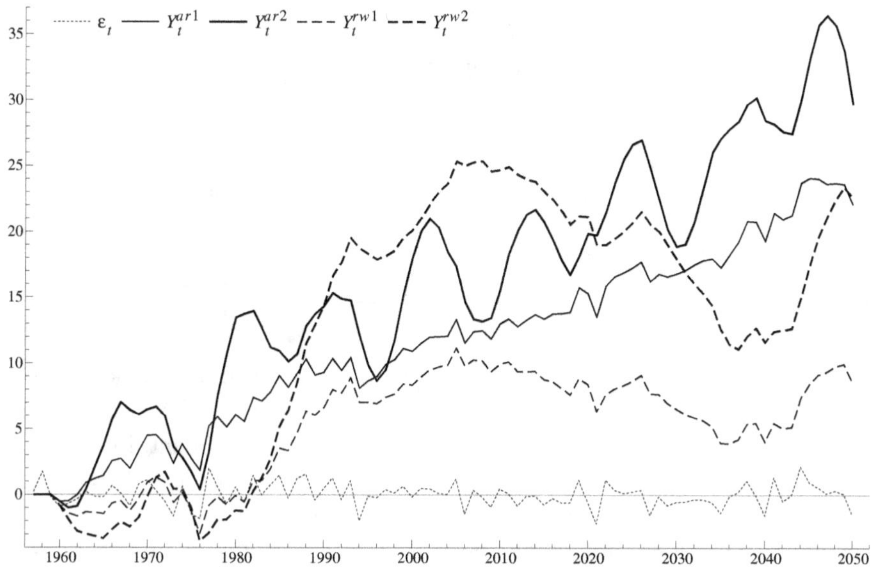

Figure 9.5. Time plots of five computer-generated time series (see Box 9.3 for details).

Box 9.3. Generated data series with trends

Figure 9.5 shows time plots of the following five time series:

$$\varepsilon_t \sim N(0,1), \text{ Gaussian white noise}$$
$$Y_t^{ar1} = 0.6Y_{t-1}^{ar1} + 0.1t + \varepsilon_t, \text{ AR}(1)$$
$$Y_t^{ar2} = 1.6Y_{t-1}^{ar2} - 0.9Y_{t-2}^{ar2} + 0.1t, \text{ AR}(2)$$
$$Y_t^{rw1} = Y_{t-1}^{rw1} + 0.1 + \varepsilon_t, \text{ RW}(1) \text{ with drift}$$
$$Y_t^{rw2} = 1.6Y_{t-1}^{rw2} - 0.6Y_{t-2}^{rw2} + 0.1 + \varepsilon_t, \text{ RW}(2) \text{ with drift}$$

As an example of unit-root testing, we can look at the properties of the Dickey–Fuller test when the DGP is Y_t^{ar2} in Box 9.3. When looking at the time plot in Figure 9.5, the manifest growth tendency is likely to have been noted. Under the null of a unit-root, that should lead to include constant and trend in the Dickey–Fuller regression. The conspicuous cycles could be one reason for inclusion of at least two lags in levels, which means one lag in the differences. However, for the point of illustration, we include one more,

Table 9.2. Dickey–Fuller tests for the time series Y_t^{ar2} in Figure 9.5. Deterministic terms: Constant and trend. $T = 94$ (1960–2050).

Critical values for $t_{\mathrm{DF},c+t}$: 5% = −3.46, 1% = −4.06

$p-1$	$t_{\mathrm{DF},c+t}$	$-\hat{\pi}(1)$	$t_{\phi_i^\dagger}$	[p-value]
2	−6.749**	−0.29	0.73	[0.47]
1	−8.481**	−0.27	14.4	[0.00]
0	−2.633	−0.15		

hence $p-1=2$ is the maximum lag length we consider in the Dickey–Fuller regression (9.22).

Table 9.2 shows the result of this test for the experimental data with $T = 94$ observations. The bottom row shows that with $p-1=0$ (the DF-regression with no stochastic augmentation), $t_{\mathrm{DF},c+t}$ is not negative enough to reject the unit root hypothesis (in the second column: $t_{\mathrm{DF},c+t} = -2.633$ while the 5% critical value is −3.46).

However, the simple Dickey–Fuller test is not reliable, as the entries in the cells in the two columns to the right in the table show. When the first lag of the difference is included in the regression, the t-value of $\phi_1^\dagger$ is extremely significant. Hence, we need to use the $t_{\mathrm{DF},c+t}$'s in the two rows (labelled $(p-1)=1$ or $(p-1)=2$) for valid inference. Both tests reject the unit-root at the 5% significance level, which is the right conclusion in this example.

9.8. Exercises

Exercise 9.1. How does a deterministic trend affect the analysis of dynamic multipliers?

Exercise 9.2. Explain property 4 in Table 9.1.

Exercise 9.3. Assume the simple trend-stationary model (9.1), and assume that the parameters are known. What is the expression for $\hat{Y}_{T+h|T} \equiv E(Y_{T+h} \mid \mathcal{I}_T)$, $h = 1, 2, \ldots, H$, where "$\mid \mathcal{I}_T$" means conditional on information in period T. What is the expression for the variance of the forecast error: $(Y_{t+h} - \hat{Y}_{T+h|T})$?

Exercise 9.4. What are the corresponding expressions when the true model is (9.2)?

Exercise 9.5. The derivation of (9.4) makes use of $\delta \lim_{t\to\infty} \sum_{j=1}^{t-1}(\phi_1^j) \cdot j \to \delta \frac{\phi_1}{(1-\phi_1)^2}$ (for $-1 < \phi_1 < 1$). Try to show this result.

Exercise 9.6. Assume that the DGP for Y_t is

$$Y_t = Y_{t-4} + \varepsilon_t, \tag{9.23}$$

where ε_t is white noise. How many unit-roots characterize Y_t?

Exercise 9.7. The data for the processes in Box 9.3, shown in Figure 9.5 are in the data file named *Simdata_trend_RW* on the book's internet pages. In the data file, the variable RW2Drift corresponds to Y_t^{rw2} in Box 9.3 and Figure 9.5. Try to see if the Dickey–Fuller test can be used to empirically determine this as an $I(1)$ series.

Exercise 9.8 (Exam 2015 ECON4160 UiO). We have annual data for hourly wages in Norwegian manufacturing for the period 1970 to 2013. We also have data for the value of labour productivity in this sector. In the

```
Unit-root tests
The dataset is: C:\SW20\ECON4160\H2015\Exam\LoennIndogFastland.in7
The sample is: 1972 - 2013 (44 observations and 2 variables)

LW: ADF tests (T=42, Constant+Trend; 5%=-3.52 1%=-4.19)
D-lag    t-adf       beta Y_1    sigma   t-DY_lag  t-prob
 1     -2.811       0.94888   0.01856     3.623   0.0008
 0     -4.145*      0.92148   0.02125

LZ: ADF tests (T=42, Constant+Trend; 5%=-3.52 1%=-4.19)
D-lag    t-adf       beta Y_1    sigma   t-DY_lag  t-prob
 1     -1.887       0.93151   0.03735   -0.3623   0.7192
 0     -1.915       0.93131   0.03693

Unit-root tests
The dataset is: C:\SW20\ECON4160\H2015\Exam\LoennIndogFastland.in7
The sample is: 1973 - 2013 (43 observations and 2 variables)

DLW: ADF tests (T=41, Constant; 5%=-3.52 1%=-4.20)
D-lag    t-adf       beta Y_1    sigma   t-DY_lag  t-prob
 1     -3.079       0.55138   0.02025     1.143   0.2603
 0     -2.864       0.62787   0.02033

DLZ: ADF tests (T=41, Constant+Trend; 5%=-3.52 1%=-4.20)
D-lag    t-adf       beta Y_1    sigma   t-DY_lag  t-prob
 1     -4.655**    -0.11150   0.03953    0.2770   0.7833
 0     -6.553**   -0.063503   0.03905
```

Figure 9.6. Augmented Dickey–Fuller (ADF) tests to determine the order of integration of LW_t and LZ_t.

printout from PcGive in Figure 9.6, we denote the logarithms of these two variables as LW (wages) and LZ (value of labour productivity), respectively.

Explain why the evidence in the screen capture in Figure 9.6 gives reason to conclude that both LW and LZ are integrated of order one, $I(1)$. (You can consider the degree of augmentation as a given thing).

Chapter 10

Cointegration

In Chapter 9, we introduced non-stationarity due to broad sense deterministic trends and unit-root non-stationarity. Trend stationarity poses no problems for the standard inference theory, which, however, unit-root non-stationarity does most notably in the form of spurious regression. In this chapter, we extend the theory to cointegration which can be regarded as the "flip of the coin" of spurious regression. While unit-roots make inference about relationships between variables hazardous when standard critical values are used, we can control the probability of Type-I error by the use the correct (non-standard) critical values. Series that are cointegrated have several representations that we know from the stationary case, notably equilibrium correction, VAR and moving average. And vice versa, equilibrium correction implies cointegration. The VAR representation of cointegrated variables is known as a cointegrated VAR (CVAR). A dynamic model of a CVAR can be developed along the same lines as we have seen above (e.g., as a SEM or as a recursive model), after the system has been reduced from $I(1)$ to $I(0)$ by imposing valid cointegration relationships.

10.1. Introduction

So far we have considered stationary VARs ("no unit-roots"), and non-stationary VARs ("all unit-roots"). The spurious regression example with two independent random walks is an example of a non-stationary VAR.

In this chapter, we consider *cointegration*, the case where there exist one or more linear combinations of $I(1)$ variables that are $I(0)$ variables. The linear combinations are called *cointegration relationships*. Cointegration is the "flip of the coin" of spurious regression: If we have two dependent $I(1)$ variables, they are cointegrated. We can guess that a correct distribution to use for testing cointegration will be of the Dickey–Fuller type, since that class of distributions accounts for the excess probability of estimating the largest characteristic root to be less than one when it is equal to one in the DGP. This turns out to be true, and one popular test of the absence of cointegration is based on an ECM model equation and the use of critical values of a multivariate Dickey–Fuller distribution.

However, we begin by presenting the statistical properties of systems that are characterized by cointegration. This is done under the headline *Engle's and Granger's representation theorem* and leads to the *cointegrated VAR*. We also review the estimation of cointegrated relationships, starting with the properties of the OLS estimators of the coefficients of static model equations, and then the estimation of ECM model equations in the cointegrated case.

In the second part of this chapter, we present methods for testing of the null hypothesis of absence of cointegration (i.e., how to avoid the pitfall of spurious regression). We cover both the single equation tests, and the system (i.e., VAR) approach to testing due to Johansen (1995).

10.2. Engle and Granger Representation Theorem

In an important paper, Engle and Granger (1987) presented a representation theorem for cointegrated variables that provided the framework for the analysis of systems of $I(1)$-variables that are cointegrated. In this section, we give a simplified exposition of the theorem, and with focus on the equilibrium correction representation of the cointegrated VAR.

10.2.1. Cointegration and rank reduction

Consider the bivariate first-order Gaussian VAR:

$$\boldsymbol{y}_t = \boldsymbol{\Phi}\boldsymbol{y}_{t-1} + \boldsymbol{\varepsilon}_t, \tag{10.1}$$

where $\boldsymbol{y}_t = (Y_t, X_t)'$, $\boldsymbol{\Phi}$ is a 2×2 matrix with coefficients and $\boldsymbol{\varepsilon}_t$ is a vector with Gaussian disturbances. The characteristic equation for $\boldsymbol{\Phi}$ is

$$|\boldsymbol{\Phi} - \lambda\mathbf{I}| = 0, \tag{10.2}$$

We are now interested in the case with one unit-root, and one stationary root

$$\lambda_1 = 1, \quad \text{and} \quad \lambda_2 = \lambda, \ |\lambda| < 1, \tag{10.3}$$

implying that both X_t and Y_t are $I(1)$. $\boldsymbol{\Phi}$ has full rank equal to 2. It can be diagonalized in terms of its eigenvalues and the corresponding eigenvectors:

$$\boldsymbol{\Phi} = \boldsymbol{P}\begin{pmatrix} 1 & 0 \\ 0 & \lambda \end{pmatrix}\boldsymbol{P}^{-1}, \tag{10.4}$$

where $\boldsymbol{P}$ has the eigenvectors as columns:

$$\boldsymbol{P} = \begin{pmatrix} a & b \\ c & d \end{pmatrix}. \tag{10.5}$$

Set $|\boldsymbol{P}| = 1$ without loss of generality (to simplify the expression for the inverse), then

$$\boldsymbol{P}^{-1} = \begin{pmatrix} d & -b \\ -c & a \end{pmatrix}.$$

Multiply (10.1) from the left by $\boldsymbol{P}^{-1}$. The VAR is then reexpressed as

$$\begin{pmatrix} W_t \\ \mathrm{EC}_t \end{pmatrix} = \begin{pmatrix} 1 & 0 \\ 0 & \lambda \end{pmatrix}\begin{pmatrix} W_{t-1} \\ \mathrm{EC}_{t-1} \end{pmatrix} + \boldsymbol{\eta}_t, \tag{10.6}$$

where $\boldsymbol{\eta}_t = \boldsymbol{P}^{-1}\boldsymbol{\varepsilon}_t$, and EC_t and W_t are defined as

$$W_t = dY_t - bX_t, \tag{10.7}$$

$$\mathrm{EC}_t = -cY_t + aX_t. \tag{10.8}$$

By direct inspection of (10.6), we see that $\mathrm{EC}_t \sim I(0)$ is a stationary variable (i.e., equilibrium correction variable), while $W_t \sim I(1)$ is called a common (stochastic) trend, i.e., Y_t and X_t contain the same stochastic trend.

We say that there is *cointegration* between X_t and Y_t, since EC_t is a stationary variable. It is a linear combination of X_t and Y_t. $-c$ and a are the *cointegrating parameters* in this model. There is a second linear combination of the variables as well, and that linear combination defines the common stochastic trend variable, $W_t \sim I(1)$.

We often reparametrize the VAR in (10.1) as

$$\Delta \boldsymbol{y}_t = \boldsymbol{\Pi}\boldsymbol{y}_{t-1} + \boldsymbol{\varepsilon}_t, \tag{10.9}$$

where we have used the notation that have become the custom in the literature, defining the matrix $\mathbf{\Pi}$ as

$$\mathbf{\Pi} = (\mathbf{\Phi} - \mathbf{I}). \tag{10.10}$$

Next, define two parameter vectors $\boldsymbol{\alpha}$ and $\boldsymbol{\beta}$, where both have dimensions 2×1, so that the product $\boldsymbol{\alpha}\boldsymbol{\beta}'$ gives $\mathbf{\Pi}$:

$$\mathbf{\Pi} = \boldsymbol{\alpha}\boldsymbol{\beta}'. \tag{10.11}$$

With the notation introduced above, we write the product as (see Exercise 10.1)

$$\mathbf{\Pi} = \underbrace{\begin{pmatrix} -(1-\lambda)b \\ -(1-\lambda)d \end{pmatrix}}_{\boldsymbol{\alpha}} \underbrace{(-c \quad a)}_{\boldsymbol{\beta}'},$$

and then (10.9) can be expressed as

$$\begin{pmatrix} \Delta Y_t \\ \Delta X_t \end{pmatrix} = \boldsymbol{\alpha}\boldsymbol{\beta}' \begin{pmatrix} Y_{t-1} \\ X_{t-1} \end{pmatrix} + \varepsilon_t. \tag{10.12}$$

Here $\boldsymbol{\alpha}$ is the matrix with equilibrium correction coefficients (the terms adjustment coefficients and loadings are also terminologies that are used for the same concept):

$$\boldsymbol{\alpha} = \begin{pmatrix} -(1-\lambda)b \\ -(1-\lambda)d \end{pmatrix} = \begin{pmatrix} \alpha_1 \\ \alpha_2 \end{pmatrix}, \tag{10.13}$$

and $\boldsymbol{\beta}$ is the vector with the cointegration coefficients:

$$\boldsymbol{\beta} = \begin{pmatrix} -c \\ a \end{pmatrix}. \tag{10.14}$$

We see that the two equations have $\boldsymbol{\beta}$ in common, while there are two separate coefficients in $\boldsymbol{\alpha}$, which have been denoted by α_1 and α_2 above. One of them can be zero, but not both, since that would represent a contradiction of the assumed cointegration between Y_t and X_t.

Note that, from (10.10) and (10.11), we have

$$\boldsymbol{\alpha}\boldsymbol{\beta}' = \mathbf{\Pi} = \mathbf{\Phi} - \mathbf{I}. \tag{10.15}$$

The eigenvalue problem (10.2) can therefore be reexpressed as

$$|\mathbf{\Pi} - z\boldsymbol{I}| = 0, \tag{10.16}$$

where $z \equiv \lambda - 1$.

Since $\lambda_1 = 1$ and $\lambda_2 = \lambda < 1$ by assumption, it follows that the matrix $\mathbf{\Pi}$ has reduced rank (rank = 1) since the roots are $z_1 = 0$ and $z_2 = \lambda - 1 \neq 0$. If we assume that also the second eigenvalue of $\mathbf{\Phi}$ is equal to one (i.e., $\lambda = 1$), there can, logically speaking, be no cointegration. In this case, the rank of $\mathbf{\Pi}$ is zero (i.e., $z_1 = z_2 = 0$). The autoregressive matrix becomes

$$\mathbf{\Phi} = \begin{pmatrix} 1 & 0 \\ 0 & 1 \end{pmatrix},$$

which follows from noting (see Exercise 10.1) that

$$\mathbf{\Phi} = \mathbf{I} - (1 - \lambda) \begin{pmatrix} b \\ d \end{pmatrix} (-c \quad a), \tag{10.17}$$

which gives $\mathbf{\Phi} = \mathbf{I}$ when $\lambda = 1$.

Hence, if $\mathbf{\Phi}$ is characterized by two unit-roots, the ECM-representation is reduced to

$$\begin{pmatrix} \Delta Y_t \\ \Delta X_t \end{pmatrix} = \varepsilon_t \tag{10.18}$$

which is the simplest case of a *dVAR*, meaning a VAR that only contains differences of the original variables. We see that in the case with first-order dynamics that we have here, the dVAR is a null model.

To summarize, there are three possible cases when the DGP is the Gaussian VAR in (10.1) with the equivalent formulation in (10.9):

(1) rank($\mathbf{\Pi}$) = 0 is equivalent with no cointegration. Both eigenvalues of $\mathbf{\Pi}$ are zero.
(2) rank($\mathbf{\Pi}$) = 1 is equivalent with cointegration. In this case, one of the eigenvalues of $\mathbf{\Pi}$ is different from zero (corresponding to one eigenvalue of $\mathbf{\Phi}$ being less than one).
(3) rank($\mathbf{\Pi}$) = 2, full rank, both eigenvalues of $\mathbf{\Pi}$ are different from zero and the VAR in (10.1) is stationary, i.e., the case we have studied in the earlier chapters.

10.2.2. Cointegration and weak exogeneity

Since $\lambda < 1$ is equivalent with cointegration, we see from (10.13) that cointegration implies Granger-causality in at least one direction: $(1-\lambda)b \neq 0$ and/or $(1 - \lambda)d \neq 0$.

Assume $d = 0$, from (10.13) this implies $\alpha_2 = 0$, and hence

$$\begin{pmatrix} \Delta Y_t \\ \Delta X_t \end{pmatrix} = -(1-\lambda)\begin{pmatrix} b \\ 0 \end{pmatrix}[-cY_{t-1} + aX_{t-1}] + \boldsymbol{\varepsilon}_t, \tag{10.19}$$

$$\begin{pmatrix} \Delta Y_t \\ \Delta X_t \end{pmatrix} = \begin{pmatrix} \alpha_1[-cY_{t-1} + aX_{t-1}] + \varepsilon_{y,t} \\ \varepsilon_{x,t}, \end{pmatrix}, \tag{10.20}$$

where $\alpha_1 = -(1-\lambda)b$.

The marginal model equation of ΔX_t contains no information about the cointegration parameters $(-c, a)'$. X_t is therefore weakly exogenous for the cointegration parameters $\boldsymbol{\beta}' = (-c, a)'$.

Intuitively, a test for weak exogeneity with respect to the cointegration parameters can therefore be done by testing restrictions on the $\boldsymbol{\alpha}$ vector.

10.2.3. Generalization of the ECM representation

In general, $\boldsymbol{y}_t \sim I(1)$ is an $n \times 1$ vector. $\boldsymbol{\varepsilon}_t$ is also $n \times 1$ and has a multivariate normal distribution. In the same way as above, we denote the order of the dynamics by p, and we write the (closed) VAR(p) as

$$\boldsymbol{\Pi}_v(L)\boldsymbol{y}_t = \boldsymbol{\varepsilon}_t, \tag{10.21}$$

where

$$\boldsymbol{\Pi}_v(L) = \mathbf{I} - \boldsymbol{\Phi}(L), \tag{10.22}$$

$$\boldsymbol{\Phi}(L) = \sum_{i=1}^{p} \boldsymbol{\Phi}_i L^i. \tag{10.23}$$

Equations (10.22) and (10.23) are matrix counterparts to the lag polynomials $\pi(L)$ and $\phi(L)$ that we have used several times above. Equivalently, we can write the VAR(p) as

$$\boldsymbol{y}_t = \boldsymbol{\Phi}(L)\boldsymbol{y}_{t-1} + \boldsymbol{\varepsilon}_t, \tag{10.24}$$

$$\boldsymbol{\Phi}(L) = \sum_{i=0}^{p} \boldsymbol{\Phi}_{i+1} L^i. \tag{10.25}$$

Sometimes, it is convenient to write the dynamics more explicitly:

$$\begin{aligned} \boldsymbol{y}_t &= \left(\sum_{i=0}^{p} \boldsymbol{\Phi}_{i+1} L^i\right) \boldsymbol{y}_{t-1} + \boldsymbol{\varepsilon}_t \\ &= \sum_{i=0}^{p} \boldsymbol{\Phi}_{i+1} \boldsymbol{y}_{t-1-i} + \boldsymbol{\varepsilon}_t. \end{aligned} \tag{10.26}$$

Each of the p coefficient matrices has dimension $n \times n$. In the same way as in the scalar case, the matrix lag polynomial $\mathbf{\Phi}(L)$ can be written as

$$\mathbf{\Phi}(L) = \Delta\mathbf{\Phi}^*(L) + \mathbf{\Phi}(1), \tag{10.27}$$

where $\mathbf{\Phi}(1)$ is the sum of all the p matrices with lag coefficients:

$$\mathbf{\Phi}(1) = \sum_{i=1}^{p} \mathbf{\Phi}_i, \tag{10.28}$$

and

$$\mathbf{\Phi}^*(L) = \mathbf{\Phi}_1^* + \mathbf{\Phi}_2^* L + \cdots + \mathbf{\Phi}_{p-1}^* L^{p-1}, \tag{10.29}$$

consists of $(n \times n)$-matrices $\mathbf{\Phi}_i^*$ $(i = 1, \ldots, p-1)$, where the elements are expressions of the elements in $\mathbf{\Phi}_i$ $(i = 1, \ldots, p)$.

Substitution in (10.24) gives

$$\boldsymbol{y}_t = (\Delta\mathbf{\Phi}^*(L) + \mathbf{\Phi}(1))\boldsymbol{y}_{t-1} + \boldsymbol{\varepsilon}_t,$$

and subtraction of $\mathbf{I}\boldsymbol{y}_{t-1}$ on both sides of the equality sign gives the generalization of the ECM form in (10.9) as

$$\Delta\boldsymbol{y}_t = \mathbf{\Phi}^*(L)\Delta\boldsymbol{y}_{t-1} + \mathbf{\Pi}(1)\boldsymbol{y}_{t-1} + \boldsymbol{\varepsilon}_t, \tag{10.30}$$

$$\mathbf{\Pi}(1) = \mathbf{\Phi}(1) - \mathbf{I} = \left(\sum_{i=0}^{p} \mathbf{\Phi}_{i+1} - \mathbf{I}\right). \tag{10.31}$$

In order to simplify notation, we will use $\mathbf{\Pi} \equiv \mathbf{\Pi}(1)$ and $\mathbf{\Phi} \equiv \mathbf{\Phi}(1)$ in the following.

In the case of no cointegration, $\mathbf{\Pi}$ is the null matrix:

$$\mathbf{\Pi} = \mathbf{0}, \tag{10.32}$$

while it is

$$\mathbf{\Pi} = \boldsymbol{\alpha}\boldsymbol{\beta}', \tag{10.33}$$

in the case of r cointegrating vectors (r equal to the rank of $\mathbf{\Pi}$). In the same way as in the bivariate case above, we have that $\mathbf{\Pi} = \mathbf{0}$ and $\text{rank}(\mathbf{\Pi}) = 0$ are equivalent with all eigenvalues of $\mathbf{\Phi}$ being unity, equivalent with all eigenvalues of $\mathbf{\Pi}$ being equal to zero.

It is the custom to refer to rank($\mathbf{\Pi}$) as the *cointegration rank*.

$\boldsymbol{\beta}'$, which has dimension $r \times n$, contains the r cointegrating vectors as rows, while $\boldsymbol{\alpha}$ $(n \times r)$ shows the strength of equilibrium correction in each of the equations for

$$\Delta Y_{1t}, \Delta Y_{2t}, \ldots, \Delta Y_{nt}.$$

In general, $\text{rank}(\boldsymbol{\beta}) = r$, and $\text{rank}(\boldsymbol{\Pi}) = r < n$.

If we imagine a situation where $\boldsymbol{\beta}$ is a known matrix with cointegration coefficients, the system

$$\Delta \boldsymbol{y}_t = \boldsymbol{\Phi}^*(L)\Delta \boldsymbol{y}_{t-1} + \boldsymbol{\alpha}(\boldsymbol{\beta}'\boldsymbol{y}_{t-1}) + \boldsymbol{\varepsilon}_t, \tag{10.34}$$

is seen to contain only $I(0)$ variables, and the maximum likelihood estimation can be done by applying OLS to each row of the VAR (see Chapter 5). Standard asymptotic inference applies to the coefficients in $\boldsymbol{\Phi}_i^*$ $(i = 1, 2, \ldots, p-1)$ and to the coefficients in $\boldsymbol{\alpha}$. With the known cointegration restrictions imposed, (10.34) is a stationary VAR, but to keep it apart from the case with $\boldsymbol{y}_t \sim I(0)$, it is useful to call it the cointegrated VAR (CVAR).

In general, and in practice, it is not feasible to claim knowledge of all cointegration parameters. However, if the rank of $\boldsymbol{\beta}$ has been estimated by a consistent estimator, and the resulting estimate of $\boldsymbol{\beta}$ is regarded as known, the conventional asymptotic inference theory also applies to the *feasible* CVAR.

We see that the VAR provides a logical framework for moving from the non-stationary system (sometimes called $I(1)$-space) to the stationary system (i.e., $I(0)$-space).

Before cointegration was developed, conceptually and with its own inference theory (see below), the only way of making the move was by differencing the data. That procedure we now see amounts to imposing n eigenvalues equal to zero, leading logically to the *dVAR*:

$$\Delta \boldsymbol{y}_t = \boldsymbol{\Phi}^*(L)\Delta \boldsymbol{y}_{t-1} + \boldsymbol{\varepsilon}_t, \tag{10.35}$$

which generalizes the simplest dVAR in (10.18). Specifically, we see that the dVAR is not generally a (multivariate) null model.

10.2.4. The roles of the intercept and the linear trend

In Chapter 9, we saw that care must be taken when unit-root non-stationarity is combined with wide-sense deterministic trends. For example, the constant term in a stationary AR(1) process determines the expectation of the time series variable, while in the case of a unit-root, it represents the slope of a deterministic trend in the solution of the process.

In the multivariate case, $\boldsymbol{y}_t \sim I(1)$ is also due to unit-roots, hence it is not surprising that there are similar remarks to be made about the role of deterministic terms in non-stationary VARs.

We can consider this point a little more closely for the first-order dynamics, and with $n = 2$ and $r = 1$. We include two non-zero intercepts ϕ_{10} and ϕ_{20}:

$$\begin{pmatrix} \Delta Y_t \\ \Delta X_t \end{pmatrix} = \begin{pmatrix} \phi_{10} \\ \phi_{20} \end{pmatrix} + \begin{pmatrix} \alpha_{11} \\ \alpha_{21} \end{pmatrix} (\beta_{11} Y_{t-1} + \beta_{12} X_{t-1}) + \varepsilon_t. \tag{10.36}$$

It is only when $\alpha_{11} = \alpha_{21} = 0$, i.e., absence of cointegration, that the deterministic trend of Y_t simply becomes $\phi_{10} t$, and the trend in X_t is $\phi_{20} t$.

It is not always that the variables contain trends. In such cases, it may be relevant to impose a certain structure on the intercepts in the VAR, namely,

$$\begin{pmatrix} \phi_{10} \\ \phi_{20} \end{pmatrix} = -\begin{pmatrix} \alpha_{11} \\ \alpha_{21} \end{pmatrix} \mu_0. \tag{10.37}$$

With (10.37), (10.36) can be written as

$$\begin{pmatrix} \Delta Y_t \\ \Delta X_t \end{pmatrix} = \begin{pmatrix} \alpha_{11} \\ \alpha_{21} \end{pmatrix} (\beta_{11} Y_{t-1} + \beta_{12} X_{t-1} - \mu_0) + \varepsilon_t.$$

If we apply the expectation on both sides of the equality sign, we obtain

$$E\begin{pmatrix} \Delta Y_t \\ \Delta X_t \end{pmatrix} = \begin{pmatrix} \alpha_{11} \\ \alpha_{21} \end{pmatrix} [E(\beta_{11} Y_{t-1} + \beta_{12} X_{t-1}) - \mu_0].$$

$E(\beta_{11} Y_{t-1} + \beta_{12} X_{t-1})$ is the expectation of a stationary variable, which is a unique parameter, we find it as

$$\mu_0 = E(\beta_{11} Y_{t-1} + \beta_{12} X_{t-1}),$$

μ_0 in (10.37) is the mean of the cointegration relationship, hence it follows that

$$E\begin{pmatrix} \Delta Y_t \\ \Delta X_t \end{pmatrix} = \begin{pmatrix} 0 \\ 0 \end{pmatrix},$$

when (10.37) holds. One way to express this is by saying that the variables of the VAR are non-trending when the intercept is in the *cointegration space*.

In the following we refer to cases like (10.36) as models with unrestricted intercepts (i.e., unrestricted constant terms). When the intercept is in the cointegration space, i.e., (10.37) applies, we have a cointegrated VAR with restricted intercepts.

It is also possible to include a trend in the cointegration space. The cointegration relationships then become trend-corrected, and there is no squared trend in the solution for the individual variables (which would be the case if the VAR includes an unrestricted deterministic trend).

As we shall see in the following, when we test the hypothesis of absence of cointegration, there are different critical values for the case of unrestricted and restricted constant terms in the VAR.

10.2.5. Conditional cointegration, exogenous I(1) variables in the VAR

We are often interested in studying cointegration in a VAR which is conditional on one or more non-modelled $I(1)$ variables. Ideally, the exogeneity assumptions (i.e., zero restrictions on the relevant α-coefficients of the closed VAR) should be empirically verified. However, in practice, that may often be difficult because the closed VAR is misspecified, while the conditional VAR has acceptable diagnostics tests.

How should we think about rank reduction in an open system if we have decided to use one? We answer by again considering the bivariate case: $\boldsymbol{y}_t = (Y_t, X_t)'$ above.

Assume that $\alpha_{21} = 0$, then X_t is weakly exogenous for $\boldsymbol{\beta}$. With Gaussian disturbances $\varepsilon_t \sim \text{IIN}(\mathbf{0}, \boldsymbol{\Sigma})$, where the elements of $\boldsymbol{\Sigma}$ are the covariances (i.e., σ_{ij}) and the variances (i.e., σ_{ii}^2), we can derive the conditional model for ΔY_t:

$$\Delta Y_t = \underbrace{\sigma_{21}\sigma_{22}^{-2}}_{\beta_0}\Delta X_t + \alpha_{11}\boldsymbol{\beta}'\begin{bmatrix} Y_{t-1} \\ X_{t-1} \end{bmatrix} + \underbrace{\varepsilon_{1t} - \sigma_{21}\sigma_{22}^{-2}\varepsilon_{2t}}_{\epsilon_t} \tag{10.38}$$

i.e., a single equation ECM. If we write it as

$$\Delta Y_t = \beta_0 \Delta X_t + \alpha_{11}\beta_{11}Y_{t-1} + \alpha_{11}\beta_{12}X_{t-1} + \epsilon_t,$$

we see that $\boldsymbol{\Pi} = \alpha_{11}\beta_{11} \neq 0$, i.e., the $\boldsymbol{\Pi}$ "matrix" has full rank.

In the open VAR, the $I(1)$-trend is now the observable exogenous variable X_t, while in the closed VAR above, it was the non-cointegrating linear combination that defines W_t,

The generalization is straightforward. Assume that the VAR contains n_1 endogenous $I(1)$ variables and n_2 non-modelled $I(1)$ variables. As noted above, we call it an open system or VAR-EX. Cointegration is then consistent with

$$0 < \text{rank}(\mathbf{\Pi}) \leq n_1. \tag{10.39}$$

Said in different words, in open systems, the cointegration rank($\mathbf{\Pi}$) may be full, i.e., the maximum rank consistent with cointegration is equal to the number of endogenous $I(1)$ variables in the system.

10.3. Estimating a Single Cointegrating Vector

In this section, we look at methods for estimating a single cointegration vector, and for testing the null hypothesis of absence of cointegration against the alternative of a single cointegration vector.

We concentrate on the static cointegration regression, due originally to Engle and Granger, and the estimation test based on a single equation equilibrium correction models (see Ericsson and MacKinnon, 2002).

10.3.1. The cointegrating regression

As noted, when rank($\mathbf{\Pi}$) $= 1$, the cointegration vector is unique, subject only to normalization (i.e., setting one of the cointegrating coefficients to 1). Hence, without loss of generality, we can set $n = 1$ and write $\boldsymbol{y}_t = (Y_t, X_t)$ as in a usual regression. The cointegration parameter β can be estimated by applying OLS to

$$Y_t = \beta X_t + u_t, \tag{10.40}$$

where the error term $u_t \sim I(0)$ by assumption of cointegration. For simplicity, we abstract from the constant term. The bias of the OLS estimator $\hat{\beta}_{\text{EG}}$ is

$$(\hat{\beta}_{\text{EG}} - \beta) = \frac{\sum_{t=1}^{T} X_t u_t}{\sum_{t=1}^{T} {X_t}^2}. \tag{10.41}$$

Since $X_t \sim I(1)$, we are in a situation which is similar to the one we studied for the univariate model above with autoregressive parameter equal to one.

In direct analogy, we need to multiply $(\hat{\beta} - \beta)$ by T in order to obtain a non-degenerate asymptotic distribution:

$$T(\hat{\beta}_{\mathrm{EG}} - \beta) = \frac{\frac{1}{T}\sum_{t=1}^{T} X_t u_t}{\frac{1}{T^2}\sum_{t=1}^{T} X_t^2}, \tag{10.42}$$

and it follows that $(\hat{\beta}_{\mathrm{EG}} - \beta)$ converges to zero at rate T instead of $\sqrt{T}$ (the standard rate for stationary variables). This result is often referred to as the Engle–Granger super-consistency theorem (see Engle and Granger, 1987; Stock, 1987). The result was surprising when we consider that exactly the same type of model equation gave rise to nonsense regression in the case of no cointegration between X_t and Y_t. Box 10.1 summarizes another interesting aspect of the super-consistency of the OLS estimator of the cointegration parameter of a two-variable system, given that it exists.

Box 10.1. Simultaneous I(1)-system

Consider the simultaneous equation model for (X_{1t}, X_{2t}):

$$X_{1t} + bX_{2t} = u_{1t}, \quad u_{1t} = u_{1t-1} + \varepsilon_{1t},$$

$$X_{1t} + \beta X_{2t} = u_{2t}, \quad u_{2t} = \rho u_{2t-1} + \varepsilon_{2t}, |\rho| < 1.$$

ε_{1t}, ε_{2t} are assumed to be two independent white noise processes. Neither b nor β are identified on the order condition. Nevertheless, when we write the bias expression of $\hat{\beta}_{\mathrm{EG}}$ as

$$\hat{\beta}_{\mathrm{EG}} - \beta = \beta - (\beta - b)\frac{\frac{1}{T}\sum u_{2t}^2 - \frac{1}{T}\sum u_{1t}u_{2t}}{\frac{1}{T}\sum u_{1t}^2 - 2\frac{1}{T}\sum u_{1t}u_{2t} + \frac{1}{T}\sum u_{2t}^2},$$

we note that $\frac{1}{T}\sum u_{1t}^2 \underset{T\to\infty}{\to} \infty$, while the other terms converge to finite numbers. Hence, we have that $\hat{\beta}_{\mathrm{EG}}$ is a consistent estimator of β, which is therefore identified. There can be only one cointegrating relationship between the two $I(1)$-variables, hence b is not identified.

The distribution of the Engle–Granger estimator $\hat{\beta}_{\mathrm{EG}}$ is, however, non-standard and that makes it impractical for inference. For example, it has been shown that $\hat{\beta}_{\mathrm{EG}}$ is not normally distributed asymptotically (it is so called mixed-normal). The same applies to the t-value of $\hat{\beta}_{\mathrm{EG}}$: It does *not* have an asymptotic normal distribution (even under the assumption of cointegration). This means that it is impractical to use the static regression for making inference about β, i.e., test a hypothesis $\beta = 1$, or of $\beta = 0$. The drawback becomes even more severe in the case of a DGP with higher order dynamics due to residual autocorrelation as a result of dynamic misspecification.

In order to be more precise about the asymptotic distribution of $T(\hat{\beta}_{\text{EG}} - \beta)$, we need to specify more of the DGP for the two variables Y_t and X_t. For the DGP:

$$Y_t = \beta X_t + u_t,\ u_t \sim N(0, \sigma_u^2), \quad \forall t,$$
$$\Delta X_t = \varepsilon_{xt},\ \varepsilon_{xt} \sim N(0, \sigma_\varepsilon^2), \quad \forall t,$$
$$E(u_t \varepsilon_t) = \sigma_{u\varepsilon},$$

the following result has been shown:[1]

$$T(\hat{\beta}_{\text{EG}} - \beta) \xrightarrow{L} \frac{\frac{\sigma_{u\varepsilon}}{2}(B_\varepsilon(1)^2 + 1) + \sigma_\varepsilon \cdot h \cdot N(0, \int_0^1 [B_\varepsilon(r)]^2 dr)}{\sigma_\varepsilon^2 \int_0^1 [B_\varepsilon(r)]^2 dr}, \tag{10.43}$$

where $h = \sqrt{\sigma_u^2 - \sigma_{u\varepsilon}^2/\sigma_\varepsilon^2}$.

In the case of $\sigma_{u\varepsilon} = 0$, the non-centrality disappears from the numerator, but the bias is still a function of the Wiener processes in the numerator and in the denominator. This implies that neither $\hat{\beta}_{\text{EG}} - \beta$ nor the t-value are asymptotically normal in the case of cointegration. As just noted above, this reduces how useful the cointegration regression is for making statistical inference.

$\sigma_{u\varepsilon} \neq 0$ creates what is known as second-order bias. The correlation between the regressor and the equation disturbance does not destroy the super-consistency property, but it nevertheless creates a bias for a finite sample. If the error term of the cointegration regression is autocorrelated, the bias will become exacerbated. These results generalize to more realistic cointegration regressions that include a constant and other deterministic terms.

The method based on the cointegration regression has, however, been further developed and modified in different ways that aim to correct the second-order bias. The most successful is maybe Phillips' and Hansen's fully

[1]See Banerjee *et al.* (1993, Section 6.2.2). Hamilton (1994) includes other, more general results for the cointegration regression, e.g., Proposition 19.2 and the following discussion, and Section 19.3, pp. 601–608.

modified estimator, which estimates the bias components and then modifies $\hat{\beta}_{\text{EG}}$. The resulting modified estimator has an asymptotic distribution which is normal, and therefore standard methods can be used to make statistical inference about β (see Pesaran, 2015, Section 22.3.3; Patterson, 2000, Section 9.4).

Saikkonen's (1991) estimator is based on

$$Y_t = \beta X_t + \gamma_1 \Delta X_{t+1} + \gamma_2 \Delta X_{t-1} + \varepsilon'_t,$$

and higher order dynamics, if that is required to ensure that the disturbance ε'_t is white noise (see, e.g., Davidson and MacKinnon, 2004, p. 630).

10.3.2. The ECM estimator

As we have seen, one implication of the Engle–Granger representation theorem is that the dynamics of cointegrated variables are characterized by equilibrium correction dynamics. Therefore, the estimation of long-run (steady-state) coefficients from an ECM, represents a logical way of also estimating the cointegration parameters. Moreover, exactly because it is a dynamic model specification, the ECM can avoid the second-order bias of the EG estimator.

With $n = 2$, $p = 1$ and weak exogeneity of X_t with respect to the cointegration parameter, the cointegrated VAR can be rewritten as the conditional model (10.38) and a marginal model for ΔX_t:

$$\Delta Y_t = \beta_0 \Delta X_t + \underbrace{\pi}_{\alpha_{11}\beta_{11}} Y_{t-1} + \underbrace{\gamma}_{\alpha_{11}\beta_{12}} X_{t-1} + \epsilon_t, \tag{10.44}$$

$$\Delta X_t = \varepsilon_{2t}, \tag{10.45}$$

where β_0 is the regression coefficient, and ϵ_t and ε_{2t} are uncorrelated normal variables. Normalization on Y_{t-1} by setting $\beta_{11} = -1$, and defining $\beta_{12} = \beta$, for comparison with the EG estimator, gives:

$$\Delta Y_t = \beta_0 \Delta X_t - \alpha_{11}(Y_{t-1} - \beta X_{t-1}) + \epsilon_t.$$

The ECM estimator $\hat{\beta}_{\text{ECM}}$ is obtained from OLS on (10.44):

$$\hat{\beta}_{\text{ECM}} = \frac{\hat{\gamma}}{-\hat{\pi}}. \tag{10.46}$$

Here $\hat{\beta}_{\text{ECM}}$ is consistent if both $\hat{\gamma}$ and $\hat{\pi}$ are consistent. OLS "chooses" the $\hat{\gamma}$ and $\hat{\pi}$ that give the best predictor $(Y_{t-1} - \hat{\beta} X_{t-1})$ for ΔY_t. Therefore, as T grows towards infinity, the true parameters γ, π and β will be found. In fact, $\hat{\beta}^{\text{ECM}}$ is also super-consistent, and it has better small sample properties than the EG estimator, since it is based on a well-specified econometric model as noted.

The distributions of $\widehat{\gamma}$ and $\widehat{\pi}$ (again, maintaining cointegration) can be shown to be the so-called *mixed normal* for large T, which means that the empirical variances converge towards stochastic variables rather than fixed parameters. However, the OLS-based t-values of $\widehat{\gamma}$ and $\widehat{\pi}$ are asymptotically $N(0,1)$. $\hat{\beta}_{\text{ECM}}$ is also mixed normal, and the t-value has an asymptotic normal distribution:

$$t_{\hat{\beta}_{\text{ECM}}} = \hat{\beta}_{\text{ECM}} / \sqrt{\text{Var}(\hat{\beta}_{\text{ECM}})} \underset{T \longrightarrow \infty}{\longrightarrow} N(0,1). \tag{10.47}$$

$\text{Var}(\hat{\beta}^{\text{ECM}})$ can be found by using the Delta method. The proof that this method, devised for the long-run coefficients in models with stationary variables, extends to the case of $I(1)$ variables is found in Johansen (1992). The generalization to $n-1$ explanatory variables, intercept and dummies is also unproblematic. However, as noted, the efficiency of the ECM estimator depends on the assumed weak exogeneity of the explanatory variables with respect to the cointegration parameters.

10.4. Testing Rank Zero Against Rank Equal to One

We have now reached the point where we can show how to do a valid test of the hypothesis of no relationship between $I(1)$ variables, and hence how to avoid the pitfall of spurious regression. We begin with the case where the alternative to absence of cointegration (rank $= 0$) in the sense explained above is that there is at the most one cointegration relationship (rank ≤ 1). The extension of the theory needed to tackle multiple cointegration relationships is found in Section 10.5.

10.4.1. The EG test

The easiest approach is to use an ADF regression to test the null hypothesis of a unit-root in the residuals $\hat{u}_t$ from the hypothesized cointegrating regression (10.40). Since the time series tested for a unit-root consists of the residuals from an Engle–Granger regression, the ADF test is referred to as the EG test of absence of cointegration. The motivation for the augmentation by $\Delta\hat{u}_{t-j}$ terms is the same as in the unit-root case, namely, to have a not misspecified ADF regression.

The critical values of the test statistics are, however, shifted to the left as deterministic terms, and/or more $I(1)$ variables in the regression are added to the (potential) cointegration regression (see Davidson and MacKinnon, 2004, Figures 14.4 and 14.5). A table with critical values was published in MacKinnon (1991). However, MacKinnon (2010) contains extended results and is therefore practical to use.

10.4.2. The ECM test

As we have seen above, $r = 0$ corresponds to $\pi = 0$ in the *ECM* model in (10.44):

$$\Delta Y_t = \beta_0 \Delta X_t + \pi Y_{t-1} + \gamma X_{t-1} + \epsilon_t. \tag{10.48}$$

It also comes as no surprise that the t-value $t_{\pi=0}$ has a Dickey–Fuller type distribution, and that the location of the distribution is shifted to the left compared to the unit-root version as a result of X_{t-1} being added to the model equation. Ericsson and MacKinnon (2002) provided the critical values for up to 11 conditioning variables, and with constant and linear trend.

The literature shows that in terms of Type-I error probabilities, there is little difference between the EG test and the ECM test. However, in general, Type-II error probabilities are smaller for the ECM test than for the EG test (i.e., the power of that test is better). Let t_π^{ECM} denote the t-value of the OLS estimated π in (10.46), and let t_τ^{EG} denote the ADF obtained by estimating

$$\Delta \hat{u}_t = \tau \hat{u}_{t-1} + e_t, \tag{10.49}$$

where $\hat{u}_t$ denotes an OLS residual from the cointegration regression (10.40). Kremers *et al.* (1992) showed that

$$t_\pi^{\text{ECM}} \cong \frac{\sigma_e}{\sigma_\epsilon} t_\tau^{\text{EG}}, \tag{10.50}$$

where σ_ϵ and σ_e are the standard deviations of ϵ_t and e_t, respectively. The two t-values become equivalent if $\sigma_e = \sigma_\epsilon$. We can get a better understanding of this special case by writing the ECM-regression model in the ADL form:

$$Y_t = \beta_0 X_t + (1+\pi) Y_{t-1} + (\gamma - \beta_0) X_{t-1} + \epsilon_t,$$

which we can write in lag-operator form as

$$(1 - (1+\pi)L) Y_t = (\beta_0 + (\gamma - \beta_0)L) X_t + \epsilon_t. \tag{10.51}$$

If we assume that the following common factor restriction (see Section 6.5.2) holds:

$$(\gamma - \beta_0) = -\beta_0(1 + \pi), \tag{10.52}$$

so that:

$$\frac{(\beta_0 + (\gamma - \beta_0)L)}{(1 - (1 + \pi)L)} = \beta_0, \tag{10.53}$$

the ECM equation is "reduced to"

$$Y_t = \beta_0 X_t + \frac{1}{(1 - (1 + \pi)L)}\epsilon_t,$$

i.e., a static model equation with an AR(1) error term:

$$\begin{aligned} Y_t &= \beta_0 X_t + e_t, \\ e_t &= (1 + \pi)e_{t-1} + \epsilon_t,\ \pi < 0. \end{aligned}$$

Hence, the ECM equation, made subject to the common-factor restriction, corresponds to a specific cointegration regression. Moreover, as the cointegration parameter is unique, we can logically set $\beta_0 \equiv \beta$.

We can also insert the common-factor restriction in the ADL equation (10.51) along with $\beta_0 \equiv \beta$ to obtain

$$Y_t = \beta X_t + (1 + \pi)Y_{t-1} - \beta(1 + \pi)X_{t-1} + \epsilon_t, \tag{10.54}$$

or:

$$\Delta Y_t - \beta \Delta X_t = \pi(Y_{t-1} - \beta X_{t-1}) + \epsilon_t. \tag{10.55}$$

If we substitute β by $\hat{\beta}_{\text{EG}}$, we see that the ECM (10.48) in fact implies the Dickey–Fuller regression:

$$\underbrace{\Delta Y_t - \hat{\beta}_{\text{EG}} \Delta X_t}_{\Delta \hat{u}_t} = \pi \underbrace{(Y_{t-1} - \hat{\beta}_{\text{EG}} X_{t-1})}_{\hat{u}_{t-1}} + \epsilon_t,$$

and that the τ coefficient in the EG Dickey–Fuller regression (10.49) is therefore equivalent with the equilibrium correction coefficient π.

However, these results are subject to the assumption that the common-factor restriction (10.52) is valid empirically. If the restriction in (10.52) does *not* hold, the EG test is based on a misspecified model, and one consequence is that $\sigma_e > \sigma_\epsilon$ and therefore the power of the EG test is generally lower than the ECM test as noted.

10.4.3. A bounds test for the existence of a long-run relationship

There are other tests of absence of cointegration that makes use of ECM and ADL equations. For example, a natural test situation could be to test H_0: $\pi = \gamma = 0$ in (10.48). However, this joint hypothesis cannot be tested by using the F-distribution, due to the unit-root present in the DGP under H_0 (see Pesaran and Youngcheol, 1998). Pesaran *et al.* (2001) provided the appropriate critical values for testing the joint null hypothesis (see also Pesaran, 2015, Section 22.3.1). In Kripfganz and Schneider (2018), critical values that are accurate for realistic finite samples are available. The bounds test has the attractive feature that it does not require that a researcher decides the order of integration of the variables prior to testing for the existence of a long-run relationship. If the value of the F-statistic falls outside the critical value bounds, a conclusion is reached about the existence of a long-run relationship without needing to know whether (or which) of the variables are $I(1)$ or $I(0)$. However, if the test value is within the tabulated bounds, there is a need to establish more about the order of integration of the variables in the putative long-run relationship.

10.4.4. Resolving spurious regression

We now revisit the DGP in Example 9.1 to see whether the ECM test can help us reveal that there is no relationship between the two random walks YA_t and YB_t.

We first estimate equation (9.15) by OLS using one of the 1000 datasets generated in the Monte Carlo analysis. The results with a sample of 100 observations become

$$\begin{aligned}\Delta\mathrm{YA}_t = \underset{(0.094)}{0.009}\,\Delta\mathrm{YB}_t - \underset{(0.054)}{0.142}\,\mathrm{YA}_{t-1} - \underset{(0.029)}{0.065}\,\mathrm{YB}_{t-1} \\ \underset{(0.013)}{-0.011} \\ \text{OLS},\ T = 100\ (\text{Sample } 2-101),\ \hat{\sigma}^2_{\varepsilon} = 0.08836.\end{aligned}$$

Since the estimated model is correctly specified, the diagnostic tests are satisfactory and they are not reported to save space.[2] The ECM test for no

[2]The dataset is: spurious_ADLmodel_d.xls, and the PcGive batch file is: ECM-test_SpuriousADLmodel.fl, on the internet page with data to Chapter 10.

relationship is seen to be

$$t_\pi^{\mathrm{ECM}} = \frac{-0.142}{0.054} = -2.63,$$

i.e., an ordinary t-value. As we have seen, the difference lies in which critical values are used. The standard t-distribution gives a p-value of 0.009, when the t-value is -2.63. However, we now know that the standard inference is invalid. Using Table 3 in Ericsson and MacKinnon (2002), we find that the asymptotic 1% critical value is -3.79, and that the 5% critical value is -3.21. Hence, the use of the formally correct statistical inference theory is seen to give the correct conclusion in this case: the relationship is spurious.

The EG test also gives the correct conclusion in this case, with $t_\tau^{\mathrm{EG}} = -2.01$ against the 5% critical value of -3.34 (see MacKinnon, 1991, Table 1).

However, the result of the one-off test could be a fortunate coincidence. In order to show the statistical properties of the ECM test, we can rerun the Monte Carlo experiment for the spurious regression Example 9.1. Recall that panel (a) in Figure 9.4 showed rejection rates for the standard t-test that are almost 10 times larger than 0.05 (which was the chosen significance level). The column labelled No cointegration (*rank* = 0) in Table 10.1 shows that the rejection rates for the ECM test of no cointegration are very close to 0.05. Hence, the use of the ECM test of the null hypothesis of no cointegration does resolve the spurious regression problem. We see that the

Table 10.1. Monte Carlo simulated rejection rates for the ECM test (t_π^{ECM}) in the case of no cointegration (rank = 0) and cointegration (rank = 1); 5% significance levels. In the rank = 0 case, the DGP is the same as in Example 9.1. In the rank = 1 case, the DGPs have $\mathrm{Cov}(\epsilon_{At}, \epsilon_{Bt}) = 0.2$ and $\sigma_A^2 = \sigma_B^2 = 0.01$. λ_1 and λ_2 denote the eigenvalues of the autoregressive matrix. The rejection rates are the averages of 1000 simulations.

		Cointegration (rank = 1)	
T	No cointegration (rank = 0)	$\lambda_1 = 1, \lambda_2 = 0.95$	$\lambda_1 = 1, \lambda_2 = 0.7$
25	0.05	0.087	0.312
50	0.053	0.462	0.862
75	0.049	0.795	0.994
100	0.040	0.985	1
150	0.042	1	1
200	0.048	1	1

Type-I error probabilities are close to the chosen nominal significance level for all the sample sizes included in the table.

The two other columns in the table show rejection rates in cases where the null hypothesis of no cointegration is not true. Hence, in these columns, we expect to see rates that are larger than 0.05, i.e., if the ECM test has statistical power. In the first of these cases, the cointegration in the DGP is relatively weak in the sense that the stable root is large, i.e., $\lambda_2 = 0.95$. We see that the ECM test has power for this DGP, as the rejection rates are above 0.05 for quite moderate sample sizes. It is also increasing in the sample size, and the statistical power is near full for a sample with 100 observations. The third column with rejection rates shows the second case with stronger cointegration in the DGP, i.e., $\lambda_2 = 0.7$. In this experiment, the test has full power already for $T = 75$, and has high power also for smaller sample sizes.

10.5. Multiple Equation Cointegration

Often, the research purpose leads us to the formulation of VARs that can theoretically contain more than one cointegration vector. In such situations, even though the cointegration rank is always identified, the cointegration vectors may not be identified. As we shall see, identification of cointegration vectors raises the same type of logical problem as the identification of equations in a SEM. For that reason, the practical way to "check identification" is to apply the rank and order conditions that we presented in Chapter 7. In the subsequent sections, we present a maximum likelihood-based method that gives a practical method of estimating cointegration rank in a way that is statistically consistent and efficient.

10.5.1. Identification

As we have seen, when $\text{rank}(\mathbf{\Pi}) = 1$, the cointegration vector is unique (subject only to normalization). Hence, if $n = 2$, cointegration implies $\text{rank}(\mathbf{\Pi}) = 1$, and there is one cointegration vector:

$$(\beta_{11},\ \beta_{12})',$$

which is uniquely identified after normalization. For example with $\beta_{11} = -1$, the unique ECM variable becomes

$$\text{ecm}_{1t} = -Y_{1t} + \beta_{12}Y_{2t} \sim I(0).$$

However, when $n > 2$, we can have rank($\mathbf{\Pi}$) > 1, and in these cases the cointegrating vectors are not automatically identified. To see this, we can assume that $\mathbf{\Pi}$ is known (in practice, consistently estimated), and that $\boldsymbol{\beta}$ is an $n \times r$ cointegrating matrix:

$$\mathbf{\Pi} = \boldsymbol{\alpha\beta}'.$$

However, for an $r \times r$ non-singular matrix $\mathbf{\Theta}$:

$$\mathbf{\Pi} = \boldsymbol{\alpha}\mathbf{\Theta}\mathbf{\Theta}^{-1}\boldsymbol{\beta}' = \boldsymbol{\alpha}_{\Theta}\boldsymbol{\beta}'_{\Theta},$$

showing that $\boldsymbol{\beta}'_{\Theta}$ is also a matrix with cointegrating vectors. This identification problem is equivalent to the identification problem of simultaneous equation models (SEMs) that we know from the stationary case (see Hsiao, 1997a). Assume, for example, that rank($\mathbf{\Pi}$) $= 2$ for an $n = 3$ VAR, which we can express as

$$-Y_{1t} + \beta_{12}Y_{2t} + \beta_{13}Y_{3t} = \text{ecm}_{1t},$$

$$\beta_{21}Y_{1t} - Y_{2t} + \beta_{13}Y_{3t} = \text{ecm}_{2t},$$

where $\text{ecm}_{it} \sim I(0)$, $i = 1, 2$. By simply viewing these as a pair of simultaneous equations, we see that they are not identified on the order condition. Exact identification requires one linear restriction on each of the equations. For example, $\beta_{13} = 0$ and $\beta_{21} + \beta_{13} = 0$ give exact identification. The inclusion of non-modelled (exogenous) variables in the cointegration relationship does not change anything: the identification problem is still analogous to the SEM case.

Hence, we are reminded that the identification of parameters of systems of equations is a logical property which cannot be resolved from the data alone, or by the use of statistics only. Economic theory often comes in as a necessary ingredient in the discussion about identification. It is worth keeping this in mind when we next turn to a statistical method for estimating (any) cointegrating rank consistently. The statistical method gives identification of that rank, but does not by itself alone give identification of the coefficients of multiple cointegration vectors.

10.5.2. Maximum likelihood estimation of cointegration rank

We now consider the general case where the vector $\boldsymbol{y}_t$ consists of n variables. Without loss of generality, we consider the case with first-order dynamics, and hence the Gaussian VAR(1) can be written as

$$\Delta \boldsymbol{y}_t = \boldsymbol{\Pi} \boldsymbol{y}_{t-1} + \varepsilon_t, \tag{10.56}$$

$$\varepsilon_t \sim \text{IIN}(\mathbf{0}, \boldsymbol{\Sigma}). \tag{10.57}$$

We can abstract from higher order dynamics since we can always regress $\Delta \boldsymbol{y}_t$ and $\boldsymbol{y}_{t-1}$ on $\Delta \boldsymbol{y}_{t-1}, \ldots, \Delta \boldsymbol{y}_{t-(p-1)}$, and then form residual vectors that can be written as a VAR(1). This is (yet) another example of the usefulness of the Frisch–Waugh theorem.

We are interested in both the cointegrating case:

$$0 < \text{rank}(\boldsymbol{\Pi}) < n, \tag{10.58}$$

and the case with no cointegration:

$$\text{rank}(\boldsymbol{\Pi}) = 0. \tag{10.59}$$

As we have seen, rank($\boldsymbol{\Pi}$) is given by the number of non-zero eigenvalues of $\boldsymbol{\Pi}$. But can we decide from data the number of eigenvalues that are significantly different from zero? Fortunately, this problem has a solution. An eigenvalue of $\boldsymbol{\Pi}$ is a special kind of squared correlation coefficient, known as a canonical correlation coefficient in multivariate statistics, Anderson (2003, Chapter 12).

The modern development of this approach is to a large extent due to the Danish statistician Søren Johansen, and is therefore often called the Johansen method (to cointegration). Two main references are therefore Johansen (1991, 1995), but see also Davidson (2000, Chapter 16), Burke and Hunter (2005), Juselius (2007), Banerjee *et al.* (1993, Section 8.2), Pesaran (2015, Sections 22.6–22.7) among others.

The log-likelihood function can be written as

$$\mathcal{L}(\boldsymbol{\Pi}, \boldsymbol{\Sigma}) = -\frac{Tn}{2} \ln(2\pi) - \frac{T}{2} \ln |\boldsymbol{\Sigma}| - \frac{1}{2} \sum_{t=1}^{T} \varepsilon_t' \boldsymbol{\Sigma}^{-1} \varepsilon_t, \tag{10.60}$$

where the conditioning on $\mathbf{y}_0$ has been suppressed in the notation to save space.

Equation (10.60) is the multivariate counterpart to expression (4.52) for the log-likelihood function of the AR(1) model in Section 4.6.3. In particular, the first term is a constant term, since π in this context denotes the number 3.14159.

As usual, when faced with a difficult problem like the maximization of (10.60), we can seek a solution by breaking the big problem up into smaller ones. Specifically, if we manage to maximize the second expression in (10.60) under the restrictions represented by $\boldsymbol{\alpha\beta}'$, we can see ourselves as maximizing the last term in the expression in a last step that makes use of residuals in the usual way.

Hence, we focus on the second term in (10.60). Insertion from (10.56) allows us to define the (partial) log-likelihood function $\mathcal{L}^c(\mathbf{\Pi})$:

$$\mathcal{L}^c(\mathbf{\Pi}) = -\frac{T}{2}\ln\left|\frac{1}{T}\sum_{t=1}^{T}(\Delta\mathbf{y}_t - \mathbf{\Pi}\mathbf{y}_{t-1})(\Delta\mathbf{y}_t - \mathbf{\Pi}\mathbf{y}_{t-1})'\right|. \qquad (10.61)$$

If $\mathbf{\Pi}$ was unrestricted, a conventional regression estimator would result. However, we are now interested in the solution that results when the restriction $\mathbf{\Pi} = \boldsymbol{\alpha\beta}'$ is imposed. The expression that we seek to maximize with respect to $\boldsymbol{\alpha}$ and $\boldsymbol{\beta}$ is therefore

$$\mathcal{L}^c(\boldsymbol{\alpha},\boldsymbol{\beta}) = -\frac{T}{2}\ln\left|\frac{1}{T}\sum_{t=1}^{T}(\Delta\mathbf{y}_t - \boldsymbol{\alpha\beta}'\mathbf{y}_{t-1})(\Delta\mathbf{y}_t - \boldsymbol{\alpha\beta}'\mathbf{y}_{t-1})'\right|. \qquad (10.62)$$

The expression inside the determinant can be written as

$$\underbrace{\frac{1}{T}\sum_{t=1}^{T}\Delta\mathbf{y}_t\Delta\mathbf{y}_t'}_{\mathbf{S}_{00}} + \boldsymbol{\alpha\beta}'\underbrace{\frac{1}{T}\sum_{t=1}^{T}\mathbf{y}_{t-1}\mathbf{y}_{t-1}'}_{\mathbf{S}_{11}}(\boldsymbol{\alpha\beta}')'$$
$$-\boldsymbol{\alpha\beta}'\underbrace{\frac{1}{T}\sum_{t=1}^{T}\mathbf{y}_{t-1}\Delta\mathbf{y}_{t-1}'}_{\mathbf{S}_{10}} - \underbrace{\frac{1}{T}\sum_{t=1}^{T}\Delta\mathbf{y}_{t-1}\mathbf{y}_{t-1}'}_{\mathbf{S}_{01}}(\boldsymbol{\alpha\beta}')'$$

giving the "partial" log-likelihood function as

$$\mathcal{L}^c(\boldsymbol{\alpha},\boldsymbol{\beta}) = -\frac{T}{2}\ln\left|\mathbf{S}_{00} + \boldsymbol{\alpha\beta}'\mathbf{S}_{11}\boldsymbol{\beta\alpha}' - \boldsymbol{\alpha\beta}'\mathbf{S}_{10} - \mathbf{S}_{01}\boldsymbol{\beta\alpha}'\right|. \qquad (10.63)$$

If we consider $\boldsymbol{\beta}$ as a fixed matrix, we find $\boldsymbol{\alpha}(\boldsymbol{\beta})$ from the first-order condition:

$$\frac{\partial L^c(\boldsymbol{\alpha},\boldsymbol{\beta})}{\partial\boldsymbol{\alpha}} = 0,$$

which implies (see Exercise 10.5)

$$\boldsymbol{\alpha}(\boldsymbol{\beta}) = \mathbf{S}_{01}\boldsymbol{\beta}(\boldsymbol{\beta}'\mathbf{S}_{11}\boldsymbol{\beta})^{-1}. \qquad (10.64)$$

We can see that behind the notational veil, this is an OLS expression. Substitution in L^c gives a new log-likelihood function

$$\mathcal{L}^{cc}(\boldsymbol{\beta}) = -\frac{T}{2}\ln|\mathbf{S}_{00}-\mathbf{S}_{01}\boldsymbol{\beta}(\boldsymbol{\beta}'\mathbf{S}_{11}\boldsymbol{\beta})^{-1}\boldsymbol{\beta}'\mathbf{S}_{10}|. \tag{10.65}$$

By defining

$$\boldsymbol{\Psi}(\boldsymbol{\beta}) = |\mathbf{S}_{00}-\mathbf{S}_{01}\boldsymbol{\beta}(\boldsymbol{\beta}'\mathbf{S}_{11}\boldsymbol{\beta})^{-1}\boldsymbol{\beta}'\mathbf{S}_{10}|, \tag{10.66}$$

we can seek $\boldsymbol{\beta}$ which minimizes $\boldsymbol{\Psi}(\boldsymbol{\beta})$, and which therefore maximizes the log-likelihood function $\mathcal{L}^{cc}(\boldsymbol{\beta})$.

We are now at the heart of the matter, and we can see that it is not straightforward to work out the first-order conditions. However, we can use a trick. The determinant of a 2×2-matrix can be written as

$$\begin{vmatrix} a & b \\ c & d \end{vmatrix} = ad - bc = \begin{cases} d(a-bd^{-1}c), \\ a(d-ba^{-1}c), \end{cases}$$

and the same can be done for partitioned matrices. By choosing suitable definitions for a, b, c and d, we can formulate the determinant:

$$\begin{vmatrix} \mathbf{S}_{00} & \mathbf{S}_{01}\boldsymbol{\beta} \\ \boldsymbol{\beta}'\mathbf{S}_{10} & \boldsymbol{\beta}'\mathbf{S}_{11}\boldsymbol{\beta} \end{vmatrix} = \begin{cases} \boldsymbol{\Psi}(\boldsymbol{\beta})\cdot|\boldsymbol{\beta}'\mathbf{S}_{11}\boldsymbol{\beta}|, \\ |\mathbf{S}_{00}||\boldsymbol{\beta}'\mathbf{S}_{11}\boldsymbol{\beta}-\mathbf{S}_{01}\boldsymbol{\beta}\mathbf{S}_{00}^{-1}\boldsymbol{\beta}'\mathbf{S}_{10}|. \end{cases} \tag{10.67}$$

Note that we have a formulation where $b = c'$, which allows us to write

$$\mathbf{S}_{01}\boldsymbol{\beta}\mathbf{S}_{00}^{-1}\boldsymbol{\beta}'\mathbf{S}_{10} = \boldsymbol{\beta}'\mathbf{S}_{10}\mathbf{S}_{00}^{-1}\mathbf{S}_{01}\boldsymbol{\beta},$$

and use the equivalence of the two determinant expressions on the right-hand side of (10.67) to obtain

$$\frac{\boldsymbol{\Psi}(\boldsymbol{\beta})}{|\mathbf{S}_{00}|} = |\boldsymbol{\beta}'\mathbf{S}_{11}\boldsymbol{\beta}|^{-1}|\boldsymbol{\beta}'\mathbf{S}_{11}\boldsymbol{\beta}-\boldsymbol{\beta}'\mathbf{S}_{10}\mathbf{S}_{00}^{-1}\mathbf{S}_{01}\boldsymbol{\beta}|. \tag{10.68}$$

Since $\mathbf{S}_{00}$ is independent of $\boldsymbol{\beta}$, minimization of $\boldsymbol{\Psi}(\boldsymbol{\beta})$ is equivalent to minimization of

$$\frac{|\boldsymbol{\beta}'\mathbf{S}_{11}\boldsymbol{\beta}-\boldsymbol{\beta}'\mathbf{S}_{10}\mathbf{S}_{00}^{-1}\mathbf{S}_{01}\boldsymbol{\beta}|}{|\boldsymbol{\beta}'\mathbf{S}_{11}\boldsymbol{\beta}|}.$$

This problem has a solution in multivariate statistical analysis, which is to estimate the columns of $\boldsymbol{\beta}$ by the eigenvectors that correspond to the r largest eigenvalues $\rho_1 \geq \rho_2 \geq \cdots \geq \rho_r \geq \cdots \geq \rho_n \geq 0$ in the (generalized) eigenvalue problem:

$$|\rho \boldsymbol{S}_{11} - \boldsymbol{S}_{10}\boldsymbol{S}_{00}^{-1}\boldsymbol{S}_{01}| = 0 \tag{10.69}$$

(see Johansen, 1995, Section 6.1). The complete set of eigenvalues is

$$[\rho_i \mathbf{S}_{11} - \mathbf{S}_{10}\mathbf{S}_{00}^{-1}\mathbf{S}_{01}]\mathbf{v}_i = \mathbf{0}, \quad i = 1, 2, \ldots, n, \tag{10.70}$$

and the matrix $\mathbf{V}$ which has the $\mathbf{v}_i$ vectors as columns satisfies the normalization

$$\mathbf{V}'\mathbf{S}_{11}\mathbf{V} = \mathbf{I}_{n \times n}, \tag{10.71}$$

by virtue of being so-called *canonical variates* (i.e., variables).

Finally, we can define a selection matrix $\boldsymbol{\Lambda}' = [\mathbf{I}_{r\times r}, \mathbf{0}']$ that collects the relevant eigenvectors:

$$\hat{\boldsymbol{\beta}} = \mathbf{V}\boldsymbol{\Lambda}, \tag{10.72}$$

where

$$\hat{\boldsymbol{\beta}}'\mathbf{S}_{11}\hat{\boldsymbol{\beta}} = \mathbf{I}_{r \times r}. \tag{10.73}$$

The normalization in (10.73) is convenient from a mathematical point of view, and it has the advantage that such normalizations can be made (e.g., in a computer program) without assuming anything about which variables cointegrate, i.e., without normalizing $\boldsymbol{\beta}$ (Johansen, 1995, p. 94). That (hopefully economically meaningful) normalization can be done as part of the discussion about identification *after* the cointegration rank has been decided.

The MLE of $\boldsymbol{\alpha}$ is obtained by substitution in (10.64). Because of the normalization in (10.73), the expression for $\hat{\boldsymbol{\alpha}}$ simplifies to

$$\hat{\boldsymbol{\alpha}} = \mathbf{S}_{01}\hat{\boldsymbol{\beta}}. \tag{10.74}$$

Mathematically, the r vectors of the $\hat{\boldsymbol{\beta}}$ matrix (10.72) span the cointegration space. In the case of $r > 1$, the cointegrating vectors in $\boldsymbol{\beta}$ are, however, subject to further inspection for identification, as discussed above. It follows from (10.73) that

$$\hat{\boldsymbol{\beta}}'\frac{1}{T}\sum_{t=1}^{T}\mathbf{y}_{t-1}\mathbf{y}_{t-1}'\hat{\boldsymbol{\beta}} = \frac{1}{T}\sum_{t=1}^{T}\hat{\boldsymbol{\beta}}'\mathbf{y}_{t-1}\mathbf{y}_{t-1}'\hat{\boldsymbol{\beta}} = \mathbf{I}_{r\times r},$$

which shows that the equilibrium correction terms, which are $I(0)$, have unit variance, and that they are mutually orthogonal variables. However, this is a technical normalization, which does not change the above conclusion about underidentification when $r > 1$. What Johansen's method gives us is a statistical method for the identification of the size of the cointegration space. Identification of the individual vectors is a logical property of the theoretical multiple long-run equation model.

10.5.3. Canonical correlation analysis

For some readers, it can aid the understanding of the Johansen method to spend some time to study canonical correlations and canonical variates (i.e., variables); see Dhrymes (1974, Section 2.1), Krzanowski (1988, Section 14.5), or the complete, and more demanding, exposition in Anderson (2003, Chapter 12). We start by collecting the T observations of $\Delta\mathbf{y}_t$ and $\mathbf{y}_{t-1}$ in a $2n \times T$ matrix $\mathbf{X}$:

$$\mathbf{X}_{2n\times T} = \begin{pmatrix} \mathbf{X}_0 \\ \mathbf{X}_1 \end{pmatrix}, \tag{10.75}$$

where $\mathbf{X}_0$ holds the observations of the differenced data, and the levels are in $\mathbf{X}_1$. Assume that we want to reduce the dimension by finding the two linear combinations of $\Delta\mathbf{y}_t$ and $\mathbf{y}_{t-1}$ that have the highest correlation among all possible pairs of linear combinations. For this purpose, we define two new variables:

$$\mathbf{u} = \mathbf{a}'\mathbf{X}_0, \tag{10.76}$$

and

$$\mathbf{z} = \mathbf{b}'\mathbf{X}_1, \tag{10.77}$$

where $\mathbf{a}$ and $\mathbf{b}$ are $1 \times n$. By using the definitions of variance and covariance of linear combinations, we obtain

$$\mathrm{Cov}(\mathbf{u}, \mathbf{z}) = \mathbf{a}'\mathbf{S}_{01}\mathbf{b} = \mathrm{Cov}(\mathbf{z}, \mathbf{u}) = \mathbf{b}'\mathbf{S}_{10}\mathbf{a}, \tag{10.78}$$

$$\mathrm{Var}(\mathbf{u}) = E(\mathbf{u}'\mathbf{u}) = \mathbf{a}'\mathbf{S}_{00}\mathbf{a}$$

and

$$\mathrm{Var}(\mathbf{z}) = E(\mathbf{z}'\mathbf{z}) = \mathbf{b}'\mathbf{S}_{11}\mathbf{b}. \tag{10.79}$$

We define the first pair of canonical variates as the $\hat{\mathbf{u}}_1$ and $\hat{\mathbf{z}}_1$ which has variance equal to 1 and which maximizes $\mathrm{Corr}(\mathbf{u}, \mathbf{z})$. We can formalize this as a Lagrange problem. Choose $\mathbf{a}$ and $\mathbf{b}$ such that the function

$$L = \mathbf{a}'\mathbf{S}_{01}\mathbf{b} - l_1(\mathbf{a}'\mathbf{S}_{00}\mathbf{a} - 1) - l_2(\mathbf{b}'\mathbf{S}_{11}\mathbf{b} - 1) \tag{10.80}$$

is maximized (l_1 and l_2 denote Lagrange multipliers). The first-order conditions are

$$\mathbf{S}_{01}\mathbf{b} - 2l_1\mathbf{S}_{00}\mathbf{a} = \mathbf{0}, \tag{10.81}$$

$$\mathbf{S}_{10}\mathbf{a} - 2l_2\mathbf{S}_{11}\mathbf{b} = \mathbf{0}. \tag{10.82}$$

Premultiplication by $\mathbf{a}'$ in (10.81), and by $\mathbf{b}'$ in (10.82) gives

$$\mathbf{a}'\mathbf{S}_{01}\mathbf{b} = 2l_1,$$

$$\mathbf{b}'\mathbf{S}_{10}\mathbf{a} = 2l_2,$$

since the variances are 1. Then,

$$\mathbf{a}'\mathbf{S}_{01}\mathbf{b} = \mathbf{b}'\mathbf{S}_{10}\mathbf{a} = \mathrm{Corr}(\mathbf{u}, \mathbf{z}) \equiv R,$$

a correlation coefficient between the $\mathbf{u}$ and $\mathbf{z}$ variables. Hence, we have

$$\mathbf{a}'\mathbf{S}_{01}\mathbf{b} = R = 2l_1 = 2l_2,$$

and (10.81) and (10.82) can be expressed as

$$\mathbf{S}_{01}\mathbf{b} = R\mathbf{S}_{00}\mathbf{a}, \tag{10.83}$$

$$\mathbf{S}_{10}\mathbf{a} = R\mathbf{S}_{11}\mathbf{b}. \tag{10.84}$$

By normalizing (10.83) on $\mathbf{a}$,

$$\mathbf{a} = \frac{1}{R}\mathbf{S}_{00}^{-1}\mathbf{S}_{01}\mathbf{b}, \tag{10.85}$$

and substituting in (10.84), we obtain

$$\left[\mathbf{S}_{10}\mathbf{S}_{00}^{-1}\mathbf{S}_{01} - R^2\mathbf{S}_{11}\right]\mathbf{b} = \mathbf{0}. \tag{10.86}$$

The converse normalization gives

$$\mathbf{b} = \frac{1}{R}\mathbf{S}_{11}^{-1}\mathbf{S}_{10}\mathbf{a},$$

and

$$[\mathbf{S}_{01}\mathbf{S}_{11}^{-1}\mathbf{S}_{10} - R^2\mathbf{S}_{00}]\mathbf{a} = \mathbf{0}. \tag{10.87}$$

Hence, R^2 can be uniquely determined from

$$|\mathbf{S}_{10}\mathbf{S}_{00}^{-1}\mathbf{S}_{01} - R^2\mathbf{S}_{11}| = |\mathbf{S}_{11}^{-1}\mathbf{S}_{10}\mathbf{S}_{00}^{-1}\mathbf{S}_{01} - R^2\mathbf{I}_{nxn}| = 0, \qquad (10.88)$$

i.e., R^2 is the eigenvalue of the matrix $\mathbf{S}_{11}^{-1}\mathbf{S}_{10}\mathbf{S}_{00}^{-1}\mathbf{S}_{01}$ (or $\mathbf{S}_{00}^{-1}\mathbf{S}_{01}\mathbf{S}_{11}^{-1}\mathbf{S}_{10}$). Given that result, the eigenvector $\mathbf{b}$ is determined by (10.86).

The matrix $\mathbf{S}_{11}^{-1}\mathbf{S}_{10}\mathbf{S}_{00}^{-1}\mathbf{S}_{01}$ has n eigenvalues, but since $R = \mathbf{a}'\mathbf{S}_{01}\mathbf{b}$ is the expression that we want to maximize, the solution is to choose the largest eigenvalue, R_1^2, and the associated eigenvectors $\mathbf{b}_1$ and $\mathbf{a}_1$. The two first canonical variates are therefore

$$\mathbf{u}_1 = \mathbf{a}_1'\mathbf{X}_0, \qquad (10.89)$$

$$\mathbf{z}_1 = \mathbf{b}_1'\mathbf{X}_1, \qquad (10.90)$$

and are characterized by

$$\text{Corr}(\mathbf{u}_1,\mathbf{z}_1) \equiv R_1.$$

R_1 is called the first canonical correlation coefficient. The remaining $n-1$ pairs with canonical variates are defined in the same way as the first pair, and can be ordered by the size of their respective eigenvalues (i.e., squared canonical correlation coefficients, R_i^2).

10.5.4. Canonical correlations and MLE

The eigenvalue problem (10.88) is the same problem that the maximum likelihood approach led us to consider, and which is given by (10.69) above (i.e., multiply both sides of (10.69) by -1). It follows that the estimators of ρ_i ($i = 1, 2, \ldots, n$) required in the MLE can be defined as

$$\hat{\rho}_i \equiv R_i^2, \quad i = 1, 2, \ldots, n,$$

where R_i ($i = 1, 2, \ldots, n$) are the canonical correlation coefficients that we have defined above. Hence, if we have a method for doing valid statistical testing of a null hypothesis like H_0: $\rho_i = 0$, based on R_i^2, the logical next step would be to decide the dimension of $\mathbf{\Lambda}$ in (10.72) by the number r for which the null hypothesis can be rejected:

$$\hat{\boldsymbol{\beta}} \equiv [\mathbf{b}_1, \mathbf{b}_2, \ldots, \mathbf{b}_r] = [\mathbf{b}_1, \mathbf{b}_2, \ldots, \mathbf{b}_r, \ldots, \mathbf{b}_n]\mathbf{\Lambda} \equiv \mathbf{V}\mathbf{\Lambda},$$

and finally

$$\mathbf{V}'\mathbf{S}_{11}\mathbf{V} = \mathbf{I}_{n\times n} \quad \text{and} \quad \hat{\boldsymbol{\beta}}'\mathbf{S}_{11}\hat{\boldsymbol{\beta}} = \mathbf{I}_{r\times r},$$

because (10.71) and (10.73) hold for canonical variables that are uncorrelated and have unit variance.

Canonical correlation analysis is not limited to the case where there are the same number of variables in the two groups $\mathbf{X}_0$ and $\mathbf{X}_1$. If there are n_1 variables in $\mathbf{X}_0$ and n variables in $\mathbf{X}_1$, the maximum number of eigenvalues becomes $\min\{n_1, n\}$. To be more concrete, we can imagine that we have a VAR-EX and that the lagged levels of the n_2 non-modelled $I(1)$-variables are included in the $\mathbf{X}_1$ matrix. Hence, $n_1 < n \equiv n_1 + n_2$ and the maximal number of cointegration vectors is therefore given by n_1. This corresponds to the case where the $\mathbf{\Pi}$ matrix may have full rank, as noted above.

Before we turn to how we can test hypothesis about the number of non-zero canonical correlations, we note that the empirical canonical correlations can be interpreted as generalizations of usual correlations coefficients.

In the case of $n_1 = 1$ and $n > 1$, there is one squared canonical correlation coefficient, which is identical to the ordinary multiple correlation coefficient in a regression between the (single) differenced endogenous variable and all the lagged levels variables.

However, with $n_1 > 1$, the largest R_1^2 may be larger than the R-squared of any of the single equation regressions. The intuition is that there may be more than one variable that equilibrium corrects, i.e., adjusts with respect to past disequilibria. This information, about multivariate adjustment, is not taken into account by single equation models, and is related to the inefficiency of the ECM estimator of $\boldsymbol{\beta}$ when weak exogeneity with respect to the cointegration parameters does not hold, see Section 10.2.2.

10.5.5. Inference about cointegration rank

Abstracting from additive constants, the maximized likelihood is

$$\mathcal{L}^* = -\frac{T}{2} \ln |\hat{\boldsymbol{\beta}}'(\mathbf{S}_{11} - \mathbf{S}_{10}\mathbf{S}_{00}^{-1}\mathbf{S}_{01})\hat{\boldsymbol{\beta}}|, \tag{10.91}$$

where we have dropped the superscripts used above to indicate concentrated likelihood. By using (once again)

$$\hat{\boldsymbol{\beta}}'\mathbf{S}_{11}\hat{\boldsymbol{\beta}} = \mathbf{I}_{r\times r},$$

and

$$\hat{\boldsymbol{\beta}}(\boldsymbol{S}_{10}\boldsymbol{S}_{00}^{-1}\boldsymbol{S}_{01})\hat{\boldsymbol{\beta}} = \boldsymbol{\rho}_{rxr},$$

where $\boldsymbol{\rho}_{rxr}$ is the diagonal matrix with the eigenvalues of $\boldsymbol{S}_{10}\boldsymbol{S}_{00}^{-1}\boldsymbol{S}_{01}$, we can reexpress (10.91) as

$$\begin{aligned}\mathcal{L}^* &= -\frac{T}{2}\ln\left|\mathbf{I}_{r\times r} - \hat{\boldsymbol{\rho}}_{rxr}\right| \qquad (10.92)\\ &= -\frac{T}{2}\sum_{i=1}^{r}\ln(1-\hat{\rho}_i).\end{aligned}$$

When $\boldsymbol{\Pi}$ is estimated without restrictions, we have

$$\mathcal{L}^{**} = -\frac{T}{2}\sum_{i=1}^{n}\ln(1-\hat{\rho}_i). \qquad (10.93)$$

The likelihood ratio test of the hypothesis that there are at most r cointegrating vectors $0 \leq r < n$, and $n - r$ unit-roots becomes

$$\begin{aligned}\eta_r &= 2(\mathcal{L}^{**} - \mathcal{L}^*)\\ &= -T\sum_{i=r+1}^{n}\ln(1-\hat{\rho}_i), \quad r = 0, 1, 2, \ldots, n-1, \qquad (10.94)\end{aligned}$$

and is called the *Trace test* (or Trace statistic) (Johansen, 1995, Section 6.1).

The testing is sequential and begins by testing the null hypothesis of $r = 0$ against the alternative of $r > 0$ by using the available critical values from the distribution of η_0 (under the null of no cointegration). Intuitively, for the null hypothesis $r = 0$ to be rejected, the largest eigenvalue (a squared correlation coefficient) must be of some magnitude, otherwise η_0 will be too close to zero to allow rejection at conventional significance levels. However, if the largest correlation coefficient and the first trace test value are large enough to allow rejection of the first H_0, we proceed to the next test situation, which is the null hypothesis of $r = 1$ against the alternative of $r > 1$ by the use of a critical value for η_1. We continue in this way until the conclusion about non-rejection is reached. If, for example, η_1 is the last significant value of the trace statistic, the conclusion is that there are two cointegrating vectors. Hence, more generally, we conclude by finding $r + 1$ cointegrating vectors if the last significant test value is for η_r $(r = 0, 1, 2, \ldots, n-1)$.

If the test situation is formulated in such a way that the null hypothesis is that the number of cointegration vectors is a specific number, and the alternative is that there is one more of such vectors, the *Max-eigenvalue test* can be used:

$$\zeta_r = -T\ln(1-\hat{\rho}_{r+1}), \quad r = 0, 1, 2, \ldots, n-1. \qquad (10.95)$$

However, it is the trace test which has become the preferred test to use for testing the cointegration rank.

In the same way as for the Dickey–Fuller tests, the EG test and the ECM test above, the trace statistic η_r is a function of Wiener-processes, and it is not Chi-square distributed asymptotically. Another complication that the trace statistic has in common with the Dickey–Fuller statistic is that the asymptotic distribution depends on which deterministic terms are included in the VAR. As noted in Section 10.2.4, whether the constant term is restricted to be in the cointegration space or not also plays a role. For these reasons, there are several tables with asymptotic critical values for the different deterministic augmentations of the VAR (see, e.g., Juselius, 2007, Appendix A).

The point that a deterministic trend affects the asymptotic critical values of the trace test tables inference extends to dummy variables (Johansen *et al.*, 2000; Doornik *et al.*, 1998; Juselius, 2007, Section 8.3). The inclusion of step indicator variables, e.g., $(\ldots 0, 0, 0, 1, 1, 1, \ldots)$, is the most consequential case. Intuitively, this is because a step dummy integrates to become a broken linear trend under the null of no cointegration. In applications with such variables in the VAR (restricted or unrestricted), formally correct inference about cointegration rank may require simulation critical values for each individual case. Indicator variables that do not integrate to (broken) trend, e.g., $(\ldots 0, 0, 0, 1, 0, -1, 0, \ldots)$ are, however, not likely to influence the asymptotic critical values of the trace test.

The number of tables is further increased because the distributions of the trace statistics are affected if we condition on non-modelled $I(1)$ variables, i.e., when the determination of cointegration rank is done in an open system (VAR-EX), (see Harbo *et al.*, 1998). Consolidated sets of tables are available in, e.g., Pesaran *et al.* (2000), Doornik (2003) (based on Doornik (1998)). In practice, the inference can be aided by the use of software programs that report p-values for the main formulations of the VAR, see e.g., Doornik and Hendry (2013c).

One issue which often comes up in practice is how one should treat non-modelled levels variables, that are stationary if it had not been for deterministic location shift, and which are economically meaningful to include in long-run relationships of the model. One example is wage and price modelling, where the rate of unemployment is conditioned on, and it makes economic sense to include it in a long-run wage curve; see Bårdsen and Nymoen (2003) and Bårdsen *et al.* (2005, Section 5.4) among others.

If such a variable is clearly without a unit-root, a pragmatic method is to include it in the short-run dynamics (together with the differences of the $I(1)$ variables), and hence to omit it from the part of the model that determines which critical values are used to determine the cointegration rank. After the rank has been decided, and the system has been reduced from $I(1)$ space to $I(0)$ space, the modelling can continue within the framework of the CVAR, and the variable can be included in the long-run relationships. Another more formally correct method is to include the cumulated sum of the $I(0)$-variable together with the $I(1)$ variables; see Seo (1998) and Rahbek and Mosconi (1999).

Finally, after all the complications that needs attention, it may be encouraging to be reminded that another generalization that we will usually need in practice, namely, from VAR(1) to VAR(p), poses no new problems for the asymptotic inference. As noted above, this is because a VAR(p) can be reexpressed as a VAR(1). With reference to the Frisch–Waugh theorem, we "regress out" the effect of the $p-1$ differences from $\Delta\mathbf{y}_t$ and $\mathbf{y}_{t-1}$ and apply the trace test to the OLS residuals.[3]

10.5.6. Examples of rank determination

To illustrate the Johansen testing and estimation procedure, we look at the two cointegrated datasets generated by the DGPs that were used in Table 10.1.

We first consider the case where the stable root of the companion matrix (i.e., the autoregressive matrix in this first-order case) is $\lambda_2 = 0.7$. Using a sample from period 2 to 101 ($T = 100$) to estimate a first-order VAR for YA_t and YB_t, the largest canonical correlation (ρ_1) is estimated to be 0.28, and the second (ρ_2) is estimated to be 0.02. The estimates are shown in Table 10.2 together with the corresponding values of the trace test. Using the formula above, it is easy to check the values of the trace test in the table:

$$\eta_0 = -100(\ln(1 - 0.28271) + \ln(1 - 0.014840)) = 34.723,$$

$$\eta_1 = -100(\ln(1 - 0.014840)) = 1.4951.$$

[3] As noted above, this can be formalized as another step in the concentration of the likelihood function of the VAR.

Table 10.2. Eigenvalues and trace tests for a VAR(1) with the two variables $(\text{YA}_t, \text{YB}_t)$, generated by the DGP with $\lambda_1 = 1$, $\lambda_2 = 0.7$ in Table 10.1. $T = 100$.

Eigenvalues (sq. correlations)		Trace test		
		H_0: rank $= r$	η_r	p-value
ρ_1	0.28271	0	34.722	0.000
ρ_2	0.014840	1	1.4951	0.221

Note: p-value based on unrestricted constant.

Table 10.3. Eigenvalues and trace tests for a VAR(1) in the two variables $(\text{YA}_t, \text{YB}_t)$, generated by the DGP with $\lambda_1 = 1$, $\lambda_2 = 0.95$ in Table 10.1. $T = 100$.

Eigenvalues (sq. correlations)		Trace test		
		H_0: rank $= r$	η_r	p-value
ρ_1	0.50040	0	70.095	0.000
ρ_2	0.0069670	1	0.6991	0.040

Note: p-value based on unrestricted constant

The value of η_0 value is large enough to clearly reject H_0: rank $= 0$. However, the value of η_1 does not allow H_0: rank $= 1$ to be rejected at the 5% or 10% levels, and the conclusion of the test is therefore that the rank is decided to be one.

We can also illustrate the rank determination procedure for the dataset generated by the DGP with $\lambda_2 = 0.95$ (see Table 10.3). It may be surprising that the canonical correlation is even higher for this dataset, which we characterized as weakly correlated above, with reference to stable root being so close to one. The reason is that the trace test is not necessarily a declining function of the stable root. Exercise 10.6 invites you to calculate the trace tests for this case.

In the same way as for many of the other tests of cointegration reviewed in this chapter, the distributions of the test statistics are asymptotic. To secure a test with a correct size (i.e., correct Type-I error probability), one can apply a small sample of Bartlett corrections, developed in Johansen (2002).[4] For small to moderate long samples (e.g., 50–60 observations), the corrections can become quite large.

[4]This method has been implemented in CATS, Dennis *et al.* (2006), and has also become part of OxMetrics 8.

10.5.7. Reduction to $I(0)$-system

We continue with the example (i.e., with $\lambda_1 = 1$, $\lambda_2 = 0.95$): Having decided the cointegration rank to be one, we can estimate the cointegrated VAR (subject to $r = 1$ being true) to obtain

$$\hat{\mathbf{\Pi}} = \hat{\boldsymbol{\alpha}}\hat{\boldsymbol{\beta}}' = \begin{pmatrix} -0.050319 \\ 0.0044730 \end{pmatrix} (1 \quad -7.7713), \tag{10.96}$$

where $\hat{\boldsymbol{\beta}}$ has been normalized on the first variable in the $\mathbf{y}_t$ vector (i.e., YA_t in this example). Following this step, we can write $\hat{\mathbf{\Pi}}\mathbf{y}_{t-1}$ as

$$\hat{\mathbf{\Pi}}\mathbf{y}_{t-1} = \hat{\boldsymbol{\alpha}}\hat{\boldsymbol{\beta}}'\mathbf{y}_{t-1} = \begin{pmatrix} \underset{(0.0053472)}{-0.050319} \\ \underset{(0.0055148)}{0.0044730} \end{pmatrix} \left(\text{YA}_{t-1} - \underset{(0.37519)}{7.7713}\,\text{YB}_{t-1}\right) \tag{10.97}$$

where we have added estimated standard errors below the point estimates of the adjustment coefficients in $\hat{\boldsymbol{\alpha}}$, and the cointegration parameter in $\hat{\boldsymbol{\beta}}'$ (see Exercise 10.6. These results suggest that the second coefficient in the $\boldsymbol{\alpha}$-vector is zero in the DGP. The relevant statistic to test the weak exogeneity of YB_t with respect to the cointegration coefficients is an LR test, which has an asymptotic Chi-square distribution under the null hypothesis of weak exogeneity. Hence, we can use the formula:

$$\text{LR} = -2(\mathcal{L}_R - \mathcal{L}_U),$$

where $\mathcal{L}_R$ denotes the log-likelihood under weak exogeneity of YB_t (i.e., with the zero restriction on the second element of $\boldsymbol{\alpha}$), and $\mathcal{L}_U$ is the unrestricted likelihood. As shown in Exercise 10.6, the test value is 0.66436, which is statistically insignificant when critical values of the Chi-square distribution with one degree of freedom ($\chi^2(1)$) are used.[5]

The use of the $\chi^2(1)$ distribution in the testing of exogeneity reflects that after the determination of cointegration rank, the unit-root non-stationary has been removed from the VAR, and it can therefore be made subject to further econometric treatment by the use of the estimation procedures and testing methods that we have studied in the earlier chapters. This includes the estimation methods for simultaneous equations, specifically GIVE and 2SLS; see Hsiao (1997b), Johnston and Dinardo (1997, p. 317). In brief, we

[5]For information, in the data generation, weak exogeneity was imposed, and the long-run derivative coefficient of YA with respect to YB was 8.

can say that the system has been "reduced from" an $I(1)$-system to an $I(0)$ system (i.e., without unit-roots).

To represent the $I(0)$ system explicitly, we can define the equilibrium correction variable as follows:

$$\text{ecm}_t = (1 \quad -7.8)\mathbf{y}_t = \text{YA}_t - 7.8\text{YB}_t \sim I(0), \tag{10.98}$$

where we have dropped decimals of the cointegration parameter for simplicity, and write the cointegrated $I(0)$ VAR as

$$\Delta\text{YA}_t = \phi_{10} + \alpha_{11}\text{ecm}_{t-1} + \varepsilon_{1t}, \tag{10.99}$$

$$\Delta\text{YB}_t = \phi_{10} + \alpha_{21}\text{ecm}_{t-1} + \varepsilon_{1t}, \tag{10.100}$$

$$\text{ecm}_t = \text{ecm}_{t-1} + \Delta\text{YA}_t - 7.8\Delta\text{YB}_t, \tag{10.101}$$

where the third line is an identity (i.e., no error term).

The estimation results for the two reduced-form equations in the $I(0)$-system become

$$\Delta\text{YA}_t = \underset{(0.012)}{-0.001} - \underset{(0.005)}{0.05}\,\text{ecm}_{t-1}, \tag{10.102}$$

$$\Delta\text{YB}_t = \underset{(0.013)}{0.016} - \underset{(0.005)}{0.005}\text{ecm}_{t-1}, \tag{10.103}$$

with a log-likelihood which is slightly lower than in the VAR that we started out with (192.8 against 193.2) (see Exercise 10.7). This is a consequence of the reduction from the $I(1)$ system to the $I(0)$ system with fewer parameters. Again, in (10.103), the weak exogeneity of YB_t with respect to the cointegration parameter is confirmed, as the t-value of ecm_t is 1.0 in that equation (see Exercise 10.7).

Based on the validity of the weak exogeneity restriction, we know from Chapter 7 that the system can be estimated as a "conditional plus marginal model", which gives

$$\Delta\text{YA}_t = \underset{(0.012)}{-0.005} + \underset{(0.01)}{0.237}\Delta\text{YB}_t - \underset{(0.005)}{0.051}\text{ecm}_{t-1}, \tag{10.104}$$

$$\Delta\text{YB}_t = \underset{(0.0096)}{0.009}, \tag{10.105}$$

which gets a log-likelihood of 192.5. The coefficient of ΔYB_t is close to the covariance of the VAR disturbances, as it should be, as it is a regression coefficient. Note that the two constant terms in the model are statistically insignificant and can also be restricted to zero. The resulting model will then have incorporated all the properties of the DGP: cointegration, weak exogeneity no drift in the two-levels variables, and zero mean in the long-run relationship.

Although we have used a simple example to illustrate both rank determination and transition from $I(1)$ to $I(0)$, there is considerable generality in the example as well. With more complex systems, there are two additional issues. First, when the rank is decided to be two or larger, the long-run relationships need to be identified as explained above. Second, for the model representation of the $I(0)$ system, simultaneous equation models are often relevant, depending on theory and the outcome of statistical tests of exogeneity.

10.6. Exercises

Exercise 10.1. Show the decomposition of $\mathbf{\Pi}$ in terms of factors $\boldsymbol{\alpha}$ and $\boldsymbol{\beta}$ in (10.2.1). (Hint: Remember the simplifying assumption $|\boldsymbol{P}| = 1$ in the main text).

Exercise 10.2 (Exam 2015 ECON4160 UiO). We refer to Exercise 9.8.

According to the theory, the system of collective wage bargaining in Norway is a form of rent sharing which creates a long-run dependency between the hourly wage and the manufacturing firms' ability to pay, as measured by the value of labour productivity.

To test this theory, we estimate the following Engle–Granger regression by OLS:

$$LW_t = \beta_0 + \beta_1 LZ_t + u_t, \quad t = 1970, \ldots, 2013, \tag{10.106}$$

where u_t is the disturbance. In Figure 10.1, the time series with the residuals from the Engle–Granger regression has been labelled as *EGLWresiduals*.

Use the results in Figure 10.1 to form a conclusion about whether the theory of a long-run relationship between LW and LZ is supported or not. The critical values of the Engle–Granger test of no long-run (cointegrating) relationship are: 5% = −3.33, and 1% = −3.90. As part of your answer, explain why you use these critical values, instead of the critical values for the ADF tests given in Figure 9.6.

Exercise 10.3 (Exam 2015 ECON4160 UiO). An alternative test of the null hypothesis of no long-run relationship can be based on a conditional equilibrium correction model (ECM). You find estimation results for such a model in Figure 10.2. In Figure 10.2, the variables DLW and DLZ are the

```
EQ(1) Modelling LW by OLS
      The dataset is: C:\SW20\ECON4160\H2015\Exam\LoennIndogFastland.in7
      The estimation sample is: 1970 - 2013

                  Coefficient  Std.Error  t-value  t-prob Part.R^2
Constant            -0.172383    0.04508    -3.82  0.0004   0.2582
LZ                   0.963630   0.008637     112.  0.0000   0.9966

sigma               0.0504044  RSS              0.106705506
R^2                  0.996637  F(1,42) =    1.245e+04 [0.000]**
Adj.R^2              0.996557  log-likelihood       70.0479
no. of observations        44  no. of parameters          2
mean(LW)              4.78569  se(LW)              0.859032

Unit-root tests
The dataset is: C:\SW20\ECON4160\H2015\Exam\LoennIndogFastland.in7
The sample is: 1973 - 2013 (43 observations and 1 variables)

EGLWresiduals: ADF tests (T=41; 5%=-1.95 1%=-2.62)
D-lag    t-adf      beta Y_1    sigma   t-DY_lag  t-prob
 1      -2.853**    0.61462  0.03731     0.5051  0.6163
 0      -2.935**    0.64303  0.03696
```

Figure 10.1. Results for an Engle–Granger regression between LW_t and LZ_t, and unit-root tests for the disturbance of that regression.

```
EQ(2) Modelling DLW by OLS
      The dataset is: C:\SW20\ECON4160\H2015\Exam\LoennIndogFastland.in7
      The estimation sample is: 1972 - 2013

                 Coefficient  Std.Error  t-value  t-prob Part.R^2
DLW_1               0.247629    0.09799     2.53  0.0163   0.1581
Constant         -0.00492564    0.03616   -0.136  0.8925   0.0005
DLZ                 0.100648    0.05653     1.78  0.0839   0.0853
DLZ_1             0.00917294    0.05715    0.160  0.8734   0.0008
LW_1               -0.250837    0.04727    -5.31  0.0000   0.4530
LZ_1                0.237388    0.04547     5.22  0.0000   0.4449
DLKPI               0.567936     0.1122     5.06  0.0000   0.4297
DLNH               -0.685046     0.2384    -2.87  0.0070   0.1953

sigma              0.0124393  RSS             0.00526103907
R^2                 0.911595  F(7,34) =      50.08 [0.000]**
Adj.R^2             0.893394  log-likelihood        129.092
no. of observations       42  no. of parameters           8
mean(DLW)          0.0691441  se(DLW)             0.0380983

AR 1-2 test:       F(2,32)   =   4.2391 [0.0233]*
ARCH 1-1 test:     F(1,40)   =   1.9135 [0.1743]
Normality test:    Chi^2(2)  =  0.33955 [0.8439]
Hetero test:       F(14,27)  =   1.3089 [0.2652]
Hetero-X test: not enough observations
RESET23 test:      F(2,32)   =   3.0802 [0.0598]
```

Figure 10.2. Results for ECM of LW_t.

differences of LW and LZ, for example, DLW = LW − LW_1, where LW_1 denotes the first lag of LW.

The ECM of LW also includes two other conditioning variables: DLKPI, which is the inflation rate, and DLNH, which is the change in the length of the normal working day. It is relevant to condition on these two variables because compensation for increases in the cost of living, and for shorter hours it is part of the bargaining between the unions and the firms. We base our analysis on the assumption that DLKPI and DLNH are $I(0)$ variables.

(1) Based on the results in Figure 10.2, and the information that the relevant 1% critical value for the ECM test of no relationship is −3.29, explain why it is reasonable to conclude that LW is cointegrated with LZ.
(2) Can you give some intuition on why the evidence in support of cointegration may be stronger when we use the ECM test than when the Engle–Granger test is used?
(3) Use the results to find the estimated long-run elasticity of the wage level (W) with respect to the value of labour productivity (Z). The estimated standard error of the long-run elasticity can be shown to be 0.032. Is a long-run elasticity of 1 supported empirically if you use a significance level of 5%?
(4) How could the standard error be calculated? Explain in words.

Exercise 10.4 (Exam 2015 ECON4160 UiO). As a way of imposing a long-run elasticity of 1, we define the variable

$$ECMwage = LW - LZ,$$

which we assume to be $I(0)$ from now on, and reestimate the ECM for wages. Figure 10.3 shows the results. Figure 10.4 shows the result for a marginal model of DLZ.

(1) Explain how you can test the weak exogenity of LZ with respect to the cointegration parameters with the aid of the information given. What does the evidence indicate?
(2) Assume that you are asked to estimate the dynamic effects on wages of a shock to average labour productivity. Could you use the results reported in Figures 10.3 and 10.4 to give an answer? Explain how you would motivate your answer.
(3) A colleague suggests that to appropriately address Question 4 (b), an SVAR model needs to be considered. Do you think using an SVAR is suitable to deal with this question?

```
EQ(3) Modelling DLW by OLS
      The dataset is: C:\SW20\ECON4160\H2015\Exam\LoennIndogFastland.in7
      The estimation sample is: 1972 - 2013

                      Coefficient  Std.Error  t-value  t-prob Part.R^2
DLW_1                    0.333612    0.09621     3.47  0.0014   0.2557
Constant               -0.0768366    0.01971    -3.90  0.0004   0.3027
DLZ                      0.134225    0.05796     2.32  0.0265   0.1329
DLZ_1                   0.0570952    0.05652     1.01  0.3193   0.0283
DLKPI                    0.681517     0.1071     6.36  0.0000   0.5365
DLNH                    -0.582600     0.2485    -2.34  0.0249   0.1357
ECMwage_1               -0.210894    0.04668    -4.52  0.0001   0.3683

sigma                   0.0131938  RSS              0.00609264708
R^2                      0.897621  F(6,35) =     51.14 [0.000]**
Adj.R^2                   0.88007  log-likelihood          126.01
no. of observations            42  no. of parameters            7
mean(DLW)               0.0691441  se(DLW)              0.0380983

AR 1-2 test:       F(2,33)   =   2.7736 [0.0770]
ARCH 1-1 test:     F(1,40)   =0.00067955 [0.9793]
Normality test:    Chi^2(2)  =   1.9124 [0.3844]
Hetero test:       F(12,29)  =  0.84777 [0.6042]
Hetero-X test:     F(27,14)  =   1.4910 [0.2185]
RESET23 test:      F(2,33)   =   3.5640 [0.0397]*
```

Figure 10.3. Results for an ECM of LW_t with cointegration imposed in the form of the variable ECMwage.

```
EQ(4) Modelling DLZ by OLS
      The dataset is: C:\SW20\ECON4160\H2015\Exam\LoennIndogFastland.in7
      The estimation sample is: 1972 - 2013

                      Coefficient  Std.Error  t-value  t-prob Part.R^2
DLZ_1                    0.105475     0.1616    0.653  0.5180   0.0117
Constant                 0.130999    0.05231     2.50  0.0169   0.1484
DLW_1                    0.558570     0.2605     2.14  0.0389   0.1132
DLKPI                   -0.144616     0.3070   -0.471  0.6404   0.0061
DLNH                    0.0181977     0.7147   0.0255  0.9798   0.0000
ECMwage_1                0.284411     0.1256     2.26  0.0297   0.1247

sigma                    0.037941  RSS               0.0518226244
R^2                      0.452038  F(5,36) =      5.94 [0.000]**
Adj.R^2                  0.375932  log-likelihood         81.0541
no. of observations            42  no. of parameters            6
mean(DLZ)               0.0693511  se(DLZ)              0.0480278

AR 1-2 test:       F(2,34)   =  0.18983 [0.8280]
ARCH 1-1 test:     F(1,40)   =  0.44294 [0.5095]
Normality test:    Chi^2(2)  =  0.31240 [0.8554]
Hetero test:       F(10,31)  =  0.60697 [0.7958]
Hetero-X test:     F(20,21)  =   1.6381 [0.1349]
RESET23 test:      F(2,34)   =   4.8045 [0.0145]*
```

Figure 10.4. Results for a marginal model of DLZ_t.

Exercise 10.5. Show expression (10.64).

Exercise 10.6. Use the dataset called weakly_cointegrated_ADLmodel_d found on the book's internet page. Formulate a VAR(1) for the two endogenous variables YA_t and YB_t with an unrestricted constant. Use the estimation sample period 2–101 and replicate the results in Table 10.3, and in equations (10.96) and (10.97).

Exercise 10.7. Continue the analysis in the answer to Exercise 10.6, and reproduce the results for the $I(0)$ system in (10.102)–(10.103), and (10.104)–(10.105).

Chapter 11

Automatic Variable Selection

In practice, specification of empirical econometric models relies on search. Researchers use both general-to-specific (Gets) and specific-to-general searches. The chapter explains how Gets can be semiautomatized to aid economists in making decisions about model specification. We first assume that the aim of model specification is to conclude with an empirical model which is a close approximation to the local data generating process (LDGP). Gets represents a sensible strategy that hinges on the premise that the LDGP is contained within the general unrestricted model (GUM), which is the starting point of the specification search. Over the past decades, Gets has evolved to become a theoretically well-founded methodology, and recently has also been supported by computer algorithms that make automatized variable selection possible. In this chapter, we review the main concepts and theory needed to use Gets, manually, or with the aid of an computer algorithm such as *Autometrics*. In the last part of this chapter, we discuss the usefulness of automatic Gets when the LDGP is not necessarily contained within the GUM, and show that the method can deliver a meaningful approximation to the LDGP in this case also with the aid of extended methods such as *Impulse Indicator Saturation* (IIS).

11.1. Introduction

As we have seen above, empirical modelling requires model specification, which in turn involves many choices and decisions: which variables to be included in the modelling exercise; and which in practice will involve clarification of operational variable definitions and of measurement issues. Thereafter, a longer list of choices needs to be taken, including sample length, variable transformations, lag order, significance levels and small or large final model to report; see Granger (1990, 1999), Kennedy (2002), Hendry (1993, 2018), Hansen (1996) among others.

Some of the modelling decisions can be approached by the use of search methods, whereby the consequences of several alternatives are evaluated. According to Hendry and Doornik (2014, Section 7.2), the history of search methods in econometric methodology goes back to Anderson (1962) who determined the order of a polynomial. He showed that starting from a polynomial of relatively high order and reducing the order by the use of tests was optimal compared to starting from a null polynomial and then expanding by statistically significant polynomial orders. This was an early comparison of two search procedures that have become known as general-to-specific (Gets), and specific-to-general (i.e., expanding from a small model, to a larger final model) (Kennedy, 2008, Chapter 5). The theoretical foundations of Gets belongs to the theory of reductions of a general data generating process; see Florens *et al.* (1990), Hendry (1987) and Hendry and Richard (1982) among others. The theoretical foundation of Gets methodology was also strengthened by the development of weak, strong and super exogeneity, which we reviewed in Chapter 8.

Also associated with Gets was the requisite validation step of the econometric model building that we have encountered several times above: Is a model which is linear in the parameters flexible enough to describe the fluctuations of the data? What about the assumed constancy of parameters, does it hold over the sample that we have at hand? And the Gaussian distribution of the errors, is that a tenable assumption for the statistical testing of the economically interesting hypotheses that we want to investigate?

The main intellectual rationale for the model validation aspect of macroeconometrics is exactly that the assumptions of the statistical model require separate attention; see Granger (1992) and Spanos (2008) among others. As noted above, one important step in model validation is to make the hypothesized statistical model subject to a battery of misspecification tests using the residuals as data.

To aid that evaluation, "batteries of diagnostic tests" have become standard in econometric software programs. Not surprisingly, producers of macroeconometric models took heart from these developments and started (re)developments of models that placed dynamic specification at the centre of the development process (Bårdsen *et al.*, 2005).

Despite these advances, many practitioners found the application of Gets modelling quite difficult. On top of that, many macroeconomists and econometricians came to attach great weight to the unfavourable results for (a version of) Gets obtained in the Monte Carlo experiments in Lovell (1983), whereby the pejorative term data mining became associated with Gets. However, what the Lovell experiments essentially showed was that the model selection based on maximum adjusted R-squared, $\bar{R}^2$, leads to overfitting. Hoover and Perez (1999) revisited Lovell's experiments, and implemented an automated multi-path (test tree-based) search. The results of Hoover and Perez changed the picture of the merits of Gets completely. In their experiments, the imaginary practitioner adopting the Gets approach did very well.

Since Gets modelling involves search which is time consuming also for trained model developers, it was perhaps inevitable that automatization would at some point replace (at least in part) manual modelling decisions, and lead to a jump forward in feasible Gets modelling (see Hendry and Nielsen, 2007, Chapter 19). In the course of the first 10–15 years of the new millennium, automated variable selection as an aid to empirical modelling has come of age. Hendry and Krolzig (2000, 2001) managed to improve on Hoover and Perez, and documented the algorithm that was included in PcGive. Doornik (2009) reviewed many of the developments between that version, and the newest version of automated Gets in PcGive, which is called *Autometrics*.

We focus on Autometrics as implemented in PcGive in this chapter. Autometrics is well suited for developing an understanding of the problems associated with Gets modelling, and to what extent they can be solved by using a good algorithm. There is no attempt in this chapter to compare Autometrics with other algorithms that are available as automated variable selection procedures. Several methods have a common ground in regression shrinkage and forward selection of regressors; see e.g., Ghysels and Marcellino (2018, Section 1.9). To get some intuition, suppose that the objective is to determine empirically the relationship between a single variable, Y, and a large set of variables in the data matrix $\mathbf{X}$. A starting point is to regress Y on the single X variable that has the largest correlation coefficient with Y, call it X_1, and to store the residuals, $\boldsymbol{\epsilon}_1$. Next, from the correlations between $\boldsymbol{\epsilon}_1$ and each of the remaining X-variables, select the variable with highest correlation and calculate a second residual $\boldsymbol{\epsilon}_2$, and so on. By application of a stopping rule, an algorithm built along these lines will deliver a final selection of X-variables to use in a model equation for Y. As a method of search, this procedure, and the generalization called Least Angle Regression (Efron *et al.*, 2004), has a definite air of specific-to-general (i.e., small to large) about it.

Hendry and Doornik (2014, Chapter 17) compare the variable selection aspects of different approaches, when implemented as automatic algorithms. Among these are RETINA, Perez-Amaral *et al.* (2003) and *Lasso*, Tibshirani (1996), both of which are widely used. The wider field of statistical learning is connected with automatic variable selection, and one accessible textbook is, for example, James *et al.* (2013). Recently, a package in the statistical system *R* developed by Pretis *et al.* (2018), implements automatic Gets, also allowing for specification of ARCH errors.

It may be noted that these developments provide the researcher with the "log section" that Magnus (2002) argued should accompany any published empirical econometric model, which echoes the point made earlier by Edward Leamer, that the job of a researcher is to report informatively the mapping from assumptions into inference ("The mapping in the message", Leamer (1983, p. 38)).

In Sections 11.2–11.6, the main concepts of Gets modelling are presented, and its theoretical properties in automatized form are illustrated using simulated data. In Sections 11.7 and 11.8, we briefly discuss two important extensions of Gets. First, automatized decisions about structural breaks, by impulse indicator saturation (IIS). Second, the application of Gets in "under-specified settings", i.e., when the GUM is not taken to include the LDGP, or when a separate decision has been made about keeping some (a subset) of the variables away from selection, maybe because we want to make sure that a few "theory variables" are retained in the final model. In both cases, the structured search plays a central role in making sure that the maintained variables are robust to the under-specification relative to the LDGP.

Box 11.1. Big Data and automatic search

Arrival of "Big Data" combined with computing power has led to a surge in interest about automatic ways to find "patterns in the data", "predictors of behaviour", "significant factors", etc.

Box 11.1 (*Continued*)

However, analyzing large datasets to discover a few substantive relationships among vast numbers of spurious relationships requires a methodological approach: Mountains of data and abundance of computing power alone do not provide defense against many false positives, Harford (2014).

Several issues that now become connected with Big Data have been analyzed and understood before in the context of econometric model specification, in particular, the importance of well-researched and tested algorithms for automatic variable selection (Doornik and Hendry, 2015). The survey by Varian (2014) also argues that automatic methods can be important for progress in Big Data research activities.

11.2. Terminology and Basic Gets Concepts

As we have mentioned above, empirical modelling in economics is based on specification, and misspecifications of models are a concern. However, to state that a model is misspecified entails that there exists an object for which it is not the correct specification. That object is referred to as the local data generating process (with the acronym LDGP), namely, the process by which the variables chosen for analysis has been generated. The LDGP is relative to the modelling purpose that motivates the choice of the variable. Hence, while we can imagine one grand DGP for the whole economy, there are many LDGPs for different modelling purposes.[1]

The logical relationship between the DGP that operates in the real world and the LDGG is covered by the theory of reduction (Hendry and Doornik, 2014, Chapter 6). We do not go into the details of that theory here, but note that at some stages of the reduction there may be considerable information loss, at other stages, there is no information loss. Data partitioning (of the DGP) determines which variables to include and which to omit from the General Unrestricted Model (GUM) that will be the starting point of the Gets modelling exercise. It is not a decision that lends itself to automatization. Usually, the researcher will refer to economic theory, past empirical modelling, data availability and quality (which is changing

[1]Elsewhere in the book, we refer to the data generating mechanism as the DGP, however, in this chapter, the conceptual distinction between DGP and LDGP is needed.

over time). Given the complexity of real-world DGPs and the specificity of economic theory, this represents the most consequential specification decision (in terms of failure or success). This also implies that, while we highlight automatic variable selections in this chapter, real life modelling will at best be semi-automatic, as human intellectual input is essential for the specification of the GUM.

In most of this chapter, we will assume that the LDGP is the target of the model selection. This does not imply that the practical usefulness of Gets hinges on always finding the LDGP, and that all other final models necessarily represent failures that do not have any value for the modelling purpose. Because of the complexity of the actual economy, and the difficulties of assessing all the consequences of reduction from the DGP to the GUM, a more reasonable position to take is that any (final) model will be an approximation to the LDGP. It follows that in practice there may exist more than one model at the same time, and they may be approximations to the same LDGP.

As mentioned above, in this chapter, we will assume that Gets is applied in a single equation regression context, which simplifies the exposition. However, note that Autometrics can be used for specification of VARs for example, Doornik (2009).

In Table 11.1, we list three of the central concepts used in Gets methodology, with corresponding model equations in a regression context.

In all practical modelling situations, the LDGP is unknown. Nevertheless, a necessary requisite for having a possibility of finding it after a search is that we are able to formulate a GUM that contains the LDGP. Therefore, the number of variables in the GUM, k_{gum}, must be at least as large as the number of variables of the LDGP: $k_{\text{gum}} \geq k_{\text{dgp}}$, where k_{dgp} denotes the number of LDGP variables.

The premise that search has to commence from a larger model than the local data generating process has sometimes been presented as an absolute obstacle to Gets modelling in practice. For example, Magnus (1999, p. 61)

Table 11.1. GUM, LDGP and selected model in a regression context.

Concept	Model equation	
GUM	$Y_t = \sum_{i=0}^{k_{\text{gum}}} \gamma_i X_{it} + u_t$	
LDGP	$Y_t = \sum_{i=0}^{k_{\text{dgp}}} \beta_i X_{it} + \epsilon_t,$	$k_{\text{dgp}} \leq k_{\text{gum}}$
Selected model	$Y_t = \sum_{i=0}^{k} \delta_i X_{it} + \eta_t,$	$k \leq k_{\text{gum}}$

stated categorically that it "does not work. If you try to estimate such a large model, that has everything in it that you can think of, you get nonsensical results".

Magnus has a point when a "nonsensical" search algorithm is used, for example, maximization of the adjusted R-squared. However, by the use of a good algorithm, the probability of retaining nonsensical results is very low, as we shall see examples of below. Moreover, the "impossibility of Gets" position also seems to downplay the conceptual distinction between DGP and LDGP. The important relationship for getting Gets to work is the relationship between the GUM and LDGP. The formulation of the GUM in practice does not require the researcher to think about everything imaginable. What is needed is a good view to the variables that are likely to be relevant for research purposes. That of course is a difficult task, but not an impossibility.

Given that the LDGP is "inside the GUM", the aim is to select variables in such a way that (with a relatively high probability) the final model equation contains the same number of variables as the LDGP ($k = k_{\text{dgp}}$), and that those variables are the same as in the LDGP. Moreover, the estimated coefficients of the included variables are close to the true values of these coefficient in the LDGP. If the selected model contains irrelevant variables, the corresponding coefficients will of course be biased as the true values are zero in light of the LDGP. Note that in cases where the LDGP is not found, a lot of learning about the LDGP can still be attained, consider eliminating eight of nine variables correctly, for example.

Gets algorithms can be tested and evaluated by Monte Carlo experiments to assess the costs of having to make many decisions incurred by either contracting or expanding searches. Following Hendry and Doornik (2014), the distinction between costs of inference and costs of search helps to clarify the source from which mistakes can arise.

Costs of inference are inevitable, which is easily seen by considering the case when search begins with the LDGP, but the model producer is uncertain whether that specification of the GUM is indeed correct. Unless all t-values of the estimated GUM are manifestly significant, the probability is quite large that a search process will drop variables that in fact are in the LDGP. For example, some of the estimated coefficients may have $|t| < 0.1$ at the available sample size so would rarely be retained even when the GUM was the LDGP. Costs of search are additional owing to commencing from a GUM that is more general than the LDGP. The costs of search are really due to selection. As just noted, the costs of inference would also confront a modeller who managed to begin from the LDGP.

Perhaps surprisingly, it is the costs of inference that represent the largest costs incurred by good search algorithms (see Hendry and Doornik, 2014, Chapter 7). Despite the inevitable accumulation of Type-I error probability (see Section 11.4) as a result of performing many tests, Monte Carlo experiments show that the retention rate of irrelevant variables after selection (dubbed *gauge* in Autometrics) can be controlled by choosing a suitably low overall significance level at the start of the algorithm. In Autometrics, this parameter set in the algorithm is called *Target size* and in the following we will denote it by α. Hence, more often than not, there is little efficiency loss in examining many candidate variables that transpire to be irrelevant. This is not to say that there cannot be constellation where the costs of search can become larger. Assume, for example, that the GUM includes irrelevant variables that are more highly correlated with the relevant regressor, than the latter is with the dependent variable. In this case, the final model after commencing from the GUM will frequently be incorrect, while starting from the LDGP will represent a better chance of retaining the correct variables.

However, in all constellations, a desirable property of a search algorithm is a high tendency of keeping relevant variables, i.e., high rejection rate for irrelevant variables, referred to as *potency*.

11.3. The Search Tree

It is easy to imagine one modelling situation where the search costs can be made exactly zero by applying a thought-trough Gets strategy. The case we have in mind is when all the regressors of the GUM are mutually uncorrelated (Hendry and Doornik, 2014, Chapter 8). An efficient strategy for deciding which variables to drop would then be to rank the absolute values of t-values of the estimated GUM from highest to lowest, and to drop from the GUM the variables that have t-values below the critical value for the chosen significance level (α). In this case, the cost of search associated with Gets is zero simply because no search was needed to decide on the final model.

However, real-life GUMs consist of correlated variables. Hence, to be able to believe in feasible Gets modelling with low search cost, we need to show that although genuine search is required in practice, a structured search is sufficient for keeping the cost of search acceptably low. The search tree, or test tree, is a concept that aids the understanding of what we mean by a structured search, and it also helps to clarify many of the challenges of

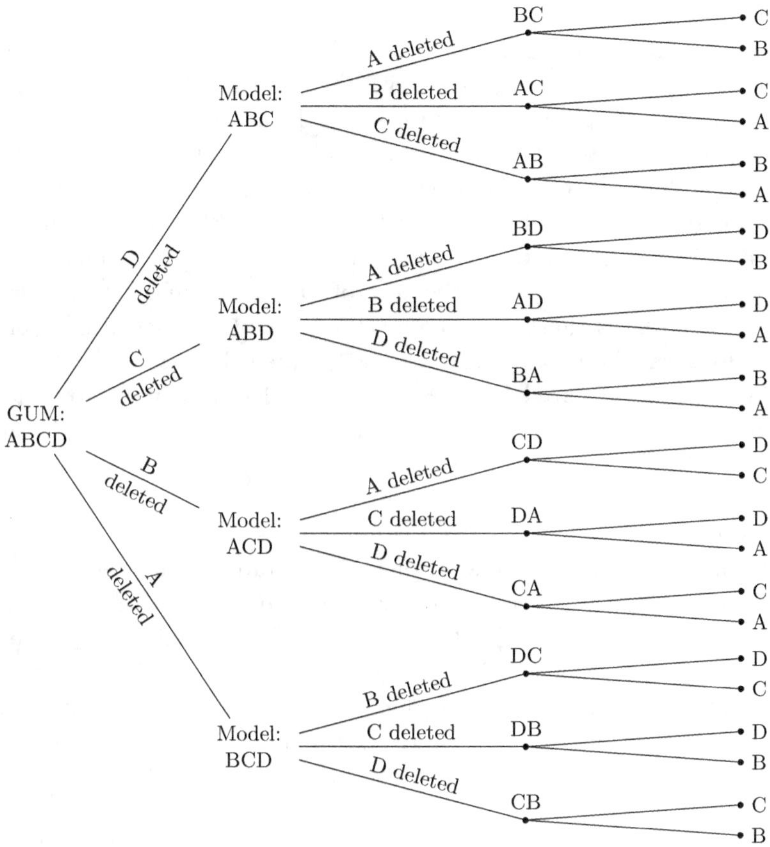

Figure 11.1. Search tree: Models starting from a GUM with regressors A, B, C, D.

making a search algorithm both efficient and reliable, see Doornik (2009), who also used the search tree to illustrate many of the features of his Autometrics algorithm.

Figure 11.1 shows (a rather chubby) tree lying on its side. The Gets interpretation of the figure is obtained by moving through the tree from left to right. The left-hand side of the tree shows the GUM which consists of one dependent variable (not labelled) and four explanatory variables, labelled A, B, C and D. The branches of the tree are defined by variables that become deleted from the GUM as part of the search process, i.e., they represent search paths. We assume that statistical tests are used to decide whether to stop the search along a given path, or to advance further down that path. For concreteness, we can think of t-values being assessed at each node (although an advanced algorithm like Autometrics also implements other criteria). The search stops at a node (model) where all variables are significant. If we begin with the branch (path) at the top of the figure, the first hypothesis tested is that D is an irrelevant variable. If the test does reject the null hypothesis, the search along that branch ends. The algorithm then goes back to the GUM and attempts a search along another main branch, for example, it tests whether C can be deleted from the GUM. The other possibility is that the test of D's irrelevance does not reject the null hypothesis that D can be dropped. The Gets algorithm therefore continues down the first path, to the node labelled Model ABC, and tests the hypotheses indicated by the three subnodes. Depending on the test outcomes, the algorithm may then deliver models BC and/or AC and/or AB, as well as stopping at model ABC.

At the two-variable nodes, each of the three models BC, AC and AB may be further simplified, and six simple regression models can be found, as indicated by the tips (leaves) of the first branch. In practice, a Gets algorithm must go one step further, and test the relevance of the remaining variable (be it A, B or C). Hence, the search may end with an empty model (i.e., no relationship between the dependent variable and the four explanatory variables). As noted above (Section 6.5.6), an empty model, where the dependent variable is only regressed on a constant, is often called a *null model*. The null models are not shown in the search tree due to lack of space.

Figure 11.1 shows all possible final models in the tree. The importance of *multiple path search* is clearly demonstrated: Assume that the LDGP is Model CD for example. By only searching the first (and the second) branch of the tree, that LDGP will not be found. When doing manual Gets, missing one or two search paths is easily done. Computer programs are much better at following a plan, and at keeping order of which paths have been investigated, and which remain unexplored. This is one reason why computer automatization of Gets is a valuable tool for model developers.

The test tree in Figure 11.1 also brings out that the different final models are sometimes identical. For example, a model with A and C as regressors can be discovered by starting from the first branch, but also by starting from the third, i.e., deleting B initially and then discovering CA. Moreover, among the leaves of the tree, there are six that contain C as the single variable (and six of the other single explanatory variable models as well). Hence, visiting every node (model) in the tree is not an efficient use of computer time, and with larger GUMs even today's machines can become bogged down. Hence, developers of automatic Gets algorithms must put weight on structured and efficient tree searches.

A structured search can begin by ranking the magnitudes of all t-values in the GUM. The first search path is entered by deleting the variable with the lowest absolute t-value, say D in Figure 11.1. The second branch deletes the second least significant variable, and so on. At each subnode, the variables can be reordered with the least significant variables first.

A natural aim for efficiency is that the search process only visits nodes with unique models. Figure 11.2 shows an example. Assume, for example, that the search down the first path ends at Model AB. In the second path, commencing with deletion of C leading to model ABD, there is no need to

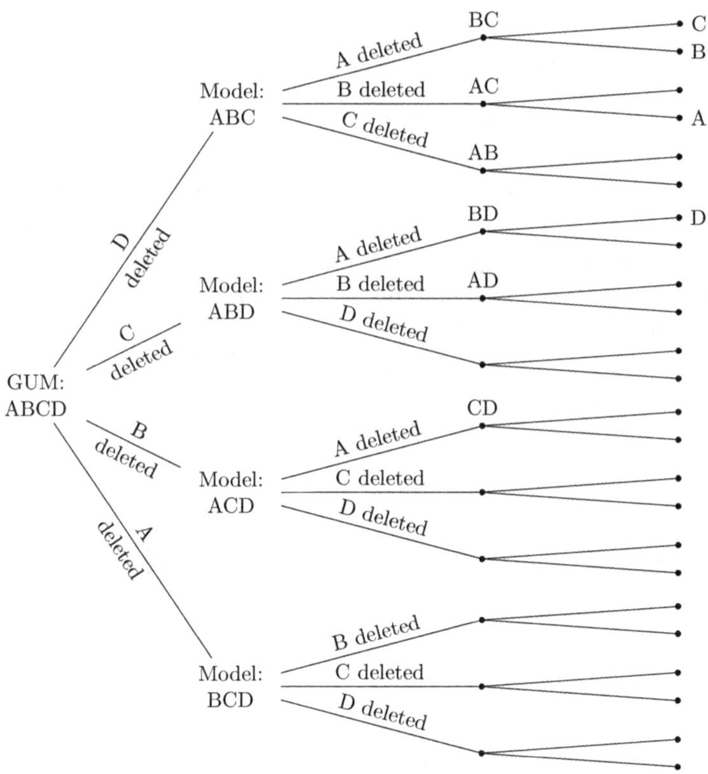

Figure 11.2. Search tree: All unique models starting from a GUM with regressors A, B, C, and D.

visit the AB node of that branch, since that model has already been found as a candidate model.

The priority of efficiency is also easy to understand by noting how the number of unique models increases when we move from stylized GUMs with only a few variables to larger GUMs that we typically will want to use in practice. With $k_{\text{gum}} = 20$, the number of unique models (nodes) with five variables ($k = 5$) is

$$\frac{20!}{5! \times 15!} = 15504,$$

by the use of the formula from combinatorics

$$\text{Number of models} = \frac{k_{\text{gum}}!}{k!(k_{\text{gum}} - k)!} \tag{11.1}$$

(see Sydsæter *et al.* 2005, Chapter 32). In a multiple path search, we do not want to omit any unique models from search. In the case of $k_{\text{gum}} = 20$, this gives

$$\text{Number of models } (k_{\text{gum}} = 20) = \sum_{k=0}^{20} \frac{20!}{k!(20-k)!} = 1.048576 \times 10^6.$$

Said in other words, almost 1.05 million unique models!

If we should visit all nodes, this already immense number becomes even larger due to the multiplicity of "arrivals" at any unique model. According to Doornik (2009, p. 93), "Autometrics implements several strategies to skip nodes and move effectively through the tree." Hence, we can understand why an automatic search algorithm like Autometrics must necessarily be complicated in order to be efficient (and at the end of the day, to be useful in practice). Therefore, evaluation of the algorithm's performance in experiments is essential. Broad evaluations are found, e.g., in Castle *et al.* (2011, 2013), Hendry and Doornik (2014, Chapter 17), and a simple example is given later in this chapter.

Box 11.2. Number of models by Newton's binomial formula

The expression for the number of unique models given in (11.1) can be simplified by the use of Newton's binomial formula (see, e.g., Sydsæter and Hammond, 2002, pp. 61–63):

$$\sum_{k=0}^{k_{\text{gum}}} \binom{k_{\text{gum}}}{k} a^{k_{\text{gum}}-k} b^k = (a+b)^{k_{\text{gum}}}.$$

Box 11.2 (*Continued*)

For the special case of $a = 1$ and $b = 1$, we obtain

$$\sum_{k=0}^{k_{\text{gum}}} \binom{k_{\text{gum}}}{k} 1^{k_{\text{gum}}-k} 1^k = (1+1)^{k_{\text{gum}}},$$

and

$$\sum_{k=0}^{k_{\text{gum}}} \binom{k_{\text{gum}}}{k} = 2^{k_{\text{gum}}} = \text{number of models},$$

where the binomial coefficient is

$$\binom{k_{\text{gum}}}{k} = \frac{k_{\text{gum}}!}{k!(k_{\text{gum}}-k)!}.$$

One point worth mentioning in particular is that there may be multiple terminal models, i.e., more than one terminal model that cannot be simplified any further with the use of the implemented criteria. In such cases, the model builder must of course be able to inspect the terminal models because she may have good theoretical or other reasons for preferring one model over another. On the other hand, a fully automated procedure must decide on a final model, and needs to include a tiebreaker. Best fit has been used as a tiebreaker, as well as the three information criteria AIC, HQ and SC mentioned above. A more advanced strategy is to delete terminal models that fail standard diagnostic tests. A second is to form the union of terminal models (as a new GUM), and try to arrive at a unique final model. Autometrics implements all these advanced features (Doornik, 2009).

11.4. Overall Test Size and the Retention Rate of Irrelevant Variables

As noted above, the two main success criteria for a search algorithm are that it should be good at removing irrelevant variables while at the same time it should be good at keeping relevant variables. As noted above, "being good at" needs to be related to the LDGP. If the t-values of all relevant variables in the LDGP equation are below 1, finding the

LDGP is an impossible requirement even if we begin the search from the LDGP.

To make the point, consider again the example of a GUM where all the k_{gum} variables are mutually orthogonal. An efficient strategy for deciding which variables to drop would then be to rank the absolute values of t-values of the estimated GUM from highest to lowest, and to drop from the GUM the variables that have t-values below the critical value for the chosen significance level (α). If each of the k_{dgp} relevant variables has a $|t| < 1$, the decision will be that the k_{gum} variables are dropped. Conversely, if the LDGP is characterized by strongly significant variables ($|t| > 3$), the same procedure will deliver the LDGP as the chosen model even at very low nominal significance levels, e.g., 0.0025 (0.25%).

Note that in each of these two examples, there was only one decision, even though k_{gum} could be arbitrary large. This is of course due to the assumed orthogonality of the explanatory variables, only then is the deletion of some variables without consequences for the estimation of the coefficients of retained variables. Hence, as there was no genuine search involved, the search cost is zero in both cases, and in the failed case (basically impossible case), the whole cost is again due to inference. In the successful case, there are no costs of either inference or search.

The one-cut decision establishes a baseline for understanding why Gets modelling can succeed. It can be viewed as going down just one branch in the test tree, for example, the first branch in Figure 11.2, where the variable D has the lowest t-value. Due to the orthogonality, there is no need to reorder the variables at each subnode, and the search can therefore be collapsed into a single decision.

However, to use value in practice, Gets needs to be able to succeed also for non-orthogonal variable selection problems, where t^2-values can change markedly as different regressors are eliminated. The test tree approach with efficient multiple path searches suggests itself as the best choice for automatization (see Doornik, 2009).

Nevertheless, as many simplification paths need to be explored, an old argument that threatens to pull the rug away under the feet of automatic Gets comes to mind. It is the argument that multiple testing will necessarily lead to inflated Type-I error probability levels. Although the significance level of a single test is set to the conventional level of 5%, the overall significance level (i.e., the test size) after having done two or more such tests will be larger.

To see this, consider again the example with a GUM with four variables, $k_{\text{gum}} = 4$. The test situation is that we do four tests of the type

$$\text{Reject } \beta_j = 0, \quad \text{when } t_j \geq c_\alpha, \quad \text{for } j = 1, 2, 3, 4,$$

where c_α denotes the critical value of the relevant t-distribution. In the case where the t-value of variable j is independent of the other t-values if $\beta_j = 0$ (i.e., under the null hypothesis), the probability that none of the tests reject is $(1-\alpha)^4$. Hence, the overall Type-I error probability (of at least one erroneous rejection) becomes

$$\begin{aligned} &P(\text{Type-I error} \mid \beta_j = 0 \text{ for all } j) \\ &\quad = 1 - (1-\alpha)^4 = 4\alpha - \binom{4}{2}\alpha^2 + \binom{4}{3}\alpha^3 - \alpha^4. \end{aligned} \tag{11.2}$$

Setting $\alpha = 0.05$, gives

$$P(\text{Type-I error} \mid \beta_j = 0 \text{ for all } j) = 1 - (1-0.05)^4 = 0.18549,$$

which is only a little less than $4 \cdot 0.05 = 0.20$ due to the switching signs of the terms on the right-hand side of the last equality sign in (11.2). But it means that $4 \cdot 0.05 = 0.20$ is a good approximation to the true Type-I error probability of a sequence of four independent tests.

The general formula for independent tests, when the number of tests is k_{gum}, is

$$\begin{aligned} &P(\text{Type-I error} \mid \beta_j = 0 \text{ for all } j) \\ &\quad = 1 - (1-\alpha)^{k_{\text{gum}}} \\ &\quad = k_{\text{gum}}\alpha - \binom{k_{\text{gum}}}{2}\alpha^2 + \binom{k_{\text{gum}}}{3}\alpha^3 - \cdots - \alpha^{k_{\text{gum}}}, \end{aligned} \tag{11.3}$$

and with $k_{\text{gum}}\alpha$ as a good approximation:

$$P(\text{Type-I error} \mid \beta_j = 0 \text{ for all } j) < k_{\text{gum}}\alpha. \tag{11.4}$$

This shows that in order to control the overall size, α needs to be calibrated against the number of tests that one realistically expects will come into play.

Hence, with $k_{\text{gum}} = 20$, the 0.05 overall significance level is secured by solving

$$0.05 = 1 - (1-\alpha)^{20}, \tag{11.5}$$

for α, giving

$$\alpha = 1 - 0.95^{1/20} = 0.00256, \tag{11.6}$$

as the *Target size.* The simpler (approximate) calculation, using (11.4), gives the Target size as $\alpha = 0.0025$, which requires a t-value of 3.0 for rejection, rather than the conventional critical value of 2.0.

However, care must be taken in how we interpret this formal result in the context of variable selection. Consider again the case where the LDGP is the null model (i.e., the dependent variable regressed on a constant), and the GUM includes k_{gum} irrelevant regressors (without the investigator knowing that for a fact in advance). To simplify, assume that the variables are independent. Following Hendry and Nielsen (2007, Section 19.3), for each variable, the decision to retain it can be modelled as a Bernoulli (i.e., binomial) distributed variable. With k_{gum} independent tests, the number of retained irrelevant variables (false positives) will be

$$k^{\text{irr}} = k_{\text{gum}}\alpha, \tag{11.7}$$

for example, with $k_{\text{gum}} = 40$, and $\alpha = 0.01$, $\alpha k_{\text{gum}} = 0.4$, which immediately strikes us as an acceptably low number of irrelevant variables on average. It is equally true, however, that the probability that no test will reject is $(1 - 0.01)^{40} \approx 0.67$, with the implication that the wrong model is selected 33% of the time. The explanation of this paradox is that although in every trial there is a high probability that a large number of variables become correctly deleted from the GUM, there is also a noticeable probability that one or two variables are retained by chance. It may sound poor that the wrong model is selected 33% of the time. However, that view fails to reflect the large increase in knowledge (i.e., learning) resulting from the discovery that almost every candidate variable can be omitted from the final model (Hendry and Doornik, 2014, p. 105).

Hence, the practical guide to the choice of significance level of the individual tests may be to focus on an acceptable average number of irrelevant variables in the final model. For example, if we decide that $k^{\text{irr}} = 1$ is an acceptable number of irrelevant variables on average, and k_{gum} is 40, the significance level is set to $\alpha = 0.025$. $k^{\text{irr}} = 2$ and $k_{\text{gum}} = 100$, implies $\alpha = 0.02$, and so on. This then represents a rule of thumb for setting the Target size (α) in Autometrics.

It is also important to realize that when we select under the null model, the largest t-value, $t^2_{(1)}$, will typically be found to be close to the chosen critical value c_α. For example, when $\alpha = 0.01$, using 2-sided tests for

$T = 100$, then $c_\alpha \approx 2.6$, whereas a t-value outside the interval ± 3 will occur only 0.34% of the time. The event that irrelevant variables obtain absolute t-values equal to 4 is extremely unlikely (0.01%, or once for every 10,000 irrelevant variable tried).

As an example, Exercise 11.3 invites you to determine a final model for the variable Ya by starting from a GUM in ADL form with four lags in the dependent variable and in the four regressors. Hence, there are 24 regressors and a constant term. The regressors are both autocorrelated and mutually correlated, so the 1-cut decision is not reliable in this case. The number of possible unique models is $2^{25} = 33.554432$ million. Nevertheless, Autometrics decides on a model in a split of a second, and after estimating only 22 models, which proves the efficiency of the algorithm.[2] The final model, estimated with the 100 observations available for the estimation of the GUM, is

$$Ya = \underset{(0.0893)}{0.9762},$$

in other words, the null model, which also is the DGP in this artificial dataset. The true value of the constant term is 1, so it is not a completely negligible error, albeit not larger than what would be the error if we had started from the DGP.

However, finding the GUM could be a stroke of luck. And the theory we have reviewed tells us that even though we can expect that a good Gets algorithm will omit many irrelevant variables, the probability of discovering that the DGP is the null model may be in the region of 80%, i.e., $(1 - 0.01)^{25} \approx 0.78$ with a Target size 1%, with the implication that the wrong model is selected 22 times out of 100.

We can illustrate these points by simulating how Autometrics selects using 1000 replications, as reported in Table 11.2. The retention rate column

Table 11.2. Monte Carlo simulation of the DGP in Exercise 11.3.

α	Retention rate of irrelevant (gauge)	LDGP found
1%	1.8%	76%
5%	6.0%	34%

[2]Autometrics version 1.5g.

in the table contains the retention frequency in the simulation as an average of the retention frequencies of all the variables in the GUM (the gauge of the algorithm). It is a little higher than the Target size (i.e., nominal significance level), which shows that selecting among correlated variables induces a certain cost of selection. Nevertheless, Autometrics correctly eliminates all 24 regressors in 340 of 1000 simulations when the nominal significance level is set to 5% (i.e., a more liberal level than recommended), and in 76% of the simulations when the tighter 1% level is used.

There it is then, the background for the conclusion made by Hendry and Krolzig (2005), that the cost of search associated with Gets will be low in almost all cases. The analysis goes a long way towards debunking the widely held view that Gets is based on "Test, Test, Test" (Kennedy, 2008, Chapter 5) in a way that fills up empirical econometric modes with irrelevant explanatory variables; see Lovell (1983) and Denton (1985).

In addition to the principles, there are also contributions to low search cost through efficient multi-path searches. The real difficulty is to get the algorithm to retain the variables that matter. Economic LDGPs are seldom null models, hence it is important to consider that issue.

11.5. Retaining Relevant Variables

The biggest challenge to Gets modelling is not, as it was long thought to be, the accumulation of Type-I error probabilities. As we have seen, that problem is solved by efficient search (in particular, not investigating every unique model) and a guided choice of a relatively tight nominal significance level. The real problem is to retain variables that are relevant in the LDGP. If the signal-to-noise ratio of the LDGP is low, giving rise to many t-values between 1 and 2 in absolute value, even commencing the search from it will result in some relevant variables being excluded (i.e., a cost of inference, not a cost of search).

An algorithm's tendency to drop variables that belong to the LGDP is negatively related to the chosen nominal significance level, α. What makes the discovery of relevant variables possible, while retaining a reasonably low false retention rate, is the nonlinearity of critical values. As recorded in Table 11.3, the significance level is reduced by a factor of 1/50, from 0.05 to 0.001 the critical value is only raised by a factor of 1.71. Nevertheless, a variable that has a so-called non-centrality parameter of 2, corresponding to $t^2 = 4$, there is only a 50–50 probability of keeping it in the model when $c_{0.05} = 1.98$ is used (see Hendry and Doornik, 2014, p. 107). The chance

Table 11.3. Significance levels and corresponding critical values for t_{100}.

α	0.05	0.01	0.005	0.0025	0.001
c_α	1.98	2.61	2.87	3.1	3.4

Table 11.4. Monte Carlo simulation for the case where Ya is given by (11.8) and DGP for $(Za, Zb, Zc, Zc)_t$ is the same as in Exercise 11.4.

	Retention rate		
α	of irrelevant (gauge)	of relevant (potency)	LDGP found
1%	2.4%	85%	42%
5%	7.2%	88%	45%

of retaining four such variables is as low as 6%, i.e., 0.5^4. However, rejection frequencies rise rapidly with a variable's t^2 as a consequence of the nonlinearity just noted.

As an illustration of the trade-off between retaining irrelevant variables by chance, and dropping relevant ones, we consider the same LDGP for the regressors as in Exercise 11.3, but instead of the null model, the relationship for Ya_t is now

$$Ya_t = 1 + 0.5Ya_{t-1} + 0.7Za_t + 0.4Zb_t + 0.3Zc_t + 1.2Zd_t + \epsilon_t, \quad (11.8)$$

with $\epsilon_t \sim \text{IIN}(0,1)$. Table 11.4 shows that the two gauges (retention rates of irrelevant variables) change only little compared to the simulation of selection under the (true) null model. The retention rates, i.e., potency, for relevant variables are 85% and 88% for the two choices of the significance levels. In this experiment, the potency is practically 1 for Ya_{t-1} and Zd_t, 0.95 for Za_t, and 0.68 and 0.77 for Zc and Zd, respectively.

By working with Exercise 11.4, you can judge how Gets will perform on a single realization of this DGP.

11.6. The Roles of $I(1)$-variables and of Misspecification Testing

The reader may wonder why there has been no mentioning of either unit root non-stationarity, or of misspecification testing, so far in the discussion of automatic variable selection. After all, the earlier chapters have emphasized that both of these issues require careful consideration. Moreover, after having introduced the concept of cost of inference, it is clear that the problem of spurious regression between independent $I(1)$ variables can be interpreted as cost of inference that may be huge (i.e., damaging for the validity of results).

First, regarding unit-roots, it might be noted that, for example, Autometrics conducts inference using standard $I(0)$ critical values. On the basis of Chapter 10, it stands to reason that this will work if unit-roots have been removed by differencing or by rank determination (i.e., cointegration analysis) prior to the selection. More generally, most selection tests remain valid when applied in $I(1)$ processes; see Hendry and Doornik (2014, Section 3.10), who refer to Sims *et al.* (1990).

In the case where the GUM includes $I(1)$ variables that are cointegrated, the challenge is not spurious selection, but to keep the relevant variables that combine into $I(0)$ variables. When the GUM is an ADL model equation, the coefficient of the lagged endogenous variable will be relatively close to unity, so the null will almost always be rejected. The current and lagged regressors (assuming that it is relevant) are also likely to be retained in the final model (typically with opposite signs). Hence, we can expect that, on average, the final model will be interpretable as a potential long-run relationship although a formal test may require us to manually use the correct critical values for testing the absence of cointegration.

A more problematic setting is when several lags of an irrelevant $I(1)$ variable are included in the GUM. It can then happen that all but one of the lags have been eliminated during selection, and in this case a t-test on the last one cannot be written in the way Sims *et al.* (1990) proposed. The practical solution is again to use a tighter significance level, thus approximating what would happen if the correct Dickey–Fuller critical values had been used.[3]

Box 11.3. Effect of selection on estimators

This chapter focuses on selection of variables, relevant and irrelevant. A separate issue is the statistical properties of the estimators for variables that have "been through" a search process. The estimators of the selected model do not have the same properties as if the LDGP had

[3]Of course, this remark applies for algorithms that do not, yet, implement the correct critical values for reduction from $I(1)$ to $I(0)$.

Box 11.3 (*Continued*)

been estimated (without any search). Intuitively, conditional on selection, coefficient estimates are biased away from zero as variables are retained only when $t^2 \geq c_{\alpha}^2$. Bias correction is, however, relatively straightforward in the context of Gets; see Hendry and Nielsen (2007, Section 19.6), Castle *et al.* (2011), Hendry and Doornik (2014, Chapter 10).

The distinction between the inferential and model validation facets of modelling is due to Spanos (2008), who dispelled the charge that misspecification testing represents an illegitimate "reuse" of the data already used to estimate the parameters of the statistical model, see also Hendry (1995a, pp. 313–314).

Misspecification testing is nevertheless important in Gets algorithms. Early installations used misspecification testing at every stage of the selection (so-called diagnostic tracking). However, in this context, the warning against repeated testing becomes relevant as the probability of false rejection (e.g., of the null of no residual autocorrelation) may then become large as the number of times we test the null hypothesis increases (Hendry and Doornik, 2014, Section 7.8).

One consequence for the performance of automatic Gets may be that some irrelevant variables are being retained because they fix a chance departure from the null of one of the misspecification tests, hence increasing the gauge (Hendry and Doornik, 2014, Chapter 12). To avoid that happening, the current best practice is to test the GUM for misspecification, select without diagnostic tracking, and then check the final model for misspecification. The motivation is that if the GUM is well specified, then valid reductions too should be, i.e., residual autocorrelation for example should not ideally be a consequence of variable selection. However, as we have seen, chance deletion of relevant variables is inevitable for most LDGPs, hence there is a need to check the residual properties of the final model decided by the algorithm.

Hence, it is seen that the characterization that Gets specifications are "continually respecified until a battery of misspecification tests allows the researcher to conclude that the model is satisfactory" (Kennedy, 2008, p. 73), considerably overstates the role of misspecification testing in the automated versions of variable selection process.

11.7. Automatic Detection of Structural Breaks

Development of an algorithm called impulse indicator saturation (IIS) for detection of structural breaks represents a major step forward in the automatization of modelling decisions; see Hendry *et al.* (2008), Hendry and Doornik (2014), Castle *et al.* (2013).

Autometrics has the feature that the GUM can be extended by one indicator variable for each observation, hence there is an even larger GUM which is saturated by impulse indicators (i.e., dummies). Since the GUM then has one indicator variable for each observation in the sample, there are more variables than observations (even if the GUM is the null model). However, the algorithm has an elegant solution to the problem of more variables than observations. In the simplest case, it is to add the indicators in blocks of $T/2$ noting that all the indicators are mutually uncorrelated. The algorithm then adds half of the indicators to the GUM (e.g., the null model in the simplest case) and selects as usual, records the outcome and drops that first indicator set. Next, add the second set of $T/2$ indicators and select again. Then the retained indicators from the first two selections are combined and added to the GUM, and the selection algorithm is run again as is if we commenced with a number of indicators well below T (see Hendry and Doornik, 2014, Chapter 15).

In this approach, αT indicators will be retained by chance, on average. Choosing nominal significance level $\alpha = 0.01$ therefore implies that one irrelevant dummy is kept on average ($T = 100$). This amounts to losing only one observation of the sample, which is a low efficiency loss.

In practice, of course, the GUM will not be the null model, but will include regressors. In this case, IIS will work in exactly the same way as above. The only difference is that indicators for observations that are lost due to lagged variables are not needed in the indicator saturated GUM. The final model may then contain both retained economic variables and one or more significant indicators. The estimators of retained economic variables have been shown to have an interpretation as robust estimators statistically speaking (see Johansen and Nielsen, 2009).

Used in combination with economically interesting GUMs, IIS therefore has several important areas of application. For example, it greatly improves the scope of exogeneity testing, as marginal model equations can be objectively (and in a way that is reproducible for other researchers) tested for breaks. Any significant break variables can be included in the GUM for the conditional model, and if they are not selected, there is evidence for autonomy (ie super exogeneity) of the regressors of that model with respect to the breaks in the marginal model; see Hendry and Santos (2009) and Castle *et al.* (2014) among others.

11.8. Gets When the GUM is Under-specified, and Keeping Theory Variables

So far, we have taken as an assumption that the GUM encompasses the LDGP. Of course, in practice it is not possible to assert 100% that the GUM is large enough or uses the right functional forms and variable transformation, so that the LDGP is truly "in" the test-tree. Hence, it is important to consider whether Gets, and in particular automatic variable selection, can have any use value when the GUM is under-specified relative to the LDGP.

Intuitively, even though we cannot find the DGP in this case, the selected model may represent an approximation (Castle and Hendry, 2014a). Imagine, for example, the case where the test tree above is under-specified by one main branch (one variable). Depending on the data correlation matrix of the LDGP, that under-specification will affect all, some or none of the estimates of the coefficients of the final model. Moreover, indication of under-specification may reveal itself in the diagnostic testing of the GUM as well as in the final model. Hence, another role of the *IIS* methodology is found in this context, as the retained indicator set can proxy the effects of the economic variables that were omitted from the GUM. Another way to look at this is that *IIS* can correct parameter non-constancy induced by location shifts in omitted variables.

A related setting which is of considerable interest is when we decide to keep one or more variables in the GUM away from the selection process. In the test trees above, this can be visualized as the "chopping off" of a main branch, e.g., the one labelled "A-deleted" if variable A is decided to always be present in the model. Consequently, all the subbranches that involve testing the null that A is irrelevant are also dropped from the search. The motivation for keeping a set of variables away from selection may be that we want to estimate a theoretically clean core model, and also want to control the estimates for the influence of other variables that are either supplementary to the core theory, or may represent an alternative theory.

The reason for always retaining variables can also be directly linked to the research purpose. Consider, for example, the estimation of the relationship between the central bank interest rate and the market interest rate that we considered in Section 6.7. Given that purpose, a final model of the bank loan interest (RL) without the central bank rate (RNB) in the model is irrelevant. Hence, a more purposeful strategy in this case is to commence from a GUM where the RNB is not selected over, but where other candidate variables (e.g., an international interest rate and its lags) are selected over, together with IIS. The result of the selection is then a model where the estimated coefficient of the central bank rate is robust, both with respect to included variables in the GUM as well as to variables that are not included directly, but may be correlated with the retained indicator variables, see Exercise 11.5.

More generally, we embed a theory model that specifies a set of k_a relevant variables, $\boldsymbol{x}_a$, within a larger set of $k_a + k_b$ candidate variables, $\boldsymbol{x}_a + \boldsymbol{x}_b$, but only select over the variables in $\boldsymbol{x}_b$. When the theory is complete and correct, so the $\boldsymbol{x}_b$ are in fact irrelevant, selection can be undertaken without affecting the theory parameters' estimator distributions (see Hendry and Johansen, 2015). This strategy keeps the theory variables estimates when the theory is correct, yet protects the investigator against presenting an under-specified model to the user when some of the variables $\boldsymbol{x}_b$ are relevant.

11.9. Exercises

Exercise 11.1. Use the expansion

$$(1+x)^m = \binom{m}{0} + \binom{m}{1}x + \binom{m}{2}x^2 + \cdots,$$

which is valid for $-1 < x \leq 1$ (formula (8.26) in Sydsæter *et al.* (2005, 2006)) to show the second equality in (11.2).

Exercise 11.2. Assume that $k_{\text{gum}} = 10$, independent tests, and that we decide that an acceptable overall probability for Type-I error is 0.10. What is the implied target size, and what is the implication for the number of irrelevant variables on average?

Exercise 11.3. Use the dataset in DGPisNullModel_Zvariables_are_correlated_d.zip to estimate a VAR(1) for $(Za, Zb, Zc, Zd)_t$. Use the full available sample length, and confirm that the time series are mutually correlated, as well as individually autocorrelated.

Next, formulate a GUM with Ya_t as the dependent variable, and with four lags in $Ya_{t-1}, Za_t, Zb_t, Zc_t, Zd_t$. Include a constant term in the GUM, and decide on a final model.

Exercise 11.4. Use the dataset in DGPisADL_Zvariables_are_correlated_d.zip to determine a final model for Ya_t by commencing from a GUM with four lags in $Ya_{t-1}, Za_t, Zb_t, Zc_t, Zd_t$. Include a constant term in the GUM.

Exercise 11.5. Use the dataset NAMdataMay17.zip found in the dataset to Chapter 6, to estimate a GUM which is an ADL(2,2,2) model for RL, with RNB (the policy rate) and RW (a foreign rate) as regressors, for the sample 1994(1)–2016(3). Try to decide on a final model from this GUM using manual or automatic Gets.

Chapter 12

Model-Based Forecasting

Forecasting is a time-oriented activity, and forecasting is therefore an important area of application of dynamic econometric models. In this chapter, the theory of model-based forecasting is presented, and its relevance for applied forecasting is illustrated. The field of forecasting is large, stretching far beyond the scope of this chapter in a non-specialized textbook. The choice of topics and emphasis has been made with applied forecasting in mind, in particular the theory that any would-be macroeconomic forecaster is well advised to have as a background. One message is that several forecasting methods have a common ground in the VAR. Hence, methods that are often presented as alternative, nevertheless, have shared strengths and weaknesses, and that they may be better described as complementary forecasting methods. A second main theme in this chapter is the large impact that structural changes in the macroeconomy have on the properties of forecast errors. Since the empirical evidence, in the form of the forecast records of resourceful forecasters, shows that forecasts failures are common, we need a theory that explains why this is so. This seems to be a requisite not only for working theoretically toward improved forecast methods, but also for improving the robustness and use value of the forecasting methods that are available today.

12.1. Introduction

Forecasting is an important purpose of statistical and econometric model building. However the forecasting field is not restricted to statistical and econometric models. Experts, with their judgements of macroeconomic news and trends, are major players in economic forecasting. Forecasting from indicators, rather than from variables that have been systematized in the model equation form, has a long history in economics, and has recently received renewed attention and research interest, much thanks to the increased capability of collecting and processing both numerical data and text in near real time, see Morgan (1990, Part I) for a historical account, and Larsen and Thorsrud (2018) for a modern business cycle index based on media coverage of the economy.

The chapter focuses on statistical forecasting methods that make use of model equations. We show that forecasting methods that often have been presented as alternative and competing, for example, univariate time series models and larger systems of equations, in fact have much in common. For example, the forecasting function for a variable in a dynamic system, small or large, has a *glide path* interpretation. Its origin is an observed (or "nowcasted") starting point, and the end point of the glide path is the estimated long-run mean (i.e., mathematical expectation of the variable). The glide path of linear models is continuous between the starting point and the end point, but it is not monotonous in general. If the variable being forecasted is $I(1)$ non-stationary, only the starting point is well defined. However, a cointegrating linear combination of $I(1)$-variables follows a well-defined glide path when forecasted.

The future is uncertain, the best we can hope for is that we know what the uncertainties are, and that we can model them by the law of statistics. Hence, forecast errors are inevitable. The wider consequences of forecast errors depend on the purpose of the forecast. For investors in the financial market, one single large and unforeseen event can break (or make) a fortune. In macroeconomics, if a forecast is made to aid policy decisions, a single forecast mistake that becomes corrected may not have consequences. However, repeated and large forecast errors may make it difficult to reach good policy decisions.

In this way, it is the large and persistent forecast errors, forecast failures, see Clements and Hendry (2006), that represent the most serious challenge to macroeconomic forecasting. Such forecast failures should be rare if the typical real-life forecasting situation is that the model is reasonable approximation to the DGP, and that the DGP is wide-sense stationary. Said differently, there are no structural breaks in the period, which is being forecasted.

However, the forecast record shows that forecast failures occur relatively frequently, and no forecasting method seems to be able to claim a "clean sheet". This goes far beyond economics, as the now classic study by Tetlock (2005) shows. Nevertheless, the assumption that the future evolution of the economy will in part be governed by laws that can be empirically discovered by using data from the past, seems to be a requisite for having success with systematic forecasting based on model equations.

Research work is going on in several disciplines with the aim of devising methods and measurements that can give a forecaster information about the future's "unknown unknowns": the parameter shifts that we do not know today, but which will affect the future outcome of the variable. In the natural sciences, much can be predicted with great precision, but forecasting an active volcano's eruption is still extremely difficult. In economics, forecasting structural breaks is by and large "music of the future". Hence, in practice, we must try to build a forecasting theory and a practice on the basis that unanticipated shocks to the economy will often occur after the preparation and publication of the forecast. Luckily, not all structural breaks are equally damaging. Empirically, the most potent breaks are in the underlying means of the process being forecasted. If this description of the situation is correct, it follows that adaptation in the forecast process, once a break has occurred, is all important for avoiding a sequence of very poor forecasts (i.e., forecast failure).

It is against this background that this chapter has been written. In Section 12.2, we review the basic concepts of the forecasting theory, and the result about the optimality of the conditional expectation as a predictor of future values of a random variable from a stationary DGP. In Section 12.3, the algebra of the conditional expectation predictor is given for model that belongs to the VAR class of econometric systems: commencing with the simplest AR(1) case and ending with the SEM-based forecasts. We show that the forecasts from all these models have the glide path interpretation mentioned above. Section 12.4 includes an illustration of the basic theory using the macromodel example from Chapter 1 (and 7) and simulated data.

In Section 12.5, we turn to the realistic case, where the economy is subject to regime shifts (parameters change). We show that a *post-forecast* location shift, a change in the unconditional expectation of the forecasted variable occurring in the forecasting period will imply a forecast failure for any forecast derived from a VAR-type model. More surprisingly, a location shift which has taken place *before* the preparation and publication of the forecasts, but which has been left unnoticed by the forecaster, will imply systematic forecast errors as well. As clarified in the important contributions of Michael Clements and David Hendry, the forecasting function does not automatically "error correct" for a location shift that has already occurred, Clements and Hendry (1999, Chapter 12). However, as noted above, it seems to be reasonable to expect that forecasters, by the use of relevant methods, can reduce the damage that *pre-forecast* structural breaks would otherwise do to economic forecasts.

Sections 12.7–12.9 then discuss various strategies that can be used to improve on the "raw" model forecasts. Among the techniques available are intercept-correction (i.e., add-factors) and combination with forecasts produced by other methods, including the so-called *naive forecasts*, which simply state that the future will be a continuation of the past either in levels or in rate of change form. Using the random walk as a tool for forecasting is an example of a naive forecast. Despite its name, it provides a certain form of robustness with respect to location shifts which the "raw" model forecast does not give.

In Section 12.10, we summarize the pros and cons for using an empirical macromodel to forecast, instead of a less costly univariate model or a naive forecast. We point out that the pro arguments gain in importance when there is a link between forecasting and policy decisions. There are many issues which typically come up in policy discussions, but about which simple forecasting methods have nothing to say. Economists armed with empirical macroeconometric models can give answers to many such questions. The answers can be communicated and debated by economists, the public and decision makers, thus contributing to rational decision making.

12.2. Basic Concepts and Results from Forecasting Theory

In Section 5.5, we noted that the solution of an endogenous variable of a VAR can be applied to produce a forecast for that time series, conditional on the last periods of the sample period. In line with the notation introduced in Section 5.5, we denote the variable to be forecasted by $Y_{i,T+h}$, where $i = 1, 2, \ldots, n$, is an index for the number of endogenous variables which are jointly forecasted, and T indicates the time period which the forecast is conditioned on.[1] $h = 1, 2, \ldots, H$ denotes how many periods into the future we forecast. $Y^f_{i,T+1}$ is called a *one-step forecast*. A synonymous terminology is that $Y^f_{i,T+1}$ is a *static forecast*. A *multi-step forecast* for $h > 1$ periods ahead is denoted by $Y^f_{i,T+h}$ for $h > 1$. Whenever a multi-step forecast is obtained by simulation (i.e., solution) of a system of model equations, we use the term *dynamic forecast*. This will be the main method that we have in mind below. An alternative way of producing a multi-step (or multi-period) forecasts is to first estimate a specified relationship between $Y_{i,t}$ and $Y_{i,t-h}$ and other pre-determined variables that are lagged $h > 1$ periods. We see that, in principle, this corresponds to estimating the implied *final form equation* for $Y_{i,t}$, and then using the empirical relationship to forecast more than one period ahead (see Section 12.8 for a discussion).

Since the variable being forecasted, $Y_{i,T+h}$, is a random variable, it can be characterized by its probability density function, which is a function conditional on information available in period T. We let $\mathcal{I}_T$ denote the information set used to produce the forecast. If the probability density function $f(y_{i,T+h} \mid \mathcal{I}_T)$ is available, then all other properties of Y_{iT+h}, such as the conditional expectation $E(Y_{i,T+h} \mid \mathcal{I}_T)$ can be easily found.

However, in practice, it is too ambitious to hope to characterize fully $Y_{i,T+h}$, and one attempts to find a single value (i.e., a point forecast), which we denoted by Y^f_{iT+h} above, or a confidence band that gives the "best feasible" representation of the random variable $Y_{i,T+h}$.

The idea of a *cost function*, where the forecast error is the argument, plays an important role in the forecasting theory. In principle, the cost function can be closely connected to the decision that the forecast is part of an information gathering process for, Granger (1969a). Let e^f_{iT+h} denote the forecast error defined by

$$e^f_{iT+h} \underset{\text{def}}{=} Y_{iT+h} - Y^f_{i,T+h}. \tag{12.1}$$

Suppose that one can quantify the imputed cost of an error to be $C(e^f_{iT+h})$, with $C(0) = 0$, and $C(e^f_{iT+h}) > 0$ for $e^f_{iT+h} \neq 0$. Given such a cost function,

[1] In general, the forecasting function will be dynamic of higher order, implying that the forecast will be conditional on $T-1$, $T-2$, and so on. Hence, in general, period T denotes the latest (most recent) conditioning period in the information set.

it is fairly natural to choose the point forecast for which the expected cost $E\{C(e^f_{iT+h})\}$ is minimized. It is the custom to refer to the cost minimizing forecast as an optimal point forecast. The particular cost function,

$$C(e^f_{iT+h}) = a(e^f_{iT+h})^2, \tag{12.2}$$

where a is a positive constant gives tidy and much referenced solutions. For example, the optimal point forecast is the conditional expectation of Y_{iT+h}, i.e.,

$$Y^f_{i,T+h|T} = E(Y_{i,T+h} \mid \mathcal{I}_T). \tag{12.3}$$

We have already referred to this classical result in Section 5.5. Since (12.2) corresponds to a least squares criterion, the result says that the conditional expectation of $Y_{i,T+h}$ has the minimum mean squared forecast error (MSFE) among all conditional predictors; see e.g., Clements and Hendry (1998, Sections 2.1 and 2.7.2) for proofs.

As we shall see, this classical result is very useful as a reference point. It requires about the conditional density function only that the first two moments exist. But it does depend of the cost function being on the form (12.2), i.e., quadratic, or at least symmetric. The actual value of the parameter a is, however, unimportant, and one typically sets it to $a = 1$ for simplicity.

The assumption of symmetry of the cost function is clearly not always acceptable, at least not for the individual decision maker (consider being 30 minutes early at you flight's gate against being 30 minutes late). However, the importance of non-symmetries for macroeconomic decision making is less obvious. If relevant, so that there is greater cost attached to, say, under-prediction than to over-prediction, an optimal forecasting rule would on average over-predict.[2] This suggest, in practical model-based forecasting, to set some of the future disturbances to positive values. Below, we refer to this practice as correction of "raw" forecasts by intercept-correction (also know as the use of *add-factors*).

As summarized in Granger and Newbold (1986, p. 127), the practical relevance of these considerations seems to be that working with a least

[2]For example, if the purpose of the forecasting is to aid decisions about regulations that reduce the risk of financial crisis and disruptive effects on the macroeconomy, the cost to society of under-predicting future bank losses and defaults may be larger than over-predicting them.

squares criterion is much more general and defensible than might originally have been thought. This chapter uses the conditional expectation as the workhorse predictor and reference forecasting function. Apart from the asymmetry mentioned above, the main reason for using other point forecasting generators is that another premise of the classic optimality may not hold in many practical forecasting situations. It has to do with the, seemingly innocuous, detail that the expectation operator in (12.3) is not dated by a "t" subscript.

The undated expectation operator reflects the assumption that the conditional probability density functions of $Y_{iT+1}, Y_{iT+1}, \dots$ (the future) are identical to the probability density functions of $Y_{i,T}, Y_{i,T-1}, \dots$ (the past). However, it is only for the second set of functions that we can estimate the parameters empirically. The correct probability distribution for the *future* values of Y_{it} cannot be known at the time of preparing a genuine (real-life) forecast. Hence, the omission of a time subscript on E in (12.3) is actually an expression for an assumption saying that (with the exception of the initial conditions) the parameters of the distributions for the random variable are the same in the future (i.e., forecasting period) as they have been in the past. Said in other words, the assumption about no structural breaks in the forecasting period is mentioned in the introduction to the chapter.

Hence, despite the usefulness of the classical result about optimality of the conditional expectation function as a forecasting device, there are also several qualifications to be made due to the broad-sense non-stationarity that typically characterizes the random variables that we are interested in forecasting.

Nevertheless, we continue the chapter with a review of the basic algebra of VAR-based forecasts, and of the properties of the associated forecast errors when the assumption about broad-sense stationarity holds. This reference case will prove to be useful also for discussing the challenges that face us as forecasters of a non-stationary economy.

12.3. Reference Properties of VAR-Based Forecasts

As we have seen above, the simplest case of the VAR, with $n = 1$ and $p = 1$, is the AR(1) process. We first establish the forecast algebra for the AR(1) case. Despite its simplicity, AR(1) forecasting holds a lot a generality, as the subsequent treatment of AR(p), VAR and SEM type forecasts will show.

12.3.1. AR(1) forecasting

In this case, we do not need the subscript i for the variable number in a system, hence we write the process Y_t; $t = 0, 1, 2, \ldots, T$ as

$$Y_t = \phi_0 + \phi_1 Y_{t-1} + \varepsilon_t, \tag{12.4}$$

where the symbols take the same meaning as earlier in the book, and ε_t is assumed to be Gaussian white noise with variance σ_ϵ^2.

As noted above, the key assumption of the reference case is that the parameters $(\phi_0, \phi_1, \sigma_\epsilon^2)$ are the same in the forecast period Y_{T+h}; $h = 1, 2, 3, \ldots, H$, as they were in the past Y_t; $t = 0, 1, 2, \ldots, T$.

By the use of repeated insertion, the solution for Y_{T+h} (conditional on Y_T) is found as

$$Y_{T+h} = \phi_0 \sum_{j=0}^{h-1} \phi_1^j + \phi_1^h Y_T + \sum_{j=0}^{h-1} \phi_1^j \varepsilon_{T+h-j}, \quad h = 1, 2, \ldots, H. \tag{12.5}$$

Clearly, Y_{T+h} is a random variable due to $\sum_{j=1}^{h} \phi_1^{j-1} \varepsilon_{T+j}$, which is a linear combination of random variables.[3] The initial condition, Y_T, is a parameter in the expression, the other parameters are the coefficients ϕ_0 and ϕ_1^h.

We next assume weak stationarity, i.e., $-1 < \phi_1 < 1$. The first term in the solution can then be expressed as

$$\phi_0 \sum_{j=0}^{h-1} \phi_1^j = \phi_0 \frac{1 - \phi_1^h}{1 - \phi_1},$$

with reference to the result for summation of the first h terms in a finite geometric progression. In order to keep the exposition in the chapter self-contained, we retrace some of the steps from Section 3.3 (as the observant reader will have noticed). Hence, the solution for Y_{T+h} can be reexpressed as

$$\begin{aligned} Y_{T+h} &= \phi_0 \frac{1 - \phi_1^h}{1 - \phi_1} + \phi_1^h Y_T + \sum_{j=0}^{h-1} \phi_1^j \varepsilon_{T+h-j} \\ &= \frac{\phi_0}{1 - \phi_1} + \phi_1^h \left(Y_T - \frac{\phi_0}{1 - \phi_1} \right) + \sum_{j=0}^{h-1} \phi_1^j \varepsilon_{T+h-j}. \end{aligned} \tag{12.6}$$

[3] A well-behaved one-sided filter in the case of $-1 < \phi_1 < 1$.

In the same way as above, we let Y^* denote the unconditional mean of Y_t (i.e., the expectation):

$$Y^* \underset{\text{def}}{=} \frac{\phi_0}{1-\phi_1} \equiv E(Y_t),$$

which gives a compact expression for Y_{T+h} in the stationary case ($-1 < \phi_1 < 1$):

$$Y_{T+h} = Y^* + \phi_1^h(Y_T - Y^*) + \sum_{j=0}^{h-1} \phi_1^j \varepsilon_{T+h-j}, \quad h = 1, 2, \ldots, H, \tag{12.7}$$

or

$$Y_{T+h} = (1 - \phi_1^h)Y^* + \phi_1^h Y_T + \sum_{j=0}^{h-1} \phi_1^j \varepsilon_{T+h-j}, \quad h = 1, 2, \ldots, H. \tag{12.8}$$

As noted above, we use the conditional expectation:

$$Y^f_{T+h|T} = E(Y_{T+h} \mid \mathcal{I}_T), \tag{12.9}$$

as our workhorse predictor. From (12.7), it is given as

$$Y^f_{T+h|T} = E(Y_{T+h} \mid \mathcal{I}_T) = Y^* + \phi_1^h(Y_T - Y^*), \quad h = 1, 2, \ldots, H, \tag{12.10}$$

since, given the assumption that the process is unchanged in the forecast period, we have $E(\varepsilon_{T+j} \mid \mathcal{I}_T) = 0$ for $h = 1, 2, \ldots, H$.

Equation (12.10) is a genuine forecasting *function*. The single argument of the function is h, which is decided by the forecaster. Y^*, Y_T and ϕ_1 are the parameters of the function.

The parameter Y_T is observable. Given the assumptions of the Gaussian AR(1) process, the parameters Y^* and ϕ_1 can be estimated consistently from the available time series data, as the earlier chapters have shown.

Below, we will discuss the consequences of the fact that, in practice, initial conditions are not perfectly observed. For example, national accounts data for any given year or quarter are subject to revisions, in particular, in the first periods after the first release. Finite sample bias of estimated coefficient also plays a role for real-life forecast errors. However, given the assumption that the model is a good approximation to the DGP (in the sample period), we can abstract from estimation issues in order to bring out what the main challenge of model-based economic forecasting is. As we shall soon see, it is not the estimation, by itself, that explains why model-based forecasters run the danger of producing large forecast errors.

When we assume that Y^* and ϕ_1 are known numbers, the properties of the forecasting function become particularly clear. For positively autocorrelated data ($0 < \phi_1 < 1$), the 1-step forecast $Y^f_{T+1|T}$ will be above the long-run mean Y^* if initially $(Y_T - Y^*) > 0$. It will be lower if $(Y_T - Y^*) < 0$. Finally, $Y^f_{T+1|T} = Y^*$ in the case where the initial period is characterized by equilibrium, i.e., $Y_T = Y^*$. When we consider dynamic forecasts ($h > 1$), the impact of the initial condition is reduced (due to stationarity) and the values of the forecasting function approach Y^* as h is increased. Hence, the forecasts of the (stationary) AR(1)-process equilibrium are correct.

The properties of the forecasting function are also illustrated by using (12.8), and writing it as

$$Y^f_{T+h|T} = (1 - \phi_1^h)Y^* + \phi_1^h Y_T, \quad h = 1, 2, \ldots, H, \tag{12.11}$$

which brings out the *glide path* interpretation: The forecast starts with the number $\phi_1 Y_T$, and glides (smoothly, if ϕ_1 is positive) towards the final value $(1 - \phi_1^H)Y^* + \phi_1^H Y_T$, as h is increased. For long forecast horizons, which can be approximated by setting $H \to \infty$, the glide path is between $\phi_1 Y_T$ (starting point) and Y^* (end point).

The AR(1) forecast errors:

$$e^f_{T+h|T} = Y_{T+h} - Y^f_{T+h|T}, \quad h = 1, 2, \ldots, H, \tag{12.12}$$

follow from the above expressions, and are given by

$$e^f_{T+h|T} = \sum_{h=1}^{h} \phi_1^{h-1} \varepsilon_{T+h}, \quad h = 1, 2, \ldots, H. \tag{12.13}$$

For all choices of h, the forecast error has expectation zero: $E(e^f_{T+h|T}) = 0$ (unbiased forecasts), and the variance is

$$\operatorname{Var}(e^f_{T+h|T}) = \sigma^2_\varepsilon \frac{1 - \phi_1^{2h}}{1 - \phi_1^2}. \tag{12.14}$$

Said differently, the variance of a forecast error is identical to the variance of the variable itself (Y_{T+h}, cf. (4.17)). This, of course, is a consequence of the deterministic nature of the forecasting function. Hence, for long forecast horizons:

$$\operatorname{Var}(e^f_{T+h|T}) \underset{h \to \infty}{=} \frac{\sigma^2_\varepsilon}{1 - \phi_1^2} = \operatorname{Var}(Y_t), \tag{12.15}$$

saying that the forecast error variance becomes identical to the unconditional variance of the variable Y_t.

12.3.2. AR(p) forecasting

In Chapter 3, we obtained (3.42) as the solution of Y_t when the generating process is an autoregressive process of order p. We can use that result to write the solution for Y_{T+h} when the solution is conditional on the p initial conditions $\{Y_T, Y_{T-1}, \dots, Y_{T-(p-1)}\}$:

$$\begin{aligned} Y_{T+h} &= b_{11}^{(h)} Y_T + b_{12}^{(h)} Y_{T-1} + \cdots + b_{1p}^{(h)} Y_{T-(p-1)} \\ &\quad + \phi_0(1 + b_{11}^{(1)} + b_{11}^{(2)} + \cdots + b_{11}^{(h-1)}) \\ &\quad + b_{11}^{(h-1)} \varepsilon_{T+1} + b_{11}^{(h-2)} \varepsilon_{T+2} + \cdots + b_{11}^{(1)} \varepsilon_{T+h-1} + \varepsilon_{T+h}, \quad (12.16) \\ h &= 1, 2, \dots, H. \end{aligned}$$

We refer to the definitions and expressions given in Section 3.4, which show that $b_{1i}^{(j)}$ $(i = 1, \dots, p)$ is a linear combination of powers j of the p characteristic roots (see Equation (3.51)). Above, we also defined:

$$b_{11}^{(0)} \underset{\text{def}}{=} 1,$$

so that we can write (12.16) more compactly as

$$Y_{T+h} = \sum_{k=1}^{p} b_{1k}^{(h)} Y_{T-(k-1)} + \phi_0 \sum_{j=0}^{h-1} b_{11}^{(j)} + \sum_{j=0}^{h-1} b_{11}^{(j)} \varepsilon_{T+h-j}, \quad (12.17)$$

which has the same status as the solution (12.5) for AR(1), i.e., it holds also outside the stationary case.

When the process is a stationary AR(p) process, all the p roots are inside the unit-circle. We therefore have that, in parallel to (3.56):

$$\phi_0 \lim_{h\to\infty} \sum_{j=0}^{h-1} b_{11}^{(j)} = Y^* \underset{\text{def}}{=} E(Y). \quad (12.18)$$

Moreover, in the stationary case, the second term on the right-hand side in (12.17) can be expressed as

$$\begin{aligned} \phi_0 \sum_{j=0}^{h-1} b_{11}^{(j)} &= \phi_0 \lim_{h\to\infty} \left[\sum_{j=0}^{h-1} b_{11}^{(j)}\right] - \phi_0 \sum_{j=0}^{\infty} b_{11}^{(h+j)} \\ &= Y^* - R^{(h)}, \end{aligned} \quad (12.19)$$

where

$$R^{(h)} \underset{\text{def}}{=} \phi_0 \sum_{j=0}^{\infty} b_{11}^{(h+j)}.$$

Using these expressions, we can rewrite (12.17) in a way that generalizes (12.7):

$$\begin{aligned} Y_{T+h} = & \left[1 + \sum_{k=1}^{p} b_{1k}^{(h)}\right] Y^* - R^{(h)} + \sum_{k=1}^{p} b_{1k}^{(h)} [Y_{T-(k-1)} - Y^*] \\ & + \sum_{j=0}^{h-1} b_{11}^{(j)} \varepsilon_{T+h-j}, \qquad (12.20) \\ & h = 1, 2, \ldots, H. \end{aligned}$$

The conditional expectation predictor, i.e., the forecasting function, for AR(p) is therefore:

$$\begin{aligned} Y^f_{T+h|\mathcal{I}_T} = & \left[1 + \sum_{k=1}^{p} b_{1k}^{(h)}\right] Y^* - R^{(h)} + \sum_{k=1}^{p} b_{1k}^{(h)} [Y_{T-(k-1)} - Y^*], \qquad (12.21) \\ & h = 1, 2, \ldots, H. \end{aligned}$$

In the same way as in the AR(1) case, $Y^f_{T+h|\mathcal{I}_T}$ is a function of h. The p initial values are parameters that define the starting value of the function, for $Y^f_{T+1|\mathcal{I}_T}$, and the equilibrium parameter Y^* defines the end point. This basic property is a consequence of the stationarity assumption (all roots inside the unit-circle), which implies

$$R^{(h)} \underset{h\to\infty}{\to} 0, \quad \text{and}$$

$$\sum_{k=1}^{p} b_{1k}^{(h)} \underset{h\to\infty}{\to} 0, \quad \text{and}$$

$$\sum_{k=1}^{p} b_{1k}^{(h)} [Y_{T-(k-1)} - Y^*] \underset{h\to\infty}{\to} 0.$$

The path between the starting point and the end point of the forecast is continuous, but it is not necessarily a monotonous glide path (i.e., due to complex characteristic roots).

The AR(p) forecast errors become

$$e^f_{T+h|\mathcal{I}_T} = \sum_{j=0}^{h-1} b_{11}^{(j)} \varepsilon_{T+h-j}, \quad h = 1, 2, \ldots, H, \qquad (12.22)$$

with $E(e^f_{T+h|\mathcal{I}_T}) = 0$ for all h, and variance:

$$\operatorname{Var}(e^f_{T+h|\mathcal{I}_T}) = \sigma_\varepsilon^2 \sum_{j=0}^{h-1} b_{11}^{(j)^2} \underset{h\to\infty}{=} \operatorname{Var}(Y_t). \tag{12.23}$$

12.3.3. VAR and VAR-EX forecasting

Consider the case where the variable being forecasted is an endogenous variable in a VAR with n endogenous variables. In Section 5.5, we mentioned forecasting as the main objective for the use of VARs in macroeconomics. We also introduced fan-charts as a way of illustrating forecast uncertainty using the cobweb model simulated data as an example.

In this chapter, the focus is on the glide path interpretation. Hence, we reintroduce the notation with subscript i for an endogenous variable, Y_{it}, $i = 1, 2, \ldots, n$. As shown in Chapter 5, a VAR implies n final form equations (one for each endogenous variable) with identical homogeneous parts, but with distinct non-homogeneous parts (constant term and random disturbances). It follows that the conditional predictor:

$$Y^f_{iT+h|\mathcal{I}_T} = E(Y_{iT+h} \mid \mathcal{I}_T), \quad i = 1, 2, \ldots, n, \tag{12.24}$$

has the same mathematical form as in the AR(p) case, i.e., (12.21):

$$\begin{aligned} Y^f_{iT+h|\mathcal{I}_T} &= \left[1 + \sum_{k=1}^{p} b_{1k}^{(h)}\right] Y_i^* - R_i^{(h)} \\ &\quad + \sum_{k=1}^{p} b_{1k}^{(h)} [Y_{iT-(k-1)} - Y_i^*], \quad i = 1, 2, \ldots, n. \end{aligned} \tag{12.25}$$

As shown above, the lag length p in (12.20) is given by the dimension of the VAR (n) multiplied by the order of the VAR. It follows that the VAR forecast errors also share the properties of the AR(p) errors. In particular, the forecast error variances are

$$\operatorname{Var}(e^f_{iT+h|\mathcal{I}_T}) \underset{h\to\infty}{=} \operatorname{Var}(Y_{it}), \quad i = 1, 2, \ldots, \tag{12.26}$$

for an n-dimensional stationary VAR.

The above algebra can also be modified to cover forecasts from a VAR with exogenous variables, i.e., a VAR-EX. The system we have in mind is one where one or more random variables appear on the right-hand side of the VAR, and none of these variables is Granger-caused by the endogenous variables. How we proceed will depend on the purpose of the forecasting project. If the purpose is to make the best (in the MSFE sense) forecast of the Y-variables (i.e., the purpose we have assumed so far), we can use a separate VAR for the X-variables to obtain forecasts that are used as input in the VAR forecast for Y.

Without loss of generality, consider the case with only one exogenous X_t in the VAR-EX. The forecasting function (12.25) may then be modified to

$$\begin{aligned} Y^f_{iT+h|\mathcal{I}_T} = {} & \left[1 + \sum_{k=1}^{p} b_{1k}^{(h)}\right] Y_i^*(X^*) - R_i^{(h)} + \sum_{k=1}^{p} b_{1k}^{(h)} [Y_{iT-(k-1)} - Y_i^*(X^*)] \\ & + \sum_{j=0}^{h-1} b_{11}^{(j)} X^f_{T+h-j}, \qquad (12.27) \\ & i = 1, 2, \ldots, n; \; h = 1, 2, \ldots, H, \end{aligned}$$

where X^f_{T+h-j} on the right-hand side denotes the forecasted values of the exogenous variable.[4] The other modification of (12.20) is that, since X_t is a forcing variable in the system, Y_i^* is associated with the long-run expectation of X_t. Therefore, we have written $Y_i^*(X^*)$ in expression (12.27).

Sometimes, the objective can be different than to produce the best MSFE forecast. For example, the purpose may be to illustrate a possible, though not very likely, future development of the economy, i.e., a *scenario analysis* as explained below. In this type of application, the extrapolation of X_t into the future can be made without the use of a VAR for the X-variable. Nevertheless, the future path of the endogenous Y-variables follows the same functional form as above:

$$\begin{aligned} Y^f_{iT+h|\mathcal{I}^{sc}_T} = {} & \left[1 + \sum_{k=1}^{p} b_{1k}^{(h)}\right] Y_i^*(X^{sc}) - R_i^{(h)} \\ & + \sum_{k=1}^{p} b_{1k}^{(h)} [Y_{iT-(k-1)} - Y_i^*(X^{sc})] + \sum_{j=0}^{h-1} b_{11}^{(j)} X^{sc}_{iT+h-j}, \qquad (12.28) \\ & i = 1, 2, \ldots, n; \; h = 1, 2, \ldots, H, \end{aligned}$$

where the superscript *sc* is used to indicate the chosen scenario path for X, and the associated long-run level for that specific scenario.

---

[4]Since we assume that X^f_{T+h-j} is forecasted from a separate VAR, it can be associated with a forecasting function which is similar to the AR(p) case above.

12.3.4. SEM forecasting

A dynamic simultaneous equation model has a reduced form which is a VAR, usually a VAR-EX. Hence, the above forecasting functions capture the gist of SEM-type forecasts as well as of VAR forecasts.

However, there are other benefits from choosing a SEM to forecast the macroeconomy. For example, national accounting identities, as well as other definitions, can be included as separate equations in the model. When the model is used for forecasting, the forecasted variables automatically satisfies those identities and definitions.

12.4. An Illustration of the Reference Case

We can illustrate the formulas above by the use of simulated data for the simple SEM macromodel used in earlier chapters, namely (1.27)–(1.29). According to the above forecasting theory, the endogenous variables have final equations with identical homogeneous parts. For C_t, the final equation is found in expression (1.32) above, which can alternatively be written as:

$$C_t = C^* + \phi_1 [C_{t-1} - C^*] + \frac{\epsilon_{Ct} + b\epsilon_{Jt}}{1-b}. \tag{12.29}$$

Since $\text{GDP}_t = C_t + J_t$, we have by insertion for C_t and J_t (Exercise 12.2):

$$\text{GDP}_t = \text{GDP}^* + \phi_1 [\text{GDP}_{t-1} - \text{GDP}^*] + \frac{\epsilon_{Ct} + b\epsilon_{Jt}}{1-b} - \phi_1 \epsilon_{Jt-1}, \tag{12.30}$$

which already shows that the two conditional forecasting functions will have different starting points (the initial values) and ending points (i.e., C^* and GDP^*), but that the dynamics (glide path) will be the same for the two variables.

Capital formation, i.e., investment, J, does not depend on GDP or C. Formally, J_t is therefore predetermined in a separate subsystem, and the final equation for J_t is the same as the model equation (1.29). Hence, the forecasting function for J_{T+h} is simply $J^f_{T+h|\mathcal{I}_T} = J^*$.

We illustrate the behaviour of the forecasting functions with the aid of simulated data for 20 time periods. We consider forecasts that are conditional on period $T = 100$. Hence the forecast period $T+h$ is $100+h$, $h = 1, 2, \ldots, H$, $H \leq 120$. In period 1–100 (sample available for estimation), the DGP parameters that are of importance for the forecasting functions have been set to:

$$a = -1, \quad b = 0.25,$$
$$c = 0.6, \quad J^* = 40, \tag{12.31}$$

implying:

$$\phi_1 = \frac{0.65}{1 - 0.25} = 0.8. \tag{12.32}$$

We let the parameters a, b, c (and therefore ϕ_1) be unchanged in the forecast period (101–120). We also assume in this section that J^* is unchanged (with value 40) in the forecast period. Below, we will see how the forecasts are affected if the value of J^* changes in the forecast period (i.e., a structural break).

Figure 12.1 shows the forecasts when we assume that the parameters in (12.31) are known to the forecaster at the time of running the model in period $T = 100$, producing forecasts for period $T + h = 101, \ldots, 120$.

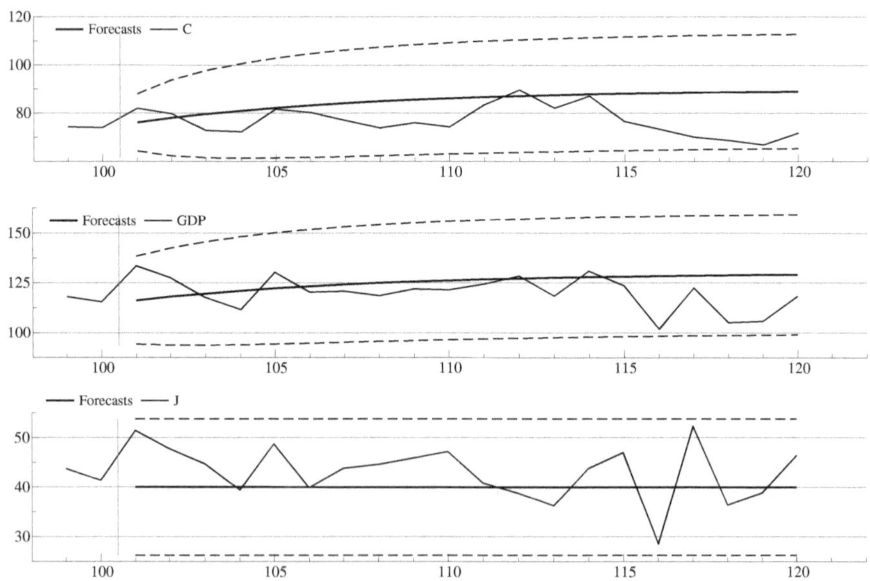

Figure 12.1. Forecasts with bounds (95%) as dashed lines, and actuals for the three variables of the Keynesian macromodel with simulated data. The true historical coefficients of the forecasting functions are assumed to be known in period $T = 100$ when the forecast is assumed to have been produced.

With the parameters in (12.31), the unconditional expectation of C_t is 90, and for GDP_t it is 130 (cf. Exercise 12.3). In the data, the values of both C_{100} and GDP_{100} are lower than the long run means. According to the theory above, due to the positive first-order autocorrelation of the final equations (i.e., $\phi_1 = \frac{0.65}{1-0.25} = 0.8$), the forecast functions of the two variables should increase monotonically towards the long-run values. That property is clearly illustrated by the graphs. Note also that all the actual values of the variables are inside the forecast intervals (indicated by dashed bounds in the graphs). Again, this is as the theory predicts: If we define a *forecast failure* as an event where the actual value is outside an interval with high confidence degree (e.g., 95%), then forecast failures should be rare events.

What happens to the forecast accuracy if we change the assumption about known coefficients to the more realistic assumption about estimation of the coefficients on a sample that ends in period $T = 100$? We can answer this question by comparing the Root Mean Squared Forecast Errors (RMSFEs) of the forecasts shown in Figure 12.1 with the RMFEs of the forecasts that use the estimated coefficients. The RMSFE is a much used descriptive measure of forecast accuracy, Klein (1983, Chapter 3). For an H-period forecast, it is defined as

$$\text{RMSFE} = \sqrt{\frac{1}{H}\sum_{h=1}^{H}(e^{f}_{T+h|\mathcal{I}_T})^2}, \tag{12.33}$$

where we have simplified the notation by dropping the subscript for the variable number being forecasted. The square of the RMSFE is the Mean Squared Forecast Error (MSFE), which can be decomposed in terms of the variance of the forecast-error ($\widehat{\text{Var}}(e_{T+H})$) and the squared bias of the forecasts ($(\widehat{\text{Bias}}Y_{T+H})^2$):

$$\text{MSFE} = \widehat{\text{Var}}(e_{T+H}) + (\widehat{\text{Bias}}Y_{T+H})^2 \tag{12.34}$$

(see Exercise 12.10). Table 12.1 shows the RMSFEs for the forecasts and outcomes in Figure 12.1 in the row labelled Known parameters. The second row, labelled estimated parameters, show the RMSFEs for the case where the SEM has been estimated (with FIML) using the 99 observations from period 2 to period 100. Note that the RMSFEs for the two sets of forecasts are practically the same. This illustrates that estimation, by itself, does not represent a threat to forecast accuracy in economics. Of course, in this

Table 12.1. RMSFE of the forecasts in Figure 12.1. Dynamic forecasts for 20 periods ($H = 20$) conditional on $T = 100$.

	RMSFE		
	C	GDP	J
Known parameters	11.2	11.7	6.5
Estimated parameters	11.2	11.9	6.5

case, the model *is* the DGP, and under that assumption we know that the estimation biases are not very large. The problem of deciding on a good empirical model is, however, a difficult one, as we has seen above. However, given that it has be resolved reasonably well, forecasting with the chosen empirical model is not fundamentally endangered by estimation bias.

Box 12.1. Statistical tests of forecast accuracy

As noted, MSFE and RMSFE are descriptive measures of forecast accuracy. Other descriptive measures are Average absolute error, and Average absolute percentage error. A concise introduction to formal statistical test is Clements (2005). A popular test of the comparative forecast accuracy of two forecast methods is the Diebold-Mariano (1995) test, and the modified test proposed by Harvey *et al.* (1997). The basic entities in both tests are pairs of h-steps ahead forecast errors, e.g., e_1 and e_2. The tests are based on the observed sample mean:

$$\bar{d} = \frac{1}{m}\sum_{\tau=1}^{m}(e_{1\tau}^2 - e_{2\tau}^2), \tag{12.35}$$

where m denotes the number of pairs of forecast errors (the number of observations in the test). Hence, the comparison is between two records of say h-period ahead forecasts produced at different point in time. For $h > 1$, the series made up of $d_\tau = e_{1\tau}^2 - e_{2\tau}^2$ is generally autocorrelated, and the DM test therefore takes into account that the variance of the mean $\bar{d}$ is affected by the autocovariance of d_τ.

12.5. Forecasting in a Non-stationary World

In addition to parameter estimation, there are several other differences between the reference forecasting situation, which is kind of an ideal situation, and the realities of real-life forecasting. As mentioned, mismeasurement of initial conditions is one, which will in the main affect the forecast errors for short horizons. Misspecification of functional forms (nonlinearities) is another. However, given that it is feasible (though difficult) to decide on empirical models that are relatively congruent with the historical data, the most important difference from the reference case becomes non-stationarity in the DGP. If a non-stationarity, in the form of a structural break, manifests itself just before the period of publishing the forecast, or in the forecast period itself, it is near impossible to avoid that the forecasts will be biased. Not all structural breaks are equally damaging though, as we will see in the following.

However, before turning to the most perilous forms of non-stationarity, we note that the above forecasting theory can be modified to $I(1)$-variables by noting that although the end point of the glide path is not defined for an $I(1)$-variable, the glide path still starts from known initial conditions, and it follows an increasing (or declining) path which is dominated by the unit-root, cf. (12.17). Moreover, for variables that are differences of $I(1)$ variables (generated from a VAR with unit-roots), the above theory holds unabridged. The same is true for valid ECM-terms, which are $I(0)$ as implied by cointegration.

12.5.1. Location shift after the forecast origin

The really challenging types of non-stationarity for forecasting are structural breaks, particularly in the long-run unconditional means of the variables. We can illustrate this point by forecasting from the example macromodel under the assumption that (12.31) represents the parameters in the period up to and including $T = 100$, and that the parameter J^* changes to 20 in period $T + 1 = 101$. Since J^* affects the unconditional means of both C_t and GDP_t, it represents a *location shift* in the DGP. However, the location shift taking place in the economy early in period $T + 1$ may not be detectable for the forecaster (it cannot be made part of $\mathcal{I}_T$). Hence, the forecasting functions will be unaffected by the regime shift, whereas the economy will change, and the implication of this may easily be forecast failures, as illustrated by Figure 12.2. The interpretation is that the economy in this case equilibrium-corrects towards:

$$J^{*\text{new}} = 20,$$

$$C^{*\text{new}} = 40,$$

$$\text{GDP}^{*\text{new}} = 60,$$

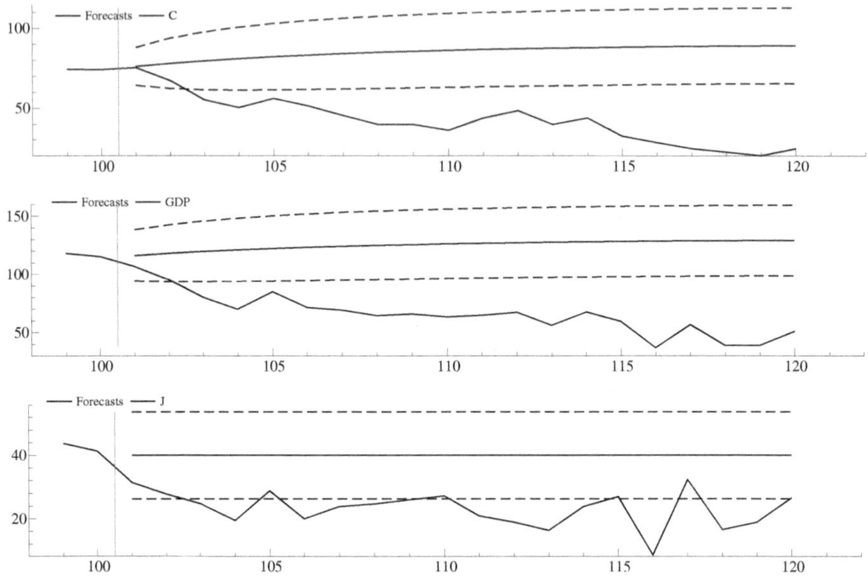

Figure 12.2. Forecasts with bounds (95%) as dashed lines, and actuals for the three variables of the Keynesian macromodel with simulated data. The true historical coefficients of the forecasting functions are known in period $T = 100$ when the forecast is produced. In the DGP, the parameter J^* changes from 40 to 20, so that actuals are affected for $T + h = 101, 102, \ldots, 120$.

Table 12.2. Root mean squared errors of the forecasts in Figure 12.1 and 12.2. Dynamic forecasts for 20 periods ($H = 20$) conditional on $T = 100$.

	RMSFE		
	C	GDP	J
Without break at the start of period 101	11.2	11.7	6.5
With break at the start of period 101	46.4	63.1	17.8

the forecasting functions correct towards the equilibrium values of the *pre-break* DGP, which in the current example are $C^* = 90$ and $\text{GDP}^* = 130$.

Table 12.2 shows the RMSFEs for the two sets of dynamics forecasts that we have considered so far. It documents the large increase in squared forecast errors for all three variables in the model even though only one of the variables (i.e., J_t) is directly affected by the structural break. The algebra of the biases in Figure 12.2 follows directly from the AR(1) case above. Hence, for Y_i (where Y_i can correspond to C

or GDP in the figure), we have that the forecast function conditional on $\mathcal{I}_T$ is

$$Y^f_{iT+h|T} = E(Y_{iT+h} \mid \mathcal{I}_T) = Y^* + \phi_1^h(Y_{iT} - Y_i^*), \quad h = 1, 2, \ldots, H. \tag{12.36}$$

However, the expectation of Y_{iT+h}, conditional on the information set which includes the parameter change that occurs at the start of the first forecast period, denoted by $\mathcal{I}_T^{\text{new}}$, is

$$E(Y_{iT+h} \mid \mathcal{I}_T^{\text{new}}) = Y_i^{*\text{new}} + \phi_1^h(Y_{iT} - Y_i^{*\text{new}}), \quad h = 1, 2, \ldots, H. \tag{12.37}$$

Hence, the expectations of the forecast errors e^f_{iT+1} will not be zero as in the case without structural break. Instead, we get the forecast bias function:

$$E(Y_{iT+h} \mid \mathcal{I}_T^{\text{new}}) - Y^f_{iT+h|T} = Y_i^{*\text{new}} - Y_i^* - \phi_1^h(Y_i^{*\text{new}} - Y_i^*), \quad h \geq 1. \tag{12.38}$$

With $0 < \phi_1 < 1$, the bias is positive for all h, and the magnitude is increasing with h, approaching $Y_i^* - Y_i^{*\text{new}}$ for long forecast horizons. We see that the biases for C and GDP shown in Figure 12.2 illustrate this function.

The algebra for the forecast bias generalizes to the forecasts from any (implied) AR(p) model (Exercise 12.4):

$$\begin{aligned} &E(Y_{iT+h} \mid \mathcal{I}_T^{\text{new}}) - Y^f_{iT+h|T} \\ &\quad = \left[1 + \sum_{k=1}^{p} f_{1k}^{(h)}\right](Y_i^{*\text{new}} - Y_i^*) - (R^{\text{new}(h)} - R^{(h)}) \\ &\qquad - \sum_{k=1}^{p} f_{1k}^{(h)}(Y_i^{*\text{new}} - Y_i^*), \end{aligned} \tag{12.39}$$

where the term $(R^{\text{new}(h)} - R^{(h)})$ is required since both $R^{(h)}$ and Y_i^* in the general expressions depend on ϕ_0. However, the first term on the right-hand side tends to dominate, and for dynamic forecasts ($h > 1$) the bias becomes well approximated by $(Y_i^* - Y_i^{*\text{new}})$, just as in the AR(1) case.

The above result for the biases in dynamic forecasts can be extended to situations where a location break in the DGP (i.e., in the real world) occurs later in the forecast period rather than in the first period after the forecast has been produced. Assume, for example, that we have $H = 20$, as in Figure 12.2, and that the change from J^* to $J^{*\text{new}}$ occurs for $h = 5$ rather than for $h = 1$. In such case, the forecasts for private consumption and GDP will be unbiased for $h = 1, 2, 3, 4$, but from period $h = 5$, the bias-driving forces will begin to damage the forecasts, creating an increasing bias. Since location breaks can happen anywhere in a dynamic economic system, and that the forecasts for all variables in a system are, in principle, affected, it is more or less inevitable that dynamic forecasts will be damaged by structural breaks in the forecasting period. The longer the forecast horizon, the larger the probability that a forecast failure will occur.

12.5.2. Location shifts before the forecast origin

Returning to the case where the location shift occurs at the start of period $T+1$, we note that, in practice, a variable is not forecasted once and for all. Instead, updated macroeconomic forecasts are continuously published, as new information becomes available. This is the same as with weather forecasts: Today's forecast for the day after tomorrow will be replaced tomorrow by a forecast for tomorrow's weather. Sometimes, there are important differences between two forecasts for the same day, notably when a sudden atmospheric change has been picked up by the meteorological measurement system, and the new measures have been put into the weather forecasting model (i.e., a revised initial condition).

It is reasonable to ask how forecast-updating in economics will affect the forecast biases that are caused by regime shifts? The answer depends on how much information about the regime shift the forecaster manages to build into the information set for the updated forecast.

Consider a situation where new data have been released, so that we can condition on period $T + 1$, and use the model to forecast $T + 2, T + 3, \ldots, T + 1 + H$. Since the location shift is now in the information set of the forecast, in the sense that the initial condition Y_{T+1} is affected by the change from Y^* to $Y^{*\text{new}}$, a first thought may be that the model forecasts that conditions on Y_{T+1} will be less biased than the forecasts that were conditional on Y_T.

Unfortunately, that intuition is wrong, which we next show (without loss of generality) for the AR(1)-case. The updated forecasting function can be written as:

$$\begin{aligned} Y^f_{iT+1+h|T+1} &= E(Y_{iT+1+h} \mid \mathcal{I}_{T+1}) \\ &= Y^* + \phi_1^h (Y_{iT+1} - Y_i^*), \quad h = 1, 2, \ldots, H, \quad (12.40) \end{aligned}$$

where we note that the new initial condition is a function of the new equilibrium value for Y_{it}:

$$Y_{iT+1} = Y^{*\text{new}} + \phi_1(Y_{iT} - Y_i^{*\text{new}}) + \varepsilon_{T+1}, \quad h = 1, 2, \ldots, H.$$

Nevertheless, since the unbiased conditional expectation is

$$E(Y_{iT+1+h} \mid \mathcal{I}_{T+1}^{\text{new}}) = Y^{*\text{new}} + \phi_1^h(Y_{iT+1} - Y_i^{*\text{new}}), \quad h \geq 1 \qquad (12.41)$$

the biases are given by the same function as in (12.38), only with new subscripts for the dating of the variables on the left-hand side of the equation:

$$\begin{aligned} E(Y_{iT+1+h} \mid \mathcal{I}_{T+1}^{\text{new}}) - Y_{iT+1+h|T+1}^{f} \\ = (Y_i^{*\text{new}} - Y_i^*) - \phi_1^h(Y_i^{*\text{new}} - Y_i^*), \quad h \geq 1. \end{aligned} \qquad (12.42)$$

Hence, even when the model-based forecast is conditioned on initial conditions that have the new location parameter "baked into" them, the forecast errors have the same bias as when the regime shift occurred after the preparation of the forecast. The glide path of the forecasting function and that of the actual economy have the same starting point but the end points are different. Both equilibrium-correct, but with respect to two different equilibria: the old (forecast), and the new (real-world economy).

Unfortunately, updated model-based forecasts do not automatically correct previous forecast errors. In order to be put on the right glide path, model-based forecasts need to be corrected by the forecaster: either by discovering what the new value $Y^{*\text{new}}$ is or by the use of the so-called *add-factors* (intercept corrections), which means setting the disturbances to non-zero values in the forecast period. We comment on this measure below along with alternative forecasting functions that produce forecasts that are more robust to changes in equilibrium means than uncorrected model forecasts are.

Above, we have only analyzed one type of regime shift that might damage model-based forecast. We have referred to it as change in long-run equilibrium mean, or location shift. However, since we have maintained that all the characteristic roots are the same in the forecast period as in the historical conditioning period, the interpretation is that it is the intercept (the constant term) of the forecasting function that is the source of the location shift.

As documented in Clements and Hendry (1999), changes in other parameters of the DGP than the long-run means will also affect the forecast errors. In practical forecasting, there may also be a combination of types of parameter changes. However, location shifts seem to be a dominant source of the type of large prediction errors that we call forecast failures, Clements and Hendry (2006), Hendry (2001).

12.5.3. Black swans and macroeconomic forecasting

Since Nassim Taleb's books, Taleb (2004, 2010), the black swan has become a metaphor for the unknown. In our context, a single black swan represents that a future observation may be more likely than indicated by the bounds of the forecast interval based on the standard normal distribution (see Section 2.2.3). As noted, macroeconomic forecasting, unlike for financial investors, a single outlier observation (black swan) hidden in the tails of a non-normal (but still symmetric) distribution may not represent a large issue.

David Hendry has likened location shifts to a flock of black swans (Hendry, 2018). Persistent changes in parameters can shift the location of the distribution, and then forecast failures will occur. When such unanticipated shifts occur, today's model-based conditional expectation of events tomorrow can be biased. More generally, today's expectation can be a poor estimate of tomorrow's outcome. Below, we shall see that when location shifts occurs, the conditional expectation can become dominated by other predictors, some of them may be quite poor approximations of the economy's DGP, but they may be quick to adapt to location shifts. One practical (informal) procedure that can guide a model-based forecast to go at least in the right direction after a location shift is the intercept correction just mentioned. Below, that remedy is explained as one way of making the forecast more robust to location-breaks.

12.6. Forecast Failures in Practice

Although the above analysis is stylized, it reflects some important traits that are easy to spot in the forecast records of professional forecasters. One practical example of that can be found in the forecasts of inflation which became part of the inflation targeting monetary policy that many countries adopted before and just after the new millennium.

In March 2001, Norway formally introduced an inflation targeting monetary policy regime. The Central Bank of Norway committed itself to stabilization of the annual inflation at 2.5%. During the first years of the new monetary policy regime, the operational target was defined as the forecasted

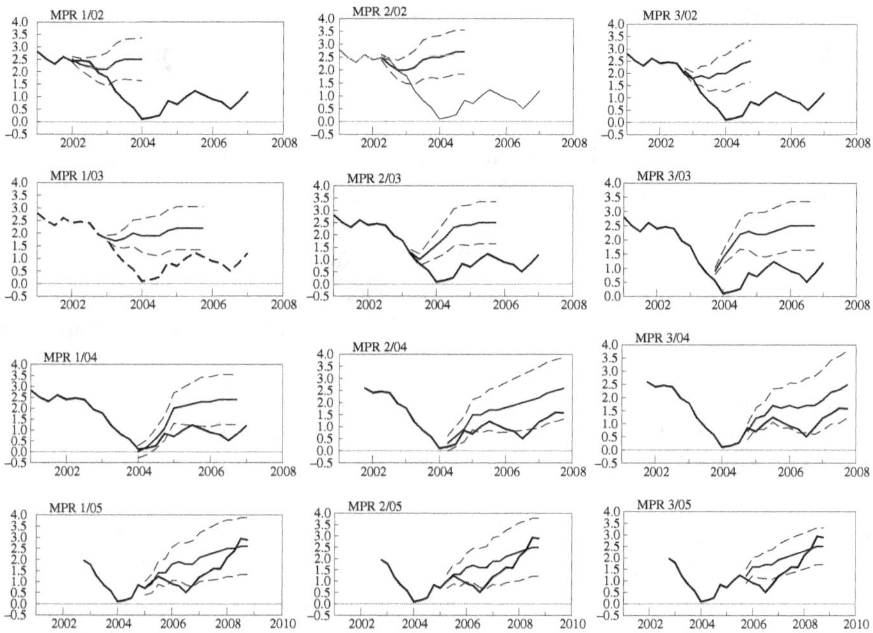

Figure 12.3. Norges Bank's inflation forecasts with 90% confidence bounds (dashed lines), and actual CPI-AET inflation shown in the thicker line graphs (in percent). The forecasts were published in Monetary Policy Report 1/02 to MPR 3/05.

rate of inflation 2 years ahead. In 2004, the policy horizon was changed to 1–3 years. The operational measure of core inflation has been based on the official consumer price index adjusted for the influence of energy prices and indirect taxes, denoted by CPI-ATE.

Forecasts from 12 Monetary Policy Reports (MPRs) from the years 2002–2005 are shown in Figure 12.3. In each panel, there are graphs for the dynamic inflation forecasts together with the 90% forecast confidence bounds, and also the actual inflation rate. There are several examples of forecast failure. For example, in MPR 2/02, the first four inflation outcomes are within the forecast confidence interval, but the continued fall in inflation in 2003 (the second year of the forecast horizon) constitutes a forecast failure. Forecast failure became more evident in the two other forecasting rounds in 2002, and all the three forecasts produced in 2003 predicted significantly higher inflation than the actual outcome. Specifically, the forecast confidence interval of MPR 3/03 did not even cover the actual inflation in the first forecast period.

The seventh panel shows that the forecasted zero rate of inflation for 2004(1) in MPR 1/04 turned out to be accurate. The change from the MPR 3/03 forecast is evident, and can be interpreted as an adaptation to a lower inflation level. That process continued in MPR 2/04, where the effect of the lengthening of the forecasting and policy horizon mentioned above is clearly visible. Although the MPR 2/04 forecasts became too high, only one of them represents a forecast failure, as we have defined the phenomenon. The last four panels in Figure 12.3 show many of the same features. The 1-step, and sometimes also the 2-step forecasts are accurate, but otherwise the forecasted inflation rate is too high. The MPR 1/05-3/05 forecasts for the end-of-horizon are accurate though as the actual inflation was a little higher than 2.5%.

In summary, the early inflation forecasts record of Norges Bank can be divided into two phases: before and after 2004. Before 2004, the monetary policy report forecast errors bear the marks of slow adaptation to a reduction of the inflation rate that became manifest during 2003. After 2004, there are fewer very large forecast errors. The above forecasts were analyzed in Falch and Nymoen (2011), who ran a parallel sequence of dynamic inflation forecasts (i.e., in real time, not *ex post*) and concluded that the central bank's forecasting in that period suffered from the use of a forecasting function that gave too little weight to the foreign inflation rate. As the start of inflation targeting (and policy-oriented forecasting) coincided with China's new roles as the world's main workshop for manufactures, that weakness of the bank's macromodel contributed significantly to the forecasts not being adaptive enough to changes in the foreign inflation rate.

12.7. Add-Factors and Intercept Corrections

It follows from the above that the routine of forecasting with all future equation disturbances set to zero is only optimal when the future becomes like the past has been. *Ex post*, when the forecast becomes evaluated against the actual values of the variables that the economy produced, it is often clear that the forecasts would have been less biased if one had been able to assign a reasonable non-zero value to one or more of the models' disturbance terms in the forecasting period. The assignment of non-zero values to disturbances is known as *add-factor* usage, or *intercept correction*. The first name is descriptive for what the forecasting economist is actually doing: She includes an additive term with non-zero values for the forecasting period in one or more of the model equations. Technically, this is the same as correcting the constant term (i.e., intercept) in the model equations, hence the name intercept correction. In the following, we use the two terms interchangeably as is usual among forecasters.

The use of add-factors is well known among practitioners as a method that can robustify forecasts against structural breaks. In his early overview of the field, Klein (1968) included "the assignment of values to residuals in prediction" (p. 48) in a chapter titled *The improvement of prediction.* Subsequently, intercept correction became heavily criticized, and has also been derogatorily relabelled as con-factor, cheat-term and *ad hoc* adjustment. It is still not uncommon that add-factor usage is pointed out as a threat to the ideal of clean or objective use of econometric models in forecasting.

On the other hand, one might ask whether the alternative of leaving the forecast unadjusted with respect to deterministic shifts that have occurred, really is defensible, if the lowest feasible forecast RMSFE is the criterion that one had in mind in the first place. In practice, intercept correction has long been known to improve forecast performance, see, e.g., Turner (1990) *inter alia.* Interestingly, correction of "raw" forecasts (for example, from a macromodel) played an important role in the theory of policy decision making under uncertainty that the Norwegian economist Leif Johansen developed (see Johansen, 1978, Section 8.9).

Clements and Hendry (1998, Chapter 8) provide a complete theory of the theory of intercept correction, and Clements and Hendry (1999, Chapter 6) investigate the usefulness of intercept correction strategies for offsetting deterministic shifts that have happened prior to the forecast origin. Since the time series are then stationary in the forecast period, the different forms of intercept corrections can be assessed in terms of squared-error loss. One of their main results is that add-factor usage in general reduces the bias of the forecast errors, but at the cost of increased forecast error variance.

We can now illustrate the impact of intercept correction on the forecast errors of our example macromodel. In Table 12.3, the row labelled *Conditional on period 100* shows, as reference, the RMSFEs in the "with break" row in Table 12.2, i.e., the RMSFEs in the case where the change in the mean of J_t happened after the preparation and publication of the forecast (after the forecast origin). The row labelled *Conditional on period 101* contains RMSFEs for two different post-break forecasts. The first (*Without add-factors*) is for the updated forecasts, where period 101 is conditioned on, and the first period forecasted is period 102, but where both

Table 12.3. Root mean squared errors of dynamic forecasts for 20 periods ($H = 20$) from the Keynesian model with and without add-factors.

	RMSFE		
	C	GDP	J
Conditional on period 100	46.4	63.1	17.8
Conditional on period 101			
Without add-factors	46.8	64.3	17.7
With add-factor for J_t	32.3	40.6	10.0
Conditional on period 102			
Without add-factors	46.5	63.1	19.9
With add-factor for J_t	24.4	29.5	7.4

the consumption and investment disturbances are set to zeros in the forecast period (which is from 102 to 121, keeping the forecast horizon at 20 as before). The post-break RMSFEs are practically unchanged from the pre-break RMSFEs, confirming what the theory in Section 12.5 indicated, namely, that being able to condition on the period where the break happened does not improve the "raw" model-based forecasts.

The row labelled *With add-factors*, however, shows a marked reduction in RMSFEs of all three variables. In this forecast, we have assigned the value -8.6 to the ϵ_{JT+1+h} ($h = 1, 2, \ldots, 20$) disturbances, effectively changing J^* from 40 to 31.4 for the length of the forecast period. Where does the intercept correcting number -8.6 come from? It is the error $J_{101} - J^f_{101|100}$ that becomes an observable entity when we are in period 102, and we are able to condition on the actual observation for period 101. Even though this feasible correction is far from perfect (which would have been to subtract -20), we see that the improvement in the RMSFE is notable. For example, the RMSFE for the consumption forecast is reduced by 30%.

The last two rows in the table shows the RMSFEs when the model forecast is conditioned on period 102, two periods after the location shift started to change the evolution of the variables. Again, the "raw" forecasts are not aided by the conditioning on data from two periods with the new regime. The forecasts with add-factor for investment are much better, the intercept-correction being in this case -12.3, which is the observed error $J_{102} - J^f_{102|101}$.

It is possible to imagine that through conditioning on new post-break forecast-errors as they become observable entities, the model-based forecast will adapt to the new equilibrium. Of course, in this example, the task of correcting the "raw" forecasts is made easier by the simple structure of the model, and by the large and permanent location-shift that takes place. In practice, in a larger multiple equation model, the task of identifying where a structural break has occurred will be much more difficult.

There is clearly a danger of over-treatment in the form of assignment of non-zero values to disturbance terms that should have been left with zeros. In practice, there will also be the issue about the permanency of a break. If the location shift is thought to be temporary instead of permanent, the correct adjustment of an equation error will be to have the largest numerical add-factors for $h = 1$, and let them tamper off toward zero as h is increased. In brief, constant add-factor use is best suited for correcting the end point of the glide path, while a reduced add-factor use (as h increases) is more geared towards correction of the starting point of the glide path (suspected mismeasurement of initial condition, or a temporary location shift).

In practice, in the preparation of a new forecast, not only will the latest forecast-error become available as a correction of the "raw" forecasts, the rational forecaster will also reestimate the coefficients of her model using the extended dataset. Although standard estimation methods may adjust slowly to regime shifts in the DGP, this practice will correct the updated forecast in the right direction. In addition, impulse indicator saturation (IIS), as explained in Chapter 11, is available as an aid in deciding whether recent forecast errors represent significant breaks or not. In summary, there are several methods now available that can be used to make model-based forecast more robust to location shifts than the "raw" forecasts are.

12.8. Combination of Forecasts

Just as it has been a "well-known secret" that add-factors can be used to correct "raw" forecasts, it has also been recognized for a long time that the combination of forecasts based on different methods can lead to forecasts that are more accurate in the MSFE sense than forecasts based on a single method; see Bates and Granger (1969), Granger and Newbold (1986), Timmermann (2006).

We need not go further than to the add-factor corrected forecast above, which clearly has an interpretation of a combined forecast: the "raw" model forecast and the judgemental correction of the equation disturbance.

However there are several other methods that can be used to form combined forecasts, especially by institutions that have the resources, Gerdrup *et al.* (2009).

In addition to expert judgement, which together with surveys about expectations clearly can play a role in the correction of "raw forecasts", a list of forecasting methods may contain the following: Univariate time series models, Exponential smoothing methods, Multi-step (or Multi-period) forecasting, Leading indicators, Factor models, Nonlinear models, State Space Representation and the Kalman filter, and Naive forecasts. Even this list is not complete, and new methods are continuously put forward in the lively field of economic forecasting.

Although all these methods are counted as different in applications, cf Ghysels and Marcellino (2018), there are also important similarities between some of them that should not be forgotten. Univariate time series models are specifications of ARMA models as defined in Chapter 4. Hence, the forecasts from these models will have the same fundamental properties as the VAR-based forecasts presented above. However, the inclusion of MA terms means that the forecasting function of, e.g., ARMA$(1,1)$ will behave differently from AR(1), but only for short forecast horizons though.

Following the influential book by Box and Jenkins (1976), a separate forecasting practice became established around the Box–Jenkins model selection. This branch of forecasting methods is well covered in several books (also textbooks) on forecasting, Granger and Newbold (1986, Chapter 5), Enders (2010, Chapter 2) among others. One practical side of this method has always been the differencing of the variables *before* the estimation of the time series models used in the forecasting. For this reason, there is an interesting connection between the comparative success of using Box–Jenkins methods to forecast macroeconomic series, and the robustness of so-called *Naive forecasts* to location shifts (see below).

Various types of Exponential smoothing, see Granger and Newbold (1986, Section 5.3), tend to be competitive with Box–Jenkins models, and part of the reason for that might be that there is in fact a close connection between the implied forecasting functions from ARMA models for differenced data, and exponential smoothing (see Harvey, 1993, Chapter 5).

Multi-step forecasting is also closely connected to the theory of dynamic forecasting above. In the simplest case, where the DGP is Gaussian AR(1), i.e., as given in (12.4), we can express the solution equation for Y_{t-h} as

$$Y_{t+h} = \beta_{0h} + \beta_{1h} Y_{t-h} + e_{t+h}, \tag{12.43}$$

where the disturbance term e_t is

$$e_{t+h} = \sum_{j=0}^{h-1} \phi_1^j \varepsilon_{t+h-j}, \tag{12.44}$$

and the two coefficients are

$$\beta_{0h} = \phi_0 \frac{1-\phi_1^h}{1-\phi_1}, \tag{12.45}$$

$$\beta_{1h} = \phi_1^h, \tag{12.46}$$

from the results above. If we denote the OLS estimates by $\hat{\beta}_{0h}$ and $\hat{\beta}_{1h}$, the direct forecast for Y_{T+h} conditional on Y_T becomes

$$Y_{T+h}^{fm} = \hat{\beta}_{0h} + \hat{\beta}_{1h} Y_T. \tag{12.47}$$

Note, however, that $\hat{\beta}_{0h}$ and $\hat{\beta}_{1h}$ will be biased, as (12.44) shows that the e_t disturbance is an MA variable. Hence, corrections for autocorrelation might be considered in practice.

More generally, a multi-period forecast Y_{T+h}^{fm} with regressors can be thought of as starting with an ADL model for Y_t, lagging all right-hand side variables h-periods, and using the estimated equation to give the point forecast.

We see that if we combine a dynamic h-period forecast with a direct h-period forecast, we, in principle, use two estimators of the start point, and of the end point of the forecast glide path. Since one of the estimators (from the multi-period regression) is more biased than the other, it is not clear why this should be an improvement. However, in applications, it might well be that the multi-period regression model might include additional variables, so that the information used for the dynamic forecasts and for the multi-period forecast is no longer the same. Hence, in general, it is an empirical question whether a combination of the two will improve on the dynamic h-step forecast.

A leading indicator is any variable whose outcome is known in advance of a related variable which is desired to forecast. A composite leading index is a combination of such variables. For example, the US Commerce Department states that its leading indicator is constructed to lead at cyclical turning points. In practice, the composition of indicator systems gets altered frequently (about every 2.2 years in the US) suggesting that elements do not lead systematically for prolonged periods, see Emerson and Hendry (1996), for a discussion of several aspects of Leading indicators.

Factors models are related to the methods in multivariate statistical analysis known as principal components methods. The idea is to commence from a large assembly of potential predictors of Y_t. In fact, the assembly may be so large that a conventional model between Y_t and all the variables in the assembly is not feasible. Instead, principal component analysis is used to reduce the dimensionality down to number for *factors* small enough to allow estimation of a relationship between Y_t and the factors, Stock and Watson (2011).

Econometric models that are nonlinear in parameters are held by many as the most promising route to models that can adjust relatively fast to location breaks. Nonlinear models are often regarded as extensions of the approximation to the DGP that was achieved by linear modelling (see Granger and Teräsvirta, 1993). Hence, nonlinear model specification has been seen as specific-to-general. However, recent developments include Gets algorithms for selecting models by commencing from a GUM that included nonlinear terms (see Hendry and Doornik, 2014, Chapter 21).

As the above shows, many of the alternatives to the equilibrium correcting VAR class of forecasting models require modelling decisions, and so may be costly to specify and maintain, though maybe not as resource binding as a large macroeconometric model. On the other side of the spectrum, we find forecasts that require hardly any modelling decisions. Clements and Hendry (2006) give the theoretical background for the role of the Naive forecasts mentioned above, and it is now time to discuss that class of forecast method more closely.

12.9. Naive Forecasts

As noted, it is important to understand forecasting methods that have a certain degree of robustness with respect to structural breaks that have happened prior to the forecast period. Such methods can aid decisions about use of add-factors in a model, and they can deliver predictions that can be part of an ensemble (i.e., combined) forecasts. One method for mean-robustification is to make use of differenced data. Consider, for example, the Naive forecast:

$$\Delta Y_{iT+1|T}^{nf} = \Delta Y_{iT}, \tag{12.48}$$

which implies that the 1-step ahead forecast of the level of Y_i becomes

$$Y_{iT+1|T}^{nf} = Y_{iT} + \Delta Y_{iT}. \tag{12.49}$$

With little loss of generality, we consider the case where also the DGP has first-order dynamics. As a reference, we first look at the forecast errors when there is no location shift at the start of period $T+1$, i.e., the DGP is

$$Y_{iT+1} = Y^* + \phi_1(Y_{iT} - Y_i^*) + \varepsilon_{iT+1}, \tag{12.50}$$

or equivalently

$$\Delta Y_{iT+1} = (\phi_1 - 1)(Y_{iT} - Y_i^*) + \varepsilon_{iT+1}. \tag{12.51}$$

The 1-step forecast error of (12.48) becomes (see Exercise 12.5)

$$e^{nf}_{iT+1|T} = (\phi_1 - 1)\Delta Y_{iT} + \varepsilon_{iT+1} - \varepsilon_{iT}. \tag{12.52}$$

There is a bias in this forecast, as $E(e^{nf}_{iT+1|T} \mid \mathcal{I}_T) \neq 0$, which is not surprising, since the Naive forecast is not the optimal forecasting method in this case (where the DGP is wide-sense stationary). However, unconditionally (imagine repeated use of the forecast method across many replications of the DGP), there is no bias because $E(Y_{iT} - Y_i^*) = 0$.

Next, consider the case with a location shift in the DGP occurring at the start of period $T+1$:

$$Y_{iT+1} = Y^{*\text{new}} + \phi_1(Y_{iT} - Y_i^{*\text{new}}) + \varepsilon_{iT+1}. \tag{12.53}$$

The 1-step forecast error of the Naive forecast is

$$e^{nf}_{iT+1|T} = (1-\phi_1)(Y^{*\text{new}} - Y^*) + (\phi_1 - 1)\Delta Y_{iT} + \varepsilon_i T + 1 - \varepsilon_{iT}, \tag{12.54}$$

which has a bias which is due to the unanticipated change from Y^* to $Y^{*\text{new}}$.

However, when we consider the Naive forecast for $T+2$, conditionally on period $T+1$, i.e.,

$$Y^{nf}_{iT+2|T+1} = Y_{iT+1} + \Delta Y_{iT+1},$$

and the actual Y_{iT+2} generated by the DGP:

$$Y_{iT+2} = Y^{*\text{new}} + \phi_1(Y_{iT+1} - Y_i^{*\text{new}}) + \varepsilon_{iT+2},$$

the expression for the 1-step forecast error becomes

$$e^{nf}_{iT+2|T+1} = (\phi_1 - 1)\Delta Y_{iT+1} + \varepsilon_{iT+2} - \varepsilon_{iT+1}, \qquad (12.55)$$

which is likely to be without systematic positive or negative values. The error for the Naive forecasts can be compared to the forecast error from using the conditional expectation with the old equilibrium parameter Y^*, i.e., from (12.42):

$$e^{f}_{iT+2|T+1} = (Y_i^{*\text{new}} - Y^*) - \phi_1(Y_i^{*\text{new}} - Y_i^*) + \varepsilon_{iT+2}, \quad h \geq 1. \qquad (12.56)$$

Again, this error will be biased due to the lack of adaptation to the new equilibrium $Y_i^{*\text{new}}$ in the "raw" model forecasts.

Hence, the Naive forecast can be mean-robust to location breaks that have happened before the forecast origin (it is in the information set). There may be, in this sense, a tendency of automatic error correction in Naive forecasts. Note, however, that the variance of the errors of the Naive forecasts will have a tendency to be large, due to the unit-root it imposes, and the extra change term in (12.48).

The above discussion also sheds light on the empirical success of other procedures that difference the data before modelling and forecasting. This includes the Box–Jenkins methodology mentioned above, which typically differences the data prior to deciding the ARMA model used for the forecasting. Discussion of the forecasting properties of two versions of a larger scale macroeconometric model, in ECM-form and in dVAR-form, are found in Eitrheim *et al.* (1999) and Bårdsen *et al.* (2005, Chapter 11). The results show that the RMSFE for the ECM version of the model tends to be lower than those of the differenced version of the model in periods with few location-breaks. After a period with location shifts, the RMSFE was more favourable for the dVAR. This pattern is understandable when we remember the decomposition of the square of the RMSFE into a bias term and a variance term, cf. (12.10). We expect that dVARs get inflated variance terms when the economy is without shocks. However, when there are structural breaks, the RMSFEs for the ECM get larger because of the bias terms.

12.10. Some Pros and Cons of Model-Based Forecasting

An econometric model provides one way of making economic forecasts, but as we have seen above, many other methods are available. The accuracy of forecasts, irrespective of the method used to produce them, depends on the following (Hendry, 2001):

a there are regularities to be captured,
b the regularities are informative about the future,
c the proposed method captures those regularities, and yet
d it excludes non-regularities.

a and **b** are characteristics of the economic system (formally the DGP whose variables we attempt to forecast). As we have seen above, both stationary and non-stationary DGPs contain regularities that can be captured though the specification and estimation of an empirical econometric model. Those regularities are also informative about the future, in particular when the DGP is covariance stationary, realistically after using differencing and cointegration transformations. For $I(1)$ variables, forecast can also be based on past regularities, but the uncertainty of the forecast increases with the length of the forecast horizon.

When the DGP is broad-sense non-stationary and is subject to intermittent structural breaks, the regularities that we can learn about with statistical methods only serve as a rough guide to the future. Nevertheless, **c**, where a relatively congruent model has been decided on, using the relevant estimation and test methods above, remains a requisite for feasible optimality of "raw" forecasts'.

d entails that a forecasting method should be robust to irregularities, for example, stemming from regime shifts prior to the origin of the forecast. As we have seen, **c** and **d** jointly can be difficult to attain in practice, and this provides one explanation for why intercept correction of a model-based forecast performs better than the "raw" forecasts. By the same token, it explains why univariate models (using differencing) can perform well in forecast comparisons.

An overall strategy for forecasting with a multiple equation econometric model may be to rely on the "raw" forecasts only when the last residuals are acceptably small, and when there is no other evidence of a location-shift in the system of equations. Otherwise, intercept-correction is recommended. Castle *et al.* (2015) discuss various ways to use a differenced version of the model to forecast in such cases.

Nevertheless, a view that emerges from the above discussion is that if the primary purpose of macroeconomic forecasting is to produce the best MSFE forecasts for GDP, and a few other other headline economic variables, the gain in forecast accuracy of a costly macroeconometric model compared to cheaper forecasting methods is not likely to be large enough to make the investment in modelling worthwhile.

However, the motivation for building a macroeconometric model is usually a wider one than to enter a forecast competition about, e.g., GDP. The interest of both the model builder and the model user also typically lies with the relationships between variables rather than with an ensemble of loosely connected headline variables. During the lead-up to a policy decisions, what is needed is often system thinking, and then the advantages of econometric models become clearer. These pro-arguments arise because a univariate time series model, or a survey or an indicator system is seldom enough to satisfy a customer or model user who are interest in more than the flash news. In macroeconomics in particular, the forecaster must always be prepared to answer follow-up questions. Armed with a macromodel, the answer can often be based on the representation of the working of the complex economy that the model gives. The time series modeller or a processor of large amounts of now-casting data can often be left struggling for an answer.

Consider, for example, a scenario where several macroeconomic forecasts show that a recent hike in inflation is likely to be start of an upward turning wage price spiral. The central bank governor is alarmed by this and decides to prepare an increase in interest rates. But she wants to know how this will affect the inflation forecasts, and turns to her team of forecasters for answers (as an economist, she more or less expects that there is more than one answer!). Our macromodel operator taps in a few changes in the program code that drives the model and immediately produces a revised forecast. By contrast, the time series forecaster can only reply that there is no change to the forecasts because the forecasting model does not include the policy interest rate in the first place.

Modelling of the VAR in VECM and SEM forms also increases the information content of forecasts in other ways. One important implication of cointegration is that the h-step forecasts will obey cointegration restrictions.

> Thus, the forecasts of levels of co-integrated economic variables will "hang together" in a way likely to be viewed as sensible by an economist. Granger and Newbold (1986, p. 226).

It is not to be expected that forecasts produced in other ways, such as by individual Box–Jenkins models, will combine in the same interpretable way.

Another advantage of multiple equation models, especially SEM-type models, is that they allow easy handling of accounting identities as well as other and definitional relationships. In that way, the vector with multivariate forecasts becomes internally consistent, and "hangs together" also in other interesting ways than through cointegration. The forecasted GDP expenditure components in a SEM not only sum to total demand, an accountable model also makes sure that the forecasted GDP "supplied" plus forecasted imports balance the forecasted demand in a way that makes economic sense.

More generally, the empirical multiple equation model enables us to conduct simulations under different states of the economy (often referred to as scenario analysis). The main purpose is then not to make the best forecast in the MSFE sense, but to aid decision makers or regulators to understand the impact that factors which are outside their control may have on the variables that they have as their business, or duty or mandate, to monitor and control.

We note that the validity of these wider uses of a dynamic macroeconometric model for forecasting and scenario analysis does not hinge on the model's success in forecast competitions. In the inflation example above, the time series model may have "topped the table" after the last rounds of inflation forecasting competitions. The advantage of the macroeconometric model lies elsewhere: namely, in being multivariate and multiple equation. What is a requisite however, is that there is sufficient *invariance* in the parameters that govern the difference between the model solutions for the two scenarios. Mathematically, this boils down to a requirement about the coefficients of the homogeneous difference equations being invariant to shifts in the non-homogeneous part of (at least one) model equation. One simple example is that the coefficients a, b, c in the macromodel are reasonably invariant with respect to a shift in J^*.

The algebra for a scenario forecast was given in (12.28). Substraction of the baseline solution, which we for simplicity can take from (12.27), gives the difference between the scenario and the baseline as

$$
\begin{aligned}
Y^f_{iT+h|\mathcal{I}^{sc}_T} - Y^f_{iT+h|\mathcal{I}_T} &= [Y^*_i(X^{sc}) - Y^*_i(X^*)] \\
&\quad + \sum_{j=0}^{h-1} b^{(j)}_{11}(X^{sc}_{iT+h-j} - X^f_{iT+h-j}), \qquad (12.57)
\end{aligned}
$$

There is nothing in the model assumptions that logically hinder that the coefficients $b_{11}^{(j)}$, which "come from" the homogeneous equation, are invariant to the difference in the long-run means $[Y_i^*(X^{sc})-Y_i^*(X^*)]$. But there is also nothing guaranteeing that the requisite invariance holds. In any practical scenario analysis therefore, the realism of the invariance assumption needs to qualified as best as one can. However, we also note that, without a model, such important questions cannot be even tentatively answered.

12.11. Exercises

Exercise 12.1. Show that the expression in (12.20) covers the special case of $p = 1$.

Exercise 12.2. Show the expression in (12.30).

Exercise 12.3. Check the values for C^* and GDP* in the case where the parameters of the DGP are the same in the forecast period as they are in the sample (conditioning) period.

Exercise 12.4. Show (12.39).

Exercise 12.5. Give an expression for the 1-step forecast-error of the Naive forecast (12.48) when there is no structural break and the DGP has first-order dynamics.

Exercise 12.6. Show (12.54).

Exercise 12.7. Show (12.55).

Exercise 12.8. Assume that, instead of (12.48), the Naive forecasts are generated by applying the forecasting rule:

$$\Delta Y_{T+1|T}^{nf} = 0.$$

What is the 1-step forecast-error bias for $T+1$ when the DGP is

$$Y_{T+1} = Y^* + \phi_1(Y_T - Y^*) + \varepsilon_{iT+1}?$$

Exercise 12.9. Assume that there is a location shift from Y^* to $Y^{*\text{new}}$ at the start of period $T+1$.

What is the expected forecast error for Y_{T+2} when

$$\Delta Y_{T+2|T-1}^{nf} = 0,$$

is used for forecasting?

Exercise 12.10. Show the identity:

$$\frac{1}{H}\sum_{h=1}^{H}(Y_{T+h} - Y^f_{T+h})^2 = \widehat{\text{Var}}(e_{T+H}) + (\widehat{\text{Bias}}\, Y_{T+H})^2.$$

(To simplify the notation, the conditioning on the information set of period T has been omitted.)

Appendix A

A Growth Model and RBC Theory

This appendix is a self-contained presentation of the Solow growth model, and of a real business cycle (RBC) model. It illustrates that macrodynamics can be derived from completely different theoretical starting points than the Keynesian view that we used for simplicity in Chapter 1. Hence, the econometric time series methods that we present in this book are applicable to different theoretical schools of thought, and they can be used to test competing macroeconomic models.

A.1. The Solow Model in Discrete Time

Growth theory is often the economics student's first encounter with a dynamic model, and here we briefly review the basic version of Solow's growth model using the framework of discrete time dynamics.[1] The first equation of the model is the macro production function of the Cobb–Douglas type

$$Y_t = K_t^{\gamma} N_t^{1-\gamma}, \quad 0 < \gamma < 1, \tag{A.1}$$

where Y_t is GDP in period t, K_t denotes the capital stock, and N_t is employment in period t. In the basic version of the model, we define N_t as the number of employed persons, which in turn is identical to the size the population. Hence, full employment is assumed, and we abstract from

[1]A good reference to both the basic version of the Solow model, and to the different extensions of the model with, e.g., technological progress is the textbook by Birch Sørensen and Whitta-Jacobsen (2010).

variations in working time. The size of the population is assumed to grow with a constant rate n:

$$\frac{N_t}{N_{t-1}} - 1 = n, \quad n \geq 0. \tag{A.2}$$

We need to be precise about the dating of the capital stock since the third equation of the model links the evolution of the capital stock to the flow of investment. We define K_t as the amount of capital available at the start of period t. We next assume that all saving, S_t, in period t is invested so that the "law of motion" for the capital stock is

$$K_t = (1 - \delta)K_{t-1} + S_{t-1}, \quad 0 < \delta \leq 1, \tag{A.3}$$

where δ is the rate of depreciation of capital. In the Solow model, an essential assumption is that saving is proportional to income, hence

$$S_t = sY_t, \quad 0 \leq s < 1, \tag{A.4}$$

where s is the fraction saved out of income in each period.

Let us first see what the steady-state solution of this dynamic model looks like, assuming that a unique and stable steady-state solution exists. To formulate the *long-run model*, we first note that if we want to write the model in terms of variables that are independent of time in the steady state, we cannot use Y, N and K directly since the population is growing with rate n in steady state, by assumption. Instead, let us make the initial guess that capital intensity $k_t = K_t/N_t$ is a variable that is a constant $\bar{k}$ in the steady state. If this is true, the long-run model, i.e., the model for the steady state, takes the form

$$\bar{y} = (\bar{k})^{\gamma}, \tag{A.5}$$

$$\bar{k} = \frac{1}{(\delta + n)} s \cdot \bar{y}, \tag{A.6}$$

where the GDP per capital is denoted $y = Y/N$, and $\bar{y}$ is the steady-state value of GDP per capita. If (A.5) and (A.6) characterize the steady state, we can combine the two equations to obtain the following equation for $\bar{y}$:

$$\bar{y} = \left[\frac{1}{(\delta + n)} s \cdot \bar{y}\right]^{\gamma}, \tag{A.7}$$

which shows that a permanent increase in the saving rate s has the following long-run effect on the GDP per capita:

$$\frac{d \ln \bar{y}}{d \ln s} = \frac{\gamma}{1 - \gamma} > 0, \tag{A.8}$$

or in the derivative form:

$$\frac{d\bar{y}}{ds} = \frac{\bar{y}}{s}\frac{\gamma}{1-\gamma}, \tag{A.9}$$

which says that a permanent increase in the saving rate has a positive long-run effect on GDP per capita, which is increasing in the initial $\bar{y}$ the initial steady-state situation.

Next, we check whether the long-run model made up of (A.5) and (A.6) does indeed represent a stable steady-state solution of the dynamic system (A.1)–(A.4). For that purpose, we need to derive the final equation for the dynamic system. We start with equation (A.3) and divide on both sides by N_{t-1}:

$$\frac{K_t}{N_{t-1}} = (1-\delta)\frac{K_{t-1}}{N_{t-1}} + \frac{S_{t-1}}{N_{t-1}}.$$

On the left-hand side, multiply by N_t/N_t, and use (A.2) and (A.4) to obtain

$$k_t(1+n) = (1-\delta)k_{t-1} + s\,y_{t-1}, \tag{A.10}$$

where $k_t = K_t/N_t$ and $y_t = Y_t/N_t$, consistent with the variables of the long-run model. From the production function (A.1): $y_t = k_t^{\gamma}$ so that the dynamic equation for the capital intensity variable k_t becomes

$$k_t = \frac{1}{(1+n)}\left\{(1-\delta)k_{t-1} + s\,k_{t-1}^{\gamma}\right\}. \tag{A.11}$$

If it were not for the last term on the right-hand side in (A.11), this equation would have been an autoregressive (AR) model, with AR parameter $\alpha = (1-\delta)/(1+n)$. In terms of economic interpretation, this corresponds to the case of $s = 0$, so that all income is consumed in every period. Since $0 < \alpha < 1$, it would then follow that $k_t \to \bar{k} = 0$ in the asymptotically stable solution, and the interpretation would be that from any given initial capital intensity $\bar{k}_0$, the combination of capital depreciation and population growth would drive the capital intensity towards zero. Consequently, GDP per head is also zero. Hence, to avoid such a dismal steady state, a strictly positive saving fraction is logically necessary.

With $0 < s < 1$, we see that the second term on the right-hand side of (A.11) is indeed essential. This term represents the positive contribution from saving to the capital stock, and if it is large enough the capital intensity k_t can grow from one period to the next in spite of capital depreciation and population growth. Because of the nature of the production function (A.1), this part of the final equation is a nonlinear function of k_t, meaning that (A.11) becomes a nonlinear AR model, unlike the linear models we make use of elsewhere in this book.

Despite the nonlinearity, it is straightforward to understand the conditions for stability of k_t. Reexpressing (A.11) as

$$(1+n)\Delta k_t = -(\delta+n)k_{t-1} + s\,k_{t-1}^{\gamma}, \tag{A.12}$$

shows that

$$\begin{aligned}
\Delta k_t > 0 &\Longleftrightarrow s\,k_{t-1}^{\gamma} > (\delta+n)k_{t-1},\\
\Delta k_t < 0 &\Longleftrightarrow s\,k_{t-1}^{\gamma} < (\delta+n)k_{t-1},\\
\Delta k_t = 0 &\Longleftrightarrow s\,k_{t-1}^{\gamma} = (\delta+n)k_{t-1}.
\end{aligned} \tag{A.13}$$

The first line in (A.13) states that the capital intensity is growing in all time periods where saving per capita is larger than the amount of saving required to compensate for capital depreciation and population growth. Conversely, line two states that the capital intensity is falling if saving per capita is less than that required amount. Finally, $\Delta k_t = 0$ so that $k_t = k_{t-1} = \bar{k}$ if and only if $s\,k_{t-1}^{\gamma} = (\delta+n)k_{t-1}$.

The nonlinearity is most important when the initial capital intensity is "far from" the steady-state value. For initial capital intensities that are close to the steady-state value, we can therefore approximate the dynamics of k_t with the aid of a linear dynamic model.

To illustrate this point, we use an approximation to the term inside the brackets in (A.11). With the aid of a first-order Taylor expansion of that term (see Sydsæter *et al.*, 2005, p. 50), we obtain a linearization of the whole expression which gives the approximate dynamics of k_t.

Define the function

$$f(k_{t-1}) = s\,k_{t-1}^{\gamma}.$$

A first-order Taylor expansion around the steady state gives

$$\begin{aligned}
f(k_{t-1}) &\approx f(\bar{k}) + f'(\bar{k})(k_{t-1}-\bar{k})\\
&= s\,\bar{k}^{\gamma} + \gamma s\bar{k}^{\gamma-1}(k_{t-1}-\bar{k}).
\end{aligned} \tag{A.14}$$

Replacing $s\,k_{t-1}^{\gamma}$ in (A.11) by the expression in the second line in (A.14), and collecting terms, gives

$$k_t \approx \left(\frac{1-\delta}{1+n} + \frac{s}{1+n}\gamma\bar{k}^{\gamma-1}\right)k_{t-1} + s\frac{1-\gamma}{1+n}\bar{k}^{\gamma}, \tag{A.15}$$

which is a first-order linear difference equation. Assuming that the AR coefficient is between 0 and 1, (A.15) is consistent with dynamic stability in the neighbourhood of the steady-state capital intensity $\bar{k}$.

Solow's growth model is the standard model for economic analysis with a time horizon that goes beyond the length of the typical business cycle of 5–10 years. In order to be able to explain the facts of economic growth the basic model that we have presented here obviously needs to be replaced by a model that includes more growth explaining factors. As one example, GDP per capita in Norway has grown by a factor of 16 since 1900, while the basic Solow model indicates zero growth in the steady state. However, we leave it to a course in economic growth theory to show that inclusion of technological progress is one of the modifications that helps reconcile the theory's predictions with the growth statistics. Instead, we turn to a model that applies the Solow model's framework to a much shorter time horizon than was originally intended.

A.2. Real Business Cycle Model

The real business cycle (RBC) approach applies the framework of the Solow model to the business cycle. Hence, unlike the Solow model, where the time period t typically refers to a 5 or 10 years averages, the time period t in the RBC refers to years or quarters of a year.

The Keynesian income–expenditure model and the RBC model are regarded as contesting explanations of short-run macroeconomic fluctuations. This is because of the differences in the assumption about the labour market. In the Keynesian model, there is involuntary unemployment, the real wage does not correspond to the market clearing real wage of a perfectly competitive labour market, and the business cycle is regarded as disequilibrium phenomenon. In the RBC model, there is no genuine involuntary unemployment. Instead, measured unemployment is regarded as something of a misnomer, for intertemporal substitution of working time for leisure, and the business cycle is an equilibrium phenomenon.

The first equation of the RBC model is the macroproduction function (A.1), augmented by a technology variable A_t

$$Y_t = K_t^{\gamma}(A_t N_t)^{1-\gamma}, \quad 0 < \gamma < 1, \tag{A.16}$$

and where we, because of the change of time horizon and the change in focus to the business cycle fluctuations, change the interpretation of N_t from persons employed to the total number of hours worked, i.e., the number of workers' times the average length of the working day. This specification of the production function is referred to as the labour augmenting technical progress since an increase in A_t implies that the GDP is increased without any increase in the capital stock (i.e., labour becomes more productive). It is important in the following that the technical progress is modelled as the sum of two parts: one completely deterministic part and a second part which is random. The deterministic part is a given rate of technological progress g_A multiplied by time, which we write as $g_A t$, and the random part is denoted as $a_{s,t}$. Hence, the RBC model's theory of technological progress is given by

$$\ln A_t = g_A t + a_{s,t}, \quad 0 < g_A < 1, \tag{A.17}$$

where the random part is given by the difference equation

$$a_{s,t} = \alpha a_{s,t-1} + \varepsilon_{a,t}, \quad 0 \leq \alpha < 1, \tag{A.18}$$

where $\varepsilon_{a,t}$ is a completely unpredictable technology shock. We can amalgamate the two technology equations into one by lagging (A.17) one period, and then multiplying by α on both sides of the lagged equation

$$\alpha \ln A_{t-1} = \alpha g_A (t-1) + \alpha a_{s,t-1}. \tag{A.19}$$

Subtraction of equation (A.19) from (A.17) gives

$$\ln A_t = \alpha g_A + g_A(1-\alpha)t + \alpha \ln A_{t-1} + \varepsilon_{a,t}, \tag{A.20}$$

which shows that the technological progress $\ln A_t$ is implied to follow a first-order process augmented by a deterministic trend $\alpha g_A(t-1)$. We can rewrite (A.20) as

$$\ln A_t - \ln A_{t-1} = \alpha g_A + g_A(1-\alpha)t + (\alpha - 1)\ln A_{t-1} + \varepsilon_{a,t}, \tag{A.21}$$

and define a steady state as a situation where all shocks are zero, i.e., $\varepsilon_{a,t} = 0$ for all t. Let $\ln \bar{A}_t$ denote the steady-state productivity. From (A.20) with $\varepsilon_{a,t} = 0$, we note that $\ln \bar{A}_{t-1}$ is given by

$$g_A = \alpha g_A + g_A(1-\alpha)t + (\alpha - 1)\ln \bar{A}_{t-1},$$

or

$$\ln \bar{A}_{t-1} = -g_A + g_A t.$$

Since $\ln \bar{A}_t = g_A + \ln \bar{A}_{t-1}$ we have

$$\ln \bar{A}_t = g_A t \tag{A.22}$$

showing that (A.17) can alternatively be written as

$$\ln A_t = \ln \bar{A}_t + a_{s,t}, \tag{A.23}$$

as long as the restriction on g_A is observed.

The RBC model also makes use of the saving equation (A.4), and the capital evolution equation (A.3), which we, however, simplify by setting $\delta = 1$, meaning that capital equipment lasts for only one period, so that

$$K_t = S_{t-1}. \tag{A.24}$$

It is the infallible mark of RBC models that the labour marked is assumed to be in equilibrium in each period. Labour supply, N_t^S, is assumed to be a function of the relative wage $w_t/\bar{w}_t$

$$N_t^S = \bar{N}\left(\frac{w_t}{\bar{w}_t}\right)^{\epsilon}, \quad \epsilon > 0, \tag{A.25}$$

where $\bar{w}_t$ is the steady-state wage, and ϵ is the labour supply elasticity. When the wage is equal to the steady-state wage, the labour supply is also equal to its steady-state value. Though simple in appearance, equation (A.25) is representing optimizing behaviour by households and individuals: They choose to supply labour in excess of the long-run level determined by demography and sociological norms and legislature when the real wage w_t is higher than the steady-state real wage $\bar{w}_t$, and to substitute labour for leisure in times when the real wage is low relative its long-run level. For simplicity of exposition, we set $\bar{N} = 1$ in the following, since in (A.25) this is merely a choice of units.

Labour demand is obtained by assuming optimizing behaviour by a "macro producer", and the marginal product of labour is therefore set equal to the real wage

$$w_t = (1-\gamma)\left(\frac{K_t}{A_t N_t}\right)^{\gamma} A_t = (1-\gamma)\left(\frac{Y_t}{N_t}\right). \tag{A.26}$$

The assumption of equilibrium in the labour market means that $N_t^S = N_t$, and we can solve (A.25) and (A.26) for real wage and for employment. First, note that from (A.25)

$$w_t = N_t^{\frac{1}{\epsilon}} \bar{w}_t. \tag{A.27}$$

Next, note that the ratio $K_t/A_t N_t$ in (A.26) is a generalization of the capital intensity variable k_t of the Solow model. The generalization is due to the inclusion of the productivity variable A_t in the production function, hence we define $k_{A,t} = K_t/A_tN_t$ as the productivity corrected capital intensity. Moreover, with reference to the Solow model above, we define $\bar{k}_A$ as the steady-state value of the productivity corrected capital intensity. The corresponding steady-state real wage, from (A.26), is

$$\bar{w}_t = (1-\gamma)\bar{k}_A^{\gamma}\bar{A}_t. \tag{A.28}$$

Remember that both $\bar{w}_t$ and $\bar{k}_A$ refer to the situation with $\varepsilon_{a,t} = 0$ (there are no shocks in the steady state). Using (A.27) and (A.28), we obtain

$$w_t = N_t^{\frac{1}{\epsilon}}(1-\gamma)\bar{k}_A^{\gamma}\bar{A}_t. \tag{A.29}$$

At this point, we take the natural logarithms on both sides of (A.26) and (A.29):

$$\ln w_t = \ln(1-\gamma) + \ln Y_t - \ln N_t,$$
$$\ln w_t = \frac{1}{\epsilon}\ln N_t + \ln((1-\gamma)\bar{k}_A^{\gamma}\bar{A}_t).$$

Using these two expressions to solve for $\ln N_t$ gives

$$\ln N_t = \frac{\epsilon}{1+\epsilon}\{\ln Y_t - \ln(\bar{k}_A^{\gamma}\bar{A}_t)\}. \tag{A.30}$$

Substitution of this expression together with (A.24) and (A.4) into the log of the production function, (A.16) gives

$$\ln Y_t = \gamma\ln(sY_{t-1}) + (1-\gamma)\left(\frac{\epsilon}{1+\epsilon}\{\ln Y_t - \ln(\bar{k}_A^{\gamma}\bar{A}_t)\}\right) + (1-\gamma)\ln A_t,$$

$$\frac{1+\gamma\epsilon}{1+\epsilon}\ln Y_t = \gamma\ln s + \gamma\ln(Y_{t-1}) + (1-\gamma)\left(\frac{-\epsilon}{1+\epsilon}\ln(\bar{k}_A^{\gamma}\bar{A}_t)\right)$$
$$+ (1-\gamma)\ln A_t,$$

and, eventually

$$\ln Y_t = \frac{\gamma(1+\epsilon)}{1+\gamma\epsilon}\ln s + \frac{\gamma(1+\epsilon)}{1+\gamma\epsilon}\ln Y_{t-1} - \frac{(1-\gamma)\epsilon}{1+\gamma\epsilon}\ln(\bar{k}_A^{\gamma}\bar{A}_t)$$
$$+ \frac{(1-\gamma)(1+\epsilon)}{1+\gamma\epsilon}\ln A_t. \tag{A.31}$$

Note that this is the *final equation* for $\ln Y_t$ in the RBC model: it expresses $\ln Y_t$ by its lag and by exogenous variables. Noting that $\ln \bar{A}_t$ and $\ln A_t$ are linked through equation (A.23), and that $\ln \bar{A}_t = g_A t$ in (A.22), the final equation for $\ln Y_t$ can be written as

$$\ln Y_t = \frac{\gamma(1+\epsilon)}{1+\gamma\epsilon}\ln s - \frac{(1-\gamma)\epsilon}{1+\gamma\epsilon}\ln(\bar{k}_A^{\gamma}) + \frac{\gamma(1+\epsilon)}{1+\gamma\epsilon}\ln Y_{t-1} + \frac{(1-\gamma)}{1+\gamma\epsilon}g_A t + \frac{(1-\gamma)(1+\epsilon)}{1+\gamma\epsilon}a_{s,t}, \tag{A.32}$$

where $a_{s,t}$ follows the AR process in equation (A.18).

There are a couple of points to be made about (A.32). First, dynamic stability of (A.32) is satisfied, since

$$\frac{\gamma(1+\epsilon)}{1+\gamma\epsilon} = \frac{\gamma(1+\epsilon)+1-1}{1+\gamma\epsilon} = 1 - \frac{1-\gamma}{1+\gamma\epsilon},$$

is a number between 0 and 1 based the assumptions of the model. Second, given the stability, there is a deterministic steady-state growth path for Y_t with growth rate g_A. Third, and heuristically speaking, the only difference between (A.32) and the implied equation for the log of the steady-state GDP, $\ln \bar{Y}_t$, is that the equation for $\ln \bar{Y}_t$ does not contain the stochastic technology shock term.[2] Hence, the equation for $\ln \bar{Y}_t$ is

$$\ln \bar{Y}_t = \frac{\gamma(1+\epsilon)}{1+\gamma\epsilon}\ln s - \frac{(1-\gamma)\epsilon}{1+\gamma\epsilon}\ln(\bar{k}_A^{\gamma}) + \frac{\gamma(1+\epsilon)}{1+\gamma\epsilon}\ln \bar{Y}_{t-1} + \frac{(1-\gamma)}{1+\gamma\epsilon}g_A t, \tag{A.33}$$

meaning that the dynamics of the logarithm of the *output gap*, defined as $(\ln Y_t - \ln \bar{Y}_t)$, is given by the AR equation

$$(\ln Y_t - \ln \bar{Y}_t) = \frac{\gamma(1+\epsilon)}{1+\gamma\epsilon}(\ln Y_{t-1} - \ln \bar{Y}_{t-1}) + \frac{(1-\gamma)(1+\epsilon)}{1+\gamma\epsilon}a_{s,t}. \tag{A.34}$$

We can simplify the notation by setting

$$\phi_1 = \frac{\gamma(1+\epsilon)}{1+\gamma\epsilon} \quad \text{and} \quad \upsilon = \frac{(1-\gamma)(1+\epsilon)}{1+\gamma\epsilon}. \tag{A.35}$$

[2]This can be made precise by taking the mathematical expectation of (A.32).

Equation (A.34) shows that, according to the RBC model, the typical evolution of GDP over time will be characterized by periods of economic booms (positive output gap), and troughs (negative output gap). This is implied even if the initial situation is characterized by $\ln Y_t = \ln \bar{Y}_t$. The explanation is that there is a flow of technology shocks that are propagated into persistent deviations from the steady state by saving and investment dynamics, and by workers' willingness to supply more labour in good times, and to substitute work by leisure in economic downturns. Hence, unlike the Keynesian income–expenditure model, periods with below capacity output, and below average recorded employment, is an equilibrium phenomenon in the RBC model — it is a theory of equilibrium business cycles. Figure A.1 simulates the GDP gap. The solution assumes that the output gap is zero in the initial year, which we have set to "1900" in the figure. Due to negative productivity shocks in the first years of the solution period (and positive autocorrelation), the output gap is negative for the first 10 years before there is a brief upturn after 12–13 years. The first more lasting boom starts in the mid-"1920's" and lasts for more than 25 years. It is followed by a long period where the GDP is lower than the steady state (i.e., equilibrium).

Figure A.1. A simulated series of the logarithm of the output gap, i.e., (A.34) with $\epsilon = 4$ and $\gamma = 0.5$ (giving $\phi_1 = \upsilon = 0.83$). The standard deviation of the technology shock variable ε_{at} is 0.01 in the data generation.

It gives rise to thought that a simple RBC model can generate economic upturns and downturns that are of such long duration as shown in Figure A.1. One lesson may be that one should not jump to conclusions about economic disequilibria or imbalances in the economy on the basis of 10 years of above or below trend economic performance—further analysis is required to decide whether the business cycle is an equilibrium phenomenon or a disequilibrium phenomenon.

Appendix B

Spectral Analysis

Time series analysis in the time domain has a classical counterpart in spectral analysis in the frequency domain. In this appendix, the emphasis is on the theoretical population power spectrum and on the impact of filtering and variable transformations, on the power spectrum. Specifically, we give the background to the famous characterization of economic time series in terms of the *typical spectral shape.*

B.1. Introduction

In the frequency domain, interest is centred on the contributions of different periodic components to the overall variation of a time series. Some economic series are dominated by variation at the seasonal frequency, or at a business cycle frequency. Many macroeconomic series are, however, dominated by low frequency variability, a phenomenon so usual (once recognized) that it has been dubbed the "typical spectral shape" (see Granger, 1966; Granger and Newbold, 1986, Section 2.7).

Spectral analysis is also referred to in the theory of integrated and cointegrated variables, and the field of time series econometrics generally assumes some familiarity with the central concepts used in the frequency domain analysis, for example, "low frequency unit-root".

This appendix has been included to allow the reader to connect to these important references without having to look it up in a separate textbook. It has been influenced by the exposition in Schumway (1988). The more recent title by Schumway and Stoffer (2000) has about the same mathematical level.

B.2. Frequency and Period

As noted in Chapter 3, the cosine function $\cos(x)$ takes all its values for values of x between 0 to 2π, i.e., $\cos(x) = \cos(x + 2\pi)$. The sine function has the same property. x is measured in radians, but we can change the unit of measurement by writing $x = \vartheta t$, where ϑ is called the *frequency* and is measured in radians and t is time. $\cos(\vartheta t)$ is a periodic function of time, and we have $\cos(\vartheta t) = \cos(\vartheta t + 2\pi)$.

More flexibility can be added by introducing the amplitude A and the phase φ, as in

$$f(t) = A\cos(\vartheta t - \varphi) = a\cos(\vartheta t) + b\sin(\vartheta t), \tag{B.1}$$

where $a = A\cos(\varphi)$ and $b = A\sin(\varphi)$, from the properties of the cosine of a sum of two variables (ϑt and $-\varphi$ here). A can be determined as $A = \sqrt{a^2 + b^2}$ and $\varphi = \tan^{-1}(b/a)$.

In the same way as in Chapter 3, *period* can be defined as the length in time taken to complete one full cycle (but now including the phase-parameter in the expressions):

$$\textit{period} = \frac{\varphi + 2\pi}{\vartheta} - \frac{\varphi}{\vartheta} = \frac{2\pi}{\vartheta}.$$

If *period* (wavelength) is two years, the number of cycles per year is $1/2$. With quarterly data, a two-year cycle means that the number of cycles per quarter is $1/8 = 0.125$. We define *frequency* as *the number of cycles per unit of time*, hence $v = 1/\textit{period}$.

We choose to define frequency as v rather than ϑ because it is practical and intuitive. Still, there are no strong conventions here, and several leading textbooks and software programs measure frequency in radians.

As noted above, the relationship between the two definitions of frequency is

$$\vartheta = 2\pi v.$$

In the following, we will study functions of v in the interval $[-1/2, 1/2]$. $v = 1/2$ is called the Nykvist-frequency (also called the folding frequency). It is the highest frequency that we can identify with the use of discrete observations.

B.3. Discrete Fourier Transformation and the Periodogram

Let $\{x_t\}$ denote a time series with observations $x_0, x_2, \ldots, x_{T-1}$.[1] Heuristically, it is interesting to approximate this time series as closely as possible by a linear combination of cosine functions, as suggested by the equation:

$$x_t = a_0 + \sum_{j=1}^{P} \{a_j \cos(\vartheta_j t) + b_j \sin(\vartheta_j t)\} + \mathit{remainder},$$

This problem turns out to have a solution (in the so-called Fourier analysis) leading to a the *discrete Fourier transform* (DFT) of the time series $\{x_t\}$

$$X(k) = X_C(k) - iX_S(k), \tag{B.2}$$

where $v_k = k/(2T)$; $k = 0, 1, 2, \ldots, T-1$, and $X_C(k)$ and $X_S(k)$ are called the cosine and sine transformations of $\{x_t\}$

$$X_C(k) = T^{-1/2} \sum_{t=0}^{T-1} x_t \cos(2\pi v_k t), \tag{B.3}$$

and

$$X_S(k) = T^{-1/2} \sum_{t=0}^{T-1} x_t \sin(2\pi v_k t). \tag{B.4}$$

Since $\cos(2\pi v_k t) - i\sin(2\pi v_k t) = \exp\{-2\pi v_k it\}$, we have that $X(k)$ can be written as

$$X(k) = X_C(k) - iX_s(k) = T^{-1/2} \sum_{t=0}^{T-1} x_t \exp\{-2\pi v_k it\}, \tag{B.5}$$

which define $X(k)$ as complex numbers associated with the frequencies v_k. An important property of the DFT is that given (B.5), we also have the inverse transformation

$$\begin{aligned} x_t &= T^{-1/2} \sum_{k=0}^{T-1} X(k) \exp\{2\pi v_k it\} \\ &= T^{-1/2} \sum_{k=0}^{T-1} X(k)\{\cos(2\pi v_k t) + i\sin(2\pi v_k t)\}, \end{aligned} \tag{B.6}$$

[1] In this appendix, it is practical to depart from the convention used above, namely, that a time series variable is denoted by an upper case letter, and to instead use the lower case letter.

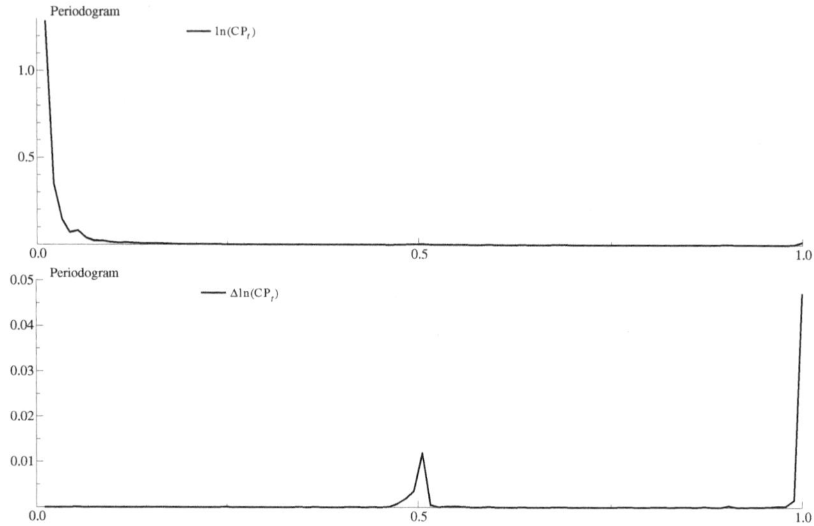

Figure B.1. Periodograms for log of private consumption ($\ln(\text{CP}_t)$) and the first difference of $\Delta\ln(\text{CP}_t)$. CP_t is measured in million kroner. Fixed 2015 prices. The data are quarterly and the sample used is 1971(1)–2017(2).

which brings out that DFT gives what we hoped for, namely, a decomposition of $\{x_t\}$ in terms of cosine waves, with $X(k)$ as weights for the different frequencies. Since $X(k)$ is complex, the real numbered contribution from a frequency v_k is defined as follows:

$$P_x(k) = X(k)\overline{X(k)} = |X(k)|^2 = X_C(k)^2 + X_S(k)^2, \tag{B.7}$$

where $\overline{X(k)}$ is the conjugate, and $|X(k)|$ is the norm of $X(k)$. $P_x(k)$ is real and $\sqrt{P_x(k)}$ is proportional to the amplitude of the cosine function with frequency v_k. The plot of $P_x(k)$ against v_k is called the *periodogram*. Figure B.1 gives two examples of periodograms.

The periodogram gives a basis for the estimation of the power spectral density (PSD) function, and is discussed briefly in the last paragraph of this appendix.

Box B.1. Frequency conventions

As noted above, the periodogram is symmetric between $-\pi$ and π, and in the graph it is plotted for $[0, \pi]$; 1 on the horizontal axis stands for ϕ, 0.5 for 0.5ϕ, etc. This is the convention used in OxMetrics, the program used to produce the graph. Compared to the definition used above,

Box B.1 (*Continued*)

cycles per time period, we have

v	Radians	Frequency in OxMetrics
0	0	0
1/4	$\pi/2$	1/2
1/2	π	1

This means that the peak in the periodogram for $\Delta \ln C_t$ at OxMetrics-frequency 1/2 corresponds to $v = 1/4$ and a period of four quarters, which reflects the strong seasonal pattern in the first difference of this time series.

B.4. Infinite Fourier Transformation

The DFT has properties that are very similar to the results of Fourier transformations of more general functions a_t defined over $t = 0, \pm 1, \pm 2, \ldots$.

If $\sum_{s=-\infty}^{\infty} |a_s| < \infty$, the *infinite Fourier transformation* (IFT) of $\{a_s\}$ is defined as

$$A(v) = \sum_{t=-\infty}^{\infty} a_t \exp(-2\pi i v t), \tag{B.8}$$

with the inverse

$$a_t = \int_{-1/2}^{1/2} A(v) \exp(2\pi i v t) dv. \tag{B.9}$$

Note that v is without a subscript, since v is a continuous frequency in this representation.

An application of this result gives the spectral representation of the autocovariance function $\gamma_x(m)$ for a stationary time series x_t:

$$\gamma_x(m) = E[(x_{t+m} - \mu)(x_t - \mu)], \tag{B.10}$$

where $\mu = E[x_t]$. Stationarity means that

$$\sum_{m=-\infty}^{\infty} |\gamma_x(m)| < \infty. \tag{B.11}$$

The IFT associated with the autocovariance function $\{\gamma_x(m)\}$ is then

$$f_x(v) = \sum_{m=-\infty}^{\infty} \gamma_x(m)\exp(-2\pi ivm), \tag{B.12}$$

and

$$\gamma_x(m) = \int_{-1/2}^{1/2} f_x(v)\exp(2\pi ivm)dv, \tag{B.13}$$

where $f_x(v)$ is called the population power spectrum.

B.5. Power Spectral Density Function

The power spectral density (PSD) function $f_x(v)$ is unique and real if x_t is real. $f_x(v)$ is also positive and symmetric. We can therefore write:

$$x_t \text{ real} \quad \Rightarrow \quad f_x(v) = f_x(-v) \quad \Rightarrow \quad \gamma_x(m) = 2\int_0^{1/2} f_x(v)\exp(2\pi ivm)dv, \tag{B.14}$$

which tells us that both $\gamma_x(m)$ and $f_x(v)$ are completely described by the frequencies in the interval $0 \leq v \leq 1/2$.

Note that, by setting $m = 0$ in (B.13), we have that the variance of x_t can be written as

$$\text{Var}(x_t) = \gamma_x(0) = \int_{-1/2}^{1/2} f_x(v)dv, \tag{B.15}$$

showing that $f_x(v)dv$ is interpretable as the contribution to the variance from each frequency.

Box B.2. White noise

If x_t is white noise, the autocovariance function is

$$\gamma_x(m) = \begin{cases} \sigma^2, & m = 0, \\ 0, & m = \pm 1, \pm 2, \ldots. \end{cases}$$

Equation (B.12) gives

$$f_x(v) = \sigma^2, \quad -1/2 \leq v \leq 1/2$$

Box B.2 (*Continued*)

showing that for a white noise process, the PSD function is constant and equal on all frequencies. A time series which is made up of components from all frequencies, and where all frequencies contribute equally much to the variance of the series, is called white noise in analogy with white light where all colours in the spectrum are present.

B.6. PSD of ARMA Series

We start by giving an important theorem for the relationship between an *input* time series x_t and a filtered (*output*) series y_t in the spectral domain.

Theorem B.1 (PSD of ARMA). *Let* $\{x_t\}$ *be stationary with* $E(x_t) = 0$ *and autocovariance function* $\gamma_x(m)$, *and spectral density* $f_x(v)$. *Let*

$$y_t = \sum_{s=-\infty}^{s=\infty} a_s x_{t-s} = a(L)x_{t-s},$$

where $\sum |a_s| < \infty$, *be a filter,* $a(L) = \sum_{s=-\infty}^{s=\infty} a_s L^s$. *Let* $A(v)$ *denote the IFT for this filter:*

$$A(v) = \sum_{s=-\infty}^{\infty} a_s \exp(-2\pi i v s) = a(\exp(-2\pi i v)). \tag{B.16}$$

$A(v)$ *is called the frequency-response function. The PSD for* $\{y_t\}$ *is*

$$f_y(v) = |A(v)|^2 f_x(v) = |a(\exp(-2\pi i v)|^2 f_x(v). \tag{B.17}$$

This relationship shows that the power spectrum of the input series is changed by filtering, and that the effect of the change takes the form of a multiplication by the squared magnitude of the frequency response function (B.16) at each frequency v.

We can sketch a proof for this important theorem. First, apply the definition of the autocovariance function to express $\gamma_y(m)$ by the spectral density $f_x(v)$:

$$\begin{aligned}\gamma_y(m) = E(y_{t+m}y_t) &= \sum_{j,k=-\infty}^{\infty} a_j a_k \gamma_x(m-j+k)\\ &= \sum_{j,k=-\infty}^{\infty} a_j a_k \int_{-1/2}^{1/2} f_x(v)\exp(2\pi i v(m-j+k))dv,\end{aligned}$$

where we have made use of $\gamma_x(m-j+k) = \int_{-1/2}^{1/2} f_x(v)\exp(2\pi iv(m-j+k))dv$ according to the IFT. We can change the places of $\sum$ and $\int$ in this expression to obtain

$$\begin{aligned}
\gamma_y(m) &= \int_{-1/2}^{1/2}\left\{\sum_{j,k=-\infty}^{\infty} a_j a_k \exp(-2\pi ivj)\exp(2\pi ivk)\right\}\exp(2\pi ivm)f_x(v)dv \\
&= \int_{-1/2}^{1/2}\left\{\sum_{j=-\infty}^{\infty} a_j \exp(-2\pi ivj)\sum_{k=-\infty}^{\infty} a_k \exp(2\pi ivk)\right\} \\
&\quad \times \exp(2\pi ivm)f_x(v)dv \\
&= \int_{-1/2}^{1/2} A(v)\overline{A(v)}\exp(2\pi ivm)f_x(v)dv \\
&= \int_{-1/2}^{1/2} |A(v)|^2 \exp(2\pi ivm)f_x(v)dv.
\end{aligned}$$

At the same time, from the IFT

$$\gamma_y(m) = \int_{-1/2}^{1/2} f_y(v)\exp(2\pi ivm)dv,$$

where $f_y(v)$ is unique. Hence,

$$f_y(v) = |A(v)|^2 f_x(v).$$

With the aid of this theorem, we can find the spectral density function of variables that follow (stationary) ARMA models. Let $y_t \sim \mathsf{ARMA}[p,q]$, i.e.,

$$\phi(L)y_t = \theta(L)\varepsilon_t, \quad \varepsilon_t \sim \mathrm{IIN}(0,\sigma^2), \tag{B.18}$$

with $\phi(L) = 1-\phi_1 L - \phi_2 L^2 - \cdots - \phi_p L^p$ and $\theta(L) = 1+\theta_1 L + \theta_2 L^2 + \cdots + \theta_p L^q$.

Without loss of generality, consider a causal ARMA(p,q), i.e., the characteristic equation $\lambda^p - \phi_1\lambda^{p-1} - \cdots - \phi_p = 0$ has all its roots inside the unit-circle.

First, set $x_t = \phi(L)y_t$; and second set $x_t = \theta(L)\varepsilon_t$, and use the theorem twice to give

$$f_x(v) = |\phi(\exp(-2\pi iv)|^2 f_{y,\mathrm{ARMA}[p,q]}(v),$$

and

$$f_x(v) = |\theta(\exp(-2\pi iv)|^2 f_\varepsilon(v),$$

so that

$$f_{y,\text{ARMA}[p,q]}(v) = \frac{|\theta(\exp(-2\pi iv)|^2}{|\phi(\exp(-2\pi iv)|^2}\sigma^2, \tag{B.19}$$

since $f_\varepsilon(v) = \sigma^2$ for a white noise process.

B.6.1. PSD of AR(1)

Let $\phi(L) = 1 - \phi_1 L$ and $\theta(L) = 1$ i (B.18). We have

$$|\theta(\exp(-2\pi iv)|^2 = 1,$$

and

$$\begin{aligned}|\phi(\exp(-2\pi iv)|^2 &= \{1 - \phi_1 \exp(-2\pi iv)\}\{1 - \phi_1 \exp(2\pi iv)\} \\ &= 1 - \phi_1(\exp(-2\pi iv) - \exp(2\pi iv)) + \phi_1^2 \\ &= 1 - 2\phi_1 \cos(2\pi v) + \phi_1^2,\end{aligned}$$

since $\exp(-2\pi iv) + \exp(2\pi iv) = 2\cos(2\pi v)$. Substitution in the general expression (B.19) gives

$$f_{y,\text{ARMA}(1,\,0)} = \frac{\sigma^2}{1 - 2\phi_1 \cos(2\pi v) + \phi_1^2}. \tag{B.20}$$

Note that $v^* = \min_v[1 - 2\phi_1 \cos(2\pi v) + \phi_1^2] = 0$ when $\phi_1 > 0$ and $0 \leq v \leq 1/2$. The PSD has a peak in $v = 0$ and declines with increasing v until $v = 1/2$. If $\phi_1 < 0$, $v^* = 1/2$ and the spectral density is increasing in v (see Granger and Newbold, 1986, p. 56). Figure B.2 plots the PSD functions for the cases of $\phi_1 = 0.5$ and $\phi_1 = -0.5$.

B.6.2. PSD of ARMA(1, 1)

By using the general expression in (B.18), it is also relatively straightforward to find the expressions of other commonly used ARMA processes, for example, ARMA(1, 1) in which case we have $\phi(L) = 1 - \phi_1 L$ and

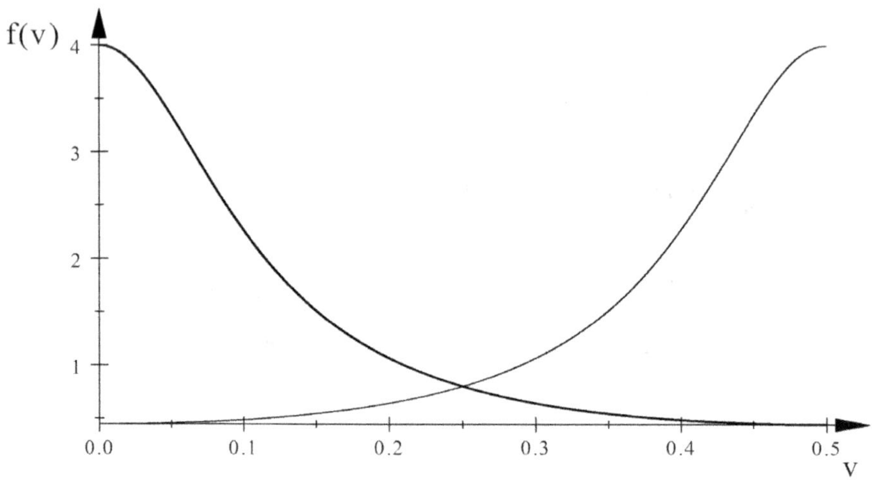

Figure B.2. Graph of theoretical PSD functions for AR(1) with coefficient $\phi_1 = 0.5$ (thicker line) line, and $\phi_1 = -0.5$ (thinner line). $\sigma^2 = 1$ in both graphs.

$\theta(L) = 1 + \theta_1 L$:

$$\begin{aligned}|\phi(\exp(-2\pi iv)|^2 &= [1 - \phi_1 \exp(-2\pi iv)]\,[1 - \phi_1 \exp(2\pi iv)]\\ &= 1 - \phi_1\,[\exp(-2\pi iv) + \exp(2\pi iv)] + \phi_1^2\\ &= 1 - 2\phi_1 \cos(2\pi v) + \phi_1^2,\end{aligned}$$

where we use that $|z|^2 = z\bar{z}$ and $\exp(-2\pi iv) + \exp(2\pi iv) = \cos(2\pi v)$ from the general mathematical formulas.

$$\begin{aligned}|\theta(\exp(-2\pi iv)|^2 &= [1 + \theta_1 \exp(-2\pi iv)]\,[1 + \theta_1 \exp(2\pi iv)]\\ &= 1 + 2\theta_1 \cos(2\pi v) + \theta_1^2.\end{aligned}$$

Hence, the expression for the PSD becomes

$$f_{y,\mathrm{ARMA}[1,1]}(v) = \sigma^2 \frac{1 + \theta_1 2\cos(2\pi v) + \theta_1^2}{1 - 2\phi_1 \cos(2\pi v) + \phi_1^2}. \tag{B.21}$$

In the case where the coefficients are set to $\phi_1 = 0.95$ and $\theta_1 = 0.5$, the PSD becomes as graphed in Figure B.3. Also, this PSD is strongly peaked at a frequency close to zero, and the wavelength of the ARMA(1, 1) series is therefore very long.

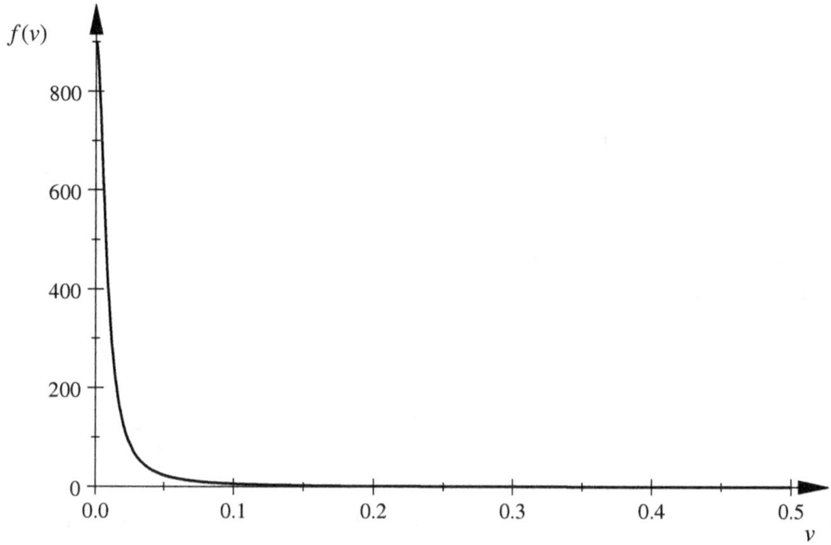

Figure B.3. Graph of theoretical PSD function for ARMA(1, 1) with coefficient $\phi_1 = 0.95$ and $\theta_2 = 0.5$, and $\sigma^2 = 1$.

B.6.3. PSD of ARMA(2, 1)

The power spectrum of $y_t \sim \mathsf{ARMA}(2,1)$,

$$y_t - \phi_1 y_{t-1} - \phi_2 y_{t-2} = \varepsilon_t + \theta_1 \varepsilon_{t-1},$$

is also easily found. The numerator in the expression is the same as for ARMA(1, 1) while the denominator becomes

$$\begin{aligned}|\phi(\exp(-2\pi iv)|^2 &= |1 - \phi_1 \exp(-2\pi iv) - \phi_2 \exp(-4\pi iv)|^2 \\ &= [1 - \phi_1 \exp(-2\pi iv) - \phi_2 \exp(-4\pi iv)] \\ &\quad \times [1 - \phi_1 \exp(2\pi iv) - \phi_2 \exp(4\pi iv)] \\ &= 1 - \phi_1^2 - \phi_2^2 - 2\phi_1(1 - \phi_2)\cos(2\pi v) - 2\phi_2 \cos(2\pi v).\end{aligned}$$

Hence, the expression for the PSD is

$$f_{y,\mathrm{ARMA}[2,\,1]}(v) = \sigma^2 \frac{1 + \theta_1 2\cos(2\pi v) + \theta_1^2}{1 + \phi_1^2 + \phi_2^2 - \phi_1(1 - \phi_2)2\cos(2\pi v) - \phi_2 2\cos(4\pi v)},$$

a function which is dominated by the denominator, which is all about the autoregressive (AR) part of the series. Figure B.4 graphs the PSD

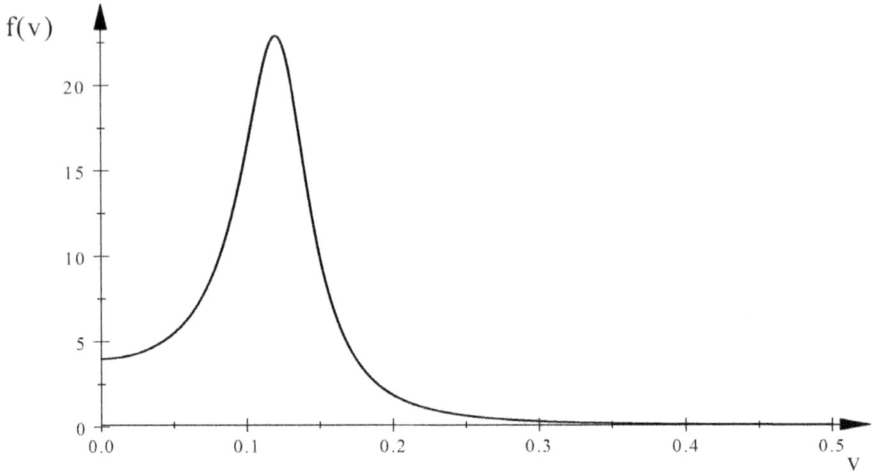

Figure B.4. Graph of theoretical PSD function for ARMA(2, 1) with coefficient $\phi_1 = 1.2$, $\phi_2 = -0.7$, $\theta_1 = 0$ and $\sigma^2 = 1$.

for the case where $\phi_1 = 1.2$ and $\phi_2 = -0.7$. The root is the complex pair 0.6 ± 0.58310 with modulus 0.83659. The spectrum has a marked peak near the 0.12 frequency. This means that the series is dominated by a cycle of with a length of approximately eight periods.

B.7. Linear Filters, Power-Shift and Phase-Shift

Let x_t denote a stationary time series with ACF $\gamma_x(m)$ and PSD $f_x(v)$. Let

$$y_t = \sum_{s=-\infty}^{s=\infty} a_s x_{t-s}, \quad \text{where} \sum_{s=-\infty}^{s=\infty} |a_s| < \infty.$$

The IFT of the filter $\{a_s\}$ is, as we have seen:

$$A(v) = \sum_{s=-\infty}^{\infty} a_s \exp(-2\pi i v s).$$

$A(v)$ is the frequency response function and the filter a_s ($s = 0, \pm 1, \pm 2, \ldots$) is often called the "impulse-response function" in the literature (as we have seen, the same term is also used about dynamic responses to shocks). Since $A(v)$ often is complex, it is useful to write $A(v)$ on polar coordinate form:

$$A(v) = |A(v)| \exp(i\kappa(v)),$$

where the norm $|A(v)|$ is called the power-shift and $\kappa(v)$ is called phase-shift. It can be shown that symmetric filters have no phase-shifting effect but that one-sided filters a_s $(s = 0, 1, 2, \ldots)$ have such an effect.

In the following we concentrate on power-shifts. From (B.17) we have

$$f_y(v) = |A(v)|^2 f_x(v), \tag{B.22}$$

showing that a filter can amplify or weaken certain frequencies in the input series x_t. Filters are often classified as *low pass* or *high pass* depending on whether high or low frequencies are amplified by the filter.

Let $y_t = \Delta x_t$ which implies $a_0 = 1$, $a_1 = -1$, $a_s = 0$ for other values of s. The IFT gives us

$$A(v) = \exp(-2\pi iv \cdot 0) - \exp(-2\pi iv) = 1 - \exp(-2\pi iv),$$

and therefore

$$\begin{aligned} |A(v)|^2 &= A(v)\,\overline{A(v)} = (1 - \exp(-2\pi iv))(1 - \exp(2\pi iv)) \\ &= 1 - \exp(-2\pi iv) - \exp(2\pi iv) + \exp(0) = 2(1 - \cos(2\pi v)). \end{aligned}$$

A plot of $|A(v)|^2 = 2(1 - \cos(2\pi v))$ will show a curve that starts in 0 and increases in v. If x_t has a root close to 1 at the zero frequency, this root will be removed from the filtered series: The differenced series will be "more stationary" than the level series itself.

One-sided filters a_s $(s = 0, 1, 2, \ldots)$ can often be defined recursively as

$$y_t = \sum_{s=0}^{s=\infty} a_s x_{t-s}, \tag{B.23}$$

which is the result of repeated substitution in

$$y_t = \sum_{s=1}^{p} b_s y_{t-s} + x_t + \sum_{s=1}^{q} c_s x_{t-s}, \tag{B.24}$$

or more compactly

$$b(L)y_t = c(L)x_t, \tag{B.25}$$

where $b(L) = 1 - b_1 L - \cdots - b_p L^p$ and $c(L) = 1 + c_1 L + \cdots + c_q L^q$. Next, we define

$$z_t = b(L)y_t = c(L)x_t. \tag{B.26}$$

Using (B.17) twice then gives

$$f_z(v) = |B(v)|^2 f_y(v) = |C(v)|^2 f_x(v),$$

where $B(v)$ and $C(v)$ are the IFTs of the two filters. This gives

$$f_y(v) = \frac{|C(v)|^2}{|B(v)|^2} f_x(v),$$

showing that the power-shift of the one-sided filter a_s $(s = 0, 1, 2, \ldots)$ in (B.23) is given by

$$|A(v)|^2 = \frac{|C(v)|^2}{|B(v)|^2}. \tag{B.27}$$

B.8. Regression in the Spectral Domain: The Cross-Spectrum and Coherency

Let $\mathbf{w}_t' = (x_{t1}, x_{t2}, \ldots, x_{tp})$ denote a weakly stationary p-dimensional vector time series. The autocovariance matrix is defined as

$$\gamma(m) = E((\mathbf{w}_{t+m} - \boldsymbol{\mu})(\mathbf{w}_t - \boldsymbol{\mu}))'. \tag{B.28}$$

This matrix is not symmetric, however,

$$\gamma_{ij}(m) = \gamma_{ji}(-m) \Rightarrow \gamma'(m) = \gamma(-m).$$

If $\sum_{m=-\infty}^{\infty} |\gamma_{ij}(m)| < \infty$, we can use the IFT on all the components in $\gamma(m)$

$$f_{ij}(v) = \sum_{m=-\infty}^{\infty} \gamma_{ij}(m) \exp(-2\pi i v m) \tag{B.29}$$

and

$$\gamma_{ij}(m) = \int_{-1/2}^{1/2} f_{ij}(v) \exp(2\pi i v m) dv. \tag{B.30}$$

$f_{ii}(v)$ are usual PSD functions, while $f_{ij}(v)$ are known as cross-spectral density functions. We have

$$f_{ij}(v) = f_{ji}(v). \tag{B.31}$$

Note that $f_{ii}(v)$ is real-valued if the time series are real, while $f_{ij}(v)$ may be complex valued. The matrix that contains all $f_{ii}(v)$ and $f_{ij}(v)$ is called the spectral matrix of $\{\mathbf{w}_t\}$. We write this matrix as $\mathbf{f}_{\mathbf{w}}(v)$. With reference to (B.30) we can write

$$\gamma(m) = \int_{-1/2}^{1/2} \mathbf{f}_{\mathbf{w}}(v) \exp(2\pi ivm)dv, \tag{B.32}$$

where the integral is taken over all the elements in the matrix $\gamma(m)$.

In the rest of this section, we consider the case of two variables ($p = 2$), x_t and y_t. The spectral matrix becomes

$$\mathbf{f}_w(v) = \begin{bmatrix} f_x(v) & f_{xy}(v) \\ f_{yx}(v) & f_y(v) \end{bmatrix}. \tag{B.33}$$

Since $f_{xy}(v)$ may be complex, it can be written as

$$f_{xy}(v) = |f_{xy}(v)|^2 \exp(i\gamma_{xy}(v)). \tag{B.34}$$

With the aid of a theorem called the multiple Cramer-representation theorem, which we will not give here, it is possible to show that $|f_{xy}(v)|$ measures the strength of the relationship between the two periodic components $P_x(v_j)$ and $P_y(v_j)$ in $\{x_t\}$ and $\{y_t\}$. $\gamma_{xy}(v_j)$ measurers the phase-shift. Heuristically, $f_{xy}(v)$ provides a frequency-based measure of the linear relationship between y_t and x. In order to give a justification of this claim, we look briefly into the tasks associated with the construction of a filter for x_t:

$$z_t = \sum_{s=-\infty}^{\infty} a_s x_{t-s},$$

that gives the best explanation of y_t in the least square sense, namely,

$$\min E\{y_t - z_t\}^2.$$

Alternatively, we can regard the filter as determined by a disturbance:

$$\epsilon_t = y_t - \sum_{s=-\infty}^{\infty} a_s x_{t-s}, \tag{B.35}$$

which is uncorrelated with $\{x_t\}$, i.e.,

$$E(\epsilon_t x_{t-k}) = 0. \tag{B.36}$$

Equations (B.35) and (B.36) give

$$\gamma_{yx}(k) = \sum_{s=-\infty}^{\infty} a_s \gamma_x(k-s), \quad k = 0, \pm 1, \pm 2, \ldots \tag{B.37}$$

directly. From (B.29), we have a relationship between $f_{yx}(v)$ and $\gamma_{yx}(k)$ which we can make use of. Substitution from (B.37) in (B.29) gives, after some manipulation,

$$f_{yx}(v) = \sum_{s=-\infty}^{\infty} a_s \exp(-2\pi i v s) \times \sum_{k=-\infty}^{\infty} \exp(-2\pi i(k-s))\gamma_x(k-s),$$

the first term on the right-hand side is the IFT of $\{a_s\}$, while the second term is the definition of the spectral density $f_x(v)$. This means that we have obtained

$$f_{yx}(v) = A(v) f_x(v), \quad A(v) = \sum_{s=-\infty}^{\infty} a_s \exp(-2\pi i v s). \tag{B.38}$$

Since ϵ_t is uncorrelated with z_t in $y_t = z_t + \epsilon_t$ we can write

$$f_y(v) = f_z(v) + f_\epsilon(v) \tag{B.39}$$

From

$$z_t = \sum_{s=-\infty}^{\infty} a_s x_{t-s},$$

it follows that

$$f_z(v) = |A(v)|^2 f_x(v),$$

which after substitution in (B.39)

$$f_y(v) = |A(v)|^2 f_x(v) + f_\epsilon(v).$$

In order to define formally the notion of frequency-dependent correlation, we now define the *squared coherence function* of y with respect to x as

$$\text{coh}_{yx}^2 = \frac{f_z(v)}{f_y(v)} = \frac{|A(v)|^2 f_x(v)^2}{f_x(v) f_y(v)} = \frac{|f_{yx}(v)|^2}{f_x(v) f_y(v)},$$

where the last equality holds with reference to (B.38).

The squared coherency is always real, while this is not the case for the cross-spectral density. We see that

$$0 \leq \text{coh}_{yx}^2 \leq 1$$

and $\text{coh}_{yx}^2 = 1$ if $f_\epsilon(v) = 0$.

B.9. The Power Spectrum of ARIMA Series: The Typical Spectral Shape

Experience tells us that many non-stationary variables can be modelled as stochastic (local) trends models. Such variables that become stationary after differencing (i.e., by use of the filter $1 - L$) are called integrated variables and belong to the class of ARIMA models. It is important therefore to establish the PSD for this model class.

We found above the PSD of an AR(1) process (see equation (B.20)). When $\phi_1 = 1$ the PSD becomes

$$f_{y,\text{RW}}(v) = \frac{\sigma^2}{2(1 - \cos(2\pi v))}, \tag{B.40}$$

which is infinite near the zero-frequency and declines sharply with increasing frequency v. This means that all the information in the series is located at the low frequencies—the series is dominated by super long waves.

Figure 9.1 in Chapter 9 graphed the theoretical PSD function for the case where the time series is generated by a random walk, and the plot of the PSD for a stationary AR(1) model was also included for comparison.

It may be noted that, formally, we are on thin ice here, since spectral analysis assumes stationarity in the first place. However, if we abstract from some problems near zero, (B.40) can be interpreted as a spectrum.

We can find the PSD to a general ARIMA$[p, 1, q]$ by using the results in Appendices B.6 and B.7.

Let $z_t \sim$ ARMA$[p, q]$ so that

$$\varphi(L)z_t = \theta(L)\varepsilon_t, \quad \varepsilon_t \sim \text{IIN}(0, \sigma^2). \tag{B.41}$$

Next, let z_t be the difference of y_t: $z_t = \Delta y_t = (1 - L)y_t$, so that

$$f_z(v) = |A(v)|^2 f_y(v), \tag{B.42}$$

where $A(v)$ is the IFT to the filter $a_0 = 1$, $a_1 = -1$, $a_s = 0$ for all other s. From the example of a low-pass filter above, we have

$$|A(v)|^2 = 2(1 - \cos(2\pi v)), \tag{B.43}$$

while Appendix B.6 showed the result

$$f_z(v) = \frac{|\theta(\exp(-2\pi i v)|^2}{|\varphi(\exp(-2\pi i v)|^2}\sigma^2. \tag{B.44}$$

Combining (B.42), (B.43) and (B.44), we obtain the PSD of $y_t \sim$ ARIMA$[p,1,q]$ as

$$f_{y,\mathrm{ARIMA}[p,1,q]}(v) = \frac{\sigma^2}{2(1-\cos(2\pi v))}\frac{|\theta(\exp(-2\pi i v)|^2}{|\varphi(\exp(-2\pi i v)|^2}, \tag{B.45}$$

which we can write as

$$f_{y,\mathrm{ARIMA}[p,1,q]}(v) = f_{y,\mathrm{RW}}(v) \cdot f_{z,\mathrm{ARMA}[p,q]}(v), \tag{B.46}$$

where $z_t = (1-L)y_t$. Since $f_{z,\mathrm{ARMA}[p,q]}(v)$ is finite for all frequencies, the PSD of ARIMA$[p,q]$ will be dominated by the *random walk* component $f_{y,\mathrm{RW}}(v)$ which is infinite at the zero frequency.

As noted, since the economic time series as a rule can be represented by estimation of ARIMA$[p,q]$ models, we expect to find that empirical PSDs typically have a marked peak at the zero frequency and maybe smaller peaks located at, for example, the seasonal frequencies. This shape of the PSD is known as the *typical spectral shape.*

B.10. Seasonal Integration

Above, we assumed that the non-stationarity is due to low frequency components. However, with quarterly or monthly series there are other possibilities.

B.10.1. Seasonally integrated series

Let y_t be generated by

$$y_t = -y_{t-1} - y_{t-2} - y_{t-3} + \varepsilon_t, \quad \varepsilon_t \sim \mathrm{IIN}(0,\sigma^2), \tag{B.47}$$

which has three characteristic roots: 0 and a complex pair: $-\frac{1}{2} \pm i\frac{\sqrt{3}}{2}$. The complex roots have modulus 1.

We can write (B.47) as

$$S(L)y_t = \varepsilon_t, \tag{B.48}$$

where $S(L) = 1 + L + L^2 + L^3$. We can interpret $S(L)$ as a filter and use the results above to give a characterization of y_t in the frequency domain.

We begin by defining

$$w_t = S(L)y_t = \varepsilon_t,$$

with $f_w(v) = \sigma^2$ and $f_w(v) = |A(v)|^2 f_y(v)$, where $A(v)$ is the IFT associated with the filter $S(L)$. The implied power-shift is

$$\begin{aligned}|A(v)|^2 &= \{1 + \exp(-2\pi iv) + \exp(-4\pi iv) + \exp(-6\pi iv)\} \\ &\quad \cdot \{1 + \exp(2\pi iv) + \exp(4\pi iv) + \exp(6\pi iv)\} \\ &= 4 + 6\cos(2\pi v) + 4\cos(4\pi v) + 2\cos(6\pi v),\end{aligned}$$

so that the PSD of y_t becomes

$$f_y(v) = \frac{\sigma^2}{|A(v)|^2} = \frac{\sigma^2}{4 + 6\cos(2\pi v) + 4\cos(4\pi v) + 2\cos(6\pi v)}, \tag{B.49}$$

which is infinite at $v = \{0, 25, 0, 5\}$ and "flat" at the other frequencies. Since

$$\text{Var}(y_t) = 2\int_0^{1/2} f_y(v)dv,$$

we see that the variance of y_t becomes infinite, which is the hallmark of a non-stationary series. By construction, we also have that the filter $S(L)$ has a power-shift which is zero for the same frequencies ($v = \{0, 25, 0, 5\}$) so that a seasonally integrated series becomes stationary by use of this filter.

When we have quarterly data, the Δ_4-operator is often used. For the seasonally integrated process above, (B.48), the filtered series $z_t = (1-L^4)y_t$ gets the PSD

$$f_{\Delta_4 y}(v) = 2(1 - \cos(2\pi v))\sigma^2, \tag{B.50}$$

since (B.48) implies $\Delta_4 y_t = -S(L)y_{t-1} + \varepsilon_t = \Delta\varepsilon_t$.

The seasonally filtered series has a PSD which is finite for all frequencies. The graph of this PSD starts with zero and increases in v. Specifically, the PSD is finite for the frequencies $1/2$ and $1/4$.

B.10.2. Seasonal random walk

Let us now replace the generating equation (B.47) by

$$y_t = y_{t-4} + \varepsilon_t. \tag{B.51}$$

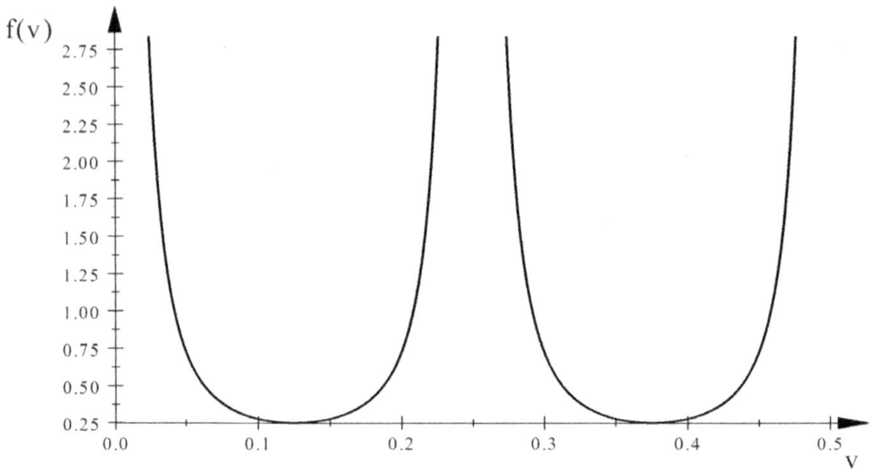

Figure B.5. Graph of theoretical PSD function for the seasonally integrated random walk process in (B.52), with $\sigma^2 = 1$.

For this model equation, we have the PSD

$$f_y(v) = \frac{\sigma^2}{2(1 - \cos(8\pi v))}, \tag{B.52}$$

which has a graph which becomes infinite at $v = 0, 1/4, 1/2$, see Figure B.5. $f_{\Delta_4 y}(v)$, on the other hand, is of course flat by construction as a result of the power-shift of the filter $1 - L^4$, which is zero at the same frequencies.

While a (plain) random walk has a single unit-root located at the zero-frequency, we need the whole unit-circle to characterize possible unit-roots of more general ARIMA models. For example, the process in (B.51) has four unit-roots, since the characteristic polynomial of $(1 - L^4)$ can be factorized as

$$(1 - z^4) = (1 - z)(1 + z)(1 + z^2),$$

with four roots: $z_1 = 1$, $z_2 = -1$, $z_3 = i$, $z_4 = -i$. All roots have modulus equal to 1 (for example, $|z_3| = |i| = \sqrt{|i|^2} = \sqrt{i\bar{i}} = \sqrt{-1(i^2)} = 1$) which satisfies the equation

$$z = \exp(i2\pi v) = \cos(2\pi v) + i\sin(2\pi v), \tag{B.53}$$

which describes the unit-circle when $0 \leq v \leq 1$. If we denote a unit-root by z_j and the corresponding frequency by v_j, we have that

$$\{z_j, v_j\} = \{1, 0;\ i, 1/4;\ -1, 1/2;\ -i, 3/4\},$$

For a random walk, we have $\{z_j,v_j\} = \{1,0\}$, while the seasonally integrated series (B.47) has roots $\{z_j,v_j\} = \{\ i,1/4;\ -1,1/2;\ -i,3/4\}$ since $S(L) = (1+L)(1+L^2)$.

B.11. Estimation

Under mild conditions (which are satisfied for causal ARMA processes), $X_c(v_k)$ and $X_s(v_k)$ from the DFT will be asymptotically independent and normally distributed with expectation 0 and variance $1/2f_x(v)$. Hence, we have

$$2\frac{X_c(k)^2}{f_x(v)} + 2\frac{X_s(k)^2}{f_x(v)} = 2\frac{P_x(v_k)}{f_x(v)} \sim \chi^2(2). \tag{B.54}$$

Therefore,

$$\mathsf{E}[P_x(v_k)] = \mathsf{E}\left[2\frac{P_x(v_k)]}{f_x(v)} \cdot \frac{f_x(v)}{2}\right] = 2\frac{f_x(v)}{2} = f_x(v) \tag{B.55}$$

is an unbiased estimator of the population PSD. The periodogram does not necessarily give a consistent estimator.

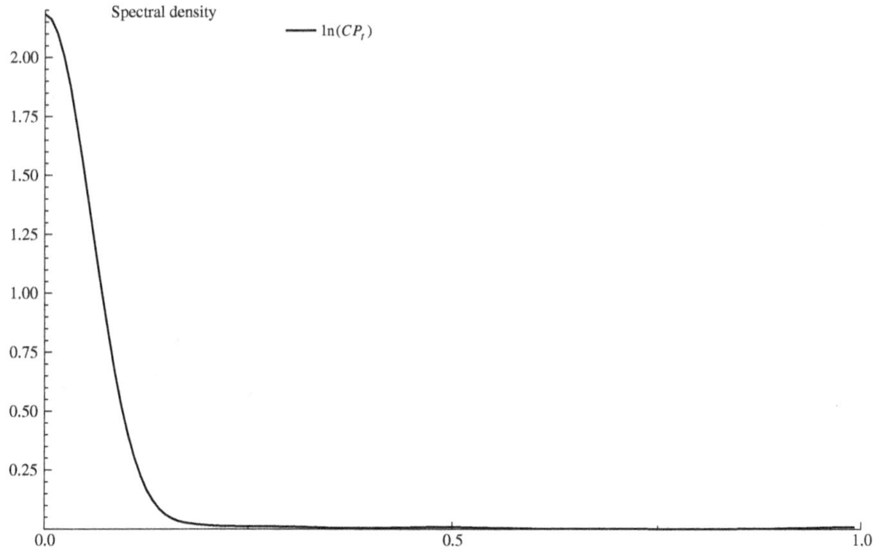

Figure B.6. Estimated PSD function for log of private consumption ($\ln(\mathrm{CP}_t)$). CP_t is measured in million kroner. Fixed 2015 prices. The data are quarterly and the sample is 1971(1)–2017(2).

However, estimators that are based on modifications of the periodogram have been developed, and these modified estimators are consistent and have good properties also for moderate sample sizes. They are implemented in Oxmetrics and other programme packages, see Figure B.6 which has been produced by OxMetrics. Clearly, this graph, for the natural logarithm of private consumption expenditure in Norway, is a case of a typical spectral shape.

It might be noted that the uncertainty is usually larger at the low frequencies than elsewhere (the "leakage" phenomenon), and this can be a problem for the interpretation of empirical PSDs for the economic time series.

Estimators that are based on the periodogram are often called non-parametric estimators.

A direct parametric approach to estimation is to estimate a well-specified ARIMA model first, and obtain the power spectrum by using the estimated parameters in the formulaes given above.

Appendix C

Answer Notes to Exercises

C.1. Chapter 1 Answers

Exercise 1.1. Renormalize (1.1) P_t:

$$P_t = \frac{1}{a}Q_t - \frac{b_t}{a}, \quad a < 0 \tag{$*$}$$

and substitute Q_t by right-hand side of (1.2):

$$P_t = \frac{c}{a}P_{t-1} + \frac{d - b_t}{a}, \quad a < 0.$$

Finally, write $(*)$ for P_{t-1},

$$P_{t-1} = \frac{1}{a}Q_{t-1} - \frac{b_{t-1}}{a}, \quad a < 0$$

and substitute in (1.2):

$$Q_t = \frac{c}{a}Q_{t-1} + \frac{da - cb_{t-1}}{a}.$$

Define $\phi_1 = \frac{c}{a}$ as the autoregressive (AR) coefficient.

Exercise 1.2 (Suggestion). In this case, the demand and (long-run) supply curves have the same slope (with opposite signs). If we repeat the thought experiment with a permanent positive (horizontal) demand shock, starting from an initial stationary state (P_{10}, Q_{10}), P_{12} will be equal to P_{10}, and P_{13} will be equal to P_{10}, with no dampening of the oscillations.

Exercise 1.3.

(1) In the software you use, make sure that the lag of the price series P_STOCH is used as a regressor together with a constant term and STEP11. Choose sample period 2–60.
(2) Obtain the "short-sample" results by choosing period 20 as the last period of the sample. Notes on differences between the two results: The estimated coefficient of the lagged endogenous variable is smallest in the sample size 59 results. Hence, the estimation error is largest when the short sample is used. Another notable difference from the full sample results is that the standard errors of the coefficients are larger. Hence, the estimated distribution around the true parameter is wider for the shortest of the two samples. Both differences can be rationalized with reference to the consistency of OLS estimators in this case (lagged-dependent variable, but the regression errors are not autocorrelated).

```
EQ( 1) Modelling P_STOCH by OLS
       The dataset is: C:dgp_determandstoch.in7
       The estimation sample is: 2 - 60

                 Coefficient  Std.Error  t-value  t-prob
P_STOCH_1          -0.755135    0.05296    -14.3  0.0000
Constant             4.22118     0.1279     33.0  0.0000
STEP11              0.745192    0.02721     27.4  0.0000
```

Figure C.1. Screen capture of regression output for (1.21), from PcGive.

```
EQ( 2) Modelling P_STOCH by OLS
       The dataset is: C:dgp_determandstoch.in7
       The estimation sample is: 2 - 20

                 Coefficient  Std.Error  t-value  t-prob
P_STOCH_1          -0.735282    0.09234    -7.96  0.0000
Constant             4.17352     0.2229     18.7  0.0000
STEP11              0.740482    0.04944     15.0  0.0000
```

Figure C.2. Screen capture of regression output for estimation of model equation (1.19), using the sample 2–20, from PcGive.

Using Stata, the dataset (file extension .dta) must first be declared as a time series dataset, or alternatively, be edited prior to estimation, so that the lagged price variable is available as a regressor.

Exercise 1.4. Substitution from the other equations into the consumption function gives

$$(1-b)C_t = cC_{t-1} + a + bJ^* + \epsilon_{Ct} + b\epsilon_{Jt},$$

which after multiplication by $\frac{1}{1-b}$ gives (1.25).

Exercise 1.5. We consider the stationary state where $C_t = C_{t-1} = C^*$, $\text{GDP}_t = \text{GDP}^*$, $J_t = J^*$, and where the three random shocks $\epsilon_{Ct}, \epsilon_{Jt}$ are set to zero for all t. The stationary version of (1.22)–(1.24) can therefore be written as

$$(1-c)C^* - b\text{GDP}^* = a, \tag{C.1}$$

$$-C^* + \text{GDP}^* = J^*, \tag{C.2}$$

$$J^* \equiv J^*. \tag{C.3}$$

The last equation is a definition. Equations (C.1) and (C.2) represent a *simultaneous equation block* where J^* is exogenous. It can be solved for the endogenous variables (C^*, S^*, GDP^*) by using, for example, *Cramer's Rule* (cf. Sydsæter *et al.*, 2008, Section 1.1):

$$|A| = \begin{vmatrix} (1-c) & -b \\ -1 & 1 \end{vmatrix} = 1 - b - c$$

There is a unique solution if and only if $|A| \neq 0$, and for reasonable magnitudes of the parameters, the determinant is a positive number, $|A| > 0$, which is less than one. The solution for C^* then becomes

$$C^* = |A|^{-1} \times \begin{vmatrix} a & -b \\ J^* & 1 \end{vmatrix}$$

which can be written as

$$C^* = \frac{a + J^*b}{1-b-c}.$$

For GDP^*, we obtain the numerator from

$$\begin{vmatrix} (1-c) & a \\ -1 & J^* \end{vmatrix} = J^* + a - J^*c,$$

and the solution can be written as

$$\text{GDP}^* = \frac{J^*(1-c) + a}{1-b-c}.$$

Exercise 1.6.

$$b = r_{YX}\frac{s_Y}{s_X}.$$

The slope coefficient in the regression with X_i as the regressand, on a constant and Y_i is

$$b' = r_{YX}\frac{s_X}{s_Y}.$$

Hence, we have that

$$b = r_{YX}\frac{s_Y}{s_X},$$

$$b = r_{YX}\left(\frac{s_Y}{s_X}\right)\left(\frac{s_Y}{s_X}\right)^{-1}\left(\frac{s_X}{s_Y}\right) = b'\frac{s_X^2}{s_Y^2}.$$

Exercise 1.7.

(1) Short versions of the variable definitions should be available in at least some of the data bank formats (notably the PcGive format).
(2) Regressing *pricelevel* on a constant and its own lag (estimation sample 2–111) gives an estimated ϕ_1 of 0.743010. However, for *tots*, the estimated ϕ_1 is only 0.0935466 (again, sample 2–111).
(3) Using the same sample period, *price* gets an estimated AR coefficient of 0.762835. For *qty*, ϕ_1 is estimated to be 0.203549. Note that since we have applied a nonlinear (i.e., log) transformation, there was no reason that the estimated autoregressions should be the same.

All in all, there is no support for negative autocorrelation, so the cobweb model is probably not the most relevant model for this market. A difference from that model which is easy to think of is that the supply of fish is likely to be inelastic with respect to price also when we look beyond the short run. It is plausible that the quantity supplied is strongly related to the fishing capacity (number and size distributions of fishing boats (with a licence) in the area), which is more or less fixed in the short run. Below, we will develop these, and other, ideas in exercises.

C.2. Chapter 2 Answers

Exercise 2.1. The mathematical expectation of a random variable is a first-order moment of the variable's probability distribution function (that function can be a marginal distribution function or a conditional distribution function). The mean of a sample of observations (realizations) of a variable is an empirical first-order moment. The mathematical variance (or the standard deviation) is a theoretical second-order moment. The empirical variance is an empirical second-order moment.

Exercise 2.2.

$$\text{Var}(X) = E[(X - \mu_X)^2] = E(X^2 - 2X\mu_X + \mu_X^2) = E(X^2) - \mu_X^2.$$

No, the smallest value possible for $E(X^2)$ is μ_X^2 in which case X is a constant.

Exercise 2.3. It is the change in the first-order moment that causes as location-shift of the distribution. An interesting inference question is whether location-shifts can be reliably estimated from the available data. Interestingly, for time series, the answer is yes.

Exercise 2.4. Even if the model only contains one explanatory *variable*, in the sense that X_i has genuine variation (take different values) over the sample, it is also true that the model contains two regressors, only that the first regressor is a "variable" with no variation in it. It is equal to 1 for every i. To make the point clear, we could write the model equation as

$$Y_i = \beta_0 \iota_i + \beta_1 X_i + \varepsilon_i,$$

and define $\iota_i = 1$ for all i. Another notation could be

$$Y_i = \beta_0 X_{0i} + \beta_1 X_i + \varepsilon_i,$$

where $X_{0i} = 1$ for all i, which comes close to how we represent the intercept when we use matrix notation as a row in a matrix with the regressors.

We can call the model equation without X_i (i.e., assuming $\beta_1 = 0$) "regression on a constant" or regression model with an intercept (only) (see Hendry and Nielsen, 2007, Chapter 3). Of course, many readers will have been presented with this model in a course in statistics, under the heading "estimation of the mean (expectation) of a random variable" (for example, see Stock and Watson, 2012, Chapter 3).

Exercise 2.5. We can write $\text{Var}(\epsilon \mid X)$ as

$$\text{Var}(\epsilon_i \mid X_i) = \text{Var}(Y_i - E(Y_i \mid X_i) \mid X_i) = \text{Var}(Y_i \mid X_i) = \sigma^2_{Y|X_i},$$

by the use of the rule for the variance of a sum, i.e., since $E(Y_i \mid X_i)$ as a fixed parameter has variance zero.

Exercise 2.6. If X and Y have a joint probability function which is normal, i.e., Gaussian, the expression of the joint pdf can be written as

$$f_{XY}(x,y) = \frac{1}{\sigma_Y \sigma_X 2\pi \sqrt{(1-\rho_{XY}^2)}} \times \exp\left[-\frac{1}{2} \frac{\left(z_Y^2 - 2\rho_{XY} z_Y z_X + z_X^2\right)}{(1-\rho_{XY}^2)} \right], \tag{C.4}$$

where z_X and z_Y are used to keep the expression compactly. They are often called standardized variables since they are defined as follows:

$$z_X = \frac{x-\mu_X}{\sigma_X} \quad \text{and} \quad z_Y = \frac{y-\mu_Y}{\sigma_Y}$$

(see, e.g., Hendry and Nielsen, 2007, Section 3.2). The rest of the notation is explained in the main text, but we define the symbols again to make the answer self-contained.

μ_X and μ_Y are the two expectations. σ_X and σ_Y are the standard deviations of the two variables: $\sigma_X = \sqrt{\sigma_X^2} \underset{\text{def}}{=} \text{Var}(X)$ and $\sigma_Y = \sqrt{\sigma_Y^2} \underset{\text{def}}{=} \text{Var}(Y)$. The correlation coefficient ρ_{XY} is

$$\rho_{XY} = \frac{\sigma_{YX}}{\sigma_Y \sigma_X},$$

where σ_{YX} is the covariance of X and Y:

$$\sigma_{YX} = \text{Cov}(Y,X) = E\left[(Y-\mu_Y)(X-\mu_X)\right].$$

From the statistical theory, we use the following result without proof: the two marginal pdfs are also normal. For the random variable Y, the pdf is

$$f(y) = \frac{1}{\sigma_Y\sqrt{2\pi}} \exp\left[-\frac{1}{2}\left(\frac{y-\mu_Y}{\sigma_Y}\right)^2 \right], \tag{C.5}$$

meaning that the answer to the first part of the question is that the first-order moment of Y is the parameter μ_Y in (C.5), and the second-order moment is the parameter σ_Y in (C.5).

In order to answer the second part of the question, we need the expression for the conditional pdf of Y given X. We can find that expression by using (C.4) together with

$$f(x) = \frac{1}{\sigma_X \sqrt{2\pi}} \exp\left[-\frac{1}{2}\left(\frac{x-\mu_X}{\sigma_X}\right)^2\right], \tag{C.6}$$

in the general expression:

$$f_{Y|X}(y \mid x) = \frac{f_{XY}(y,x)}{f(x)}.$$

The first step is to simplify common factors and form one common exponential:

$$\begin{aligned}
&f_{Y|X}(y \mid x)\\
&= \frac{\frac{1}{\sqrt{2\pi\sigma_Y^2\left(1-\rho_{XY}^2\right)}} \times \exp\left[-\frac{1}{2}\frac{\left(z_Y^2-2\rho_{XY}z_Y z_X+z_X^2\right)}{\left(1-\rho_{XY}^2\right)}\right]}{\exp\left[-\frac{1}{2}\frac{\left(1-\rho_{XY}^2\right)z_X^2}{\left(1-\rho_{XY}^2\right)}\right]}\\
&= \frac{1}{\sqrt{2\pi\sigma_Y^2\left(1-\rho_{XY}^2\right)}}\\
&\quad \times \exp\left\{-\frac{1}{2(1-\rho_{XY}^2)}[(z_Y^2-2\rho_{XY}z_Y z_X+z_X^2)-(1-\rho_{XY}^2)z_X^2]\right\}\\
&= \frac{1}{\sqrt{2\pi\sigma_Y^2\left(1-\rho_{XY}^2\right)}}\\
&\quad \times \exp\left\{-\frac{1}{2(1-\rho_{XY}^2)}[z_Y^2-2\rho_{XY}z_Y z_X+\rho_{XY}^2 z_X^2]\right\}.
\end{aligned}$$

The argument in the exponential function is

$$[z_Y^2-2\rho_{XY}z_Y z_X+\rho_{XY}^2 z_X^2] = (z_Y-\rho_{XY}z_X)^2,$$

and we can begin to see that the conditional pdf "looks like" a normal pdf, except for the presence of the correlation coefficient ρ_{XY}:

$$f_{Y|X}(y \mid x) = \frac{1}{\sqrt{2\pi\sigma_Y^2\left(1-\rho_{XY}^2\right)}} \times \exp\left\{-\frac{(z_Y-\rho_{XY}z_X)^2}{2\left(1-\rho_{XY}^2\right)}\right\}.$$

The role of $\rho_{XY} = \frac{\sigma_{YX}}{\sigma_Y \sigma_X}$ becomes clearer if we express the pdf in terms of X and Y:

$$f_{Y|X}(y \mid x) = \frac{1}{\sqrt{2\pi\sigma_Y^2(1-\rho_{XY}^2)}} \times \exp\left\{ -\frac{\left(\frac{y-\mu_Y}{\sigma_Y} - \frac{\sigma_{YX}}{\sigma_Y\sigma_X}\frac{x-\mu_X}{\sigma_X}\right)^2}{2(1-\rho_{XY}^2)} \right\}$$

$$= \frac{1}{\sqrt{2\pi\left(\sigma_Y^2 - \sigma_Y^2 \frac{(\sigma_{YX})^2}{\sigma_Y^2\sigma_X^2}\right)}}$$

$$\times \exp\left\{ -\frac{1}{2} \frac{\left[y - \left(\mu_Y - \frac{\sigma_{YX}}{\sigma_X^2}\mu_X + \frac{\sigma_{YX}}{\sigma_X^2}x\right)\right]^2}{\sigma_Y^2 - \sigma_Y^2\frac{(\sigma_{YX})^2}{\sigma_Y^2\sigma_X^2}} \right\}.$$

If we define

$$\beta_1 \equiv \frac{\sigma_{YX}}{\sigma_X^2}, \quad \text{and}$$

$$\beta_0 \equiv \mu_Y - \beta_1\mu_X,$$

we obtain the conditional pdf of Y given X with conditional expectation $\mu_{Y|X} \equiv \beta_0 + \beta_1 x$, and conditional variance $\sigma_{Y|X}^2 \equiv \sigma_Y^2 - \frac{(\sigma_{YX})^2}{\sigma_X^2}$:

$$f_{Y|X}(y \mid x) = \frac{1}{\sqrt{2\pi\left(\sigma_Y^2 - \frac{(\sigma_{YX})^2}{\sigma_X^2}\right)}} \times \exp\left\{ -\frac{1}{2}\frac{[y-(\beta_0+\beta_1 x)]^2}{\sigma_Y^2 - \frac{(\sigma_{YX})^2}{\sigma_X^2}} \right\}$$

$$= \frac{1}{\sqrt{2\pi\sigma_{Y|X}^2}} \times \exp\left[-\frac{1}{2}\left(\frac{y-\mu_{Y|X}}{\sigma_{Y|X}}\right)^2 \right].$$

The answer to the second part of the question is therefore that the first-order moment is $\mu_{Y|X}$, and the second-order moment is $\sigma_{Y|X}^2$, with the definitions given above.

Exercise 2.7. We refer to Hendry and Nielsen (2007, Section 5.2) and Stock and Watson (2012, Section 4.2) among others.

From the first-order conditions:

$$\overline{Y} - \hat{\beta}_0 - \hat{\beta}_1\overline{X} = 0,$$

$$\sum_{i=1}^{n} X_iY_i - \hat{\beta}_0\sum_{i=1}^{n} X_i - \hat{\beta}_1\sum_{i=1}^{n} X_i^2 = 0.$$

The first of these equations gives

$$\hat{\beta}_0 = \overline{Y} - \hat{\beta}_1 \overline{X},$$

which is the same as the expression for $\hat{\beta}_0$ in the main text. Substitution in equation number two gives

$$\begin{aligned}
\sum_{i=1}^{n} X_i Y_i - (\overline{Y} - \hat{\beta}_1 \overline{X}) \sum_{i=1}^{n} X_i - \hat{\beta}_1 \sum_{i=1}^{n} X_i^2 = 0 \\
\hat{\beta}_1 \left(\overline{X} \sum_{i=1}^{n} X_i - \sum_{i=1}^{n} X_i^2 \right) &= - \sum_{i=1}^{n} X_i Y_i + \overline{Y} \sum_{i=1}^{n} X_i \\
\hat{\beta}_1 \sum_{i=1}^{n} (\overline{X} X_i - X_i^2) &= - \sum_{i=1}^{n} X_i Y_i + \overline{Y} \sum_{i=1}^{n} X_i \\
\hat{\beta}_1 \sum_{i=1}^{n} (\overline{X} - X_i) X_i &= - \sum_{i=1}^{n} X_i (Y_i - \overline{Y}) \\
-\hat{\beta}_1 \sum_{i=1}^{n} (X_i - \overline{X}) X_i &= - \sum_{i=1}^{n} (Y_i - \overline{Y}) X_i,
\end{aligned}$$

which gives $\hat{\beta}_1$ as

$$\hat{\beta}_1 = \frac{\sum_{i=1}^{n} X_i (Y_i - \overline{Y}_i)}{\sum_{i=1}^{n} (X_i - \overline{X}) X_i}.$$

In the numerator, $\sum_{i=1}^{n} X_i (Y_i - \overline{Y})$ is identical to $\sum_{i=1}^{n} Y_i (X_i - \overline{X})$. In the denominator: $\sum_{i=1}^{n} (X_i - \overline{X}) X_i = \sum_{i=1}^{n} (X_i - \overline{X})^2$. Hence, the expression for $\hat{\beta}_1$ is identical to the one we obtained (more directly) in the main text.

Exercise 2.8. Under the assumptions of the model, the statistical theory states that

$$\frac{1}{\sigma^2} \sum_{i=1}^{n} \hat{\epsilon}_i^2 \overset{D}{\sim} \chi^2(n-2),$$

$$E \Bigg(\underbrace{\frac{1}{n} \sum_{i=1}^{n} \hat{\epsilon}_i^2}_{\hat{\sigma}^2} \Bigg) = \frac{\sigma^2}{n} E \left(\frac{1}{\sigma^2} \sum_{i=1}^{n} \hat{\epsilon}_i^2 \right) = \frac{\sigma^2 (n-2)}{n} < \sigma^2,$$

while $\tilde{\sigma}^2 = \frac{1}{n-2} \sum_{i=1}^{n} \hat{\epsilon}_i^2$ is an unbiased estimator based on the assumptions of the model.

Exercise 2.9. We write (2.50) as

$$\frac{1}{n}\sum_{i=1}^{n}(Y_i - \hat{\alpha} - \hat{\beta}_1(X_i - \bar{X})) = 0.$$

Taking the summation through, and multiplying all terms by $\frac{1}{n}$ gives

$$\frac{1}{n}\sum_{i=1}^{n}Y_i - \hat{\alpha} - \hat{\beta}_1\frac{1}{n}\sum_{i=1}^{n}(X_i - \bar{X}) = 0,$$

which gives $\hat{\alpha} = \bar{Y}$ (since $\frac{1}{n}\sum_{i=1}^{n}(X_i - \bar{X}) \equiv 0$). Substitution of $\hat{\epsilon}_i$ by $Y_i - \hat{\beta}_0 - \hat{\beta}_1 X_i$ in (2.51), we get

$$\frac{1}{n}\sum_{i=1}^{n}(Y_i - \hat{\beta}_0 - \hat{\beta}_1 X_i)(X_i - \bar{X}) = 0$$

$$\iff \frac{1}{n}\sum_{i=1}^{n}Y_i(X_i - \bar{X}) - \hat{\beta}_1\frac{1}{n}\sum_{i=1}^{n}X_i(X_i - \bar{X}) = 0,$$

and solving for $\hat{\beta}_1$ gives

$$\hat{\beta}_1 = \frac{\frac{1}{n}\sum_{i=1}^{n}Y_i(X_i - \bar{X})}{\frac{1}{n}\sum_{i=1}^{n}X_i(X_i - \bar{X})},$$

which is the same as the OLS/ML estimator, since $\sum_{i=1}^{n}X_i(X_i - \bar{X}) \equiv \sum_{i=1}^{n}(X_i - \bar{X})^2$.

Exercise 2.10. Under the assumptions of the regression model, the (conditional) distribution of the disturbance term is IID (or, somewhat stronger: Gaussian), and under that assumption, the two OLS estimators $\hat{\beta}_0$ and $\hat{\beta}_1$ are consistent as follows:

$$\text{plim}(\hat{\beta}_0) = \beta_0,$$
$$\text{plim}(\hat{\beta}_1) = \beta_1.$$

From the properties of the probability limits, it follows that

$$\text{plim}(\hat{\theta}) = \frac{\text{plim}\,\hat{\beta}_0}{\text{plim}\,\hat{\beta}_1} = \theta,$$

showing that $\hat{\theta}$ is a consistent estimator.

Exercise 2.11. If you use PcGive, the results in the results window are as follows:

```
EQ(1) Modelling INF by OLS
      The dataset is: C:NORPCMa.in7
      The estimation sample is: 1981 - 2005

                 Coefficient  Std.Error  t-value  t-prob Part.R^2
Constant             10.5088      1.639     6.41  0.0000   0.6413
U                   -1.83147     0.4613    -3.97  0.0006   0.4067

sigma                2.64904  RSS                161.400248
R^2                 0.406675  F(1,23) =     15.76 [0.001]**
Adj.R^2             0.380878  log-likelihood       -58.7861
no. of observations       25  no. of parameters           2
mean(INF)            4.35213  se(INF)               3.36667

AR 1-2 test:      F(2,21)   =   14.820 [0.0001]**
ARCH 1-1 test:    F(1,23)   =   26.590 [0.0000]**
Normality test:   Chi^2(2)  =   1.1618 [0.5594]
Hetero test:      F(2,22)   =   2.7322 [0.0871]
Hetero-X test:    F(2,22)   =   2.7322 [0.0871]
```

Figure C.3. Screen capture of PcGive estimation results for the simple PCM in (2.56).

and other programs will give the same estimation of the coefficients and their standard errors, but there will be some differences in how the rest of the output is organized. Specifically, PcGive reports a battery of standard misspecification tests below the other output (see the following exercise).

In order to obtain the covariance needed in the Delta method: Test Menu → Further output → Covariance matrix of estimated parameters.

In PcGive, nonlinear estimation is perhaps done the easiest way by running the following script:

```
// Batch code for EQ( 2)
module("PcGive");
package("PcGive", "Non-linear");
usedata("NORPCMa.in7");
nonlinear
{
actual=INF;
fitted=&1*(U-&2);
&1=-0.01;&2=2;
}
estimate("NLS", 1981, 1, 2005, 1);
```

Figure C.4. PcGive batch language code (also called "script") for NLS estimation of PCM.

In this code, the coefficients are specified as &1 and &2, and it is easy to see that &1 corresponds to β_1, and &2 to U^{nat} in (2.57). If you use PcGive, the result window of the program shows the following:

```
EQ(2) Modelling actual by NLS
      The dataset is: C:NORPCMa.in7
      The estimation sample is: 1981 - 2005

                  Coefficient  Std.Error  t-value  t-prob Part.R^2
&1                   -1.83149     0.4613    -3.97  0.0006   0.4067
&2                    5.73786     0.6647     8.63  0.0000   0.7641

sigma                 2.64904  RSS               161.400248
log-likelihood       -58.7861
no. of observations        25  no. of parameters          2
mean(actual)          4.35213  se(actual)           3.36667

Standard errors based on information matrix
BFGS/warm-up using numerical derivatives (eps1=0.0001; eps2=0.005):
Strong convergence

AR 1-2 test:      F(2,21)    =   14.820 [0.0001]**
ARCH 1-1 test:    F(1,23)    =   26.589 [0.0000]**
Normality test:   Chi^2(2)   =   1.1618 [0.5594]
Hetero test:      F(2,22)    =   2.7321 [0.0871]
Hetero-X test:    F(2,22)    =   2.7321 [0.0871]
```

Figure C.5. Screen capture of PcGive estimation results for the simple PCM in (2.56), using NLS.

Exercise 2.12. The last four lines in the above screen capture the OLS/NLS estimation results containing the misspecification tests. These tests (for residual autocorrelation, heteroskedasticity and non-normality) can be found in any introductory course in econometrics, and for completeness, Section 2.8 includes a self-contained (but brief) explanation all the tests.

The line `AR 1-2 test` shows the F-version of the test of residual autocorrelation, which has an F-distribution with 2 and 21 degrees of freedom (i.e., `F(2,21)`). The p-value, in (hard) brackets at the end of the line, strongly indicates that the residuals are autocorrelated. Of course, this is not surprising, since we gave a static model equation here and, as noted in the introduction, dynamic specifications are usually required to make progress with empirical modelling in macroeconomics.

It is possible to investigate the matter a little more closely. For example, redoing the test with only first-order autocorrelation gives `F(1,22) = 30.640` which is highly significant, while testing for second-order autocorrelation (only) gives: `F(1,22) = 12.589` which is lower, but still statistically significant.

ARCH heteroskedasticity (the default is the first order) is tested by `F(1,23) = 26.59` in the second line with tests. Also, the null of no ARCH effects in the residuals is therefore rejected at practically any significance level we might choose. One explanation is that the variance of inflation (as well as the level) is high at the start of the sample period, and low at the end, but this feature of the data is not captured by the model.

The two last tests shown, the Jarque-Bera test of normality (i.e., χ^2_{norm} above), and White's heteroskedasticity test (i.e., F_{het} above), are both insignificant. The normality test is called `Normality test Chi2(2)` in the regression output. White's test is reported as `Hetero test: F(2,224)` in the screen capture. Note that you would reject the null hypothesis at the 10% level based on this evidence, but not reject at the 5% level. Since we have only one regressor, the version of the test that includes cross-products ($F_{\text{het}-x}$), which would appear as `Hetero-X test: F(2,44)`, becomes identical to the first test.

Exercise 2.13. Define a new parameter INF^{it}. The expression for the natural rate of unemployment is seen to be derived for $\text{INF}^{\text{targ}} = 0$. More generally, we can set $\text{INF}_i = \text{INF}^{\text{it}}$ and solve the estimated PCM for $(\hat{U}^{\text{it}})$. With $\text{INF}^{\text{it}} = 2.5$, we obtain:

$$\text{IT-rate } \hat{U}^{\text{it}} = \frac{(8.37527 - 2.5)}{1.36632} = 4.3001.$$

As the inflation target is a known parameter, the estimated variance of the inflation target rate of unemployment obtained by the use of the Delta method is the same as variance calculated in the main text.

Exercise 2.14.

$$\begin{aligned}(\mathbf{y} - \mathbf{X}\boldsymbol{\beta})'(\mathbf{y} - \mathbf{X}\boldsymbol{\beta}) &= (\mathbf{y}' - \boldsymbol{\beta}'\mathbf{X}')(\mathbf{y} - \mathbf{X}\boldsymbol{\beta}) \\ &= \mathbf{y}'\mathbf{y} - \boldsymbol{\beta}'\mathbf{X}'\mathbf{y} - \mathbf{y}'\mathbf{X}\boldsymbol{\beta} + \boldsymbol{\beta}'\mathbf{X}'\mathbf{X}\boldsymbol{\beta} \\ &= \mathbf{y}'\mathbf{y} - 2\mathbf{y}'\mathbf{X}\boldsymbol{\beta} + \boldsymbol{\beta}'\mathbf{X}'\mathbf{X}\boldsymbol{\beta}\end{aligned}$$

Note that the two middle terms in the second line have the same scalar (number), and they appear as $\mathbf{2y'X}\boldsymbol{\beta}$ in the third line.

In order to find the first-order condition for a minimum, we do as usual: Find the first derivative and set the result to zero. From the rules of differentiation of matrices, we have

$$\frac{\partial}{\partial \boldsymbol{\beta}}(2\mathbf{y}'\mathbf{X}\boldsymbol{\beta}) = 2\mathbf{X}'\mathbf{y}.$$

and

$$\frac{\partial}{\partial \boldsymbol{\beta}}(\boldsymbol{\beta}'\mathbf{X}'\mathbf{X}\boldsymbol{\beta}) = \boldsymbol{\beta}'\{(\mathbf{X}'\mathbf{X}) + (\mathbf{X}'\mathbf{X})'\} = 2(\mathbf{X}'\mathbf{X})\boldsymbol{\beta},$$

noting that this is for a quadratic form (cf. Sydsæter *et al.*, 2005, Section 23). We have chosen the vector variant of organizing the derivatives (rather than the row version $2\boldsymbol{\beta}'(\mathbf{X}'\mathbf{X})$) because it is convenient.

Hence the first-order condition for minimum is

$$-2\mathbf{X}'\mathbf{y} + 2\mathbf{X}'\mathbf{X}\hat{\boldsymbol{\beta}} = \mathbf{0}.$$

The common scalar 2 in the first-order conditions cancels, and we can write the conditions as

$$\mathbf{X}'\mathbf{X}\hat{\boldsymbol{\beta}} = \mathbf{X}'\mathbf{y}.$$

Assuming that $\mathbf{X}'\mathbf{X}$ is invertible (has full rank), we get our result as

$$\hat{\boldsymbol{\beta}} = (\mathbf{X}'\mathbf{X})^{-1}\mathbf{X}'\mathbf{y}.$$

An alternative to the use of differentiation is to base the solution of the "least-square problem" on the principle of orthogonality between predicted values and the information in $\mathbf{X}$ (see, e.g., Sydsæter *et al.*, 2016, Section 15.8).

Exercise 2.15. We can write $\mathbf{X}$ as

$$\mathbf{X} = [\mathbf{x}_0 \quad \mathbf{x}_1 \quad \cdots \quad \mathbf{x}_k],$$

where $\mathbf{x}_j$ $(j = 0, 1, \ldots, k)$ are vectors of length n. We write individual random variables with capital letters, so $\mathbf{x}_j' = [X_{0j} \quad X_{1j} \quad \cdots \quad X_{nj}]$. This means that the typical element in $\mathbf{X}'\mathbf{X}$ is

$$\mathbf{x}_j'\mathbf{x}_l = \sum_{i=1}^{n} X_{ij}X_{il},$$

for $j, l = 0, 1, 2, \ldots, k$ and that the typical element in $\mathbf{X}'\mathbf{y}$ is

$$\mathbf{x}_j'\mathbf{y} = \sum_{i=1}^{n} X_{ij}Y_i,$$

for $j = 0, 1, 2, \ldots, k$. This means that the typical elements in $n^{-1}\mathbf{X}'\mathbf{X}$ and $n^{-1}\mathbf{X}'\mathbf{y}$ are the (uncentred) second-order empirical moments.

Exercise 2.16.

$$\begin{aligned}\mathbf{y} &= \mathbf{X}\boldsymbol{\beta} + \boldsymbol{\varepsilon} \\ &= \boldsymbol{\iota}\beta_1 + \bar{\mathbf{X}}_2\boldsymbol{\beta}_2 + (\mathbf{X}_2 - \bar{\mathbf{X}}_2)\boldsymbol{\beta}_2 + \boldsymbol{\epsilon} \\ &= \boldsymbol{\iota}\beta_1 + \boldsymbol{\iota}\bar{\mathbf{x}}_2'\boldsymbol{\beta}_2 + (\mathbf{X}_2 - \bar{\mathbf{X}}_2)\boldsymbol{\beta}_2 + \boldsymbol{\epsilon},\end{aligned}$$

since $\bar{\mathbf{X}}_2\boldsymbol{\beta}_2 = \boldsymbol{\iota}\bar{\mathbf{x}}_2'\boldsymbol{\beta}_2$. But then we can set $\boldsymbol{\iota}\beta_1 + \boldsymbol{\iota}\bar{\mathbf{x}}_2'\boldsymbol{\beta}_2 = \boldsymbol{\iota}(\beta_1 + \bar{\mathbf{x}}_2'\boldsymbol{\beta}_2) = \boldsymbol{\iota}\alpha$.

Exercise 2.17. Using the partitioning of $\mathbf{X}$, the first $\mathbf{X}'\hat{\boldsymbol{\varepsilon}} = \mathbf{0}$ can be written as

$$\begin{pmatrix} \boldsymbol{\iota}' \\ \mathbf{X}_2' \end{pmatrix} \hat{\boldsymbol{\varepsilon}} = \begin{pmatrix} \boldsymbol{\iota}'\hat{\boldsymbol{\varepsilon}} \\ \mathbf{X}_2'\hat{\boldsymbol{\varepsilon}} \end{pmatrix} = \begin{pmatrix} 0 \\ \mathbf{0} \end{pmatrix}.$$

In the first part, the sum of the residuals is zero:

$$\boldsymbol{\iota}'\hat{\boldsymbol{\varepsilon}} = 0 \text{ (scalar)}, \tag{C.7}$$

and we also have that $\bar{\mathbf{X}}_2'\hat{\boldsymbol{\varepsilon}} = \mathbf{0}$ (matrix with zeros). Hence we can write the second part of the restrictions as

$$(\mathbf{X}_2 - \bar{\mathbf{X}}_2)'\hat{\boldsymbol{\varepsilon}} = \mathbf{0} \tag{C.8}$$

We can now perform the multiplications in (C.7) and (C.8) using the partitioning in the expression for $\hat{\boldsymbol{\varepsilon}}$:

$$\hat{\boldsymbol{\varepsilon}} = \mathbf{y} - \boldsymbol{\iota}\hat{\alpha} + (\mathbf{X}_2 - \bar{\mathbf{X}}_2)\hat{\boldsymbol{\beta}}_2. \tag{C.9}$$

This gives first (for (C.7)):

$$\boldsymbol{\iota}'\hat{\boldsymbol{\varepsilon}} = \boldsymbol{\iota}'\mathbf{y} - \boldsymbol{\iota}'\boldsymbol{\iota}\hat{\alpha} + \boldsymbol{\iota}'(\mathbf{X}_2 - \bar{\mathbf{X}}_2)\hat{\boldsymbol{\beta}}_2 = \boldsymbol{\iota}'\mathbf{y} - \boldsymbol{\iota}'\boldsymbol{\iota}\hat{\alpha}, \tag{C.10}$$

since $\boldsymbol{\iota}'(\mathbf{X}_2 - \bar{\mathbf{X}}_2)\hat{\boldsymbol{\beta}}_2 = 0$. Equation (C.10) implies $\sum_{i=1}^{n} Y_i = n\hat{\alpha}$, and hence we get $\hat{\alpha} = \bar{Y}$.

For (C.8), we get

$$(\mathbf{X}_2 - \bar{\mathbf{X}}_2)'\hat{\boldsymbol{\varepsilon}} = (\mathbf{X}_2 - \bar{\mathbf{X}}_2)'\mathbf{y} - (\mathbf{X}_2 - \bar{\mathbf{X}}_2)'\boldsymbol{\iota}\hat{\alpha} + (\mathbf{X}_2 - \bar{\mathbf{X}}_2)'(\mathbf{X}_2 - \bar{\mathbf{X}}_2)\hat{\boldsymbol{\beta}}_2,$$

and since $(\mathbf{X}_2 - \bar{\mathbf{X}}_2)'\boldsymbol{\iota}\hat{\alpha} = \mathbf{0}$, we can solve for $\hat{\boldsymbol{\beta}}_2$, and obtain the expression in (2.163), equation (6.18) in the main text.

Exercise 2.18. Multiplication of $Y_i = \beta_0 + \beta_1 X_i + \epsilon_i$ by $\sqrt{X_i}$ gives the transformed model

$$\frac{1}{\sqrt{X_i}} Y_i = \frac{1}{\sqrt{X_i}} \beta_0 + \beta_1 \frac{1}{\sqrt{X_i}} X_i + \frac{1}{\sqrt{X_i}} \epsilon_i, \tag{C.11}$$

which, by consequence of the assumed form of heteroscedasticity, is without an intercept. With the notation in the main text, we have (we drop the conditioning to save notation):

$$\begin{aligned}
\operatorname{Var}(\boldsymbol{\varepsilon}_*) \\
&= E(\boldsymbol{\epsilon}_*\boldsymbol{\epsilon}_*') \\
&= E\begin{pmatrix} X_1^{-1}\epsilon_1^2 & X_1^{-1/2}X_2^{-1/2}\epsilon_1\epsilon_2 & \cdots & X_1^{-1/2}X_n^{-1/2}\epsilon_1\epsilon_n \\ X_2^{-1/2}X_1^{-1/2}\epsilon_2\epsilon_1 & X_2^{-1}\epsilon_2^2 & \cdots & X_2^{-1/2}X_n^{-1/2}\epsilon_2\epsilon_n \\ \vdots & \vdots & \ddots & \vdots \\ X_n^{-1/2}X_1^{-1/2}\epsilon_n\epsilon_1 & X_n^{-1/2}X_2^{-1/2}\epsilon_n\epsilon_2 & \cdots & X_n^{-1}\epsilon_n^2 \end{pmatrix} \\
&= \begin{pmatrix} X_1^{-1}\operatorname{Var}(\epsilon_1) & 0 & \cdots & 0 \\ 0 & X_2^{-1}\operatorname{Var}(\epsilon_2) & \cdots & 0 \\ \vdots & \vdots & \ddots & \vdots \\ 0 & 0 & \cdots & X_n^{-1}\operatorname{Var}(\epsilon_n) \end{pmatrix}.
\end{aligned}$$

Since $\operatorname{Var}(\epsilon_i) = \sigma^2 X_i$ for all i, we get

$$\operatorname{Var}(\boldsymbol{\varepsilon}_*) = \sigma^2\mathbf{I},$$

showing that homoskedasticity is reinstalled by the suggested weights. In the light of (2.124), the weights can be collected in the matrix $\mathbf{\Psi}'$:

$$\mathbf{\Psi}' = \begin{pmatrix} X_1^{-1/2} & 0 & \cdots & 0 \\ 0 & X_2^{-1/2} & \cdots & 0 \\ \vdots & \vdots & \ddots & \vdots \\ 0 & 0 & \cdots & X_n^{-1/2} \end{pmatrix}.$$

Conversely, the assumed heteroskedastiticy, $\text{Var}(\epsilon_i \mid X_i) = \sigma^2 X_i$, can be written as

$$\text{Var}(\boldsymbol{\varepsilon}) = \sigma^2 \mathbf{\Omega},$$

where $\mathbf{\Omega}$ has X_i $(i = 1, 2, \ldots, n)$ along the diagonal, and zeros everywhere else. The inverse $\mathbf{\Omega}^{-1}$ has X_i^{-1} $(i = 1, 2, \ldots, n)$ along its diagonal, and zeros elsewhere. Now,

$$\mathbf{\Psi}'\mathbf{\Psi} = \mathbf{\Omega}^{-1},$$

implying that OLS on (C.11) gives the identical estimator of β_0 and β_1 as the GLS estimator.

C.3. Chapter 3 Answers

Exercise 3.1. For example, (a) $\phi_1 = 0.5$, $\phi_2 = 0.2$ (b) $\phi_1 = 1.6$, $\phi_2 = -0.5$ and (c) $\phi_1 = 1.6$, $\phi_2 = -0.6$.

Exercise 3.2. We first show the result for $p = 2$. We can simplify the notation somewhat by writing $c_1 = \{g_{11}g^{11}\}$ and $c_2 = \{g_{12}g^{21}\}$, so that

$$\begin{aligned} b_{11}^{(j)} &= \{d_{11}d^{11}\}\lambda_1^j + \{d_{12}d^{21}\}\lambda_2^j \\ &= c_1\lambda_1^j + c_2\lambda_2^j. \end{aligned}$$

We then obtain

$$\begin{aligned} \left[\sum_{j=1}^{t-1} b_{11}^{(j)} + 1\right] &= \sum_{j=1}^{t-1}(c_1\lambda_1^j + c_2\lambda_2^j + 1) \\ &= c_1\sum_{j=1}^{t-1}\lambda_1^j + c_2\sum_{j=1}^{t-1}\lambda_2^j + 1 \end{aligned}$$

$$= c_1 \left(\sum_{j=0}^{t-1} \lambda_1^j - 1 \right) + c_2 \left(\sum_{j=0}^{t-1} \lambda_2^j - 1 \right) + 1$$

$$= c_1 \sum_{j=0}^{t-1} \lambda_1^j + c_2 \sum_{j=0}^{t-1} \lambda_2^j,$$

where we have used that $-(c_1 + c_2) = -1$ from (3.52). We now assume stability: $|\lambda_1| < 1$ and $|\lambda_2| < 1$:

$$\left[\sum_{j=1}^{t-1} b_{11}^{(j)} + 1 \right] \underset{t \to \infty}{\longrightarrow} c_1 \frac{1}{1 - \lambda_1} + c_2 \frac{1}{1 - \lambda_2}, \quad |\lambda_1| < 1, \ |\lambda_2| < 1.$$

Furthermore,

$$c_1 \frac{1}{1 - \lambda_1} + c_2 \frac{1}{1 - \lambda_2} = \frac{c_1(1 - \lambda_2) + c_2(1 - \lambda_1)}{(1 - \lambda_1)(1 - \lambda_2)} = \frac{c_1 + c_2 - c_1\lambda_2 - c_2\lambda_1}{1 - (\lambda_1 + \lambda_2) + \lambda_1\lambda_2}.$$

Viètes rule gives us $\lambda_1 + \lambda_2 = \phi_1$ and $\lambda_1\lambda_2 = -\phi_2$, and by the use of $c_1 + c_2 = 1$, we can show that

$$\left[\sum_{j=1}^{t-1} b_{11}^{(j)} + 1 \right] \underset{t \to \infty}{\longrightarrow} \frac{1 - c_1\lambda_2 - c_2\lambda_1}{1 - \phi_1 - \phi_2} = \frac{1}{1 - \phi_1 - \phi_2},$$

where the equality follows from

$$c_1 = \frac{\lambda_1}{\lambda_1 - \lambda_2},$$

$$c_2 = \frac{-\lambda_2}{\lambda_1 - \lambda_2},$$

in accordance with (3.59) and (3.60).

For the case of general p, it is possible to make a more direct argument. The elements in the sum are

$$b_{11}^{(t)} = \{d_{11}d^{11}\}\lambda_1^t + \{d_{12}d^{21}\}\lambda_2^t + \cdots + \{d_{1p}d^{p1}\}\lambda_p^t \quad \text{for } t > 0,$$

and $b_{11}^{(0)} = 1$ for $t = 0$ (since $\sum_{i=1}^{p} d_{1i}d^{i1} = 1$).

Clearly, no matter how large the constants $\{d_{1i}d^{i1}\}$ are, $b_{11}^{(t)} \underset{t \longrightarrow \infty}{\longrightarrow} 0$ if and only if $|\lambda_i| < 1$ for all i. By direct reasoning, we can therefore continue *as if*:

$$\left(\sum_{j=1}^{t-1} b_{11}^{(j)} + 1 \right) \equiv \left(\sum_{j=0}^{t-1} b_{11}^{(j)} \right)$$

is an ordinary geometric progression. Hence,

$$\lim_{t\to\infty}\left(\sum_{j=1}^{t-1} b_{11}^{(j)} + 1\right) \equiv \left(\sum_{j=0}^{t-1} b_{11}^{(j)}\right) = K,$$

where K denotes a constant which is yet to be determined.

First, we can take the limit on both sides of (3.42):

$$\lim_{t\to\infty} Y_t = \lim_{t\to\infty}\left(\sum_{i=1}^{p} b_{1i}^{(t)} Y_{-(i-1)}\right) + \phi_0 \lim_{t\to\infty}\left(\sum_{j=0}^{t-1} b_{11}^{(j)}\right) + \lim_{t\to\infty}\left(\sum_{j=0}^{t-1} b_{11}^{(j)}\varepsilon_{t-j}\right).$$

If all roots are less than one in magnitude (modulus less than one), the first term on the right-hand side is zero (cf. (3.55)), and using $(\sum_{j=0}^{t-1} b_{11}^{(j)}) = K$, we get

$$\lim_{t\to\infty} Y_t = \phi_0 K + \lim_{t\to\infty}\left(\sum_{j=0}^{t-1} b_{11}^{(j)}\varepsilon_{t-j}\right).$$

For simplicity, but without loss of generality, we evaluate the limit for the particular case where all disturbances are set to zero. Hence, we get the particular solution of (3.42) as

$$\lim_{t\to\infty} Y_t = \phi_0 K \underset{\text{def}}{=} Y^*.$$

From the uniqueness of a solution of a difference equation, Y^* has to fit in (3.9) (in the case where we set $\varepsilon_t = 0$), i.e.,

$$Y^* = \phi_0 + \phi_1 Y^* + \phi_2 Y^* + \cdots + \phi_p Y^*,$$

giving

$$Y^* = \frac{\phi_0}{1 - \phi_1 - \phi_2 - \cdots - \phi_p}.$$

Substitution of Y^* in the $\phi_0 K = Y^*$ gives K as

$$K = \frac{1}{1 - \phi_1 - \phi_2 - \cdots - \phi_p},$$

which is what we wanted to show.

Exercise 3.3. The solution in the second line of (3.108) for Y_{t-1} is

$$Y_{t-1} = (1/a_{21})X_t - (a_{22}/a_{21})Y_{t-1} - (1/a_{21})\varepsilon_{xt}.$$

Insertion in the equation in the first line gives

$$Y_t = \frac{a_{11}}{a_{21}}X_t + \left(a_{12} - a_{11}\frac{a_{22}}{a_{21}}\right)X_{t-1} - \frac{a_{11}}{a_{21}}\varepsilon_{xt} + \varepsilon_{yt},\ a_{21} \neq 0.$$

From the second line, we get, by writing the equation for period $t+1$:

$$X_{t+1} = a_{21}Y_t + a_{22}X_t + \varepsilon_{xt+1},$$

which after insertion gives

$$\begin{aligned} X_{t+1} = {} & a_{21}\left(\frac{a_{11}}{a_{21}}X_t + (a_{12} - a_{11}\frac{a_{22}}{a_{21}})X_{t-1} - \frac{a_{11}}{a_{21}}\varepsilon_{xt} + \varepsilon_{yt}\right) \\ & + a_{22}X_t + \varepsilon_{xt+1} \\ = {} & (a_{11} + a_{22})X_t + (a_{21}a_{12} - a_{11}a_{22})X_{t-1} + \varepsilon_{xt+1} - a_{11}\varepsilon_{xt} + a_{21}\varepsilon_{yt}. \end{aligned}$$

Hence, the equation for period t is

$$X_t = \phi_1 X_{t-1} + \phi_2 X_{t-2} + e_{xt},$$

where the coefficients ϕ_1 and ϕ_2 are given in (3.112) and (3.113). We see that the characteristic equation associated with this final equation will be identically the same as (3.116). However, the disturbance of this equation is

$$e_{xt} = \varepsilon_{xt} - a_{11}\varepsilon_{xt-1} + a_{21}\varepsilon_{yt-1},$$

which is different from e_{yt} in (3.114). As we shall see below, this means that the impulse-response functions are different for the two time series.

Exercise 3.4. With $p = 3$, we have

$$\mathbf{y}_t = [Y_{1t}, Y_{2t}, Y_{3t}]',$$

and (3.120) becomes

$$\begin{pmatrix} \mathbf{y}_t \\ \mathbf{y}_{t-1} \\ \mathbf{y}_{t-2} \end{pmatrix} = \begin{pmatrix} \mathbf{\Phi}_1 & \mathbf{\Phi}_2 & \mathbf{\Phi}_3 \\ \boldsymbol{I} & \mathbf{0} & \mathbf{0} \\ 0 & \boldsymbol{I} & \mathbf{0} \end{pmatrix} \begin{pmatrix} \mathbf{y}_{t-1} \\ \mathbf{y}_{t-2} \\ \mathbf{y}_{t-3} \end{pmatrix} + \begin{pmatrix} \boldsymbol{\varepsilon}_t \\ \mathbf{0} \\ \mathbf{0} \end{pmatrix}.$$

By multiplying out, we get back (3.119):

$$\begin{aligned}\mathbf{y}_t &= \mathbf{\Phi}_1\mathbf{y}_{t-1} + \mathbf{\Phi}_2\mathbf{y}_{t-2} + \mathbf{\Phi}_3\mathbf{y}_{t-3} + \varepsilon_t,\\ \mathbf{y}_{t-1} &= \mathbf{y}_{t-1} + \mathbf{0},\\ \mathbf{y}_{t-2} &= \mathbf{y}_{t-2} + \mathbf{0},\end{aligned}$$

where

$$\mathbf{\Phi}_{\boldsymbol{i}} = \begin{pmatrix} \phi_{i,11} & \phi_{i,12} & \phi_{i,12} \\ \phi_{i,21} & \phi_{i,22} & \phi_{i,23} \\ \phi_{i,31} & \phi_{i,32} & \phi_{i,33} \end{pmatrix},$$

with an extra subscript indicating a lag number between 1 and 3.

Exercise 3.5. Formulate the equation:

$$4 + (x-1)^2 = x^2 - 2x + 5 = 0,$$

and find the roots in the usual way as

$$x_{1,2} = \frac{1}{2}(2 \pm \sqrt{(4 - 4 \cdot 5)} = 1 \pm \frac{1}{2}\sqrt{-16} = 1 \pm 2\sqrt{-1} = 1 \pm 2i.$$

The polynomial can now be factorized as

$$x^2 - 2x + 5 = (x - r_1)(x - r_2) = (x - 1 - 2i)(x - 1 + 2i),$$

which can be checked by multiplication on the right-hand side (we can assume that standard algebraic rules apply):

$$\begin{aligned}(x-1-2i)(x-1+2i) &= (x-1)^2 + (x-1)2i - 2i(x-1) - 4i^2\\ &= (x-1)^2 - 4(-1) = (x-1)^2 + 4.\end{aligned}$$

Exercise 3.6. Let $z_k = a_k + ib_k$ $(k = 1, 2)$. We then have

$$\begin{aligned}z_1 z_2 &= (a_1 + ib_1)(a_2 + ib_2)\\ &= a_1 a_2 + i(a_1 b_2 + a_2 b_1),\end{aligned}$$

so the norm of the product becomes

$$\begin{aligned}|z_1 z_2| &= \sqrt{a_1^2 a_2^2 + b_1^2 b_2^2 - 2a_1 a_2 b_1 b_2 + a_1^2 b_2^2 + a_2^2 b_1^2 + 2a_1 b_2 a_2 b_1}\\ &= \sqrt{(a_1^2 + b_1^2)(a_2^2 + b_2^2)} = |z_1|\,|z_2|\,.\end{aligned}$$

Exercise 3.7. The property follows directly: The distance to origo (i.e., zero) for the complex number z^j is given by $|z^j| = |z|^j$ which converges to 0 as $j \longrightarrow \infty$.

C.4. Chapter 4 Answers

Exercise 4.1. ε_t is a stationary process with constant (time independent) variance, expectation and autocorrelation function (ACF). It then follows by the use of algebra that also Y_t has expectation and variance that are constant parameters. Also, the autocovariance function of Y_t is independent of time.

Exercise 4.2. The conditional solution is

$$Y_t = \phi_0 \sum_{i=0}^{t-1} \phi_1^i + \phi_1^t Y_0 + \sum_{i=0}^{t-1} \phi_1^i \varepsilon_{t-i}.$$

By using the formulae for the sum, the t first terms in a geometric progression:

$$\sum_{i=0}^{t-1} \phi_1^i = \frac{1-\phi_1^t}{1-\phi_1},$$

hence the solution can be written as

$$Y_t = \phi_0 \frac{1-\phi_1^t}{1-\phi_1} + \phi_1^t Y_0 + \sum_{i=0}^{t-1} \phi_1^i \varepsilon_{t-i}.$$

The conditional expectation of Y_t given Y_0 is therefore (4.14).

The conditional variance is also found by taking the operator through the conditional solution:

$$\begin{aligned}\operatorname{Var}(Y_t \mid Y_0) &= \operatorname{Var}\left(\sum_{i=0}^{t-1} \phi_1^i \varepsilon_{t-i}\right) = \sigma^2 \sum_{i=0}^{t-1} \phi_1^{2i} \\ &= \sigma^2 \frac{1-\phi_1^{2t}}{1-\phi_1^2}.\end{aligned}$$

Exercise 4.3. From (4.21), we have the expression:

$$\zeta_j = \frac{\operatorname{Cov}(Y_t, Y_{t-j})}{\operatorname{Cov}(Y_t)} = \phi_1 \frac{\gamma_{j-1}}{\operatorname{Var}(Y_t)} \equiv \phi_1 \zeta_{j-1}, \quad j = 1, 2, \ldots.$$

Setting $j = 1$, we get

$$\zeta_1 = \phi_1 \zeta_0.$$

By definition, $\zeta_0 = \frac{\gamma_0}{\gamma_0} = \frac{\text{Var}(Y_t)}{\text{Var}(Y_t)} = 1$, hence:

$$\zeta_1 = \phi_1. \tag{C.12}$$

Setting $j = 2$:

$$\zeta_2 = \phi_1 \zeta_1 = \phi_1^2 \tag{C.13}$$

and so on, showing that in general:

$$\zeta_j = \phi_1^j. \tag{C.14}$$

The two graphs will show monotonous decline for the case of 0.5 and dampened oscillations for -0.5.

Exercise 4.7. We commence from

$$\hat{\phi}_1 = \frac{\sum_{t=1}^{T} Y_t(Y_{t-1} - \bar{Y}_{(-)})}{\sum_{s=1}^{T}(Y_{s-1} - \bar{Y}_{(-)})^2}. \tag{C.15}$$

Substitute Y_{t-1} by $\phi_0 + \phi_1 Y_{t-1} + \varepsilon_t$ in the numerator and simplify the expression:

$$\begin{aligned}
&\sum_{t=1}^{T} Y_t(Y_{t-1} - \bar{Y}_{(-)}) \\
&\quad = \sum_{t=1}^{T}(\phi_0 + \phi_1 Y_{t-1} + \varepsilon_t)(Y_{t-1} - \bar{Y}_{(-)}) \\
&\quad = \phi_0 \sum_{t=1}^{T}(Y_{t-1} - \bar{Y}_{(-)}) + \phi_1 \sum_{t=1}^{T} Y_{t-1}(Y_{t-1} - \bar{Y}_{(-)}) \\
&\qquad + \sum_{t=1}^{T} \varepsilon_t(Y_{t-1} - \bar{Y}_{(-)}) \\
&\quad = \phi_0 \sum_{t=1}^{T}\left(Y_{t-1} - T^{-1}\sum_{t=1}^{T} Y_{t-1}\right) + \phi_1 \sum_{t=1}^{T} Y_{t-1}(Y_{t-1} - \bar{Y}_{(-)}) \\
&\qquad + \sum_{t=1}^{T} \varepsilon_t(Y_{t-1} - \bar{Y}_{(-)}) \\
&\quad = \phi_0 \left(\sum_{t=1}^{T} Y_{t-1} - T^{-1}T\sum_{t=1}^{T} Y_{t-1}\right) + \phi_1 \sum_{t=1}^{T} Y_{t-1}(Y_{t-1} - \bar{Y}_{(-)})
\end{aligned}$$

$$+\sum_{t=1}^{T}\varepsilon_t(Y_{t-1}-\bar{Y}_{(-)})$$

$$=\phi_1\sum_{t=1}^{T}Y_{t-1}(Y_{t-1}-\bar{Y}_{(-)})+\sum_{t=1}^{T}\varepsilon_t(Y_{t-1}-\bar{Y}_{(-)}).$$

Simplify in the numerator:

$$\sum_{s=1}^{T}(Y_{s-1}-\bar{Y}_{(-)})^2=\sum_{s=1}^{T}(Y_{s-1}-\bar{Y}_{(-)})(Y_{s-1}-\bar{Y}_{(-)})$$

$$=\sum_{s=1}^{T}(Y_{s-1}(Y_{s-1}-\bar{Y}_{(-)}).$$

By noting that the only difference between the two are the symbols used for the indicator (t and s), and then doing the division, we get

$$\hat{\phi}_1=\phi_1+\frac{\sum_{t=1}^{T}\varepsilon_t(Y_{t-1}-\bar{Y}_{(-)})}{\sum_{s=1}^{T}(Y_{s-1}-\bar{Y}_{(-)})^2}.$$

As noted, in the main text, it is very seldom that you see authors using two summation indicator symbols. Later, we will just use t in the numerator as well and just write

$$\hat{\phi}_1=\phi_1+\frac{\sum_{t=1}^{T}\varepsilon_t(Y_{t-1}-\bar{Y})}{\sum_{t=1}^{T}(Y_{t-1}-\bar{Y})^2}.$$

Exercise 4.8. With two lags, the available sample is from day 1 to day 111. The OLS estimation results are as follows:

```
EQ(1) Modelling price by OLS
      The dataset is: C:fish.in7
      The estimation sample is: 3 - 111

                 Coefficient  Std.Error  t-value  t-prob
price_1             0.914789    0.09562     9.57  0.0000
price_2            -0.196642    0.09602    -2.05  0.0430
Constant          -0.0519600    0.02754    -1.89  0.0620

sigma               0.249324  RSS                6.5892251
R^2                 0.586944  F(2,106) =     75.31 [0.000]*
Adj.R^2             0.579151  log-likelihood       -1.7420
```

Inspection of the battery of diagnostic tests will show that, with the possible exception of the ARCH 1–1 test, there is nothing that indicates significant departures from normality, hence the coefficient estimates can be regarded as approximate ML estimators. For *qty*, the results are as follows:

```
EQ( 2) Modelling qty by OLS
       The dataset is: C:fish.in7
       The estimation sample is: 3 - 111

                  Coefficient  Std.Error  t-value  t-prob
qty_1                0.241930    0.09533     2.54  0.0126
qty_2               -0.152380    0.09520    -1.60  0.1124
Constant              7.76387      1.026     7.57  0.0000

sigma                 0.72425  RSS                55.6009652
R^2                 0.0673973  F(2,106) =      3.83 [0.025]*
Adj.R^2              0.049801  log-likelihood       -117.978
no. of observations       109  no. of parameters           3
mean(qty)              8.5266  se(qty)              0.742987
```

One observation is that the positive first-order autocorrelation is larger for *price* than for *qty*. If the data are generated by a first-order VAR, such as in Section 4.9, should the two estimated AR polynomials be more equal? On the other hand, finite sample issues may intervene and can be responsible for some of the differences.

One thing we can say with considerable certainty: there is no cobweb pattern here, since there is a clear dominance of positive, not negative, autocorrelation in both equations. There can be several explanations. Despite fish being a perishable product, short-run replenishment of supply may nevertheless be possible through trade between regional markets? Another realistic point is that supply is more closely connected to the fishing boat capacity (which can be fixed in the short-run), than to last period's (i.e., yesterday's) price. Hence, supply is likely to be much "smoother" than in the canonical cobweb model (but still responsive to changing weather).

Exercise 4.9. In "equation form" the results from OLS estimation are (standard errors below the coefficients) as follows:

$$\begin{aligned} price_t = {} & \underset{(0.096)}{0.8297}\, price_{t-1} - \underset{(0.0931)}{0.1637}\, price_{t-2} - \underset{(0.0324)}{0.1113} \\ & + \underset{(0.0543)}{0.166}\ stormy_t + \underset{(0.141)}{0.1271}\ hol_t \end{aligned}$$

$$qty_t = \underset{(0.0866)}{0.1181}\ qty_{t-1} - \underset{(0.0843)}{0.09723}\ qty_{t-2} + \underset{(0.912)}{8.497}$$
$$-\underset{(0.137)}{0.3371}\ stormy_t - \underset{(0.385)}{1.998}\ hol_t$$

The weather variable *stormy* is significant in both equations, while *hol* only affects quantity. Another impact is that the two second-order AR coefficients become reduced numerically, and for *qty*, also the first AR coefficient is reduced by the introduction of the two dummies. In summary, the empirical AR(2) models may suggest a more "ordered" system than a VAR, maybe of the recursive type that we investigate below?

C.5. Chapter 5 Answers

Exercise 5.1. By combining (5.7) and (5.8) with the information in Table 5.1, we get

$$\begin{vmatrix} 0.0270^2 & (-0.958)0.0270 * 0.0338 \\ (-0.958) * 0.0270 * 0.0338 & 0.0338^2 \end{vmatrix}.$$

The determinant is 6.8489×10^{-8}.

$$\ln(6.8489 \times 10^{-8}) = -16.497$$
$$-16.497 + 2 * 6/96 = 16.372$$

Because of rounding errors, there are some differences at the second and third decimal points, but with one decimal point we then get AIC value in Table 5.1.

Exercise 5.2. In the data to the VAR example, it is the step indicator variable $S11_t$ that represents the demand shift, which is symbolized by b_t in the cobweb model in Chapter 1. b_t is the time-dependent "constant term" in the linearized demand equation of the model. According to the theory, a shift in demand affects the price in the same period as the shock occurs, and quantity in the period after the shock, and then in response to the change in price. This is brought out in (1.16). Hence, according to the theory, there should be no direct effect of $S11_t$ in the Q_t-equation of the VAR. That restriction is not imposed in the restricted reduced form (RRF) that we estimated in Section 5.3. However, if we let $\gamma_{2,2}$ denote the coefficient of $S11_t$ in the second row of the VAR, we can test $H_0{:}\gamma_{1,2} = 0$ separately by calculating the t-ratio, either from the URF, which gives $0.06/0.04 = 1.50$, or from the RRF, which gives $0.04/0.024 = 1.83$.

With reference to Box 5.2, we can perform an asymptotic test with the use of critical values of the standard normal distribution, but a t-test can have better properties in small samples. A t-value of 1.83 has a p-value of 0.0672 (two-sided test) when the normal distribution is used, and 0.0704 when the t-distribution with 94 degrees of freedom is used. Hence we would not reject H_0:$\gamma_{1,2} = 0$ at the 5% level, but at the 10% level. Hence, a too liberal significance level would lead to a Type-I inference error in this example (a false positive).

Exercise 5.3. We give answer notes to this exercise for Oxmetrics/PcGive and Eviews.

Oxmetrics/PcGive

Oxmetrics/PcGive has a command language that can be used to execute structured collections of (batches) of algebraic operations (typically for data transformation) estimation and reporting (results and graphs). The code in Figure C.6 can be copied into the batch editor window of the program and saved with the file extension .fl for easy retrieval. The code loads the dataset and then uses it for estimation of the system that is specified inside the curly brackets (you can also load in the dataset before you try to run the batch code). The last line sets the estimation method, and the sample size (annual observations, starting with year 5 and ending with year 100). Alternatively, everything can be done with the program's easy-to-use menu system, but for documentation and answer notes, the batch program capability is better.

```
// Batch code VAR of cobweb model data

module("PcGive");
package("PcGive", "Multiple-equation");
usedata("dgp_determandstoch.in7");
system
{
   Y = P_STOCH, Q_STOCH;
   Z = P_STOCH_1, Q_STOCH_1, STEP11;
   U = Constant;
}
estimate("OLS", 5, 1, 100, 1);
```

Figure C.6. Batch code that replicates the results in Table 5.1.

```
SYS(1) Estimating the system by OLS
       The dataset is: C:\dgp_determandstoch.in7
       The estimation sample is: 5 - 100

URF equation for: P_STOCH
                     Coefficient  Std.Error  t-value  t-prob
P_STOCH_1              -0.716148    0.03941    -18.2  0.0000
Q_STOCH_1              0.0214920    0.03217    0.668  0.5058
STEP11                  0.723390    0.02908     24.9  0.0000
Constant      U          4.09420     0.1229     33.3  0.0000

sigma = 0.0269697   RSS = 0.06691768018

URF equation for: Q_STOCH
                     Coefficient  Std.Error  t-value  t-prob
P_STOCH_1               0.935183    0.04942     18.9  0.0000
Q_STOCH_1             -0.0290313    0.04034   -0.720  0.4736
STEP11                 0.0619949    0.03647     1.70  0.0925
Constant      U        -0.834143     0.1542    -5.41  0.0000

sigma = 0.0338214   RSS = 0.1052378374

log-likelihood       523.805425  -T/2log|Omega|      796.241624
|Omega|          6.24832599e-08  log|Y'Y/T|         -8.32522615
R^2(LR)                0.999742  R^2(LM)               0.919032
no. of observations          96  no. of parameters            8
```

Figure C.7. Screen capture of results for unrestricted cobweb-VAR estimation, compare with Table 5.1.

After the batch code has been run, the result window fills up with parameter estimates, associated estimated standard errors and summary statistics. A screen-capture is given in Figure C.7.

The coefficient estimates and standard errors are easily recognized with several more decimals points than in Table 5.1 in the text. The maximized log-likelihood, denoted $\mathcal{L}_U^*$, in Table 5.1 is easily found, as is the minimized value of the determinant of the residual covariance matrix, $\frac{T}{2}\ln|\hat{\mathbf{\Sigma}}_U|$. There are several more summary statistics in the screen capture. Some of them may be self-explanatory, but all of them are documented as explained in the second volume of the PcGive book, Doornik and Hendry (2013c) (a pdf version comes together with the program).

The three information criteria in Table 5.1 are not part of the standard output, but they are easily obtained by using the menu system (Test Menu → Further Output → Information Criteria).

```
// Batch code for MOD(2)
module("PcGive");
package("PcGive", "Multiple-equation");
usedata("dgp_determandstoch.in7");
system
{
   Y = P_STOCH, Q_STOCH;
   Z = P_STOCH_1, Q_STOCH_1, STEP11;
   U = Constant;
}
model
{
   "P_STOCH" = "P_STOCH_1", "STEP11";
   "Q_STOCH" = "P_STOCH_1", "STEP11";
}
estimate("FIML", 5, 1, 100, 1);
```

Figure C.8. Batch code that can be run to replicate the RRF (restrictions $\phi_{1,12} = \phi_{1,22} = 0$) shown in equation (5.9).

In order to replicate the LR test of the zero restrictions on the two AR coefficients, we first show in the PcGive batch code for estimating equation (5.9), the RRF. The code is shown in Figure C.8. Note that Figure C.8 (restricted VAR) contains more codes than Figure C.6 (unrestricted VAR). This is because in PcGive, testing restrictions on the VAR is a step in the development of a model of the VAR. Hence in Figure C.6, the system is specified first in the code (as you can see, this is simply the same in the unrestricted system in Figure C.6), and it is followed by the model specification inside curly brackets. Note that the model is given in terms of two equations, and it is understood that the first equation is normalized on P_STOCH and the second is normalized on Q_STOCH. In that aspect, there is change from the unrestricted VAR system. The difference between the model and the system is that model omits the lags of Q_STOCH in both equations.

PcGive switches to FIML estimation as the default for model estimation.[1]

[1]However, in this case where the two restrictions only apply within equations, there are no cross-equation restrictions, we could have specified the model equally well as a VAR

```
MOD(2) Estimating the model by FIML
       The dataset is: C:\dgp_determandstoch.in7
       The estimation sample is: 5 - 100

Equation for: P_STOCH
                    Coefficient  Std.Error  t-value  t-prob
P_STOCH_1              -0.729082    0.03422    -21.3  0.0000
STEP11                  0.738094    0.01895     38.9  0.0000
Constant      U          4.15506    0.08230     50.5  0.0000

sigma = 0.0268893

Equation for: Q_STOCH
                    Coefficient  Std.Error  t-value  t-prob
P_STOCH_1               0.952655    0.04293     22.2  0.0000
STEP11                 0.0421332    0.02378     1.77  0.0797
Constant      U        -0.916345     0.1033    -8.87  0.0000

sigma = 0.0337336

log-likelihood      523.533083  -T/2log|Omega|     795.969281
no. of observations         96  no. of parameters           6

LR test of over-identifying restrictions: Chi^2(2)  =  0.54468 [0.7616]
```

Figure C.9. Screen capture of results for the model that represent the cobweb model, with the restrictions $\phi_{1,12} = \phi_{1,22} = 0$, imposed.

The results from FIML estimation are shown in Figure C.9. The maximum value of the restricted likelihood is 523.533083. In Figure C.7, it is 523.805425. This gives an LR test statistic of 0.544684. Allowing for rounding errors, it is the same value as in the main text. Note that it also reported in the last line of Figure C.9, where it appears in the line labelled: *LR test of over-identifying restriction*. Hence, whenever we specify a multiple equation model in PcGive, the program automatically checks whether the model is identified, and tests the validity of any over-identifying restrictions by a likelihood ratio test.

Eviews. As noted, VARs are easy to estimate in all software programs. Figure C.10 shows the URF estimated in Eviews. Here, we have used the predefined VAR object in Eviews, and it is not possible to test restriction directly in that object. However, Eviews also contains a flexible

with only P_STOCH_1 on the right-hand side, and estimated it with OLS for each row, with the same results as with FIML.

Vector Autoregression Estimates
Date: 03/18/19 Time: 18:25
Sample: 5 100
Included observations: 96
Standard errors in ( ) & t-statistics in [ ]

	P_STOCH	Q_STOCH
P_STOCH(-1)	-0.716148	0.935183
	(0.03941)	(0.04942)
	[-18.1726]	[18.9233]
Q_STOCH(-1)	0.021492	-0.029031
	(0.03217)	(0.04034)
	[0.66807]	[-0.71960]
C	4.094204	-0.834143
	(0.12293)	(0.15416)
	[33.3048]	[-5.41082]
STEP11	0.723390	0.061995
	(0.02908)	(0.03647)
	[24.8742]	[1.69987]

Figure C.10. Screen capture of results for unrestricted cobweb-VAR estimation, estimated in Eviews.

SYSTEM object, where the URF can be estimated first, and then restrictions imposed.

Exercise 5.4. Substitution of (5.14) and (5.15) in the third line of (5.18) gives

$$\begin{aligned} & b_{11}^{(j)} e_{1t} + b_{11}^{(j-1)} e_{1t+1} + \cdots + b_{11}^{(1)} e_{1t+j-1} + e_{t+j} \\ &\quad = b_{11}^{(j)}(\varepsilon_{1t} - \phi_{1,22}\varepsilon_{1t-1} + \phi_{1,12}\varepsilon_{2t}) \\ &\qquad + b_{11}^{(j-1)}(\varepsilon_{1t+1} - \phi_{1,22}\varepsilon_{1t} + \phi_{1,12}\varepsilon_{2t+1}) + \cdots \end{aligned}$$

Calculating the partial derivatives of $\frac{\partial Y_{1t+j}}{\partial \varepsilon_{1t}}$, from (5.18) with this in mind gives (5.19), and $\frac{\partial Y_{1t+j}}{\partial \varepsilon_{1t}}$ gives (5.15).

Exercise 5.5. The question is to analyze the responses of price to a shock to ε_{1t} of size 1. In the period of the shock the only response is that P_t

increases by 1. In the first period after the shock, there is no new impulse, and P_{t+1} therefore changes by -0.716 (compared to the solution where there was no shock) due to the initial increase by 1 in the previous period. Q_{t+1} is changed by 0.935 (compared to the baseline without the shock):

$$\begin{aligned} P_{t+1} \text{ change:} &\quad -0.716 \cdot 1, \\ Q_{t+1} \text{ change:} &\quad 0.935 \cdot 1. \end{aligned}$$

In the second period after the shock, the changes are:

$$\begin{aligned} P_{t+2} \text{ change:} &\quad -0.716 \cdot (-0.716) + 0.021 \cdot (0.935) = 0.53229, \\ Q_{t+2} \text{ change:} &\quad 0.93 \cdot (-0.716) - 0.029 \cdot (0.935) = -0.69300. \end{aligned}$$

Using (5.19) to check the result for P_{t+1}, We need the estimated $\mathbf{B}$ matrix:

$$\widehat{\mathbf{B}} = \begin{pmatrix} \hat{\phi}_1 & \hat{\phi}_2 \\ 1 & 0 \end{pmatrix}.$$

We have from (5.12) and (5.13), and Table 5.1, that $\hat{\phi}_1$ and $\hat{\phi}_2$ are as follows:

$$\begin{aligned} &\hat{\phi}_1 = (-0.716 + (-0.029)) = -0.745, \\ &\hat{\phi}_2 = \phi_{1,12}\phi_{1,21} - \phi_{1,22}\phi_{1,11} = 0.02 \cdot (0.94) - (-0.03) \cdot (-0.72) = -0.0028. \end{aligned}$$

Hence, element $(1,1)$ in $\widehat{\mathbf{B}}$ is: $\widehat{b_{11}^{(1)}} = -0.745$. Using the expression in (5.19) to calculate $\frac{\partial P_{1t+1}}{\partial \varepsilon_{1t}}$, we get:

$$\frac{\partial P_{1t+1}}{\partial \varepsilon_{1t}} = \widehat{b_{11}^{(1)}} - \widehat{b_{11}^{(0)}}\hat{\phi}_{1,22} = -0.745 - 1 \cdot (-0.029) = 0.716$$

confirming the "direct reasoning" above. For the second period after the shock, we first calculate $\widehat{b_{11}^{(2)}}$ from

$$\begin{aligned} \widehat{\mathbf{B}}^2 &= \begin{pmatrix} -0.745 & -0.0028 \\ 1 & 0 \end{pmatrix} \cdot \begin{pmatrix} -0.745 & -0.0028 \\ 1 & 0 \end{pmatrix} \\ &= \begin{pmatrix} 0.55223 & 2.086 \times 10^{-3} \\ -0.745 & -0.0028 \end{pmatrix} \end{aligned}$$

and then use the formula

$$\frac{\partial P_{1t+2}}{\partial \varepsilon_{1t}} = \widehat{b_{11}^{(2)}} - \widehat{b_{11}^{(1)}}\hat{\phi}_{1,22} = 0.55223 - (-0.745) \cdot (-0.029) = 0.53063,$$

where there is numerical difference from the "direct reasoning"result (but only at the third decimal position though). Figure C.11 contains plots of the two impulse response functions.

Exercise 5.6. The VAR consistent with the AR(2) equations for *qty* and *price*, with *stormy* and *hol* in both equations, is a VAR(1) with *stormy* and *hol* included in each of the two rows (i.e., they are in D_t). Using estimation sample $2 - 111$, we obtain log-likelihood $\mathcal{L}_R = -86.6891544$. There is no indication of residual misspecification. The eigenvalues of the estimated companion matrix are 0.62 and 0.18, and are therefore supportive of stationarity.

Adding *mixed* in each row gives $\mathcal{L}_U = -83.1138072$. The variable is marginally significant since the value of the LR-test becomes $-2(-86.6891544 - (-83.1138072)) = 7.15$, with a p-value of 0.0280 in the $\chi^2(2)$ distribution. With two decimals, the eigenvalues are unchanged.

The estimated contemporaneous residual covariance matrix for the VAR that includes the three dummies (*stormy*, *hol*, *mixed*) is:

$$\widehat{\mathbf{\Sigma}} = \begin{pmatrix} (0.61955)^2 & -0.43737 \\ -0.43737 & (0.23662)^2 \end{pmatrix}.$$

The variance of *qty* is in element $(1,1)$, and the residual variance of *price* is in $(2,2)$.

C.6. Chapter 6 Answers

Exercise 6.1. By definition:

$$\epsilon_t = Y_t - E(Y_t \mid X_t, X_{t-1}, Y_{t-1}),$$

where $E(Y_t \mid X_t, X_{t-1}, Y_{t-1})$ is given in, for example, (6.7).

$$\begin{aligned}\epsilon_t &= \phi_{10} + \phi_{11}Y_{t-1} + \phi_{12}X_{t-1} + \varepsilon_{yt} \\ &\quad - \phi_{10} + \frac{\sigma_{xy}}{\sigma_x^2}\phi_{20} - \frac{\sigma_{xy}}{\sigma_x^2}X_t - \left(\phi_{12} - \frac{\sigma_{xy}}{\sigma_x^2}\phi_{22}\right)X_{t-1} \\ &\quad - \left(\phi_{11} - \frac{\sigma_{xy}}{\sigma_x^2}\phi_{21}\right)Y_{t-1}\end{aligned}$$

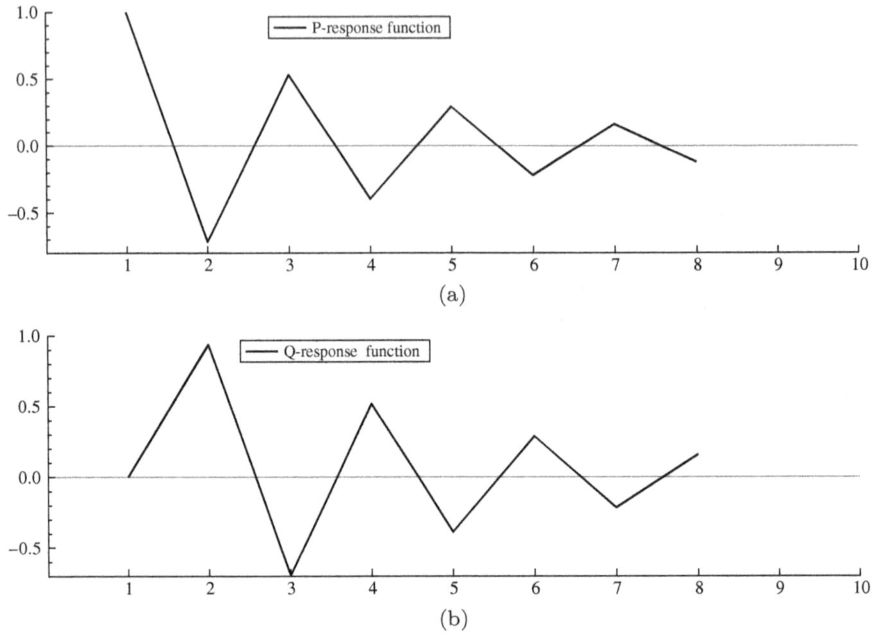

Figure C.11. Impulse-response function for price (panel (a)) and quantity (panel (b)), for the cobweb VAR in Table 5.1 with respect to shock to ε_{1t}.

$$= \varepsilon_{yt} + \frac{\sigma_{xy}}{\sigma_x^2}\phi_{20} - \frac{\sigma_{xy}}{\sigma_x^2}X_t + \frac{\sigma_{xy}}{\sigma_x^2}\phi_{22}X_{t-1} + \frac{\sigma_{xy}}{\sigma_x^2}\phi_{21}Y_{t-1}$$

$$= \varepsilon_{yt} - \frac{\sigma_{xy}}{\sigma_x^2}\varepsilon_{xt}$$

where we have used that

$$\varepsilon_{xt} = X_t - \phi_{20} - \phi_{21}Y_{t-1} - \phi_{22}X_{t-1},$$

from the second row in the VAR.

Exercise 6.2.

$$\mathrm{Var}(\epsilon_t) = \mathrm{Var}\left(\varepsilon_{yt} - \frac{\sigma_{xy}}{\sigma_x^2}\varepsilon_{xt}\right) = \sigma_y^2 + \left(\frac{\sigma_{xy}}{\sigma_x^2}\right)^2\sigma_x^2 - 2\frac{\sigma_{xy}^2}{\sigma_x^2}$$

$$= \sigma_y^2 - \frac{\sigma_{xy}^2}{\sigma_x^2} = \sigma_y^2 - \sigma_y^2\frac{\sigma_{xy}^2}{\sigma_x^2\sigma_y^2} = \sigma_y^2(1 - \rho_{xy}^2),$$

which shows (6.15).

Exercise 6.3. With $p = 2$, we have

$$\beta(L) = \beta_0 L^0 + \beta_1 L + \beta_2 L^2,$$
$$\delta(L) = \delta_0 L^0 + \delta_1 L^1 + \delta_2 L^2 + \cdots .$$

Collection of terms in the product $\delta(L)\beta(L)$ gives

$$\begin{aligned}(\delta_0 L^0 + \delta_1 L^1 + \delta_2 L^2 + \cdots)(\beta_0 L^0 + \beta_1 L + \beta_2 L^2)\\ = \delta_0\beta_0 L^0 + (\delta_0\beta_1 + \delta_1\beta_0)\, L + (\delta_0\beta_2 + \delta_1\beta_1 + \delta_2\beta_0)\, L^2\\ + \cdots + (\delta_{j-2}\beta_2 + \delta_{j-1}\beta_1 + \delta_j\beta_0)\, L^j + \cdots .\end{aligned}$$

Exercise 6.4. Setting the disturbance term to zero, and rearranging the ADL, we have

$$\Delta Y_t = \phi_0 + (\phi_1 - 1)Y_{t-1} + \beta_0 \Delta X_t + (\beta_0 + \beta_1)X_{t-1},$$

which must hold for a steady-state path. Hence,

$$\Delta Y_t^* = \phi_0 + (\phi_1 - 1)Y_{t-1}^* + \beta_0 g_X + (\beta_0 + \beta_1)X_{t-1}^*,$$

where $\Delta X_t^* = g_X$ has been substituted in. Rearranging on the right-hand side gives

$$\begin{aligned}\Delta Y_t^* &= \phi_0 + \beta_0 g_X + (\phi_1 - 1)\left[Y_{t-1}^* - \underbrace{\frac{\beta(1)}{\pi(1)}}_{S_1} X_{t-1}^*\right]\\ &= \phi_0 + \beta_0 g_X + (\phi_1 - 1)S_0 + (\phi_1 - 1)\left[Y_{t-1}^* - S_0 - S_1 X_{t-1}^*\right].\end{aligned}$$

Hence S_1 is determined as

$$S_1 = \frac{\beta(1)}{\pi(1)} = \beta_*,$$

where β_* denotes the long-run multiplier, i.e., (6.3), in the main text. Moreover, since $Y_{t-1}^* - S_0 - S_1 X_{t-1}^* = 0$ along the steady-state path, we have from the ADL:

$$\Delta Y_t^* = \phi_0 + \beta_0 g_X + (\phi_1 - 1)S_0.$$

On the other hand, by differencing on both sides of $Y_t^* = S_0 + S_1 X_t^*$, we get

$$\Delta Y_t^* = S_1 \Delta X_t^* = S_1 g_X.$$

Hence, we determine S_0 from the equation:

$$S_1 g_X = \phi_0 + \beta_0 g_X + (\phi_1 - 1) S_0$$
$$S_0 = \frac{1}{(\phi_1 - 1)} \left[-\phi_0 + (S_1 - \beta_0) g_X \right],$$

giving

$$S_0 = \frac{1}{(\phi_1 - 1)} \left[-\phi_0 + (\beta_* - \beta_0) g_X \right].$$

Exercise 6.5. The results in (6.22) include $\mathcal{L}_{P-\mathrm{ADL},U} = 332.861$ for $T = 95$, which represent the unrestricted maximum. Estimation of a static model equation (omitting P_STOCH_1 and Q_STOCH_1) gives a restricted log-likelihood value of 332.857. This gives a LR statistic of 0.008, i.e., $(-2(332.857 - 332.861))$. The relevant distribution for this asymptotic test is the Chi-square with two degrees of freedom. Since the p-value is larger than 0.99, joint null hypothesis is very far from being rejected.

If we instead use the unrestricted and restricted residual of squares, the test becomes $F(2, 91) = 0.0040895[0.9959]$, which is again a clear non-rejection.

Exercise 6.6. The two tests for the validity of a static equation in the place of (6.22) give: $\chi^2(2) = 490.34[0.0000] **$ and $F(2, 92) = 245.17[0.0000] **$.

Exercise 6.7. Writing the Comfac-model for period $t-1$, multiplied by ϕ_1, gives:

$$\phi_1 Y_{t-1} = \phi_1 \eta + \phi_1 \beta_0 X_t + \phi_1 u_{t-1}.$$

Subtracting this equation from $Y_t = \eta + \beta_0 X_t + u_t$ gives

$$Y_t = \eta(1 - \phi_1) + \beta_0 X_t - \phi_1 \beta_0 X_{t-1} + \phi_1 Y_{t-1} + \epsilon_t.$$

The impact multiplier of this equation is β_0, and the first dynamic multiplier is $-\phi_1\beta_0 + \phi_1\beta_0 = 0$. Consequently, all the higher order multipliers are also zero. It follows that the long-run multipliers is identical to the impact multiplier.

Exercise 6.8. First, write (6.65) in terms of the level variable Y:

$$Y_t = \phi_0 + Y_{t-1} + \beta_0 \Delta X_t + \epsilon_t. \tag{C.16}$$

We now need to be precise about assuming independence between ΔX_t and the history of Y, i.e., between ΔX_t and Y_{t-1} or further back in time. Without that assumption, a stationary solution for Y_t cannot be ruled out, although the mathematical form of such a solution cannot be found from (6.65) alone.

Under the assumption that ΔX_t is such an independent process, we see that formally there is no difference between ΔX_t and ϵ_t. Hence, we can treat the sum $\beta_0 \Delta X_t + \epsilon_t$ as a joint white noise process. With reference to the earlier chapters, and in particular Theorem 4.2, we can therefore conclude that the difference equation for the Y_t process has a single characteristic root, and that root is on the unit-circle. Hence, there is no stationary solution.

Exercise 6.9. Equation (6.1) can be written as

$$\Delta Y_t = \phi_0 + (\phi_1 - 1)Y_{t-1} + \beta_0 \Delta X_t + \epsilon_t.$$

Also, from (6.1), Y_{t-1} can be expressed as

$$Y_{t-1} = \phi_0 + \phi_1 Y_{t-2} + \beta_0 \Delta X_{t-1} + \epsilon_{t-1}.$$

Insertion in the first equation gives

$$\begin{aligned} \Delta Y_t &= \phi_0 + (\phi_1 - 1)\left[\phi_0 + \phi_1 Y_{t-2} + \beta_0 \Delta X_{t-1} + \epsilon_{t-1}\right] + \beta_0 \Delta X_t + \epsilon_t \\ &= \phi_1(\phi_1 - 1)Y_{t-2} + (\phi_1 - 1)\beta_0 \Delta X_{t-1} + \epsilon_t + (\phi_1 - 1)\epsilon_{t-1} \\ &\quad + \beta_0 \Delta X_t + \phi_0 + (\phi_1 - 1)\phi_0. \end{aligned} \tag{C.17}$$

By writing the first equation (in the answer) for period $t-1$, we get

$$(\phi_1 - 1)Y_{t-2} = \Delta Y_{t-1} - \beta_0 \Delta X_{t-1} - \phi_0 - \epsilon_{t-1},$$

which inserted in (C.17) gives equation (6.66):

$$\begin{aligned} \Delta Y_t &= \phi_1\left[\Delta Y_{t-1} - \beta_0 \Delta X_{t-1} - \phi_0 - \epsilon_{t-1}\right] + (\phi_1 - 1)\beta_0 \Delta X_{t-1} + \epsilon_t \\ &\quad + (\phi_1 - 1)\epsilon_{t-1} + \beta_0 \Delta X_t + \phi_0 + (\phi_1 - 1)\phi_0 \end{aligned}$$

$$= \phi_1 \Delta Y_{t-1} - \beta_0 \Delta X_{t-1} + \beta_0 \Delta X_t + \epsilon_t - \epsilon_{t-1}$$
$$= \phi_1 \Delta Y_{t-1} + \beta_0 \Delta^2 X_t + \Delta \epsilon_t,$$

which we were asked to show.

Exercise 6.10. We want to estimate the slope of the long-run Phillips curve associated with model equation (6.49), and use the dataset in NORPCMb.zip. As noted in the exercise text, the variable $D80$ needs to be included in the model equation as well, and the estimation period should start in 1980 and end in 2005.

In order to estimate the ECM form (6.50) of the Phillips curve we need to create the variable ΔINF_t, the change in the inflation rate. Depending on your software you may also have to create INF_{t-1} as a separate variable, but that is not necessary in PcGive, it is created automatically when we specify the model equation, and is given the name INF_1.

Using PcGive for estimation with OLS, we obtain the results shown in Figure C.12. Replication of the point estimate $\hat{\beta}_*$ is straightforward from

```
EQ(1) Modelling DINF by OLS
      The dataset is: C:\NORPCMb.in7
      The estimation sample is: 1980 - 2005

                  Coefficient  Std.Error  t-value  t-prob Part.R^2
INF_1               -0.251924    0.08702    -2.89  0.0084   0.2758
U                   -0.657243     0.2640    -2.49  0.0208   0.2198
D80                   5.22782      1.427     3.66  0.0014   0.3788
Constant              3.02485      1.184     2.55  0.0181   0.2288

sigma                 1.29734  RSS                   37.027944
R^2                  0.609383  F(3,22) =      11.44 [0.000]**
Adj.R^2              0.556117  log-likelihood         -41.4889
no. of observations        26  no. of parameters             4
mean(DINF)          -0.123164  se(DINF)                1.94724

AR 1-2 test:      F(2,20)    =  0.30445 [0.7409]
ARCH 1-1 test:    F(1,24)    =  0.71456 [0.4063]
Normality test:   Chi^2(2)   =   4.2721 [0.1181]
Hetero test:      F(4,20)    =   1.0535 [0.4050]
Hetero-X test:    F(5,19)    =   2.4801 [0.0686]
RESET23 test:     F(2,20)    =  0.72842 [0.4950]
```

Figure C.12. Empirical version of the Phillips curve in the ECM form. The left-hand side variable DINF is the same as ΔINF_t in (6.50) and the right-hand side variable INF_1 is identical to INF_{t-1}.

these results. By using the correct numbers in the *Covariance matrix of estimated parameters*, you can also confirm the use of the Delta method in the main text of the chapter.

We can demonstrate a convenient feature of PcGive that shows that the Delta-method is built in that program, albeit as a special tool that needs to be used with care. The point is that if an ADL model equation is estimated (*without* the reparameterization to ECM), in our case:

$$\text{INF}_t = \underset{(0.087)}{0.7481}\text{INF}_{t-1} + \underset{(1.18)}{3.025} - \underset{(0.264)}{0.6572}U_t + \underset{(1.43)}{5.228}\text{D80}_t \tag{C.18}$$

we can use PcGive's Test Menu → Dynamic analysis → Static long-run solution, and the program reports the long-run slope coefficients as directly estimated, see Figure C.13 and with the same standard error that we obtained by using the Delta method on the ECM form of the PCM model equation.

Finally, we consider the option of nonlinear least squares estimation for this problem. Running the script gives &3 as the slope parameter.

Exercise 6.11.

$$\begin{aligned}\Delta Y_t = \phi_0 + \sum_{i=1}^{3}\phi_i^{\ddagger}\Delta Y_{t-i} + \sum_{i=0}^{3}\beta_i^{\dagger}\Delta X_{t-i}\\ - \pi(1)Y_{t-1} + \beta(1)X_{t-4} + \epsilon_t,\end{aligned} \tag{C.19}$$

and, using the notation of lag-polynomials:

$$\begin{aligned}\Delta Y_t = \phi_0 + \phi^{\ddagger}(L)\Delta Y_{t-1} + \beta^{\dagger}(L)\Delta X_{t-i}\\ - \pi(1)Y_{t-1} + \beta(1)X_{t-4} + \epsilon_t,\end{aligned} \tag{C.20}$$

```
Solved static long-run equation for DINF
                 Coefficient  Std.Error  t-value  t-prob
INF                -0.251924    0.08702    -2.89  0.0084
U                  -0.657243     0.2640    -2.49  0.0208
D80                  5.22782      1.427     3.66  0.0014
Constant             3.02485      1.184     2.55  0.0181
Long-run sigma = 1.29734
```

Figure C.13. PcGive output after estimation of (C.18) and choosing Menu → Dynamic analysis → Static long-run solution.

where

$$\phi^{\ddagger}(L) = \sum_{i=1}^{3} \phi_i^{\ddagger} L^i,$$

$$\beta^{\dagger}(L) = \sum_{i=0}^{3} \beta_i^{\dagger} L^i.$$

Exercise 6.12. The ARCH process is

$$\sigma_{\varepsilon t}^2 = \varkappa^2 + \sum_{j=1}^{\infty} \varrho_j \varepsilon_{t-j}^2.$$

The geometric lag distribution that we used in Section 6.6 can be applied to the ARCH coefficients:

$$\varrho_j = \alpha \varsigma^j, \quad 0 \leq \varsigma < 1,$$

which gives

$$\sigma_{\varepsilon t}^2 = \varkappa^2 + \alpha \sum_{j=1}^{\infty} \varsigma^j \varepsilon_{t-j}^2.$$

Using the transformation in Section 6.6:

$$\varsigma \sigma_{\varepsilon t}^2 = \varsigma \varkappa^2 + \alpha \sum_{j=2}^{\infty} \varsigma^j \varepsilon_{t-j}^2,$$

$$\sigma_{\varepsilon t}^2 - \varsigma \sigma_{\varepsilon t-1}^2 = \varkappa^2(1 - \varsigma) + \alpha \varsigma \varepsilon_{t-1}^2,$$

```
// Batch code for NLS estimation of ECM form of PCM

module("PcGive");
package("PcGive", "Non-linear");
usedata("NORPCMb.in7");
nonlinear
{
actual=DINF;
fitted=-&1*(INF[-1]-&2-&3*U)+&4*D80;
&1=-0.3;&2=5;&3=-1.0;&4=5.23;
}
estimate("NLS", 1980, 1, 2005, 1);
```

Figure C.14. PcGive code (script) for NLS estimation of the ECM version (6.50) of the Phillips curve.

by defining symbols for GARCH coefficients as $\tau = \alpha\varsigma$ and $\sigma^2 = \varkappa^2(1-\varsigma)$, we get the (first-order) GARCH:

$$\sigma_{\varepsilon t}^2 = \sigma^2 + \tau\varepsilon_{t-1}^2 + \varsigma\sigma_{\varepsilon t-1}^2,$$

in the main text.

C.7. Chapter 7 Answers

Exercise 7.1. The answer does not depend on the sample chosen, but of course it has to be the same for the VAR estimation as for the estimation of (7.5)–(7.7). Choosing the sample 2–101, and formulating the VAR-EX as prescribed, estimate and obtain the following correlations for the VAR residuals $\hat{\varepsilon}_{1t}$, $\hat{\varepsilon}_{2t}$, $\hat{\varepsilon}_{3t}$ (standard deviations on diagonal):

1.0499	0.22246	0.45458
0.22246	1.0041	−0.42415
0.45458	−0.42415	0.95746

There are 100 observations used, and PcGive counts 15 parameters. The maximized log-likelihood should be −382.034584.

When the system (7.5)–(7.7) is estimated, and with "Equation-by-equation OLS (1SLS)", the correlations $\hat{\epsilon}_{1t}$, $\hat{\epsilon}_{2t}$, $\hat{\epsilon}_{3t}$ become

0.80598	0	0
0	0.91414	0
0	0	0.96254

and the log-likelihood is −382.034584 with 100 observations and 18 parameters in the model.

Exercise 7.2. (1.15)–(1.16) is a VAR for the vector $\mathbf{y}_t = (P_t,\ Q_t)'$. Premultiplying that VAR by

$$\mathbf{A} = \begin{pmatrix} 1 & \dfrac{1}{-a} \\ 0 & 1 \end{pmatrix},$$

gives

$$P_t + \left(\frac{1}{-a}\right) Q_t = \frac{c}{a} P_{t-1} + 0Q_{t-1} + \frac{d-b_t}{a} + \frac{\epsilon_{st}-\epsilon_{dt}}{a} - \frac{1}{a}(d+\epsilon_{st}),$$

$$Q_t = cP_{t-1} + d - \epsilon_{st}.$$

The first row can be rearranged as

$$P_t + \left(\frac{1}{-a}\right)Q_t = \frac{c}{a}P_{t-1} + 0Q_{t-1} + \frac{-b_t}{a} + \frac{-\epsilon_{dt}}{a},$$

which is identical to the demand equation (1.13) after changing the normalization variable from Q_t to P_t. The second row already contains the supply equation (1.14).

If we want to, we can present the structural form as

$$\underbrace{\begin{pmatrix} 1 & \left(\frac{1}{-a}\right) \\ 0 & 1 \end{pmatrix}}_{\mathbf{A}} \begin{pmatrix} P_t \\ Q_t \end{pmatrix}$$

$$= \underbrace{\begin{pmatrix} \frac{c}{a} & 0 \\ 0 & c \end{pmatrix}}_{\mathbf{A}\boldsymbol{\Phi}_1} \begin{pmatrix} P_{t-1} \\ Q_{t-1} \end{pmatrix} + \underbrace{\begin{pmatrix} 1 & \left(\frac{1}{-a}\right) \\ 0 & 1 \end{pmatrix}}_{\mathbf{C}} \begin{pmatrix} \frac{d-b_t}{a} + \frac{\epsilon_{st}-\epsilon_{dt}}{a} \\ d - \epsilon_{st} \end{pmatrix}.$$

Exercise 7.3.

$$\begin{aligned} \mu_1 &= a_{10}, \\ \mu_2 &= a_{20} - a_{21}a_{10}, \\ \sigma_1^2 &= \omega_1^2, \\ \sigma_2^2 &= \omega_2^2 + a_{21}^2\omega_1^2, \\ \sigma_{12} &= -a_{21}\omega_1^2, \end{aligned}$$

giving

$$a_{21} = -\frac{\sigma_{12}}{\sigma_1^2},$$

and

$$a_{20} = \mu_2 + a_{21}a_{10}.$$

Hence, the model with a lower-triangular contemporaneous coefficient matrix (in combination with a diagonal $\boldsymbol{\Omega}$) is also exactly identified.

Exercise (Exam 2015 ECON4160 UiO).

(1) $\frac{\partial}{\partial X_i}E(Y_i \mid X_i)$ is the partial derivative of $E(Y_i \mid X_i)$, which is linear in parameters, and therefore, $E(Y_i \mid X_i) = \beta_0 + \beta_1 X_i$ and $\frac{\partial}{\partial X_i}E(Y_i \mid X_i) =: \beta_1$ for example. Based on the assumptions given, the MLE of β_1 is therefore the OLS estimator $\hat{\beta}_1 = \sum_{i=1}^{n}(X_i - \bar{X})Y_i / \sum_{i=1}^{n}(X_i - \bar{X})^2$.

ε_i is the disturbance term in the model equation $Y_i = \beta_0 + \beta_1 X_i + \varepsilon_i$. $\text{Var}(\varepsilon_i \mid X_i) = \sigma^2$ says that the conditional variance of the disturbance is independent of X (homoscedasticity). Based on the information given, the MLE of σ^2 is therefore $\hat{\sigma}^2 = n^{-1}\sum \hat{\varepsilon}_i^2$ where $\varepsilon_i =: Y_i - \hat{\beta}_0 - \hat{\beta}_1 X_i$ with OLS estimators $\hat{\beta}_0$ and $\hat{\beta}_1$.

(2) With heteroscedastic error of this particular type, the MLE estimator can be found by estimating the following model equation by OLS

$$\underbrace{\frac{Y_i}{X_i}}_{V_i} = \beta_0 \underbrace{\frac{1}{X_i}}_{W_i} + \beta_1 + \underbrace{\frac{\varepsilon_i}{X_i}}_{e_i}$$

this is because $\text{Var}(\frac{\varepsilon_i}{X_i} \mid X_i) = \text{Var}(\frac{\varepsilon_i}{X_i} \mid X_i) = \frac{1}{X_i^2}\text{Var}(\varepsilon_i \mid X_i) = \sigma^2$, meaning that in the model that regresses V_i on W_i and a constant "back" in the homoscedastic model of (1). The efficient estimator of β_1 is therefore the OLS estimator, the so-called $\tilde{\beta}_1$, of the constant term in the transformed model. This estimator is also known as Weighted Least Squares, which is an example of GLS.

It can be written as (but this is not asked for)

$$\tilde{\beta}_1 = \bar{V} - \tilde{\beta}_0 \bar{W},$$

where $\tilde{\beta}_0$ is the OLS estimator of the slope coefficient in the transformed model.

(3) (a) A discussion of identification is based on a classification of variables as endogenous and exogenous. In this case, a reasonable classification is that Y and Z are endogenous, while X (as a conditioning variable) is exogenous. Based on that, and since the covariance between the disturbances is unrestricted, (1) and (2) form a "system of regression equations" (it could be the reduced form of a simultaneous equations model (SEM) for Y_i and Z_i, for example). β_2 is identified in this case and the simple OLS estimator of the parameter is consistent and efficient (since the right-hand side variable is the same in both equations, in fact GLS "reduces to" and becomes identical with OLS in this case).

(b) In this case, the reasonable classification is that Y and X are endogenous. However, since $\omega_{12} = 0$, the rank and order conditions do not apply. (1) and (3) are equations of a recursive model, and again OLS on (1) gives a consistent estimator of β_1.

(c) There are two equations in the model and five variables: Y, X, Z_1, Z_2 and *Constant*. We base our answer on the premise that Y and X are endogenous, while Z_1 and Z_2 are exogenous and uncorrelated with both disturbances. Since the correlation between the two disturbances is unrestricted, the rank and order conditions apply. If both $\gamma_2 \neq 0$ and $\gamma_3 \neq 0$, equation (1) is over-identified on the rank condition. 2SLS is then a consistent estimator of β_1 which uses the two instrumental variables in an optimal way (combine them in a way that gives the best linear predictor of X_i). 2SLS is, however, not statistically efficient, since it does not take account of the correlation between the disturbances. Based on an (extra) normality assumption, FIML is more efficient than 2SLS.

(4) Yes, in (b), because of recursiveness. No, in (c), by order and rank conditions.

Exercise 7.5. The estimation equation becomes

$$Y_t = b_0 X_t + u_t,$$

where the expression for u_t is

$$\begin{aligned} u_t &= \epsilon_t - b_0(X_t - E(X_t \mid \mathcal{I}_{t-1})) = \epsilon_t - b_0(\phi_{22}X_{t-1} + \varepsilon_{xt} - \phi_{22}X_{t-1}) \\ &= \epsilon_t - b_0\varepsilon_{xt}. \end{aligned}$$

The OLS estimator is

$$\hat{b}_0 = \frac{\sum_{t=1}^T X_t Y_t}{\sum_{t=1}^T X_t^2} = b_0 + \frac{\sum_{t=1}^T X_t u_t}{\sum_{t=1}^T X_t^2},$$

and the probability limit of the bias term is

$$\begin{aligned} \text{plim}\left(\frac{\sum_t X_t u_t}{\sum_t X_t^2}\right) &= \frac{1}{\text{Var}(X_t)}\text{plim}\left(\frac{1}{T}\sum_t(\phi_{22}X_{t-1} + \varepsilon_{xt})(\epsilon_t - b_0\varepsilon_{xt})\right) \\ &= \frac{1}{\text{Var}(X_t)}(-b_0\sigma_x^2), \end{aligned}$$

giving

$$\text{plim}(\hat{b}_0 - b_0) = \frac{1}{\frac{\sigma_x^2}{1-\phi_{22}^2}}(-b_0\sigma_x^2) = -b_0(1-\phi_{22}^2),$$

as in (7.103).

Exercise 7.6.

(1) The results in (6.25) and (7.45) are directly reproduced by choosing the variable C in the datasets as endogenous and *C_1* and GDP as regressors, and choosing sample 2–101 (i.e., $T = 100$).

It can aid intuition to plot the three time series in the two datasets to see visually how the two different variances for C in the data generation affect C and *GDP*.

(2) Using the order condition, the consumption function excludes one variable in our two-equation model, namely, J. Since, J has a coefficient of 1 in the general budget equation GDP $= C + J$, the rank condition holds.

(3) In PcGive, using the dataset *Keynes_closed_notax_nobreakA.in7*, and using single-equation dynamic modelling and IVE with J as instrumental variable (A: Additional instrument) reproduces the estimation results in (7.71). Changing to the use of multiple-equation dynamic modelling, mark GDP and an identity variable (I:Identity), specify the general budget equation as the second equation in a SEM and estimate by 2SLS, 3SLS and FIML. Because we are estimating an exactly identified structural equation, all methods logically give the same point estimates of the coefficients.

Exercise 7.7. We first reestimate the VAR from the answer to Exercise 5.6, with log-likelihood: $\mathcal{L}_{\text{VAR}} = -83.1138072$. We next specify the two-equation SEM in accordance with the description of the theory given in the exercise text.

In the first equation, the SEM is normalized on *qty*, and embeds the identifying and over-identifying assumptions about the structural supply equation: qty_{t-1} and $price_{t-1}$ do not appear. The second is normalized on qty_t, and is specified in accordance with the exercise text: *stormy* and *mixed* are excluded from the demand equation.

We estimate by 2SLS, the results are in (C.21) and (C.22), with standard error below the coefficients.

$$\begin{aligned} qty_t = \underset{(0.275)}{0.5034}\, price_t \; &+ \underset{(0.15)}{8.961} - \underset{(0.203)}{0.6783}\, stormy_t \\ &- \underset{(0.169)}{0.3039}\, mixed_t - \underset{(0.405)}{2.219}\; hol_t, \end{aligned} \tag{C.21}$$

$$\begin{aligned} price_t = -\underset{(0.119)}{0.4464}\, qty_t \; &+ \underset{(0.078)}{0.8544}\, price_{t-1} + \underset{(0.938)}{3.508} \\ &+ \underset{(0.041)}{0.03482}\, qty_{t-1} - \underset{(0.293)}{0.8068}\, hol_t, \end{aligned} \tag{C.22}$$

with $\mathcal{L}_{\text{SEM,2SLS}} = -85.47709$, and estimated SEM residual covariance matrix:

$$\widehat{\mathbf{\Omega}} = \begin{pmatrix} (0.68702)^2 & 0.49269 \\ 0.49269 & (0.27330)^2 \end{pmatrix}.$$

The variance of *qty* is in element $(1, 1)$, and the residual variance of *price* is in $(2, 2)$.

The degree of over-identification is 1 in each of the two equations, hence the LR-test of over-identifying restriction is as follows:

$$\begin{aligned} &\text{LR test of over-identifying restriction} \\ &\quad = -2(\mathcal{L}_{\text{SEM,2SLS}} - \mathcal{L}_{\text{SEM,VAR}} \\ &\quad = -2(-85.47709 - (-83.1138072)) = 4.7266, \end{aligned}$$

gets a p-value of 0.0941 in the $\chi^2(2)$ distribution with two degrees for freedom.

Hence, the over-identifying restrictions of the theory are not rejected at the 5% level, and marginally rejected at the 10% level of significance. The signs of the coefficient estimates of the structural model are consistent with the theory. In model equation (C.22) in particular, we note the correct negative signed coefficient of qty_t, which is also precisely estimated. The coefficient of $price_t$ in (C.21) also has the theoretically correct sign, but it is less precisely estimated. This is not a large inconsistency with theory though, since the main hypothesis is that the supply is determined by catch-capacity and weather, so the statistically uncertain coefficient on $price_t$ is not problematic by itself.

It is of interest to impose other economically meaningful restrictions, and to test their statistical acceptability, for example, excluding qty_{t-1}

from (C.22). Since there the estimated $\mathbf{\Omega}$ matrix has quite large off-diagonal elements, it is also of interest to estimate by FIML.

C.8. Chapter 8 Answers

Exercise 8.1. Building on the answer to Exercise 6.10, use the dataset with the created inflation variable INF and estimate equation (8.6); remember to use the 1981–2005 sample. Save the residuals and estimate the marginal equation for U_t with the following result:

$$U = \underset{(0.133)}{0.9199U_t} + \underset{(0.617)}{0.1164} + \underset{(0.0463)}{0.04917}\ \mathrm{INF}_{t-1}.$$

Save the residual from this equation, and add that variable to the estimated model for INF. Estimate the augmented INF-equation, the "DWH-regression", with the results:

$$\mathrm{INF} = \underset{(0.0927)}{0.7749}\ \mathrm{INF}_{t-1} + \underset{(1.41)}{2.369} - \underset{(0.32)}{0.5U_t} - \underset{(0.572)}{0.5006}\ \mathrm{residuals}_t,$$

where residuals$_t$ is the residual from the marginal equation for U_t.

Exercise 8.2. Using U_{t-1} as an instrumental variable, we obtain the IV estimates as follows:

$$\mathrm{INF} = -\underset{(0.321)}{0.5}\ U_t + \underset{(0.0929)}{0.7749}\ \mathrm{INF}_{t-1} + \underset{(1.41)}{2.369},$$

which has coefficient estimates that are identical to the corresponding ones in the DWH regression in the previous answer.

This is not surprising because the OLS estimators of the coefficients of the INF model in the DWH regression are identical to the 2SLS estimates, which in this exactly identified case are equivalent to the IV estimates.

In order to see this, we can look at an example:

$$Y_{1t} = \beta_1 X_{1t} + \beta_2 X_{2t} + \varepsilon_{1t},$$
$$X_{2t} = \gamma_1 X_{1t} + \gamma_2 Z_t + e_{2t},$$

where Z_t in the marginal equation is assumed to be a valid instrument.

The DWH regression is

$$Y_{1t} = b_1 X_{1t} + b_2 X_{2t} + \lambda \hat{e}_{2t} + v_{1t}. \tag{C.23}$$

Note that, by using $X_{2t} \equiv \hat{X}_{2t} + \hat{e}_{2t}$ ($\hat{X}_{2t}$ and $\hat{e}_{2t}$ refer to OLS estimation of the marginal equation), the DWH regression can be written as

$$Y_{1t} = b_1 X_{1t} + b_2 \hat{X}_{2t} + (b_2 + \lambda)\hat{e}_{2t} + v_{1t}. \tag{C.24}$$

From the properties of OLS residuals, we have $\mathrm{Cov}(\hat{e}_{2t}, X_{1t}) = \mathrm{Cov}(\hat{e}_{2t}, \hat{X}_{2t}) = 0$. But this means that the OLS estimates for b_1 and b_2 from the DWH-regression must be identical to the OLS estimates obtained for

$$Y_{1t} = b_1 X_{1t} + b_2 \hat{X}_{2t} + v'_{1t},$$

which is the second stage of 2SLS.

C.9. Chapter 9 Answers

Exercise 9.1. The analysis of dynamic multipliers is not affected by the inclusion of deterministic trends. This is true for ARs, ADLs and VARs. The reason is that the deterministic terms belong to the particular part of the difference equation that defines the AR- and VAR-generated time series. The multiplier expressions only involve coefficients from the homogeneous part.

In ADL model equations and in VAR-EX systems, the multipliers of course depend on the distributed lag coefficients. But also these coefficients are separate from the deterministic part.

Exercise 9.2. In, for example, Section 3.6, we used expressions that are valid independently of whether the characteristic roots are located inside the unit-circle or not. These expressions showed that the impulse-response functions are dominated by the largest root of the characteristic polynomial. Using the definition of an $I(1)$-series, we understand that since the largest root is $+1$, the responses will never "die out", unlike the stationary case, where they become zero asymptotically, as we have seen.

Exercise 9.3.

$$\hat{Y}_{T+h|T} \equiv E(Y_{T+h} \mid \mathcal{I}_T) = \phi_0 + \delta(T+h), \quad h = 1, 2, \ldots, H,$$

which implies that the forecast function is monotonously increasing if $\delta > 0$, and declining if $\delta < 0$.

$$\mathrm{Var}(Y_{t+h} - \hat{Y}_{T+h|T}) = \sigma_\varepsilon^2,$$

which means that the forecast uncertainty is the same irrespective of whether the forecast horizon is long or short.

Exercise 9.4.

$$
\begin{aligned}
\hat{Y}_{T+1|T} &= \phi_0 + \phi_1 Y_T + \delta(T+1) \\
\hat{Y}_{T+2|T} &= \phi_0 + \phi_1 \left[\phi_0 + \phi_1 Y_T + \delta(T+1)\right] + \delta(T+2) \\
&= \phi_0(1+\phi_1) + \phi_1^2 Y_T + \phi_1\delta(T+1) + \delta(T+2) \\
&= \phi_0(1+\phi_1) + \phi_1^2 Y_T + \delta(1+\phi_1)T + \delta(\phi_1+2) \\
\hat{Y}_{T+2|T} &= \phi_0 + \phi_1[\phi_0(1+\phi_1) + \phi_1^2 Y_T + \delta(1+\phi_1)T + \delta(\phi_1+2)] + \delta(T+3) \\
&= \cdots \delta\phi_1(\phi_1+2) + \delta(T+3) + \cdots \\
&= \delta(\phi_1^2 + \phi_1 2 + 3)
\end{aligned}
$$

Exercise 9.5. Define in general s as the infinite sum:

$$s = 1 + 2x + 3x^2 + 4x^3 + \cdots \quad \text{for } -1 < x < 1$$

(x is a given number), and the product of x and s as

$$x \cdot s = x + 2x^2 + 3x^3 + 4x^4 + \cdots.$$

By taking the difference between s and xs, and by collecting terms with the same power $(x^0, x^1, x^2, x^3, \ldots)$ we obtain

$$s - xs = 1 + x + x^2 + x^3 + \cdots = \frac{1}{1-x}.$$

On the other hand, $s - xs = (1-x)s$, and therefore,

$$(1-x)s = \frac{1}{1-x},$$

and hence we can write the infinite sum s as

$$s = \left(\frac{1}{1-x}\right)^2.$$

In our case, we have

$$
\begin{aligned}
\delta \lim_{t\longrightarrow\infty} \sum_{j=1}^{t-1} (\phi_1^{2j}) \cdot j &= \delta(1\phi_1^2 + 2(\phi_1^2)^2 + 3(\phi_1^2)^3 + 4(\phi_1^2)^4 + \cdots) \\
&= \delta(x + 2x^2 + 3x^3 + 4x^4 + \cdots) = x \cdot s,
\end{aligned}
$$

where we used $x = \phi_1^2$. But then, we also have

$$\delta \lim_{t \longrightarrow \infty} \sum_{j=1}^{t-1} (\phi_1^{2j}) \cdot j = \delta \phi_1^2 \left(\frac{1}{1-\phi_1^2} \right)^2 = \delta \frac{\phi_1^2}{(1-\phi_1^2)^2}$$

which is the result that we wanted to show.

Exercise 9.6. Equation (9.23) can be expressed as

$$(1 - L^4)Y_t = \varepsilon_t.$$

The characteristic polynomial of the homogeneous equation $(1 - L^4)Y_t = 0$ can be factorized as

$$(1 - z^4) = (1 - z)(1 + z)(1 + z^2),$$

with four roots: $z_1 = 1$, $z_2 = -1$, $z_3 = i$, $z_4 = -i$. All roots have modulus (norm) equal to 1 (i.e., $|z_3| = |i| = \sqrt{|i|^2} = \sqrt{i\bar{i}} = \sqrt{-1(i^2)} = 1$) and each one is therefore a solution of the equation:

$$z = \exp(i2\pi v) = \cos(2\pi v) + i\sin(2\pi v), \tag{C.25}$$

which defines the unit-circle when $0 \leq v \leq 1$.

Exercise 9.7. In order to do the investigation, we need both the level series (which are available as RW2Drift) and the first difference DRW2Drift, which can be created in algebra. For a sample 1961–2050 (93 observations) and from 0 to 2 lags in the differences, none of the t-ADF values reject the null of unit-root non-stationarity. The t-ADF with one lagged difference is the most relevant one. It is -1.477 while the 5% critical value is -3.46 (Constant + trend).

For the first difference, both the t-DF (no lags, -4.7) and the t-ADF with one lag (-4.8) reject the null hypothesis of a unit-root (we get the same conclusion if we only use a constant term as deterministic augmentation of the Dickey–Fuller regression).

Hence, the Dickey–Fuller test procedure identifies correctly RW2Drift as an $I(1)$ series.

Exercise 9.8 (Exam 2015 ECON4160 UiO). In the upper part of the table, the null hypothesis is that LW and LZ are $I(1)$. By using the relevant t-ADF values (for LW, in particular the D-lag 1 row column) we conclude that the unit-root hypothesis is not rejected for any of the variables. Although not shown in the question, many readers will have noted that both series have a manifest trend, so it would give extra marks to comment on the role of deterministic augmentation (Constant + trend) as a way of obtaining a well-behaved test, for example, allowing for a trend in the series both under the null and the alternative. In the bottom part the null hypothesis, the differences of LW and LZ are $I(1)$, and this hypothesis is rejected for both. So, the overall conclusion is that LW and LZ are both $I(1)$.

C.10. Chapter 10 Answers

Exercise 10.1. Using (10.4) and the expressions for $\boldsymbol{P}$ (cf. (10.5)) and $\boldsymbol{P}^{-1}$, we get

$$\boldsymbol{\Phi} = \begin{pmatrix} ad - cb\lambda & -ab + \lambda ab \\ cd - cd\lambda & -cb + da\lambda \end{pmatrix}$$

$$= \begin{pmatrix} ad - cb\lambda & -(1-\lambda)ab \\ (1-\lambda)cd & -cb + da\lambda \end{pmatrix}.$$

The simplification we motivated in the main text, namely, $|\boldsymbol{P}| = 1$, implies that

$$ad = bc + 1,$$

and using this to reexpress element $(1,1)$ and element $(2,2)$ in $\boldsymbol{\Phi}$ gives

$$\boldsymbol{\Phi} = \begin{pmatrix} (1-\lambda)bc + 1 & -(1-\lambda)ab \\ (1-\lambda)cd & -(1-\lambda)ad + 1 \end{pmatrix}.$$

But then, $\boldsymbol{\Pi}$ can be written as

$$\boldsymbol{\Pi} = \boldsymbol{\Phi} - \boldsymbol{I} = \begin{pmatrix} (1-\lambda)bc & -(1-\lambda)ab \\ (1-\lambda)cd & -(1-\lambda)ad \end{pmatrix},$$

which, by inspection, can be expressed as

$$\boldsymbol{\Pi} = \begin{pmatrix} -(1-\lambda)b \\ -(1-\lambda)d \end{pmatrix} (-c \quad a),$$

or

$$\boldsymbol{\Pi} = \boldsymbol{\alpha}\boldsymbol{\beta}',$$

with the symbols used in the main text.

Exercise 10.2 (Exam 2015 ECON4160 UiO). The null hypothesis of no cointegration implies that u_t is $I(1)$, so a relevant test is an ADF test. However, in place of the unobservable u_t, we use the OLS residuals, and this explains why the critical values are larger in absolute value here than in an ADF for an observable variable. Briefly explained, this is because, also under the null of no relationship, the residuals will "look more" stationary since OLS always finds the best fitting linear relationship in any given sample. Therefore, the location of the Engle–Granger test of no relationship is shifted to the left as more regressors are included in the hypothesized cointegration regression. Failure to account for this is one aspect of the spurious regression case. In this case, the test does not reject the null hypothesis of no relationship.

Exercise 10.3 (Exam 2015 ECON4160 UiO).

(1) The value of the ECM-test for no cointegration is found as -5.31, which is strongly significant when judged against the 1% critical value of -3.29.
(2) As noted above, there are common factor restrictions that are implicit in the Engle–Granger test. This restriction essentially entails that the short-run effect of an increase in LZ is the same as the long-run effect. From the results, we see it is far from being the case here. A known implication of invalid common factor restrictions is that the power of the Engle–Granger test will be lower than the power of the ECM test. Another feature worth noting is that DLKPI (in particular) and also DLH are highly significant. Inclusion of these variables may also increase the power of the test.
(3) $0.237388/0.250837 = 0.9464$ (with four decimals). The upper limit of an approximate 95% confidence interval becomes $0.9464 + 2 \times 0.032 = 1.0104$, which is somewhat larger than 1. Hence, the unit long-run elasticity is supported by this constructed confidence interval.
(4) The long-run elasticity is a ratio of two estimated parameters. The standard-error of that ratio can be calculated by the use of the Delta method. It requires that we have the access to the estimated covariance of the estimated parameters of LW_1 and LZ_1. Alternatively, with the use of PcGive (or similar), we can reparametrize the ECM as an ADL, reestimate it and obtain the standard error from the menu with Dynamic analysis.

Exercise 10.4 (Exam 2015 ECON4160 UiO).

(1) The relevant statistic to look at here is the t-value of *ECMwage1* in the equation for DLZ, this is with reference to Grangers-representation

theorem for example. The evidence suggests rejection of weak exogeneity at least at the 5% level.

(2) To answer the question, we need an empirical model of the relationship between productivity and wages. Figures 10.3 and 10.4 give such a model. For example, LZ can be decomposed as $LZ_t = LP_t + LQ_t$, where LP is the log of the producer price index and LQ is log of average labour productivity, so LZ increases one-to-one with an increase in productivity. Then, one possibility is to use EQ(3) in Figure 10.3. That the residual misspecification tests are insignificant (with a possible exception for the RESET-test) is relevant to mention, since this implies that the statistical evidence is reliable. Hence, one relevant answer is to report the dynamic multipliers of LW with respect to a change in LZ that we can calculate from EQ(3) in Figure 10.3. However, Figures 10.3 and 10.4 show evidence of two-way causality between LZ and LW, and that goes in the direction of not (only) relying on the single equation dynamic multipliers from EQ(5), but also the impulse-responses of LW with respect to a shock to the EQ(4) in Figure 10.4.

(3) The answer is "YES" because it is important to have identified dynamic multipliers, or impulse responses, and using a SVAR is one coherent way of securing that kind of identification. It is relevant to mention the possibility of formulating a SEM model for DLW and DLZ, derive the reduced form, and point out that the VAR residuals are correlated, then introduce recursiveness/Cholesky-decomposition.

Exercise 10.5. Since $\mathbf{S}_{10} \equiv \mathbf{S}_{01}$:

$$\mathcal{L}^c(\boldsymbol{\alpha},\boldsymbol{\beta}) = -\frac{T}{2}\ln\left|\mathbf{S}_{00} + \boldsymbol{\alpha}\boldsymbol{\beta}'\mathbf{S}_{11}\boldsymbol{\beta}\alpha' - \boldsymbol{\alpha}\boldsymbol{\beta}'\mathbf{S}_{10} - \mathbf{S}_{10}\boldsymbol{\beta}\boldsymbol{\alpha}'\right|. \tag{C.26}$$

In analogy with ordinary rules of derivation, we get

$$\frac{\partial L^c(\boldsymbol{\alpha},\boldsymbol{\beta})}{\partial\boldsymbol{\alpha}} = -\frac{T}{2}\frac{1}{\left|\mathbf{S}_{00} + \boldsymbol{\alpha}\boldsymbol{\beta}'\mathbf{S}_{11}\boldsymbol{\beta}\alpha' - \boldsymbol{\alpha}\boldsymbol{\beta}'\mathbf{S}_{10} - \mathbf{S}_{10}\boldsymbol{\beta}\boldsymbol{\alpha}'\right|} \times \frac{\partial\left|\mathbf{S}_{00} + \boldsymbol{\alpha}\boldsymbol{\beta}'\mathbf{S}_{11}\boldsymbol{\beta}\alpha' - \boldsymbol{\alpha}\boldsymbol{\beta}'\mathbf{S}_{10} - \mathbf{S}_{10}\boldsymbol{\beta}\boldsymbol{\alpha}'\right|}{\partial\boldsymbol{\alpha}}$$

$$\frac{\partial\boldsymbol{\alpha}\boldsymbol{\beta}'\mathbf{S}_{11}\boldsymbol{\beta}\alpha'}{\partial\boldsymbol{\alpha}} = \boldsymbol{\beta}'\mathbf{S}_{11}\boldsymbol{\beta}\alpha' + (\boldsymbol{\alpha}\boldsymbol{\beta}'\mathbf{S}_{11}\boldsymbol{\beta})' = 2\boldsymbol{\beta}'\mathbf{S}_{11}\boldsymbol{\beta}\alpha'$$

$$\frac{\partial\boldsymbol{\alpha}\boldsymbol{\beta}'\mathbf{S}_{10}}{\partial\boldsymbol{\alpha}} = \boldsymbol{\beta}'\mathbf{S}_{10}$$

$$\frac{\partial \mathbf{S}_{10}\boldsymbol{\beta}\boldsymbol{\alpha}'}{\partial \boldsymbol{\alpha}} = (\mathbf{S}_{10}\boldsymbol{\beta})' = \boldsymbol{\beta}'\mathbf{S}_{10}.$$

$$\frac{\partial L^c(\boldsymbol{\alpha},\boldsymbol{\beta})}{\partial \boldsymbol{\alpha}} = 0,$$

therefore, implies

$$2\boldsymbol{\beta}'\mathbf{S}_{11}\boldsymbol{\beta}\boldsymbol{\alpha}' - 2\boldsymbol{\beta}'\mathbf{S}_{10} = 0$$
$$\boldsymbol{\alpha}\boldsymbol{\beta}'\mathbf{S}_{11}\boldsymbol{\beta} = \mathbf{S}_{10}\boldsymbol{\beta}$$
$$\boldsymbol{\alpha} = \mathbf{S}_{10}\boldsymbol{\beta}(\boldsymbol{\beta}'\mathbf{S}_{11}\boldsymbol{\beta})^{-1},$$

showing expression (10.64).

Exercise 10.6. Make a time plot of the two data series to begin with. Note that cointegration is not so obvious in this dataset as YA drifts far away form YB. A second point is that there no clear deterministic drift in any of the two series. Hence, to secure a similar test of cointegration rank, it appears to be sufficient to include an unrestricted constant term in the VAR. The estimated VAR is given in Figure C.15:

```
SYS( 3) Estimating the system by OLS
       The dataset is: C:weakly_cointegrated_ADLmodel_d.xls
       The estimation sample is: 2 - 101

URF equation for: Ya
                 Coefficient  Std.Error  t-value  t-prob
Ya_1                0.947929   0.008677     109.  0.0000
Yb_1                0.396367    0.04660     8.51  0.0000
Constant      U  0.000443287    0.01327   0.0334  0.9734

sigma = 0.093506    RSS = 0.8481073365

URF equation for: Yb
                 |Coefficient  Std.Error  t-value  t-prob
Ya_1              -0.00128607   0.008921   -0.144  0.8857
Yb_1                0.982731    0.04791     20.5  0.0000
Constant      U     0.0195575   0.01364     1.43  0.1549

sigma = 0.0961356    RSS = 0.8964784957

log-likelihood       193.214225  -T/2log|Omega|       477.001931
|Omega|          7.19140699e-05  log|Y'Y/T|          -1.28349191
R^2(LR)                 0.99974  R^2(LM)                0.898961
no. of observations         100  no. of parameters             6
```

Figure C.15. The VAR used in Table 10.3.

Empirically, the roots of the companion matrix form a complex pair with modulus 0.97, hence the magnitude of the root is almost right, although the DGP has two real roots 1 and 0.75. Note also, from the statistical output, that the estimated covariance matrix for the VAR disturbances is

$$\hat{\boldsymbol{\Sigma}} = \begin{pmatrix} 0.093506 & 0.23270 \\ 0.23270 & 0.093506 \end{pmatrix}.$$

The results of the cointegration tests are shown in Figure C.16.

```
I(1) cointegration analysis, 2 - 101

  eigenvalue     loglik for rank
                  158.1669    0
     0.50040       192.8647    1
   0.0069670       193.2142    2

  H0:rank<=  Trace test [ Prob]
     0           70.095 [0.000] **
     1          0.69914 [0.403]

Asymptotic p-values based on: Unrestricted constant
Unrestricted variables:
Constant
Number of lags used in the analysis: 1
```

Figure C.16. Eigenvalues and trace test for the VAR in Figure C.15.

```
beta
Ya              1.0000
Yb             -7.7713

alpha
Ya          -0.050319
Yb          0.0044730

Standard errors of alpha
Ya          0.0053472
Yb          0.0055148
```

Figure C.17. Estimated $\boldsymbol{\alpha}$ and $\boldsymbol{\beta}$ from the VAR in C.15, with estimated standard errors.

Next, based on the tests, reestimate the system as a cointegrated VAR with rank equal to 1 ($r = 1$). The results for $\boldsymbol{\alpha}$ and $\boldsymbol{\beta}$ are shown in Figure C.17.

The screen capture in Figure C.17 shows the estimates of the adjustment coefficient and cointegration parameter in (10.96) and (10.97) in the main text.

As noted, the results clearly indicate weak exogeneity of YB_t, and testing that restriction on the cointegrated VAR gives

$$\text{LR-test of restrictions: } \chi^2(1) = 0.66436[0.4150],$$

which can also be calculated directly as:

$$-2(192.532475 - 192.864655) = 0.66436.$$

```
SYS(2) Estimating the system by OLS
       The dataset is: C:\weakly_cointegrated_ADLmodel_d.xls
       The estimation sample  is: 2 - 101

URF equation for: DYa
                    Coefficient  Std.Error  t-value  t-prob
ecm_1                -0.0500082   0.005316    -9.41  0.0000
Constant      U    -0.000922521    0.01242  -0.0743  0.9409

sigma = 0.0930714   RSS = 0.848903077

URF equation for: DYb
                    Coefficient  Std.Error  t-value  t-prob
ecm_1                0.00446744   0.005481    0.815  0.4170
Constant      U       0.0157486    0.01280     1.23  0.2216

sigma = 0.0959734   RSS = 0.9026672202

log-likelihood       192.863542  -T/2log|Omega|      476.651249
|Omega|          7.24202226e-05  log|Y'Y/T|         -8.83909172
R^2(LR)                0.500393  R^2(LM)               0.250196
no. of observations         100  no. of parameters            4

correlation of URF residuals (standard deviations on diagonal)
                 DYa           DYb
DYa         0.093071       0.23432
DYb          0.23432      0.095973
```

Figure C.18. Estimated version of (10.99)–(10.100), replicating (10.104)–(10.105).

```
MOD( 2) Estimating the model by 1SLS
       The dataset is: C:\weakly_cointegrated_ADLmodel_d.xls
       The estimation sample is: 2 - 101

Equation for: DYa
                     Coefficient  Std.Error  t-value  t-prob
ecm_1                 -0.0510234   0.005212    -9.79  0.0000
DYb                     0.227239    0.09572     2.37  0.0195
Constant       U     -0.00450122    0.01223   -0.368  0.7135

sigma = 0.0904801

Equation for: DYb
                     Coefficient  Std.Error  t-value  t-prob
Constant       U      0.00884232   0.009581    0.923  0.3583

sigma = 0.0962981

log-likelihood      192.525775  -T/2log|Omega|     476.313482
no. of observations        100  no. of parameters           4
```

Figure C.19. Estimation results for the conditional plus marginal model of the $I(0)$-system, (10.104)–(10.105) in the main text.

Exercise 10.7. The variable ecm has to be created. Once that has been done, the $I(0)$-system is estimated as shown in Figure C.18. To estimate the econometric model of the system, we formulate a recursive model which is efficiently estimated by equation-by-equation OLS (1SLS in the estimation menu in PcGive). The results are shown in the screen capture in Figure C.19. The treatment of identities varies between software programs. In PcGive, the variable ecm_t can be labelled as an identity variable (ecm_{t-1} is already in the model as a predetermined variable), and the program will then estimate the exact identity $\text{ecm}_t = \Delta\text{YA}_t - 7.8\Delta\text{YB}_t + \text{ecm}_{t-1}$. In other software packages (or in other contexts), the identity will need to be hardcoded.

C.11. Chapter 11 Answers

Exercise 11.1. We set $m = 4$ and $x = (-\alpha)$:

$$(1 + (-\alpha))^4 = \binom{4}{0} + \binom{4}{1}(-\alpha) + \binom{4}{2}(-\alpha)^2 + \binom{4}{3}(-\alpha)^3 + \binom{4}{4}(-\alpha)^4.$$

The binomial coefficient $\binom{4}{0} = 1$, by definition, and

$$\binom{4}{1} = \frac{4!}{1!3!} = 4, \quad \text{and} \quad \binom{4}{4} = 1,$$

$$(1-\alpha)^4 = 1 - 4\alpha + \binom{4}{2}\alpha^2 - \binom{4}{3}\alpha^3 + \alpha^4.$$

Hence,

$$\begin{aligned} 1-(1-\alpha)^4 &= 1 - \left[1 - 4\alpha + \binom{4}{2}\alpha^2 - \binom{4}{3}\alpha^3 + \alpha^4\right] \\ &= 4\alpha - \binom{4}{2}\alpha^2 + \binom{4}{3}\alpha^3 - \alpha^4, \end{aligned}$$

showing the equality.

Exercise 11.2. Using (11.3):

$$\begin{aligned} 0.10 &= 1-(1-\alpha)^{10} \\ (1-\alpha)^{10} &= 0.90 \\ \alpha &= 1 - 0.90^{\frac{1}{10}} = 0.0105, \end{aligned}$$

the optimal target size on this reckoning is $\alpha = 0.01$ (with two decimals). Using the approximation in (11.4):

$$0.10 = \alpha 10$$

for the calculation, the answer becomes $\alpha = 0.01$. Setting the target size to 0.01 implies that the number of irrelevant variables on average becomes $0.01 \cdot 10 = 0.1$. Hence, even though we will select a wrong model in 10% of the times, we follow this strategy (under the null hypothesis that the null model is the LGDP), every variable in the GUM is correctly removed in the final model.

Exercise 11.3. Using sample 2–104, the estimated VAR(1) for the four variables Za_t, Zb_t, Zc_t, Zd_t, gives *log-likelihood* $= -456.269307$ and the correlation matrix in Figure C.20. The matrix of the VAR residuals shows that the series are contemporaneously correlated, and the inspection of the

```
correlation of URF residuals (standard deviations on diagonal)
                 Za           Zb           Zc           Zd
Za          0.90262      0.49377      0.25511      0.71992
Zb          0.49377      0.99664     -0.33220    0.0049175
Zc          0.25511     -0.33220       1.1252      0.26711
Zd          0.71992    0.0049175      0.26711      0.82134
```

Figure C.20. Correlation matrix for the four VAR residuals.

VAR coefficient matrix shows examples of joint Granger causation as well as of significant autoregression. Since each variable is entered in the GUM for Ya with four lags, this means that there is multi-collinearity among the regressors.

The estimation equation for the GUM takes the form:

$$Ya_t = \text{Constant} + \sum_{i=1}^{4} \phi_i Ya_{t-i} + \sum_{i=0}^{4} \beta_{1i} Za_{t-i} + \sum_{i=0}^{4} \beta_{2i} Zb_{t-i}$$
$$+ \sum_{i=0}^{4} \beta_{2i} Zc_{t-i} + \sum_{i=0}^{4} \beta_{2i} Zd_{t-i} + \epsilon_t$$

Using the 100 observations (5–104), you get $\hat{\sigma}^2 = 0.923875$ and RSS $=$ 64.0158917, with 25 parameters (including the constant). Note that, although the dataset is multi-collinear, the 1-cut procedure would lead to correct elimination of all variables here: The highest t^2 is found for the constant term, which is also statistically significant. The next highest t-value for Ya_{t-3}, has p-value of 0.14, so already that variable will be deleted.

Exercise 11.4. Using the 100 observations (5–104), you get $\hat{\sigma}^2 = 0.926663$ and RSS $= 64.4027878$, with 25 parameters (including the constant). From the details of the output, it would be relatively easy to decide to include $Ya_{t-1}, Za_t, Zc_t, Zd_t$, and you would perhaps consider Ya_{t-3}, Ya_{t-4} and Za_{t-4}, since their t-values are close to significance at the $\alpha = 0.10$ level. Zb_t, which is in the DGP, is difficult to decide to include in the model in this data realization. In the case that we instead start from the DGP equation for Ya_t, Autometrics retains also Zb_t, with $\alpha = 0.05$ though, not with $\alpha = 0.01$.

Exercise 11.5. The GUM shown in the screen capture is an ADL(2, 2, 2), i.e., there are two lags in the endogenous variable RL and the two regressors,

RNB and RW, have distributed lags of order 2. From Chapter 6, we recognize RL as the Norwegian bank loan rate and RNB as Norges Bank's policy interest rate. The variable RW is a foreign interest rate. Estimation of this model (GUM) shows that each of the tests in the test battery is significant with the exception of the autocorrelation test. Hence, the GUM is not congruent. Taking cue from Chapter 6, we can create $(I:1998(3), I:1998(3))$ in algebra (or calculator) and include them to the ADL$(2,2,2)$.

Estimation of the extended GUM shows improved diagnostics, now only the heteroskedasticity tests are significant at the 1% significance level. The residual heteroskedasticity could be due to volatility, which can be addressed separately, as noted in Chapter 6. If we try a 1-cut selection, using a 1% level, only RW is dropped. Compared to equation (6.71), this gives a model with five extra parameters. In fact, (6.71) was chosen by commencing from ADL$(2,2,2)$ and using Autometrics with IIS and $\alpha = 0.001$. The low α explains why Autometrics keeps fewer variables.

Note also that in this example, one variable which is relevant to keep away from the selection is the constant term, as dropping it would imply that in a steady state the market rate in identical to the policy rate, which would be not be a helpful model.

As can be expected, the transmission mechanism model is quite sensitive to the estimation sample. The decision to start in 1994(1) was perhaps a little naive (but helped to illustrate volatility modelling). Choosing the start of formal inflation targeting in Norway, which would be 2001(2), and commencing from ADL$(2,2,2)$ as before, Autometrics with IIS and $\alpha = 0.001$, and keeping the constant term away from the selection, gives the final model as follows:

$$\begin{aligned}\mathrm{RL} = &\underset{(0.0373)}{0.9776}\,\mathrm{RL}_{t-1} + \underset{(0.0333)}{0.8837}\,\mathrm{RNB}_t - \underset{(0.0489)}{0.861}\,\mathrm{RNB}_{t-1}\\ &+ \underset{(0.116)}{0.05777}.\end{aligned}$$

Note that compared to (6.71), the constant term is much lower, and would obviously have been dropped in a selection. Nevertheless, the long-run relationship becomes

$$\mathrm{RL} = 2.6 + 1.01\mathrm{RNB},$$

while (6.71) implies a similar sized mark-up coefficient of 2.9.

C.12. Chapter 12 Answers

Exercise 12.1. For the $p = 1$ case, we have from, e.g., Section 3.4 that $b_{11}^{(j)} = 1 \cdot \phi_1^j = \phi_1^j$:

$$\left(1 + \sum_{i=1}^{p} b_{1i}^{(h)}\right) Y^* = (1 + \phi_1^h) Y^*,$$

$$R^{(h)} = \phi_0 \sum_{j=0}^{\infty} \phi_1^{h+j} = \phi_0 \phi_1^h \sum_{j=0}^{\infty} \phi_1^j = \phi_1^h Y^*,$$

$$\sum_{i=1}^{p} b_{1i}^{(h)} [Y_{T-(i-1)} - Y^*] = \phi_1^h [Y_T - Y^*],$$

$$\left(1 + \sum_{i=1}^{p} b_{1i}^{(h)}\right) Y^* - R^{(h)} = (1 + \phi_1^h) Y^* - \phi_1^h Y^* = Y^*.$$

Inserting these results in (12.22) gives (12.11).

Exercise 12.2. From Chapter 1, we have

$$\begin{aligned}
\text{GDP}_t &= C^* + J^* + \phi_1 \left[C_{t-1} - C^*\right] + \frac{\epsilon_{Ct} + b\epsilon_{Jt}}{1-b} + J_t - J^* \\
&= \text{GDP}^* + \phi_1 \left[\text{GDP}_{t-1} - J_{t-1} - \text{GDP}^* + J^*\right] + \frac{\epsilon_{Ct} + b\epsilon_{Jt}}{1-b} \\
&= \text{GDP}^* + \phi_1 \left[\text{GDP}_{t-1} - \text{GDP}^* - \epsilon_{Jt-1}\right] + \frac{\epsilon_{Ct} + b\epsilon_{Jt}}{1-b} \\
&= \text{GDP}^* + \phi_1 \left[\text{GDP}_{t-1} - \text{GDP}^*\right] + \frac{\epsilon_{Ct} + b\epsilon_{Jt}}{1-b} - \phi_1 \epsilon_{Jt-1}.
\end{aligned}$$

Exercise 12.3. From Chapter 1, we have expressions for C^* and GDP^*:

$$C^* = \frac{a + bJ^*}{(1-b-c)},$$

$$\text{GDP}^* = \frac{J^*(1-c) + a}{1-b-c}.$$

Using the parameter values in (12.32), we get

$$C^* = \frac{-1 + 0.25 \cdot 40}{(1 - 0.25 - 0.65)} = 90,$$

$$\text{GDP}^* = \frac{40 \cdot (1 - 0.65) - 1}{1 - 0.25 - 0.65)} = 130.$$

Exercise 12.4. Using the formulae in Section 12.3.2, we can define

$$Y^f_{T+h|\mathcal{I}_T} = \left[1 + \sum_{k=1}^{p} f_{1k}^{(h)}\right] Y^* - R^{(h)} + \sum_{k=1}^{p} f_{1k}^{(h)} [Y_{T-(k-1)} - Y^*],$$

$$E(Y_{iT+h} \mid \mathcal{I}_T^{\text{new}}) = \left[1 + \sum_{k=1}^{p} f_{1k}^{(h)}\right] Y^{*\text{new}} - R^{\text{new}(h)}$$
$$+ \sum_{k=1}^{p} f_{1k}^{(h)} [Y_{T-(k-1)} - Y^{*\text{new}}],$$

where

$$R^{\text{new}(h)} \underset{\text{def}}{=} \phi_0^{\text{new}} \sum_{j=0}^{\infty} f_{11}^{(h+j)}$$

is defined so that it conforms with $Y_i^{*\text{new}}$. The expression (12.40) then follows.

Exercise 12.5. The naive forecast using (12.49) is

$$Y^{nf}_{iT+1|T} = Y_{iT} + \Delta Y_{iT},$$

while the DGP for period $T+1$ is

$$Y_{iT+1} = Y^* + \phi_1 (Y_{iT} - Y_i^*) + \varepsilon_{iT+1}.$$

The forecast error becomes

$$\begin{aligned} e^{nf}_{iT+1} &= Y_{iT+1} - Y^{nf}_T \\ &= Y_{iT+1} - (Y_{iT} + \Delta Y_{iT}) \\ &= Y^* + \phi_1 (Y_{iT} - Y_i^*) + \varepsilon_{T+1} - (Y_{iT} + \Delta Y_{iT}) \end{aligned}$$

$$= Y^* + \phi_1(Y_{iT} - Y_i^*) + \varepsilon_{T+1} - (Y^* + \phi_1(Y_{iT-1} - Y_i^*) + \varepsilon_{iT}) - \Delta Y_{iT}$$
$$= \phi_1(Y_{iT} - Y_{iT-1}) - \Delta Y_{iT} + \varepsilon_{T+1} - \varepsilon_T$$
$$= (\phi_1 - 1)\Delta Y_{iT} + \varepsilon_{T+1} - \varepsilon_T.$$

Exercise 12.6.

$$\begin{aligned} e^{nf}_{iT+1|T} &= Y^{*\text{new}} + \phi_1(Y_{iT} - Y_i^{*\text{new}}) + \varepsilon_{T+1} \\ &\quad - (Y^* + \phi_1(Y_{iT-1} - Y_i^*) + \varepsilon_{iT}) - \Delta Y_{iT} \\ &= Y^{*\text{new}} + \phi_1(Y_{iT} - Y^{*\text{new}}) + \varepsilon_{T+1} \\ &\quad - (Y^* + \phi_1(Y_{iT-1} - Y_i^*) + \varepsilon_{iT}) - \Delta Y_{iT} \\ &= (1 - \phi_1)(Y^{*\text{new}} - Y^*) + (\phi_1 - 1)\Delta Y_{iT} + \varepsilon_{T+1} - \varepsilon_T. \end{aligned}$$

Exercise 12.7.

$$\begin{aligned} e^{nf}_{iT+2|T+1} &= Y^{*\text{new}} + \phi_1(Y_{iT+1} - Y_i^{*\text{new}}) + \varepsilon_{iT+2} - (Y_{iT+1} + \Delta Y_{iT+1}) \\ &= Y^{*\text{new}} + \phi_1(Y_{iT+1} - Y_i^{*\text{new}}) + \varepsilon_{iT+2} - Y^{*\text{new}} \\ &\quad - \phi_1(Y_{iT} - Y_i^{*\text{new}}) - \varepsilon_{iT+1} - \Delta Y_{iT+1} \\ &= \phi_1(Y_{iT+1} - Y_i^{*\text{new}}) + \varepsilon_{iT+2} - \phi_1(Y_{iT} - Y_i^{*\text{new}}) \\ &\quad - \varepsilon_{iT+1} - \Delta Y_{iT+1} \\ &= \phi_1\Delta(Y_{iT+1} - Y_i^{*\text{new}}) + \varepsilon_{iT+2} - \varepsilon_{iT+1} - \Delta Y_{iT+1} \\ &= (\phi_1 - 1)\Delta Y_{iT+1} + \varepsilon_{iT+2} - \varepsilon_{iT+1}. \end{aligned} \tag{C.27}$$

Showing (12.55).

Exercise 12.8. The expected forecast error is

$$\begin{aligned} E(Y_{iT+1} \mid \mathcal{I}_T) - Y^{nf}_{T+1|T} &= Y^* + \phi_1(Y_T - Y^*) - Y_{T-1} \\ &= Y^* + \phi_1(Y_T - Y^*) + Y_T - Y_T - Y_{T-1} \\ &= Y^*(1 - \phi_1) - (1 - \phi_1)Y_T + \Delta Y_T \\ &= (1 - \phi_1)(Y^* - Y_T) + \Delta Y_T, \end{aligned}$$

which is non-zero in general.

Exercise 12.9. In $T+2$, the DGP is

$$Y_{iT+2} = Y^{*\text{new}} + \phi_1(Y_{iT+1} - Y_i^{*\text{new}}) + \varepsilon_{iT+2},$$

while the forecast is

$$Y_{T+2}^{nf} = Y_{T+1} = Y^{*\text{new}} + \phi_1(Y_T - Y^{*\text{new}}) + \varepsilon_{T+1},$$

giving the forecast error:

$$\begin{aligned} Y_{iT+2} - Y_{iT+2}^{nf} &= \phi_1(Y_{T+1} - Y^{*\text{new}}) - \phi_1(Y_T - Y^{*\text{new}}) + \varepsilon_{T+2} - \varepsilon_{T+1} \\ &= \phi_1 \Delta Y_{T+1} + \varepsilon_{T+2} - \varepsilon_{T+1}, \end{aligned}$$

Conditional on period $T+1$, the expected error is

$$E(Y_{iT+2} - Y_{iT+2}^{nf} \mid \mathcal{I}_T) = \phi_1 \Delta Y_{T+1} - \varepsilon_{T+1},$$

which will not be systematically positive or negative.

Exercise 12.10. Since

$$\text{MSFE} = \frac{1}{H}\sum_{h=1}^{H}(Y_{T+h} - Y_{T+h}^f)^2,$$

the question is to show that

$$\widehat{\text{Var}}(e_{T+H}) + (\widehat{\text{Bias}}\, Y_{T+H})^2.$$

The average of $Y_{T+h} - Y_{T+h}^f$ is $(\bar{Y}_H - \bar{Y}_H^f)$. We add and subtract $(\bar{Y}_H - \bar{Y}_H^f)$ inside the parenthesis:

$$\begin{aligned} &\frac{1}{H}\sum_{h=1}^{H}(Y_{T+h} - Y_{T+h}^f)^2 \\ &\quad = \frac{1}{H}\sum_{h=1}^{H}[Y_{T+h} - Y_{T+h}^f + (\bar{Y}_H - \bar{Y}_H^f) - (\bar{Y}_H - \bar{Y}_H^f)]^2 \\ &\quad = \frac{1}{H}\sum_{h=1}^{H}[\{(Y_{T+h} - Y_{T+h}^f) - (\bar{Y}_H - \bar{Y}_H^f)\} + (\bar{Y}_H - \bar{Y}_H^f)]^2 \\ &\quad = \frac{1}{H}\sum_{h=1}^{H}[\{Y_{T+h} - Y_{T+h}^f - (\bar{Y}_H - \bar{Y}_H^f)\} + (\bar{Y}_H - \bar{Y}_H^f)]^2. \end{aligned}$$

We see that when the expression on the right-hand side is written out, it will contain

$$-2\frac{1}{H}\sum_{h=1}^{H}[\{Y_{T+h} - Y^f_{T+h} - (\bar{Y}_H - \bar{Y}^f_H)\}(\bar{Y}_H - \bar{Y}^f_H)]$$

$$= -2\frac{1}{H}(\bar{Y}_H - \bar{Y}^f_H)\sum_{h=1}^{H}[\{Y_{T+h} - Y^f_{T+h} - (\bar{Y}_H - \bar{Y}^f_H)\}] = 0.$$

Hence, we have the identity:

$$\frac{1}{H}\sum_{h=1}^{H}(Y_{T+h} - Y^f_{T+h})^2$$

$$= \underbrace{\frac{1}{H}\sum_{h=1}^{H}[Y_{T+h} - Y^f_{T+h} - (\bar{Y}_H - \bar{Y}^f_H)]^2}_{\widehat{\text{Var}}(e_{T+H})} + \underbrace{[\bar{Y}_H - \bar{Y}^f_H]^2}_{\widehat{\text{Bias}}\, Y^2_{T+H}},$$

where $\widehat{\text{Var}}(e_{Y+h})$ denotes the empirical variance of the forecast error, and $\widehat{\text{Bias}}\, Y^2_{T+H}$ denotes the square of the estimated bias of the forecasts.

Bibliography

Agresti, A. (2015). *Foundations of Linear and Generalized Linear Models*. Wiley Series in Probability and Statistics. Wiley, New Jersey.

Aitken, A. C. (1935). On the Least Squares and Linear Combinations of Observations. *Proceedings of the Royal Society of Edinburgh*, *55*, 42–48.

Akram, Q. F. and R. Nymoen (2009). Model Selection for Monetary Policy Analysis — How Important is Empirical Validity? *Oxford Bulletin of Economics and Statistics*, *71*, 35–68.

Aldrich, J. (1989). Autonomy. *Oxford Economic Papers*, *41*, 15–34.

Aldrich, J. (1995). Correlations. Genuine and Spurious in Pearson and Yule. *Statistical Science*, *10*(4), 364–376.

Almon, S. (1965). The Distributed Lag Between Capital Appropriations and Expenditures. *Econometrica*, *33*, 178–196.

Anderson, T. W. (1962). The Choice of the Degree of a Polynomial Regression as a Multiple Decision Problem. *Annals of Mathematical Statistics*, *33*, 255–265.

Anderson, T. W. (2003). *An Introduction to Multivariate Statistical Analysis*. Wiley, New Jersey, 3rd edn.

Andrews, D. W. K. (1993). Tests for Parameter Instability and Structural Change with Unknown Change Point. *Econometrica*, *61*, 821–856.

Andrews, D. W. K. (2003). Tests for Parameter Instability and Structural Change with Unknown Change Point: A Corrigendum. *Econometrica*, *71*, 395–397.

Angrist, J., K. Graddy and G. Imbens (2000). The Interpretation of Instrumental Variables Estimators in Simultaneous Equations Models with an Application to the Demand for Fish. *Review of Economic Studies*, *67*(3), 499–527.

Banerjee, A., J. J. Dolado, J. W. Galbraith and D. F. Hendry (1993). *Co-integration, Error Correction and the Econometric Analysis of Non-stationary Data*. Oxford University Press, Oxford.

Bårdsen, G. (1989). Estimation of Long-Run Coefficients in Error-Correction Models. *Oxford Bulletin of Economics and Statistics*, *51*, 345–350.

Bårdsen, G., Ø. Eitrheim, E. S. Jansen and R. Nymoen (2005). *The Econometrics of Macroeconomic Modelling*. Oxford University Press, Oxford.

Bårdsen, G., E. S. Jansen and R. Nymoen (2003). Econometric Inflation Targeting. *Econometrics Journal*, *6*, 429–460.

Bårdsen, G., E. S. Jansen and R. Nymoen (2004). Econometric Evaluation of the New Keynesian Phillips Curve. *Oxford Bulletin of Economics and Statistics*, *66*(Suppl.), 671–686.

Bårdsen, G. and R. Nymoen (2003). Testing Steady-State Implications for the NAIRU. *Review of Economics and Statistics*, *85*(3), 1070–1075.

Bårdsen, G. and R. Nymoen (2009). Macroeconometric Modelling for Policy. In Mills, T. and K. Patterson (eds.), *Palgrave Handbook of Econometrics*, Vol. 2, Chap. 17, pp. 851–916. Palgrave Macmillan.

Bårdsen, G. and R. Nymoen (2011). *Introductory Econometrics* [*Innføring i økonometri*]. Fagbokforlaget, Bergen.

Bårdsen, G. and R. Nymoen (2014). *Topics in Econometrics* [*Videregående emner i økonometri*]. Fagbokforlaget, Bergen.

Bates, J. M. and C. Granger (1969). The Combination of Forecasts. *Operations Research Quarterly*, *20*, 451–468.

Bernanke, B. S. (1986). Alternative Explanations of the Money-Income Correlation. *Carnegie-Rochester Conference Series on Public Policy*, 49–100.

Bjerkholt, O. (2007). Writing "The Probability Approach" with Nowhere to Go: Haavelmo in the United States. 1939–1944. *Econometric Theory*, *23*(5), 775–837.

Bjerkholt, O. and D. Qin (2011). *Teaching Economics as a Science: The Yale Lectures of Ragnar Frisch*. Routledge, Milton Park.

Bjørnland, H. C. and L. A. Thorsrud (2015). *Applied Time Series for Macroeconomics*. Gyldendal Akademisk, Oslo.

Blanchard, O. and M. W. Watson (1986). Are Business Cycles All Alike? In Gordon, R. J. (ed.), *The American Business Cycle: Continuity and Change*, NBER Studies in Business Cycle, Vol. 25, Chap. 2, pp. 123–180. University of Chicago Press, Chicago.

Blanchard, O. J. and C. M. Kahn (1980). The Solution of Linear Difference Models under Rational Expectations. *Econometrica*, *48*, 1305–1310.

Blanchard, O. J. and D. Quah (1989). The Dynamic Effects of Aggregate Demand and Supply Disturbances. *American Economic Review*, *79*, 655–673.

Bollerslev, T. (1986). Generalized Autoregressive Conditional Heteroskedasticity. *Journal of Econometrics*, *32*, 307–327.

Box, G. E. P. and G. M. Jenkins (1976). *Time Series Analysis, Forecasting and Control*. Holden-Day, San Francisco.

Brockwell, P. Y. and R. A. Davies (1991). *Time Series: Theory and Method*. 2nd edn. Springer, New York.

Burke, S. P. and J. Hunter (2005). *Modelling Non-stationary Time Series. A Multivariate Approach*. Palgrave Texts in Econometrics. Palgrave Macmillan, Houndmills.

Cartwright, N. (1999). *The Dappled World: A Study of the Boundaries of Science*. Cambridge University Press, Cambridge.

Cartwright, N. (2007). *Hunting Causes and Using Them*. Cambridge University Press, Cambridge.

Cartwright, N. (2009). Causality, Invariance and Policy. In Kincaid, H. and D. Ross (eds.), *The Oxford Handbook of the Philosophy of Economics*. Oxford University Press, Oxford.

Castle, J. L., M. P. Clements and D. F. Hendry (2015). Robust Approaches to Forecasting. *International Journal of Forecasting*, *31*(1), 99–112.

Castle, J. L., J. A. Doornik and D. F. Hendry (2011). Evaluating Automatic Model Selection. *Journal of Time Series Econometrics*, *3*(1), Article 8.

Castle, J. L., J. A. Doornik, D. F. Hendry and R. Nymoen (2014). Mis-specification Testing: Non-invariance of Expectations Models of Inflation. *Econometric Reviews*, *33*(5–6), 553–574. DOI:10.1080/07474938.2013.825137.

Castle, J. L. and D. F. Hendry (2014a). Model Selection in Underspecified Equations with Breaks. *Journal of Econometrics*, *178*, 286–293.

Castle, J. L. and D. F. Hendry (2014b). Semi-automatic Non-linear Model Selection. In Haldrup, N. and P. Saikkonen (eds.), *Essays in Non-linear Time Series Econometrics*, pp. 163–197. Oxford University Press, Oxford.

Castle, J. L. and D. F. Hendry (2017). Clive W.J. Granger and Cointegration. *European Journal of Pure and Applied Mathematics*, *10*(1), 58–81.

Castle, J. L., X. Quin and W. R. Reed (2013). Using Model Selection Algorithms to Obtain Reliable Coefficient Estimates. *Journal of Economic Surveys*, *27*, 269–296.

Chow, G. C. (1960). Tests of Equality between Sets of Coefficients in Two Linear Regressions. *Econometrica*, *28*(4), 591–605.

Christiano, L. J., M. Eichenbaum and C. Evans (1996). The Effects of Monetary Policy Shocks: Evidence from the Flow of Funds. *Review of Economics and Statistics*, *78*, 16–34.

Clements, M. P. (2005). *Evaluating Econometric Forecasts of Economic and Financial Variables*. Palgrave Texts in Econometrics. Palgrave, Houndmills.

Clements, M. P. and D. F. Hendry (1998). *Forecasting Economic Time Series*. Cambridge University Press, Cambridge.

Clements, M. P. and D. F. Hendry (1999). *Forecasting Non-stationary Economic Time Series*. The MIT Press, Cambridge, MA.

Clements, M. P. and D. F. Hendry (2006). Forecasting with Breaks. In Elliot, G., C. W. J. Granger and A. Timmermann (eds.), *Handbook of Economic Forecasting*, Vol. 1. Elsevier, Amsterdam.

Davidson, J. (2000). *Econometric Theory*. Blackwell Publishers, Oxford.

Davidson, R. and J. G. MacKinnon (2004). *Econometric Theory and Methods*. Oxford University Press, Oxford.

Dennis, J. G., H. Hansen, S. Johansen and K. Juselius (2006). *CATS in RATS. Cointegration Analysis of Time Series, Version 2*. Estima, Evanstone.

Denton, F. (1985). Data Mining as an Industry. *Review of Economics and Statistics*, *67*, 124–127.

Dhrymes, P. J. (1974). *Econometrics. Statistical Foundations and Applications*. Springer, New York.

Diebold, F. X. and R. Mariano (1995). Comparing Predictive Accuracy. *Journal of Business and Economic Statistics*, *13*, 253–263.

Doornik, J. A. (1998). Approximations to the Asymptotic Distribution of Cointegration Tests. *Journal of Economics Surveys*, *12*, 573–593.

Doornik, J. A. (2003). Asymptotic Tables for Cointegration Tests Based on the Gamma-Distribution Approach. Unpublished Paper, University of Oxford.

Doornik, J. A. (2009). Autometrics. In Castle, J. and N. Shephard (eds.), *The Methodology and Practice of Econometrics*, Chap. 8, pp. 88–121. Oxford University Press, Oxford.

Doornik, J. A. and H. Hansen (1994). A Practical Test of Multivariate Normality. Unpublished Paper, University of Oxford.

Doornik, J. A. and H. Hansen (2008). An Omnibus Test for Univariate and Multivariate Normality. *Oxford Bulletin of Economics and Statistics*, *70*, 927–939.

Doornik, J. A. and D. F. Hendry (2013a). *Empirical Econometric Modelling PcGive* 14, Vol. 1. Timberlake Consultants, London.

Doornik, J. A. and D. F. Hendry (2013b). *Interactive Monte Carlo Experimentation in Econometrics. PcNaive* 6. Timberlake Consultants, London.

Doornik, J. A. and D. F. Hendry (2013c). *Modelling Dynamic Systems PcGive* 14, Vol. 2. Timberlake Consultants, London.

Doornik, J. A. and D. F. Hendry (2015). Statistical Model Selection with "Big Data". *Cogent Economics and Finance*, *3*, 1–15.

Doornik, J. A., D. F. Hendry and B. Nielsen (1998). Inference in Cointegration Models: UK M1 Revisited. *Journal of Economic Surveys*, *12*, 533–672.

Doornik, J. A., D. F. Hendry and M. Ooms (2013). Time Series Models (ARFIMA). In Doornik, J. A. and D. F. Hendry (eds.), *Econometric Modelling. Pc-Give* 14, Vol. 3, Chaps. 11–13. Timberlake Consultants.

Efron, B., T. Hastie, I. Johnstone and R. Tibshirani (2004). Least Angle Regression. *The Annals of Statistics*, *32*, 407–499.

Eika, K. H., N. R. Ericsson and R. Nymoen (1996). Hazards in Implementing a Monetary Conditions Index. *Oxford Bulletin of Economics and Statistics*, *58*(4), 765–790.

Eitrheim, Ø., T. A. Husebø and R. Nymoen (1999). Equilibrium-Correction versus Differencing in Macroeconomic Forecasting. *Economic Modelling*, *16*, 515–544.

Eitrheim, Ø., E. S. Jansen and R. Nymoen (2002). Progress from Forecast Failure: The Norwegian Consumption Function. *Econometrics Journal*, *5*, 40–64.

Emerson, R. A. and D. F. Hendry (1996). An Evaluation of Forecasting Using Leading Indicators. *Journal of Forecasting*, *15*(4), 271–291.

Enders, W. (2010). *Applied Econometric Time Series*, 3rd edn. Wiley, NJ.

Engle, R. F. (1982). Autoregressive Conditional Heteroscedasticity with Estimates of the Variance of United Kingdom Inflation. *Econometrica*, *50*, 987–1007.

Engle, R. F. and C. W. J. Granger (1987). Co-integration and Error Correction: Representation, Estimation and Testing. *Econometrica*, *55*, 251–276.

Engle, R. F. and D. F. Hendry (1993). Testing Super Exogeneity and Invariance in Regression Models. *Journal of Econometrics*, *56*, 119–139.

Ericsson, N. R. (1992). Cointegration, Exogeneity and Policy analysis: An Overview. *Journal of Policy Modelling*, *14*, 251–280.

Ericsson, N. R., E. S. Jansen, N. A. Kerbeshian and R. Nymoen (1999). Understanding a Monetary Conditions Index. Technical Report, Paper Presented at ESEM 1997, Toulose.

Ericsson, N. R. and J. G. MacKinnon (2002). Distributions of Error-Correction Tests for Cointegration. *Econometrics Journal*, *5*, 285–318.

Evans, G. and S. Honkapoja (2001). *Learning and Expectations in Macroeconomics*. Princeton University Press, Princeton, NJ.

Falch, N. S. and R. Nymoen (2011). The Accuracy of a Forecast Targeting Central Bank. *Economics: The Open-Access, Open-Assessment E-Journal*, *5*(15), 1–36.

Favero, C. and D. F. Hendry (1992). Testing the Lucas Critique: A Review. *Econometric Reviews*, *11*, 265–306.

Florens, J. P., M. Mouchart and J. M. Rolin (1990). *Elements of Bayesian Statistics*. Marcel Dekker, New York.

Frisch, R. (1929). Statikk og dynamikk i den økonomiske teori. *Nationaløkonomisk Tidsskrift*, *67*, 321–379. Translated (Section 1–3) as 'Statics and Dynamics in Economic Theory', *Structural Change and Economics Dynamics*, 3 (1992):391–401.

Frisch, R. (1933). Propagation Problems and Impulse Problems in Dynamic Economics. In *Economic Essays in Honour of Gustav Cassel*, pp. 171–205. Allen and Unwin, London.

Frisch, R. and F. V. Waugh (1933). Partial Time Regression as Compared with Individual Trends. *Econometrica*, *1*, 387–401.

Fuller, W. A. (1976). *Introduction to Statistical Time Series*. John Wiley & Sons, New York.

Galí, J. and M. Gertler (1999). Inflation Dynamics: A Structural Econometric Analysis. *Journal of Monetary Economics*, *44*(2), 233–258.

Gerdrup, K., A. Jore, C. Smith and L. Thorsrud (2009). Evaluating Ensemble Density Combination — Forecasting GDP and Inflation. Working Paper 19/2009, Norges Bank, Oslo.

Ghysels, E. and M. Marcellino (2018). *Applied Economic Forecasting Using Time Series Methods*. Oxford University Press, Oxford.

Godfrey, L. G. (1978). Testing for Higher Order Serial Correlation When the Regressors Include Lagged Dependent Variables. *Econometrica*, *46*, 1303–1313.

Graddy, K. (1995). Testing for Imperfect Competition at the Fulton Fish Market. *RAND Journal of Economics*, *26*, 75–92.

Graddy, K. (2006). The Fulton Fish Market. *Journal of Economic Perspectives*, *20*, 207–220.

Graddy, K. and P. Kennedy (2010). When Are Supply And Demand Determined Recursively Rather Than Simultaneously? *Eastern Economic Journal, 36*(3), 188–197.

Granger, C. (1969a). Prediction with Generalized Cost of Error Function. *Operational Research Quarterly, 20*, 199–207.

Granger, C. W. J. (1966). The Typical Spectral Shape of an Economic Variable. *Econometrica, 34*, 150–161.

Granger, C. W. J. (1969b). Investigating Causal Relations by Econometric Models and Cross-spectral Methods. *Econometrica, 37*(3), 424–438.

Granger, C. W. J. (1990). General Introduction: Where are the Controversies in Econometric Methodology? In Granger, C. W. J. (ed.), *Modelling Economic Series. Readings in Econometric Methodology*, pp. 1–23. Oxford University Press, Oxford.

Granger, C. W. J. (1992). Fellow's Opinion: Evaluating Economic Theory. *Journal of Econometrics, 51*, 3–5.

Granger, C. W. J. (1999). *Empirical Modeling in Economics. Specification and Evaluation*. Cambridge University Press, Cambridge.

Granger, C. W. J. and P. Newbold (1974). Spurious Regressions in Econometrics. *Journal of Econometrics, 2*, 111–120.

Granger, C. W. J. and P. Newbold (1986). *Forecasting Economic Time Series*. Academic Press, San Diego.

Granger, C. W. J. and T. Teräsvirta (1993). *Modelling Non-linear Economic Relationships*. Oxford University Press, Oxford.

Greene, W. (2012). *Econometric Analysis*. Pearson, Harlow, 7th edn.

Haavelmo, T. (1940). The Inadequacy of Testing Dynamic Theory by Comparing Theoretical Solutions and Observed Cycles. *Econometrica, 8*(4), 312–321.

Haavelmo, T. (1943a). The Statistical Implications of a System of Simultaneous Equations. *Econometrica, 11*, 1–12.

Haavelmo, T. (1943b). Statistical Testing of Business-Cycle Theories. *Review of Economics and Statistics, 25*, 13–18.

Haavelmo, T. (1944). The Probability Approach in Econometrics. *Econometrica, 12*(Suppl.), 1–118.

Hamilton, J. D. (1994). *Time Series Analysis*. Princeton University Press, Princeton.

Hansen, B. E. (1996). Methodology: Alchemy or Science? *Economic Journal, 106*, 1398–1413.

Hansen, B. E. (2017). *Econometrics*. University of Wisconsin. Book Manuscript. URL: http://www.ssc.wisc.edu/bhansen/econometrics/.

Hansen, L. P. (1982). Large Sample Properties of Generalized Method of Moments Estimators. *Econometrica, 50*, 1029–1054.

Harbo, I., S. Johansen, B. Nielsen and A. Rahbek (1998). Asymptotic Inference on Cointegrating Rank in Partial System. *Journal of Business & Economic Statistics, 16*, 388–399.

Harford, T. (2014). Big Data: Are We Making a Big Mistake? *Financial Times*. March 28.

Harvey, A. C. (1981). *The Econometric Analysis of Time Series*. Philip Allan, Oxford.

Harvey, A. C. (1990). *The Econometric Analysis of Time Series*, 2nd edn. Philip Allan, Oxford.

Harvey, A. C. (1993). *Time Series Models*, 2nd edn. Harvester Wheatsheaf, Hempstead.

Harvey, D., S. Leyborne and P. Newbold (1997). Testing the Equality of Mean Squared Errors. *International Journal of Forecasting*, *13*, 281–291.

Hendry, D. F. (1984). Monte Carlo Experimentation in Econometrics. In Griliches, Z. and M. D. Intriligator (eds.), *Handbook of Econometrics*, Vol. 2, Chap. 16, pp. 937–976. North-Holland, Amsterdam.

Hendry, D. F. (1987). Econometric Methodology: A Personal Perspective. In Bewley, T. W. (ed.), *Advances in Econometrics*, pp. 29–48. Cambridge University Press, Cambridge.

Hendry, D. F. (1988). The Encompassing Implications of Feedback Versus Feedforward Mechanisms in Econometrics. *Oxford Economic Papers*, *40*, 132–149.

Hendry, D. F. (1993). *Econometrics. Alchemy or Science?* Blackwell, Oxford.

Hendry, D. F. (1995a). *Dynamic Econometrics*. Oxford University Press, Oxford.

Hendry, D. F. (1995b). Econometrics and Business Cycle Empirics. *The Economic Journal*, *105*, 1622–1636.

Hendry, D. F. (2001). How Economists Forecast. In Ericsson, N. R. and D. F. Hendry (eds.), *Understanding Economic Forecasts*, Chap. 2, pp. 15–41. The MIT Press, Cambridge, MA.

Hendry, D. F. (2009). Methodology of Empirical Econometric Modelling. In Mills, T. C. and K. Patterson (eds.), *Palgrave Handbook of Econometrics. Applied Econometrics*, Vol. 2, Chap. 1, pp. 3–67. Palgrave Macmillan, Basingstoke.

Hendry, D. F. (2018). Deciding Between Alternative Approaches in Macroeconomics. *International Journal of Forecasting*, *34*(1), 119–135.

Hendry, D. F. and J. A. Doornik (2014). *Empirical Model Discovery and Theory Evaluation. Automatic Selection Methods in Econometrics*. Arne Ryde Memorial Lectures. MIT Press, Cambridge, MA.

Hendry, D. F. and S. Johansen (2015). Model Discovery and Trygve Haavelmo's Legacy. *Econometric Theory*, *31*, 93–114.

Hendry, D. F., S. Johansen and C. Santos (2008). Automatic Selection of Indicators in a Fully Saturated Regression. *Computational Statistics*, *23*, 317–335 and Erratum 337–339.

Hendry, D. F. and H. M. Krolzig (2000). Improving on Data Mining Reconsidered by K.D. Hoover and S.J. Perez. *Econometrics Journal*, *2*, 202–219.

Hendry, D. F. and H. M. Krolzig (2001). *Automatic Econometric Model Selection Using PcGets* 1.0. Timberlake Consultants, London.

Hendry, D. F. and H. M. Krolzig (2005). The Properties of Automatic Gets Modelling. *Economic Journal*, *115*, C32–C61.

Hendry, D. F. and G. E. Mizon (1978). Serial Correlation as a Convenient Simplification, Not a Nuisance: A Comment on a Study of the Demand for Money by the Bank of England. *The Economic Journal*, *88*(351), 549–563.

Hendry, D. F. and B. Nielsen (2007). *Econometric Modeling*. Princeton University Press, Princeton.

Hendry, D. F. and J. F. Richard (1982). On the formulation of Empirical Models in Dynamic Econometrics. *Journal of Econometrics*, *20*, 3–33.

Hendry, D. F. and C. Santos (2009). An Automatic Test of Super Exogeneity. In Watson, M. W., T. Bollerslev and J. Russell (eds.), *Volatility and Time Series Econometrics*, pp. 164–193. Oxford University Press, Oxford.

Hill, R. C., W. Griffiths and G. Lim (2012). *Principles of Econometrics*, 4th edn. Wiley, NJ.

Hoover, K. (2001). *Causality in Macroeconomics*. Cambridge University Press, Cambridge.

Hoover, K. D. and S. J. Perez (1999). Data Mining Reconsidered: Encompassing and the General-to-Specific Approach to Specification Search. *Econometrics Journal*, *2*, 1–25.

Hsiao, C. (1997a). Cointegration and Dynamic Simultaneous Equations Model. *Econometrica*, *65*(3), 647–670.

Hsiao, C. (1997b). Statistical Properties of the Two Stage Least Squares Estimator Under Cointegration. *Review of Economic Studies*, *67*, 385–398.

Hurwicz, L. (1950). Least Squares Bias in Time Series. In Koopmans, T. C. (ed.), *Statistical Inference in Dynamic Economic Models*, Cowles Commission Monograph, Vol. 10, Chap. 15. John Wiley & Sons, New York.

James, G., D. Witten, T. Hastie and R. Tibshirani (2013). *An Introduction to Statistical Learning*. Springer, Berlin.

Jarque, C. M. and A. K. Bera (1980). Efficient Tests for Normality, Homoscedasticity and Serial Independence of Regression Residuals. *Economics Letters*, *6*, 255–259.

Johansen, L. (1978). *Lectures on Macroeconomic Planning. Part 2. Centralization, Decentralization, Planning Under Uncertainty*. North-Holland, Amsterdam.

Johansen, S. (1991). Estimation and Testing of Cointegrating Vectors in Gaussian Vector Autoregressive Models. *Econometrica*, *59*, 1551–1580.

Johansen, S. (1992). Cointegration in Partial Systems and the Efficiency of Single-Equation Analysis. *Journal of Econometrics*, *52*, 389–402.

Johansen, S. (1995). *Likelihood-Based Inference in Cointegrated Vector Autoregressive Models*. Oxford University Press, Oxford.

Johansen, S. (2002). A Small Sample Correction for the Test of Cointegrating Rank in the Vector Autoregressive Model. *Econometrica*, *70*, 1929–1961.

Johansen, S., R. Mosconi and B. Nielsen (2000). Cointegration Analysis in the Presence of Structural Breaks in the Deterministic Trend. *Econometrics Journal*, *3*, 216–249.

Johansen, S. and B. Nielsen (2009). Analysis of the Indicator Saturation Estimator as a Robust Regression Estimator. In Castle, J. L. and N. Shephard (eds.), *The Methodology and Practise of Econometrics*. Oxford University Press, Oxford.

Johnston, J. and J. Dinardo (1997). *Econometric Methods*. McGraw-Hill, New York, 4th edn.

Jordà, O. (2005). Estimation and Inference of Impulse Responses by Local Projections. *American Economic Review*, *95*(1), 161–182.

Juselius, K. (2007). *The Cointegrated VAR Model: Methodology and Applications*. Oxford University Press, Oxford.

Kennedy, P. (2002). Sinning in the Basement: What are the Rules? The Ten Commandments of Applied Econometrics. *Journal of Economic Surveys*, *16*, 569–589.

Kennedy, P. (2008). *A Guide to Econometrics*. Blackwell Publishing, Oxford, 6th edn.

Kiviet, J. F. (1986). On the Rigor of Some Mis-specification Tests for Modelling Dynamic Relationships. *Review of Economic Studies*, *53*, 241–261.

Klein (1983). *Lectures in Econometrics*, Advanced Textbooks in Econometrics, Vol. 22 North-Holland, Amsterdam.

Klein, L. R. (1968). *An Essay on the Theory of Economic Prediction*. Yrjö Jahnsson Lectures. The Academic Book Store, Helsinki.

Koyck, L. M. (1954). *Distributed Lags and Investment Analysis*. North-Holland, Amsterdam.

Kremers, J. J. M., N. R. Ericsson and J. J. Dolado (1992). The Power of Cointegration Tests. *Oxford Bulletin of Economics and Statistics*, *54*, 325–348.

Kripfganz, S. and D. C. Schneider (2018). Response Surface Regressions for Critical Value Bounds and Approximate *p*-Values in Equilibrium Correction Models. Unpublished Paper. University of Exeter Business School and Max Planck Institute for Demographic Research.

Krzanowski, W. J. (1988). *Principles of Multivariate Analysis: A User's Perspective*. Clarendon Press, Oxford.

Larsen, V. H. and L. A. Thorsrud (2018). Business Cycle Narratives. Working Paper 3/2018, Norges Bank.

Lay, D. (2003). *Linear Algebra and its Applications*, 3rd edn. Addison-Wesley, Boston.

Leamer, E. E. (1983). Let's Take the Con Out of Econometrics. *American Economic Journal*, *73*, 31–43.

Lewbel, A. (2017). The Identification Zoo-Meanings of Identification in Econometrics. *Journal of Economic Literature*. Forthcoming.

Lovell, M. C. (1983). Data Mining. *Review of Economics and Statistics*, *65*, 1–12.

Lucas, R. E., Jr. (1976). Econometric Policy Evaluation: A Critique. In Brunner, K. and A. H. Meltzer (eds.), *Carnegie-Rochester Conference Series on Public Policy: The Phillips Curve and Labor Markets*, Vol. 1, 19–46.

Lütkepohl, H. (2007). *New Introduction to Multiple Time Series Analysis*. Springer, Berlin.

MacKinnon, J. G. (1991). Critical Values for Cointegration Tests. In Engle, R. F. and C. W. J. Granger (eds.), *Long-Run Economic Relationships: Readings in cointegration*, Chap. 13. Oxford University Press, Oxford.

MacKinnon, J. G. (2010). Critical Values for Cointegration Tests. Queen's Economics Department Working Paper 1227/1-2010, Queen's University. January 1990. Reissued January 2010 with Additional Results.

Magnus, J. R. (1999). The Success of Econometrics. *De Economist*, *147*, 55–75.

Magnus, J. R. (2002). The Missing Tablets: Comment on Peter Kennedy's Ten Commandments. *Journal of Economic Surveys*, *16*, 605–609.

Mandelbrot, B. B. (1963). The Variation of Certain Speculative Prices. *The Journal of Business*, *36*(4), 394–419.

Martin, V. L., S. Hurn and D. Harris (2012). *Econometric Modelling with Time Series. Specification, Estimation and Testing*. Cambridge University Press, Cambridge.

Morgan, M. S. (1990). *The History of Econometric Ideas*. Cambridge University Press, Cambridge.

Myers, D. E. (1989). To be or Not to Be ... Stationary? That is the Question. *Mathematical Geology*, *21*(3), 347–362.

Nymoen, R., A. R. Swensen and E. Tveter (2012). Interpreting the Evidence for New Keynesian Models of Inflation Dynamics. *Journal of Macroeconomics*, *35*(2), 253–263. Online version: http://dx.doi.org/10.1016/j.jmacro.2012.01.008.

OECD (2017). Labour market resilience: The role of structural and macroeconomic policies. In *Employment Outlook 2017*. OECD Publishing, Paris.

Pagan, A. (1984). Model Evaluation by Variable Addition. In Hendry, D. F. and K. F. Wallis (eds.), *Econometrics and Quantitative Economics*, Chap. 5. Basil Blackwell, Oxford.

Patterson, K. (2000). *An Introduction to Applied Econometrics. A Time Series Approach*. Macmillan, Basingstoke.

Patterson, K. (2011). *Unit Root Tests in Time Series*. Palgrave Macmillan, Houndsmills.

Perez-Amaral, T., G. M. Gallo and H. White (2003). A Flexible Tool for Model Building: The Relevant Transformation of the Input Network Approach (RETINA). *Oxford Bulletin of Economics and Statistics*, *65*, 821–838.

Pesaran, M. (1987). *The Limits to Rational Expectations*. Basil Blackwell, Oxford.

Pesaran, M. and S. Youngcheol (1998). An Autoregressive Distributed Lag Modelling Approach to Cointegration Analysis. In Strøm, S. (ed.), *Econometrics and Economic Theory in the 20th Century: The Ragnar Frisch Centennial Symposium*, Econometric Society Monograph Series, No. 32, Chap. 16, pp. 499–527. Cambridge University Press, Cambridge.

Pesaran, M. H. (2015). *Time Series and Panel Data Econometrics*. Oxford University Press, Oxford.

Pesaran, M. H., Y. Shin and R. J. Smith (2000). Structural Analysis of Vector Error Correction Models with Exogenous I(1) Variables. *Journal of Econometrics*, *97*, 293–343.

Pesaran, M. H., S. Youngcheol and R. Smith (2001). Bounds Testing Approaches to the Analysis of Level Relationships. *Journal of Applied Econometrics*, *16*, 289–326.

Pretis, F., J. Reade and G. Sucarrat (2018). General-to-Specific (GETS) Modelling and Indicator Saturation with the R Package Gets. *Journal of Statistical Software*, *86*(3), 1–44.

Quandt, R. (1960). Tests of the Hypothesis that a Linear Regression System Obeys Two Separate Regimes. *Journal of the American Statistical Association*, *55*, 324–330.

Rahbek, A. and R. Mosconi (1999). Cointegration Rank Inference with Stationary Regressors in VAR Models. *Econometrics Journal*, *2*, 76–91.

Reed, W. R. (2015). On the Practice of Lagging Variables to Avoid Simultaneity. *Oxford Bulletin of Economics and Statistics*, *77*, 897–905.

Rhodes, R. (1986). *The Making of the Atom Bomb*. Simon & Schuster, New York.

Rødseth, A. (2000). *Open Economy Macroeconomics*. Cambridge University Press, Cambridge.

Romer, P. (2016). The Trouble with Macroeconomics. *The American Economist*. Forthcoming.

Saikkonen, P. (1991). Asymptotically Efficient Estimation of Cointegration Regressions. *Econometric Theory*, *7*, 1–21.

Sargan, J. D. (1958). The Estimation of Economic Relationships Using Instrumental Variables. *Econometrica*, *26*, 393–415.

Sargan, J. D. (1964). Wages and Prices in the United Kingdom: A Study of Econometric Methodology. In Hart, P. E., G. Mills and J. K. Whitaker (eds.), *Econometric Analysis for National Economic Planning*, pp. 25–63. Butterworth Co., London.

Sargent, T. J. (1987). *Macroeconomic Theory*. Academic Press, San Diego.

Sbordone, A. M. (2002). Prices and Unit Labor Costs: A New Test of Price Stickiness. *Journal of Monetary Economics*, *49*, 265–292.

Schumway, R. H. (1988). *Applied Statistical Time Series Analysis*. Prentice-Hall International Editions, London.

Schumway, R. H. and D. S. Stoffer (2000). *Time Series Analysis and its Applications*. Springer-Verlag, New York.

Seo, B. (1998). Statistical Inference on Cointegration Rank in Error Correction Models with Stationary Co-variates. *Journal of Econometrics*, *85*, 339–385.

Sims, C. A. (1980). Macroeconomics and Reality. *Econometrica*, *48*, 1–48.

Sims, C. A. (1986). Are Forecasting Models Usable for Policy Analysis. *Bank of Minneapolis Quarterly Review*, 2–16.

Sims, C. A., J. M. Stock and M. W. Watson (1990). Inference in Linear Time Series Models with Some Unit Roots. *Econometrica*, *58*, 113–144.

Spanos, A. (1995). On Theory Testing in Econometrics: Modelling with Non-Experimental Data. *Journal of Econometrics*, *67*, 189–226.

Spanos, A. (1999). *Probability Theory and Statistical Inference. Econometric Modelling with Observational Data*. Cambridge University Press, Cambridge.

Spanos, A. (2008). Sufficiency and ancillarity revisited: testing the validity of a statistical model. In Castle, J. L. and N. Shephard (eds.), *The Methodology and Practice of Econometrics*. Oxford University Press, Oxford.

Stewart, M. B. and K. F. Wallis (1981). *Introductory Econometrics*. Basil Blackwell, Oxford.

Stock, J. and M. W. Watson (2012). *Introduction to Econometrics*, 3rd edn. Addison-Wesley, Boston.

Stock, J. H. (1987). Asymptotic Properties of Least Squares Estimators of Cointegrating Vectors. *Econometrica*, *55*, 1035–1056.

Stock, J. H. and M. W. Watson (2011). Dynamic Factor Models. In Clements, M. P. and D. F. Hendry (eds.), *Oxford Handbook of Economic Forecasting*, Chap. 2. Oxford University Press.

Sydsæter, K., A. A. Strøm and P. Berck (2005). *Economists' Mathematical Manual.* Springer, Berlin.

Sydsæter, K. and P. Hammond (2002). *Essential Mathematics for Economic Analysis*, 2nd edn. Prentice-Hall Person Education, Harlow.

Sydsæter, K., P. Hammond, A. Seierstad and A. Strøm (2008). *Further Mathematics for Economic Analysis*, 2nd edn. Prentice-Hall International Editions, Harlow.

Sydsæter, K., P. Hammond, A. Strøm and A. Carvajal (2016). *Essential Mathematics for Economic Analysis*, 2nd edn. Prentice-Hall International Editions, Harlow.

Sydsæter, K., A. Seierstad and A. Strøm (2004). *Matematisk Analyse. Bind 2*, 2nd edn. Universitetsforlaget, Oslo.

Taleb, N. (2004). *Fooled by Randomness*. Penguin Books, London.

Taleb, N. N. (2010). *The Black Swan: The Impact of the Highly Improbable: With a New Section: "On Robustness and Fragility"*, 2nd edn. Penguin Random House, London.

Tetlock, P. (2005). *Expert Political Judgement*. Princeton University Press, Princeton.

Tibshirani, R. (1996). Regression Shrinkage and Selection via the Lasso. *Journal of the Royal Statistical Society. Series B (Methodological)*, *58*(1), 267–288.

Timmermann, A. (2006). Forecast Combinations. In Elliot, G., C. W. J. Granger and A. Timmermann (eds.), *Handbook of Economic Forecasting*, Vol. 1, Chap. 4, pp. 135–196. Elsevier, Amsterdam.

Turner, D. (1990). The Role of Judgement in Macroeconomic Forecasting. *Journal of Forecasting*, *9*, 315–345.

Varian, H. R. (2014). Big Data: New Tricks for Econometrics. *Journal of Economic Perspectives*, *28*, 3–18.

Wallis, K. F. (1977). Multiple Time Series Analysis and the Final Form of Econometric Models. *Econometrica*, *45*, 1481–97.

White, J. (1980). A Heteroskedasticity-Consistent Covariance Matrix Estimator and a Direct Test of Heteroskedasticity. *Econometrica*, *48*, 817–838.

Wold, H. (1938). *A Study in the Analysis of Stationary Time Series Data*. Almquist and Wicksell, Stockholm.

Wold, H. and L. Juréen (1953). *Demand Analysis: A Study in Econometrics*, 2nd edn. Wiley, New York.

Yule, G. U. (1926). Why do we sometimes get Nonsense Correlations between Time-Series? — A Study in Sampling and the Nature of Time-Series. *Journal of the Royal Statistical Society*, *89*, 1–64.

Index

M

N

O

Z

www.ingramcontent.com/pod-product-compliance
Lightning Source LLC
LaVergne TN
LVHW052014200926
848481LV00005B/1491